TESTAMENTS
OF TIME

TESTAMENTS OF TIME

*The Search
for Lost Manuscripts
and Records*

BY LEO DEUEL

New York: Alfred·A·Knopf

1965

L. C. catalog card number: 65–11118

THIS IS A BORZOI BOOK,
PUBLISHED BY ALFRED A. KNOPF, INC.

FIRST EDITION

In Memory of My Brother

HANS DEUEL

"And why," I asked myself, "why should I have learned that this precious book exists, if I am never to possess it—never even to see it? I would go to seek it in the burning heart of Africa, or in the icy regions of the Pole if I knew it were there. But I do not know where it is. I do not know if it be guarded in a triple-locked iron case by some jealous bibliomaniac. I do not know if it be growing mouldy in the attic of some ignoramus. I shudder at the thought that perhaps its torn-out leaves may have been used to cover the pickle-jars of some housekeeper."

ANATOLE FRANCE: *The Crime of Sylvestre Bonnard*

FOREWORD

*The history of the manuscripts through which we know
what little is known of the ancient world is one of the
most interesting chapters in the record of human endeavor.*

DOUGLAS C. McMURTRIE[1]

SINCE writing came into use in the Near East some five to six
thousand years ago, the survival of human records has constantly been threatened. Destruction came from the elements, and
from man's own negligence and bigotry. Books were put to lowly
uses, willfully burned, or allowed to rot. Whole civilizations vanished from the face of the earth, and the written word, which
alone could have perpetuated their names and traditions, was
obliterated. The books and documents not only of remote and forgotten peoples but of all ages and cultures even beyond the invention of printing have vanished. The ancient Hebrews registered
the loss of the Book of Jasher; most of the literature of the Anglo-
Saxons has disappeared; there are gaps in the Elizabethan drama;
today we possess but a fraction of the works of Hellenic and Latin
authors.

For a long time men cared little for ancient texts. In the
early Renaissance, however, a few Humanist scholars began
seriously to hunt for ancient documents, and during our modern
age of exploration a widespread interest in human origins has
made the recovery of lost documents one of the triumphs of
archaeology. Inevitably, such a search instilled a concern for their
preservation.

Whether the scholars were moved by the wish to recover lost
classics or by a concern with the beginnings of Christianity and
the authenticity of scripture, they were always led to search for
buried books. Each effort that succeeded inspired further quests.
As the achievements of Egypt, Mesopotamia, and the adjacent
countries of the Fertile Crescent came increasingly to light, their
all but forgotten writings were also rediscovered. The decipher-

---

[1] Douglas C. McMurtrie: *The Book: The Story of Printing and Bookmaking,* third revised edition (New York: Oxford University Press; 1943), p.
80.

ment of strange scripts made it possible to restore unknown literatures and the history of millennia. Sometimes the vibrant life of people, whose very existence had been hidden from our great-grandparents, was recaptured in amazing detail. After the Egyptians and the Assyrians, the Sumerians, Hittites, Hurrians, Mitannis, Canaanites, and many more began to speak to us. Before long the manuscript trail was extended far into the heart of Asia and, as we shall see, into the New World.

The story of such literary and documentary resurgences is the subject of my work. This is, in short, a book about books and about the scholars who searched for and discovered lost manuscripts and who interpreted and deciphered them. In my account I have concentrated on the efforts made since the Renaissance. The hunt for manuscripts, as I view it, reflects our increasing curiosity about the past. It parallels other antiquarian pursuits in our race to recover the fruits of human ingenuity and skill.

The tracking down of records in the dust of the ages is in itself a true story of detection, in many ways comparable to the excavation of treasure-laden tombs. Indeed, actual excavation, with its dangers and suspense, was often involved, besides the tedium of a long, uncertain search. More than once, risky forays into foreign countries provided the stuff of true epic stories of scholar-adventurers.

The recovery of lost works helped to revolutionize our civilization and changed many of our modes of thought. Entirely new avenues opened up to scholarship. Newly unearthed manuscripts enabled us to communicate with bygone eras, to reconstruct history, and to gauge the spirit, mind, and genius of our remote ancestors. Our heritage was enriched by works embodying the supreme expressions of the ancients in literature, religion, and science. These works have thrown light on the roots of our traditions and institutions and have posed exciting new problems.

Strange to say, the story of the pursuit of these manuscripts has never been told except in a fragmentary way. It was the discovery of the so-called Dead Sea scrolls after World War II that stirred the world, but the finding of these ancient Hebrew documents, while notable on all counts, was far from unique. It is in the hope of focusing attention on the strangely neglected area of what might be called the "archaeology of books" that I have written this volume.

Surely, this phase of research deserves its due. A lost civilization, no matter how splendid the monuments it may yield to the excavator, reveals its inner fabric only through written documents. From the Sumerians of Mesopotamia to the Mixtecs of Middle America, deciphered texts mark the breakthrough in the reconstruction and revival of past cultures.

How haphazard would our knowledge of Egypt have remained without Champollion's passkey to its script and the rich harvest of papyri from the sand wastes along the Nile. The clay tablets dug from Ikhnaton's capital at Tell el Amarna illuminated a whole epoch. The most glittering of all Egyptian finds, the tomb of Tutankhamen, most likely would never have been made had not inscriptions and texts alerted scholars to the existence of the boy king and set them on the search for his burial site. Inscribed seals led Arthur Evans to unearth the Minoan civilization in the rubble of Crete.

The most memorable incident in the career of Leonard Woolley, excavator of Ur in Mesopotamia, was the finding of a gray tablet inscribed with archaic cuneiform symbols. It was a short record, but it identified, as he wrote, "the first king of that First Dynasty of Ur which scholars have rejected as a mythological invention, and here was his name and that of his son on a contemporary document to prove that the supposed myth was sober history. . . ."[2]

An account of so vast a topic as the archaeology of writing must necessarily be limited in scope and time. Principal consideration will be given to books, that is, to compact compositions of fairly well defined contents and considerable length, possessing cultural, historical, or literary significance. With a few exceptions, I regretfully bypassed a vast body of vital epigraphic data: inscriptions on tombs, stones, buildings, metal plaques, potsherds. Moreover, I shall discuss only books dating from before the introduction of printing in the West. Such fascinating finds as the Boswell papers, an early novel by Proust, the memoirs of Caulaincourt, and the diary of Anne Frank fall outside our compass. The emphasis will be on early manuscripts from the literature of classical Greece and Rome, the ancient Near East, and the Judeo-Christian orbit. A concluding section on the resurrected texts from Inner Asia and pre-Columbian America rounds out the extensive geographical range of the material.

Most of the discoveries I shall consider took place within the past hundred and fifty to two hundred years. The Renais-

---

[2] Leonard Woolley: *Spadework in Archaeology* (New York: Philosophical Library; London: Butterworth Press; 1953), p. 92.

sance, which launched the first systematic campaign to resurrect literary texts, serves as a prelude to the problems and challenges of modern manuscript hunters. Throughout my book I have tried to project something of the meaning and background of the recovered texts.

In my selections I have included examples of the different writing materials, the multiple modes of transmission, and the equally varied ways in which they were recovered. On occasion I have digressed to discuss less well known aspects of cultural contacts, decipherment of scripts, physical characteristics of bookmaking, manufacture of writing materials, textual criticism, classical scholarship, and related topics. Even fraud and forgery played a prominent role in the study of manuscripts and will command our attention from time to time.

In theme and subject matter, the present work cuts across many disciplines and cannot be neatly classified under either palaeography or archaeology. The former, dealing with decipherment and with the evolution and changes of ancient scripts, bears but occasionally on our topic and hence is not treated systematically. The latter, at least in the generally accepted sense, touches only partly on the materials and methods which will here be considered.

To avoid retelling the familiar, I omitted well-reported archaeological bonanzas, particularly those from Mesopotamia, in favor of the lesser known sites of Dura-Europos, Ras Shamra-Ugarit, and Chinese Turkestan. Likewise, the inevitable limitation of length forced me to disregard some first-rate materials recovered in Egypt and elsewhere.

It need hardly be stressed that the ways and means of restoring buried texts reach far beyond dirt archaeology. Much of the "digging" may be carried out in the hidden recesses of far-flung libraries or in the national museums of a bustling modern metropolis. The shock of recognition may come from infrared light thrown on a faded, twice-written parchment. The identification of authorship and the decipherment of wording and meaning are important, if not decisive, phases of most recoveries. Thus the bookhunter, like the armchair archaeologist, may concentrate on homework and leave expeditions to alien lands to colleagues of a more peripatetic temperament.

Sites other than those of Cathay and Troy had their Marco Polos and Schliemanns. And these men loom large in our story. The semi-biographical approach may not comprise the whole historical truth, but in a highly selective survey it has the advantage of imposing a vivid and plausible framework.

One word of caution. I am well aware of the controversy over such concepts as the Renaissance—to name just one of the categories around which the material is grouped. If anything, the "Renaissance" is a historical construct. To inquire whether it was rather "the last flowering of the Middle Ages" than the true awakening of modern man, or to argue about Petrarch's place in it, is not the purpose of this book. Admittedly, there are those, like Lynn Thorndike, who have declared the very word "Renaissance" taboo. Others, more recently, have re-embraced the classical thesis of Burckhardt. Historians are notoriously revisionists. The triteness of yesteryear may well turn out to be the sophistication of tomorrow. However, this is a work of popularization. It shuns academic debates, just as it avoids discursive footnotes (the scholar's saving alibis and afterthoughts) and excessive qualifying statements.

Finally, it should be mentioned that I have been impressed by one underlying and unifying theme: the interdependence of human culture throughout most of the globe since the neolithic dawn. Thus I have dwelt on common roots, mutual borrowings, interpenetrations, continuity in time and space, rather than on the "unique" glory of Egypt, Greece, and Israel, or schematic systems of separate rising and falling civilizations. This is not to trace all manifestations of civilization to one single cradle. But there is, nevertheless, as William H. Prescott put it a long time ago, "one great brotherhood of nations . . . knit together by sympathies, that make the faintest spark of knowledge, struck out in one quarter, spread gradually wider and wider, until it has diffused a cheering light over the remotest."[3] This outlook lies back of the principal topics discussed in these pages: from modes of writing, forms of books, and their literary or religious contents to the meeting points of ancient civilizations where so much documentary evidence has been discovered. Hence, in a very modest way, this book on books is also a book on the history of one world.

In a work ranging over several civilizations, continents, and ages and extending beyond the mere romance of hunting ancient manuscripts, my task was the more hazardous and difficult because I had little general literature to guide me. For my data

---

[3] William H. Prescott: *History of the Conquest of Mexico* and *History of the Conquest of Peru* (New York: Random House–The Modern Library; n.d.), p. 54.

I frequently had to enter the thickets of professional journals, proceedings, symposia, *Festschriften,* research papers, and institutional reports in more than half a dozen languages. Since no one expert could possibly be at home in all the ground covered, I was bold enough to venture into the domains of many specialists, even at the risk of committing errors in judgment and fact. My goal was to inform my curiosity. My hope is that some of my enthusiasm for the world of books—living, lost, reborn, and yet-to-be-born—will prove equally compelling to my readers.

A NOTE ON SPELLING

As to the spelling of foreign names, particularly of places and persons of Greece, the ancient Near East, and Central Asia, I soon realized that the one sin is pedantry, or rather consistency. More often than not, one must choose between a bewildering number of alternates, all more or less sound. Instead of following one authority or standard reference work, I tried, above all, to settle on common and recognizable usage. Within such limits, I gave priority to the spellings employed by the men chiefly discussed and quoted in my book.

ACKNOWLEDGMENTS

A work that has been in the making for several years, and which has grown from the continuous absorption in the reports, studies, and narratives of many scholars, owes its very substance to other men. Though it would be impossible to single out even a fraction of my debt to them, I feel that my book is, no matter how insufficiently, a tribute to the explorers, historians, archaeologists, antiquarians, palaeographers, philologists, and bibliophiles whose researches were an inspiration to me. A few of these I was able to discuss at length. Many more are listed in the bibliography or, regretfully, remain unnamed.

My warmest thanks go to Mr. Harold Strauss, editor in chief of Alfred A. Knopf, who has taken a discerning interest in my work since its inception as a very brief and tentative outline. His assistant, Mrs. Sophie Wilkins, and the copy editor, Miss Carmen Gomezplata, helped with valuable editorial suggestions.

It is a special pleasure to express my gratitude to friends who have offered advice and criticism, in particular Dr. Geraldine Pelles Ross, Mrs. Barbara Wheatley Murray, Mrs. Shirley Zimmerman, and Mr. Charles Blackwell. The late Dr. Maria Loewe not only gave encouragement when sorely needed, but assisted with the research material.

I also wish to record my thankfulness to Dr. Herbert and Dr. Heidi Deuel-Zogg, St. Gall, Mr. and Mrs. G. Philipp of Johannesburg, and Mrs. Gertrud Deuel of Zurich for their readiness in procuring literature and illustrations. Regarding the latter, I am appreciative of courtesies rendered by Miss Valerie Vondermuhl of *Life* and Mr. Leverett Norman of the library of New York's City College.

CONTENTS

PLATES

FIGURES

MAPS

Book One

A RENAISSANCE
PRELUDE

·I·

THE QUEST FOR

CICERO: PETRARCH

I certainly will not reject the praise which you bestow upon me for having stimulated in many instances, not only in Italy but perchance beyond its confines, the pursuit of studies such as ours, which have suffered neglect for so many centuries. I am indeed one of the oldest among us who are engaged in the cultivation of these subjects.

PETRARCH TO BOCCACCIO[1]

A WORRIED FATHER set out from Avignon one day on a surprise visit to his teen-age son, a law student at the medieval university of Montpellier in southern France. Like any upright middle-class parent, Ser Petracco di Parenzo, himself a lawyer, was eager for his offspring to succeed in the profession he had imperiously, though well-meaningly, chosen for him. Was his Francesco squandering time and money on juvenile pastimes like most of the university youth of the fourteenth and many another century? True, Francesco had been studious since boyhood; he was the brightest pupil his teacher, the minor Italian poet Convennevole, had had. But was Francesco advancing in jurisprudence? Ser Petracco knew that his son had shown little enthusiasm for the law, and he was resolved to tolerate no nonsense.

Francesco knew only too well that his pursuit of the newly discovered delights of classical literature at the expense of dreary

---

[1] James Harvey Robinson and Henry Winchester Rolfe, eds.: *Petrarch. The First Modern Scholar and Man of Letters*, second revised edition (New York: G. P. Putnam's Sons; 1914), pp. 12–13.

law studies could hardly meet with his father's approval. In anticipation of a sudden appearance by his father, he had hidden his
few precious copies of Latin works.

But now his father had entered the modest room, and, to
Francesco's horror, quickly spotted the contraband. He seized the
books and flung them into the blazing fireplace. Francesco burst
into sobs. Ser Petracco relented, and dashing to the fire, snatched
out two charred tomes, Vergil's *Aeneid* and Cicero's *Rhetoric*.
These he held out to Francesco, saying: "Take the first one as an
occasional relaxation for your mind and the second as an aid
to your law studies." The boy gratefully took back "these restored
comrades—so few, but so eminent."[2]

The elder Petracco's aversion to the reading of the classics
was fairly common in an age that held scant respect for books—
an attitude that had persisted for many centuries.

Ancient literature had fallen into neglect with the eclipse
of the Roman order in the West. Barbarian tribes poured into the
collapsing empire and destroyed libraries and seats of learning.
Meanwhile the Church professed little affection for the books of
the heathen Greeks and Romans. A sixth-century historian of the
Franks, Gregory of Tours, dryly observed: "The study of letters
has perished."[3] Typically enough, he had no regrets. Instead, he ex-
horted the faithful: "Let us shun the lying fables of the poets . . .
lest we incur the doom of endless death by sentence of our Lord."[4]

Even the most learned Christian teachers of the "Dark Ages"
were wont to expiate their occasional lapses into reading classical
literature. St. Augustine, whom Petrarch revered, professed to hate
the Greek language and to curse the time he had wasted poring
over Vergil. And Pope Gregory the Great, contemporary of his
namesake of Tours, though he had been born into an old Roman
family scorned classical learning, boasted of his ignorance, and
fostered irrationalism. In Spain, the most respected scholar was
Archbishop Isidore of Seville, one of the tireless compilers whom
the early Middle Ages brought forth in profusion. Yet he forbade
his churchmen and monks to read any ancient authors except
grammarians. The rhetorical works of Cicero and Quintilian he

---

[2] Pierre de Nolhac: *Petrarch and the Ancient World* (Boston:
Humanists' Library; 1907), p. 44.

[3] Richard C. Jebb: "The Classical Renaissance," *Cambridge Medieval
History* (Cambridge: Cambridge University Press; 1902), Vol. I, p. 534.

[4] John Addington Symonds: *Renaissance in Italy*, Vol. II of *The Revival of Learning* (New York: G. P. Putnam's Sons–Capricorn Books;
1960), p. 43.

dismissed as "too diffuse to be read"[5]— a flagrant case of the darkest of pots calling the kettle black. Is it any wonder that the classics were forgotten, and many manuscripts were lost?

Yet, not all was darkness in the medieval "millennium." Some religious houses continued to care for the works of ancient literature, just as Carolingian scribes in the eighth and ninth centuries copied various classics and thus helped to transmit them to a later age.

Woodcut of medieval scribe. *Calendrier des Bergers* (PARIS, 1500)

By the eleventh century, with the growth of trade and cities, learning was no longer in disrepute. Cathedral schools and universities had become intellectual centers. Contacts with the more advanced Islamic civilization in Sicily and Spain had brought several Aristotelian treatises and other, mostly scientific and philosophical works into the West by way of translations from the Arabic. However, scholars concentrated almost exclusively on theology. Because of this preoccupation, the rising tide of the

---

[5] Henry Hallam: *Introduction to the Literature of Europe* (London: John Murray; 1873), Vol. I, p. 27.

scholastic movement retarded rather than furthered a knowledge of classical literature. And the monasteries—once prime guardians of manuscripts—tended to lose to other institutions the little intellectual zeal they ever had.

A few men, nevertheless, did read the ancients—John of Salisbury, for instance, and Gerbert, who later became Pope Sylvester II, and Abélard, who straddled the thin borderline of heresy. But only a limited body of works was available to them. Seldom was an author read *in toto*. Classical texts appeared and vanished like shooting stars. Some, like Halley's Comet, would reappear suddenly, perhaps in remote Scandinavia or Hungary. Others, whose existence we know of because they are mentioned in medieval records, subsequently disappeared for good. An author read or esteemed in one part of Western Europe—or in just one monastery—might be altogether unknown in another.

In sum, the Middle Ages lacked what we call a classical tradition—a more or less established, consciously perpetuated canon of literary works. Barely any of the classics formed part of the stream of culture,[6] and people had the most muddled notions about the writers and poets of antiquity. One authority attributed the *Iliad* to Pindar; Homer and Vergil were likely to be depicted as contemporaries and friends. A prominent professor at the University of Bologna, with whom Petrarch corresponded, referred to Cicero as one of the ancient poets.[7] In some parts of medieval Italy, legend had raised Cicero to a great warlord who had besieged and stormed a fortress city held by the rebel chieftain "Catellina."[8]

This was the situation when Petrarch appeared on the scene.

We are concerned here with the mature Petrarch, the man of letters, rather than the young Petrarch, the supreme lyricist of the *Canzoniere*—his love songs to Laura in Italian. Our Petrarch was above all a writer in Latin, counselor of kings and cardinals, Italian patriot, author of the epic *Africa*—which in Vergilian verse sang the glory of all-conquering Rome—and the sworn enemy of scholasticism, astrology, and medical quackery. He inaugurated a movement known as Humanism which was to refashion European culture.

Petrarchan Humanism emphasized man's role in this world

---

[6] Frederick B. Artz: *The Mind of the Middle Ages*, third edition (New York: Alfred A. Knopf; 1959), p. 435.

[7] Robinson and Rolfe: op. cit., p. 35.

[8] L. Patrick Wilkinson, ed.: *Letters of Cicero* (London: Arrow Books; 1949), pp. 18–19.

and looked to the long-neglected freedoms of the past. In classical antiquity Petrarch and his followers found ideals of truth and beauty which they urged the Western world to reclaim. The past was the key to progress. If one upheld the worth and perfectibility of man, one had a stake in the revival of classical learning. If one would develop one's personality, become a rational being, adopt a proper style in public and private conduct, achieve the highest skill in speaking and writing, lead and train men—one must read the ancients.

But how to get hold of the classic authors? Few of the great works were readily accessible, and some were known only in pitiful fragments. Petrarch must have suffered frustration many times as he came across references to ancient masterpieces which apparently had vanished. He would then cry out in anger over the losses inflicted by the "barbarian" successors of Rome. "For every illustrious name that I invoke," he once wrote, "I call to mind a crime of the dark ages that followed! As if their own sterility had not been shame enough, they left the books born of the vigils of our fathers [the ancient Latins!], and the fruits of their genius to perish utterly. That epoch, which produced nothing, did not fear to squander the paternal heritage."[9] It was singular good fortune to obtain even one copy of the work of one illustrious ancient writer. And then, more often than not, the manuscript had been so ineptly transcribed that Cicero, or Livy, would not have recognized his own work.[1]

Should one despair? What chance was there to track down lost works? Where could one hope to find fairly well preserved manuscripts? These questions burned in the mind of the budding fourteenth-century scholar. And thus it was that Petrarch, who had collected and loved books since he could read, and who had tasted "forbidden fruit" at Montpellier, grew up to be the first systematic hunter of manuscripts in the West.

When his father died, in 1326, Petrarch was at last free to pursue his own literary interests. He returned to Avignon and made it a point to cultivate the company of venerable bibliophiles attached to the papal court there, but their appetites ran toward legal texts. If only he had lived in antiquity! Since that could not be, he did the next best thing: he tried to recapture the past.

One way to delve into antiquity was to travel to the seats of ancient culture. Petrarch was on the move constantly, a wander-

---

[9] Nolhac: op. cit., p. 18.   [1] Robinson and Rolfe: op. cit., p. 25.

ing scholar ranging over Western Europe, going from city to city—
each of which, at one time or another, he declared he loathed. He
would reside in one town—Milan, Padua, Mantua, Ferrara, Parma,
Venice—for a few years and then he would be off again. Another
way to reach into the past was through books, and the search for
lost books motivated many trips. Everywhere he went he searched.
He followed up rumors, made inquiries, bought, transcribed, had
copies made. Once in a while he managed to lay his hands on
what was to him "more valuable merchandise than anything
offered by the Arabs or the Chinese."[2]

In all his searching, Cicero was uppermost in his mind: Cicero
led him into the ancient world. Almost every phase of the Humanist movement, therefore, came to bear the stamp of Cicero. Petrarch
would not stop until he knew Cicero the whole man—stylist, orator,
philosopher, witness of Rome's great political crisis.

Portrait of Cicero after an ancient bust

The affinities between the two men, separated by thirteen
centuries, are understandable. Both were primarily sensitive, civilized, humane men of letters; vivid synthesizers rather than profound thinkers; admirers of style and eloquence rather than prop-
agators of originality. Petrarch's love for the Roman orator led
him to "converse" with him every so often, and to invent a new
literary genre, the writing of letters to a man long since dead.
Before he ever set eyes on Laura and long after his infatuation for
her had cooled, he was in pursuit of Cicero. The rescue of all the
master's works became a veritable obsession that runs through

---

[2] Quoted in Will Durant: *The Renaissance* (New York: Simon and
Schuster; 1953), p. 8.

his entire life. From the classical literature he read, he gleaned a long list of Cicero's works that his contemporaries knew little about. He poured time, energy, and money into his mission to gather the remains of classical literature. But it was always Cicero first.

Petrarch came to know people of influence in all the Western countries, and pressed them into service. He carefully kept up good relations with lovers of books everywhere. If a rare item came into somebody's possession and Petrarch learned of it, he would write to the person, whoever he was. If it was something by Cicero, he would be particularly persuasive. "The rumor runs," he wrote once, "that Cicero lodges under your roof and that you have many and rare works of his genius. Oh, happiness a hundred times greater than that of Evander's who received Alcides! If you deem me worthy, permit me to bask in the presence of such a guest."[3]

He coaxed a friend: "If you love me, commission some trustworthy and educated persons to wander about Tuscany to forage among the bookshelves of monks and other friends of study, and endeavor to find something which will appease—though it may irritate—my thirst. Although you know well enough in what waters I am used to fish, and in what woods I like to hunt, yet that you may not go wrong, I enclose in my letter the list of what I particularly desire. . . ."[4]

When Petrarch borrowed a precious manuscript, he would find it well-nigh impossible to part with it. He kept one of Cicero's orations for four years on the grounds that he could not find a competent person to copy it; in the end, as he often did, he transcribed it himself. His efforts to hunt down manuscripts were far-flung: "Ah, the prayers I have addressed, the money I have sent, not only to Italy, but to France, to Germany, even to Spain and England—nay, would you believe it?—to Greece!"[5] Greece, though it proved barren of Ciceronian material, yielded a Greek manuscript of Homer and, later, sixteen dialogues of Plato. It was a source of great distress to Petrarch that he could not master Greek: most of the Greek authors would remain shadows for him. But knowledge of Greek was rare in Western countries. Only in Petrarch's later years did a crude translation of the *Iliad*, undertaken by Boccaccio with the help of a Calabrian who knew Greek, make Homer accessible. Even though he was denied entry into

---

[3] Nolhac: op. cit., p. 69.   [4] Ibid., pp. 72–3.   [5] Ibid., p. 72.

that holy land, however, he could inspire others to go into it. Ultimately, the rescue of Greek classics from oblivion in the West
was also due to Petrarch's influence.

Petrarch made the prize discoveries himself. As soon as he
saw the walls of a monastery on the horizon his excitement rose,
and "immediately turning aside, I would make my way towards it,
always hoping to find some of the works for which I was greedily
searching."[6] And off he went to knock on the cloister door and
charm the brethren into helping him.

One gratifying find he made before he turned thirty. In 1333
he went on a long journey to Paris and farther north into what
are now the Low Countries and Western Germany. He went from
monastery to monastery until, at Liège, he had the fortune to discover two speeches of Cicero's, one of them the *pro Archia*. With
permission, he copied one and enlisted a companion to transcribe
the other. The only complaint he had: "In that good barbarous
town we had endless trouble to get a little ink, and when we got it,
it was like saffron."[7] But he could now proclaim like a conquering
Roman: "Through me Italy has received them both [the two lost
orations]."[8]

Four years later he visited Rome for the first time, and saw
with dismay that the walls, the palaces, the temples were a
shambles. Nobody seemed to care. The Rome of old, Petrarch
wrote sadly to a friend, was nowhere as little known as in Rome
itself. And the wretched Romans had sunk so low that they were
selling marble pillars and monuments to decadent Naples in the
south. With this kind of treatment, he predicted, all the splendid
ruins would vanish altogether before long.[9]

Undeterred, Petrarch continued hunting books. Within a few
days he had acquired a fine text, and in another ten days he had
located more. On a subsequent trip back from Rome, he stopped
at his native Arezzo and there found a hopelessly fragmented
Quintilian. Shortly after, in Mantua, he acquired the Elder Pliny's
Natural History. The supreme discovery of his life came in Verona
in the spring of 1345: a collection of Cicero's *Letters to Atticus*,
and Cicero's correspondence with his brother Quintus and with

---

[6] Maud F. Jerrold: *Francesco Petrarca. Poet and Humanist* (London:
J. M. Dent; 1909), pp. 34–5.
[7] Nolhac: op. cit., p. 49.
[8] Jerrold: op. cit., p. 35.
[9] Georg Voigt: *Die Wiederbelebung des classischen Alterthums* . . . ,
fourth edition (Berlin: W. de Gruyter; 1960), Vol. I, p. 49.

Brutus—both of which had apparently been unknown to scholars for generations, though they may have been glimpsed from time to time by local men in Verona. There is in existence no other copy as complete, and, but for Petrarch's transcript, the priceless collection might never have come to light. The original Verona

Renaissance image of classical ruins. Francesco Colonna: *Hyp-nertomachia Polyphili* (1499)

codex has long since disappeared; it was already in a decayed state when Petrarch saw it, buried in what he called an "unexpected place," probably in the library attached to the cathedral.

That this all happened in Verona is of interest. Verona was the city richest in Roman remains in northern Italy. Its attractions for Petrarch were obvious. It was the birthplace of Catullus; it boasted a number of ancient structures, the most splendid of which was a vast, well-preserved amphitheater dating back to the first century A.D., with a seating capacity of 25,000 spectators. Its ancient cathedral library, in which the epistles were probably found, is one of the world's oldest.

Verona in the late Middle Ages

Petrarch had long wanted these letters. They shed light both on Cicero's personality and on the pulsating life of the declining Roman republic, assailed by gangster politicians. Petrarch, though ailing, copied the entire Verona codex in his own hand, and he never tired of telling his friends about the strain and the joy of it.[1] The resulting tome was oversized, too large to fit with any of the other manuscripts in his library. Not knowing what else to do with the bulky, heavy volume, he placed it on the floor, where it soon proved to be something of an occupational hazard. One day, as Petrarch entered the room, his flowing gown caught on the volume and tumbled it heavily against his shins. This happened again the next day, and repeatedly thereafter. By the time Petrarch at last removed the book to a less obtrusive spot, his much abused leg was swollen and infected. Severe pains set in and doctors gloomily predicted permanent damage. Some months later, however, Petrarch was on the way to complete recovery.[2] And these epistles of Cicero overshadowed everything else in his possession;

---

[1] Nolhac: op. cit., p. 119.   [2] Ibid., pp. 62–3.

he guarded them so jealously that he permitted no one to borrow or copy them.

Verona yielded him additional treasures; foremost among these, a Catullus and a Propertius. Indeed, it is likely that all subsequent texts of Propertius are descended from Petrarch's personal copy. The Verona "archetype" was eventually lost.

Petrarch's discovery of the Cicero correspondence at Verona was one of the great events in the cultural history of the Renaissance. The letters brought before the world the hitherto little-known character of the great Roman orator, with all its weaknesses and virtues. Perhaps nothing as self-revealing appeared on the European literary scene again until Rousseau's *Confessions*.[3] The letters came to be among the favorite reading of Renaissance men, and not only because of their content. The elegant but colloquial style revolutionized the Latin that Humanists were struggling to free from medieval corruptions, jargon, and antiquarian mannerisms. Thanks to Cicero's example, letter writing itself became perhaps the most popular medium of Humanist literature; it was Cicero's correspondence which inspired Petrarch to write his first letter to a classical author, and other letters, addressed to Varro, Livy, Quintilian, Horace, and Homer, followed.

Petrarch's first "Letter to Cicero" was evidently composed in Verona after a perusal of the collection, for it bears the marks of his excitement over the find as well as a certain shock at some of its disclosures. "Your letters," Petrarch wrote to Marcus Tullius, "I sought for long and diligently; and finally, where I least expected it, I found them. At once I read them, over and over, with the utmost eagerness. And as I read I seemed to hear your bodily voice, O Marcus Tullius, saying many things, uttering many lamentations, ranging through many places of thought and feeling. I long had known how excellent a guide you have proved for others; at last I was to learn what sort of guidance you gave yourself.

"Now it is your turn to be the listener. Hearken, wherever you are, to the words of advice, or rather of sorrow and regret that fall, not unaccompanied by tears, from the lips of one of your successors, who loves you faithfully and cherishes your name. . . ."[4] There follows Petrarch's reproach to Cicero for his numerous faults (they "make me blush for you"). Cicero's excessive vanity and lack of resolution when faced with the great

---

[3] Wilkinson: op. cit., p. 18. [4] Robinson and Rolfe: op. cit., pp. 239–40.

issues of his time saddened Petrarch, who was himself a mass of contradictions but could not accept human failings in his paragon. A shadow was cast on Cicero's admirable philosophy, for the master had not always practiced what he so eloquently preached. Petrarch's moralistic, rather self-conscious, address is no match for Cicero's epistolary grace and ease. A second Letter to Cicero is more felicitously phrased, however, and happily renews the friendship. Petrarch includes an interesting digression in it on the great Republican's reputation in Petrarch's day. The neglect of learning and the loss of books Petrarch blames, as Petronius did the decadence of Rome, on "the love of money [which] forces our thoughts in other directions. . . . We must waste and spoil through our cruel and insufferable neglect, the fruits of your labors, too, and of those of your fellows as well, for the fate that I lament in the case of your own books has befallen the works of many another illustrious man."[5]

Petrarch then goes on to speak of the books of Cicero whose loss is most regrettable: among others, the *Republic*, the Roman's major political treatise; the *Praise of Philosophy;* and the essays on the *Care of Property,* on the *Art of War,* on *Consolation,* and on *Glory.* As to the surviving volumes, Petrarch is distressed by the huge gaps and the mutilations. He is reminded of a great battle, in which "we had to mourn noble leaders slain, and others lost or maimed."[6]

All the attempts to find Cicero's *Republic* ("De republica") were of no avail; Petrarch at last gave up the search.[7] But in his youth he had had the treatise on *Glory,* which he had lent to his teacher Convennevole. Convennevole had pawned it in a time of extreme want, and none of Petrarch's offers to buy it back were of any avail. The old teacher, embarrassed, promised to redeem it himself, but in the end the book vanished from Avignon. Petrarch never gave up the hope of recovering the precious manuscript, but *De gloria* has remained lost to this day.

Modern scholars have on occasion questioned Petrarch's claims that he once owned this work of Cicero's. But there is no compelling reason to doubt his word, even though the treatise has never been found. Several major works of antiquity were transmitted in single copies, which were as likely as not to have been destroyed. Indeed, their chances were negligible until the Renaissance was well on its way. And even then, only immediate copying

---

[5] Ibid., pp. 250–1.   [6] Ibid., p. 251.   [7] Voigt: op. cit., p. 38.

could assure their survival. A number of books that were still extant during the Middle Ages eventually disappeared. Many more may have been destroyed than ever came down to us, and these losses continued beyond Petrarch's own lifetime.

CICERO.bruto.GL Fungerer officio quo tu fiictuif ef in meo luc
tu toq: per Literaf confolarer.' nifi fcurem yf remedyf quibuf mei
dolorem tulouaffef re in tuo non egere': ac uelim facil uuf q' in tuo

From a Renaissance copy of Cicero's *Letters*

Petrarch's second Letter to Cicero may have given a grim picture of the fate of books in his own time. But it also throws into graphic relief his ardent campaign to reverse the trend. He was indeed the first of those who "loved dead letters with a living love, and found again in ancient dust the spark of eternal beauty."[8] Not only did he bring back lost and forgotten works, but he set up new standards for the study and love of literature and converted others to his enthusiasm. In all this he succeeded so splendidly that a whole new generation of Humanist bookhunters sprang up who saved almost all that remained to be saved on European soil.

---

[8] Nolhac: op. cit., p. 16.

·II·

HUMANISTS IN ACTION: BOCCACCIO AND SALUTATI

As the Franks deemed themselves thrice blest if they returned with relics from Jerusalem, so these new Knights of the Holy Ghost, seeking not the sepulchre of a risen God, but the tombs wherein the genius of the ancient world awaited resurrection, felt holy transports when a brown, begrimed, and crabbed copy of some Greek or Latin author rewarded their patient quest. Days and nights they spent . . . till the treasure-trove became the common property of all who could appreciate its value.

JOHN ADDINGTON SYMONDS[1]

NOTHING is as contagious as a great example. Already within the lifetime of Petrarch, Italians were seized by a fever of exploration into the literary unknown. After his death the search for lost, hidden, or neglected classics became a passion in its own right.

Of all his contemporaries, Petrarch had no more fervent a follower than Boccaccio, his junior by some ten years. Between the two, Humanism was taking shape.

Like Petrarch before him, Boccaccio, the half-French author of the *Decameron* and one of the founding fathers of Italian litera-

---

[1] Symonds: op. cit., p. 96.

ture, turned fom popular, sensuous works in the Tuscan tongue to scholarship, affecting to look down on his earlier creations, on which his popular fame happens to rest. Petrarch converted him to manuscript hunting, and in the end, Boccaccio's successes were to outshine those of Petrarch.

Giovanni Boccaccio was born in Paris in 1313, the natural child of an unknown Frenchwoman and a Florentine moneylender, Boccaccio di Chellino. As an infant he was taken to Florence by his father, by then an affluent and respected citizen. Owing to his father's connections with the great banking house of the Bardi, young Giovanni in about 1328 secured a position in Naples. He was on his own in the gayest city of Italy, and he threw himself with gusto into its sultry life. It was there that he met Fiammetta, who was perhaps an illegitimate daughter of Robert d'Anjou, the King of Naples. And there he found the themes for his richly colored stories and verse.

The carefree fling came to a sudden end when his father's business failed. Boccaccio had to return to Florence—and poverty. However, misfortune proved a good taskmaster for the budding poet and future scholar. Thenceforth he concentrated on his literary projects, and within a few years several of his best-known books were completed. He might have continued in this vein, had it not been for his encounter with Petrarch.

Probably the first meeting of the two men took place in the Jubilee Year of 1350. Petrarch was on a pilgrimage to Rome to gain indulgences,[2] and Boccaccio welcomed him at the gates of Florence, the city that had banished Petrarch's father. Henceforth they maintained a close friendship that lasted until Petrarch's death. In his will Petrarch left his friend fifty gold florins, "to buy a winter gown for his studies and nocturnal meditations"—and he said he was embarrassed to leave so little to such a great man.[3]

Boccaccio, though he lived in dire poverty most of his life, gave freely to others. He was liberal with his time, his knowledge, his books—and he made Florence a center of Humanist studies. In the course of earning his livelihood, which he made by tedious copying, he transcribed for Petrarch lengthy texts of Cicero's and Varro's. Soon after they had become friends, Boccaccio regaled Petrarch with a sumptuous copy of St. Augustine's *Commentary*

---

[2] Edward Hutton: *Giovanni Boccaccio: A Biographical Study* (London: J. Lane; 1910), p. 150.
[3] Jerrold: op. cit., p. 243.

on the Psalms and a manuscript, in his own hand, of Dante's *Divina Commedia.* The latter was grudgingly accepted by the great man, who found it easier to worship the ancients than a modern rival to his own fame.

Once Petrarch had expressed a desire to read an obscure religious work, which he had been unable to obtain: the *Life of*

View of Florence. From a 1490 chronicle

Peter Damian. The saint interested him because of his praise of solitude, a subject Petrarch was about to treat in *De vita solitaria* ("The Life of Solitude"). Could the book perhaps be found in Ravenna, the saint's native town? Boccaccio made it a point to get to that city and start a search. Neither the monks nor any laymen knew of a copy. At last, however, an old man directed Boccaccio to his house, which harbored a pile of dirty, rotting volumes. As Boccaccio burrowed through the moldy lot, his hopes sank. And then, just as he was reaching the bottom, he glimpsed a badly decayed booklet, the *Life of Peter Damian.* Triumphantly he bore it away and set to copy it, even though, on examination, he wondered what Petrarch could see in it. But who was he to question Petrarch's motives?[4]

In his rise as an advocate of Humanism, Boccaccio had to overcome the handicap of an indifferent education. Yet in his mature years his learning was well ahead of that of most of his

---

[4] Nolhac: op. cit., p. 67.

contemporaries. When he was fluent in Latin, he turned, with Petrarch's encouragement, to Greek, and eventually he surpassed Petrarch by far in that ancient tongue. Petrarch applauded his progress and urged him to render Homer in Latin: this was to be the first modern translation of the Greek national epics.

The way was thorny. There were no manuals to aid him and hardly any original texts. Competent teachers were at least as scarce. Petrarch had gotten nowhere with his teacher Barlaam, a Greek monk from southern Italy, who had no sympathy for classical learning. Boccaccio, however, enlisted the services of Leontius Pilatus, a Calabrian who loved to pose as a Greek— Boccaccio's association with Leontius did not lack touches of the bizarre. The man was an unsavory adventurer. A by no means flawless command of Greek could hardly make up for his sleazy character and ill temper. His appearance was equally repellent: a face "covered with bristles of black hair, an untrimmed beard completing the effect; and his ragged mantle only half covered his dirty person."[5] Petrarch, who pressed him into his manuscript searches, called Leontius "a great beast" (*magna belua*). But Boccaccio with forbearance took Leontius into his house and secured him a lectureship in Greek at the University of Florence. For the cause of Humanism, Boccaccio put up with Leontius and later on with many a sullen monk who possessed precious parchments.

Boccaccio's Latin translation of Homer, based on Petrarch's Greek manuscript, was completed after years of labor. According to tradition, Petrarch was found dead slouched over a copy of Boccaccio's Latin version, which he had been annotating in his last hours.

Boccaccio's career in Humanist learning suffered a serious setback occasioned by one of those religious crises which so often beset the "new men" hesitatingly crossing the threshold from the Middle Ages. Shaken by a communication he received in 1362 from a dying monk, Boccaccio was about to take orders himself, renounce his studies, burn his own works, and dispose of his library. Petrarch, who despite his sincere piety was supremely practical in ordering his own life to suit his talents, was perturbed when he heard of Boccaccio's conversion. It needed all his eloquence to reconcile his friend to both the religious and the Humanist viewpoints: "Neither the love of virtue nor the thought of approaching death ought to divert us from the study of letters,

---

[5] Hutton: op. cit., p. 194.

which, if it is carried on with good intentions, awakens the love of virtue, and diminishes and destroys the fear of death. . . . Try to quote me the greatest saint you can who was ignorant of letters, and I will undertake to match him with a learned man who shall be still more holy."[6] Petrarch went on to urge Boccaccio to seek solace in the service of ancient texts. The appeal was successful, and Boccaccio from then on applied himself to the classics with greater zeal, but he gave up Italian poetry and risqué stories.

In 1363 he retired to Certaldo, the little Tuscan town which was his father's birthplace and which, along with Florence, he considered his home. Though barely fifty, he seems to have resigned himself to premature old age, forsaken the pleasures of the flesh, and burnt the midnight oil. Occasionally he broke the gloom by undertaking embassies for the Florentines to places as far distant as Avignon and Rome.

In 1370 he accepted the invitation of a friend to visit Naples, and stayed into 1371. It was during this trip that he made his most notable discoveries. The site was Monte Cassino, the ancient Benedictine monastery. Perched high on a hill overlooking the strategic inland road from Rome to Naples, the convent had been one of Christianity's foremost centers of learning in the West since the sixth century. Its abbey was repeatedly rebuilt after having been

Seal of the monastery of Monte
Cassino showing the ancient basilica

laid waste successively by barbarian invaders and natural catastrophes. Some twelve years before Boccaccio's coming, it was damaged by an earthquake. (It was to suffer its most violent assault in World War II when the Allies, assuming the buildings to be a defensive position in the German Gustav Line, pulverized it.)

Oddly enough, we know of Boccaccio's adventure among the manuscripts of Monte Cassino through a note tucked away in the

---

[6] Jerrold: op. cit., p. 232.

commentary of his disciple, Benvenuto da Imola, on Dante's *Paradiso*. On his way to Naples, Boccaccio decided to stop at the monastery. It was winter—the time of December rains—when he climbed up to the massive, though battered, structures.[7] His prime interest was the library. "Desirous of seeing the collection," writes Benvenuto, "which he understood to be a very choice one, he modestly asked a monk—for he was always most courteous in manners—to open the library, as a favor, for him. The monk answered stiffly, pointing to a steep staircase, 'Go up; it is open.' Boccaccio went up gladly; but he found that the place which held so great a treasure, was without a door or key. He entered, and saw grass sprouting on the windows, and all the books and benches thick with dust. In his astonishment he began to open and turn the leaves of first one tome and then another, and found many and divers volumes of ancient and foreign works. Some of them had lost several sheets; others were snipped and pared all round the texts, and mutilated in various ways." At length he left the library sadly. "Coming to the cloister, he asked a monk whom he met, why those valuable books had been so disgracefully mangled. He was told that the monks, seeking to gain a few *soldi*, were in the habit of cutting off sheets and making psalters [of them], which they sold to boys. The margins too they manufactured into charms, and sold to women." Benvenuto closes with a sardonic note: "So then, O man of study, go to and rack your brains; make books, that you may come to this!"[8]

Benvenuto da Imola's report gives a lively picture of what these early explorers were up against. Conditions were little short of scandalous even in the very cradle of Benedictine monasticism, which had enjoyed such a high reputation for learned activities.

Though we know of Boccaccio's visit to Monte Cassino, unfortunately we lack any direct information on his transactions there. Bookhunters in the Renaissance had an exasperating habit of obscuring the sources of their manuscripts, and often would keep to themselves what they had found. They apparently had their reasons for this secretiveness: it undoubtedly kept rivals from rushing to the scene. Besides, it was always wise not to let the former owners know the true value of the manuscripts that had been taken off their hands so unceremoniously. To put it bluntly, these good Humanists were not beyond theft. They contended that

---

[7] Francis MacManus: *Boccaccio* (London: Sheed & Ward; 1947), p. 235.
[8] Symonds: op. cit., pp. 97–8.

the rightful owner was too ignorant to be worthy of his possession, and to give the business legalistic sanction improvised elegant Latin formulas—such as: *si ius violandum est, librorum gratia violandum est* ("if the law is to be broken, let it be broken for the sake of books").[9] On similar grounds, national museums and dilettanti would in a later age enlarge their collections. And in the manner of many a self-styled rescuer of antiquities from Greece and the Near East in more modern days, the fourteenth- and fifteenth-century Italians felt that expropriation of antiquities from their place of deposit meant their heroic salvation.

Recent bibliographic research leaves little doubt that Boccaccio "acquired" from Monte Cassino one of the most notable manuscripts recovered in the Renaissance—the manuscript of major portions of Tacitus' *Annals* (Books XI–XVI) and *History* (Books I–V). No modern before Boccaccio had any knowledge of this grand master of Roman historians, a vital source on the Roman Empire from Tiberius to Nero. After 1370, however, Boccaccio quotes Tacitus copiously. Yet he said nothing about his acquisition, even to Petrarch. And the mystery persisted after the death of Boccaccio. It was then that the manuscript came into the possession of two second-generation Florentine Humanists, Lionardo Bruni and Niccolò de' Niccoli—how, nobody knows. Since they too maintained strict secrecy, it has been suggested that they in turn stole the manuscript from Boccaccio's heirs. If so, it was in a way a happy move because the bulk of Boccaccio's library was ruined by fire in the fifteenth century. Some fifty years after Boccaccio's death, in a letter of 1427, Poggio Bracciolini, who borrowed the Tacitus codex from Niccoli, assures the latter that he kept his pledge not to utter a word about it to anyone.[1] This is highly unusual in Poggio, who always opposed secrecy in these matters. He himself lent his most precious manuscripts freely, often with unfortunate consequences. However, with Niccoli's Tacitus, it seems, he had no choice but to follow the stipulations of the "owner."

Speculation over the recovery of the Tacitus continued for a long time. Since the manuscript appeared to be unknown until Poggio's reported reading of it, a nineteenth-century English

---

[9] From letter of Bruni to Niccoli, quoted in Albert C. Clark: "Sabbadini's 'Finds of Latin and Greek Manuscripts,'" *The Classical Review*, Vol. XX (1906), p. 225.

[1] Clark: op. cit., p. 225.

scholar advanced the ingenious theory that the *Annals* had been forged by none other than Poggio himself. The theory is clearly absurd. Boccaccio had already quoted from the *Annals* before Poggio was born. And earlier parts of the work (Books I–VI) were discovered in a German monastery half a century after Poggio's death. However, like many other demonstrably false theories, the Poggio "fake" has been revived from time to time.

Brief passage from Tacitus codex or Mediceus II (*Annals*, Books XI–XVI; *Histories*, Books I–V) which Boccaccio probably took from Monte Cassino. Bound with a copy of Apuleius' *Golden Ass*, it is now at the Laurenziana library of Florence. The writing is in the Beneventan or South Italian minuscule, believed to have been executed in the eleventh century at Monte Cassino.

By Boccaccio's last years, classical literature had been enriched with works whose authors were almost completely unknown to the most learned men of the Middle Ages and even to Dante and Petrarch. His Tacitus is only the first of a list of notables. No Humanist before Boccaccio had been able to read Varro's essay on the Latin language. Other classics discovered by Boccaccio are Martial, the satiric poet, Ovid and his *Ibis*, the fourth-century A.D. Gallo-Roman man of letters Ausonius, and the collection of unblushing erotic poems, *Priapeia* ("Irreproachable in versification," says *The Oxford Classical Dictionary* of them, but "marked by extreme, even repulsive, obscenity"), of which the oldest surviving copy in Boccaccio's own hand is preserved in the Laurentian Library of Florence. Ironically, Ovid and the *Priapeia* brought up themes which Boccaccio had relished in his lusty youth, when the capricious Neapolitan beauty Fiammetta inspired him to write the *Decameron*, ancestor of the European novel. He had come a long way since.

When Boccaccio heard that Petrarch was dead, he drew up his will, and one year later, in December 1375, he too was laid to rest. His death prompted the chancellor of Florence to declare that "both of the luminaries of the new eloquence had been extinguished."[2] The man who delivered this eulogy was Coluccio Salutati, the statesman-scholar, who after Petrarch and Boccaccio was the third and youngest in the great "Florentine triad" of early Humanists. He was first of many urbane men of affairs and patrons of learning who, as assiduous and affluent collectors of books, stimulated the discovery of lost manuscripts by others, though they did not themselves engage actively in field work.

Salutati was a man of the stern cast of a Roman Republican. He translated Dante into Latin, wrote biographies of Dante, Petrarch, and Boccaccio, and was an accomplished stylist. Well-known is the remark ascribed to Gian Galeazzo Visconti, the Milanese strongman, that the writings of the chancellor had been more injurious than a Florentine army.[3] Ciceronian Latin was forged by him into a tool of diplomacy.

After Petrarch's death Salutati, just promoted to high office in Florence, got in touch with the poet's son-in-law to gain access to the manuscript collection. Petrarch had not been particularly communicative about the works he had in his possession. His codices of Catullus and Propertius had not been made available; even their existence among the dead man's papers was by no means certain. The negotiations dragged on, but in the end Salutati managed to get a transcript of some sixty letters of Cicero. As a result—*l'appetit vient en mangeant*—he wanted all the letters, which he knew Petrarch had copied from a Verona codex. Just then Gian Galeazzo, the Milanese warrior, received some ancient manuscripts from recently conquered cities in northern Italy. Among these were the Veronese parchments. Though Milan was at war with Florence, Salutati was able to get a copy of Cicero's letters. He had not lost touch even with his enemy, for these were the happy centuries before the savage efficiency of total war was conceived of. As a rule, military action did not imply the disruption

---

[2] John Edwin Sandys: *History of Classical Scholarship* (Cambridge: Cambridge University Press; 1908), Vol. II, p. 15.

[3] Symonds: op. cit., p. 76.

of cultural relations. Renaissance princes and generals would have endorsed Louis XIV, who is supposed to have said, in a similar situation: "We are at war with England but not with humanity."

When Salutati began leafing through the manuscript, he could not believe his eyes. None of the letters resembled those he had seen previously. They were not directed to Quintus, Atticus, or Brutus. Was somebody playing a trick on him? Further inquiries cleared up the puzzle. Gian Galeazzo had sent him transcripts not of the Verona codex but of another one, "annexed" from the town of Vercelli. And this had not even been known to exist! The Vercelli manuscript contained an additional, hitherto unheard of collection of letters, the *Ad Familiares*. Salutati was as elated as Petrarch had been over his discovery of Cicero's letters, and as grateful. He called the manuscript a "gift from Heaven." To read it was ecstasy, he confessed, beyond anything he had thought he could ever feel. It afforded still deeper insight into the great Roman's personality![4] Yet, Salutati yearned for the remaining

An Italian classroom of the fifteenth century. Perothus: *Regulae Sypontinae* (Venice, 1492–93)

Veronese letters—for which he had to wait for years. Then at long last he became the proud owner of both collections of Cicero's correspondence.[5]

Salutati instigated a number of other recoveries as well, among them the elder Cato's essay *On Agriculture*. This Latin text

---

[4] Georg Voigt: op. cit., p. 208.   [5] Ibid.

was based on a Carthaginian treatise, the only work the Romans chose to preserve from an entire national literature when they ruthlessly vanquished their African rivals in 148 B.C. In true Humanist tradition, Salutati was not merely a collector but also a critic and a philologist. He proved, for example, that an essay (*De differentia*) once ascribed to Cicero was spurious. And he was the principal agent in bringing to Florence Chrysoloras, the Byzantine Greek scholar, whose labor of teaching in Italy is considered of far-reaching importance in the classical revival. Salutati's accomplishments were thus crowned by his selfless patronage of Greek studies. It was also due to his personal intervention that young Florentine Humanists (like himself, most were not of Florentine birth) received decisive encouragement and reward—foremost among them, Lionardo Bruni and Poggio Bracciolini, both of whom sat at the feet of Chrysoloras and were one day to occupy the chancellorship of Florence.

After Salutati, manuscript hunting reached a high-water mark. Excitement rose to a peak at the renewed contact with a free, rational humanity from which, so it was alleged, medieval bigotry and scholastic dogmatism had shut themselves off. Our story would be incomplete without a brief reminder of the exuberant temper in which the recovery of manuscripts was carried on. Drama was not lacking, nor a touch of braggadocio. The joys of discovery were colored by the expansive outlook of the Renaissance, so much akin to that of the navigators sailing into uncharted seas. The manuscript hunters who reclaimed sunken or lost continents of human expression, on expeditions ranging from Spain to Scandinavia and into the Near East, might be considered the true predecessors of da Gama, Columbus, Amerigo, and Cabot—just as Humanist studies helped to prepare the mariners intellectually. We should not forget that both Columbus and Copernicus, in their reliance on classical texts, were Humanists.

All over the Italian peninsula, not only men of letters, but townsmen, tyrants, churchmen, and princes were electrified by the success of the bookhunters. "The acquisition of a province could not have given so much satisfaction as the discovery of an author little known, or not known at all."[6] To restore a treatise by Cicero or Quintilian was a feat second only to having written it. The Florentine Humanist Lionardo Bruni, on receiving from Poggio Brac-

---

[6] Isaac D'Israeli: *Curiosities of Literature* (New York: Widdleton; 1865), Vol. I, p. 69.

ciolini news of a recently discovered manuscript, dashed off a congratulatory note that rose to the occasion: "The republic of letters has reason to rejoice not only in the works you have discovered, but also in those you have still to find. What a glory for you it is to have brought to light by your exertions the writings of the most distinguished authors! Posterity will not forget that manuscripts which were bewailed as lost beyond the possibility of restoration, have been recovered, thanks to you. As Camillus was called the second founder of Rome, so you may receive the title of the second author of the works you have restored to the world. Through you we now possess Quintilian entire; before we only boasted of half of him, and that defective and corrupt in text. O precious acquisition! O unexpected joy! And shall I, then, in truth be able to read the whole of that Quintilian which, mutilated and deformed as it has hitherto appeared, has formed my solace? I conjure you send it me at once, that at last I may set eyes on it before I die."[7]

A true pioneering spirit fired this passion, and men were ever ready to make sacrifices to increase human knowledge and to rescue as much as possible at any price. Giovanni Aurispa, a Sicilian manuscript hunter, remembers "having given up my clothes to the Greeks in Constantinople in order to get codices—something for which I feel neither shame nor regret!"[8] And Niccolò de' Niccoli of Florence, who became a kind of director general and central agent for manuscript hunters in the field, sold his farms to finance additions to his collection. He ran into further debt, however, and in return for assistance, Cosimo de' Medici reserved the right to take most of Niccoli's books after his death.

At the slightest hint of a potential find, the Humanist bookman of the times would take off, although, more often than not, it was on a blind lead. Aged Petrarch, on hearing that Leontius Pilatus had been killed on his return voyage from Constantinople, rushed to the port to search the dead man's belongings, but his hopes of finding a Euripides or a Sophocles were unrealized.[9]

The scholars were sometimes joined by condottieri, dukes, cardinals, and merchant-capitalists who would sponsor and finance exploration, though, to Poggio's disgust, they were, like most philanthropists, fickle in their help. Europe was combed for trophies

---

[7] Symonds: op. cit., p. 100.
[8] Alfred Hessel: *A History of Libraries* (New Brunswick, N.J.: The Scarecrow Press; 1955), p. 41.
[9] Edward Gibbon: *The History of the Decline and Fall of the Roman Empire*, J. B. Bury, ed., ninth edition (London: Methuen & Co.; 1932), Vol. VII, p. 120.

of the classical muses. Popes Nicholas V and Leo X sent special agents across the Mediterranean to Syria and Asia Minor, and north as far as Sweden and Denmark. Poggio Bracciolini braved the elements, crossed snowbound passes, and ascended mountains

Profile of a scholar. Paoli Attavanti: *Breviarum totius juris canonici* (Milan, 1497)

to browse in the decrepit library of a remote Alpine monastery. Of him a contemporary (Francesco Barbaro) has said: "No severity of winter cold, no snow, no length of journey, no roughness of roads, prevented him from bringing the monuments of literature to light."[1]

---

[1] Symonds: op. cit., p. 100.

·III·

THE PASSIONATE

BOOKHUNTER:

POGGIO BRACCIOLINI

These pioneers, when they ransacked libraries for manuscripts, felt as if they were liberating the master-spirits of old from captivity.

SIR RICHARD C. JEBB[1]

IN ONE OF THE Renaissance tales of the nineteenth-century Swiss writer Conrad Ferdinand Meyer, "Plautus in the Nunnery," Poggio Bracciolini gets himself into some ticklish situations while extricating twelve comedies of Plautus from a convent in Switzerland's Appenzell. The piquant episode in the nunnery has little basis in fact, though Poggio was at least indirectly involved in reclaiming lost plays of the Roman dramatist. However, Meyer's version of the exploits reflects Poggio's legendary fame as knight-errant book sleuth.

Poggio Bracciolini (1380–1459), the poor boy from the little town of Terranuova near Arezzo, epitomizes the Humanist type of manuscript hunter. As an underpaid scribe in Florence, Poggio caught the eye of Salutati, and before long was deep in the New Learning. While still in his early twenties, he rose to prominence in the papal curia, where he excelled in the composition of apostolic letters—which did not keep him from sharply criticizing abuses

---

[1] Richard C. Jebb: op. cit., p. 553.

of the Church. In 1414 he was made papal secretary, and for nearly half a century he served Rome. Then, when he was over seventy, he was named, like Salutati before him, to the post of chancellor of Florence. His reputation was constantly enhanced as he grew into one of the age's most prolific and combative men of letters. He wrote a more polished Latin than either Petrarch or Salutati, and only Niccoli was his equal when it came to deciphering difficult Latin scripts. He advanced beyond Boccaccio in mastering Greek and contributed a number of translations. Poggio's own literary productions, as well as his mode of life, have a modern, even a profligate ring, though he was by no means the unabashed epicurean he is often portrayed to have been.

There is the episode of his attempt to copy an ancient stone inscription in the outskirts of Rome while engaged in conversation with some of the female passersby. Niccoli was forever hinting that Poggio was too attentive to the fair sex, so Poggio hastened to assure him that at least in this case the initiative had not been his. The beauteous women of Rome were amused at seeing a gentleman, in the summer heat, clearing a stone of ivy; and chivalry bade him enlighten them.[2] This incident, by the way, shows Poggio as an archaeologist and epigrapher. He pioneered the charting of the antiquities of Rome—Gibbon acknowledges his debt to Poggio's survey—and made many field trips in the Roman Campagna for this purpose. He collected ancient coins and statues too. Typically, when he took Frontinus' work on Roman aqueducts from Monte Cassino in 1429, he also carried away a fragment of a statue—a female torso—which had just been excavated near the monastery.[3]

Like other Humanists, Poggio had his morose moments and sometimes lapsed into a "medieval" disdain for life. But such seizures were relatively brief and did not keep him from taking to wife, in his old age, an eighteen-year-old Florentine girl of gentle birth and raising eight sons. As Symonds points out, he was no mere bookworm but a man "whose eyes and mind were open to the world around him."[4]

Poggio earned his spurs as a manuscript hunter on a visit with Lionardo Bruni to Monte Cassino in 1407. Here he extricated a

---

[2] Ernst Walser: *Poggius Florentinus, Leben und Werke* (Leipzig: B. G. Teubner; 1914), p. 142.
[3] Ibid., p. 143.
[4] Symonds: op. cit., p. 167.

fragment from Livy, *ex vetustissima scriptura* ("from a very ancient script").[5] Livy and Monte Cassino mark both the beginning of his quest and the end, for his last active campaign took him once more to the ancient monastery. To recover the lost books of Livy's *History* always remained an obsession with him. Poggio traveled all over Italy, crisscrossed France, Germany, and Switzerland, and resided

Renaissance scribe. Francesco Colonna:
Hypnertomachia Polyphili

for nearly five years in England. Under his guidance, the systematic search for manuscripts was extended beyond the Alps, and the yield was prodigious. But it was during the Council of Constance that Poggio's discoveries reached their peak.

Constance, an old German Imperial city on the lake of the same name near the present Swiss border, had been chosen as the site of a Church Council to settle the Great Schism, confirm a new Pope, introduce reforms, and stamp out the heresies of the Hussites in Bohemia. The picturesque town was soon filled with people from all Christendom. Across the crowded stage passed popes, antipopes, cardinals, an emperor, princes, and an army of aides, as well as heretics, mountebanks, and courtesans. Not unexpectedly, it was hard to reach any agreement. The international congress procrastinated.

Poggio had been dispatched to Constance in 1414 as secretary to John XXIII shortly to be deposed by the Council. Despite his

[5] Clark: op. cit., p. 225.

status, Poggio did not seem to be unduly perturbed by the issues at stake. But he enjoyed the spectacle, which he could watch with ease in an official capacity that barely taxed his energies. The gathering broadened his horizons. Moreover, a number of scholars were there too, foremost among them the great Chrysoloras, his teacher. Unfortunately, however, he died suddenly, and was buried in a local church. There were many Italian scholars, and not a few cardinals, most of them attached to an ecclesiastical delegation or in Constance simply for the fun of it. Several had studied with Poggio in Florence.

Seal of medieval Constance, 1254

The Italians were not a little surprised to find among the foreigners men of considerable culture. The contact and exchange between men of learning from different lands was of incalculable importance,[6] for one of the Council's most significant achievements was the spread of the seeds of Humanism across Western Christendom. Before Poggio and his fellow Humanists crossed the Alps, they had given little thought to the "barbarian" lands as having ever had much knowledge of ancient literature. But the closeness of Constance to several renowned Benedictine monasteries and discussions with non-Italian churchmen soon opened their eyes. Was it possible that transalpine monasteries housed ancient masterpieces no longer available in Italy herself?

Poggio decided to find out for himself. During the Council he undertook four trips out of Constance. He was by no means the only explorer in the field, but he was perhaps the one best prepared, considering his vast knowledge of classical literature. His previous studies enabled him to detect more manuscripts and to decipher them; he knew what to look for. Manuscripts he could not take along he copied quickly and expertly. At times he employed his own

---

[6] Voigt: op. cit., p. 234.

copyist at Constance.[7] In addition, he kept in constant touch with his friends in Florence and elsewhere in Italy. They assisted him in many ways and liberally dispensed that stimulus which any Humanist worth his salt needed most: encouragement and adulation.

Poggio himself was an ideal traveler who could cover much ground despite the enormous transportation difficulties of the age. In a matter of importance, he was immune to discomforts, and tolerant of foreign ways. He would pick up all kinds of information and impressions, and wrote delightful letters home about his experiences in the strange lands across the Alps. There are no livelier Renaissance documents than Poggio's letters from Constance. Justly famous is the letter on the trial and heroic death of Jerome of Prague, a Hussite, whose Socratic self-defense and fortitude Poggio, though a papal emissary, truly admired. In a lighter vein is the long epistle on his visit to the thermal springs of Baden, the Swiss spa near Zurich, where he found guests of both sexes bathing and frolicking together.

Fortunately for Poggio, the Council adjourned from time to time. While the Apostolic See remained vacant, from May 1415 to November 1417, Poggio's services as secretary to the Pope were not required and he was free to do as he pleased. The first book-hunting trip, perhaps originally undertaken on behalf of John XXIII's lost cause, brought him to the once proud Cluny in French Burgundy, several days' journey away from Constance. Possibly Poggio turned to Cluny on the advice of French colleagues at the Council. There, in 1415, he found an old manuscript of five speeches of Cicero's. Two of these—*pro Murena* and *pro Sexto Roscio*—had been entirely unknown in Italy. The monks let him take the codex along, though it was dismally dilapidated. Poggio dispatched it promptly to Niccoli, who with his fellow Humanists received it jubilantly but had considerable trouble reading and transcribing the ancient hand. Their difficulties sprang not only from the spelling and the script—and from the tattered state of the codex—but from the fact that old manuscripts rarely indicated divisions of words and sentences. Nevertheless, the speeches were speedily copied in Florence that same year and began to circulate in Italy.[8]

---

[7] Ibid., p. 235.

[8] Curt S. Gutkind: "Poggio Bracciolinis geistige Entwicklung," *Die Vierteljahrsschrift für Literaturwissenschaft und Geistesgeschichte,* Vol. X (1932), p. 568. See also Walser: op. cit., p. 49.

The following summer, Poggio made his way to St. Gall, accompanied by several Italian friends. The abbey of St. Gall, founded by Irish monks in the seventh century, was not far from Constance. In Poggio's time St. Gall enjoyed considerable prestige, and its abbots were ruling princes of the Holy Roman Empire. But their power was mainly political. A thirteenth-century abbot with the commanding name of Rumo von Ramstein could not even read or write[9]—a considerable difference from the early Middle Ages, when the abbey was one of the liveliest intellectual centers of the German world and counted several renowned authors among its brethren. The abbots then had taken pride in their library and added to it constantly; a few relics from these better days had been preserved. The situation, then, was comparable to that at Monte Cassino, except that Poggio and his companions, unlike Boccaccio, left accounts of their finds. They minced no words about what they saw at St. Gall. One of them, Agapito Cenci, said that they all cried at the sameful spectacle, and he added for good measure a curse on the German barbarians.[1] Poggio's own letter is a mixture of sober reportage and Humanist pathos.

"The monastery of S. Gallen," he wrote to his friend Guarino, another prominent Florentine Humanist, "lies at the distance of some twenty miles from that city [Constance]. Thither, then, partly for the sake of amusement and partly of finding books, whereof we heard there was a large collection in the convent, we directed our steps. In the middle of a well-stocked library, too large to catalogue at present, we discovered Quintilian, safe as yet and sound, though covered with dust and filthy with neglect and age. The books, you must know, were not housed according to their worth, but were lying in a most foul and obscure dungeon at the very bottom of a tower, a place into which condemned criminals would hardly have been thrust; and I am firmly persuaded that if anyone would but explore those *ergastula* [dungeons] of the barbarians wherein they incarcerate such men, we should meet with like good fortune in the case of many whose funeral orations have long ago been pronounced. . . ."[2]

Italian Humanists often referred to the northerners as barbarians, though there is no indication that the manuscripts retained on the Italian peninsula fared much better. But it suited the chau-

---

[9] James Westfall Thompson, et al.: *The Medieval Libraries* (Chicago: Chicago University Press; 1939), p. 196.

[1] Voigt: op. cit., p. 237.

[2] Symonds: op. cit., p. 99.

vinism of the Italian Renaissance to underline the barbarian dis-
respect for ancient learning. By stamping the transalpine creatures
as aliens to the classical legacy and desecrators of it, the Italians
assumed full right to take back to their own country what had
never belonged to the uncouth foreigners in the first place.

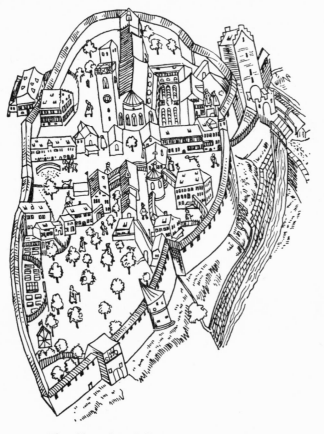

The abbey of St. Gall. A late medieval sketch

Poggio, though not as crude as Cenci, was no exception in
this respect. However, with the Humanists it is always difficult to
tell where rhetoric ends and sincerity begins. Poggio's description
of his prize find, the Quintilian, probably owes more to the former.
Thus, in the anthropomorphic vein dear to Petrarch, he refers to
the "martyred" manuscript he has saved: "I verily believe that, if
we had not come to the rescue, he [Quintilian] must speedily have
perished; for it cannot be imagined that a man magnificent, polished, elegant, urbane, and witty could much longer have endured

the squalor of the prison-house in which I found him, the savagery of his jailers, the forlorn filth of the place. He was indeed right sad to look upon, and ragged, like a condemned criminal, with rough beard and matted hair, protesting by his countenance and garb against the injustice of his sentence. He seemed to be stretching out his hands, calling upon the Romans [i.e., Italians], demanding to be saved from so unmerited a doom. . . ."[3]

Poggio goes on in his letter to mention that he and his friends also exhumed the first three and a half books of the *Argonautica,* an epic poem by Valerius Flaccus, and the valuable *Commentaries* of Asconius Pedianus on various orations of Cicero. Poggio's copy of the *Commentaries* is the only surviving "archetype," since the St. Gall manuscript itself no longer exists. However, at the time, the Quintilian excited the greatest interest in Italy and was, as we have seen, ecstatically hailed by fellow Humanists. Salutati and others had vainly searched for it. One Humanist, Gasparino da Barzizza, had even undertaken to reconstruct the pieces missing from Petrarch's fragmented copy.[4]

Petrarch had found the first known codex, which was badly torn and contained barely half the treatise. In his posthumous Letter to Quintilian he described the "dismembered letters of a beautiful body," and the "admiration mingled with grief" which seized him when he unearthed it. Prophetically, he added: "Even at this moment, indeed, thy work may be resting intact in someone's library, and, what is worse, with one who perhaps has not the slightest idea of what a guest he is harboring unawares. Whosoever more fortunate than I will discover thee, may he be sure that he has gained a work of great value, one which, if he be at all wise, he will consider among his chief treasures."[5]

Bias against the "barbarians," however, did not prevent Poggio from remaining on good terms with St. Gall. One of Poggio's amiable traits was that he shunned diplomatic subtleties or subterfuges. He made no attempt to abscond with the precious manuscript. Instead he obtained the abbot's permission to borrow it, in addition to other texts, to have them copied at Constance. And he seems to have returned them promptly. Otherwise, he would hardly have been able to undertake further visits to the abbey library.

---

[3] Ibid., pp. 98–9.
[4] Voigt: op. cit., p. 236.
[5] M. E. Cosenza, tr.: *Petrarch's Letters to Classical Authors* (Chicago: Chicago University Press; 1910), p. 84.

At the same time, Poggio was casting about for new sources of literary treasures. Again his attention was directed to the Swabian and Swiss monasteries (Reichenau and Weingarten?) within reasonable proximity of Constance. And after New Year's, 1417, despite the winter snow, he was on his way. Besides visiting St. Gall, he paid calls on several unidentified monasteries. Like Petrarch before him, he was stimulated by the mere sight of a monastery: as yet unseen manuscripts sprang before his eyes. One such monastery was an *erimitarium in visceribus Alpinum* ("a hermitage in the entrails of the Alps"), which might have been Einsiedeln. Others on his itinerary could only be reached, as he wrote, "after crossing rocks and crevices, mountain brooks and forests."[6]

Excerpt from Niccolò Niccoli's handwritten copy (now at the Biblioteca Nazionale, Florence) of a work by Ammianus Marcellinus, a Roman historian, which was found by Poggio in a transalpine monastery. The cursive strokes reflect the zest and dispatch with which recovered texts were transcribed by Florentine Humanists—factors which may have helped to forge the new "Italic" writing style.

This trip was as gratifying as the previous ones and yielded far more uncommon finds. But it is impossible to say what came from St. Gall, what from the other convents. There was the didactic poem *On the Nature of Things* by Lucretius—expounding Epicurus' philosophy—which had sunk so far into oblivion that it had ceased to be the object of any search. Yet it had been highly regarded in antiquity. Some moderns, following Cicero, consider it of greater poetic merit than Vergil's *Aeneid*. Also found were the works of Ammianus Marcellinus, last of Rome's outstanding his-

---

[6] Walser: op. cit., p. 55.

torians, who, in the words of Gibbon, was "without the prejudices and passions which usually affect the mind of a contemporary";[7] and the longest Latin poem, Silius Italicus' *Punica*, a valuable record of Rome's life and death struggle with Carthage.

No sooner had Poggio returned to Constance in the summer of 1417 than he embarked on his fourth transalpine venture. Lionardo Bruni, in the congratulatory letter concerning Quintilian, had begged him to keep his eyes out for Cicero above all. And now he was able to reclaim some of Cicero's lost works. This time his trip took him far from the Church Council, northward along the Rhine into Germany and France. How far he followed up tips or trusted his own instincts it is impossible to say. At a Cluniac monastery on the Marne, at Langres, he found a manuscript of six of Cicero's speeches under a waste pile.[8] One was the unknown *pro Caecina*. Shortly after, at Cologne in Germany, he made the discovery he was most proud of:[9] seven then entirely unknown orations by the venerated Roman.

Poggio, an experienced scribe, copied in 1428 Cicero's treatise *De oratore*, a Renaissance favorite, in a beautiful Roman book hand that consciously went back to earlier models.

At first Cologne proved a bitter disappointment. Poggio was barred from the ancient cathedral library which had been installed under Charlemagne. However, he managed to gain access to the affiliated *libreria nova*, and there he was amply compensated by the Cicero codex he found. The only sour note was that the manuscript allegedly had been copied by nuns, and Poggio and his Florentine associates credited them with the occasional confusion and

---

[7] "Ammianus Marcellinus," *The Oxford Classical Dictionary* (Oxford: Clarendon Press; 1949), p. 43.

[8] Voigt: op. cit., p. 243.

[9] Walser: op. cit., p. 58.

illegibility of the text. As is so often the case with Renaissance finds, the manuscript which the Humanists had originally located and transcribed has since vanished, and it is through Poggio's copy that three of the speeches have come down to us. One of the three, the *Oratio in L. Pisonem* (against Caesar's father-in-law Lucius Calpurnius Piso) was to serve as a key to manuscript discoveries made some three hundred years after Poggio's visit to Cologne.

Somewhere on the way, Poggio picked up a curious collection of Latin inscriptions from Rome—many, as he realized, copies of inscriptions long vanished—and, in addition, an eighth-century map of the Eternal City. It so excited his antiquarian's palate that Poggio, who liked to wear priestly garments though he had not taken even minor orders, let it slip into the hospitable long sleeves of his ecclesiastic tunic.

When the Church Council at last ended the schism by electing Martin V, Constance lapsed back into insignificance. Poggio had hoped for preferment from the new Pope, but this failed to materialize and he ill-advisedly accepted an invitation to go to England as the guest of the mighty Duke of Beaufort, John of Gaunt's ambitious son, whom he had met at the Council. That visit was to mark the most miserable period of his life. His patron treated him haughtily and with negligence. He loathed the climate and the people. The English, he thought, were little interested in Humanist culture and much given to gluttony. His cheerfulness deserted him, and he took refuge in reading the Church Fathers. Still, he shrewdly observed the social mobility of the country, where the aristocracy was constantly renewed by influx from the lower classes. Occasionally he carried out reconnaissances in search of manuscripts, and it was thus that he must have come upon a fragment from Petronius.

Once he had left England, Poggio's natural curiosity and liveliness returned. True, he now painted the pursuit of manuscripts as a costly, time-consuming enterprise, far beyond the means of a footloose scholar. But he was not unemployed for very long. Soon he was back in the saddle in Rome.

On his return trip to Italy, Poggio made some new acquisitions in Paris and Cologne. It was probably in Cologne that he obtained the major fragment of Petronius' satirical novel, which he lent to a friend, who kept it for years. The fragment describing Trimalchio's famous banquet, presumably found in England, seems to have been stolen and was lost sight of until a transcription of it was discovered in a Croatian monastery in the mid-seventeenth century.[1] So thin were the threads on which hung the survival of precious classical works, even in an age that appreciated them.

At this point it may be well to touch briefly on the occasional attempts of historians to deride the importance of the contributions of Poggio and others in rescuing manuscripts. The value of the works rescued is belittled, and it is usually argued that the manu-

Cologne, Woodcut from *Fasciculus Temporum* (Cologne, 1474)

scripts—themselves copied in the Middle Ages—were always partially known and never really lost. Hence it was absurd to say that they had to be "discovered." There is some truth to this: the tendency has been to call any manuscript not familiar to Renaissance Florence a discovery.[2] One cannot deny a note of exaggeration in the claims of these volatile Latins of the Renaissance, many of whom were immoderate, vainglorious, and arrogant. Their practice of overpraising their own efforts, their excess adulation for each other, their petty intrigues and rivalries show little of the classical dignity they claimed to admire. Nevertheless, the critics forget that many works came down in only one copy, that these rare codices were often disintegrating, and that it was due to their timely recovery that they survived at all. Manuscripts vanished constantly; many of the very manuscripts that the Humanists managed to track down and copy disappeared subsequently. Some books reported extant in the Middle Ages, or even in the Renaissance, did not survive into our times. Granted that the concept of "discovery" is fraught with semantic ambiguities, nevertheless, in the case of Tacitus, Lucretius, Petronius, and several of Cicero's treatises and speeches—all unknown to Petrarch—nothing short of "discovery"

---

[1] Albert C. Clark: "The Trau Manuscript of Petronius," *The Classical Review*, Vol. XXII (August 1908), pp. 178–79.
[2] Voigt: op. cit., p. 242.

would adequately describe the Humanist contribution in making them available once more.

Poggio's activities with regard to the manuscripts, directed from his headquarters at the papal curia, were now of a more sedentary kind. He sent out feelers to Trier (Trèves), Utrecht, and remote Portugal for other Cicero texts.[3] His dealings with visiting churchmen gave him a strategic advantage, for there were innumerable opportunities for him to use his influence on behalf of some foreign canon or prior if he in turn would be willing to show his appreciation by reporting on the manuscripts in the possession of his diocese, abbey, or convent. Most rewarding of all was Poggio's relationship with a German ecclesiastic, Nicolas of Trier (now believed to have been Nicholaus of Cusa or Cusanus, the illustrious philosopher and cardinal-to-be). In 1429 Nicolas sent a list of manuscripts so impressive that Poggio at once enlisted the help of a Roman cardinal, of the noble house of Orsini, to assure the success of the venture. The transaction took some time and not all the titles given by the German churchman could be verified, but the story had a happy ending with the appearance of a text of Plautus' comedies, twelve of which (C. F. Meyer was right in this detail) were entirely new. The only difficulty was caused by the cardinal, who claimed proprietary rights to the codex and refused to let anybody even look at it.

"I have not been able to get possession of Plautus," Poggio wrote bitterly to Niccoli. "Before the cardinal's departure, I begged him to send you the book, but he refused to comply with my request. I do not understand what the man means. He seems to think that he has done something great, though in fact he has not had the least part in the discovery of the book. It was found by another, but it is hidden by him. I told both him and his people, that I would never again ask him for the book, and I shall be as good as my word. I had rather unlearn what I have learnt, than acquire any knowledge by means of his books."[4]

Gentle pressure by the Medici at last persuaded the cardinal to release the manuscript temporarily to Niccoli in Florence for copying. Poggio was deprived of his reward, but he took it in stride.

Even more frustrating were Poggio's dealings with the so-

---

[3] Sandys: op. cit., p. 31.
[4] Rev. William Shepherd: *The Life of Poggio Bracciolini* (Liverpool: J. Cadell; 1802), p. 104.

called monk of Hersfeld, a German monastery near Fulda rumored to possess several shorter works of Tacitus, the *Agricola, Germania,* and *Dialogus.* Negotiations had begun in 1425 to get the monk to spirit the manuscripts off to Rome, but each time the monk came to Rome he was empty-handed. Each time he promised to do better on the next occasion. Then nothing more was heard from him. However, some thirty years later a Humanist pope, Nicholas V—himself once an obscure scribe like Poggio, named Tommaso Parentucelli—sent a special envoy to Hersfeld and obtained these great texts. They, too, were the only copies of these works we have ever known.

IλΜΤΙΒΙΙΙΙλΥϢλΕΙϚΝΟ
RΑΝΙΙλSλΕCΟΙλRISΒΟ
ΝλΟΓΙΝλΙϢROSΊΕΝϽλ⁻

A few lines from a famous Livy manuscript at Vienna. It was written in the fifth century in uncial letters (rounded majuscules).

In comparison to the Plautus and Tacitus episodes, Poggio's efforts on behalf of Livy, the Roman historian, were ill-starred, if not quixotic. The quest for the lost books of Livy had been nearly as persistent a theme of Italian Humanism as the hunt for lost works of Cicero. And Poggio, encouraged by other finds, hoped to do as well by Livy, who had been fairly popular in the Middle Ages (though it is uncertain how many of his 142 "books" were known). By Poggio's time only some thirty-five books were accessible. Petrarch and Salutati had made great efforts to find more of Livy's work, but failed. Poggio, however, had greater resources, and much more persistence. And rumors continued to reach his ears. First there was a man from Chartres. Then there was a Dane who appeared in Rome in 1424, solemnly declaring that he had seen three giant volumes of Livy's history at the Cistercian monastery of Soröe near Roskilde. He even gave detailed descriptions of the ancient script. Poggio got busy at once. Through Niccoli, he persuaded Cosimo de' Medici to dispatch his agent at Lübeck to the Danish monastery. But back came the report that no such books could be located.

Poggio became wary after this letdown, but the Livian phantom gave him no peace. News cropped up all the time. Like a stock-market speculator, he swore he would never be taken in again. But when another traveler from the north reported that he had seen all the "decades" of Livy in a Danish monastery, the skeptic caught fire once more—only to be disappointed anew. He bitterly denounced "the swindlers" and would hear no more talk of Livy. Still another northerner confirmed his compatriot's account, but Poggio called him a cheat outright. Yet the story persisted, perhaps nourished by the Humanists' desire that it be true. Finally, Pope Nicholas V again dispatched his agent northward.

Sketch after Donatello's statue of Poggio Bracciolini in the Duomo of Florence

By that time Poggio was back in Florence. Close to death, he wrote a Latin history of his adopted city, peppered with imaginary speeches of Ciceronian eloquence in the classical manner. When Poggio died, the Florentines commissioned a statue of him by Donatello to be placed outside the cathedral of Santa Maria del Fiore. Some hundred years later, during alterations, the statue was accidentally removed from its original site and placed inside the church among the Twelve Apostles. Visitors may still behold the sparse, agile figure, with its chiseled features, thus enshrined— resembling rather an ancient Roman writer or jurist than a devout disciple of Christ, Gian Francesco Poggio Bracciolini, manuscript hunter extraordinary.[5]

Poggio was not alone, but he is representative of the other Humanists whose discoveries followed his. After Poggio, there were fewer finds and they lacked the continuity that made a kind of relay race of the efforts of Petrarch, Boccaccio, Salutati, and Poggio.[6] Still, a number of contributions of the first order were to be made in the following century. In 1500 Fra Giocondo of Verona discovered in Paris the correspondence of Pliny the Younger with Trajan, which includes one of the earliest nonevangelical testimonies of Christianity. Then, in 1508, half a century after Poggio's death, and possibly as a result of one of his long-range negotiations in Germany, the first six books of Tacitus' *Annals* were brought to Italy under the auspices of Giovanni de' Medici, soon to be Leo X. Most surprising of all, in 1527, when the sack of the Holy City by the Imperial troops dealt a death blow to Italian Humanism, the German abbey of Lorsch at long last produced a few lost books of Livy: the first five (XLI–XLV) of the fifth decade.

With relatively few notable exceptions, the classics that were known by the second quarter of the sixteenth century—particularly in the field of Latin literature—are the classics we have today. Clearly, the losses far outweighed the survivals, to the sorrow of all. After 1527, only once in a while were there evidences of the passionate involvement of Humanism with lost classical manuscripts. In sheer volume nothing could compare with the discovery, in 1713, of the remains of the Verona library, where centuries earlier a Catullus had been located even before Petrarch appeared on the scene to call forth Cicero. In the eighteenth century, the Marquis Scipio Maffei was urged by friends to compile a guide book to Verona. He had not gone very far in his preliminary research when he became puzzled about the once famous cathedral library, presumably the site of Petrarch's finds and now completely vanished. Jean Mabillon, the French Benedictine scholar, had inquired in vain about the whereabouts of the library some fifty years earlier. Maffei was not satisfied with the explanations of its disappearance. Because of later evidence, it seemed unlikely that Gian Galeazzo or some other man of arms had removed it in its entirety in the early Renaissance. Nor was there any indica-

---

[5] Ibid., p. 458. (Walser; op. cit., p. 314, disputes the identity of the statue.)

[6] Sandys: op. cit., p. 35.

tion that it had been destroyed through war or catastrophe. Maffei would not rest until he had searched the darkest recesses of the cathedral buildings, and he had the help of the aged canon Carinelli.

On an October day in 1713, Carinelli summoned Maffei to the cathedral, and there, in one of the adjuncts used as administrative quarters, he directed Maffei to a cabinet filled with chancery papers. Carinelli had noticed that this closet contained a high compartment that abutted the ceiling. Maffei now climbed up to it and beheld an exciting sight: an enormous pile of ancient manuscripts. How these got there, no one could tell. It is possible that they were placed in the cabinet for safety at a time of impending floods, and consequent outbreaks of the plague, deaths, and the passing of time obliterated all memory of this treasure.[7]

A

IISIATVAQVIDIOSITIAVMSIADIAOLLIACOGL
BISIAMITALOSHOSLISHIAECAIIERAAIOIDIAA

a

Epircopimanuminnocentei
guamnonadfulriloguumcoc
nactionemanteriorirtenenti

b

nifquiaudicuerbumregni ecnonimcellage
uenicmalui e crapicquod fominacumefc
incordeeiuf hicefequifcaufuiamfominaauf
efc quiautemfuperpecrofafeminacuufofc
hicefequiuerbumaudic eccoranuocum

c

Scnoxeft de quar fchptrumeft, Err
noxuar dief illuminabitur.

d.

Samples of Latin scripts (A): *a*) from fifth-century Vergil manuscript (Codex Palatinus) in rustic (slightly rounded) capital letters showing debt to lettering of stone inscriptions; *b*) early-sixth-century "half uncial" script with incipient minuscule characters, perhaps introduced from grafitti and nonliterary papyri; *c*) selection from Alcuin Bible in graceful Carolingian minuscules of the ninth century; *d*) a twelfth-century text in stylish "Lombardic" book hand developed in Italy

---

[7] Thompson: op. cit., pp. 152–4. See also Ludwig Traube: *Vorlesungen und Abhandlungen* (Munich: C. H. Beck; 1909), Vol. I, p. 44.

The "library," upon examination, did not appear to contain any notable lost masterpieces, but it furnished abundant specimens of Latin script in an almost unbroken time sequence going back to Theodoric (474–526)—the barbarian king who resided at Verona—several years before Monte Cassino was founded. To Maffei these manuscripts suggested the beginning of a virtually

B

Samples of Latin scripts (B) of increasingly cursive, and illegible, hands used in charters, bulls, etc.: (*a*) Merovingian diplomatic document, seventh century; (*b*) Bull of Pope John VIII, A.D. 876, in round, bold strokes derived from the official Roman hand; (*c*) minuscule papyrus from Ravenna, A.D. 572

new science, palaeography. The evidence clearly indicated that there was no such thing as distinct types of Latin scripts separately designed and introduced, but one chain of development with imperceptible transitions. This was a novel thesis and in the history of ideas it may well rank as one of the earliest evolutionary approaches to science. In completeness and orderliness, none of the data submitted by later historians, sociologists, naturalists, or archaeologists surpassed this continuous series.

The titles of the manuscripts found by Carinelli and Maffei are not known, since unfortunately they failed to catalogue them and in later days the books were incorporated with those of the parish library. It is impossible to tell, therefore, whether another noted find was part of Maffei's treasure—although the likelihood is that it was. In 1816 B. G. Niebuhr, the Danish-German historian, discovered the fourth book of the *Institutes* by the Roman jurist Gaius. The manuscript was a palimpsest—that is, written over earlier, effaced text and rendered legible through various, not always well advised treatments, which have earned it the epithet of "illustrious martyr of palaeography." The restoration of the Gaius parchments was all the more interesting because it was not supposed to have survived. Tradition had it that Justinian had ordered the destruction of all sources for his legal code—the Gaius work among them. Gibbon had denied this and now he was vindicated.[8]

NLIMINME
SAMPOSSESSI·
qUAMESIHK
fORIUNATY
PUTANÒLIS
CLIJSOLUERE
LICEATOMNI·

From Cicero's long-lost political work, *De republica* (Cod. Vat. 5757). The fourth- or fifth-century copy was discovered at the beginning of last century by the Italian bibliographer and Vatican librarian Angelo Cardinal Mai in a palimpsest under St. Augustine's work on the Psalms, which was from the seventh century.

Palimpsests for a while constituted the greater part of the additions to the list of known classics, for the earlier texts on "twice-written" manuscript pages were often ancient works that could be made visible. Particularly in the beginning of the nineteenth century, a number of recoveries were made in this manner. Angelo Cardinal Mai and his followers, for example, rescued large sections of Cicero's lengthy political treatise *De republica*, which

---

[8] Thompson: op. cit., p. 148. See also "Gaius," *The Oxford Classical Dictionary*, pp. 375–6.

Petrarch and Salutati had long sought. Yet, except for a few other lesser finds (including fragments from Livy), the anticipated flood of literary resurrections from this source did not materialize. All in all, European ecclesiastic libraries failed to add significantly to the classical texts unearthed in the Renaissance. Was it conceivable that there were still "paths untrodden" by the restless manuscript hunters of the Humanist springtime?

So far, in this Renaissance prelude to the modern discovery of lost books, we have chiefly discussed the Latin classics. Before we move on, a brief supplementary note on Greek authors is called for.

Their "recovery" was begun at about the same time and was inspired by the same Humanist movement. In its interest in Greek texts, the Renaissance clearly distinguished itself from any previous medieval classical revival. Nevertheless, the earliest Humanists had only a vague knowledge of Greek literature and its greatness, not to mention the language itself. Petrarch was convinced that the Greeks were secondary to the best of the Roman authors. Both he and Boccaccio denied categorically that Plato could ever have banished Homer from his ideal state. Their negligible knowledge of Plato was matched by their inability to check original sources.

With the Greek classics the Humanists had to start from scratch. Next to nothing had been copied, studied, or preserved in the West during the Middle Ages, with the exception of Aristotle (who was brought in largely by the Arabs in the twelfth century, and then in fragments), Plato's *Timaios* (greatly mutilated), the fables of Aesop, an occasional work of Ptolemy, some medical treatises, and the Eastern Church Fathers. True, a few men in the Middle Ages studied Greek, but they did not establish a tradition. As a rule, even learned men were at a loss when they came across Greek quotations and scribes simply substituted for them the standard formula: *Graeca sunt, ergo non legenda* (they are Greek and therefore incomprehensible).

Under these conditions, Greek language and literature had to come into Western Europe as an alien import. With a profounder study of the Latin classics, scholars—starting with Petrarch and Boccaccio—began to thirst for the Greek roots and models. The coming of Chrysoloras was the turning point. It was then that Lionardo Bruni, with true Renaissance enthusiasm, wrote: "The knowledge of Greek was revived, after an interval of seven cen-

turies. Chrysoloras of Byzantium . . . brought us Greek learning.
. . . I gave myself to his teaching with such ardor, that my dreams
at night were filled with what I had learned from him by day."⁹
The Humanists of the West embarked on a love affair with the
Greek language, of which Gibbon once remarked that "it gives a
soul to the objects of sense and a body to the abstractions of philosophy."¹ Cultivation of Greek led to a full-scale traffic in Greek
texts. Chrysoloras was among the first to bring in important works.

Socrates. After a Roman mosaic at Cologne

Many of the Greek books were fairly easy to procure in
Constantinople, on the Greek or Asia Minor mainland, and in the
islands, since the Greek language—corrupted, but closer to the
ancient idiom than Tuscan was to Latin—was still spoken. Besides,
Byzantium too had undergone a revival of learning. But again,
only a fraction of the ancient texts had survived, and some of the
books existed only in single copies. To what extent the acquisitions of the Humanists were actually discoveries rather than
more or less routine purchases, however, it is now almost impossible to say. Hence the difficulty of assessing the achievements
of such men as Guarino da Verona or Francesco Filelfo, contemporaries of Poggio, who went to Constantinople to study Greek
and returned laden with manuscripts unknown at least in Italy.
Guarino's hair was said to have turned white when a part of his
shipment of Greek books was swallowed by the sea.²

Giovanni Aurispa, a Sicilian and no stranger to the search
for Latin manuscripts, is credited with having done for the Greek

---

⁹ Jebb: op. cit., p. 542.   ¹ Gibbon: op. cit., Vol. VI, p. 116.
² Symonds: op. cit., p. 102.

classics what Poggio did for the Latin. From Constantinople he sent Niccoli the famous Medici Codex—now at the Laurentian Library of Florence—which contained six tragedies of Aeschylus, seven tragedies of Sophocles, and the *Argonautica* by Apollonius Rhodius. The beautifully written manuscript has become the sole surviving archetype for two of Aeschylus' dramas,[3] and a reliable authority for the plays included in it. The Byzantine Emperor Manuel II is reported to have regaled Aurispa with various rare codices, but Aurispa was also accused by the Byzantines of "having robbed them of holy books."[4] When Aurispa returned from Constantinople in 1423, he brought with him crates containing

From a Greek manuscript of Demosthenes at Florence. Early eleventh century

238 books—which amounted, in the words of Voigt, to the "transplantation of an entire literature to a new and fertile soil."[5] However, unlike Poggio, Aurispa was much more a trader than a collector and seems to have undertaken his operations primarily for profit. He did not care to retain any of the manuscripts for his own delectation. His dealings were at best obscure; a Greek ambassador to Florence called him a crook outright. Poggio undoubtedly has a far better claim to have rescued works that might otherwise have perished. Few of the books brought in by Aurispa were as rare.

It has been counted one of the supreme good fortunes of civilization that Italy was able to absorb the bulk of the Greek legacy before the fall of Constantinople and all of Greece to the Turks. "What had not previously been rescued," declared Voigt, "has perished almost without exception under the banner of the

---

[3] Édouard Tièche: "Die Wiederentdeckung der antiken Bücher im Zeitalter der Renaissance," *Bibliothek der schweizerischen Bibliophilen*, Ser. II, Heft 7 (Berne, 1936), p. 13.

[4] Voigt: op. cit., p. 264.

[5] Ibid.

Crescent."[6] Yet, Ottoman Constantinople in the fifteenth century was no doubt more cultured than most of Western Europe; and its treasure of Greek works probably continued to outshine that of Italy for some time.[7] Throughout the period of Turkish rule and into our own age, Greek monasteries have preserved countless precious manuscripts.

Although the Aurispas and Filelfos of their day may have been neither discoverers nor rescuers of the Greek classics, their contribution is invaluable, for they made these works available to the West when it was most receptive, and thereby immeasurably broadened the classical basis of Humanism. In time, Greek literature became fully acclimated in Western Europe, and when Nicholas V launched his program to translate all Greek classics into Latin, Filelfo proclaimed: "Greece did not perish. It migrated to Italy, the country which since ancient times bore the name 'Magna Graecia.' "[8] Thus, just as Greek literature was losing ground in the East, it was becoming an object of study and investigation in the West, and it was the large-scale transfer of manuscripts that made the new flowering possible. From then on, the hope of expanding the dwindled legacy of Greece would never die out.

---

[6] Ibid., p. 266.
[7] R. R. Bolgar: *The Classical Heritage and Its Beneficiaries* (Cambridge: Cambridge University Press; 1954), p. 459.
[8] Tièche: op. cit., p. 16.

Book Two

THE PERMANENCE OF PAPYRUS AND CLAY

A: *Classics*

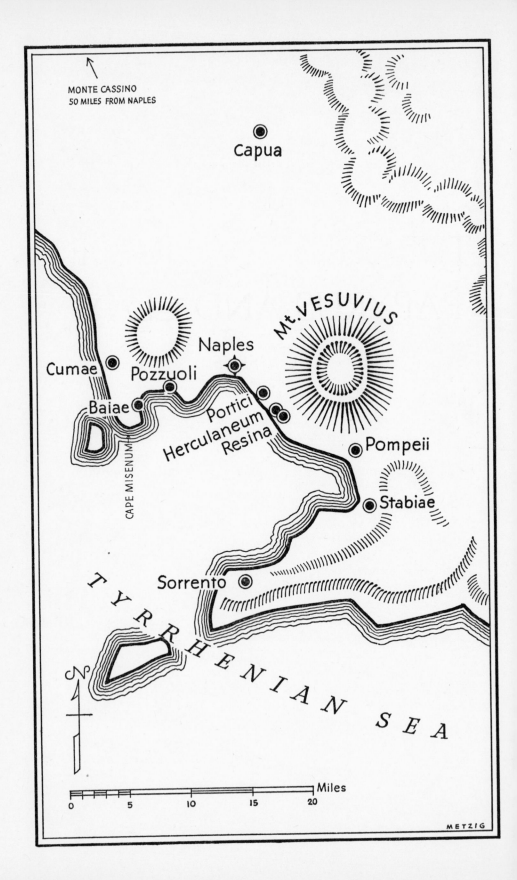

MONTE CASSINO
50 MILES FROM NAPLES

Capua

Mt. VESUVIUS

Naples

Cumae
Pozzuoli

Baiae
Portici
Herculaneum
Resina

Pompeii

Stabiae

CAPE MISENUM

Sorrento

T Y R R H E N I A N   S E A

N

Miles

0   5   10   15   20

METZIG

·IV·

ROLLS AND A VILLA

O ye, who patiently explore
The wreck of Herculanean lore
What rapture! could ye seize
Some Theban fragment, or unroll
One precious, tender-hearted, scroll
Of pure Simonides!
WILLIAM WORDSWORTH

IN DECEMBER 1754, the Royal Society of London published in its *Transactions* a letter from an Italian painter, Camillo Paderni, who was assisting in the excavations then being carried out on the fringes of the buried city of Herculaneum. "As yet we have only entered one room . . ." the correspondent wrote about the work in progress. "It appears to have been a library, adorned with presses, inlaid with different sorts of wood, disposed in rows, at the top of which were cornices, as in our own times. I was buried in this spot more than twelve days, to carry off the volumes found there, many of which were so perished, that it was impossible to remove them. Those which I took away amounted to the number of 337, all of them, at present, incapable of being opened. These all are written in Greek characters. . . ."[1]

The learned world thus received one of the first hints of a surprise find which opened entirely new prospects for the return of lost masterpieces. The news raised the pulse of lovers of the classics. Would Pindar speak to them through an unknown ode of his adored Olympian victors? Or a Sophocles unfold another of his tragedies in which man endured fate with steadfast nobility?

---

[1] Edward Edwards: *Memoirs of Libraries* (London: Trübner & Co.; 1859), Vol. I, p. 63.

Did Herculaneum shelter the lost books of Livy, the poems of Sappho?

Johann Joachim Winckelmann, the German art historian, who appeared on the scene four years later, expressed such thoughts when he speculated on the recovery of "ancient historians such as Diodorus, Theopompus and Ephorus; Aristotle's survey of the

Roman countryside. After a sketch at Eton

dramatic arts; the missing pieces of Sophocles, Euripides, Menander and Alexis; the rules of symmetry composed by Pamphylius for the use of painters."[2] Few manuscript discoveries ever caused as much suspense. And if Herculaneum did not quite fulfill the expectations it aroused, it did offer ample rewards.

Only an unusual combination of physical circumstances can account for the preservation of the papyri at Herculaneum. In the two hundred years since the striking of the Herculanean lode, no other site excavated in Italy has yielded papyri. Pompeii, much larger than Herculaneum, victim of the same holocaust, and far more extensively probed by archaeologists, has failed to produce a single shred of manuscript—only some wax tablets and inscriptions on lead. The reason lies in the different manner of their burial. Herculaneum was drowned by an avalanche of mud and mire, which quickly solidified, whereas Pompeii was covered by a much thinner and more porous layer of volcanic ashes and lapilli.

---

[2] Johann Joachim Winckelmann: *Critical Account of the Situation and Destruction by the First Eruptions of Mount Vesuvius, of Herculaneum, Pompeii, and Stabiae* ["Sendschreiben"] (London: n.p.; 1771), p. 116.

The rediscovery of Herculaneum had begun some forty years before Paderni's report, when a farmer in the little town of Resina on the Gulf of Naples deepened a dried-up well on his land and came upon marble structures. Marble blocks were then in demand by builders and sculptors, and word of this fine material reached an Austrian officer, the Prince d'Elbeuf, who was building a countryhouse for himself near adjacent Portici. But when he saw the pieces, d'Elbeuf quickly gave up the idea of using them for housing. Instead he bought the peasant's land and started excavating.[3]

A Pompeian mural depicting Mount Vesuvius before the fatal eruption in A.D. 79. The volcano was then considered extinct. Note vegetation (grapevines?) on slope.

As luck would have it, he immediately struck a large underground edifice, the Herculaneum theater, which was richly ornamented with columns, statues, and vases. Most of these objects he removed to his new house. But within a few years d'Elbeuf was recalled, and the excavation came to rest until the late 1730's, when the king of Naples, Charles III, who had acquired the Portici

---

[3] Marcel Brion: *Pompeii and Herculaneum* (New York: Crown Publishers; 1960), pp. 41–2.

mansion, launched a systematic campaign. This revealed the identity of the buried city from an inscription at the theater. Soon another, more extensive town nearby was uncovered: Pompeii.

The names of Herculaneum and Pompeii brought back the memory of those fatal August days of A.D. 79—vividly described in Pliny the Younger's letters to Tacitus—when the eruption of Mount Vesuvius abruptly cut off the cities' thread of life. Smothered and sealed by volcanic matter and soil-forming vegetation, they had been bypassed by history. For many centuries they were forgotten. But in violent death they suffered the paradoxical fate of being immortalized, their extinct civilization preserved for future ages. Actually, these towns were of comparatively little significance in their own time. Their greatest claim to historical status is, like that of the boy pharaoh of the Eighteenth Dynasty of Egypt, their extraordinary embalmment, which after more than sixteen hundred years was to bring back a spark of life from the Greco-Roman epoch to wonder-struck moderns.

The new discoveries had a profound impact on the eighteenth century. Just as the science of archaeology could be said to have made its proper beginning then, so popular excitement over archaeological discoveries was first aroused by the resurrection of Herculaneum and Pompeii. The thrill of uncovering buried cities, where time had stood still for millennia, was, after all, new to the age. In January 1751 a Belgian writer addressed the *Mercure de France:* "During the past ten years, all of Europe has suffered agonies from having been kept waiting for details of the discoveries at ancient Herculaneum."[4] Around mid-century, the Vesuvian sites were besieged by visitors. Those who were admitted were lavish in their comments on the mural paintings ("more beautiful than Raphael"), on the tripods, the stuccos, the statues, the household goods ("so much like those of modern days"), the temples, theaters, houses, baths, bordellos, wineshops, and a whole gamut of well-preserved trivia, including ubiquitous, and often crude, *graffiti.*

If anything, the interest was heightened by the veil of secrecy which the Bourbon rulers of Naples imposed. They suspiciously guarded all artifacts, some of which were declared immoral and locked away. Neapolitan authorities claimed the sole right to publish the results of excavations. Their sluggishness in this caused malicious rumors to spring up in Florence that all

---

[4] Charles Waldstein (Walston) and Leonard Shoobridge: *Herculaneum: Past, Present and Future* (London: Macmillan & Co.; 1908), p. 1.

these Neapolitan discoveries were nothing but southern humbug. Already in 1739, a French visitor found "the people who show the antiquities sullen and very jealous."[5] Any learned foreigner or visiting artist was immediately suspect, if not barred outright—like Lady Mary Wortley Montagu in 1740—from descending by torchlight into the deep subterranean shafts or from inspecting the art treasures collected at the royal palace at Portici. To make any drawings, as Goethe and his friend Tischbein were to learn as late as 1787, was out of the question. In order to gain admission, one had to be in good standing with the court or ingratiate oneself with the Neapolitan *eruditi* and antiquarians. The latter, so much a part of the rediscovery of Herculaneum, were a mixed lot of bookish men and pompous asses—querulous, vain, and obscurantist, given to the inane intrigues of the academic tribe, and liable to turn at any moment into a mob of haggling viragoes.

Not surprisingly, specific information on the manuscript finds announced by Paderni was hard to come by. Could one give any credence to the latest Neapolitan tale? If true, why should it take so long to let the world know of the contents of recovered works of literature?

Paderni's discovery had started much like the original find of Herculaneum itself. A well had been dug in 1750 in the garden of the Augustinian Fathers a few hundred yards northwest of the Herculaneum theater, off the old road between Naples and Pompeii. It was a choice location on a gentle slope overlooking the bay and cooled by west winds. Again marble was struck when the workmen cut through a considerable layer of lava deposited during the great eruption of 1631, and the hardened mud tufa or *pappamonte* underneath. Countryfolk rushed to inform the king's men. Subsequently, the labor force engaged at Herculaneum and Pompeii was shifted, and excavation began in earnest at the new site.

Using the well as an entrance, the excavators drove shafts in all directions. A whole maze of tunnels—so-called *cuniculi* (literally, rabbit warrens)—was dug, at places more than a hundred feet deep. It soon became clear that the royal engineers had encountered an ancient Roman villa of enormous dimensions. Once it was possible to trace the atrium, peristyle, and colonnades, which ended in a kind of belvedere abutting the Gulf of Naples,

---

[5] Mario Praz: "Herculaneum and European Taste," *American Magazine of Art*, Vol. XXXII (December 1939), p. 684.

its length was estimated to be over 750 feet. But the dimensions of the edifice were its least remarkable feature, though they spoke for its unusual lavishness.

As at the Herculanean theater, the original well had nearly hit the bull's eye. Laborers did not proceed very far before they began to free bronze and marble statues in bewildering succession. They found ninety in all, amounting to no less than "an ancient

Sumptuous Roman villa. After a painting in the house of M. Lucretius Fronto, discovered at Pompeii in 1900

museum of sculpture,"[6] which later became the pride of the Museo Nazionale in Naples. One can well imagine the delight when one figure after another was brought up to the surface: dancing fauns, sleeping satyrs, cupids, a Mercury in repose, a somber grouping of five female dancers, and much more. Suffice it to say that several of the statues are among the best-known from antiquity, although a number may be fine Roman copies rather than Hellenic originals. The collection ranges from the archaic Attic style, through classical examples worthy of Phidias or Lysippus, the melancholy busts of Diadochi rulers, playful and realistic treatment of children and animals in the Hellenistic manner, to the stark heads of Roman politicos.

Such a windfall justified Amadeo Maiuri, the twentieth-century Italian archaeologist, in calling this country mansion "the wealthiest and most precious villa of the ancient world."[7] However, it was yet another find that spread the fame of the villa

[6] Ethel Ross Barker: *Buried Herculaneum* (London: A. and C. Black; 1908), p. 71.
[7] Amadeo Maiuri: *Herculaneum*. Guide Books to the Museums and Monuments of Italy's Ministerio della Pubblica Istruzione, No. 53 (Rome: Istituto Poligrafico dello Stato—Libreria dello Stato; 1956), p. 74.

far and wide and, incidentally, gave it a name: *Villa dei papiri.*
In this instance, the bonanza did not become evident at once.

Two years after the excavations were begun, laborers entered
various smaller rooms of the villa. One of the rooms had portrait
busts of Epicurus, Demosthenes, Zenon of Sidon, and Hemarchus.
The preponderance of Epicurean philosophers among these sculptures appeared to indicate the leanings of the owner. It was
probably among the debris in the tablinum (dining room) that
some oddly shaped objects were first noticed. They were roughly
oblong cylinders. The workers, not unreasonably, took them for
sticks of charred wood and without paying them any further attention cast them away. A later visitor, J. J. Winckelmann, testified
to their striking resemblance to "briquettes. Only few were round.
Many have been pressed flat. Most of them are parched, and as
full of wrinkles as a ram's horn."[8]

However, as more and more of these "briquettes"—all of
approximately the same length and shape—turned up, someone
was bound to become curious and pick one up for closer examination. It was obvious that the objects consisted of several layers,
which disintegrated on touch, and it was assumed that they were
bundles of linen. A few men, however, thought they had served
as some type of fishing or hunting gear. We don't know to what
we owe this imaginative guess, but whatever the strange articles
may have been, they were once again judged useless and discarded.
The room in which a whole pile of them was found was labeled
Bottega del Carbonaio, shop of the coal dealer.

And then there came light. Perhaps at one point a roll broke
accidentally in two.[9] Perhaps the artificial illumination being used
in the subterranean areas fell on it at a favorable angle, and
someone realized that the brittle dark layers were covered with
writing. Be that as it may, it was Camillo Paderni who took all
the credit. He first announced in November 1753 the discovery of
molti volumi di papiri, which, he said, indeed resembled coal and
blackened one's fingers. None, he added, had so far been unrolled.[1]

Camillo Paderni was a mediocre painter from Rome who had

---

[8] Winckelmann: op. cit., p. 85.
[9] Edwards: op. cit., p. 64. David Diringer: *The Hand-produced Book*
(London: Hutchinson & Co.; 1953), p. 253.
[1] Karl Lebrecht Preisendanz: *Papyrusfunde und Papyrusforschung*
(Leipzig: Hiersemann; 1933), p. 43.

entered government service in Naples in 1750 as custodian of the antiquities collection at d'Elbeuf's former palace at Portici. He was thoroughly disliked by his associates and is described as an exceedingly vain ignoramus. Conceivably this unflattering picture owes something to the jealousy of his rivals at court. Winckelmann and his mentor at Portici, Father Antonio Piaggio (Piaggi), were among Paderni's chief detractors. They arrived on the scene after the papyrus rolls had already been found and recognized. What they have to say about the original discovery is little at variance with Paderni's version in the first person singular.

Paderni continued boasting to the end of his days that it was due to him alone that the priceless manuscripts were rescued from complete destruction. And to back his claims he had a spellbinding yarn to tell, which, for all we know, might have been true. As soon as he heard of the bizarre lumps scattered in one room of the villa, he maintained, he gave an order that some of the specimens be brought to him at the museum. Almost immediately he discerned written characters. In the flush of excitement, he rushed to the royal palace, and though it was an inappropriate time to call on the sovereign, brave Paderni disregarded etiquette and asked to be announced to the king, who was, by the way, an enthusiastic patron of archaeology. Admitted to the royal chamber, Paderni displayed his trophy. Then he took a sharp knife—the thought of it makes all scholars wince—and boldly cut through the dark husk. This was his bravado manner of demonstrating to the king that there were, clearly, written passages inside the carbonized husks. It also helped to dramatize the magnitude of his discovery. Having made the desired impression, he talked the king into granting him the exclusive right to handle all the rolls.

According to his own account, Paderni now spent several days from early dawn in the dark cavities underground, working continuously and single-handedly at the task of extracting the papyri. He made a great ado of the dangers under which he slaved in dim candlelight, which was liable to be extinguished at any moment. He claimed he ran the risk of getting lost in the maze of the *cuniculi* and of not finding his way out. Worse still, he was liable to be buried under a collapsing ceiling or even to "suffocate in his own sweat." But his fortitude was rewarded. Miraculously, we are led to believe, he completed his rescue action, and carried the precious manuscripts all by himself to the museum.[2]

---

[2] Christian Jensen: "Die Bibliothek von Herculaneum," *Bonner Jahrbücher*, Heft 135 (1930), p. 51.

In the following year Paderni returned to the scene and emptied what is believed to have been the actual library room. It was a report of this incident which was printed in the *Transactions* of the Royal Society of December 1754.

At least four major finds of manuscripts were made under Paderni's aegis from 1752 to 1754, followed by a few minor finds up to 1759. The cache from the library was probably the principal discovery and may have contained the favorite works of

An "armarium" with papyrus rolls. One of the most detailed renderings known of the manner in which the ancients stacked their books on wall shelves. The rolls at the Herculaneum library may have been similarly arranged. The etching was made in the seventeenth century after a Roman relief near Trier, Germany, which is no longer in existence.

the original owner. There was no mistake about the nature of the room, with its inlaid wooden bookcases lining the walls. Some of the manuscripts were still resting on the shelves, others were scattered around. Libraries from classical antiquity have been excavated from time to time, but none was ever found with ancient books still in it.

Altogether, the Roman villa yielded an estimated 1,800 manuscripts—including fragments which represented some 800 complete rolls. A great many more were no doubt destroyed before their nature had been noted. Others suffered annihilation from the crude methods used in extracting them from the hardened volcanic mass in which they were enclosed.

And what about the opening of the rolls? Did the dismal state in which they had been found allow room for hope? Scholars everywhere were afire to know about the contents, but the manuscripts had to be laboriously unrolled before anyone could begin to decipher them and establish their identity. Unfortunately, this problem was never satisfactorily solved. To make the muted voices from Herculaneum speak again from these dark, crumbling, carbonized lumps called for the utmost delicacy and ingenuity. But buried papyrus rolls were a novelty. No one had the slightest idea how to proceed—and a number of quacks volunteered their services. By their dubious tricks, many irreplaceable texts were hopelessly damaged or obliterated. No sooner were the ancient rolls recovered than their survival was threatened afresh. Father Piaggio, who was to play a part in the unrolling, likened the *poveri papiri* to a sick person whose precious life could still be saved, but who runs the greatest danger from the collegium medicum watching over him. "One gave them a dose of hemlock, the others administered mercury. Placed under a focal lens, they were exposed to burning sun rays. One has cooked them in boiling water to mud and baked them in ovens to biscuits."[3]

The monopoly bestowed on Camillo Paderni by the king was mercifully short-lived. This self-styled Sir Galahad of the Holy Papyri had devised a method for opening them in the robust manner of Alexander and the Gordian Knot. In most cases—as in the performance before the king—he just hacked lengthwise through the rolls, splitting them into longitudinal halves. He then scraped layer by layer successively from the inner core while copying as best he could (and that was worthless!) the writing on each, until he reached the outer hulls, the so-called *scorze,* which were the only pieces to outlive the ordeal and be preserved. Within no time at all, the painter-custodian—who used equally drastic measures in chopping mural paintings from walls—went through some 142 rolls, to which an equal number of empty shells are the pathetic witnesses. Since Paderni never had much confidence that more than a few disconnected lines could be rescued, we can well imagine how slipshod and utterly ruinous his copies were. Fortunately, Good King Charles of Naples called a halt to this massacre.

Admittedly, the Bourbon ruler was a man of limited intelligence and knowledge, but he took his job seriously, and next to hunting and fishing, the *scavi* (excavations) became his passion. This uncouth Nimrod never treated antiquarian research with

---

[3] Carl Justi: *Winckelmann und seine Zeitgenossen,* fifth edition (Constance: Phaidon; 1956), Vol. II, p. 219.

erratic caprice. It is told of him that when he left Naples to occupy the throne of Spain, he took from his finger a ring that he had himself found within a lava clump at Pompeii; declaring it not to be his personal property, he left it with the Portici museum. In 1755 he founded the Accademia Ercolanese, whose principal purpose was the editing of the papyri and the publication of the results. Before that, however, he turned his attention to the unrolling. It was the director of the Vatican collections who advised him to send for Father Antonio Piaggio, a Genovese monk then in the employ of the Vatican as copyist of Latin manuscripts and custodian of miniature paintings, the "only man in the world who could undertake this difficult affair."[4] Piaggio already had a reputation for mechanical ingenuity; and his skill in copying with astonishing precision all kinds of script unknown to him was something of a legend.

Papyri fragments from Herculaneum and Father Piaggio's unwinding machine. After a contemporary (1825) etching by A. de Jorio at the *officina dei papiri* in Naples

Piaggio was first sent on loan from the Vatican for two years. However, when his services to the papyri were deemed indispensable, his stay in the shadow of Mt. Vesuvius was made permanent. After his arrival at Portici he promptly constructed a machine whose operations are expounded in innumerable letters and antiquarian accounts of the day. It was likened to a loom, to the apparatus of a wigmaker, to a machine for bookbinding. The contraption is still on exhibit at the Museo Nazionale in Naples. We are told by Winckelmann that it was very simple, but he took some five pages to describe its operations, making it sound rather complicated. Considerably more tersely, a "learned gentleman from Naples" wrote to the Royal Society in 1755 that Piaggio "made a machine with which, by means of certain threads . . . gummed to the back of the papyrus . . . he begins by degrees to pull, whilst with a sort of engraver's instrument he loosens one

---

[4] Quoted in Edwards: op. cit., p. 64.

leaf from the others . . . and then makes a sort of lining to the back of the papyrus . . . and with some spirituous liquor, with which he wets the papyrus, by little and little unfolds it."[5]

Piaggo's device supplanted Paderni's guillotine. It was by no means the ideal solution which Winckelmann and latter-day popular authors would like us to believe it was. Otherwise, it seems unlikely that from time to time less orthodox methods would have been tried with the encouragement of Neapolitan officialdom. For one thing, the apparatus was tantalizingly slow. Winckelmann reported that "four or five hours are scarce enough to detach a finger's breadth; nor less than a month for a palm's breadth."[6] It took Piaggio four years to unroll and copy just thirty-nine columns of one roll. Then there came a slight improvement in output, but the going was still immensely slow. Though Piaggio received additional help, no more than eighteen rolls of varying length were disentangled during his almost forty years of active work. At this early stage he naturally selected the best-preserved pieces that would conceivably yield to a combined manual-"chemical" onslaught. Even so, the gadget, despite all caution, was liable to harm already damaged sections by gripping through a hole in the layer at the time on the surface to the one below it. None of the rolls attacked by Piaggio was opened completely. None remained fully intact.

In 1802, the Prince of Wales sent one of his court chaplains, the Reverend John Hayter, to Naples. The Prince had apparently caught the papyrus bug from English travelers to Herculaneum. He, too, dreamed of finding lost classics. A few years before, he had already begun—following the example of Sir William Hamilton, English ambassador to Naples and husband of "that woman"—to pay salaries to Piaggio and the Italian craftsmen who worked on the papyri. Now, at the Prince's own expense and with the permission of the Neapolitan government, Hayter was made supervisor of operations at the *officina dei papiri*. He was not exactly a profound scholar, and most of his restorations of missing passages are worthless. But he brought a new élan to the work, and within four years he was able to unroll some two hundred papyri by streamlining Piaggio's manipulations. Of about half of these, he and his aides made facsimiles in pencil and on copperplates.

During the Napoleonic Wars, in 1806, Hayter fled with the

[5] Ibid.   [6] Winckelmann: op. cit., p. 114.

royal family to Palermo. There he continued his labors, edited the fragments of a Latin text, and composed a tedious poem in Latin on Herculaneum, which he dedicated to the Prince of Wales. On his return to England he brought with him ninety-six pencil copies of papyri texts, which proved extremely valuable for research later, when the original papyri had suffered further decay. Some of these were misplaced at the Bodleian Library until they were rediscovered by the eminent Austrian classical scholar, Theodor Gomperz, in the 1860's.[7]

Fragment in facsimile from Philodemus' treatise *On Death*, found among the papyrus rolls of the Herculanean villa. The lead-pencil transcript was engraved on copperplate under the direction of the Reverend John Hayter at Palermo between 1806 and 1810 and was deposited at Oxford University in 1811.

England continued its active interest in the papyri when Humphrey Davy, the chemist, undertook a mission to Naples. He made two voyages to investigate the physico-chemical modification of the manuscripts and possibly to suggest remedies. In the course of his research he came to the conclusion that the carbonization of the rolls was due not so much to the action of fire or excessive heat, as was generally believed, but rather to the dampness and airtightness of their burial. Davy seems to have had some success in separating the layers of papyri by application of an alcoholic solution with a camel's-hair brush. During two months' experiments in Naples he managed to unroll, according to his own

---

[7] Heinrich Gomperz, ed.: *Theodor Gomperz: Briefe und Aufzeichnungen* (Vienna: Gerold; 1936), Vol. I, p. 354.

report, twenty-three manuscripts, most of which had apparently been declared *disperati,* hopeless cases. But little of their texts was legible. Further efforts met with manifest ill will and chicanery on the part of Neapolitan officials, and Davy then decided that it would be "both a waste of public money and compromise of character . . . to proceed any further."[8]

Davy had put high hopes in chemical techniques. If the rolls had been carbonized, why could not the chemist's art reverse the process wrought by natural agents? The list of reputable scientists who tried their hands at it—unfortunately with negative results—is long. Among them was Thomas Young, physicist and physician, known for his partial success with the decipherment of Egyptian hieroglyphics. Even a giant like Germany's Justus von Liebig, to whom in 1857 the *officina* handed over six fragments (never since accounted for), failed. Experiments were carried out into the twentieth century with paraffin, albumen, alcohol, glycerin, and water vapor, all in vain. The elixir could not be produced.

In 1903, a certain Carlo Marrè, attached to the Vatican libraries, thought he was on the right track. But by the perversity of fate, roll 266, which had withstood the eruption of Mt. Vesuvius, was consumed by a small fire. Twenty years later, an expert by the ill-fitting name of Miraglia devised another of those ingenious methods which promptly atomized a roll into nothingness. The list of these methodical destroyers is far from exhausted by these names.[9]

Next to the butchering methods of Paderni, the greatest slaughter was inflicted by a German, Dr. Sickler of Hildburghausen, on the rolls which had come into the possession of the British crown. He was the kind of charlatan and cheat who invariably crops up in great manuscript recoveries. In order to prove the effectiveness of his mysterious operation, Sickler submitted an opened fragment, allegedly from the private collection of an unnamed friend. It has been surmised that this showpiece either was stolen from the *officina* or, more likely, represented a forgery. But it helped Sickler to gain the desired end, and a parliamentary commission entrusted him with the task of applying his advertised process to the long-suffering rolls. When a committee of the House

---

[8] Edwards: op. cit., p. 70.
[9] Preisendanz: op. cit., pp. 44–5. See also Werner Liebich: "Aus der Arbeit an den Papyri von Herculaneum," *Deutsche Akademie der Wissenschaften, Wissenschaftliche Annalen,* Jahrg. II (Berlin, 1953), p. 309.

of Commons inquired into the matter in 1818, the German doctor had managed to ruin utterly seven rolls and to run through an expenditure of about £1,200. His bluff was called at last, and the few remaining rolls in British possession escaped certain destruction.

To round off the story of the losses, a considerable number of papyri were given away. George IV, when Prince of Wales, was presented with eighteen—we have just seen with what catastrophic effects. The survivors of this transaction (one other roll has somehow vanished) are now divided between the Bodleian and the British Museum. In 1806, the Neapolitan government gave six rolls to Napoleon. One roll, never heard of again, was presented at the time to a Dutch emissary in Naples, another to the commander at Portici. And some material seems to have been lost when the Bourbons fled to Palermo the first time in 1799 and took the papyri along.

The deciphering, copying, collating, editing, and publishing of the relatively few readable texts was beset with as many pitfalls as the unrolling. It took even more time. And another frustrating chapter was added to the hazards of the Herculanean rolls.

When Winckelmann appeared in Naples as early as 1758, little more than rumors and vague generalities had reached the centers of learning. He had come to gain precise knowledge of the nature of these rolls. Winckelmann was determined to break through the papyrus curtain raised by the Neapolitans' obsession with secrecy. In the course of time he became thoroughly embroiled in the local politics and eventually wrote his famous *Sendschreiben*, a *chronique scandaleuse* of the Herculanean affair, and one of the first works of popular archaeology. His principal informant was the embittered Piaggio, whom he called "the world's greatest *galantuomo*" and with whom he boarded during his four weeks' stay at Portici.

Winckelmann's many anecdotes about the tragicomedy of errors connected with the decipherment of the rolls begins with Paderni, who chopped up the rolls on the grounds that they would not yield anything but a few disconnected passages. Then there was the renowned Neapolitan antiquarian who declared all the rolls to have been written in the then unknown Oscan tongue. Thus, one was comfortably released from any obligation to disentangle them! A look at a few opened fragments could have easily dispelled his theory; or that of a confrere of his who firmly maintained that classical works had been set down in square book forms, of the kind we have today, and rolls were used only for commercial or administrative records. He argued that it would be absurd for the ancients, sagacious as they were, to have chosen for their books so inconvenient a form as rolls.

A composite of ancient writing implements, forms of books, and a book container—all taken from Pompeian and Herculanean paintings. After Sir William Gell's *Pompeiana* (1832)

These savants were like Galileo's antagonists at Padua, who refused to look through a telescope at the moons of Jupiter, since they knew for certain—no matter what they might see—that Galileo had to be wrong when matched against Aristotle, "the master of all who know." Verily, as has been said, there is no idea preposterous enough that it has not found a champion in some scholar or intellectual. Our champion of the square book form was a Signor Martorelli, who had advanced his strange views in an eight-hundred-page tome on an ancient inkpot. Winckelmann has a wonderful time making him look ridiculous. When a treatise on music was identified among the papyri, Martorelli was not at a loss. He declared that the roll dealt with a legal squabble— "perhaps," suggested Winckelmann sarcastically, "a dispute between city hall and the town band concerning church and wedding music."[1] With the prevalence of such a mentality among the Neapolitan academicians, it was little wonder that the world had to wait fifty years after the discovery of the papyri before the first volume in which their contents were officially published saw the light of day. This so-called *Collectio Prior* was completed in 1850.

Nineteen fairly comprehensive manuscripts were included in this edition, a fraction of the material unrolled or copied. The entire opus is of enormous bulk but little content, and is now

---

[1] Winckelmann: op. cit., p. 54.

considered useless because of its countless inaccuracies. In addition, the original passages are practically pushed to the wall by an avalanche of bombastic and irrelevant notes and "learned" discourses from the pens of eminent Neapolitan members of the Accademia Ercolanese. Understandably, critics could talk of a second ghastly burial of the rolls under the logomachy of pretentious scholarship. A nineteenth-century English classicist commented: "It is difficult to speak with patience of the perversity shown by them [the Neapolitan *accademici*] in treating the contents of the papyri as anything to be concealed as long as possible from the outer world, and of the opportunities irreparably lost by the careless copying of originals that have since perished; and some of their editions are almost unique as specimens of pedantic imbecility."[2]

While Piaggio tinkered with his apparatus, friends of ancient literature lived in suspense, wondering what would emerge. Like Winckelmann, each had his own favorites he longed to see restored. Although in the long run the results of the decipherments fell far short of expectations, some hopes that a vanished masterpiece would rise from among the charred lumps—about a third of which remain closed today—would not die out till late into the nineteenth century. Schiller's hexameter:

> *Im ernsten Museum liegt noch ein köstlicher Schatz seltener Rollen gehäuft* (There still lies a precious trove of rare rolls in the somber museum)

echoed through the years. Madame de Staël wrote—somewhat hysterically—that she trembled, in the presence of the rolls, lest "a mere breath could abduct the dust in which noble thoughts might still be slumbering."[3]

The awakening from all these dreams was rather harsh. Ecstasy was to give way to an overdose of romantic disillusionment. When the manuscripts were eventually put down as "third or fourth rate," "derivative," "tedious," "of little or no value as philosophy or literature," "inferior," "worthless"[4]—judgments which have prevailed since in most of the textbooks and reference works—public interest in the once legendary Herculanean library began to die out. One modern writer bluntly states: "No greater

---

[2] Walter Scott: *Fragmenta Herculensia* . . . (Oxford: Clarendon Press; 1885), p. 8.
[3] Jensen: op. cit., p. 49.
[4] Barker: op. cit., p. 117.

disappointment ever befell a patient seeker for truth."[5] Was the effort and expense really commensurate with the returns? Even Winckelmann had thought the labor on Philodemus, to whom most of the larger, originally unrolled papyri are ascribed, ill spent.

This kind of reversal is at best misinformed and outdated. But the appearance of various exceedingly interesting fragments has not modified the standard judgment. Instead, classical scholars disregarded some of the new material. The study of the Herculanean texts has become an obscure specialization—not even to be counted as a branch of papyrology[6]—a byway that students of ancient history and literature have often lost touch with. Thus, several studies of Epicurus were written without as much as a mention of the recovery of considerable portions of his magnum opus, *On Nature,* the work from which Lucretius drew his ideas.

Herculaneum may not have yielded up the lost Greek and Latin masterpieces prayed for, but it has given us some items of value; for example, the natural philosophy of Epicurus, of which more passages may yet be forthcoming. It was a work of great influence in the history of Western thought, consisting of 37 "books" written in a deliberately dry and bare style. It seems there were three copies of it in the Herculanean library. The prominence of Epicurean texts throws a significant light on the nature of the collection, which was almost exclusively restricted to philosophical works of that school and of a few of its adversaries. Only some five fragments on geometry found so far fall outside this limitation. The Latin rolls, twenty-four in all, appear to have been an addition made by a later heir or owner of the villa. The library, then, was highly specialized. It may well be regretted that its proprietor seems to have lacked broader interests such as history, poetry, and drama. But as a treasure of ancient Epicurean thought it is priceless. The variety of philosophical subjects dealt with has shown that Epicureans were not as narrowly confined to ethical thought as it was once believed; they, like the Academy and the Stoa, encompassed all major philosophical disciplines.

Another interesting glimpse, liable to change preconceptions about the "foul company" of Epicureans, is afforded through the

---

[5] Cecil Headlam: *The Story of Naples* (London: J. M. Dent-Everyman Library; 1927), p. 178.
[6] Preisendanz: op. cit., p. 40.

fragments from Epicurus' own letters, which in pre-Christian antiquity had enjoyed wide circulation. Like those of Paul, they were collected for distribution among the widely scattered Epicurean communities all around the Eastern Mediterranean. Among them is a moving letter by the sage to a child. The letters reveal the Epicureans as a quasi-religious brotherhood rather than simply men living in placid, self-indulgent withdrawal. Together with other fragments, they depict members of that school as com-

Epicurus. After a bust at the British Museum

mitted to an active participation in the political struggles of their day, and enjoying considerable public prestige. In a memorable sidelight, one of the rediscovered letters reports Epicurus' intervention with Antipater for the release of one of his disciples, who had been taken prisoner. Among the agnostic Epicurean fraternities the person of Epicurus seems to have loomed as something of a savior, and the writings and discussions of his followers were largely concerned with the exegesis of the master's words. In a way, the Herculanean papyri have enriched our knowledge of the Epicureans as much as the Dead Sea scrolls have contributed to our understanding of the Qumran sectarians.

Besides the works of Epicurus himself and Philodemus, the library included lost treatises by several other Epicurean teachers. Chrysippus is the one noted Stoic represented. In addition, we have a manuscript on the Stoa. The latter, like most of the Epicurean texts with the exception of Philodemus, has become available in useful form in recent decades only.

The bulk of the library, roughly two thirds, consists of the works of Philodemus. The first roll opened by Father Piaggio was a diatribe attacking music for enfeebling the manly virtues and demoralizing society. (This was a familar theme in antiquity; in our own days Thomas Mann has expressed some affinities with it.) In addition, we have Philodemus' compendia, each of an almost Aristotelian breadth: on rhetoric, logic, aesthetics, psychology, and theology. He even composed an essay on government. Perhaps the most valuable of these manuscripts is his outline on the teachings of Greek thinkers. John Stuart Mill was surprised to find in one treatise anticipations of modern empirical logic.[7]

These Epicurean works are in the main compilations, interpretations, and popularizations rather than the offerings of an original mind. They may have been lecture notes for an Epicurean circle or school. This is the more likely: we have some tangible proof that Philodemus was a considerable intellectual force in late Republican Rome. Much else has been preserved in Philodemus' discursive treatises, through his ample quotations from Hellenistic writings of the third- and second-century B.C., including, occasionally, such gems as an unknown passage from Euripides. In addition to being a prime source for Epicurean philosophy and the intellectual arsenal of Lucretius, the Herculanean papyri have given us valuable material on other contemporary schools and serve as a link to later writers such as Cicero, Quintilian, Seneca, and, above all, Horace.[8]

Until the discovery of thirty-odd prose works, the only known literary productions of Philodemus were an excerpt in Diogenes Laertes and some twenty poems that had been included in an ancient anthology. In marked contrast to his long-winded didactic prose, these sparkling verses are the typical product of Hellenistic eroticism and elegance, despite occasional lapses into scurrilousness. Their echo can be traced in the love poetry of Ovid and Catullus.[9] It was, then, not an entirely unknown writer whose name has become associated with the only Roman library transmitted to us. Philodemus, a Syrian "Greek" from Gadara, a little town near the Palestinian coast, was a fellow countryman of one of the outstanding Hellenistic poets, Meleager. He was known to have settled in Italy after the Mithridatic wars, around 75 B.C. Cicero mentions him several times, always with great respect, except when he is referred to along with his patron, the ex-consul L. Calpurnius Piso Caesonius, Caesar's father-in-law and one of

---

[7] Letter to Theodor Gomperz, April 30, 1865, in Heinrich Gomperz: op. cit., p. 353.

[8] J. U. Powell and E. A. Barker, eds.: *New Chapters in the History of Greek Literature* (Oxford: Clarendon Press; 1921), Vol. I, p. 26. Jensen: op. cit., pp. 57–9.

[9] "Philodemus," *Oxford Classical Dictionary*, p. 681. Jensen: op. cit., p. 56.

Cicero's most despised enemies. Then Cicero's reverence noticeably cools.

A real detective story grew from the attempt to ascertain who the owner of the villa and its library had been. No external sign or inscription had left the slightest hint. Could the library offer any clue? There was first the distinctly Epicurean character of the collection of books. Once several rolls had been identified, the obvious candidate for ownership was the poet-philosopher Philodemus himself. The suggestion that he was the proprietor of the villa has been made repeatedly, even by Winckelmann, but it has little plausibility. True, several of Philodemus' treatises contain additional notes that might well have come from his pen. And who but an author would keep so many copies of his works? However, at most this evidence makes Philodemus the owner or the compiler of the library, but not necessarily chatelain of what may be the most sumptuous Roman villa known. It is inconceivable that anyone but an exceedingly wealthy Roman, probably a Patrician, built and occupied this pleasure garden. No foreign intellectual with uncertain means of support would qualify.

Thanks to a speech of Cicero's unearthed at Cologne by Poggio Bracciolini in the fifteenth century, we know Calpurnius Piso was the patron of Philodemus. Cicero refers to this aristocratic magistrate in the most unflattering terms: in fact, Cicero tried to have him convicted for the mismanagement and plunder of Roman provinces. Like Verres, another of Cicero's arch-enemies, and the noble Brutus, Piso did well for himself in the lands he served as proconsul after his consulate in 58 B.C. The forensic wizard, a *homo novus* espousing the solid Roman virtues, accuses Piso of all manner of vices and paints a harsh picture of the wellborn Roman's unkempt appearance. Cicero's tirade would not seem to fit a man with the undeniably good taste of the proprietor or builder of the Herculaneum villa, but the profusion of Greek statuary might well have been loot carried away by Piso from the Greek mainland and Byzantium.

In any case, it is fairly certain that Piso was Philodemus' friend and sponsor and that he was wealthy, fond of good living, and had Epicurean affiliations. Since the hand of Philodemus can be seen in the library, his patron naturally comes into the picture. The two lived together for many years. From the internal evidence of the library and from the references in Cicero, we may assume with a measure of confidence that Philodemus stayed in Piso's

villa in the Campania and there assembled the books for one of
the Epicurean circles known to have existed at the time in the
resort towns of the Neapolitan countryside. Perhaps Piso even had
a library of his own at the villa. All we have is circumstantial evidence, but particularly since the definitive study by D. Comparetti
and G. de Petra, the estate has been called Piso's Villa. Only the
more cautious still refer to it as Villa Suburbana, Villa of the
Papyri, or Villa of the Humanist Collector.

In 1765 the focus of concentration was shifted to Pompeii and
because of that and because of the alleged noxious gases rising in
the subterranean passages, excavations were halted at the villa.
The people in charge of the papyri were not particularly disturbed.
They had more rolls than they could handle for a long time to come.
It was not until much later, when the expectations of a dramatic
recovery from the motley lot stored at the *officina dei papiri* finally
collapsed, that there was clamor for a renewed search. But archaeological zeal continued to favor Pompeii over Herculaneum. Inter-
mittently, new *scavi* would be taken up—none however at the villa.
In 1902, an Anglo-American archaeologist, Charles Waldstein
(Walston), organized a campaign on an international basis for the
systematic excavation of Herculaneum. He held out great hopes,
and the project was hailed on two continents. The Epicurean library, he rightly pointed out, was "hardly fully representative of
the thought or life of the age. But all the rich dwellers in the villas
of Herculaneum were not such specialists; and should we come
upon the library of an ordinary lady or gentleman of the age, we
may certainly expect to find the classical representatives of ancient
thought and literary art. . . ."[1]
Unfortunately, Waldstein's generously conceived plan failed
to materialize. Theodore Roosevelt, in a flamboyant gesture, assumed the patronage of the project—wounding Italian national
pride. In 1927 Mussolini endorsed a separate archaeological effort,
fittingly initiated by a thunderous speech, but the excavations made
little progress.
Despite all these failures, it has been firmly established that
the volcanic burial of Herculaneum and its environs helped to preserve papyri manuscripts. The town of Herculaneum itself, still
largely unexcavated (modern Resina stands on it), could well contain a treasure of writings. Indeed, a roll was found, albeit of in-

---

[1] Waldstein: op. cit., p. 8.

CRAEBERETQVESVAE·
QVALISADINSTANTIS·
SIGNATVBAF.CLASSESQ
EST.FACIES.ENVISA.LOCI

Among the few Latin papyri recovered at Herculaneum
was one of a lost poem on Augustus' triumph over Octa-
vian, *De bello Actiaco,* written early in the first century
A.D. and hence considerably later than the Greek manuscripts from the villa library. The letters are delicate
rustic capitals.

different value, in 1870.[2] And the surrounding areas, where once
proud Roman villas stood, remain largely buried and untouched, a
fertile ground for hunters of classical antiquity. Though another
land, far from Italy, has come to fulfill the cherished hopes raised
in the eighteenth century, Wordsworth's prayer—quoted at the beginning of this chapter—may yet find an answer in the Neapolitan
Campania felix.

---

[2] Preisendanz: op. cit., p. 49.

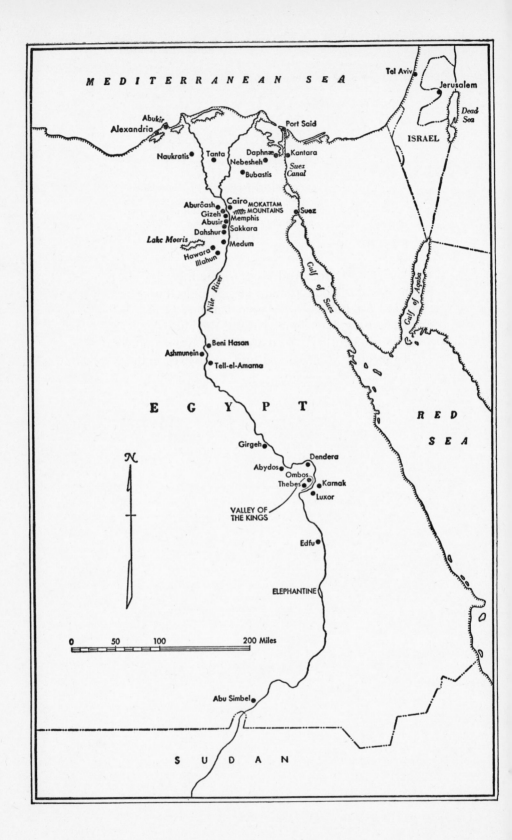

·V·

THE PAPYRUS OF EGYPT

Till to astonished realms Papyra taught
To paint in mystic colours sound and thought,
With Wisdom's voice to print the page sublime,
And mark in adamant the steps of Time.

ERASMUS DARWIN[1]

JOHANN JOACHIM WINCKELMANN had been dead ten years, and the first Herculanean rolls were yet to be published, when an incident in Egypt rekindled the dream that had been fading for scholarly enthusiasts. It shifts the scene across the Mediterranean to a land which by virtue of its climate and its cultural and political background has contributed more to the recovery of lost books and documents than perhaps any other region.

Fellahin in 1778 had come upon some fifty papyrus rolls hidden in a buried jar. The find was made, they said, at a site near Gizeh, but the claims of native diggers were even then notoriously unreliable, if not purposely misleading. In any case, the indications are that the jar's contents originated in the Fayum, the large lacustrine depression west of the lower Nile Valley, which in the Hellenistic age became a center of Greek rural settlements. The rolls, it seems, were offered to a dealer, who saw little market value in such oddities but, thanks to a flicker of curiosity, agreed to buy one of them. The rest were thereupon committed to the flames by the natives, for the sake of the pleasant fragrance emitted by burning papyri.[2] Robert Browning has recalled this alleged aroma in his well-known verses:

---

[1] From *The Loves of the Plants*, canto ii, quoted by C. H. Roberts: "The Greek Papyri," in S. R. K. Glanville, ed.: *The Legacy of Egypt* (Oxford: Clarendon Press; 1942), p. 249.

[2] James Baikie: *Egyptian Papyri and Papyrus-hunting* (London: Religious Tract Society; 1925), p. 36.

> And strew sweetness from old
> Egyptian's fine worm-eaten shroud
> Which breaks the dust when once unrolled!

The olfactory properties of papyri, by the way, have never been verified. Yet we know that the ancients sometimes impregnated papyri with cedar oil, and the root of the papyrus plant itself was used by the Egyptians as a source of perfume. Could it be that Europeans lack the cultivated sensibilities of fellahin nostrils? Luckily, Europeans are susceptible to such other endowments of the papyrus rolls as do not require their annihilation.

The lone survivor of the fifty rolls came somehow into the possession of Stefano Cardinal Borgia, who deposited it in his museum at Velletri. It was the first such document known in modern times to have become part of a European collection, though long-forgotten scraps may have reached a Basel professor two centuries earlier. It was edited promptly by a Danish philologist, Nicholas (Niels Iversen) Schow, and was published in 1788 as *Carta papyracea Graeca scripta Musei Borgiani Veletris*. Disappointingly, the Greek text, which dated from the reign of the profligate Roman Emperor Commodus, toward the end of the second century A.D., yielded little but a list of the farmers enlisted for *corvée* duties in flood control and the maintenance of canals on the Nile. Had eighteenth-century visions of literary treasures once again failed to materialize? As we now know, the Borgia roll provided a significant foretaste of things to come.

Several elements vital to later discoveries could already be discerned. Of primary importance was the realization that Egypt provided ideal conditions for the preservation of antique texts, which were likely to be in a far better state of survival there than those buried by the eruptions of Vesuvius, and indeed might well include legal and other nonliterary texts. However, Western scholars had to depend to a large extent on the accidental finds of natives, whose ignorance—coupled with the less than enlightened attitudes of dealers—as often as not impeded rather than promoted recovery of ancient manuscripts. As for the manuscripts themselves, the texts buried in the soil of Egypt would probably consist of sheets, leaves, scraps, or rolls—all made from papyrus. What was this protean material to which we owe such unexpected survivals from antiquity?

Rowing up a river in the 1880's in Sicily, Guy de Maupassant, the French novelist, paid his respects to an amazing site. "An island appeared finally, covered with strange bushes. The frail and triangular stems eight or nine feet high bore at the top round clusters of green threads, soft and flexible, like human hair. They resembled heads that had become plants, which might have been thrown into this sacred stream by one of the pagan deities who lived here in days gone by. And this was the ancient papyrus. The peasants, however, call this reed *parucca* [wig]. Farther on, a whole forest of these quivered and rustled, bending and entangling their hairy heads, looking as if they were conversing about unknown

A papyrus plant

and mysterious things. Is it not strange that this wonderful plant, which brought to our minds the thoughts of the dead and which was the guardian of human genius, should have on its ancient body an enormous mane of thick and flowing hair, such as poets affect?"[3]

This is a perceptive and accurate description of a papyrus grove, equalled only by the delightful paintings, reliefs, and sketches of Egyptian artists of three thousand and more years ago. The scene was most common in ancient Egypt. But note that Maupassant had to go outside Egypt to find its likeness. The reed marshes which for ages had been so vibrant a part of Egypt's landscape and life have almost totally disappeared in modern times. However, Egypt is closely associated with papyrus. In hieroglyphics, Lower Egypt, that is, the Delta country, is designated by a papyrus reed; and papyrus is as evocative of the ancient land of the Nile as its pyramids. Its share in the shaping of Egyptian civilization is immeasurable. Moreover, papyrus reached other Near Eastern countries, and classical Greece and Rome, through Egypt and was adopted as their principal writing material after it had already been in use along the Nile for millennia. Even to the Mesopotamians,

---

[3] Guy de Maupassant: *The Collected Works*, Alliance Française edition (New York and London: M. Walter Dunne; 1903), Vol. XII, pp. 86–7.

whose favorite medium was clay tablets, papyrus was by no means unknown.

Not only did Egypt originate the use of papyrus, but it was probably the main supplier of papyrus "paper" throughout antiquity. Parchment and modern paper have been in use but for a brief while compared to papyrus, though all three were used simultaneously for a time. It is thus befitting, but hardly inevitable, that Egypt would ultimately prove to be the main guardian of papyrus documents, which in that land turned out to be almost as lasting as monuments of stone. The anything but sturdy rolls disintegrate quickly when exposed to dampness and become brittle

The union of Upper and Lower Egypt is symbolized by tying together lily and papyrus plants, sacred to the southern and northern regions respectively.

when dry: according to Eusebius, a Father of the Church, "moth and time devoured them." But given the favorable climate and the sand of Egypt, they were endowed with unexpected durability.

However, these circumstances have come to light only during recent centuries. Classical texts from Hellenistic, Roman, and Byzantine Egypt have been uncovered in prodigious numbers, providing a continuous record of some one thousand years from the coming of Alexander, late in the fourth century B.C., to and beyond the Arab conquest in the seventh century A.D. The discovery of these records led to the birth of a new science, papyrology, which is today devoted almost exclusively to the study of Greek and Latin papyri from Egypt. The badly damaged papyrus rolls from Herculaneum have received little attention, and their survival is considered only a freak accident: the sand of Egypt rather than the mud and volcanic matter of Herculaneum was to be the great benefactor and preserver. A medievalist studying peasant life or social and economic conditions of Western Europe in the tenth century A.D. may well look with envy on the data available to his colleague who is investigating Ptolemaic Egypt in the second century B.C.

Papyrus has been in use throughout Egypt's long history and may have been first adapted to writing purposes in pre-Dynastic days. The oldest known papyrus appears to date back to the First Dynasty, at the end of the fourth millennium B.C. But it is blank.[4] In 1893 a Swiss Egyptologist, Édouard Naville, bought a written papyrus, probably from a temple at Abusir, and perhaps as old as 2700 B.C. A few other pieces in the Berlin Museum and elsewhere are assumed to be of approximately the same age.

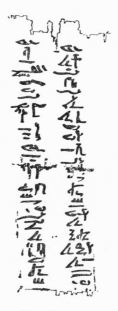

Section from a hieratic papyrus of the Berlin collection, ascribed to the Sixth Dynasty of Old Kingdom Egypt (about 2300 B.C.)

Papyrus is a reed-like water plant (*Cyperus papyrus*) of the sedge family, native to Africa. It still thrives in great profusion in and near the tropical rivers of Africa, which are sometimes clogged by its luxuriant growth. In ancient times, however, papyrus thickets grew all along the Nile and in the Delta. They were of a different variety from those found in parts of Syria, Mesopotamia, beside the

---

[4] Walter Byran Emery: *Archaic Egypt* (Harmondsworth, Middlesex: Penguin Books; 1961), p. 335.

Jordan, and in Sicily today, although these closely resemble the reeds of Egypt that were made into "paper" in antiquity.

To the ancient Egyptians, papyrus was the all-purpose plant which, like bamboo in Southeast Asia or the agave (maguey) in Mexico, furnished food, building material, clothing, footwear, floor mats, medicine, and much else besides. The favorite column in Egyptian architecture may be considered an abstraction of papyrus stems and buds—which reached gigantic proportions in the hypostyle halls of Karnak and perhaps inspired the columns of Greek temples. When Xerxes threw a bridge across the Bosporus to invade Greece, he used cables made from papyrus fiber. The swift, sturdy reed boats plying the Nile, which, curiously, resemble the reed vessels on Lake Titicaca, were made from bundles of papyri—as they are today on the great lakes of Central Africa— and so was the ark in which the child Moses was found among the (papyri) bulrushes. Papyrus could be formed into sheets and rolled up, as Emil Ludwig put it, "to await the records of wisdom and bear them down the stream of time."[5]

Papyrus writing sheets were not paper in the modern sense— an invention of the Chinese that reached Egypt in the eighth century A.D., before it came to Europe. Through Theophrastus, the successor of Aristotle at the Lyceum, and Pliny the Elder, the Roman naturalist who perished during the eruption of Vesuvius in A.D. 79, we are fairly well informed on the way the Egyptians manufactured papyrus. Typically, the process did not change noticeably in three thousand years—by following Pliny's description, we have been able to reproduce papyrus "paper," and in Sicily a minor trade has developed from the sale to tourists of postcards and rolls made from local plants.

The raw material taken from the tall plants—some as high as thirty-five feet—consisted of strips cut lengthwise from the pith of the three-sided stalks. Strips of equal length and quality were then arranged on a flat surface, in the manner of latticework, in a horizontal and vertical layer, the former representing the recto and the latter the verso side of the sheet. Through the application of pressure and water from the Nile—perhaps with the occasional addition of glue—the layers were merged into a fairly homogeneous mass, which was then exposed to the sun. After drying, the sheets were rubbed smooth with shells or ivory and perhaps whitened with chalk. Excess moisture was forced out by additional pounding.

---

[5] Emil Ludwig: *The Nile* (New York: Pyramid Books; 1963), p. 302.

The papyrus was then ready to be written on with a reed pen. As a rule, only the recto side was inscribed.

It was customary to glue together some twenty single sheets (usually five to six inches wide and eight to nine inches high) into a continuous roll on which a fairly lengthy text or document of many columns could be copied. In this form papyrus became a convenient standardized article of trade. The average length of a papyrus roll in Greek and Roman days was approximately twenty-five to thirty feet, just about the length of one of Plato's shorter

Egyptian writing pens of reed and bronze

dialogues or one of the Gospels. But some of the ancient Egyptian rolls, such as one magnificent Book of the Dead, were much longer. The Papyrus Harris I of the British Museum, which came from a tomb at Thebes, is the longest in existence. Once opened, it was found to be 133 feet long and 16¾ inches wide. Constantinople supposedly treasured in Byzantine times rolls of 150 feet which contained the entire *Iliad* or *Odyssey*.

When the technique of writing on papyrus was adopted by the Greeks is unknown. Chances are that the Egyptian material was introduced simultaneously with the Phoenician alphabet. In fact, judging by the term *byblos* (Greek for "papyrus"), the Greeks seem to have received the product from the Phoenician-Syrian port of Gebal ("Byblos"), whose name they equated with "paper." Yet the Greek word for "book," *diphthéra*, which means "skins," suggests that animal hides were first used for writing. However, by the time of Herodotus, in the Periclean Age (fifth century B.C.), papyrus was so much the standard stationery that the historian relates an incident from the Ionian past when, during a shortage of papyrus, people had to resort to the use of skins, as the "barbarians" still did in his own day. Throughout the classical period and the Hellenistic Age, papyrus remained the vehicle for Greek literary works. Books took the form of rolls of joined sheets (*kollémata*). Only gradually in the early Christian era—the stages have been obscure until recently—papyrus gave way to parchment, and the rolls were replaced by the modern codex form of folded leaves— perhaps an adaptation of ancient notebooks (*pugillares*) consisting of several wax-covered tablets joined by strings or hinges.

The Romans, as was to be expected, imitated the Greeks. Their term for papyrus was *charta* or *carta*, which, like "paper," entered into modern European languages in the words "chart" and "card." The Latin word for book, by the way, is historically as revealing as its Greek counterpart. It was *liber* and is etymologically derived from the Latin for "bark." As a writing material, bark has been used almost universally, and books from bark were particularly prominent in Central Asia and the Far East until relatively recent days. Even North American Indians seem to have used birchbark for the keeping of records. Into historic times Roman archives also employed linen (*libri lintei*), as testified by Livy. With books, neither physical shape nor material are in any way fixed. A book is a book is a book—but its form is ever changing. And it is only a matter of convenience not to call a recording or a tape or a text on film strip or micro-cards a book, though conceivably they may be the "books" of the future.

By the time of the Caesars, when Egypt became the private estate of the Emperor, as it had been of the Ptolemies, the trade and manufacture of papyrus was largely a state monopoly, and an important source of revenue. The raw product was still derived exclusively from Egypt. Indeed, according to C. H. Roberts, a British papyrologist, "Egypt supplied the whole Roman Empire from Hadrian's Wall to the Euphrates and from the Danube to the First Cataract, and papyrus was used as naturally by Irenaeus in Gaul, as by Origen in Alexandria."[6] Like cables, radio, newsprint, and other means of communication in the electronic age, papyrus helped to weave together the civilized world.

Harvesting papyrus in the Old Kingdom, Egypt. From a tomb at Memphis

With the growing refinement of the erstwhile peasant warriors of Rome, delicate and perhaps not always tangible distinctions between different types or qualities of papyrus—some flatteringly renamed for emperors and their consorts—were introduced. The ancient Egyptians had valued the hieratic, made from the center fibers of the pith, and used it for their sacred texts. Connoisseurs

[6] Roberts: "The Greek Papyri," in Glanville: op. cit., p. 251.

now distinguished almost as many kinds of papyrus as wines, each with its particular merits, hues, and stylish uses, and varying accordingly in price—and also in width and height. Some of the best papyrus came from Sebennytus in the Delta, also from Tanis and Saïs; and the *Carta Thebaica* from Thebes, in Upper Egypt had a solid reputation.[7] Other grades were named for their manufacturers. The coarsest type, *emporetica* ("merchants' paper"), was used for wrapping only.[8]

On the whole, Latin literature on papyrus has fared far worse than Greek because Latin never penetrated deeply into Egypt, except for administrative purposes during the Roman occupation. Hence Latin papyri from Egypt are at a minimum. As in most of the Eastern Mediterranean, Greek remained the official language during the Roman Empire. Roman rule may have been arrogant and predatory, but it was free of the cant of *mission civilisatrice*. Even Caesar's last words were probably spoken in Greek.

Indeed, the Roman preference for papyrus was long-lasting. After the so-called Fall of Rome, Cassiodorus, the patrician Roman Christian of the sixth century, sings the praises of the noble plant: "Here was lifted up a forest without branches; these bushes without leaves; this harvest in the waters; this ornament of the swamp."[9] As an heir of the Roman Empire, the Church continued using papyrus for its records and bulls into the eleventh century. The last document of this nature which bears a date is from the chancery of Pope Victor II, in 1057.[1]

The Latin papal documents and late Imperial and Gothic records from Ravenna were just about the only papyri known until 1752, when the Herculaneum library was found. Winckelmann and other commentators invariably resort to them as points of reference, particularly since at first there was not the slightest notion of the existence of the Egyptian treasure house. But with the Herculanean rolls the emphasis shifted from Latin to Greek. And, after 1778, Egypt became almost exclusively the chief source of Greek papyri.

In surveys of archaeology it has become something of a dogma that Egyptological research began with Napoleon's campaign in the shadow of the Pyramids ("Forty centuries are looking down upon

---

[7] Georg Ebers: "The Papyrus Plant," *Cosmopolitan*, Vol. XV (1893), pp. 679–80.

[8] David Diringer: op. cit., p. 135.

[9] Ebers: op. cit., p. 680.

[1] Roberts: op. cit., p. 251.

you"). True, Napoleon founded the Institut National at Cairo, and there followed the magnificent volumes of the *Description de l'Égypte*. One of the lucky results of the campaign was the discovery of the Rosetta Stone. But such eighteenth-century travelers as the Earl of Sandwich, Richard Pococke, James Bruce, and the Comte de Volney were as alert and inquisitive observers of Egyptian antiquities as the Frenchmen who snooped around the Nile Valley decades later under cover of a military invasion. Attempts were already being made to decipher Egyptian hieroglyphics, and the search for papyri was well on its way. Indeed, the Napoleonic effort, which differed from its predecessors in organization and financing, was itself a symptom of the newly awakened interest in ancient Egypt.

But there is no denying that the campaign added momentum, stimulating the European market for Egyptian curios, from obelisks to scarabs, from mummies to papyri. Natives and Europeans alike began to dig ruthlessly, and golden days dawned for dealers and forgers—professions that had flourished in the Near East for some time. These men catered with customary unscrupulousness to the flamboyant tastes of the national museums of Europe and of wealthy collectors, who unfortunately considered papyri one of the lesser items on their list of coveted objects. Hence, papyri were often haphazardly dealt with. Many rolls undoubtedly ended up in the glass cabinets of ignorant private owners whose bored descendants threw the rolls away or relegated them to the attic with shark's teeth, shrunken heads, and Great-great-aunt Jessica's decrepit hand loom.

The pillage—archaeology of the crudest kind—consisted mainly of the plundering of ancient mummies. Since the "orgy of spoliation"[2] was directed toward mummies of pre-Ptolemaic Egypt, most of the papyri looted in the first decades of the nineteenth century were written in Egyptian hieroglyphic and hieratic scripts, which were generally held to be forever undecipherable. This was the firm opinion of François Jomard, leader of the French mission, whose refusal to acquire additional papyri aroused the ire of young Champollion. Because of such prejudices, papyrus rolls were counted of little value as sources of knowledge of ancient times. They fed a passing curiosity and, as a rule, were hopelessly scattered throughout the world.

---

[2] Baikie: *A Century of Excavation in the Land of the Pharaohs* (London: Religious Tract Society; 1924), p. 8.

Antiquarians attached to Napoleon's *mission* claim to have been the first to realize that Egyptians in the time of the Pharoahs did indeed possess books. The proof came to the versatile Dominique Vivant Denon, gifted draftsman, author of erotica, and protégé of Josephine. "I could not help flattering myself that I was the first to make so important a discovery," he wrote self-consciously in his *Voyage dans la Basse et la Haute Égypte*, "but was much more delighted, when, some hours after, I was assured of the proof of my discovery, by the possession of a manuscript itself which I found in the hand of a fine mummy. . . . One must have the passion of curiosity, and be a traveler and collector, to appreciate the full extent of such delight." Denon was moved to intense reflection and a crisis of conscience at the sight: "I felt that I turned pale with anxiety; I was just going to scold those who, in spite of my urgent requests, had violated the integrity of this mummy, when I per-

Egyptian scribes—from an Old Kingdom tomb—pictured in typical positions: "They squat on the ground with the case for the papyrus rolls near them; the strip of the papyrus on which they are writing is held by their left hand, the reed pen in their right hand, and a reed pen in reserve is behind the ear" (D. Diringer: *The Hand-Produced Book*, p. 114).

ceived in his right hand and under his left arm the manuscript of a papyrus roll, which perhaps I should never have seen without this violation: my voice failed me; I blessed the avarice of the Arabs, and above all the chance which had arranged this good luck for me; I did not know what to make of my treasure; so much was I frightened lest I should destroy it; I dared not touch the book, the most ancient book so far known; I neither dared to entrust it to anyone, nor to lay it down anywhere; all the cotton of my bed-quilt seemed to me insufficient to make a soft-enough wrapping for it. Was it the story of this person? Did it tell the period of his life? Was the reign of the sovereign under whom he had lived inscribed there? Or did the roll contain theological dogmas, prayers, or the dedication of some discovery? Without realizing that the script of my book was not known, any more than the language in which it was written, I imagined for a moment that I held in my hand the *compendium* of Egyptian literature. . . ."[3]

Needless to say, the archaeologist—inevitably a grave robber —got the better of the moralist. Where Denon took the roll, he did not say in his travelogue, but the precious object may well have reached the Louvre. Conceivably, after he recovered from his first qualms and his initial enthusiastic speculations, and after he learned that rolls buried with mummies were anything but unique, he may have let it drift into the hands of a collector, as a latter-day Egyptologist, James Baikie, has suggested. At any rate, it is unaccounted for and we cannot be certain about its contents, but it is reasonably safe to assume that the roll represented a version of the *Book of the Dead,* of which we now possess a considerable number of variants.

Once it became common knowledge that the ancient Egyptians had a proclivity for attaching papyrus rolls to their dead, the despoliation of mummies was carried on wholesale. This sorry practice was simply a renewal of the earlier plundering by the fellahin of their remote ancestors for the sake of the so-called "mummy" (the resinous substance of mummies), long esteemed in Western medicine as an all-round panacea. "Idols of value" were a by-product, also pilfered from the desiccated cadavers by the fellahin.

Denon's exploits set a precedent, for there was increasing demand in Europe for such curios. Some twenty years later, Italian adventurers such as Passalacqua, Drovetti, and the inimitable Belzoni were playing the game. These sanguine gentlemen were little troubled by respect for the dead of three-thousand-odd years before. They acted with the aplomb of condottieri when laying siege to their archaeological fortresses and feuded with each other at gun point in the manner of the lawless American frontier. Their enterprises included the systematic and ruthless looting of the Theban necropolis.

Giovanni Belzoni, the most endearing of the lot, frankly admitted that his attention was focused on the extraction of funerary rolls: "The purpose of my researches was to rob the Egyptians of their papyri of which I found a few hidden in their breasts, under their arms, in the space above the knees, or on the legs,

[3] Dominique Vivant Denon: *Travels in Upper and Lower Egypt, During the Campaing of General Bonaparte in that Country* . . . , transl. by Arthur Aiken (New York: Heard and Forman; 1803), Vol. II, pp. 247–8. Baikie: *Egyptian Papyri and Papyrus-hunting,* pp. 48–50.

and covered by the numerous folds of cloth that envelop the mummy." The ebullient Padovese depicts his ghastly operations with unsentimental frankness: "Nearly overcome, I sought a resting place, found one and contrived to sit; but when my weight bore on the body of an Egyptian, it crushed like a bandbox; I naturally had recourse to my hands to sustain my weight, but they found no better support, so that I sunk altogether among the broken mummies, with a crash of bones, rags and wooden cases, which raised such a dust as kept me motionless for a quarter of an hour, waiting till it subsided again." He wandered farther along a passage: "It was choked with mummies, and I could not pass without putting my face in contact with that of some decayed Egyptian; but as the passage inclined downwards, my own weight helped me on [he was six foot six and a former circus strongman]; however, I could not avoid being covered with bones, legs, arms, and heads rolling from above. Thus I proceeded from one cave to another, all full of mummies piled up in various ways, some standing, some lying, and some on their heads. Every step I took I smashed a mummy in some part or other. . . ."[4]

The fertile brain of a past master of Hollywood horror movies could hardly improve upon this script. Yet it has been said: "Belzoni was an angel of light compared with some of his rivals, native or foreign."[5] Considering that the magic funerary rolls had the purpose of facilitating the dead Egyptians' passage to the other world, one cannot escape noting the macabre irony that, like the Pyramids, they helped invite the despoilment of their bearers' mortal remains.

When the dust from these ghoulish raids on the Egyptian necropolises settled, it had almost been forgotten that the first Egyptian papyrus known to the West was written in Greek. For quite a few years the unread hieroglyphic rolls from the Thebaid mummies preoccupied scholars, but in the early nineteenth century the few scattered Greek finds, if identified at all, were paid little attention. As prominent a historian of the Hellenistic Age as Germany's Johann Gustav Droysen, who showed an abiding interest in papyri, was unable to recognize the cursive Greek handwriting of several documents shipped to Berlin (he thought they

---

[4] Giovanni Belzoni: *Narrative of the Operations and Recent Discoveries within the Pyramids, Temples, Tombs, and Excavations in Egypt and Nubia* . . . (London: John Murray; 1820), pp. 157–8.

[5] Baikie: *A Century of Excavation in the Land of the Pharaohs*, p. 13.

were Arabic!). Moreover, the preponderantly legalistic and administrative contents of the known Greek papyri dampened the hopes of classicists. In 1809 a French clergyman, the Abbé Delille, wrote a poem containing the verses: *"D'Homère et de Platon, durant les premiers âges,/ Le papyrus du Nil conservait les ouvrages."*[6] This was nothing but poetic license. No one, as far as is known, had yet laid eyes on a classical Greek papyrus. But Delille, a lesser poet than Wordsworth, outstripped him as a prophet.

In June 1821, the Englishman William John Bankes visited the Nile island of Elephantine in southern Egypt near Aswan. The island was then already an important center of the trade in antiques, and there, in the company of an Italian friend, Bankes acquired from a dealer the now celebrated roll containing in beautiful second-century A.D. script seven hundred verses from the last (24th) book of the *Iliad*. This highly valued manuscript was purchased from the Bankes family in 1879 by the British Museum. It was close to a thousand years older than the oldest copy known at the time—but it turned out to be only the first of a great number of Homeric texts which, to the exasperation of later scholars, made up a high proportion of all Greek papyri. Copies of the *Iliad* were far more numerous than copies of the apparently less popular *Odyssey*. Nevertheless, in the eighteen-twenties the Bankes Homer was a treasure, and it remained a rarity until a new age in papyrological exploration dawned half a century later.

Virtually all the rolls that cropped up in the first half of the nineteenth century represented nonliterary documents of everyday affairs. Notable among these were second-century B.C. papers from the Serapeum near Memphis, dug up by fellahin in 1820, which included records concerning two sister-priestesses. These were to inspire several novels, one by a Frenchman, Brasseur de Bourbourg, of whom we shall hear later.

On the whole, archaeologists, who now appeared on the scene, were after bigger prizes: pyramids, sculptures, graves, and precious *objets d'art*. Thus, next to nothing was reported about the location and circumstances of the manuscript finds. Moreover, it became the practice to cut up manuscripts in order to increase profits, and sections of the same roll were liable to be scattered, like the murdered Osiris, all over the world, to the detriment of scientific studies. Then, toward the middle of the last century more and more papyri began to be available, at least intermit-

---

[6] Preisendanz: op. cit., p. 96.

tently. New hope flickered with the appearance of lost orations by Hyperides, a contemporary of Demosthenes; a fragment from the Spartan bard, Alcman (acquired in 1855 by Auguste Mariette for the Louvre); and what was later called the "prophetic papyrus," which eventually reached Berlin, and which contained a catalogue of works of Aristotle, among them the lost *Constitution of Athens*. This last was, in fact, recovered some fifty years later.

Notable papyrologists such as A. S. Hunt and Frederic Kenyon have dated the new era from 1877, exactly one hundred years after the discovery of the *Carta Borgiana*. It was then, as Hunt wrote in 1912, "that the great possibility of Egypt in this direction came to be realized . . . and the stream which then started has been flowing continuously ever since."[7] This chronologically elegant dividing line was actually the discovery in 1877 of the Fayum as a source of papyri. The quantities of papyri that suddenly swamped the Cairo antiquities market were staggering. Representatives of European institutions eagerly bid for them, but the bulk went via an Austrian dealer into the private collection of the Archduke Rainer of Habsburg, who deposited them in his museum in Vienna in 1884. Thereafter the archduke continually added new pieces, and by 1899, when the collection was bequeathed to the Imperial Library of Vienna, it counted some 100,000 papyri of varying length, from minute scraps to respectable rolls, the majority, however, in a rather sad state of preservation. Nearly all the papyri—including those acquired by other institutions— represented documents, that is, nonliterary texts: bills, receipts, contracts, all kinds of official decrees, wills, leases, schoolchildren's exercise books, horoscopes, letters, notes, and so on. Whole cartonfuls contained only domestic minutiae. The major portion were from the late Byzantine period, and a considerable number had been written after the victory of Islam. Almost a third of the Vienna papyri, perhaps the most valuable items in the collection, were in Arabic. A sizable number were in Coptic. Though the range was impressive, scholars at that time paid little attention to the social and economic history of antiquity. Papyri were rated according to literary content, and these were regarded as pretty mediocre. Besides, the huge quantities and the decayed state of the documents made study and sorting a difficult and lengthy process.

Arguments ensued among the experts as to the origin of the papyri. It was known that the Fayum, where the find of 1778 had probably been made, had also yielded these, but the exact site and the manner of deposit were not known. The custodian of the Rainer collection was certain that they had all come from a newly discovered ancient archive at the district capital of Medinet el Fayum, the Arsinoë or Crocodilopolis of old. But he was misled by the relative uniformity of the original Viennese purchase, which, as was later established, indeed came from one source. Even so, the disheveled state of the materials—disorderly, damp, fragmented, and torn—as well as their unofficial, private nature and their range over several centuries (some were as recent as the tenth century A.D.) should have cast doubt on the surmised origin. The custodian's article in a Vienna publication was promptly refuted by a brilliant young German Egyptologist, Adolf Erman.[8]

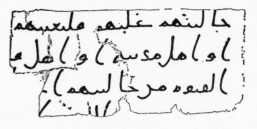

Arabic papyrus

Erman, in a bold argument, declared that all these documents had been taken from the enormous rubbish heaps (*koms*) that stretch for miles over the Fayum and most of Egypt. The precious documents had been unceremoniously discarded along with all other kinds of refuse to form successive layers of the Egyptian version of garbage dumps. Fortunately, the Egyptians were not prone to burn their papers and refuse, but rather left man-made hills like the kitchen middens of prehistoric sites. Local fellahin had always used them as a source for fertilizer, the nitrate-rich *sebakh*—there is of course no telling what invaluable treasures had thereby been obliterated. Some palaeographers nevertheless continued to uphold the archival thesis, and they were not entirely wrong: the documentary materials may well have included discarded archives.

The literary returns thus far were meager, except for parts

---

[8] Adolf Erman: "Die Herkunft der Fayum Papyri," *Hermes*, Vol. XXVI (1886), pp. 585–9.

of the lost *Hekale,* an idyllic epic by Callimachus, which was edited by Theodor Gomperz. But the fellahin had learned of the insatiable appetite of Europeans for such "rubbish," and these scraps would from now on escape utter ruin. Still, faulty methods of handling and sheer carelessness probably led to the destruction of more documents than were ever rescued. And more often than not, there was no record of where the documents had been deposited or where the various pieces could be located for reassembly. The realization that the extraction of papyri could not be left to illiterate and callous opportunists came only gradually to the experts, including archaeologists. This was to be changed, however, when W. M. Flinders Petrie pitched his tent in the Fayum in the late 1880's. He was the first to excavate for papyri scientifically, and he was to discover still another source for ancient manuscripts. With him begins the heroic age of papyrus finds.

·VI·

COFFINSFUL OF KNOWLEDGE: FLINDERS PETRIE IN THE FAYUM

The power of conserving material . . . of observing all that can be gleaned; of noticing trifling details which may imply a great deal else; of acquiring and building up a mental picture; of fitting everything into place and not losing or missing any possible clues—all this is the soul of the work, and without it excavating is mere dumb plodding.

W. M. FLINDERS PETRIE[1]

THE FAYUM, which Flinders Petrie explored from 1887 to 1890, was then a much neglected area of Egypt. Archaeologically speaking, it remained a no-man's-land until the young English excavator made the world aware of its past and established it as a prime source of Greco-Roman papyri.

Though not a part of the Nile basin, the Fayum is traditionally a province of Egypt and has been intensively cultivated during most of the country's history. It is in fact an extensive oasis (as well as a deep depression) of the Libyan Desert, situated within some fifty miles southwest of Cairo. Through a narrow gap in its hilly fringe it is joined with the Nile, to which, like all of Egypt,

---

[1] William Matthew Flinders Petrie: *Methods and Aims in Archaeology* (London: Macmillan & Co.; 1904), p. 5.

it owes its fertility. In remote times the Fayum was probably filled by a vast body of water, Lake Moeris, which has steadily receded. Long before the emergence of Dynastic Egypt, the shoreline of that marshy lake was occupied by hunting, fishing, and farming people who had strong affinities with the Mesolithic and Neolithic cultures of the North African Sahara. A long-headed Mediterranean race, they and their kinsmen in the western Delta may well have contributed the decisive impetus to civilization in Egypt.

Petrie's spadework was to show that the Fayum received particular attention from the Twelfth Dynasty pharaohs of the Middle Kingdom (*c.* 2000–1780 B.C.). It was these "engineering monarchs," greatest among them Amenemhet III, who built vast dikes to contain the lake, to reclaim land, and to direct water from the overflow of the Nile into irrigation canals. Some of the rulers made their capital here and built a number of pyramids at neighboring sites such as Hawara, Kahun, and Illahun (El Lahun)— all high points of Petrie's early archaeological ventures. When Herodotus visited the Fayum, more than a thousand years later, the colossal statues raised by Amenemhet III still stood towering over the lake, and the Greek traveler was enraptured by the enormous temple, the "Labyrinth," a structure much larger than the one at Luxor—all of it now vanished. Herodotus was equally fascinated by the local worship of the sacred crocodiles of Lake Moeris, who incarnated Sobk (Sebek or Suchos), the paramount reptilian deity of the Fayum.

Coin of Alexander the Great

After Herodotus came the Macedonian-Greek conquerors, in the wake of Alexander, and under their alien dynasty the Fayum underwent another flowering and expansion. Reclamation was resumed on a much larger scale and the new land was colonized by Macedonian veterans and other Hellenized newcomers, who built some one hundred towns bearing familiar Greek-sounding names such as Philadelphia, Theadelphia, Euhemeria, Dionysias, and Bacchias. Undoubtedly, the settlers found the Fayum to their liking. Here the monotony of the desert landscape and the riverine plain was broken by hills with verdant glens and occasional water-falls. Olives thrived and grapes ripened as well as anywhere in Attica or Thessaly. Centuries later, however, when the Roman order was rent asunder, the Fayum became a backwater; irrigation canals fell into disrepair; the desert reclaimed much of the land; and once prosperous Greek settlements turned into ghost towns.

When Flinders Petrie started his first dig in the Fayum, com-munications with Cairo were poor, and bands of bedouin robbers threatened life and property. True to the discreditable practices of the French-administered Egyptian Service des Antiquités, the most promising archaeological sites were leased to dealers of *antikas* and of *sebakh,* who, with or without legal sanction, had dug for fertilizer since time immemorial in the rubbish heaps of abandoned towns—the same people who had unearthed most of the papyri that had been shipped to Europe since the appearance of the *Carta Borgiana* a hundred years earlier.

Petrie, who became the towering figure of nineteenth-century Egyptology, had landed in Egypt in 1881 without any intention of excavating. Nor was he set on archaeology as a career. But while he was studying the construction of the pyramids and laboriously measuring them, he had witnessed the French excava-tions beside the pyramids at Gizeh. Near the Sphinx, he saw a gang of soldiers execute orders to dynamite an ancient granite temple fallen into ruins: obliteration was easier than restoration. So staggering was the mutilation and neglect of antiquities that he feared most of them would vanish within a few generations. "A year's work in Egypt," he later wrote, "made me feel it was like a house on fire, so rapid was the destruction going on."[2] Then and there he decided to act as a "salvage man."

What Petrie wanted to see rescued above all were the smaller, seemingly insignificant objects without which it would be well-nigh impossible to piece together the life and civilization of the Nile in the three or four millennia before Christ. "Perhaps," he warned the neophyte diggers eager for quick returns, "in some places nothing whatever may be found that would be worth six-

---

[2] Petrie: *Seventy Years in Archaeology* (London: Sampson Low, Marston; 1931), p. 19.

pence in the antiquity market; and yet the result from walls, and plans, and pottery, and measurements may be what historians have been longing to know about for years before."[3] There was a desperate need for regular procedures, for meticulous techniques. In Petrie's opinion, the sieve counted for more than the spade— such insight makes him the Copernicus of modern archaeology.

Petrie was an extraordinary man, even among the other eminent Victorians. Though he never attended any institution of higher learning, he made the pompous holders of a university degree look like fumbling amateurs; and in due time he was given honorary titles from dozens of academies and was appointed to England's first Chair of Egyptology, at the University of London. A man of enormous independence of mind, he lacked the disposition to deal with officialdom and often made scathing comments that of course reached the ears of his associates. Unfortunately, he was in need of official assistance, which at best was precarious. That he managed at all was due to extreme austerity and economy. His first project, the investigation of the pyramids, was estimated to entail a minimum expense of £1,300; yet he did it on less than £300. He spent next to nothing on himself and ate and slept under conditions that might well have shamed the early Christian hermits of the Egyptian desert.

Charles Breasted, son of the American Egyptologist, recalled visiting the site of one of the excavations in Egypt with his father. There was Petrie, at forty-one, "with a genial face, kindly eyes, and the agility of a boy. His clothes confirmed his universal reputation for being not merely careless but deliberately slovenly and dirty. He was thoroughly unkempt, clad in ragged, dirty shirt and trousers, worn-out sandals and no socks. It was one of his numerous idiosyncrasies to prefer that his assistants should emulate his own carelessness, and to pride himself on his own and his staff's ability to 'rough it' in the field. He served a table so excruciatingly bad that only persons of iron constitutions could survive it, and even they had been known on occasion stealthily to leave his camp in order to assuage their hunger by sharing the comparatively luxurious beans and unleavened bread of local fellahin."[4]

Though Petrie was rarely granted excavation rights at a first-rate site, he more or less created the science of Egyptian antiquities. He may have come up with comparatively few pieces of

---

[3] Ibid., p. 36.
[4] Charles Breasted: *Pioneer to the Past. The Story of James Henry Breasted* (New York: Charles Scribner's Sons; 1943), p. 75.

interest to museum directors, but he added entire new chapters to the story of man's past in the Nile Valley, throwing light on every period from the Neolithic Age and the first two dynasties—once thought to be mythological—to the Roman and Byzantine eras.

Petrie undertook the first major dig of his "Seventy Years in Archaeology" in the winter 1883 to 1884 at Tanis in the eastern Nile delta, and it was then that he had his first brush with papyri. Even today it is barely conceivable that documents could have survived in this relatively humid section of Egypt. But Petrie was ever ready for the unexpected, and when he stumbled on a pile of litter in one of the ruins, he bent down to take a closer look. Before his amazed eyes was a letter in the "finest Greek writing"— but as quickly as the written characters appeared, they vanished under the slightest touch. The house he was investigating showed traces of fire. Once again, destruction had led to preservation, for in the cellar Petrie came upon the burned remains of a "basketful of knowledge." "In a recess under the cellar stairs had been five baskets of old papyri. Though many had utterly perished by being burnt to white ash, yet one basketful was only carbonized; and tenderly undermining the precious black mass, I shifted out and carried it up to my house with fear and reverent joy. It took ten hours' work to separate safely all the documents, twisted, crushed, and squeezed together, and all as brittle as only burnt papyrus is; a bend, or a jerk, and the piece was ruined. At last, I had over a hundred and fifty documents separated; and, each wrapped apart, and put in tin boxes, they traveled safely. . . . A little more air in the burning, a little less care in the unearthing, the separation, the packing, or the opening, and these documents would have disappeared. Of course, under the usual system of leaving Arab overseers to manage excavations, all such discoveries are utterly destroyed."[5]

It is typical of Petrie to have proceeded with extreme caution, relying little on hired help, and to have improvised methods of preservation. The texts proved to be valuable, though little of consequence was in Greek. They dated from a late age. But among the Egyptian papyri was a catalogue of hieroglyphic symbols with corresponding hieratic, or cursive, signs arranged in parallel columns. The document was probably a schoolbook for the teaching of the Egyptian scripts. It was the first of its kind to be found, and

---

[5] Petrie: *Ten Years' Digging in Egypt, 1881–1891*, second edition (London: Religious Tract Society; 1893), pp. 33–5.

furnished the philologists with priceless data. Another carbonized papyrus shed light on ancient geographic concepts of Egypt and on the country's administrative division into "nomes."

Petrie was by no means discouraged when early in 1887 the Service of Antiquities offered him the Fayum for exploration. Other archaeologists may have considered the region worthless fare; no archaeologist had ventured into the Fayum for twenty-five years. To Petrie, though he had moments of bitterness, a new site was a challenge and an opportunity, and in fact the very lack of glamour and the unfamiliarity of the area were to contribute to his success. However, when he was making preparations for the venture, the satisfaction he felt was "somewhat chastened by knowing that one of the most astute Arab dealers had been turned loose in the Fayum with permission to work. . . ."[6]

Petrie's main objective in the Fayum were the pyramids. Unlike the better preserved pyramids of Gizeh, nothing whatsoever was known about these. No attempt had yet been made to determine when they had been built and by whom. Would these pyramids—always, for Petrie, the favorite monuments of Egypt—help him lift the veil that shrouded the Fayum?

Funerary portrait from Hawara, on wax panel

It did not take him long to identify the pyramids as structures of the Twelfth Dynasty. And his excavation of the pyramid of Amenemhet III and the location of the burial chamber have come to rank as among the most ingenious feats in Egyptology. He started out at Medinet el Fayum (ancient Crocodilopolis), where he surveyed the site of the temple; then he shifted to Hawara. There, too, his attention centered on the pyramid, but he found another, "least expected . . . mine of interest"—the now famous

---

[6] Petrie: *Seventy Years in Archaeology*, p. 81.

portraits of the deceased, done on wax on the mummy cases, which, together with the murals of Herculaneum and Pompeii, constitute the most vivid Greco-Roman paintings we possess. There seemed to be an inexhaustible supply of these wax panels in the local graveyard: sometimes five portraits would pour in within twenty-four hours.

One day a native boy had just reported still another portrait when a party of visitors arrived. Petrie's communications to the London journals on the work in progress were spreading word of his investigations. Among his fellow archaeologists, in the first decade of his long career he was already a legend. They studied his methods as much as his discoveries, and they urged him to expound his theories on the evolution and interrelationships of the ancient Near East. The party that now arrived at the desert camp consisted of three prominent Germans: "Schliemann, short, round-headed, round-faced, round-hatted, great round-goggled eyes, spectacled, cheeriest of beings, dogmatic, but always ready for facts. Virchow, a calm, sweet-faced man, with a beautiful gray beard, who nevertheless tried to make mischief in Cairo about my work. Schweinfurth [the ethnologist] . . ."[7] All three displayed a keen interest in the Englishman's work, but for Schliemann Petrie had, by coincidence, just the right kind of thing.

He had dug it up under extraordinary circumstances at Hawara, while plowing through the Greco-Roman cemetery. It was the mummy of a young girl, her head resting on a Greek

ωΝ ΓΛωССΑΠΟΛΥСΠΕΡ
ΟСΛΝΗΡCΗΛΛΙΝΕΤωΟ
ΕΙСΘωΚΟСΛΗСΛΛΕΝΟ

From a second century A.D. *Iliad* in an uncial script similar to the Petrie papyrus from Hawara which clearly foreshadows the style of the fourth-century vellum codices of the Bible, especially of the Vaticanus and the Sinaiticus

manuscript roll written in the fine uncials of the second century A.D. The papyrus contained a large part of the second book of the *Iliad*. More surprising than the annotated text itself—which actually added little to textual knowledge—was the manner of its deposit. Archibald Henry Sayce, the Oxford Orientalist and founder of Hittitology, who was commissioned by Petrie to publish any

---

[7] Ibid., pp. 83–4.

manuscripts found, was certain that the roll reflected the discriminating literary tastes of the mummy, "a predecessor of Tennyson's Princess." In an appendix to Petrie's report *Hawara, Biahmu, and Arsinoe* (1889), he wrote somewhat fancifully: "The roll had belonged to a lady with whom it had been buried in death. The skull of the mummy showed its possessor had been young and attractive looking with features at once small, intellectual, and finely chiselled, and belonging distinctly to the Greek type. . . . Both skull and papyrus are now in the Bodleian Library at Oxford, along with a tress of the unknown Hypatia's black hair [the skull was later transferred to the South Kensington museum]."[8]

Chances are that the Greek beauty never read the roll. The burial of Greek manuscripts with mummies served a less rational use. Probably the Greek settlers in Egypt had simply adopted—in the half-understood manner of rituals—the ancient Egyptian custom of providing the deceased with a copy of the *Book of the Dead*, and by that time the contents of the text no longer mattered. Otherwise, as a modern papyrologist has remarked, "that anyone should select a copy of Isocrates' speech *Against Nicocrates*, which was found lying between a mummy's legs, as a companion for the next world is a strain on our credulity."[9] Scholars had often wondered why incomplete rolls came from apparently unplundered sarcophagi, and it was not until many years after Petrie's dig at the Fayum that they acknowledged the fact that fragments, just as much as entire rolls—irrespective of subject matter—could serve this funerary purpose.

Whatever the meaning of the custom, a virtually untapped supply of Greek papyri had been uncovered, and in time other tombs were to yield first-rate specimens. The *Iliad* roll was the most spectacular of the papyri recovered from Hawara. Sayce refers to a harvest of about 450 fragments, the majority consisting of deeds, tax rosters, and other legal documents. Many were simply deposited in the area by the drifting sand. Petrie and his associates assumed that these various papers had formed part of a public records office which over the centuries had been scattered by the wind and buried in the desert, but it is much more likely that they simply were carried down from nearby garbage heaps. Even Petrie had not yet accepted rubbish deposits as treasure troves of papyri.

At least two exceptional literary fragments, part of an un-

---

[8] Archibald Henry Sayce, in Petrie: *Hawara, Biahmu, and Arsinoe* (London: Field & Tuer; 1889), p. 24.

[9] Roberts: op. cit., p. 253.

known historical work on Sicily, were culled from Hawara. More interesting for their mode of burial than for their subject matter were a series of Byzantine papyri dating from 512 to 513 pertaining to the sale of two monasteries. They had been carefully rolled up, tied together, and inserted in a jar—just like the Dead Sea scrolls and numerous other documents of antiquity. The Hawara papyri amply demonstrated the wealth of the Fayum in ancient documents. In addition they furnished new information on the various ways in which such texts had survived: chiefly in abandoned houses, buried with mummies, in earthenware vessels, and in the sand itself. But this, as we shall see, by no means exhausted all modes of provenance.

In the following season, 1889 to 1890, Petrie concentrated his activities at Gurob, near the eastern entry of the Fayum. And it was here that he struck his richest find, opening a new phase in the hunt for papyrus and marking the beginning of the science of papyrology.

Gurob had attracted Petrie while he was still at Hawara, when natives had brought him beads and ornaments from there. He sensed at once that the ruined town would be of interest because of its contacts with foreigners from the eastern Mediterranean during the Eighteenth Dynasty (c. 1480–1200 B.C.). True to expectations, he found a Phoenician "Venus" and the wooden figure of a Hittite harpist, but he was most impressed by an ample supply of vases, which, in a bold hypothesis, he declared to be "Aegean." Evans's discoveries in Knossos some ten years later were to prove him right. The record of contacts between Greece, Crete, and Egypt was at one stroke extended into the past by more than a millennium. Cretan civilization could be fixed in historic time by cross-dating with the Aegean (or "Minoan") artifacts from Middle and New Kingdom Egypt. This alone was one of the milestones of Near Eastern archaeology and constituted a new link in the chronology of unrecorded civilizations. Petrie, in his reports of the excavations, introduced the now fully accepted term "Aegean." However, as he was to say with characteristic sarcasm in his autobiography: "Reinach and Evans debated which of them had started the name Aegean some years later. . . ."[1]

It was almost with regret that Petrie turned at last from the buried Egyptian town to the adjacent site of the Ptolemaic

---

[1] Petrie: *Seventy Years in Archaeology*, p. 101.

settlement, with its extensive cemetery, in the north of Gurob. No matter how indifferent it looked, it could not be slighted if this was to be an exhaustive archaeological survey of the area. The initial examination confirmed Petrie's pessimistic views. The physical remains compared unfavorably with those from the time of the Pharaohs. The decline was evident even in the burial of the Ptolemaic dead, who were entombed at the edge of the desert. "Their mummies," Petrie wrote in his notes, "are destitute of

Four sketches tracing the evolution of mummy decoration in Hellenistic and Roman Egypt. The thoroughly Egyptian model of Ptolemaic times gave way to a more hybrid style, which eventually incorporated a portrait.

amulets or ornaments, and have all gone to black dust, their cartonnage coverings are without names, and of the most conventional and uninteresting kind and their coffins are of prodigious rudeness; a few are good enough to be grotesque, but others are things of which a Pacific islander would be ashamed. The noses are long triangular ridges, the eyes marked with two scores in the board, and the mouth with a third line. In some the nose is pressed on; and in others a ghastly attempt at improvement is made by painting black and white eyes. Within these grossly rough cases were comparatively fine cartonnages." However, to this dejected note he added: "But what was worthless in the days of Philadelphos is a treasure now."[2]

When he examined the "cartonnages," or mummy cases, however, he noticed, with the true instinct of the discoverer, that they consisted, not of layers of linen as in the days of the Pharaohs, but of sheets of papyrus, some of which bore recognizable traces of writing. It was the beginning of a cinderella story. The shabby,

---

[2] Petrie: *Ten Years' Digging*, p. 135.

nameless dead yielded up Greek manuscripts more valuable and far older than any so far known. Professor Sayce, once again called on by Petrie to edit them, was greatly moved. The disinterred classical papyri, he declared, were "of an age of which the most sanguine scholar had not ventured to dream."[3]

Cartonnages had long been in use as a kind of inner cover of the mummy. The Greek settlers had again copied the native Egyptians in this funerary practice, but they simplified the process —to our great benefit. Instead of folds of linen, they employed discarded papyrus, which they moistened and molded to the mummy's head, legs, chest and shoulders, and feet. Over the wet pieces was spread a thick coat of stucco, which was subsequently painted in more or less garish colors. Initially the papyri were joined by glue, but, luckily, this step was later eliminated. Actually the mummies were more durable without glue, for insects liked glue and would eat their way through one layer of the gummed papyrus to the next, leaving nothing but the stucco.

Petrie was able to despoil some thirty mummies of their cartonnages. Fortunately, most of the papyri from Gurob were unglued, but they were in a frightful state. That some survived the treatment they were accorded, after an interment of more than two thousand years, is in itself astonishing. Wherever the writing had been exposed to the stucco, it had been obliterated through the chemical action of the lime.

Where had these papyri come from? Their physical condition suggested an answer. Much of the material had been fragmentary to start with, and had probably been acquired by the ancient undertaker as rubbish. He may have been supplied regularly by a junk dealer with material collected and shipped from other places. Often one mummy case, or even several mummies, consisted of fragments from the same papers, which could be matched.[4] One lot, for example, turned out to be the private and official papers of a colonist, whose career could be reconstructed from them. On occasion, a lengthy document was employed in its entirety, particularly when fitted to a flat part of the body. Then, if luck held, "it may be taken out none the worse for its burial of over two thousand years."[5]

When all the papyri shrouds had been collected, Petrie ap-

---

[3] Sayce, in Petrie: *Illahun, Kahun and Gurob* (London: David Nutt; 1891), p. 34.
[4] Ibid.
[5] Petrie: *Illahun, Kahun and Gurob*, p. 28.

plied himself to the task of disentangling the baked pieces—by no means an easy process, and not always successful. As with the Herculanean rolls, a great deal of experimentation was necessary. Petrie relied mainly on soaking the papyri. Later on, a fairly satisfactory treatment with water vapor and chemicals was worked out. Petrie was able to extricate quite a number of readable passages. At the end of the season he took those with him to England and handed them over to Sayce, who was at his old college in Oxford for the summer. Sayce invited Professor John Pentland Mahaffy from Dublin, a student of Ptolemaic history, to share the exciting work with him during the long summer vacation of 1890. Several pieces were still unopened, but most of them were ready for preliminary sorting out, after which the major job of decipherment could begin. The writing was unfamiliar and from a period which so far had yielded no other palaeographic specimens. The meaning had to be determined, and eventually an attempt had to be made at identification. This last offered the greatest challenge— and held in store the greatest surprise—for the classical scholars. If the fragment happened to be from a lost or unknown work, it became a tremendous problem[6] to assign authorship—often defying solution.

Both Mahaffy and Sayce have written with sensitiveness of the halcyon weeks of that summer in Oxford. "Seldom," Mahaffy said, "has it fallen to the lot of modern scholars to spend such days as we spent together at Oxford in the Long Vacation of 1890; poring all day, while the sun shone, over these faint and fragmentary records; discussing in the evening the stray lights we had found and their possible significance. Gradually pieces of a Platonic dialogue emerged, which presently we determined to be the *Phaedo;* then a leaf of a tragic poem . . . and with these were many legal or official documents with dates, which arrested and surprised us. . . ."[7]

A fragment of three hundred verses from an Attic tragedy posed one of the formidable riddles. The writing was difficult to make out, and transcription proceeded slowly. At first the plot seemed obscure. The style, however, was reminiscent of Euripides. But this suspicion was too little to go by. If only the scholars could pin down the subject. Suddenly Mahaffy told Sayce: "I have an

---

[6] John Pentland Mahaffy: "The Petrie Papyri," *New Review,* Vol. VII (1892), pp. 551–2.

[7] Mahaffy: "On the Flinders Petrie Papyri," *Cunningham Memoirs* No. VIII (Dublin: Royal Irish Academy; 1891), p. 11.

inspiration: let us go to the library!" And to the library they went. "In a few minutes," Sayce later wrote, "he showed me a quotation from the lost Euripidean tragedy *Antiope* which agreed exactly with one of the lines we had been copying. The fragment was identified, and a long-lost relic of the great Athenian poet was once more in our possession."[8] The incident, by the way, is a fair illustration of the manner in which identification of a lost work usually proceeds. It has been frequently reenacted.

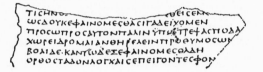

Passage from a lost tragedy by Euripides. Facsimile after Berlin papyrus of the *Melanippe*

The lost *Antiope* had been quoted by Plato in the dialogue *Gorgias*. In antiquity it was considered one of Euripides' finest plays. "Longinus," the master of ancient literary critics, referred

Third-century B.C. copy of Plato's *Phaedo*, discovered by Petrie at Gurob. Because of its early date, it probably resembles manuscripts contemporary with the great classical authors of Greece.

to one passage in the play as an example of "majestic conciseness." Mythological in theme, the play dealt with the rescue of the captive Antiope by her two children, who in turn punish her oppressor, the vile Dirce. Dirce is tied to the horns of a wild bull, as depicted in a famous Hellenistic marble group now at the National Museum of Naples. On the basis of the familiar plot, Sayce and Mahaffy were certain that the Petrie papyrus contained parts of the last act, when the young heroes Amphion and Zethus come to terms with Dirce's husband, Lycus, and claim the throne of Thebes.

---

[8] Sayce: *Reminiscences* (London: Macmillan & Co.; 1923), p. 279.

The *Phaedo*, though a known work of Plato's, was palaeo-graphically a find of the first order. It was written in a neat lapidary style, quite close to Greek stone inscriptions of the fourth century. Mahaffy and Sayce have argued that it may have been written by an Attic hand, perhaps even in Plato's lifetime, and had been taken along by a settler from his native Greece.

The *Phaedo* and the *Antiope* were the most notable discoveries among the Flinders Petrie literary papyri. But considerable interest adheres also to another fragment, which dealt with the "Contest of Homer and Hesiod." One of Mahaffy's colleagues eventually ascribed it to the *Museion* of Alcidamas, a sophist of the fourth century B.C. A version of the poem had been known since the time of the Emperor Hadrian (who is quoted in it), in the second century A.D., and had generally been considered the original until a young German scholar in two brilliant articles of philological detective work challenged the view, some twenty years before the Petrie find. With only a few hints to guide him, he suggested that the work was known long before Hadrian's days. He then boldly proposed—though he lacked conclusive proof—that the Aeolian Alcidamas was the true author, some four hundred years before Hadrian. The papyrus from the third century B.C. found by Petrie in the Fayum confirmed his thesis. "It rarely happens," wrote a critic in 1892, "to a scholar in this field to receive such an unexpected proof of the correctness of a theory, and to have it proved to be based upon such profound learning and sagacity."[9]

The name of the German classicist was Friedrich Nietzsche. Mahaffy, in his edition of the Alcidamas papyrus, mentions him, but he does not seem to be aware of Nietzsche's greater claims to fame. The author of *Zarathustra*, already in the throes of insanity, was little known at the time, even in his native Germany.

Among other literary pieces culled from Petrie's collection was, of course, a fragment from the *Iliad*. It appeared to be "a miserable scrap . . . giving us only the ends of the lines in one column and the beginnings of the next, in all thirty-five ends and openings, sufficient to identify from the 11th book of the *Iliad*, but containing five or six not known in any of our text." Since this was easily the oldest copied passage of the *Iliad* that had ever come to light, it was to spark endless disputes on the trustworthiness of the traditional text, which had been transmitted through

---

[9] Edward G. Mason: "Greek Papyri in Egyptian Tombs," *The Dial*, Vol. XIII (June 1892), p. 49.

the Alexandrine critics of a later date. "The discussion of this problem," Mahaffy wrote, "is now occupying the Germans, who send me every month a pamphlet concerning it."[1]

After the memorable summer of 1890, Sayce, whose principal interest was ancient Near Eastern languages rather than Greek literature and palaeography, with Petrie's permission handed the sole responsibility of editing and publishing the papyri over to Mahaffy. Years afterwards, Sayce was to recall nostalgically those days of intellectual delight when it seemed they were living over again the days of the Renaissance: "Now, as then, lost fragments of classical literature were constantly coming to light along with copies of existing works centuries older than any manuscripts of them previously known." How they had relished burying themselves in these texts until the dinner hour arrived, when they would have occasion to discuss "their discoveries and hopes with other scholars over the dessert and wine of the Common Room. It was an ideal time, but like all ideal times it came too soon to an end."[2]

A wooden mummy tag resembling those long in use by Egyptians for identifying their dead. This one, however, is inscribed in Greek.

For Flinders Petrie, Sayce, and Mahaffy it was a lasting joy to have shared in the first major recovery of ancient Greek papyri. Here were literary texts from the third century B.C., if not the fourth—which might almost have been written in the lifetime of Demosthenes or Euripides. Now at last the peculiarities of early Hellenistic script could be studied. Even transmitted Greek texts

---

[1] Mahaffy: "The Petrie Papyri," p. 552.
[2] Sayce: *Reminiscences*, p. 279.

became available in copies that had been made a thousand years earlier than the oldest traditional texts. And there were glimpses of works otherwise totally lost, some attributable to the greatest names in classical literature. It took four large volumes to publish the bulk of the finds, and these volumes did not even include all the Greek papyri, not to mention those in other languages. Yet Petrie's finds among the funerary trappings of Gurob marked the threshold of a renaissance in lost literary works from antiquity.

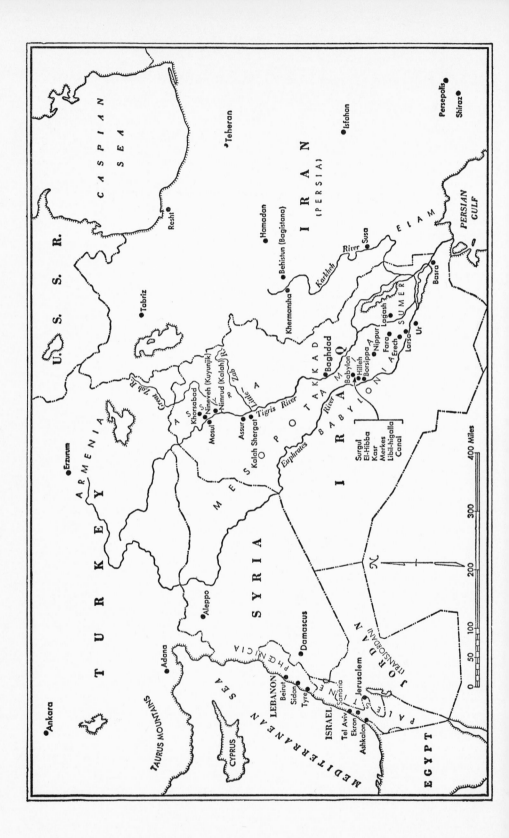

·VII·

THE TRAFFIC IN

PAPYRI: WALLIS BUDGE

*The interest which was being attracted to potsherds
had been recalled to papyri. We have substantial works
of poetry to set against the Hermes of Olympia and the
Charioteer of Delphi; we have new histories to compete
with the histories revealed by the excavations of Troy,
of Mycenae, and of Crete.*

FREDERIC G. KENYON[1]

FREDERIC G. KENYON had been a junior assistant at the British
Museum for a few months when in January 1890 he was
summoned to the manuscript room. Before him was a table
covered with papyrus rolls. The papyri had just been opened by a
skilled technician. What could he make of them? On first sight,
the material seemed entirely unfamiliar. The cursive script, though
obviously Greek, was unusual and almost illegible. Kenyon thought
that some of the rolls might be of a historical character. Others
appeared to be works of literature. Kenyon's superiors were impressed enough to hand the rolls (and sheets) over to him. When
he published them the following year—simultaneously with Sayce
and Mahaffy's "Flinders Petrie Papyri"—the restored texts established 1891 as the *annus mirabilis* of papyrology. Whereas Petrie's
mummy cases yielded manuscripts far too short to permit a full-
scale recovery of an ancient tragedy, the British Museum papyri

---

[1] Frederic G. Kenyon: "Greek Papyri and Their Contribution to Classical Literature," *Journal of Hellenic Studies,* Vol. XXXIX (1919), p. 13.

gave to the world nearly intact works. High on the list of literary discoveries were four texts which the museum released from 1891 to 1897. These were Aristotle's *The Constitution of Athens*, the *Mimes* of Herodas (Herondas), the poems of Bacchylides, and additional speeches by Hyperides.

As soon as the treatise by Aristotle was resurrected, its provenance excited enormous curiosity. Had someone had the good fortune to dig up an old library? Was the miracle of Herculaneum being repeated and outstripped in Egypt? There were little more than rumors at the time, and officials of the British Museum refused to disclose their sources. Instead, they declared that "no answer need be expected or required. . . . It is possible that there

From the oration *pro Euxenippe* by Hyperides, a contemporary and rival of Demosthenes. British Museum papyrus

may be more where this came from, and if so the authorities of the British Museum would be extremely unwise if they indicated this possible source of future treasures."[2] Naturally this secretiveness was a torment to many, not least to the Egyptian Service of Antiquities in Cairo. It also raised a good deal of suspicion. But, no doubt, the officials of the British Museum had good reason to maintain stubborn silence. Only years later did the facts come to be known. The man who was to reveal them was Ernest Alfred Thompson Wallis Budge, an outstanding Orientalist long associated with the museum as keeper of the Department of Egyptian and Assyrian Antiquities.

In a way the new finds, with which Budge was so closely connected, were a throwback to the freebooting days of the early papyrus hunters, a lamentable reversal to the shady practices of

---

[2] Kenyon: "Aristotle's Treatise on the Constitution of Athens." *Review of Reviews*, Vol. III (February 1891), p. 176.

native grave robbers and crafty dealers. Even the cloak-and-dagger touches of Belzoni's forays into Egyptian treasure domes were there. But this is an inevitable aspect of archaeology: discoveries do not always travel the road of progress or follow improved methods. On the contrary, illicit digging is encouraged by the very success of scientific excavation.

European institutions would have been foolish to turn a cold shoulder to offers from native diggers and dealers. Even Flinders Petrie and others like him, while digging for papyrus, at the same time bought documents and rolls from the fellahin. In fact, it was in this manner that Petrie had gained possession of the renowned Revenue Papyrus, which he handed over for decipherment to the young British scholar Bernard Pyne Grenfell. Grenfell and his colleague Arthur Surridge Hunt also bought papyri in later years. Long after the excavation of papyri had become a full-fledged branch of advanced archaeology, several outstanding caches reached the world through irregular, or commercial, channels.

Egypt in the 1880's was crowded with tourists, amateur excavators, and other men whose appetite for the country's buried treasures was insatiable. Into such a scene stepped Wallis Budge.

Wallis Budge, whom the British Museum sent out on some sixteen buying missions to the Near East, knew how to make a good bargain and in the process tended to stretch the letter of the law governing the export of antiquities. He thereby embroiled himself not only with the French-directed Service of Antiquities in Egypt. The Turkish authorities of Mesopotamia, as much as the British civil servants who ruled Egypt, were reputed to frown on his transactions. But "everybody did it"—Budge more successfully and more ingeniously than most. He had a way with the natives, and when it came to eluding watchful officials he could count on an "Ahmed" in Egypt and an equally quick-witted son of the Tigris ("Hassan") in Mesopotamia. And there were always a few high-placed men around to help him get out of a tight spot or circumvent a bottleneck.

His enemies were many, particularly among the other agents and representatives of rival European institutions, not excluding fellow Englishmen. Envious of his successes, they would denounce him to the authorities and also accuse him of having a secret understanding with the Service of Antiquities, of making large profits, and of taking shameless advantage of the natives. To the latter insinuation he retorted: "This was most uncomplimentary to the natives, who, as is very well known by everyone who had had dealings with them, are exceedingly clever in protecting their own interests. The truth of the matter is that the natives tried to treat me as they treated everyone else, and when they found that it did not pay, they altered their plans and began to trust me."[3]

Budge, it has been well said, had one lifelong passion, and that was the British Museum. For its sake he was ever ready to despoil the ancient Near East of its antiquities. Though one may look askance at the means he sometimes employed, it must be acknowledged that he promoted with selfless zeal the museum's greater glory. He was also convinced that he was serving the best interests of scholarship. And in fact no one suffered as a result of Budge's passion. Much that might have been irremediably lost was preserved and made available to students everywhere. Moreover, Budge was not merely a pillager and a clever buyer; he also took an active part in the actual discoveries.

Strangely, Budge has never quite become a hero to popularizers of archaeology. Yet his rescue and acquisition of the lost Aristotle and Bacchylides texts are major achievements that rank with the recoveries of Boccaccio and Poggio. Indeed, Budge was moved by much of the same zest, daring, amiable shrewdness, and

From Bacchylides papyrus written around the middle
of the first century B.C., at about the same time as the
Philodemus rolls of Herculaneum

love of letters as the men of the Renaissance. Like the greatest of the Humanists, he was a philologist as much as a traveler and diplomat. He was also somewhat of an Elizabethan in his vitality and versatility. Blunt, volatile, a first-class raconteur, full of energy, intolerant of humbug and idleness, and of a formidable physique, he cut a singular figure among men of learning. For company he preferred soldiers and men of affairs to his fellow scholars, and although he attained great eminence in Oriental

[3] Ernest Alfred Wallis Budge: *By Nile and Tigris* (London: John Murray; 1920), Vol. II, p. 327.

linguistics, he was destined to become a scholar-adventurer in the true sense.[4]

Budge was born in Cornwall in 1857. His forebears had been in the service of the East India Company, and mementos of the Orient rather than a taste for the classics pervaded his boyhood. While still in his teens, he took up Hebrew on his own initiative in order to study the Books of Kings in the original. When George Smith, the pioneer scholar of Mesopotamian texts, read his famous paper on the Assyrian account of the Deluge (based on cuneiform tablets from Nineveh), which profoundly affected Old Testament studies, young Budge was entranced. An introduction to Dr. Samuel Birch, then the leading Orientalist of the British Museum, set him on his way. Birch allowed him to copy Assyrian texts at the museum, interested Gladstone in the budding Assyriologist, and saw to it that he got a scholarship to Cambridge as a "noncollegiate" student. Afterwards came a scholarship to Christ's College and several academic prizes. While an undergraduate, at the age of twenty-one, Budge brought out his first book, *Assyrian Incantations*, which dealt with magic texts. Within a few months it was followed by another book. Budge's professor first frowned on the publications of a mere fledgling, but soon acknowledged the young man's skill in the interpretation of cuneiform. These books were only the start of a long list. Indeed, their flow was so prodigious that in sheer quantity Budge may well have outdone some of the busiest producers of popular fiction. In the end there were some 130 volumes, a list of which made the author's biographical sketch in *Who's Who* extend to a full page—the longest entry in the book.

Despite this literary output, which would have taxed the lives of several men put together, Budge had time enough to carry on a number of excavations in Mesopotamia, Egypt, and the Sudan. These he tackled with his customary energy and with nearly complete disregard of the new scientific techniques. In 1883 Budge was appointed, on the instigation of Gladstone, to the Oriental Department of the British Museum. His rise was rapid, even though the jealousy of a colleague forced him to abandon Assyriology for the time being. But he was soon as much at home in Egyptology and made a specialty of the study of hieratic texts. By 1893 he was head of the department, which he ran with notable efficiency until his retirement in 1924.

---

[4] R. Campbell Thompson: "Ernest Alfred Wallis Budge," *Journal of Egyptian Archaeology*, Vol. XXI (September 1935), p. 69.

Budge made a signal contribution to Egyptian archaeology when in 1887 he was able to trace vague rumors of cuneiform tablets supposedly dug up by a peasant woman in Upper Egypt. Thanks to his proficiency in Assyriology, he established conclusively, and against the opinion of the majority, that they were genuine records representing correspondence between the kings of Egypt and foreign powers or vassals in the second millennium B.C. True to form, he immediately effected the purchase of eighty-two of the precious clay documents from Tell el Amarna for the British Museum.

A year later, in December 1888, Budge traveled up the Nile to Asyut by slow train, stopping at various villages along the way, including Mallawi, some 185 miles south of Cairo, an early Christian center where he had purchased Coptic and Greek "magical" papyri the previous year. This time he took the trouble to prod a native about the source of the religious texts and was led across the river to a low spur of hills where there were many fine ancient rock-hewn tombs of the late Pharaonic era (26th Dynasty). On one side of a hill he was shown two rows of tombs from the Roman-Byzantine Age, probably of the fourth or fifth century A.D. A number of mummies had been removed from these, in addition to the magical papyri. Budge was quick to notice a lower tier of tombs which had been left untouched because of "the immense heaps of stone and sand that blocked up the approaches." He had high hopes that these tombs of the lower series contained important antiquities.

Budge was only on a stopover. He had little time and was unable to take charge of excavations. Besides, he lacked the equipment and the permission to dig, and anyway he recognized the prior claims of the Copts who had guided him to the place. He proposed that they ask the consent of the Service of Antiquities for opening the tombs. Budge wrote in his autobiography: "They absolutely refused to do this, saying they had no faith in that department!" One may assume, though Budge is silent on that point, that they feared that alerting the Service might well bring in others, maybe professional archaeologists or even rival dealers. Besides, the Service of Antiquities was entitled to retain valuable pieces as national treasures.

The legitimate claims of the Egyptian authorities did not seem to bother Budge. Instead, he hit on a solution agreeable to himself and to the Copts: they were to proceed with clearing the site and penetrating the crypts, while he pledged himself to purchase one half of anything they might find buried in the rocks. Should the enterprise fail to bring to light anything of value, he would defray fifty percent of the expense incurred in clearing away the stones and sand blocking the entrances to the tombs. Having reached a gentleman's agreement, Budge departed.[5] The excavations he was underwriting were much in his thoughts, however. Had his instincts guided him correctly? For a considerable time his native associates had nothing much to report. They had decided to defer the clearing operations until the coming summer, although all archaeological work is usually at a standstill at this time. But they felt the enervating sultry season was most suitable for them, because "the great heat usually paralyzed the energies of the inspectors of the Service of Antiquities, and the contents of the tombs were left to take care of themselves."[6]

By September Budge had word that entry had been made into the tombs. But the reports of the native diggers echoed the vexing adage of archaeology in the Near East: others had been there before—however, not in modern times. Tomb robbers had looted the site ruthlessly in antiquity, leaving visible signs of their raid on the mummies, which had been unceremoniously broken into many parts and lay strewn all over the area. The Copts wrote that no papyri had been found so far. But the search continued. And in November 1888, Budge, who was at that time digging along the Tigris, had word that several rolls of considerable length had been discovered in a painted box.

Arrangements were made for the Copts to meet him when his ship, coming by way of the Indian Ocean and the Red Sea, docked at Port Said in April 1889. There, on schedule, Budge and his partners got together. "We discussed," Budge relates, "the purchase of all these papyri and they named their price. The papyri reached England in due course and the Trustees [of the British Museum] bought them, and immediately some busybodies accused me of wasting the funds of the Museum by paying a 'fool-price' for the papyri, and others said I had taken advantage of the 'poor natives' and robbed them by paying for the papyri less than they were worth. As a matter of fact the natives were paid more than they asked, and they were perfectly satisfied, and did business with me for at least twenty years more, in fact as long as they had anything to sell. . . ."[7]

The Copts of Mallawi also did business with others. A few

---

[5] Budge: op. cit., p. 149.   [6] Ibid., p. 150.   [7] Ibid.

invaluable sections of *The Constitution of Athens,* the prize find of the lot, were missing, as Frederic Kenyon noticed when he set out to decipher and transcribe the text. Even if the Copts dealt fairly with Budge, of course no one would ever know what texts they had found in the rock tombs; the natives themselves could not read them. Nor could anyone be certain which texts hailed from these tombs or precisely how they had been uncovered. Nevertheless, the British Museum had good reason to be pleased with the returns from Budge's third "buying mission" of 1888–9. A detailed account submitted to the Trustees listed among others: 210 cuneiform tablets and fragments from Kuyunjik (Nineveh); 1,500 tablets, 49 cylinder seals from Abu Habba and Der in Mesopotamia; 3 rolls of papyrus inscribed on both sides in Greek (on the verso was the copy of Aristotle's work); various rolls of papyrus containing portions of the *Iliad,* magical texts, etc.; 3 hieroglyphic papyri, and 52 Arabic and Syriac manuscripts from Mosul and its neighborhood.

When Budge, on the instruction of the British Museum, returned to Egypt the next year to institute a search for the missing portions of the Aristotelian treatise, all of Egypt was seething with the news of the extraordinary discovery. The Service of Antiquities was irate that another treasure had slipped through its fingers. Though the British Museum refrained from disclosing the manner in which it had gained possession of the "literary find of the century," officials in Egypt were not for long in doubt that Wallis Budge had something to do with it, and they did not fail to show their annoyance and keep close watch on his activities.

Several of Budge's colleagues, who were less well informed, voiced different opinions. To his amusement, Budge met with gentlemen who insisted that they had identified the Greek text of the lost work. "Others claimed to have discovered the papyrus themselves and to have sold it to natives who sold it to me, and more than one archaeologist told me personally that the Trustees acquired it from him."[8] Variations of these stories continue to crop up in the literature, but since Budge broke the silence and Kenyon and the British Museum confirmed his part in the acquisition, they can be readily dismissed.

Budge's efforts to trace the missing pieces led him to a lengthy search through the villages along both sides of the Nile. At long last he was led to a man at Asyut, with whom he came quickly

---

[8] Ibid., p. 148.

to terms, but there remained the problem of getting the fragments out of the country. That the Service of Antiquities would allow their export was out of the question. Besides, Budge was being closely watched. He was not at a loss to devise an escape, however. "At length I bought a set of Signor Beato's wonderful Egyptian photographs, which could be used for exhibition in the Egyptian galleries of the British Museum, and having cut [!] the papyrus into sections, I placed these at intervals between the photo-

Sir E. A. Wallis Budge, in whom Egyptology and the British Museum found a forceful champion. Caricature by Powys Evans

graphs, tied them up in some of Madame Beato's gaudy paper wrappers, and sent the parcel to London by registered post."[9] There were a few weeks of anxious waiting. But as he was getting ready to go on to Mesopotamia, Budge received a telegram advising him of the arrival of the package and stating innocently that "its contents were exactly what had been hoped for."[1]

Budge had now succeeded in securing for the British Museum some of the most valued documents ever taken from Egypt: the papyri of Aristotle and Herodas; the Ani roll, a decorated version of the *Book of the Dead*, remarkably preserved; and part of the Tell el Amarna tablets. No wonder that the Museum sent him out

---

[9] Ibid., p. 154.   [1] Ibid.

on further field trips, with explicit instructions to acquire all manner of ancient manuscripts. Upon his arrival in Egypt in 1892, he was heartily welcomed by native diggers and dealers, who found their relations with the museum both profitable and enjoyable. From Cairo, Budge made his way to the small towns and villages of Upper Egypt, visiting dealers, gathering information, and looking into a few small digs that the natives were carrying out on his initiative. In 1892, at the old cemetery near modern Meir, from which the Aristotle had presumably come, he took an active part in the excavations with his friends from Mallawi and he was able to carry away a good many scraps of Greek papyri, several of them dated, but none of any major significance. For a few years after that, the returns diminished, and it seemed that Budge had lost his lucky touch and the papyrus resources of his native friends were gradually drying up.

In November 1896, while he was meeting with his native colleagues in Cairo to collect some Greek manuscripts, a man from Meir approached him. He had not participated in Budge's earlier ventures, but he was well acquainted with the Englishman's reputation and he announced that he had a papyrus roll to sell. According to Budge's description: "He opened the box and produced a roll of light-colored papyrus, with many fragments which had been broken off it, and when one end of the roll was laid flat, I saw that it contained several columns of Greek uncials. I had not sufficient knowledge of Greek literature to be able to identify the text, but I understood enough to see that it was a literary composition, and that it was written before the end of the second century [A.D.], and I was certain that I must do my utmost to secure it for the British Museum. But I showed no interest in the document, and we all talked about everything except the papyrus, and sipped coffee and 'drank smoke,' until the owner began to tie up his box and make ready to go. Then as a sort of afterthought, I began to talk about the papyrus and to ask his price. When I came to bargain with him I found him 'solid' and 'dry,' as the natives say, and, compared with what I had paid for Greek papyri in previous years, his price seemed preposterous."[2]

In the ensuing conversation Budge was to use all the artful devices of a seasoned bargainer in the Oriental bazaars. He had made up his mind that he would not leave without staking a claim to the papyrus. But he could not let the present owner know this.

---

[2] Ibid., p. 346.

Budge did not have the sum demanded, and he had to ascertain whether the roll was worth that much before he made his "last offer." So he first got the native's permission to copy a few lines to send to London to get approval of the price. The trick was to obtain an irrevocable option on the manuscript while waiting for word from the museum. Budge continued to ingratiate himself with the man while drinking endless cups of coffee, the Near Eastern social lubricant *par excellence*. In the course of the conversation he learned that the roll had been found in a coffin taken from a large tomb, one of many burials in a hill near Meir. The papyrus had been lying, so the man said, between the feet of a mummy and the coffin. The native then got to talking about the other objects he had found in the tomb, some of which he apparently had with him for disposal in the antiquities market. Budge knew "that nothing facilitated one difficult transaction so much as the transfer of money in connection with another," and several items quickly changed hands. "The sight of ready money had a good effect upon him"[3]—the negotiations could now return to the more vital papyrus. A price was agreed on, but Budge had to admit that he could not pay until the museum had given him the authority.

Now the native went into his act. Incensed, he packed up his goods and got ready to leave. Budge was frightened. "I felt," he wrote, "that it would be a colossal blunder on my part to let him do this, so I told him that I would give him a substantial sum of money out of my own pocket as a deposit, provided that he would place the papyrus with a native friend of mine in Cairo until I returned from Upper Egypt. He agreed to do this. . . . I then sent the copy of the few lines of the Greek text which I had made to the Principal Librarian in London, and asked for instructions. . . ."[4]

While he waited for a reply, Budge made his regular trip up the Nile to see how his other enterprises were doing. On his return to Cairo, he found a letter from the museum asking him to secure the Greek papyrus, which, the communication implied, was of considerable importance. But fresh complications arose. The man from Meir had shown the fragments to other experts, one of whom thought he recognized the lost poems of an ancient classical author. An English scholar, then at large in Cairo, confirmed this and went around town boasting about his extraordi-

---

[3] Ibid., p. 347.   [4] Ibid., p. 348.

nary discovery. The publicity increased the cash value of the roll and also its desirability. Its native owner now realized that even the "preposterous" sum he had demanded from Budge was too modest, and he extricated the roll from Budge's friend in whose keeping it had been left.

At this point Budge reentered the scene, ready to pay what he owed and take the papyrus. Instead, the man from Meir insisted on returning the down payment, declaring that he could no longer do business with Budge. Furthermore, he insinuated that the Service of Antiquities knew about the manuscript and had intimidated him. Budge could not contain himself. He could not let the British Museum down. He argued, cajoled, pleaded. How could the man think of refusing to sell him the roll when in fact he had already sold it? He would not relent, and his tenacity swayed the native in the end: "Having sat in his house with him for two days and two nights, on the evening of the third day we came to terms, and I returned to Cairo with the papyrus."[5] Whether a higher price was paid than had originally been agreed upon, we do not know.

The dangerous operation of whisking the manuscript out of the country under the very eyes of the Service of Antiquities, past railroad guards, harbor police, and customs officials, leads us into familiar realms of adventure. To Budge, by now, such an international maneuver was more or less routine, one of many carried out between various other pursuits such as writing books on the Coptic Church, the vocabulary of hieratic, the religion of ancient Egypt, and planning a new exhibit in the Babylonian room of the British Museum. But there is a note of pride in Budge's sober account of the outcome of this mission: "A fortnight later I gave the papyrus into the hands of the Principal Librarian. . . . The papyrus contained forty columns of the text of the Odes of Bacchylides, a great lyric poet who flourished in the first half of the Fifth Century B.C., and the experts thought that it was written about the middle of the First Century B.C. Sir Richard Jebb [the great classicist] told me that he thought it was worth more than all the other things I had acquired for the Museum put together! His works were hitherto unknown except for a few disjointed fragments."[6]

The British Museum's four major acquisitions of Greek papyrus manuscripts from Egypt in the 1890's deserve a few words. They

---

[5] Ibid., p. 351.   [6] Ibid., p. 355.

cover four different fields—history, poetry, oratory, and a hitherto virtually unknown medium, mime. Of all of them, the Aristotelian treatise excited the greatest attention. At last Egypt had given up an almost intact work, moreover a work of one of the giants of classical thought. For at least twelve hundred years no one had set eyes on the work, and now here they were, three unrolled, long, yellowish strips of papyrus displayed in a case in the British Museum with the proud label: "The Unique Text of Aristotle on the Constitution of Athens." The ink seemed quite fresh. Less clear, however, was the cursive Greek writing of the first century A.D., which was not of the uncial type normally used for literary works, but reflected a nonprofessional hand. The treatise had been copied on the verso of a financial account by a Greek colonial, the bailiff Didymus—in itself a document of considerable interest in the economic history of early Roman Egypt. We do not know why this notable text on the rise and fall of Athenian political institutions was transferred to the back of a local administrative record. Chances are that it was done by the bailiff himself, or by a member of his family or circle of friends, for private consumption. This would explain the unconventional resort to the verso of a used papyrus.

That Aristotle was indeed the author is today generally accepted. But how did a lost classical work come to be ascribed to him? There was no title page or credit line in the damaged manuscript, and neither the writer nor the nature of the text was immediately ascertainable when the British Museum gained possession of it. The hand of the copyist was difficult, of a kind that palaeographers had little experience with, and some passages were badly smudged or rubbed off. First of all, the crumbling rolls had to be carefully opened—a job that called for great skill. Then a scholar could embark on the slow and cautious process of deciphering the text. The fact that the writing did not correspond to any surviving text made the job much harder, though every unfamiliar line raised the pulse of the scholar in a flush of hope and suspense.

It fell to Frederic G. Kenyon to identify "the greatest literary find that has been known for centuries,"[7] in addition to other texts included in the consignment received by the museum. The task was to catapult him to instant fame. Kenyon later recalled how one of the texts, "after a little painful deciphering of its small and very cursive writing," appeared to be an unknown work of

---

[7] Kenyon: op. cit., p. 176.

Greek history. "While at Oxford I had heard of the two small fragments of the lost *Athenaion Politeia* (Constitution of Athens) of Aristotle, published by Blass and identified by Bergk at Berlin in 1885. This suggested something to look for, and after a few days' work suspicion was converted into practical certainty by the identification of one of the known quotations of the work, and early in February I was satisfied that the manuscript before me contained this much-desired treatise, mutilated no doubt in places, but at any rate comprising the main bulk of it."[8] Actually, of fifty-eight quotations from the work by Plutarch, fifty-four were found in the rescued text.[9]

The work was of uncommon interest, not only because it revealed Aristotle as a sound historian of a cautious inductive bent, quite unlike the caricature Francis Bacon and others have made of "The Philosopher" in their anti-scholastic zeal. It was the only survivor of 158 such treatises that Aristotle—perhaps with the assistance of his disciples—had compiled on various constitutions as a vast study in what one may call comparative government. The approach was strictly historical, with little of the anti-democratic bias one might expect. In a brief, masterly sweep, it took up the evolution of the Athenian government since Draco, helping to shed light on certain hitherto little-known institutions. Above all, students of Greek history were stimulated to reexamine the traditional record, where Aristotelian testimony was at variance with the rendering of Athenian history by Thucydides or Herodotus. Among the lost Greek books recovered in Egypt, the Aristotelian treatise has also the distinction of being one of the very few which have come down nearly complete.[1]

The Constitution of Athens was a work of intrinsic value, no matter who had written it. That it was almost certainly by Aristotle added to its fascination, but it could hardly contribute anything more to its author's stature, though it disclosed a new side of his personality. Quite different was the case of shadowy Herodas (or Herondas), who previously had been barely a name. In fact, even the spelling of his name remains uncertain. Yet Egyptian papyri restored to us eight of his *Mimes*, a kind of genre poetry in iambic meter (*scazon*), thus contributing a virtually new type of Greek literature and making Herodas a posthumous celebrity.

---

[8] Kenyon: *Ancient Books and Modern Discoveries* (Chicago: The Caxton Club; 1927), p. 45.

[9] Powell and Barber: op. cit., Vol. I, p. 134.

[1] Ibid., p. 133.

Indeed, some scholars would give the Herodas text greater accolades than all other literary discoveries from the sands of the Nile. Kenyon for one declared that "among all the gifts from the papyri, there is none which has so clearly enlarged our knowledge of Greek literature by the addition of new conceptions."[2]

From the papyrus of Herodas' *Mimes*, one of the notable late-nineteenth-century recoveries of Greek literature for which Budge's operations in Egypt were responsible. British Museum

The British Museum papyrus containing Herodas' humorous sketches was extraordinarily well preserved. Six of the mimes were almost complete. Their subject matter is far from the elevated themes of the great tragedies or of Homer, and they are totally devoid of poetic magnificence, but what they lack in pathos they make up in a delicious realism. In them are captured scenes from everyday life in an ancient Mediterranean town, and they can be read and enjoyed without much classical background. Like the writings of Petronius, they verge on the salacious, but the material is handled with considerable restraint. The titles are indicative: *The Bawd, The Pimp, The Women Worshippers, The Jealous Mistress.* Volatile women are almost invariably the central characters. In *The Bawd*, a young lady whose husband is away on a prolonged voyage to Egypt is visited by an elderly woman friend. After an exchange of niceties, the visitor "comforts" the younger woman by hinting at the varied attractions of Egypt, a land whose women match Paris' three goddesses. But why worry? There are desirable men right here at home. There is for instance a glorious young athlete, a five-time winner at the Pythian Games, who passionately craves to make the acquaintance of the young lady. It would be easy to arrange an introduction. However, chastity triumphs in the end: the young woman firmly resists all the arguments of the amateur procuress.

---

[2] Kenyon: "Greek Papyri and Their Contribution to Classical Literature," p. 7.

Perhaps the most amusing of the mimes is *The Schoolmaster,* in which a much tormented mother complains about her intractable son, whom she is on the point of handing over to the disciplinarian. He will send her to an early grave: he refuses to learn, mixes with the town's scum, gambles, terrorizes the whole neighborhood, and disappears for days at a time. His father, too, is at his wits' end. The schoolmaster, moved by the woman's entreaties, promptly goes to work on the boy with a strap of cowhide. The boy shrieks his promises to be good; the mother urges the schoolmaster on; and he orchestrates the proceedings with loud admonitions.

Disciplining an obstreperous boy. After a Greek vase

In contrast to the Herodas, the odes of Bacchylides, "the nightingale of Cos," were purest literature from the greatest age of classical lyrical verse. Bacchylides was not the Pindar or Simonides Wordsworth had wished for, yet he had often been ranked as nearly equal to them. He was in open competition with Pindar, and Simonides was his maternal uncle and mentor. Moreover, the Emperor Julian, among others, preferred his limpid charm to the grandiose obscurities of Pindar. Scores of complete poems by Bacchylides, about 1,200 lines in all, were now exhumed, and scholars and readers of the classics could admire the grace, good sense, elegant simplicity, and fine craftsmanship of the fifth-century Greek poet. Admittedly, Bacchylides was a minor poet—of the kind, as "Longinus" observed, who never soar to such Olympian heights or fall so precipitously as a Pindar or a Sophocles. He could be read by the many instead of being worshipped by the few. Indeed, Kenyon considered him the easiest among the Greek poets and an excellent introduction to the study of Greek lyrics.

The same virtues of style, ease, and precision characterize Hyperides, the Attic orator who was to his contemporary and oc-

casional enemy Demosthenes as Bacchylides was to Pindar. That
he was held in great esteem is again amply borne out by the frequency with which he is quoted by others in antiquity. Like Cicero,
he may be said to have been at his best in the forensic artifices of
the lawyer for the prosecution or for the defense, rather than in
the grand sonorous style of the statesman-orator. Hyperides'
resurgence is one of the most interesting in papyrological exploration, and one of the strangest. It was during the Revival of Learning, when so much classical writing had been restored, that, perversely, Hyperides was lost. One copy of his speeches survived into
the sixteenth century in the library of Matthias Corvinus, the king
of Hungary. But when the Turks laid siege to Budapest in 1526,
the library was ruined and scattered. Fragments, possibly of the
same copy, can be traced to the inventory of a bishop of Transyl-
vania in 1545, and then all of Hyperides vanishes. Yet Hyperides
clung to life after all, and speeches of his were the first lost literary
texts to turn up in Egypt. The recovery itself was as fortuitous as
it could be.

In 1847 two Englishmen, A. C. Harris and Joseph Arden,
were traveling in Egypt. Apparently unbeknown to each other, they
both bought papyrus fragments. Mr. Arden, who got his directly
from the Arabs, made the better bargain, some forty-nine continuous columns in an excellent state. Mr. Harris's purchase was
part of the same roll, and within a few years both acquisitions were
published. They consisted of three pieces: the defenses of Ly-
cophron and Euxenippus and the speech against Demosthenes, the
latter, unfortunately, badly damaged. Nine years later another
source yielded an almost complete copy of Hyperides' Funeral
Oration for those fallen in the Lamian War, regarded by "Longinus"
as among Hyperides' finest efforts. This copy, obtained by another
Englishman, the Reverend H. Stobart, was transcribed in a clumsy
schoolboy's hand on the back of a horoscope.

Additional sections from the original roll, of which Messrs.
Harris and Arden had received the lion's share, continued to turn
up under extraordinary circumstances. The dealers had apparently
retained segments of the papyrus in order to fabricate "dummy
rolls," which were then sold to gullible tourists. The trick was to get
some worthless papyrus, glue it together, and fasten to the end a
strip of genuine old writing to give the impression that it was an
ancient roll only partly opened. Several of these dummies showed
up in London and Paris, one with the actual identification "Hyperides" on the strip of genuine text. Other dummy rolls helped to

fill a few lacunae, though many more were undoubtedly lost or scattered by their purchasers. The recovery of the Hyperides texts constitutes an exciting episode in the history of manuscripts. It also illustrates the vitality of the author, by whom Egypt had done better, even before the days of the great papyrus discoveries, than by any other author of antiquity.

The hope for still more of Hyperides' work betrayed a lack of common sense. Yet in the British Museum's major acquisition, the results of which were published in 1891, there was another oration, the one against Philippides, which shows Hyperides as a much stouter patriot than the ultranationalist Demosthenes, who had become weak-kneed after the fateful battle of Chaeronea. This political speech is particularly important because of the light it sheds on little-known historical developments after the Macedonian triumphs.

At the same time that the Philippides speech was acquired, the Louvre obtained the last major work so far salvaged, a plea for the prosecution of Athenogenes, one of the liveliest of the orations. The case in question was particularly fascinating and offered the great lawyer an opportunity to display his skill at "stealing the

Sketch of an orator. After a Roman painting

verdict" by ingenious argument where appeal to the letter of the law would have been fatal. Like all great courtroom lawyers, Hyperides was an impeccable showman. "Longinus" tells of one incident from the lost speech in defense of Phryne which could well be from a contemporary Neapolitan courtroom drama. When Hyperides feared the jurors might be unsympathetic toward his attractive client, he had her exhibit her charms, thus weakening the court's resistance and winning the case.

The six now largely restored speeches in our possession represent a good sampling of Hyperides' art, his admirable persuasiveness, clarity, urbanity, and an almost Gallic *esprit*. Hyperides in his private life had the reputation of a *bon vivant* and rake, and hence makes an especially apt counterpart to Demosthenes, with his prophetic exhortations and self-righteousness. Hyperides was perhaps the lesser orator—more natural and less conscious of style, sounder but less rhetorical, less passionate and grandiose but of greater ingenuity and good sense. His speeches, nevertheless, have an eloquence of their own. They reveal to us the man as well as the age he lived in and the social and political trappings of fourth-century Athens. They are as much history as literature. And they are among the most cherished works returned to life by Egypt.

·VIII·

PEARLS FROM

RUBBISH HEAPS:

GRENFELL AND HUNT

Might it not be more satisfactory, perhaps in the long run more economical, to go to the source and to dig papyri up for oneself instead of buying them at second or third hand and thereby encouraging illicit traffic?
ARTHUR S. HUNT[1]

FLINDERS PETRIE'S campaigns at Tanis and Gurob gave us the first glimpse of scientific excavation of papyri. But no matter how remarkable Petrie's finds, they were accidents rather than the result of a well-thought-out search. To that master digger, papyri were little more than welcome byproducts of archaeological spade-work. And unless we dignify Wallis Budge's highly rewarding maneuvers with the name of archaeology, no mission had yet been undertaken by a trained archaeologist for the explicit purpose of digging up ancient texts from the sheltering sands of Egypt.

All this was to change with the appearance in Egypt of two young Oxford scholars, Bernard Pyne Grenfell and Arthur Surridge Hunt, who dominated scientific papyrology for a quarter of a century. Their work in the Fayum, at Oxyrhynchus, and at home in Oxford began a new phase in the restoration of classical manu-

---

[1] Arthur S. Hunt: "B. P. Grenfell, 1869–1926," *British Academy. Proceedings*, Vol. XII (1926), p. 359.

scripts, for they developed a specialized method for papyrus hunting. The two friends excelled equally as excavators and as decipherers. While still in their twenties, they gave to the world in
1897 the so-called *Logia*, then by far the oldest record of Christ's
life.

What brought Grenfell and Hunt to international fame started
modestly enough. The first initiative was made by the Egypt Exploration Fund (later Society), an organization until then mainly
dedicated to the support of the archaeology of Pharaonic Egypt.
Its governing members had become weary of trusting the discovery
of lost manuscripts to accident alone, especially in view of the
publications of 1891 by the British Museum and the accomplishments of Flinders Petrie. A further challenge was a large-scale
papyrus search being conducted by natives in 1890, centering
on Socnopaei Nesus, far out on the western fringe of the Fayum, which resulted in the flooding of the Cairo market with nonliterary miscellanies.

There was nothing ingenious or revolutionary in the action
of the Egypt Exploration Fund. The only surprising thing is that
it had taken Western institutions and scholars so long to come to
this. Prospective sites were dwindling at a rapid pace: Egypt was
undergoing an agricultural expansion, and unqualified diggers
were wiping out valuable evidence and materials on a gigantic
scale. Even when the fellahin became aware of the profits to be
derived from papyri, their crude methods obliterated half of the
fragile texts they uncovered. Ruthless traders and souvenir hunters
also contributed to the destruction and ruin of manuscripts.

Such considerations weighed heavily on the Fund when it
decided to sponsor a project for the excavation of papyri. As to
a site, the choice fell naturally on the Fayum, where Flinders
Petrie had made history. The Fayum had reputedly yielded the
greatest quantity of texts, and moreover it was threatened by the
immediate extension of cultivation. The Fund obtained a permit
to explore the northeast area, and by the end of 1895 a group was
ready to start operations. The men selected to direct the preliminary dig were David George Hogarth and the twenty-five-year-old
Bernard Pyne Grenfell. Hogarth's specialty was southwestern Asia
and in particular Hittite inscriptions, and he soon left papyrology.
(He later led the celebrated dig at Carchemish, with T. E. Lawrence
and Leonard Woolley as assistants.)

Despite his youth, Grenfell was well prepared to take charge.
He had been an honors student at Oxford and had been planning

to major in economics when the publication of Aristotle's *Constitution of Athens* turned him to Greek papyri. An essay on the subject won him a two-year traveling fellowship, and in the winter of 1893–94 he apprenticed himself to Flinders Petrie at a dig at Coptos in Upper Egypt. He also took up Arabic and was on hand when Petrie purchased an important nonliterary papyrus written in Greek, which gave him a chance to show his skill as editor. Eventually he acquired a missing section and other texts on his own.

Grenfell had been eager from the beginning of the Fayum project to enlist Arthur Surridge Hunt, his junior by two years and an intimate friend since undergraduate days. Hunt had succeeded to Grenfell's Oxford fellowship and was studying Latin manuscripts in Spanish libraries, but Grenfell was able to persuade him to join him in Egypt instead. Thus, "Latin palaeography's loss," as one of Hunt's eulogists has said, "was the gain of papyrology."[2]

In January 1896, Hunt followed Grenfell to the Fayum, initiating an association that a German colleague has characterized as a *schöpferische Einheit* ("creative unity"). In an obituary on his friend in 1926, Hunt wrote movingly of their relationship: "A scientific partnership more intimate and harmonious than was ours during the years 1896–1908 has perhaps not often been formed. In the winter at our Egyptian camp we seldom saw another European, in the summer months our editorial work was mostly done in the same room. Problems which arose in the field, difficulties of decipherment and interpretation, were ventilated and discussed, copies of papyri were exchanged for the purpose of collation, and whatever one wrote was revised by the other."[3] The academic brotherhood labeled them the "Oxford Dioscuri," and the "Twin Stars of Papyrology," and indeed it became impossible to single out their individual contributions. While Hunt was away on military duty in World War I, and during the long illnesses of Grenfell, no marked difference and certainly no lessening in excellence and care is noticeable. Their joint efforts—particularly in the decipherment, identification, editing, and translation of their discoveries—achieved a rare brilliance and a high degree of accuracy.

The two men were quite different in intellect and temperament, and their differences complemented and enhanced each other.

---

[2] H. Idris Bell: "Arthur Surridge Hunt, 1871–1934," *British Academy. Proceedings*, Vol. XX (1934), p. 327.

[3] Hunt: op. cit., p. 362.

The result was utmost competence. Grenfell was expansive, impetuous, intuitive. He was in his element in the company of men, in the college, on the lecturer's rostrum, at scientific gatherings. Indeed, he found it difficult to resist any invitation to give an address, and his talents were immediately recognized. "To excellent eyesight and a gift for the marshalling and lucid exposition of a complex mass of evidence he united energy, enthusiasm, and a brain at once imaginative and critical."[4] When it came to criticism, to the careful weighing of evidence and argument, to meticulous decipherment, to the microanalysis of palaeography and the checking of references, Hunt was probably Grenfell's superior. Hunt brought to bear on everything he considered the controlled discernment of solid, cool, patient, incisive scholarship. He was reserved and somewhat shy, though of great delicacy and kindness. The descendant of an old Essex family, he was the well-bred Anglo-Saxon, loyal to his class and his Church, conscientious and of high ideals, but unobtrusive. Those who got to know him well found him affectionate, not without a lighter side, and indeed a witty versifier. A friend recalled him as "the perfect scholar, so beautiful in demeanor and in feature."[5]

The 1895–6 campaign in the Fayum was organized on a small scale; its purpose was to probe the possibilities of systematic excavation, and it served as an excellent training ground for the young scholars. At ancient Karanis, where the University of Michigan was later to dig, and Bacchias, they had ample opportunity to appreciate the importance of town sites for their branch of archaeology. Egyptologists, with their interest in temples and tombs, had by and large spurned unimposing "domestic" areas as offering little promise. In heavily populated Egypt most settlements had been continuously inhabited, at least until the Arab invasion, and it was unlikely that anything of great splendor or significance would have survived from the earlier Pharaonic period.

But the situation was entirely different in the case of classical papyri of the Ptolemaic, Roman, and Byzantine periods. These town sites—especially those at the edge of the desert—would prove to be the most fertile repositories. But what the best conditions were for the discovery of papyri in these sites, no one knew.

---

[4] Bell: "Hunt, A. S.," *Dictionary of National Biography.*
[5] Bell: "Arthur Surridge Hunt, 1871–1934," p. 335.

It so happened, however, that the Fayum offered all kinds of likely papyrus deposits. Up to that time, one of the favorite targets of papyrus hunters was any house which had been abandoned abruptly but which remained more or less intact. There undamaged rolls might have been preserved in jars or stored in some other way. Unfortunately, such houses were in short supply, and the chances that one might strike it rich in a hidden cellar, as Petrie had done at Tanis, were infinitesimal.

Desert landscape of ancient Egypt. After a mosaic from Palestrina, Italy

At first Grenfell and Hunt made complete rolls the objective of their search, and so they concentrated on homesteads. Graves received as much attention, since any one of them might be the resting place of a Greek colonial interred with a lost masterpiece. There were also the papyrus burial cases from early Ptolemaic cemeteries; because of their age, they were likely to contain fragments from the greatest period of Greek literature. Perhaps because of this orientation toward Ptolemaic objects, the first Fayum campaign was not as rewarding as it might have been. Quite a few documents were brought to light, but, as Hunt put it: "The results, though encouraging, were by no means spectacular. . . .

We had, however, acquired useful experience which was to stand us in good stead later on, and the outcome appeared sufficient to justify a fresh attempt."[6]

Expectations, then, were not pitched too high when Grenfell and Hunt went on a second campaign during the following winter of 1896 to 1897. The natives might very well have done a thorough job of plundering. Had the scientists come too late?

Once again the Egypt Exploration Fund sponsored the excavations. Since the Fayum had proved somewhat disappointing, it was decided to apply for permission to dig elsewhere. The choice fell on the desert fringe of the western Nile Valley, which seemed equally favored by physical and climatic conditions for the preservation of papyrus texts. There, too, Greeks had inhabited various town sites. The Department of Antiquities gave permission to dig anywhere within the ninety-mile strip immediately south of the Fayum to Minya. The decision to concentrate on the far south of the allotted territory was Grenfell's—and his archaeological instinct proved most acute: he picked the site of ancient Oxyrhynchus, then partly occupied by a few hovels that went by the name of Behnesa (Futûh el Bahnasâ).

The capital of this old district, or nome, some 120 miles south of Cairo beside the Bahr Yusef (a western arm of the Nile, which also feeds the Fayum), has never attracted travelers. There are no magnificent buildings, no evidence of Ramesside monumentomania, no rock-hewn mausoleums, no ruined palaces of apostate kings. Well out of sight of the boats or trains speeding up to Thebes from Cairo, Oxyrhynchus does not list as a stopover for the modern tourist. Intensive excavation since the days of Grenfell and Hunt has only added a morbid air to the carcass of a desert town, as if it had been finally debased by trench warfare and land mines. But it was here that a papyrological Klondike came to life. How did Grenfell know?

Oxyrhynchus was named by the Greeks for the fish oxyrhynchus, which the local people considered sacred, as reptiles were considered in the Fayum. The name suggested to Grenfell that Greeks had settled here. Otherwise, little was known about Oxyrhynchus. It had not played a part in history, but judging by the extent of its ruins and its status as a provincial center, it must have had a sizable population of a higher cultural level. Its well-to-do, Hel-

---

[6] Hunt: "Twenty-five Years of Papyrology," *Journal of Egyptian Archaeology*, Vol. VIII (1922), p. 121.

lenized upper classes might once have owned Greek literary texts, perhaps even whole libraries.

There was another inducement. No papyrus which had appeared on the antiquities market could be traced to Oxyrhynchus. This could be taken as an indication that there were no papyri there, or it might mean that the fellahin had not indulged of late in any raids on its antiquities. The latter hypothesis was quite plausi-

Mosaic at Palestrina showing the teeming country life of Hellenistic Egypt—replete with garden, farmhouse, dovecote, boats, religious procession, and temple. The exotic scene of Egypt was a favorite subject for Roman artists.

ble: the few natives left there were under constant threat from marauding Bedouin from the adjacent desert and had little stomach for anything but abandoning the place altogether. The dilapidated remains of four handsome mosques testified to the fairly recent exodus of most of the inhabitants of Behnesa.

Still another attraction of Oxyrhynchus was that it had been an early Christian stronghold and had had a wealth of monasteries (with some 10,000 monks and 12,000 nuns) and churches. This was one of the few things known about it. Hence, might it not harbor Christian fragments in Greek, dating back beyond the oldest

New Testament manuscripts then known? "The rapid spread of Christianity about Oxyrhynchus," wrote Grenfell, "as soon as the new religion was officially recognized [in the fourth century] implied that it had already taken strong hold during the preceding centuries of persecution."[7]

Grenfell's anticipations were to be fulfilled more abundantly and more promptly than he had ever dared to hope. Provision had been made by the Egypt Exploration Fund for Grenfell and Hunt to join Flinders Petrie at Oxyrhynchus. Petrie was to explore the ancient Egyptian cemetery, while the other two men took up their search for buried papyri. After a few trial digs, however, Petrie decided that this was not a promising site for him, and turned instead to Desbasheh, forty miles to the north. Grenfell and Hunt were now alone and for the first time in full control. They started with the Greco-Roman cemetery but failed to turn up any of the coveted mummy shrouds or any of the even rarer funerary rolls. The evidence was all too clear: tomb after tomb had been plundered long ago, and the few unopened graves were in damp subsoil, which would have been ruinous to any papyrus deposited there.

Meanwhile, there was excitement of a different kind. Bedouin were wont to pay Oxyrhynchus nocturnal visits. The roaming princes of the desert were following their natural inclinations, sanctioned, so they claimed, by the Creator Himself, to supplement their miserable subsistence with a few additions from their slightly more affluent brethren. The villagers usually submitted sheepishly, but one night the marauders made an attempt to get into the explorers' hut, which was outside the village. This time, to the Bedouin's wonderment and indignation, they were fired on by the native guards, and they decamped in a hurry. "Not indeed," wrote Grenfell, "that they need have been frightened by the antique muzzle-loaders such as our worthy guardians possessed, but the Bedouin, knowing the fellahin's temperament well enough, does not expect to be resisted."[8]

After three weeks of unprofitable digging in the graveyard, Grenfell and Hunt decided on an onslaught on the "town." Like everybody else, they believed that the papyri brought in by fellahin had come for the most part from habitations rather than from cemeteries, so a logical step was to search the ancient houses of Oxyrhynchus. However, first impressions were anything but en-

---

[7] Bernard P. Grenfell: "The Oldest Record of Christ's Life," *McClure's*, Vol. IX (1897), p. 1025.
[8] Ibid.

couraging. Grenfell scrutinized the length and breadth of the site
—roughly a square mile. Only the bare outlines of a few former
edifices were visible. Everything around them was in the state
"of utter ruin to which a thousand years' use as a quarry for stone
and bricks had reduced the site."[9] The buildings were a shambles
and the sand seemed to cover little of substance. Even a thorough
search, which might take years, was unlikely to yield papyri. This
left the rubbish mounds, high walls of sand and garbage, some
seventy feet high, which crisscrossed the town and its surroundings. They contained the detritus of centuries, if not millennia.

To dig for papyri in this rubbish seemed almost an admission
of defeat. Despite the great number of papyri obtained through
the fellahin since 1877, the possibilities presented by these mounds
had hardly occurred to the Europeans. Presently, however, Grenfell
and Hunt were to show that the garbage heaps were a prime source
of ancient texts, and papyrology took, literally, to the path of dirt
archaeology.

Rarely was a document preserved unimpaired. Much of the
material so irreverently disposed of had been torn or occasionally
burnt, and only under certain special circumstances was papyrus
thus discarded kept from utter decay. At levels reached by water,
which seeped up during the annual floods, papyrus simply rotted
away. The particular make-up of the mound and what it contained
was decisive to the survival of written sheets or rolls. In many instances, for example, temporary abandonment of an adjacent
settlement bestowed a protective top layer. In time, Grenfell and
Hunt were able to recognize potential deposits of papyrus from the
stratigraphy of the man-made hills. One of the promising kinds of
layers, called by the natives *afsh*, consisted of soil mixed with straw
or twigs, and almost invariably it preserved papyrus for centuries.
To Grenfell and Hunt it suggested a parallel to gold mining: "The
gold seekers follow a vein of quartz, while the papyrus digger
has to follow a stratum, or vein, of afsh. . . ."[1]

As a rule, papyri were found in a relatively horizontal layer,
rather than scattered over the mound. By the same token, papyri
from separate layers were usually from different time periods;
consecutive layers were likely to be closely related in age. The
mounds of Oxyrhynchus fell into three main groups—Roman,
Byzantine, or Arab—and they could be distinguished according to

---

[9] Ibid., p. 1026.
[1] Grenfell, Hunt, and D. G. Hogarth: *Fayum Towns and Their Papyri*
(London: Egypt Exploration Fund; 1900), p. 24.

their location in relation to the town site. Next to nothing from the earlier Ptolemaic era came to light.

Trenches had to be cut to permit any full-scale operation, and this involved major expenditures of time and manpower, which the Oxford explorers had to keep within reasonable limits. Moreover, the diggers needed strict supervision so that the fragile texts would suffer no harm or vanish under a tunic. It was also essential to sort out the pieces according to the original place of deposit, in order to facilitate the joining of torn papyri later on and the establishment of age and content. At Oxyrhynchus, as at many other sites, it was the exception rather than the rule for papyri to have withstood the ravages of time and man: the vast bulk of rubbish heaps yielded nothing whatsoever. Archaeological digging is not at all like unlocking a well-stocked bank vault. In romantic imagination, shining treasures turn up all the time, yet the reverse is closer to the truth. In the excavation of papyrus, as in everything else, Grenfell confessed, "there are more blanks than prizes."[2]

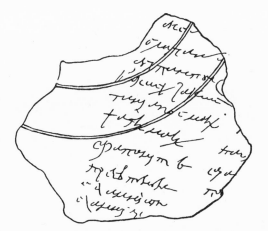

A Greek ostrakon from Egypt covered with cursive writing. Potsherds, wood, and other materials, besides papyrus, were widely used for nonliterary jottings.

The young excavators nevertheless found that life in the desert had a "fascination possessed by few other pursuits." But they did not romanticize its difficulties. They were upper-class Englishmen and valued comfort and cleanliness, though a passion for ancient literature had transplanted them to the sweltering sand wastes of the Orient—"standing all day to be half choked and

---

[2] Grenfell: "The Oldest Record of Christ's Life," p. 1030.

blinded by the peculiarly pungent dust of ancient rubbish, blended on most days with the not less irritating sand of the desert; probably drinking water which not even the East London waterworks would have ventured to supply to its consumers, and keeping incessant watch over men who, however much you may flatter yourself to the contrary, will steal if they get the chance and think it worth their while to do so."[3]

On January 11, 1897, the fateful first assault on an Oxyrhynchus rubbish heap began. In the cool of sunrise Grenfell and Hunt moved out from their hut with some seventy workmen and boys, who were immediately put to digging trenches. A low mound had been selected near an ancient temple and, in no time, papyrus scraps emerged from it in great numbers, some surprisingly long, almost complete. Nonliterary materials were the first found, among them private letters, contracts, and other legal or official documents. But then several fragments distinctly written in uncials, indicative of religious and literary texts, were uncovered.

A few days later, Hunt began to sort out the papyri. He was not a little startled to find among the scraps collected on the second day the Greek word for "mote" (KARPHOS) written in uncials on a mutilated papyrus which was covered with some twenty lines. The crumpled piece measured less than six by four inches and appeared to come from a notebook (the leaf was numbered) arranged like a modern book, in pages rather than as a roll. A papyrus book was in itself a novelty. It seemed to denote a humble document of a nonliterary nature. Yet almost at once the Greek word KARPHOS brought to Hunt's mind the well-known passage in the Gospels relating to the mote and the beam (Matthew 7:3–5; Luke 6:41). A careful reading bore out Hunt's supposition: it was indeed the Gospel verse. But this did not put an end to the surprises. Further examination disclosed eight sayings on the leaf, each one prefaced by the formula: "Jesus saith." However, only three of them were substantially identical with verses in the New Testament. Three were entirely unknown sayings here attributed to Jesus, and another two were too severely damaged to be understandable. Here is one (5:2–9)—without parallel in the New Testament—which was to be a lifetime inspiration to Hunt (it reappears in one of his poems): "Jesus saith, wherever there are two, they are not without God, and wherever there is one alone, I say, I am with him. Raise

---

[3] Ibid.

the stone, and there thou shalt find Me, cleave the wood and there am I."[4]

The little scrap was to become known as *Logia*, perhaps the most sensational literary find of its size ever to be made. The theological discussions it provoked resulted in an enormous number of articles and monographs for years to come. For one thing, the *Logia*, or *Sayings of Jesus*, copied around A.D. 200, moved back the Christian record by about a hundred and fifty years. Previously, the famous codices Vaticanus and Sinaiticus were the earliest written evidence of the life of Christ. Then suddenly the three hundred years that separated Christ's career on earth from a surviving account was cut by half.

Above all, it was the extraordinary contents of the leaf that occupied the minds of men. The three unknown sayings attributed to Jesus seemed to some to ring as true and authentic as Jesus' words in the Gospels. Did they represent a lost popular collection which originally circulated side by side with the Gospels, perhaps before the latter were accorded their exclusive, canonical status? Or was the *Logia* a remnant from a work older than the so-called Synoptic Gospels? Had it served, in addition to Mark, as source "Q" (from the German *Quelle*, spring or fountain) for Matthew and Luke? This was the opinion of several German scholars. Still other scholars saw affinities with the apocryphal "Gospels" according to the Hebrews and to Peter, or the Gospel of the Twelve. A few theologians, particularly impressed by verse five, quoted above, claimed to detect a less lively, less fresh tradition than that of the canonical Gospels. They heard overtones of "philosophized" teachings of Christ, announcing an immanent God. This view gained some strength when Grenfell and Hunt found another "Logia" text at Oxyrhynchus in 1903. Were the *Logia* then imbued with a sectarian spirit? Were they heretic?

The debate continued for a long time and remained unresolved until another manuscript find was made along the Nile—also, like that at Oxyrhynchus, in Upper Egypt—half a century later: that of lost Gnostic books, a virtual library hidden in jars, found at Chenoboskion (Nag Hammadi). This time the discovery was made by natives, so that few of the details are certain. It occurred at approximately the same time as the finding of the Dead Sea scrolls, shortly after the end of World War II, and has been unduly overshadowed by its fame. When at last the Coptic

---

[4] Grenfell and Hunt: *The Oxyrhynchus Papyri. Part I* (London: Egypt Exploration Fund; 1898), p. 2.

texts could be studied and edited scientifically, it was a French Biblical scholar, H.-C. Puech, who realized that the noncanonical sayings of Christ from the *Logia* reappeared word for word in this heretic literature and had probably been taken from there. The *Logia's* heretic association may have come as a shock. However, the argument that not all of Christ's words appear in the New Testament, that some were preserved at least in part in other religious writings, still stands unrefuted.

The finding of the *Logia* constituted a triumph for the systematic search for Greek papyri, and lent an aura to all of Grenfell's and Hunt's further efforts. In the public eye, this was the foundation of papyrus archaeology. And the two men became celebrities in the world of scholarship, which showered them with honors. Within a few months of their return to Oxford, they published a scholarly edition of the "Sayings of Our Lord," with a facsimile of the manuscript. The booklet was distributed by the Egypt Exploration Fund to announce its decision to establish a Greco-Roman branch devoted exclusively to the exploration and study of the Greek papyri from Egypt. A series of monographs followed, issued regularly by Grenfell and Hunt, and by 1908 Oxford had created the first Chair of Papyrology, which Grenfell was elected to occupy. Hunt later succeeded him.

The *Logia*, then, were the beginning. They created a favorable, receptive atmosphere, and they stimulated the two young men to further efforts. Grenfell's supposition that Oxyrhynchus would yield Christian materials was amply borne out. Indeed, a day after the discovery of the *Logia* fragment, Hunt came up with a leaf from a copy of St. Matthew's Gospel, also dating from the first decades of the third century. The early date meant that these pieces had been written prior to the recognition of Christianity in the Roman Empire. Grenfell thought they represented the remains of a Christian library whose owner may have perished in Diocletian's persecutions and whose books had been quickly disposed of.[5]

Additional Christian texts cropped up from time to time, but they by no means constituted the bulk of the recoveries. The lifework of Grenfell and Hunt was the restoration of classical works, however, and it is this that we shall now take up again, leaving the recovery of Christian manuscripts for a later section of this book.

---

[5] Grenfell: "The Oldest Record of Christ's Life," p. 1028.

For the remainder of the first Oxyrhynchus campaign, Grenfell and Hunt resolved to proceed more quickly and with greater intensity. Their labor force was increased to 110. A man working together with a boy was judged to be the most effective unit; the output of each such team was stored and packed separately. With the exception of four trained men from the Fayum, the native diggers were recruited locally—and the explorers felt they were fortunate to have "unsophisticated" laborers who were oblivious of the market value of the antique finds. No doubt the natives wondered about the absurd appetite of the foreigners for shreds of dirty old paper.

The work day consisted of about eleven hours, and in the end there were more boys than men, because they were easier to manage and more honest. All the youngsters of the neighborhood, it seemed, were clamoring to be taken on. "Some of the tiny applicants really looked as though they had only recently left their cradles, if they had ever known such luxury, which of course, they had not." Grenfell fondly recalled one such urchin, barely eight years old but the most alert of them all, "who had a wonderful eye for the right kind of soil and for finding papyri."[6]

Their forces strengthened for a renewed assault on the same mound that had produced the *Logia*, the phalanx of workmen was now moved to its northern section. And what had started as a moderate flow turned into a veritable torrent. Because of the care that had to be taken in sorting, packing, and transporting, the explorers found themselves in the happy predicament of not knowing how to cope with the unanticipated riches. Within a short time they ran out of containers. At length two men were delegated to do nothing all day long but make tin boxes for storing the papyri. Even so, after ten days they could scarcely keep up with the influx of material. And so it went on, almost continuously. Yet the amount taken from the heaps was only a fraction of what it might have been, so much had been hopelessly crushed, torn, or burnt. As a rule, the lower layers were unproductive. There, the explorers were convinced, the rolls had gone the way of all paper in most other countries but Egypt.

Judging from later work at Oxyrhynchus, the first campaign just skimmed the cream—and there one sees Grenfell's influence. The excavation was not conducted with the utmost precision and

---

[6] Ibid., p. 1030.

care. Indeed, any venture with the single objective of taking as many papyri as possible in the shortest time was bound to violate the canons of scientific archaeology. In this respect, the excavations conducted by the University of Michigan much later at Karanis brought immeasurable improvements. But who can blame these pioneers for faulty techniques or for making the most of their good fortune? There was one section of a rubbish hill, for example, "where merely turning up the surface with one's boot would sometimes disclose a roll."[7] So why drill shafts and drive trenches into depths of uncertain yield, when in this layer one could move from one vein of pure gold to another?

How to account for the fact that in the three types of mounds (Roman, Byzantine, and Arab), such a profusion of rolls were found within the same strata? A plausible assumption was that masses of papyri had been transferred from local archives. Here is Grenfell's explanation: "It was the custom in Egypt during the Roman period to carefully store up, in the record offices at each town, official documents of every kind dealing with the administration and taxation of the country; and to these archives even private persons used to send letters, contracts and other documents which they wished to keep, just as we send similar documents to a solicitor or banker. Of course, after a time, when the records were no longer wanted, a clearance became necessary, and it seems that the old papyrus rolls were put in baskets or on wicker trays, and thrown away as rubbish."[8] Such a practice, oddly remindful of the Jewish *geniza* (a kind of lumber room), proved to be a boon to papyrologists. It confirms once again the archaeological truism that destruction and disposal may confer permanence, where men's overanxious attempts to preserve are condemned to failure.

The returns from the "archives" were substantial indeed. From the early Roman period (first century and the beginning of the second century A.D.) came basketfuls of papyri. Occasionally, the rolls were still in their wicker containers. Papyri of later Roman and Byzantine times were distinguished by unusual length and documentary interest. In the middle of March, after more than two months, the greatest find, quantitatively speaking, was made in the Byzantine deposits. Grenfell and Hunt had opened a mound that had "a thick layer of almost solid papyrus." Six pairs of workers were immediately shifted to this site, and the problem now became how to get enough baskets in the Arab village to carry the

---

[7] Ibid., p. 1028.   [8] Ibid.

papyri from the mound. That day's harvest made up thirty-six baskets replete to the brim. One can imagine the joy of Grenfell and Hunt when they emptied the baskets and came across many rolls in an excellent state of preservation, several measuring up to ten feet. The baskets were needed for the following day, so the two men spent most of the night storing away the papyri. Early next morning they were out again with the laborers—and there was a repeat performance, "for twenty-five more baskets were filled before the place was exhausted."[9]

Grenfell and Hunt stayed on another month. But they were convinced that they had tapped the most promising sites. When it came to packing the papyri for shipment, they were to fill twenty-five large cases, weighing close to two tons. The task of unrolling and sorting was to be carried on at Oxford, and the study and eventual publication of the material was to take years. The first volume of the Oxyrhynchus papyri was published within eleven months after the return of the scholars to England (the twenty-fifth appeared in 1959 under UNESCO sponsorship), but a quarter of a century later several of the cases had still not been opened. However, the first volume contained enough surprises, even though none of the texts was complete, as the Aristotelian treatise had been.

Grenfell and Hunt selected 158 texts from some 1,200 documents in fairly good condition which they had been able to examine after their return from the first Oxyrhynchus campaign. Most cherished of all was a fragment of a lost poem that can almost certainly be ascribed to Sappho. There were twenty mutilated lines, sixteen of which are pretty clear and permit a reasonable restoration. The ode deals most likely with Sappho's estranged brother, Charaxus, who was returning home by sea to Lesbos. It was only the first and probably not the best of several fragments from Sappho to be recovered from the papyri. "Still Sappho is— Sappho," in Hunt's words. The lines showed unmistakably "the simple directness, the apparently effortless felicity, characteristic of the poetess"[1]—which are evident here, in Grenfell and Hunt's unassuming translation:

> *Sweet Nereids, grant to me*
> *That home unscathed my brother may return,*
> *And every end, for which his soul shall yearn,*
> *Accomplished see!*

---

[9] Ibid. [1] Hunt: "Papyri and Papryology," p. 83.

And thou, immortal Queen,
Blot out the past, that thus his friends may know
Joy, shame his foes,—nay rather, let no foe
By us be seen!

And may he have the will
To me his sister some regard to show,
To assuage the pain he brought, whose cruel blow
My soul did kill,

Yea, mine, for that ill name
Whose biting edge, to shun the festal throng
Compelling, ceased awhile; yet back ere long
To goad us came![2]

Sappho among her adoring disciples. Attic vase from the museum at Athens

To this we may add a fragment in hexameter attributable to Alcman, the seventh-century B.C. Spartan poet worthy to rank with Sappho. It reminded someone of the procession of graceful maidens on the frieze of the Parthenon.

We came to great Demeter's fane, we nine,
All maidens, all in goodly raiment clad:
In goodly raiment clad, with necklets bright
Of carven ivory, that shone like [snow].[3]

The authorship of several other poetic pieces could not be established. A considerable prose passage was part of a treatise, perhaps by Aristoxenus (a disciple of Aristotle), on metrics, with

---

[2] Grenfell and Hunt: *The Oxyrhynchus Papyri. Part I*, p. 12.
[3] Ibid., p. 13.

samples from unknown works. Another fragment, from a historical work, treats in chronological order Greek and Roman events from 355 to 315 B.C. Two columns from a lost comedy strongly suggest Menander, the Athenian master of the New Comedy. In addition, this first sampling included selections from already known works by some of the great names of antiquity, which contributed to the critical study and authentication of traditional texts. A large proportion of *Oxyrhynchus I*, as the first volume is called, consists of nonliterary documents, ranging from a declaration by a guild of workmen to the monthly meat bill of a cook and the repudiation of a betrothal. Later volumes in the Oxyrhynchus series brought to light a great many more hitherto lost texts. A list of the authors represented would look like an index to a history of Greek literature.

In the first collection, Grenfell and Hunt declared: "It is not very likely that we shall find another poem of Sappho, still less that we shall come across another page of the *Logia.*" This prediction happily turned out to be mistaken. The two scholars were nearer the truth when they added: "But we have no reason for thinking that the surprises to come will be much less exciting than those which have gone before."[4] The temptation might have been for Grenfell and Hunt to stay home and devote themselves to editing the manuscripts. The material from one campaign was sufficient to absorb their energies for years to come. But for the next ten years, until 1907, when Grenfell suffered a serious breakdown, the two dug in Egypt every winter, dividing their lives between active work and more contemplative study. To both pursuits they brought outstanding talents.

---

[4] Ibid., p. vi.

·IX·

OXYRHYNCHUS

REVISITED

. . . Helen's beauty in a brow of Egypt.
SHAKESPEARE

FROM 1898 to 1902 Grenfell and Hunt worked again in the Fayum. Oxyrhynchus had yielded an enormous amount of documents from Roman and Byzantine times, but the men were particularly eager to find earlier Ptolemaic evidence. The Fayum, supposedly rich in mummy cases of papyri, was the most likely place to search. Besides, Oxyrhynchus had been so depleted that it might not justify another full season of work.

None of the Fayum digs, however, was as rewarding as Oxyrhynchus until Tebtunis (Urum el Baragât), in the southern end of the great depression, became the target. These excavations were sponsored by the University of California under a bequest from Mrs. Phoebe A. Hurst. Tebtunis was chosen because, like Oxyrhynchus, it was somewhat off the beaten track, in a fairly inaccessible district, so that it too had largely escaped native diggers. The site was more diverse, and in addition to the mounds, there were houses, temples, a Coptic church, and cemeteries, all of which invited investigation. Quantities of scarabs, beads, and amulets from tombs of Middle and New Kingdom (Pharaonic) age were among the items uncovered by the spade. Everywhere there was evidence of the local cult of the crocodile god, and indeed one of his shrines was discovered. The ruined houses of Tebtunis yielded several excellently preserved Greek rolls, but few literary pieces of any importance. Once again it was the Ptolemaic cemetery which drew attention. It was extensive and the excavators hoped it would produce a rich harvest of third-century B.C. mummy cases, but it soon became evident that plunderers had been at work here too. In addition, humidity and salt had done a great deal of damage. However, about fifty mummy cases were salvaged.

Still, the Tebtunis venture was thus far a near failure. The whole picture changed with what was to be the most eccentric of all papyrological discoveries. A great surprise—stranger even than Petrie's "cartonnage"—awaited the excavators. And they almost missed it. They had been burrowing through the Ptolemaic cemetery, which seemed endless. Then at last they came to the area set aside for burial of crocodiles, adjacent to the human burial ground. In Egypt this was not strange, but the explorers were irritated: these odd mummies were nothing but a nuisance—a poor substitute for human cadavers, which might well yield papyrus rolls or funerary cases. The Englishmen's impatience was infectious and soon began to be felt by the native workmen too. One outburst, described by Grenfell and Hunt, made history:

"The tombs of the large Ptolemaic necropolis . . . proved in many instances to contain only crocodiles, and on January 16, 1900, a day which was otherwise memorable for producing twenty-three early Ptolemaic mummies with papyrus cartonnage—one of our workmen, disgusted at finding a row of crocodiles where he expected sarcophagi, broke one of them in pieces and disclosed the surprising fact that the creature was wrapped in sheets of papyrus."[1]

Eventually, and with reawakened enthusiasm, thousands of the crocodile remains were dug up, "ranging in size from the fully grown animals, thirteen feet long, to baby crocodiles just out of the egg, besides numerous sham crocodile mummies which when opened proved to contain merely a bit of bone or a few eggs."[2] Of the many remains excavated, only about two percent were associated with papyri. However, these creatures not only had been wrapped in papyrus sheets but had been "stuffed" with entire rolls. In order to envelop and fill out a fair-sized crocodile properly, a large amount of papyrus was required—and virtually all the sheets were in Greek. Unfortunately they were considerably damaged, but a number of extensive and valuable, though chiefly nonliterary,

---

[1] Grenfell, Hunt, and J. Gilbart Smyly, eds.: *The Tebtunis Papyri I* (London: H. Frowde; 1902), p. vi.
[2] Grenfell and Hunt: "A Large Find of Papyri," *Athenaeum*, No. 3785 (May 12, 1900), pp. 600–1.

documents were salvaged, dating mainly from the century and a half before Christ. Thanks to the Tebtunis crocodiles, then, palaeographic knowledge was extended well into the second century B.C. These papyri came to be valued greatly in later years for their documentation of Ptolemaic economic, social, and political history, and for the contribution they make to the study of Hellenistic law.

A Ptolemaic petition, dated 163 to 162 B.C. Palaeographically the cursive Greek script is noteworthy for its many ligatures.

At the headquarters of the Grenfell and Hunt expedition the crocodile cult had something of a revival; the crocodile became a symbolic figure. E. J. Goodspeed, an American visitor, reported finding the sacred animal in evidence all over the camp. Even in his tent he was honored with the presence of a few baby crocodile mummies. During his stay, an entire "crocodile house" was being constructed.[3]

In 1902, Grenfell and Hunt ventured out of the Fayum once more. Their destination was El Hibeh, along the Nile, where fellahin had recently found Ptolemaic mummy cases. Two seasons were devoted to excavations there, again under the auspices of the Egypt Exploration Fund. The harvest of Ptolemaic papyri was notable for the age of the finds (third century B.C.) and for several unusual items, particularly a fragment ascribed to Euripides, and parts of an unknown comedy and epic.

After El Hibeh, it was back to Oxyrhynchus for the pair's last five seasons in Egypt. Excavations at other sites must have made it evident that they had far from realized the potential of Oxyrhynchus. Yet, probably because of the enormous quantitites of papyri Grenfell and Hunt had taken from there in their first year, neither natives nor Europeans had bothered to reexamine the place. Only one large mound, investigated briefly by the two in 1897, had caught the eye of local men just before Grenfell and Hunt returned. The torrential flow of the first season was never quite duplicated at

---

[3] Edgar Johnson Goodspeed: "Papyrus Digging with Grenfell and Hunt," *Independent*, Vol. LVII (1904), p. 1069.

Oxyrhynchus, though the additional recoveries were impressive.
When Grenfell and Hunt left Oxyrhynchus for good, it was with
the realization that the site had by no means yielded all its treasures. Non-English scholars, especially Germans and Italians, followed—Oxyrhynchus seemed inexhaustible. As late as 1922,
Flinders Petrie—by then the grand old man of Egyptology—uncovered several hundred fragments, among them passages from
Hebrew hymns of the second or third century A.D.[4]

The Oxford Dioscuri never had reason to regret their return.
Each season was profitable and filled with surprises. During
1903–4, other *Logia* fragments were found, and in 1904–5
quantities of documents turned up, recalling "the most palmy days

Performance of a satyric drama. After a Pompeian mural

of the excavations of 1897."[5] Among the surprises that year were
Hebrew and Syriac texts and wax writing tablets on wood, which
were known from Pompeii. Portions of the lost *Oineus* of Euripides
were also unearthed. Even the most fleeting account of the
Oxyrhynchus excavations cannot fail to mention as vital a find as
the *Ichneutae* of Sophocles, one of the lost satyr plays (the curtain
raisers to Greek tragedies), which was sufficiently restored to be
staged in Germany; or the few precious fragments from the poets
Alcaeus and Ibycus, and the most extensive ones from Callimachus,
who had been put down as a pedantic querulous academic from
Alexandria and was now revealed as a poet of considerable

[4] Preisendanz: op. cit., p. 138.
[5] Grenfell and Hunt: "Excavations at Oxyrhynchus," *Archaeological Reports* of Egypt Exploration Fund. Graeco-Roman Branch, 1904–5, p. 13.

originality. The publication in 1959, in volume 25 of the Oxy-rhynchus series, of a few lyric pieces that are possibly by Simonides, the "most wanted" of all Greek poets, indicates that the flow has not yet come to an end.

Another notable find at Oxyrhynchus was a biography of Euripides by Satyrus. There were also frustrating scraps such as the so-called *sillyboi* (title tags once attached to manuscript rolls), bearing the legends: "The Female Mimes of Sophron," a work that was never found, or "The Complete Works of Pindar." To compensate for such disappointments, there were bits and pieces, not great literature in themselves but of value nevertheless, such as an epitome, in Latin, of the missing books of Livy, written on the verso of a Christian text; also a list of the Olympic victors. This last would not have been remarkable in itself, had it not enabled art historians to settle the long-disputed dates of certain classical statues depicting fifth-century B.C. athletes. The new chronological evidence refuted the opinions of several experts, including Germany's Adolf Furtwängler. It was now evident that the great creative period of the sculptor Polyclitus was earlier than had hitherto been believed. This in turn established approximate dates for Polyclitus' contemporary Myron, sculptor of the Discus Thrower. In addition, the list helped to date certain odes by Pindar and Bacchylides celebrating athletes' triumphs at Olympia. As for Bacchylides himself, it became clear that he had lived at least sixteen years longer than had previously been assumed.[6] Among the athletes, a boxer by the improbable name of Anthropos is mentioned. There is also a reference to him in Aristotle, but, because *anthropos* simply means "man" in Greek, he was thought to be a symbolic figure. Now, some two and a half millennia after his death, the man's actual existence was established.

The last two seasons at Oxyrhynchus were the most rewarding in terms of literary returns. Grenfell and Hunt, however, thought in 1905 that they had fairly exhausted the buried treasure. Indeed there were few likely sites left from Roman and early Byzantine times, and it was well known that the interest in Greek literature in Egypt declined sharply after the fourth century A.D. But the report made to the Egypt Exploration Fund after work was resumed in December 1905 stated: "Fortune . . . as the event proved, had reserved her most precious gift until the fifth season [1905–6], the results of which surpass even those of the first excavations at

---

[6] Hunt: "Twenty-five Years of Papyrology," pp. 126, 286 ("Notes and News").

Oxyrhynchus in 1897."⁷ Knowing that they might not be able to undertake another expedition, the two men had doubled their work force and planned to cover as much ground as possible. They hoped to scan even supposedly less rewarding layers of late Byzantine refuse.

One of the first finds was another Christian text in Greek, a vellum leaf (not papyrus) from a lost Gospel, depicting an apocryphal episode: a visit of Jesus to the Temple of Jerusalem. Somewhat in the manner of a Socratic dialogue, Jesus embroils a Pharisee in a discussion of purity, in the course of which a plea is made for inner purity as against meaningless outward ceremonials of purification. Grenfell and Hunt were impressed by the "cultivated literary style, picturesqueness, and vigor of phraseology, which includes several words not found in the New Testament, and the display of a curious familiarity—whether genuine or assumed—with the topography of the Temple and Jewish ceremonies of purification."⁸ After this Christian prologue to the expedition, poetry was to be foremost in the finds, including some hymns of thanksgiving by mighty Pindar himself.

On several occasions at Oxyrhynchus a load of documents was hit upon that unmistakably had belonged to a single individual or the same archive and had been disposed of in bulk. But none of these had contained literary fragments of any value. Was it conceivable that a whole library or an entire collection of books might have been discarded in the same manner? This was a secret hope the two friends never quite lost. "And on January 13," they wrote a few months later in their report, "we were at length fortunate enough to make a discovery of that nature. Shortly before sunset we reached, at about six feet from the surface, a place where in the third century A.D. a basketful of broken literary papyrus rolls had been thrown away. In the fading light it was impossible to extricate the whole find that evening; but a strong guard was posted on the spot during the night, and the remainder was safely removed in the following forenoon. Before being condemned to the rubbish-heap, the papyri had, as usual, been torn up; but amid hundreds of smaller fragments there were a couple of cores of rolls, containing ten or twelve columns, other pieces containing five or six, and many more one or two columns. The process of combining the various pieces is necessarily slow, and we have not

---

⁷ Grenfell and Hunt: "Excavations at Oxyrhynchus," *Archaeological Reports,* 1905–6, p. 8.
⁸ Ibid., p. 9.

yet had time to fit together and decipher more than about half the find. . . ."[9]

To find literary works discarded wholesale was astonishing enough—and here were two major poetical fragments from lost works of ancient authors of the first rank. Of particular interest were some 300 lines of Pindar's *Paeans,* of which nothing of any consequence had hitherto been known. This was the longest lyrical

Sillybos (or sittybos)—a title tag—to a lost collection of all of Pindar's poems. After a leather label in the possession of the Egypt Exploration Society of London

work to be taken from Egypt since the Bacchylides, and it easily ranks in value with the extensive sampling from that poet. Perhaps less grandiloquent than Pindar's other works, the *Paeans* shows him in a more readable vein, "fuller of human interest, less concerned with myth and less obscure in expression."[1] The *Ode to Delphi* has since become a familiar piece in our classical heritage. The other major recovery was a considerable portion of Euripides' *Hypsipyle,* enough to permit classicists to divine the plot of the tragedy. In addition, there were fragments from Sappho and from the little known *Meliambi* (satiric poems) of Cercidas.

Prose manuscripts were by no means lacking—in particular a new historical work that, like Aristotle's *Constitution of Athens,* made an indelible impression on classical scholars and historians. It was a fragment of about 600 lines dealing with the period from 396 to 394 B.C. in Hellenic history. As a narrative it could take its place beside Thucydides, whose work it apparently set out to continue, and Xenophon, with whom it was not always in agreement. It is generally known as the *Oxyrhynchia Hellenica,* and a heated debate is still in progress today as to the identity of its author. Ephorus is at present the leading contender.

---

[9] Ibid., p. 10.
[1] Grenfell and Hunt: *Oxyrhynchus Papyri, Part V,* p. 12.

These finds represent only the highlights of Grenfell and Hunt's greatest season, which Kenyon hailed as comparable to 1891 in the magnitude of the discoveries made. This description is the more apt because, just as in 1891, in 1905 notable papyri were also obtained from a different source. The most celebrated was the Menander codex found in a grave near Aphroditopolis by Gustave Lefèbvre, a French scholar attached to the Cairo Museum. It consisted of substantial parts of five of the vanished comedies of Menander, whose plays were models for Plautus and Terence, and hence for Molière and right on down to playwrights of the current Broadway season.

When, in 1906, Grenfell and Hunt terminated their active career in exploration, papyrus hunting had come of age and the systematic study of Greek papyri had become a science. Oxyrhynchus was then considered the most fabulous wellspring of papyri yet revealed.

Thanks to such pioneers as Petrie, Budge, and Grenfell and Hunt, Egypt, the ancient land of miracles, of pharaohs, plagues, and pyramids, could now add papyrus to its roster. Of the vital importance of the written scraps that were reaching institutions of learning in mounting quantities there could be no doubt. And the identification, from these ragged bundles, of lines of literary glory and a wealth of data on ancient civilization gave a piquant air to classical scholarship. "Papyri have infused new life into the veins of learning," declared Germany's Adolf Deissmann. J. U. Powell, an English colleague, stressed that 1891 not only had brought to light vast amounts of new material that added to our store of classical knowledge, but represented the beginning of "a new epoch in Greek scholarship."[2]

Numerous fields of research were now opening up. The gradual accumulation, for instance, of papyri covering a continuum of one thousand years made it possible to trace changes in both the Greek language and its script. This palaeographic record—more extensive than anything available to the Marchese Maffei among the Latin manuscripts of Verona—showed clearly the emergence of uncial and minuscule lettering from Greek capitals and cursives. Linguistic analysis also elucidated the evolution of the Byzantine idiom and even traced affinities with modern Greek. In the first flush of excitement scholars naturally concentrated on the literary

---

[2] Powell and Barber, eds.: op. cit., Vol. III, p. v.

fragments recovered. In their hands was proof that many a lost work had circulated in Egypt and might conceivably turn up.[3] With such knowledge came new notions on the penetration, spread, and duration of the Hellenistic influence in the Near East.

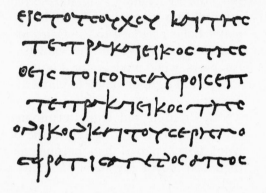

Facsimile lines of an official order in Greek from third-century B.C. Ptolemaic Egypt

Judging by the evidence we have today, there is hardly any ancient Greek writer who was not at some time or other read in Egypt. But some authors and some fields were more favored than others. Philosophy, for example, does not seem to have been explored too thoroughly in Egypt—at least in the provinces. Plato was, indeed, among the most widely copied authors, but his dialogues were probably valued as literature rather than as metaphysics or epistemology. Of Aristotle there is little trace, except for *The Constitution of Athens*, which dealt with history, not philosophy. The works of other major Greek writers, such as Aeschylus and Aristophanes, are only rarely found in papyri. Conceivably, Aeschylus lacked appeal because of his difficult, elevated style, and Aristophanes may have been too absorbed with local

Theater ticket made from bone, with the inscription "Aeschylus." It admitted bearer to stalls of the theater named for the Greek playwright.

[3] Roberts: "The Greek Papyri," in Glanville, ed.: *The Legacy of Egypt*, p. 254.

Athenian issues and personalities as targets for his satirical wit to be readily understandable in Egypt.

The notable addition in the field of the drama was the substantial segment from the New Comedy of Menander found in the now famous Cairo Codex, which was supplemented by papyri from Oxyrhynchus and elsewhere. Of Menander's work nothing but a few quotations (one in the New Testament!) had hitherto survived. Now it was possible to gain an idea of his art, which the ancients considered on a par with that of Plato and Euripides. That Hellenized Egypt took kindly to a writer of such ease and verve was to be expected. Several years before the find, Kenyon, in discussing Hyperides, had prophetically observed (1894): "There were two authors whom most scholars would have named as those, the loss of whom was most surprising, and the recovery of whom might be held most probable. The first of these was Menander, the second Hyperides. For Menander we wait still, but Hyperides was the first fruits of the new harvest."[4]

Next to Menander, perhaps the most interesting recovery in the drama was a work by Timotheus of Miletus, a kind of musical

Passage from *Persae* by Timotheus. Papyrus in a lapidary irregular hand, late fourth century B.C.

libretto entitled *Persae,* which not only introduced a new art form but turned out to be probably the oldest (fourth century B.C.) Greek literary manuscript taken from Egypt. It was found in 1902 by the German Egyptologist Ludwig Borchardt in a soldier's grave at Abusir, north of the entrance to the Fayum. Timotheus is an example of the suspense inherent in the hunt for papyri, which has brought to light some of the least-known and least expected as well as some of the best-known names in Greek literature. Other

---

[4] Kenyon: "Hyperides," *Quarterly Review,* Vol. 178 (1894), pp. 532–3.

examples were Herodas and the Boeotian poetess Corinna, an elder contemporary of Pindar, who wrote in a meter peculiar to her alone.

Lyric poetry was conspicuously enriched by the yield from the sands of Egypt. No moderately comprehensive collection of any of the Greek lyricists had been available until then. Hence the elation over the Bacchylides and Pindar manuscripts and the gems from Sappho and others. The finds made at Oxyrhynchus also helped to reinstate the Sicilian poet Ibycus, known from Schiller's ballad. Forty verses of his were uncovered, four times as much as had previously survived.

Of the known works for which Egypt furnished the oldest copies, none even approximates the popularity of Homer, in particular of the *Iliad*. The epic of the Trojan War remained a kind of Greek bible throughout Hellenistic, Roman, and early Byzantine times, and copies show up in almost perplexing profusion, provoking gentle Hunt to the impious remark: "The great popularity of the bard is indeed one of the chief trials of the excavator's patience. He sees an extra large literary fragment emerging from the soil, and wonders for a brief moment what new treasure he has found—but ten to one it is only old Homer again."[5] At an early stage in papyrological studies Kenyon observed that, next to Homer, Demosthenes had the greatest number of texts to his name, and Plato the next highest number. Aeschylus and even Sophocles were easily outdone by Euripides, with Menander close on his heels. In addition to Demosthenes, such orators as Isocrates and Lysias were favorites, as was Hyperides. But it was rare that a work of Aeschines was found. In history, Thucydides and Xenophon were in the lead, but, oddly enough, Herodotus was almost unknown. (A later study, however, did not substantiate the apparent scarcity of the works of Herodotus.) Lyric poetry must have had relatively few readers, though all the works of Pindar, Bacchylides, and Sappho seem to have been in circulation.

According to a rough estimate made by Kenyon in 1919, Egypt had so far yielded some 920 papyri of a literary nature. Of these, about 570 were texts known to us. If we subtract from this figure about 100 Biblical and patristic texts and about 270 of Homer's, we have left only 200 papyri of familiar works, as against 350 papyri of unknown works.[6] The fact that the greater number (apart

---

[5] Hunt: "Papyri and Papyrology," p. 85.
[6] Kenyon: "Greek Papyri and Their Contribution to Classical Literature," p. 3.

from Homer and Christian literature) represent lost manuscripts has been amply borne out by the more thorough surveys carried out by an American, Charles Henry Oldfather, in 1922 and in more recent years (1945, 1952) by Laura Giabbani of Italy and Roger A. Pack of Michigan. Oldfather's findings suggest that Egypt possessed a legacy of Greek literature comprising about three times the works extent today in the West. Since the great bulk of the papyri we have found, such as those from Oxyrhynchus, are from the first Christian centuries, the conclusion is warranted that each of these texts had been in circulation during that time. Indeed, throughout the Roman era virtually all of Greek literature may have been available in Egypt. The destruction of the main library at Alexandria during Caesar's campaign probably had no effect whatsoever—contrary to popular belief—on the ultimate loss of much of classical literature.

Formerly it was often assumed that by the early Christian centuries practically all that has failed to come down to us had already been lost. When a grammarian of that time would quote, for instance, from a play by Euripides, he supposedly took the lines from an anthology of selected passages rather than from the

Fragment of the *Odyssey*, from the first century A.D., at the British Museum. In contrast to the bold, angular Ptolemaic hands, the writing reflects the lighter, rounded Roman style.

original. Such misconceptions were dispelled by the papyrus discoveries. Moreover, if the Egyptian provinces had such a wealth of Greek literary works at a comparatively late date, how much more would these books—and others besides—have circulated in the great Greek-speaking urban centers of the Empire: in Alexandria, Ephesus, Antioch, Athens, or even Rome?

Do the literary papyri give us any clue to the decline of

Greek literature, just as they provide an indelible record of its popularity and longevity?

Today it is certain that at least in Egypt the decrease in available copies of Greek literary works and in their circulation set in relatively late. Without singling out first causes, it may be stated that the decline of Greek literary texts became marked at the time of the official recognition of Christianity in the fourth century, a period that coincides in Middle and Upper Egypt with severe economic setbacks and a drastic curtailment and wholesale abandonment of areas of cultivation. Nevertheless, we need not concur with Gibbon and his "triumph of barbarism and Christianity." Civilization and literacy were not simply dying out, but, as A. S. Hunt has judiciously observed: "The right-minded man would tend to replace Sappho with the Psalms and satisfy his appetite for history and romance with the lives of the saints and martyrs!"[7] The closing chapter of Greco-Roman Egypt is anything but abrupt. The Menander codex, for example, and poems of Sappho and Pindar—none of which survived into the Middle Ages—were recovered from Byzantine deposits of the sixth and seventh centuries; and Greek continued to be spoken into the period of Arab dominance. There may have been links between the old and the new, such as works on physics, written in Greek after the Arab conquest, which, while based on Aristotle, foreshadow the teachings of the Arab philosophers and of their successors, the European scholastics.[8]

Of the vast amount of ancient Greek literature in circulation

Masks worn in Greek tragedies

during the Hellenic age in Egypt, recoveries so far represent but a fraction. Greek lyric poetry, except for a few notable exceptions, remains in oblivion. Of all genres, drama fared best. However, if we consider that 7 plays of Sophocles' reputedly 113 have survived, and only 18 of Euripides' 92—and nothing to speak of from a number of tragedians whom the ancients judged to be almost

---

[7] Hunt: "Papyri and Papryology," p. 84.
[8] Roberts: "The Greek Papyri," in Glanville, ed.: *The Legacy of Egypt*, p. 261.

the equals of these two, such as Agathon, known because he appears in Plato's *Symposium*—the lacunae are still enormous.

> *Eupolis, atque Cratinus, Aristophanesque poetae,*
> *Atque alii . . .*

This Latin verse on the masters of the Old Comedy reminds us that we possess of them little but Aristophanes (with eleven comedies, and probably not his best). Of his peers, Eupolis and Cratinus, there are just a few tantalizing fragments. And the others? There were supposedly some 170 others, most of whom

Masks worn in Greek comedies

are not known to us at all. Much the same can be said about the New Comedy, pre-Socratic philosophy, and the works of Democritus and such eminent historians as Hecataeus (to whom Herodotus was indebted) and Theopompus, of whom we have barely a paragraph (unless the Oxyrhynchus historical fragments can be assigned to him).

Numerically, the loss in Latin letters is at least as shattering, though the absence may not be as deeply mourned. Yet, the missing books of Livy have been keenly sought. And who would not give a king's ransom for Hadrian's memoirs, despite Marguerite Yourcenar's superb "re-creation?"

What then is the outlook for the future? Grenfell and Hunt's golden decade at Oxyrhynchus has not yet been matched, and since the outbreak of World War I systematic papyrus hunting has lost much of its momentum, except for a few brief ventures that had only moderate results. Once again, the most spectacular finds, such as that of Chenoboskion, were made by chance. (No one seems to know the origin of Menander's *Dyskolos*, the only full-length play to be recovered in Egypt, which was acquired from a dealer by Martin Bodmer, the Swiss collector, and was first published in 1958.[9]) Nevertheless, the number of papyri, as well as

---

[9] Victor Martin, ed.: *Papyrus Bodmer IV. Ménandre: Le Dyscolos* (Cologny–Geneva: Bibliotheca Bodmeriana; 1958), p. 7. See also Gilbert Highet: " 'The Dyskolos' of Menander," *Horizon*, Vol. I, No. 6 (July 1959), pp. 78–89.

the collections of texts in the universities of Europe and the Western Hemisphere, continue to grow.

At one time the possibilities of literary discoveries in Egypt seemed limitless. Oxyrynchus showed what could be done: Menander, Aristotle, Hyperides, and Bacchylides were illustrious finds indeed. The rubbish heaps looked inexhaustible. Mummified crocodiles, cartonnages, and jars filled with papyri continued to provide valuable fragments. But wars intervened, native wages rose, foundations hesitated, Egyptian legislation blocked the export of papyri, men like Grenfell and Hunt failed to groom successors, and a handful of papyrologists had all they could handle in the vast stores deposited in collections at home. The archaeology of stone, then, rather than of paper, took the stage again in Egypt and reached a high point in Carter's opening of the tomb of Tutankhamen in 1922. No papyrus discovery in the 1920's could equal the treasure-laden mausoleum of the boy king. Papyrology, however, has remained a vigorous frontier of modern scholarship, and a resurgence of interest in papyrus discoveries may well be imminent. Just when Egypt became firmly established as the only country likely to contain repositories of papyri and parchments of lost works of classical literature, other areas—e.g., southern Palestine, northern Mesopotamia, Asia Minor, which had been ruled out or had never even been considered—began to emerge as possibilities. No one can say what the future holds in store and where a buried tragedy of Agathon, or Emperor Claudius' encyclopedic study of the Etruscans, may be discovered—though Egypt undoubtedly remains the most likely prospect. While this book was in preparation, even its writer maintained that, except for Herculaneum, Europe could not have preserved ancient manuscripts in its rain-drenched soil. Yet, in January 1962 a tomb northwest of Thessalonike, opened in the course of road construction, yielded partly burned (the reason for their preservation), but legible papyri. These are the only intact papyri on record ever found in Greece, and, moreover, they appear to antedate all the Greek documents from Egypt. It is very likely that they were written before Alexander was born. According to preliminary reports, they deal with Orphic religious myths.[1]

Are we about to experience a new springtime of manuscript discoveries in Greece itself?

---

[1] Harálambos Makarónas: "The Dherveni Crater," *Greek Heritage*, Vol. I, No. 1 (Winter, 1963), p. 5.

·X·

A BOOK

WITHOUT COVERS

Familiar letters written by eye-witnesses, and that, without design, disclose circumstances that let us more intimately into important events, are genuine history; and as far as they go, more satisfactory than formal premeditated narratives.

HORACE WALPOLE[1]

PARADOXICAL as it will seem to many, let me say that the non-literary papyri are of greater value to the historical enquirer than are the literary. We rejoice . . . when ancient books, or fragments of them, are recovered from the soil of Egypt, especially when they are lost literary treasures. But scientifically speaking the real treasure hidden in Egypt is not so much ancient art and literature . . . but all the ancient life, actual and tangible, that is waiting to be given the world once more."[2] The man who wrote these once heretical words was Adolf Deissmann, a German theologian. It was he who did most to turn attention to the non-literary papryi which were being dug up in such profusion and for which classical scholars had hitherto shown little patience. A new line of Sappho or a scene from the vanished comedies of Menander was what they were after. A crudely written letter by a Greco-Egyptian farmer expressing his annoyance with a tax

---

[1] From letter to Sir John Fenn, June 29, 1784, quoted in Betty Radice, ed.: *The Letters of the Younger Pliny* (Harmondsworth, Middlesex: Penguin Books; 1963), p. 9.

[2] Adolf Deissmann: *Light from the Ancient East. The New Testament Illustrated by Recently Discovered Texts of the Graeco-Roman World*, revised edition (London: Hodder & Stoughton; 1937), p. 39.

agent, or a contract in shorthand for the training of a slave, was looked upon with condescension. Literary fragments were on the whole speedily published. The trivia of common daily life, which made up more than ninety-five percent of all papyri, could wait.

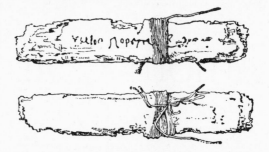

Rolled-up and inscribed papyrus letters from Egypt

Adolf Deissmann was a young lecturer at a small Protestant university when in the early 1890's he chanced to examine a fac-simile volume of the Berlin papyri collection at the Heidelberg library. In the typical flash of most simple but revolutionary dis-coveries, a cursory reading of the Greek documents put him on the track of a new evaluation of nonliterary papyri. The insight actu-ally came to him through the solution of a persistent problem of New Testament scholarship. Theologians and philologists had for long been puzzled by the type of Greek used in the original text of the New Testament. Syntax, style, meaning of words, and a great many words themselves were so patently different from the Attic dialect used by the classical writers, including their latter-day imitators, that it seemed almost another language. Being apparently *sui generis*, the strange idiom was most commonly labeled "Bible Greek" or "New Testament Greek." Some called it "Hebraic Greek," because, plausibly enough, its oddities could be attributed to the Semitic roots of the Christian religion and the fact that Christ and the Apostles, whose words the holy text re-corded, had spoken an Aramaic dialect. In this light, the Greek of the New Testament mirrored the adaptation of another idiom to the thoughts and linguistic habits of men of an alien culture, who never fully mastered Greek. Friedrich Nietzsche is a good example of the classicist's disdain for this allegedly hybrid medium when he quips: "It is strange that God found it necessary to learn Greek

in order to communicate with man, and that he learnt it so badly."[3]
More piously, another German savant attributed the Greek of the
New Testament to a "language of the Holy Ghost."[4]

And there the problem stood when young Deissmann boldly
removed both opprobrium and divine inspiration. He declared
that there was no such thing as Biblical Greek. The language of
Paul and the Evangelists was virtually identical with that used by
ordinary Greek-speaking people of the eastern Mediterranean. The
medium of the nonliterary papyrus documents was the living, colloquial Greek of the time, inevitably different, in style and
vocabulary, from the formal, stately language of the literary tradition. The vernacular spurned by the Hellenistic authors was quite
fittingly adopted by Holy Scripture. Only by choosing the everyday
tongue of the civilized world could Christianity become a world
religion. Deissmann's announcement caused almost as much stir
as the identification of Linear B with pre-Homeric Greek by
Michael Ventris some fifty years later.

The everyday language of both nonliterary papyri and the
New Testament (as well as, to a considerable degree, of the
Septuagint) was the Koine, which had a freshness, terseness,
and warmth admirably suited to the Christian message and to
the humble background of the early Church. Of the approximately
ten percent of "exotic" words in the Greek vocabulary of the New
Testament (out of a total of about 5,000), almost all were eventually matched with words in papyrus documents. The parallel also
held for peculiarities of sentence structure and grammar. This
discovery led to a fresh understanding of the original text which
was bound to affect drastically all future translations of the Bible.

To the classicists, of course, New Testament Greek could
only appear to be a deteriorated form of the Greek of Plato or
Demosthenes. It took a theologian who was also a Greek philologist and who had an abiding interest in the historical scene of the
ancient world—Greek-Roman-Byzantine-Christian—to bring about
a simultaneous change in the study of Greek and of the New Testament.

There was some "Deissmannism" before the young German

---

[3] James Underhill Powell and Eric Arthur Barber, eds.: op. cit., Vol. II,
p. 138.
[4] Richard Rothe: *Zur Dogmatik* (Gotha: F. A. Perthes; 1863), p. 238,
quoted in John Finegan: *Light on the Ancient Past* (Princeton: Princeton
University Press; 1946), p. 330.

theologian appeared on the scene. Even the *Carta Borgiana* papyrus of the late eighteenth century had suggested to its decipherers a certain verbal correspondence to the New Testament. And in 1863 an English divine, Bishop Lightfoot, was credited with the observation: "If we could only recover letters that ordinary people wrote to each other without any thought of being literary, we should have the greatest possible help for the understanding of the language of the New Testament in general."[5] But these were isolated sparks from a kind of philological underground. They failed to fire a contemporary response sufficient to work them out systematically. The traditional view of "New Testament Greek" was left unchallenged. Even after Deissmann's announcement, any "secularization" of the Bible was regarded by many ecclesiastics as sacrilege.

Deissmann, unlike his predecessors, was able to spell out his brilliant intuitions. Soon called to a chair at the University of Berlin, he gained recognition as the leading German theologian, next to Harnack, and remained the most fervent advocate of the value of the nonliterary papyri. On this subject he wrote a number of books, foremost among them his *New Light on the New Testament*. English and American universities repeatedly invited him to lecture. Though he was as thrilled as anybody by the recovery of the so-called *Logia*, lost words of Jesus, and of manuscripts of the Gospels far older than any hitherto known, and though he was a cultured European deeply appreciative of the restoration of ancient classical texts, he continued to uphold his conviction that none of these epigraphic jewels could match the gains derived from the nonliterary papyri. Deissmann was a kind of archpriest of this doctrine. His judgments are now universally accepted— though with the acknowledgment of occasional "Semiticisms" in the Greek New Testament. (Deissmann himself allowed for an Aramaic original of St. Matthew's Gospel.)

To Deismann, evidence of early Christians moving about the Greco-Roman world and speaking its universal language was little less than a revelation. The scene of Christ's apostolate was the ordinary world of the common man of the Orient during the Roman Empire. That scene, so relevant to the understanding of primitive Christianity, was brought to life by nonliterary papyri, and the papyri, because of their ordinariness, achieved a significance far beyond their Christian interest. They

---

[5] Powell and Barber: op. cit., p. 137.

were in truth "the short and simple annals of the poor" of antiquity. Much of the worth and charm of these documents derive from the fact that they were not written with an eye to an audience. They are entirely free from affectation, cant, and the artificialties of more conscious literary efforts. They ring true, particularly the letters, which may lack the polish and epistolary art of Pliny the

Lower section of a typical papyrus letter from Hellenistic Egypt. It contains a request for drugs to be sent from Alexandria. First century A.D. Now at the British Museum

Younger, Lord Chesterfield, and Rilke, but are more credible and refreshingly spontaneous. As documentation for the anonymous history of an epoch, nonliterary papyri are all one could wish for. Their variety defies classification: they are "as many-sided as life itself."[6] It has become a common practice to divide them into official and private documents, though the distinction cannot be made too rigidly. Classified as official papers are various legal records, such as tax receipts, land registers, deeds of sale, leases, documents pertaining to loans, petitions, mortgages, partnerships, marriage contracts, bills of divorce, death certificates, inventories, denunciations, and government decrees. An enormous number of magical texts and horoscopes are in a group by themselves. There are also private or personal testimonies, schoolboy exercises (some of them copies of lost literary texts), diaries, notes, and, most delightful of all, a great many letters.

Nearly every scrap sheds light on the land, the age, and the people. Here are bits that sample the passions, frailties, squabbles,

---

[6] Deissmann; op. cit., p. 36.

predicaments, virtues, and jokes of the men and women of antiquity. One man writes of a bad dream in which a runaway slave attacked him. Another tells of a crook who had cheated his mother out of a stipend. A judge passes sentence on a criminal: "You seem to me to have the soul, not of a man, but of a beast—or rather, not even that of a beast."[7] Or, in one of the Oxyrhynchus papers, a man reports that on his return to Alexandria he found that his house and the house of a friend had been searched and that there had been mass arrests of highly placed persons. Obviously, the early-morning knock at the door was not invented by the modern police state. Another perennial note is struck by a schoolboy's copy of the pedagogical pronouncement: "Take pains, boy, or you'll be skinned alive";[8] yet another, by a soldier's request for transfer from his present stint at some godforsaken outpost on the Red Sea.

Private documents are frequently mixed with official communications. A papyrus from El Hibeh may yield data on the highly organized local postal service, and a list of the poor of one town reveals that the well-to-do were pledged to contribute to the relief of their less fortunate brethren. In one of many Oxyrhynchus documents bearing on religion, a man sets down his quid-pro-quo relation to a divinity: "Know that I am not going to pay the god any attention if I do not first get my son back."[9] Another man expresses his "religious" outlook even more bluntly: "As the gods have not spared me, so will I not spare the gods."[1] In contrast, there is a believer's pious assertion: "It is Zeus who sends our daily bread."[2]

Like the last sample, many passages in the papyri will remind us of the Gospels. If not related in outlook, they display at least the same moral vigor and sparkle and introduce personalities whom we seem to have already met: the Roman prefect, the innkeeper, the tax collector, the moneylender, the thief, the prodigal, as well as a host of soldiers, peasants, scribes, artisans, and slaves. But such associations barely touch upon the significance of the Egyptian documents to the study of early Christianity. Fragments from canonical and noncanonical Christian literature

---

[7] W. G. Wadell: *The Lighter Side of the Greek Papyri* (Newcastle: Cutter; 1932), p. 19.

[8] Ibid., p. 4.

[9] Bell: "The Historical Value of Greek Papyri," *Journal of Egyptian Archaeology*, Vol. VI (1920), p. 243.

[1] Ibid.

[2] Wadell: op. cit., p. 18.

(hymns, homiletics, apocrypha, "lost gospels") abound, and a few nonliterary records illumine the Christian tradition itself.

One of the best-known bits of information taken from the papyri, however, touches on Christianity only by inference. It pertains to a legal record from A.D. 88 and quotes a Roman prefect as saying to a culprit: ". . . you deserve scourging . . . but I make a present of you to the crowd and will show myself more merciful than you."[3] This recalls immediately the incident of Barabbas in the Gospels, who was freed in the same manner by Pilate. The "promising of a condemned man to the people," it turns out, was a general Roman practice.

Another indirect piece of evidence is provided by a papyrus which deals with the taking of the Roman census in A.D. 104. It contains the stipulation of the authorities that people had to return for that purpose to their home towns. We recall from Acts and Luke that Mary and Joseph went before His birth to Bethlehem in order to comply with the approaching Roman census. Once again the historical veracity of a detail in the New Testament is borne out. Furthermore, dated papyri gave proof of a fourteen-year cycle of Roman census-taking and thereby helped to fix the likely year of Christ's birth.

A number of documents from different parts of Egypt mark the expansion of Christianity; relative reticence in some undoubtedly Christian notes may bespeak persecution. The most tangible evidence of Roman repression of the Christian faith, particularly during the reign of Emperor Decius, is furnished by the so-called *libelli*, certificates the Imperial authorities issued to any suspect after he had participated in pagan sacrifices. One such declaration, made in A.D. 250 by a certain Aurelius Gaion at Oxyrhynchus, reads: "I have always been accustomed to sacrifice and make libations and pay reverence to the gods in accordance with the orders of the divine decree, and now in your presence I have sacrificed and made libations and tasted the offering along with Taos my wife and Ammonius and Ammonianus my sons and Thecla my daughter, acting through me, and I request you to certify my statement. . . ."[4]

Other documents deal with the organization and growth of the Church (a veteran of the Roman army in the fourth century, for

---

[3] Roberts: "The Greek Papyri," in Glanville, ed.: *The Legacy of Egypt*, p. 265.
[4] Hunt and C. C. Edgar, eds.: *Select Papyri* (Cambridge, Mass.: Harvard University Press–Loeb Library; 1932), Vol. II, p. 318.

example, will leave half his property to the "holy church"); the rise of monasticism; and the private affairs of adherents of the true faith in Egypt. All these enrich our picture of the new religion.

In another category are the many papers attesting to the fascination held for the Egyptians not only by the numerous mystery cults but by Christian heresies such as Gnosticism, of which a large literature has been recovered in recent decades. Several papyri reflect the nascent crusading spirit and intolerance of the Christians when faced with a popular rival like Manichaeanism, the dualistic faith of Persian origin. Subjects such as the religious life of Greco-Roman Egypt can be pursued endlessly in the papyri. So can education, the position of women, the role of Jews, or Greek colonization—to name just a few topics on which monographs have been produced.

Despite the wealth of documents, however, the political history of a thousand years of Hellenized Egypt, as such, derives comparatively little enlightenment from the papyri, since they tend to deal with events from the perspective of ordinary people in their day-to-day life rather than from the point of view of the practicing politician or the political chronicler. Still, some data contained in the documents are of "historical" stature. To cite, again at random: one papyrus established that in 170 B.C. Egypt had been successfully invaded by the Seleucids from Syria, who deposed the Ptolemaic king. The private papers of a second-century A.D. local administrator give us considerable sidelights on the Jewish revolt at the end of Trajan's reign which spread into Egypt and necessitated military measures against the "godless Jews."[5]

Political allusions from the Roman period are fairly numerous. Of particular interest are edicts to the Alexandrians from Germanicus, in A.D. 19, which express concern over the god-like worship he received during his stay—honors due only to the reigning emperor, Tiberius. Germanicus, for good reasons, was afraid lest he antagonize the emperor and endanger his succession to the throne. In fact, he died shortly afterwards under mysterious circumstances. The Emperor Caracalla's famous edict of A.D. 242, the *Constitutio Antoniana*, which conferred citizenship on virtually all inhabitants (*peregrini*) of the Roman dominions, can now be read in an almost complete version. From the time of Diocletian come data on his desperate attempt to reform the financial and administrative structure of the tumbling empire. One official in Egypt

---

[5] Roberts: op. cit., p. 277.

got wind of a monetary devaluation before it was enacted and cunningly hedged against inflation by instructing a middleman "to make haste to spend all the Italian silver that you have on purchases, on my behalf, of goods of every description at whatever price you find them."[6]

When it comes to describing less incisive events, or long-term trends, the papyri are much more explicit. Their unbroken sequence bestows a lifelike movement to the past. In the words of F. G. Kenyon, the value of the nonliterary papyri consists "not so much in the revelation of new facts of first-rate importance, as in the accumulation of small details, in themselves not striking, but collectively forming a foundation on which the constructive historian may base his inferences."[7]

On the basis of this ample, cumulative documentation, modern historians have had little difficulty in working out in full the administrative structure of the Egyptian provinces during each stage of Ptolemaic and Roman rule. Practically all the data come from the papyri. There we learn that Ptolemaic absolutism, at least when wielded by the capable earlier rulers, restored Egypt to remarkable affluence and efficiency. A monetary and banking

"Ptolemy," rendered in demotic and hieroglyphic characters

system was built up, state granaries were established, monopolies were leased out (the oil monopoly is dealt with extensively in Grenfell's Revenue Papyrus, edited in 1896). The state fixed prices and supervised the planting and marketing of crops. The Romans transmuted the Ptolemaic system into naked exploitation. Around A.D. 60, a local tax collector reported that the population of six Fayum villages, "once numerous, has now shrunk to a few persons, because some have fled, having no means, and some have died without leaving relatives."[8]

Around the middle of the third century A.D. the decline of Egypt became all too evident. Settlements were abandoned wholesale (which incidentally led to the preservation of rubbish heaps

---

[6] Ibid., p. 273.

[7] Kenyon, ed.: *Classical Texts from Papyri in the British Museum . . .* (London: British Museum; 1891), Vol. I, p. vii.

[8] Bell: *Egypt, from Alexander to the Arab Conquest* (Oxford: Clarendon Press; 1948), p. 77.

and all kinds of remains), irrigation canals were left to dry up, large estates drove out the independent farmer and reduced him to servitude, taxpayers fled, the bottom fell out of the currency. Ruthless statist interventionism only accelerated the breakdown— the medicine prescribed was more lethal than the disease.

Of all the documents from Hellenized Egypt, nothing illuminates the entire kaleidoscopic scene better than the endless series of contracts. The long series begins with the oldest of all Greek papyri from Egypt, a marriage contract drawn up in the year 312/11 B.C. ("In the seventh year of the reign of Alexander, son of Alexander, the fourteenth year of the satrapship of Ptolemy [Ptolemy Soter, who died in 305 B.C.], in the month of Dius. Marriage contract of Heraclides and Demetria. . . ."⁹ The series continues beyond the advent of the Arabs. But by that time Greek was already a dying language in Egypt.

The wealth in numbers and subject matter of this type of papyri has led to the development of a whole branch of studies known as "legal papyrology." Greco-Egyptians were in the habit of sealing almost any settlement or transaction with a contract. This explains the quantity of documents touching on marriage, divorce, adoption, last wills, deeds, the hiring of entertainers, the instruction of children by professional teachers, and much else. One legal paper even provides for the exposure of an unwanted child by a widow's prospective mother-in-law. Another document concerns a winegrower's hiring of a musician to play during the vintage—clearly not for the entertainment of the workers but to make sure the wine treaders pounded the grapes in rhythm and did not slacken.[1] A contract of apprenticeship carries a special clause to protect the master against a boy's natural tendency to play hooky: "If the boy is truant for certain days during the term of his apprenticeship, his father shall produce him for an equal number of days after its close, or he must pay a penalty of one silver drachma for each day."[2] Statements like these, no matter how routine, bring to life the ancient scene.

A great deal can be made of the common humanity we share with the Greek colonists and the native Egyptians of 2,000-odd years ago. Yet the nonliterary papyri also serve to show up in specific, concrete detail the variety and change, the unique character, and the chequered historical context of Hellenistic Egypt. The ragged, yellowed shreds move us when we learn that as late as

---

⁹ Hunt and Edgar: op. cit., Vol. I, pp. 3–5. [1] Wadell: op. cit., p. 14.
[2] Ibid., p. 4.

A.D. 359 an effort was made to resume trade relations with India;[3] that in one area grainfields had to be surrounded by nets to protect them from gazelles; or that within a generation or two of the Greek settlements, the newcomers had adopted the native worship of crocodiles in the Fayum and were contracting brother-sister marriages. Does it much matter that they also used hot-water bottles, even as our arthritic grandmother does now in Kansas City?

Although scholars embarked on painstaking interpretations of the Egyptian documents, a number of papyri were clearly and charmingly intelligible even to the ordinary man of today. The most

Funerary portrait from the Fayum

lively of these documents are the letters, which reward the reader with a close-up view of the drama of human existence some two thousand years ago. A person forgotten by his kin perhaps a few years after his death, here comes back to life. We see the twinkle in his eye, his dismay, his pain, his pride. He strides to inspect the labors of his slaves; he quarrels with his neighbor over water rights; he hugs his little son or reprimands him. The magic of language, conveyed by a few dozen symbols, may be the closest approximation to immortality.

The letters are not all from nonentities. There are, for example, the celebrated Zenon papyri that natives dug up in the ruins of a Fayum town in 1915 after German explorers failed to unearth anything of value. Unfortunately the spoils were divided by the illicit diggers and were scattered among Egyptian, European, and American institutions. The greater part, however, reached Italy, and publication was started in 1917 in Florence. This was

---

[3] Roberts: op. cit., p. 270.

quickly recognized as a major event. The papyri are particularly valuable because of their age: they date from the second part of the third century B.C. Moreover, because they represent the private archives of one man, they possess a rare compactness and completeness. Interspersed throughout the letters are bits and pieces of a political nature which carry us back even into court circles and within close range of the throne. Several of these references have helped scholars reconstruct the chronology of early Ptolemaic Egypt.[4] Probably no other collection of Egyptian nonliterary documents has been so widely studied and written about. In addition to letters, it contains a variety of private and business documents to which M. I. Rostovtzeff devoted a major monograph. Zenon's correspondents range from Apollonius, the royal minister, to tenant farmers, artisans, petty officials, and swineherds. There is, for example, a complaint of a colonist to a bullying bureaucrat: "As for me, outrage and arrest me, if you can. I shall try to help myself; but let me tell you, you are monstrous. And the more consideration a man shows you, the more aggressive you become. And it is not only I who says this, but all who are in the city, such a favorite are you!"[5] No one whose lot it has been to meet such abusers of power among petty tyrants and megalomaniac department heads could fail to sympathize!

The owner of this private archive was a Carian Greek from southwestern Asia Minor. Zenon had risen to wealth and position as a kind of majordomo of Apollonius, a leading minister of Ptolemy II (Philadelphus). The first document, dated 260 B.C., shows Zenon traveling to Syria on behalf of the minister and perhaps the king himself. After 256 B.C. his activities concentrate on the Fayum town of Philadelphia, a new Greek settlement, where he supervised the vast estates given to Apollonius by the king. Through his multiple duties as manager of these lands—planting new crops, directing a large labor force, dealing with all kinds of men and issues—we gain a fresh image of this flourishing "frontier" of Hellenism in the Fayum. The zest with which wasteland is turned within a few years into productive farmland and orchards is indicative of the pioneering spirit of the Greek colonists. Apollonius and Zenon are actively engaged in introducing new crops: from vines and fruit trees to roses and garlic. Breeds of livestock are improved. We are reminded of Johnny Appleseed

---

[4] Bell's review of *"Papiri greci e latini," Journal of Egyptian Archaeology,* Vol. VI (1920), p. 129.
[5] Powell and Barber: op. cit., p. 133.

and the eighteenth-century agricultural "revolutionaries," like "Turnip" Townshend and Robert Bakewell. A new town rises, people arrive in droves and settle down to raise families. Schools, gymnasiums, and temples are built. All is activity, growth, life. Gurgling water rushes through newly dug canals and pours over virgin fields. Apollonius, though occupied with his royal duties at Alexandria, continues to take a hand. He writes to Zenon: "Plant fir trees, over three hundred of them if possible, and at any rate not

Egyptian landscape. After a Roman mural

less, all over the park and round the vineyard and the olive groves, for the tree has a handsome appearance and will be to the advantage of the king."[6]

As a mine of information on commerce and the like, the papyri "are full to overflowing."[7] Zenon was also in constant correspondence with a number of officials, judges, tradesmen, and local artisans. Letters from them have been preserved, even letters not addressed to Zenon. People of many races, from Asia Minor, Syria–Palestine, North Africa, and Ethiopia, flit through these documents. Diverse religious cults are mentioned. Matters of trade come up, with implications beyond the confines of Egypt. Discussions of tariff and currency yield new fiscal data. And so it goes. "Dip into the letters at random," wrote a modern commentator, "and you are sure to strike some picturesque figure or name or episode."[8]

What social historian would not delight in the description of Zenon's traveling wardrobe or of Apollonius' opulent table? One letter reports the peasants' refusal to sell their products for anything but hard currency. Another discusses the sale of female slaves. Papyrus 440 of the Italian collection tells us that those who volunteered to feed the sacred cats were exempted from other state services. In between we have a fair number of letters of a

---

[6] Bell: *Egypt, from Alexander to the Arab Conquest*, p. 47.
[7] Powell and Barber: op. cit., p. 128.
[8] Ibid., p. 130.

more personal nature, though we never learn whether Zenon was married and had a family of his own. But we hear of his father back in Caria and his brothers in Egypt. One intimate detail crops up: the death of his favorite dog, killed by a boar when out hunting with his master. Zenon had a poet write an epigraph for the tombstone of his canine friend.[9]

With the death of Ptolemy II, Apollonius disappears too. He was probably removed from his exalted office by the new king and also lost his benefices. Zenon, however, carried on at Philadelphia as a landowner in his own right and as the first citizen of the thriving provincial town. Then, for more than two thousand years, his records lay buried in the ruins of the abandoned site, until fellahin dug them up in their search for *sebakh* to fertilize perhaps the same fields which Zenon's skill had once brought to fruition.

A comprehensive collection such as Zenon's is exceptional. No other comes even close to it in scope, age, or wealth of data. Probably one must go to the archives of certain Italian Renaissance merchants to find records as rewarding.

On a much smaller scale are some collections of documents found on the crocodile mummies of Tebtunis, from about a century later. Among them are several documents relating to a

Portrait from the Fayum

certain Menches, who occupied the high-sounding office of *komogrammateus*, or scribe, at the town of Kerkeosiris, in the Fayum, in the second century B.C., and apparently also served the central authorities as an agent. Quite a few of his documents were found and published by Grenfell and Hunt on behalf of the University of California. Menches was a less impressive personage than Zenon, and some of his papers cast a shadow on his honesty: they

---

[9] Mikhail Ivanovich Rostovtzeff: *Out of the Past of Greece and Rome* (New Haven: Yale University Press; 1932), p. 107.

were certainly not meant to be preserved. In order to be reappointed to his post, which he must have found profitable, Menches distributed a few well-placed bribes. Then, during his new term in office, he had his hands full with a local outlaw (and the outlaw's son), who, though accused of murder, was not apprehended. Menches, probably a relative of the criminal, at long last sought advice from a higher official in another town. In a subsequent letter, however, he seems to have come to terms with the rogue, who showed his gratitude by warning Menches of the coming visit of a treasury inspector and counseling him "to get the books balanced." Other documents in the Menches collection complete the picture of a rather lawless town.

Visitations from government inspectors, by the way, appear to have been a constant harassment for village and temple officials. The papyri make no bones about ways and means of dealing with the troublesome envoys: Gogol's suspenseful comedy *The Inspector General* must have been enacted many a time in ancient Egypt. What a man needed was friends in the other district settlements to alert him to the government agent's approach and give him time to put his records and accounts in order. A letter from Tebtunis performed just such a service and more, quite beyond the call of friendship. It said, among other things: "You must know that an inspector of finance in the temples has arrived and intends to go to your division also. Do not be disturbed on this account, as I will get you off. So if you have time write up your books and come to me; for he is a very stern fellow. If anything detains you, send them on to me and I will see you through, as he has become my friend. If you are in any difficulty about expense and at present have no funds, write to me, and I will get you off now as I did at first. I am making haste to write to you in order that you may not put in an appearance yourself; for I will make him let you through before he comes to you. He has instructions to send recalcitrants under guard to the high-priest."[1]

A visit of an altogether different sort, also recorded by the Tebtunis papyri, has become famous. It concerns the plan of a roving Roman senator to stop at the Fayum, a must on any grand tour of Egypt because of its divine crocodiles and the Labyrinth at Hawara. The letter confirms Herodotus' and Strabo's colorful descriptions. But part of its interest lies in the respects paid to a Roman politician in Ptolemaic Egypt. Obviously Roman pressure

---

[1] Grenfell, Hunt, and Smyly: op. cit., Vol. II, p. 315.

on Egypt was already felt then, though it was more than a hundred years before the actual takeover following the battle of Actium. The letter itself is a classic example of the studied sycophancy meted out to visiting VIP's. It was forwarded from Alexandria via several middlemen to a certain Horus, secretary to a high-ranking district leader. Horus is also known to us from his correspondence with Menches. The papyrus reads: ". . . Lucius Memmius, a Roman senator, who occupies a position of great dignity and honor, is making the voyage from Alexandria to the Arsinoite nome to see the sights. Let him be received with special magnificence, and take care that at the proper spots the chambers be prepared and the landing-places to them be got ready, and that the gifts of hospitality below written be presented to him at the landing place, and the furniture of the chamber, the customary tid-bits for Petesuchus and the crocodiles, the necessary for the view of the labyrinth, and the offerings and sacrifices be provided; in general take the greatest pains in everything that the visitor may be satisfied, and display the utmost zeal. . . ."[2]

Whether the noble Roman was pleased with this treatment and with the exotic sights, we do not know. In all probability, like most perfunctory tourists he was somewhat bored, and he might well have frowned on the strange gods of the decadent Egyptians and the ready adoption of them by the Greek settlers who were their masters. He may have mumbled to himself about the need for Roman austerity and for the good old common sense of his farming ancestors. Back home, he would make an impressive report on his "fact-gathering" tour of foreign countries allied to Rome, and thereby augment his political stock. As to Horus, the man in charge of the reception, did this son of Egypt scorn the pomp and circumstance fabricated for the tourists and find the Roman politician an overbearing, humorless barbarian?

Tourism was a flourishing industry in Egypt long before the coming of Thomas Cook and Sons (and even Alexander and his generals). Around A.D. 100, one industrious sightseer took his task so seriously that he traversed the entire land, going up the Nile to its southern outpost at Syene, the present Aswan. He also took to the desert trail for a visit to the Siva Oasis, site of the oracle of Jupiter Ammon. Upon reaching the shrine, he scratched the names of his friends into the stone to have them remembered by the god.

---

2 Ibid., Vol. I, p. 128.

The ancients (for example, Herodotus) called the Egyptians the most religious of all peoples, by which they probably meant the most idolatrous. The new settlers quickly fell into the same pattern. The papyri of the Greco-Roman period provide a great many examples of the varieties of Egyptian religious experiences and practices. Of charms, incantations, oracles, and magic formulas there is no end. Local deities are consulted on any vital issue, somewhat in the manner of the ancient Chinese oracle bones. For instance, an Oxyrhynchus papyrus begs Serapis Helios, the beneficent god, "to answer four questions: Is it expedient to buy a slave? Is it granted to me to marry? Is it good to make a contract with So-and-So? Is it fated for him to depart the city?"[3] These were more or less the standard questions submitted to the deities. More interesting perhaps are the references to great religious festivals, particularly the description, in the Zenon papyri of the festival of the goddess Isis.

The papyri also shed light on a more commonplace but rarely recorded aspect of civilization: Egypt at play. When it came to entertainment, the people knew well how to escape from the daily toil and trouble and the tyranny of superiors, inferiors, rulers, and rapacious gods. Judging by the Oxyrhynchus papyri, horse racing and chariot racing were almost an obsession. Clubs of

Horse racing. After a Greeek vase

all kinds flourished and multiplied. From Tebtunis comes an account of a kind of diners' club, listing the members by number and specifying extra charges for bread, wine, and decorations.[4] An athletic club went by the fanciful name of "The Worshipful Gymnastic Club of Nomads under Imperial Patronage," though it was about as "nomadic" as some equally exotic American fraternities are Red Indians or Arab dervishes. It gained Imperial favor through its gift of a golden crown to Emperor Claudius when he won a victory in Britain. All this is disclosed in a document which

---

[3] Wadell: op. cit., p. 13.   [4] Ibid., p. 14.

conferred club membership on a boxer by the name of Herminius, in A.D. 194, upon payment of the round sum of one hundred denars.[5]

Those who look for some kind of quasi-Jungian archetypes in the social life of these Mediterranean peoples of some two thousand years ago will not be disappointed. Similarities to modern practices are so striking that there is no need to stress them. Just take a routine invitation sent from Oxyrhynchus in the second or third century A.D.: "Chaeremon requests your company at dinner, at the table of the Lord Serapis in the Serapeum, tomorrow the 15th at 3 o'clock."[6] Only the R.S.V.P. is missing. The Serapeum, the local temple to the syncretic Greco-Egyptian god, had apparently developed into a social center, like any modern church in American suburbia.

Musicians and other entertainers were well-nigh obligatory for any self-respecting host, and letters requesting their services are numerous. In A.D. 237, for example, the city fathers of the Fayum town of Bacchias wrote to an agent requesting two dancing girls for a coming festivity. On one occasion in the year A.D. 182, when castanet players had been hired to liven up a party, tragedy ensued. An eight-year-old slave boy, barred by age and rank from attending the performance, was watching from upstairs, and while climbing for a better view, fell to his death. The pitiful incident is related in a report to the governor (strategos) of the Oxyrhynchus district—an indication that even the life of a slave was held to be of some account.

The most moving and candid documents are those dealing with intimate relationships such as marriage, friendship, love, parenthood. There is, for example, the letter of Hilarion to his wife Alis, whom he addresses in the Egyptian style as "sister," which she may well have been. Hilarion had apparently gone to Alexandria to seek employment, while his wife was with child: "Hilarion to Alis his sister, heartiest greetings, and to my dear Berous and Apollonarion. Know that we are still even now in Alexandria. Do not worry if when all the others return I remain in Alexandria. I beg and beseech you to take care of the little child, and as soon as we receive wages I will send them to you. If— good luck to you!—you bear offspring, if it is male, let it live; if it is female, expose it. You told Aphrodisias, 'Do not forget me.' How can I forget you? I beg you therefore not to worry. . . ."[7]

---

[5] Ibid., p. 15.   [6] Ibid., p. 15.
[7] Hunt and Edgar: op. cit., Vol. I, p. 295.

This is a loving letter, no matter how savage the time-honored practice of disposing of unwanted children may seem to us. There are also many affectionate letters from wives—such as the letter to a man fighting Caesar's wars, in which his wife writes that she is "constantly sleepless, filled night and day with the one anxiety" for his safety; and then she goes on to implore him not to brave unnecessary dangers. It may not be the epitome of patriotism, but it bespeaks feminine realism and concern when she counsels him: "But just as the strategos [local governor] here leaves the bulk of the work to the magistrates, you do the same."[8]

There are, on the other hand, countless divorce bills and letters such as the one, from a later century, in which a Christian lady pours out her heart over the insulting behavior of her godless

Portrait from the Fayum

husband, who, like any anticlerical nineteenth-century Frenchman, was particularly irritated by her churchgoing and once even shut the door of God's house on her. Planting himself outside the church, he screamed at her: "Why did you go to the church?" adding "many terms of abuse to my face and through his nose." What could one expect from a monster like that? The long-suffering lady sadly concludes: "He kept saying, 'A month hence I shall take a mistress.' God knows this is true."[9]

Among the most spirited of the letters are those between fathers and sons, testifying to the closeness of a relationship that for the ancients was of prime importance. One justly celebrated letter scribbled by a cheeky little boy in a clumsy hand, and full of spelling errors, is a delightful example of juvenile effrontery: "Theon to Theon his father, greeting. It was *so* kind of you not

---

[8] Baikie: *Egyptian Papyri and Papyrus-hunting*, p. 295.
[9] Ibid., pp. 293–4.

to take me off with you to town! If you won't take me with you to
Alexandria, I won't write you a letter, or speak to you, or wish you
health any more. And if you do go to Alexandria, I won't take
your hand or greet you again. So that's what will happen if you
won't take me. Mother said to Archelaus, 'He's quite upsetting me:
away with him!' Oh, it was *so* kind of you to send me a present!—
such a beauty!—nothing but husks! They tricked us that day, the
12th, when you sailed. Send for me then, I beseech you. If you
don't, I won't eat, I won't drink. So there! I pray for your health."[1]

Exchanges between "Sweetest Father" and "Sweetest Son"
abound in the Oxyrhynchus texts. The sons are usually respect-
ful and obeisant, however, while the fathers dispense such advice
as: "Take care not to offend any of the persons at home, but
give your mind to your books and nothing else, devoting yourself
to learning, and so you will have profit from them."[2] One of the
most charming letters comes from Apion, a model son, who had
enlisted in the imperial armies and had been given a new Latin
name. He hastens to let his family at Philadelphia (Zenon's
town) know of his arrival in Italy after a stormy crossing, and
of an impending promotion. The letter was mailed from the
Roman naval base at Misenum on the Gulf of Naples, whence

Portrait from the Fayum

Pliny the Elder had set forth to rescue victims of Mt. Vesuvius.
It reads: "Apion to Epimachus, his father and lord, heartiest greetings. First of all, I pray that you are in health, and continually
prosper and fare well with my sister and her daughter and my
brother. I thank the lord Serapis that when I was in danger at
sea he saved me. Straightaway when I entered Misenum I re-

---

[1] Grenfell and Hunt: *The Oxyrhynchus Papyri*, Vol. I, p. 119.
[2] Ibid., Vol. III, p. 531.

ceived my travelling-money from Caesar, three goldpieces. And I am well. I beg you, therefore, my lord father, write me a few lines, first regarding your health, secondly regarding that of my brother and sister, thirdly that I may kiss your hand because you have brought me up well, and on this account I hope to be quickly promoted, if the gods will. Give many greetings to Capito, and to my brother and sister, and to Serenilla, and my friends. I send you a little portrait of myself at the hands of Euctemon. And my new name is Antonius Maximus. I pray for your good health. . . ."[3]

Women played a significant role in colonial society. Some women, apparently, even received advanced schooling. There are a considerable number of letters from mothers—though they are not as numerous as the letters from fathers—and they are not all written by scribes. In a letter from the second century B.C., a mother registers satisfaction that her son has taken up the native Egyptian language, which she hopes will bring him financial rewards. The letter is of interest because it shows not only that women concerned themselves with their children's education, but also that Greek settlers did not keep aloof from the natives but were amenable to assimilation. Not all mothers could take pride in their sons' careers, however. One papyrus letter from the second century A.D., taken from the village of Karanis in the Fayum, was written by a prodigal son who tells his mother that, because of his misfortunes, he is too ashamed to return: ". . . I am going about in rags. I write to tell you that I am naked. I beseech you, mother, be reconciled to me. Besides, I know what I have brought upon myself. I have got a lesson, as was needful. I know that I have sinned. I have heard from Postumus who met you in the Arsinoe district and told you the whole story without reserve. Don't you know I would rather become a cripple than be conscious that I am still owing any man two cents."[4]

On occasion a son, afraid of his father's harshness, followed the familiar device of appealing to his mother's softer heart, as in this shameless passage: ". . . When you receive my letter, kindly send me 200 drachmae. . . . I've spent all the money. . . . I write this to you that you may know. Send me a thick woollen cloak and a purse, and a pair of puttees and a pair of leathern cloaks, some olive-oil and the wash-basin of which you spoke and a pair of pillows. In addition, then, mother, send my monthly allowance in all haste. . . . My father came to me and gave me not a farthing,

---

[3] Hunt and Edgar: op. cit., Vol. I, p. 305.
[4] Ibid., Vol. I, pp. 317–19.

nor a purse nor anything. But they are all jeering at me, saying 'His father's a soldier and has given him nothing.' . . . So I beg you, mother, send me things: do not leave me as I am. . . ." Further notes on the margin, otherwise illegible, reiterate: "Send me". . . "send me."[5]

In contrast to this whining plea is a letter from a man who has heard that his brother was lacking in filial kindness. He writes to him: "I have been informed that you are all laying heavy burdens on our revered mother. Please, my sweetest brother, do not grieve her in anything; and if any of our brothers withstand her, you ought to box their ears. For you ought now to be called a father. . . . But don't be offended at my letter chiding you; for we ought to reverence our mother like a goddess, especially such a good mother as ours. This I have written to you, brother, because I know the sweetness of revered parents. . . ."[6]

Portrait from the Fayum

Family letters like these, so personal and so immediate, bring these people to life across the chasm of time. When there is a death in the family, we share in the human drama, in the hopelessness of those who grieve—though the loss of a close relative will try men differently. There is a stern rebuke from a good Samaritan to two heartless brothers: ". . . I am very much surprised that you went off so unfeelingly without your brother's body: you gathered up all that he had, and then you went off. From this I see that it was not for the deceased's sake you came here, but for his goods."[7] For sympathy and good sense, however, the following letter of condolence can hardly be outdone: "Irene to Taonnophis and Philo, good cheer. I was so much grieved and wept as much over

[5] Wadell: op. cit., pp. 6–7.   [6] Ibid., pp. 8–9.
[7] Powell and Barber: op. cit., pp. 143–4.

the blessed one as I wept over Didymas, and I did all that was fitting and so likewise all my household, Epaphroditus and Termuthion and Philion and Apollonius and Planras. But nevertheless one can do nothing against such things. Therefore comfort yourselves. Good fortune to you."[8]

Such stoic fortitude is conspicuously lacking in the following letter, with condolences of a different nature: ". . . That you suffered like mother Eve, like Mary; and, as God lives, my master, neither righteous women nor sinners ever suffered what you suffered; nevertheless your sins are nought. But let us glorify God because it was He who gave and He who took away; but pray that the Lord may give them rest and may vouchsafe to behold you among them in Paradise when the souls of men are judged; for they are gone to the bosom of Abraham and Isaac and of Jacob. That I exhort you, my lord, not to put grief into your soul and ruin your fortunes, but pray that the Lord may send you his blessing. For the Lord has many good things and makes the sorrowful to be of good cheer if they desire a blessing from Him; and we hope in God that through this grief the Lord may send joy to you and the lord your brother. . . ."[9]

Byzantine coin with the Christian emblem (Labarum)

A comparison between the pagan letter and the other, far wordier one mirroring the emergent Christian outlook indicates the change of heart that had taken place in Greco-Roman Egypt. Indeed, the end was near.

These few examples suggest the variety of the nonliterary papyri, though obviously they do not bear out, or at least do not bear on, Carlyle's great-man concept of history, or any of the standard textbook histories, for that matter. There is little here

---

[8] Grenfell and Hunt: *The Oxyrhynchus Papyri*, Vol. I, p. 115.
[9] Hunt and Edgar: op. cit.: Vol. I, p. 168.

about the grand-scale crimes of supermen and the fateful decisions of opportunists with second-rate talents and first-rate ambitions (to cite Justice Holmes). If anything, these everyday documents demonstrate that to the vast majority of people "history" happens on quite a different level, one seldom visited by heroes. They are of that "greater reality" which Goethe once ascribed to a farm as compared to the phantoms of rising and falling empires. They speak not of drums and thunder, not of battalions and dynasties, but of the nameless masses at their daily toil, of the farmer, the baker, the candlestick maker, the young mother, the army veteran, the estate manager, and the corrupt local politician. These forgotten voices resound with the realities of making a living and of getting by in a hard world. Here we come face to face with bureaucracy, legal institutions and law enforcement, religious practices, farming methods, economic setbacks, slavery, social classes, state intervention, public conduct and private behavior in the multifaceted social and economic world of Egypt throughout a thousand years. From these documents we can rewrite its history—largely an anonymous, internal history, fed by an almost unbroken record through which successive generations speak of themselves instead of being relegated to the silence of "human instruments" by the facile abstractions of political, military, and "philosophical" historians.

The papyri have added immeasurably to the understanding of historians—not to mention palaeographers, philologists, and theologians—of the life of Hellenistic and Roman Egypt. The Hellenistic age had for long been an entirely neglected period uncomfortably set between the meteoric career of Alexander and the advent of the Roman Caesars. Of Egypt since the eclipse of the Pharaohs, little had been known except for a few references in Herodotus (who lived before Alexander the Great) and in Strabo, Diodorus Siculus, and Plutarch. Nearly everything we know now was gleaned from the recovered documents.

Among the most zealous workers in the field of economic and social history was Mikhail Ivanovich Rostovtzeff, a refugee from Bolshevist Russia who later taught at Yale and became one of the outstanding historians of the twentieth century. He ranks high among those who restored the Hellenistic epoch to its proper place, for it was Hellenism which propagated the concept of a world community with its Koine, or world language, and which instituted far-reaching measures in law, politics, and economies. Without it the Roman Empire would not have been possible. Another modern scholar, whom we shall discuss at greater length later, is Aurel Stein, who devoted some of his early studies to the elucidation—from papyri—of the Roman administration in Egypt.

Egypt may have been a backwater during Roman times, but the Egyptian documents shed light on the greater Mediterranean world, for which we have little or no data from any other source. The thousands of fragments project a picture of such precision

Scene of Rural Egypt. After a Pompeian mural

and fullness that, in the words of Rostovtzeff, they "will some day give us an almost exact idea what life used to be" in Hellenistic and Roman Egypt.[1]

---

[1] Rostovtzeff: op. cit., p. 100.

B: *The Ancient Near East*

·XI·

THE WORLD'S

OLDEST BOOKS

*The modern world has inherited from Ancient Egypt,
as from Greece, in two different ways. In the first place
there has been single historical transmission. . . . But
secondly there has existed also a deferred mode of acquisition, in which Champollion and his successors
have played for Egypt the same role as the scholars of
the Renaissance played for Greece.*

ALAN H. GARDINER[1]

THE PAPYRI of Greco-Roman Egypt have commanded so much
interest since the last quarter of the nineteenth century that
it has become difficult to realize that these documents were after
all only those left by alien intruders—and late-comers at that.
Papyrology, with its professorships, international congresses,
learned journals, methodological treatises, and special collections,
is generally understood to comprise little else but texts in the
classical languages. Yet papyri in Greek or Latin form only one
segment of the polyglot record of more than five thousand years of
Egypt's cultural life. Side by side with the Greek and occasional
Latin texts, there were found papyri written in Aramaic, Hebrew,
Pahlavi (Persian), Syrian, Libyan, a number of Asia Minor idioms,
Coptic, Ethiopic, and Arabic. One of the curiosities was scraps in
Gothic, probably the earliest Germanic writing in existence, which
bears out the tradition of Roman employment of barbarian north-

---

[1] Alan H. Gardiner: "Writing and Literature," in S. R. K. Glanville,
ed.: *The Legacy of Egypt*, p. 53.

From Aramaic (right), Syriac (top left), and Hebrew (bottom left) papyri from Egypt. Polyglot testimonies to the cultural variety and political fortunes of the Nile Valley, which helped non-Egyptian as well as Egyptian documents to survive.

ern soldiers along the Nile, an incident familiar to readers of Charles Kingsley's novel *Hypatia*.

However, all these documents made their appearance only after the great civilization of Egypt had already been flourishing for about three millennia. And of Egypt's generous legacy not the

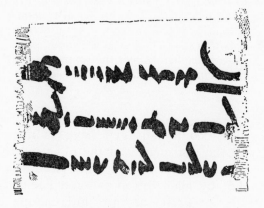

Persian papyrus from Egypt

least was papyrus itself. The use of papyrus for writing was, as we have seen, an Egyptian innovation, and the papyrus was made from a native Egyptian plant. We do not know the exact date when it came into use, but the evidence now places it before the beginning of Dynastic Egypt, about 3100 B.C.

Dwellers along the banks of the Nile, then, had been literate for all this time, longer by far than any other people, with the possible exception of the Sumerians of Mesopotamia. Unlike the Mesopotamian, the Egyptian literate culture continued virtually unbroken into the Christian era and ended only with the coming of the Arabs and the gradual eclipse of the old scripts, the pictographic hieroglyphs and their cursive variants, hieratic and demotic. Yet Coptic, the final form of the native Egyptian language, lingered on into the seventeenth century and is still used today in the rites of the Coptic Christian Church.

Once the Copts adopted a modified Greek alphabet, their ability to write and read the old scripts was soon forgotten. Only the vaguest notions of the meaning of the strange symbols were passed on. Unfortunately, even these were obscured in classical accounts, which since the days of Plato and Thales mirrored the Greeks' extravagant respect for what seemed to them the almost supernatural wisdom of the Egyptians. Lost was the key to the profuse inscriptions on temple ruins and obelisks. And lost was the knowledge of any work of ancient Egyptian literature. Indeed, skeptics doubted that, except for religious incantations, Egyptian writing had ever served any but utilitarian purposes. That Egypt possessed a literature in the modern sense, one of a surprising liveliness, mental alacrity, and variety, was unthought of until about the last hundred and fifty years.

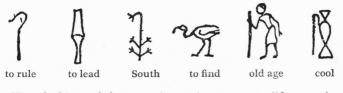

| to rule | to lead | South | to find | old age | cool |

Hieroglyphic symbols expressing various concepts (ideograms)

Speculations as to the meaning of the pictograms were rife in Europe from the days of a German Jesuit scholar, Athanasius Kircher, in the seventeenth century, but the problem seemed insoluble. Of course, thoroughly Islamized Egyptians looked upon the relics of their pagan ancestors with little but disgust and unceremoniously destroyed any artifacts of idolatry that came their way. We may be sure that they did not discriminate between various kinds of papyri, whether written in Greek or Egyptian hieratic or demotic. The Comte de Volney, traveling in Egypt and Syria before the French Revolution, heard of an auto-da-fé with some three hundred rolls "written in an unknown language," which natives had found near Damietta and which the local sheik ordered obliterated immediately. Here is a tale grimmer yet than that attending the rescue of the Greek *Carta Borgiana,* and just as revealing. This time, however, the burning did not even serve to provide olfactory titillation for fellahin nostrils.[2]

That Europeans paid any attention to Egyptian papyri earlier than to Greek ones is unlikely, though from time to time some chance finds may have drifted into private collections, to be forgotten and to gather dust. In Italy there was reported a *pezetto di papiro scritto con lettere egiziane* (a piece of papyrus written in Egyptian letters), but it too was lost.[3] To judge by their accounts, few travelers in Egypt showed an awareness of anything but the massive monuments above ground—the Pyramids of Gizeh, the halls of Karnak, and the rock tombs of the Valley of the Kings. In a way, further obstacles were provided by the finds in Herculaneum and by the *Carta Borgiana,* which led men to equate papyri with Greek records, a bias that has characterized papyrological studies ever since.

However, with the coming of Napoleon, Egyptian writing—on stone, ostraca (potsherds and limestone flakes), wood, and, not the least, papyri—struck the eyes of the French savants at every turn of their explorations. We have already alluded to the excitement felt by F. Jomard and V. Denon, and others like them, when they contemplated the beautiful penmanship and ornamentation of the funerary rolls they extricated. This was the beginning of an influx of papyri—in Egyptian and other scripts—to Europe, which was accelerated in the coming decades by the unscrupulous operations of Belzoni and the consuls-general of Western powers in Alexandria, such as Bernardo Drovetti, a veteran of Napoleon's campaign who was acting on behalf of France, Henry Salt, agent for England, Giovanni d'Anastasi, an Armenian acting for Sweden, and Jean-François Mimaut, acting for Sardinia. Through them the bases were established for the collections at Paris, London, Rome, Florence, Turin, Berlin, Leiden, and elsewhere.

But all the wonders of Egypt and its forgotten texts, reported by the French in sumptuous tomes and made evident by actual shipments of ancient objects, heightened rather than solved the mystery of a civilization already ancient before Achaean warriors sacked Troy.

How the veil came to be lifted by what was essentially the ingenuity and resolution of one man, Jean-François Champollion,

---

[2] K. L. Preisendanz: *Papyrusfunde und Papyrusforschung* (Leipzig: Hiersemann; 1933), p. 70.
[3] Ibid., p. 68.

is well known. Champollion conquered Egypt in a manner that by comparison makes the Corsican adventurer's campaign look vain and grotesque. His genius was responsible for one of archaeology's dramatic triumphs: the rolling back of millennia when the key was found to the life, history, thought, and religion of Old Egypt.

The three main Egyptian scripts: from top to bottom, hieroglyphic, hieratic, and demotic. Demotic, the most simplified and cursive of the three, probably came into use only in late Dynastic or early Ptolemaic times. Hieroglyphic was the first to be deciphered. It still causes less difficulty to scholars than its cursive variations.

Champollion's monumental achievement was the decipherment of the hieroglyphs, for which task the Rosetta Stone, one of Napoleon's trophies, constituted a valuable aid. The solution to the hieroglyphic puzzle made possible the recovery of unknown books and texts—indeed, of an entire literature. It opened up a notable epoch in the history of man which had hitherto been shrouded in silence. However, only a small fraction of what was most certainly a large body of literature has so far been recovered.[4]

From the decipherment of Egyptian scripts to a full grasp of the language was a tortuous road that has not even today been fully traversed. After all, Egyptian had undergone great changes in three or four thousand years, and the idiom of the early dynasties of the beginning of the third millennium B.C. was no longer readily understandable to the men of the Middle Kingdom a thousand years later, just as the writing of the latter presented difficulties to the people of the Eighteenth Dynasty in the second half of the second millennium B.C., and still more to their descendants. Yet, phenomenal advances were made: scholars compiled dictionaries of the Egyptian language, and texts came to be read and translated with increasing authority.

Champollion not only deciphered the script but was the pioneer student of Egyptian texts. He produced the first grammar of

---

[4] Adolf Erman: *The Literature of the Ancient Egyptians* (London: Methuen & Co.; 1927), p. xxiv.

the long-buried language, and he espoused the cause of the Egyptian papyri with prophetic zeal and fought a one-man crusade against the attitude exemplified by François Jomard, who had been pessimistic about the chances of their ever being read. (Jomard also thought that virtually all papyri represented copies of the same funerary compositions.) Champollion was particularly incensed when Jomard advised the French government to desist from further purchases. It was because of Jomard that the papyrological resources of Paris were surpassed by those of other centers, such as Turin and Berlin—the latter on the urging of Alexander von Humboldt. Before Champollion's untimely death at the age of forty-one, he studied the papyri available in France and Italy and made discoveries that may well rank with his original achievement. As a result, what had been odd curiosities became valuable documents from which it was possible to reconstruct one of the most ancient civilizations. Here were literary works whose loss had not even been mourned, for their existence was not known.

Champollion undertook numerous trips to copy papyri as they came to his knowledge. From 1824 to 1826 he traveled in Italy, and there organized the growing collection of Egyptica in the

HIEROGLYPHIC					HIEROGLYPHIC BOOK-SCRIPT	HIERATIC			DEMOTIC
2900-2800 B.C.	2700-2600 B.C.	2000-1800 B.C.	c. 1500 B.C.	500-100 B.C.	c. 1500 B.C.	c. 1900 B.C.	c. 1300 B.C.	c. 200 B.C	400-100 B.C.

Table indicating the evolution of several Egyptian hieroglyphs and their cursive equivalents. After G. Möller (1919)

Vatican, on the invitation of Angelo Cardinal Mai. He also visited Florence and other cities. At Naples' *officina dei papiri* he was much pained by the condition of the manuscripts from Herculaneum. He was convinced that the scholars to whom the charred rolls had been entrusted had been unnecessarily negligent because they believed, like Jomard, that the documents could never be read. "I maintain instead," he wrote, "that with sufficient persistence we would soon recover from the 1,700 manuscripts a considerable number of literary treasures. . . ."[5] But he saved his energies for the Egyptian papyri. His most profitable studies were carried out in Turin, capital of the Kingdom of Sardinia, which had recently acquired a cache of Drovetti's Egyptian booty after it had been spurned by authorities in Paris.

On contemplating such riches, Champollion confessed, he was "in a trance." His insight into the Egyptian language grew by leaps and bounds. At every turn the papyri revealed to him unknown facets of the history and culture of Egypt. One of his most noteworthy discoveries concerned the so-called *rituel funéraire*, or "Book of the Dead" (as Richard Lepsius, the German Egyptologist, was to call it later), which was not as standardized as had generally been believed, but had existed in various versions of different lengths and content.

He spent days transcribing these beautifully preserved treasures, and then, to his surprise, he was told that the garret of the Turin Academy housed more Egyptian manuscripts—however, because of their decayed state, they were "no longer of any use." Only after much insistence was he granted access to them. "On entering this room, which I shall henceforth call a Columbarium of History, I was spellbound. In front of me was a table, ten feet long, covered in its entire breadth with a layer at least half a foot deep of papyrus fragments. . . . I find it impossible to describe all I felt as I examined these remains of world history. Even the most sedate imagination would have been excited, for who could restrain his emotions while touching the ancient dust of centuries? I lapsed into a trance. No passage from Aristotle or Plato is so eloquent as these mounds of papyri! . . . I was able to savor dates of which history had lost all recollection, and names of gods who have had no altars in more than fifteen centuries. . . ."[6] And so he went on, in a letter to his brother Figeac.

---

[5] Hermine Hartleben: *Champollion. Sein Leben und Sein Werk* (Berlin: Weidmann; 1906), Vol. I, p. 559.
[6] Ibid., p. 526.

But not all these dusty fragments reflected grave historical matters. They also taught him, he said, "that it is only one step from the sublime to the ridiculous. . . . At the side of a government decree of Ramses the Great or of another prominent leader . . . I have seen fragments of Egyptian caricatures, a cat holding a shepherd's staff in its paw as it guards ducks, or a monkey playing the flute. . . . Here, a funerary text on the reverse of which secular concerns left a certificate of sale; there, remains of drawings whose monstrous immorality gave me a strange idea indeed of the serenity and wisdom of Egypt."[7]

Champollion quickly recovered from the shock of finding Egyptians as prone to pornography, or at least to uninhibited sensuality, as the latter-day Pompeians and Herculaneans. It was quite likely, he assured himself, that in those remote days the scrupulous Egyptian government had confiscated these "dirty" pictures.

From the Turin lists of Egyptian kings, in hieratic script. When complete, the papyrus contained the chronology and names of 300 pharaohs, together with the lengths of their reigns.

And with this he recaptured his former enthusiasm. He now told his brother of what has come to be regarded since as a major source of Egyptian history, the Turin lists of kings, which he dated back to at least the Nineteenth Dynasty (twelfth century B.C.): "I could snatch from the dust twenty bits of this precious manuscript, pieces no more than one or two thumbs wide, which however contained the more or less truncated names of seventy-seven Pharaohs. . . . Egypt alone could furnish us documents of such astonishing antiquity. You will understand that the age of the

---

[7] Ibid., p. 527.

Lagides [Ptolemies] and even of the Persians is beginning to arouse pity in me—all this dates from yesterday in comparison to what I have been holding in my hands for the last eight days."[8]

In view of the groping and fragmentary knowledge of ancient Egyptian then at his command, it is something of a miracle that Champollion learned as much as he did from the papyri in the few years left to him after he first deciphered hieroglyphics. Luckily, Champollion could plunge into the tidal wave of Egyptian papyri just arriving in the West.

At Aix-en-Provence a French private collector, M. Sallier, possessed several valuable papyri (later acquired by the British Museum) among which Champollion identified a rhapsodic poem describing an alleged victory of Ramses II at Kadesh over a people whose name Champollion read as *Scheta* and whom he held to be the Scythians. Much later it was established that they were in fact the Hittites, of whom next to nothing had been known. They had been among the greatest imperial powers of the ancient Near East.

Eventually Champollion at last set foot on Egyptian soil, and there he noticed a duplicate of the Ramses epic engraved on a wall of the Rameseum of Thebes. It was then that he took to the spade and excavated the structure of an ancient temple library at Karnak.

The flow of Egyptian papyri was probably never again quite as profuse as it had been in the first half of the nineteenth century. It diminished considerably after the tomb-robbing expeditions to the Theban necropolis and the pillage of temple ruins, and in the second half of the century it was just a trickle compared with the search for Greco-Roman papyri of a later age. Deposits of hieratic and hieroglyphic documents in rubbish heaps were extremely rare. Hence the digs, whether by native amateurs or by European professionals, added relatively little. Only demotic texts—in the Egyptian cursive that may not have originated earlier than the Ptolemaic era—cropped up in considerable amounts. But though they supplemented the Greek records, they were, on the whole, of little consequence to our knowledge of the pre-Hellenic Egyptian civilization. Moreover, except for the ventures of men like Belzoni and Drovetti, the discovery of Egyptian papyri was left entirely to chance. Unlike classical papyri, these were not sought in any systematic manner, and even today there is no

---

[8] Ibid., p. 528.

catalogue of the scores of Egyptian papyri scattered in collections around the globe. A large number deposited in reputable institutions still wait to be deciphered and published.[9]

Because of the nature of these accidental finds, usually made by natives, we know next to nothing of the places of origin and the circumstances surrounding the discovery of the majority of even the most valuable Egyptian texts. M. Sallier's papyri are said to have been acquired from an Egyptian seaman. No more is known. And even this may be questionable. Mrs. D'Orbiney, an Englishwoman, purchased the only extant copy of the celebrated *Tale of the Two Brothers* from some unknown person in Italy around 1850.

Only in rare instances do we have concrete facts, as in the case of the Great Harris Papyrus, one of the manuscripts obtained in the mid-nineteenth century by A. C. Harris, an English traveler and a resident of Alexandria, whose extraordinary collection was sold by his daughter to the British Museum in 1876. Great Harris, or Harris I, the longest Egyptian papyrus in existence (133 feet), was, on reliable evidence, dug up by fellahin near Thebes. Great Harris, by the way, well deserved its epithet not only because of its length but because of its excellent state of preservation, its fine hieratic script, and its content: a eulogistic catalogue of the accomplishments of Ramses III, which, despite its tendentious slant, has yielded significant historical information. Arabs took it from a rock tomb behind the temple of Medinet Habu. The tomb when opened was said to have been filled with mummies that had already been desecrated in antiquity. The "catalogue" consisted of some twenty rolls, but Mr. Harris was unable to buy all of them and the others unfortunately were scattered, so that it is not complete. It seems, however, that various papyri dealing with tomb robberies of the eleventh century B.C., among them the Abbott, were also taken from this site.

The origin of the equally renowned Harris 500, which is also in the British Museum—and which constitutes something of an anthology of Egyptian literature in the New Kingdom—is less certain. More is known about its later misfortunes. It was complete when purchased by Mr. Harris but was partly destroyed in an explosion in Alexandria. Harris was said to have copied the entire text before the catastrophe, but his transcript has never been lo-

---

[9] Preisendanz: "Abriss der Papyruskunde," in Fritz Milkau, ed.: *Handbuch der Bibliothekswissenschaft* (Wiesbaden: O. Harrassowitz; 1952), Vol. I, p. 51.

cated. As a result, we may have lost forever any record of several works of Egyptian literature.[1]

Fate dealt more kindly with one of the most popular pieces of Egyptian secular writing, the story of Wenamun, who went on a luckless buying trip to Syria. This work has come down to us in its entirety. In 1891 some fellahin were camping outside El Hibeh, where Grenfell and Hunt excavated a few years later. The night was cold and they decided to make a fire. Since they needed fuel, a commodity notoriously unavailable in the desert, they searched for stray pieces of wood. Luckily a fine inflammable stick protruded from the sand nearby. Upon examination, it turned out to be a written roll. In the 1890's the fellahin were well aware of the value of scraps of ancient texts, which could be turned into enough cash to keep several campfires burning. So Wenamun's tale of travel found its way to an antiquarian dealer, and shortly thereafter it was picked up, undoubtedly at an increase in price of several hundred percent, by Professor Golenisheff of St. Petersburg, who had already made singular contributions to the recovery of Egyptian literature.

Among the professional excavators who made momentous finds of hieratic papyri, a consumptive young Scottish antiquarian, H. A. Rhind, deserves honorable mention, though the famous Rhind mathematical papyrus was bought from a dealer. But again Flinders Petrie easily takes the lead. It was at Kahun and Gurob, near the Fayum pyramids, that he recovered papyri dating from the Middle and New Kingdom. Those of the Twelfth Dynasty from Kahun included letters, accounts, a medical treatise dealing with gynecology, and a magnificent hymn to Sesostris III (nineteenth century B.C.), written in the Pharaoh's lifetime. It has come down to us as "the earliest known example of poetry exhibiting rigid strophic structure"[2] and displays the "parallelism of members" and the effective metaphors so familiar from Biblical verse. Laudatory strophes to a sovereign were among the common forms of Egyptian literature. This, the oldest to survive, is unexcelled. The reader may get a taste of it from one of its six strophes:

> *Twice great is the king of his city, above a million arms:*
> *as for other rulers of men, they are but common folk.*

---

[1] James Baikie: *Egyptian Papyri and Papyrus-hunting* (London: Religious Tract Society, 1925), p. 160.

[2] James Henry Breasted: *A History of Egypt* (New York: Charles Scribner's Sons; 1937), p. 207.

*Twice great is the king of his city: he is as it were a dyke,
damming the stream in its water flood.*
*Twice great is the king of his city: he is as it were a cool
lodge, letting every man repose unto full daylight.*
*Twice great is the king of his city: he is as it were a bulwark,
with walls built of sharp stones of Kesem.*
*Twice great is the king of his city: he is as it were a place of
refuge, excluding the marauder.*
*Twice great is the king of his city: he is as it were an asylum,
shielding the terrified from his foe.*
*Twice great is the king of his city: he is as it were a shade,
the cool vegetation of the flood in the season of harvest.*
*Twice great is the king of his city: he is as it were a corner
warm and dry in time of winter.*
*Twice great is the king of his city: he is as it were a rock
barring the blast in time of tempest.*
*Twice great is the king of his city: he is as it were Sekhmet
to foes who tread upon his boundary.*[3]

Petrie found a somewhat similar panegyric in 1896 when excavating the mortuary temple of the Nineteenth-Dynasty King Merenptah (Merneptah), son and successor of Ramses II. This time the document was not on papyrus but was carved on a stela. The monument became famous because it contains the first and only reference to Israel ("Israel is desolated, her seed is not"[4]) in Pharaonic Egyptian records.

Inscriptions carved on stone, rather than set down on papyri, constitute the oldest actual remains of Egyptian literature from the Old Kingdom, though papyrus was already in use. These inscriptions are by no means limited in length on account of their physical rendering. Indeed, when collected and edited, they make up two formidable volumes of a total of more than a thousand pages. The collection goes by the name of the Pyramid Texts, since the pieces were copied from the walls of chambers of some six pyramids of the Fifth and Sixth Dynasties (c. 2450–2250 B.C.). But, like much else in the Egyptian language, particularly anything of a religious or literary nature, they probably date back to the beginning of the Old Kingdom (c. 2800 B.C.), if not to proto- and pre-Dynastic days. Some of the formulas found on the walls of pyramids reflect a much cruder age, as for example the "cannibalistic" hymn of Unas, which describes the lassoing of

---

[3] Ibid., p. 207.
[4] J. H. Breasted: *Ancient Records of Egypt: The Historical Documents* (Chicago: Chicago University Press; 1905), Vol. III, pp. 616–17.

the gods. In the manner of later Egyptian mortuary texts, the inscriptions consist of a vast number of hymns, prayers, and spells whose purpose was to facilitate the travel of the deceased to the Netherworld. This makes them the direct ancestors of the Coffin Texts (characteristic of the Middle Kingdom) and the so-called *Book of the Dead,* which evolved in the New Kingdom and was usually conveyed on a papyrus roll interred with the dead person as a kind of *passe partout.* The transcribing and translating of the archaic Pyramid Texts is considered one of the triumphs of Egyptology.

These books on stone, despite their large dimensions, had been completely buried for about four thousand years. Their discovery came quite unexpectedly. Archaeologists had long disregarded the sadly decayed and unprepossessingly small pyramids in the Sakkara area (near the Step Pyramid of King Zoser), which clearly marked a decline in comparison to the Fourth-Dynasty structures at Gizeh. But in the last year of his life, Auguste Mariette, then head of the Egyptian Antiquities Service, gave the signal to open them. The work was directed by Maspero, who rushed to the dying Mariette's bedside in January 1881 to tell him of the extraordinary find: wall after wall, even ceilings, covered with hieroglyphics of greenish pigment. Mariette himself had held all his life that pyramids bearing inscriptions—no matter what Herodotus had said of the Cheops Pyramid—were quite improbable.

The inscriptions are invaluable in the study of the evolution of Egyptian religion. As old as they are, they show unmistakable signs of deriving from a much greater antiquity. When carved into the pyramids, they had already undergone intensive modification and, if we are to believe modern scholars, the ancient copyists "were perplexed and hardly understood the texts which they had before them."[5] Though many of them, like the *Book of the Dead,* make hardly any sense to us (and they probably are little more than gibberish), passages of rude, primitive power are not lacking. Maspero, who discovered and published the texts, has said that they "contain much verbiage, many pious platitudes, many obscure allusions to the affairs of the world, and amongst all this rubbish some passages full of movement and wild energy, in which poetical inspiration and religious emotion are still dis-

---

[5] Wallis Budge: *The Book of the Dead. The Papyrus of Ani, Scribe and Treasurer of the Temples of Egypt* . . . (New York: G. P. Putnam's Sons; 1913), p. 18.

cernible through the veil of mythological expressions."[6] We must not forget that these writings on walls are "the earliest body of religious writing—the earliest bible, in fact, in the world."[7] Like the Bible itself, they are not all light nor all lofty ethics.

Among all the Egyptian papyri, the *Book of the Dead* occurs about as frequently as Homer's *Iliad* among the Greek papyri. To Egyptologists this can be equally exasperating. Nevertheless, when it comes to calligraphic skill and illumination, Egypt has not yielded finer manuscripts. And they are the pride of any museum display, since, somewhat paradoxically, the much older Egyptian papyri are on the whole better preserved and far better executed than the Greek documents. Much of the content of the *Book of the Dead* is disconcerting, however. This harsh judgment is not due entirely to modern man's lack of understanding of the religious sensibilities of the ancients.

First of all, it should be remembered that there is no such thing as *"the" Book of the Dead*, as Champollion realized. These texts are of varying length and make-up. Standard passages do recur and common sources are drawn on (some scholars trace their origins to the First Dynasty), but one can hardly speak of a

From a colored vignette in the Papyrus Ani, an Eighteenth Dynasty "Book of the Dead" acquired by Sir Wallis Budge for the British Museum. "Anubis, the jackal-headed god of the dead, adjusts the scales on which the heart of the deceased (who is on the extreme left) is being weighed against Right and Truth symbolized by the feather. Thoth, the ibis-headed god of learning, stands ready with a scribe's palette to write down the verdict of the balance" (The Metropolitan Museum of Art).

---

[6] Quoted by Francis Llewellyn and Kate B. Griffith: "Egyptian Literature," in Charles Dudley Warner, ed.: *Library of the World's Best Literature* (New York: The International Society; 1896), Vol. XIII, p. 5229.

[7] Baikie: *Egyptian Antiquities in the Nile Valley* (London: Methuen & Co.; 1932), p. 161.

canon as in other Eastern religious works. Even the most splendid funerary rolls appear to be quite haphazardly put together, with some vital chapters missing and other passages senselessly repeated. There is neither continuity nor uniformity. Errors abound. Indeed, a majority of these rolls were probably fabricated for sale and were written by professional hacks without scruples. The rogues may have displayed a refreshing touch of agnosticism, but they were certainly shortchanging their customers, whose passage to the other world they endangered. In addition, the later fashion of sumptuously illustrating the funerary rolls led to a curtailment of textual matter. In the manner of modern magazine editing, the story had to be rigorously cut to make way for appealing pictures. As a modern Egyptologist observed: "The better the pictures in the Book of the Dead the worse the text."[8]

And what the customers bargained for was at best dubious, even if conscientiously executed. The intention was to outwit the gods by a calculated wordiness and absurd formulas in order to gain access to life eternal along the lovely banks of the celestial Nile. As is obvious from what had been incongruously labeled Negative Confession ("I have not done evil to men./ I have not ill treated animals./ I have not sinned in the temple./ . . . I have not blasphemed the gods./ I have not made anyone weep./ I have not slain. . . ."[9]), the average Egyptian of 1500 B.C. wanted to play it safe. Such are the ways of a mechanical ritual, commonly found where a strong priesthood has come to power. The sale of indulgences in the West and the use of water-powered prayer mills in the East are related practices.

It must be admitted, however, that the *Book of the Dead* mirrored a deeply moral awareness and a concept of eternal justice and judgment. The whole catalogue of sins given in the Negative Confession is in itself a moral code that can be compared with the injunctions in the Ten Commandments and with Buddha's Eightfold Path, which were formulated much later. And as in the Pyramid Texts, from which it was ultimately derived, the *Book of the Dead* contains verses of genuine religious fervor and poetic sublimity, foremost among them the hymns to Osiris and other deities.

There is good reason to believe that the Pyramid Texts and

---

[8] Jaroslav Černý: *Paper and Books in Ancient Egypt* (London: University College; 1952), p. 26.

[9] James B. Pritchard, ed.: *Ancient Near Eastern Texts*, second edition (Princeton: Princeton University Press; 1955), pp. 4–5.

their direct descendants down to the *Book of the Dead* are the oldest books in existence. Egyptologists, however, generally make this claim for the Prisse Papyrus, a Middle Kingdom manuscript acquired in Egypt in 1839 by the French archaeologist Émile Prisse d'Avennes. The place of discovery is uncertain, though the Frenchman thought it likely that the fellah who sold it to him, and whom he had employed while excavating a Theban burial ground, had simply taken it from the tomb of the Eleventh-Dynasty king which was then being opened.

Compared with the *Book of the Dead*, the Prisse Papyrus is a comprehensive text of known (or ascribed) authorship. Unlike the Pyramid and the Coffin texts, it is written on papyrus and comes closer to our conventional idea of the physical nature of a book. According to the text itself, the authors of the two treatises were men of the Old Kingdom, of the Third and Fifth Dynasty respectively, royal counselors by the name of Kagemna (Kagemni) and Ptahhotep. These men are historical personages. There is no evidence against this assertion, and hence the two moralistic tracts contained in the Prisse Papyrus may well hail from the beginning of the third millennium B.C., which would separate them from Aristotle by as much time as Aristotle is removed from us.

Both treatises—Kagemna's is much the shorter one—are typical of didactic works that were in vogue throughout the history of Egypt. There are close parallels to them in the Old Testament, particularly in Proverbs and in the apocryphal Ecclesiasticus. These sensible, somewhat prosaic counsels are said to have been written down conventionally by an aging father (occasionally even by a king) to guide his son. That so much of this genre has come down to us we owe to the fact that it was copied by schoolboys— not so much for pleasure, we may be sure, as because it was a standard exercise.

There is no end to this sound parental advice, which makes even Polonius seem a paragon of the laconic statement. Respect for property, chastity, humility, and all the other familiar virtues is preached. There are admonitions not to repeat frivolous words, not to trust to fortune, to respect superiors, and to be of cheerful countenance at festivities. The advantages of marriage are duly enumerated, but there is a stern warning against women: "If thou wouldst prolong friendship in an house [to which] thou hast admittance, as master, or as brother, or as friend, into whatsoever place thou enterest, beware of approaching the women. The place where they are is not good. On that account a thousand go to perdition. . . ."[1] A final section paints a rosy future for the son who follows this excellent advice. He shall prosper and rise in the world. And in due time he will in turn pass on the instruction of his father to his children. Some of the aphorisms credited to kings, however, balance the utilitarian temperament of Ptahhotep with a good dose of mature pessimism toward human nature, and a "tragic sense of life."

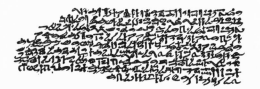

From the Prisse papyrus, a Middle Kingdom copy of two much more ancient didactic works from the Third and Fifth Dynasties (reduced). Now at the Louvre

A high moral note is struck by later writings, such as those of Amenemope (Amenemopet), which Wallis Budge bought for the British Museum in 1888,[2] but which had to wait some thirty-five years to be published (1922–24). Then they drew a good deal of attention. Budge was the first to notice the resemblance to the Biblical Proverbs of Solomon. However, it was Adolf Erman who pointed out precise parallels that could not be accidental. "Almost every verse in Prov. xxii. 17–xxiii. 14 finds its fellow in the Egyptian didactic work."[3] Quite a few sentences are essentially the same in the Egyptian treatise and in its Biblical counterpart. In the opening verse of the corresponding section of Proverbs, the Hebrew text reads: "Incline thine ear and hear my word,/ And apply thine heart to learn [them]." Amenemope reads: "Give thine ear, hearken to the things I have said,/ Give thy heart to understand them."[4]

A thorough study of Amenemope even enabled Erman to correct an obscurity in the Bible. A word previously rendered as "excellent things" has always been considered doubtful. The Hebrew alternative offered was "formerly" (*shilshôm*) or, as Hebrew scribes have suggested in the margin, "officers" (*shalîshîm*)—but neither made too much sense. The word, we now know, is

---

[1] Erman: op. cit., p. 59.
[2] British Museum: *A General Introductory Guide to the Egyptian Collections. . . .* (London: British Museum; 1930), p. 63.
[3] Gardiner: op. cit., p. 67.
[4] Ibid., p. 68.

"thirty" (shelôshîm), a reference to the number of chapters in Amenemope, which are paralleled by the thirty precepts given in the corresponding Hebrew text.[5]

Few scholars would deny the near-identity of the Hebrew and Egyptian precepts, but who copied from whom? That the Hebrew was the original is supported by the strong infusion of Semitic words into Egypt around the time of Amenemope's writing and by the ethical and monotheistic tenor of Amenemope's thought. Along with linguistic influences, so the argument runs, there must have come concepts and ideas. However, Amenemope's treatise is based on a long tradition of didactic literature that, as we have seen, goes back to the Old Kingdom and that had found a literary form long before the Hebrews emerged as a tribe from the Arabian desert. No Egyptologist can subscribe, as Alan H. Gardiner has stressed, "to such a view, which takes insufficient account of the ever-growing tendency to monotheism manifest in all Egyptian writings of post-Akhenaton times."[6] However, much of this dispute is beside the point once we overcome nationalistic fallacies in our conception of the ancient civilizations of the Near East. Egypt did not develop in isolation and of itself. Even Greece is the culmination of millennia, not a unique, isolated phase of Mediterranean culture. Since time immemorial, the lands of the eastern Mediterranean have freely exchanged their art, their religious concepts, their legends, and their deities, as much as their linguistic and racial stocks. Mediterranean peoples have borrowed from each other constantly and avidly, and ultimately they share common origins. To expect them to have qualms about "plagiarizing" is absurd.

Closely akin to wisdom literature are several other types of writing, among them letters and sermons upholding the profession of scribe. These pieces of "propaganda" proliferated in the New Kingdom, and their survival owes much to the fact that they were suitable for schoolboys and budding scribes to copy. A recurrent theme is the so-called "Satire of Trades," which has its parallel in Ecclesiasticus (the Wisdom of Jesus ben Sira).

In the *Instruction of Duauf*, a father enrolling his young son in the royal writing school ("School of Books") tells him to make the most of this grand opportunity, which will free him from the drudgery of all other trades:

---

[5] Ibid., p. 69.   [6] Ibid., p. 70.

Behold, there is no profession that is not under rule;
Only the man of learning himself ruleth. . . .
Never have I seen the engraver an ambassador,
Or the goldsmith with an embassy,
But I have seen the smith at his work
At the mouth of his furnace.
His fingers were as crocodile [hide],
He stank more than fish-roe. . . .[7]

And so it goes down the line, profession by profession. Don't be a soldier, a peasant, a husbandman, a butcher, a baker, or a barber—they wear themselves out day and night, and their rewards are a broken back, harvests ruined by plagues, debts, and confiscation of property. "I have seen him that is beaten, him that is beaten: thou art to set thine heart on books. I have beheld him that is set free from forced labor: behold nothing surpasseth books. . . . Would that I might make thee love books more than thy mother, would that I might bring their beauty before thy face. It is greater than any calling. . . ."[8] Only the scribe has a genteel trade with minimal risks to health and comfort. And, no matter how humble his origins, his calling raises him above his class and may even bring him to the threshold of the mighty. In short, the schoolboy carries in his satchel the seal of the vizier, the staff of the field marshal, perhaps even a scepter. And there is a record of such meteoric careers in Ancient Egypt. The way to power was not through the sword but through the pen. Scribes commanded armies, and in every age there came forth model scribes who achieved fame and glory.[9] To be portrayed in the customary position of the scribe was much favored by high officials. The Egyptians' respect for writing and learning remind us of the attitude of Chinese mandarins. For both ancient peoples this reached the dimensions of a cult and may have fostered the less pleasant byproducts of social conceit and intellectual aridity.

Elaborate hieroglyphic abstraction of papyrus roll with ribbon tied around it. From an inscription at Beni Hassan

---

[7] Griffith: op. cit., p. 5342.
[8] Erman: op. cit., p. 67.
[9] British Museum: op. cit., *A General Introductory Guide to the Egyptian Collections . . .* , p. 61.

Texts like the *Instruction of Duauf* served as favorite school-books, yet all their admonitions and exemplary passages frequently had little effect. According to Erman, the copies made by students were often very bad. Of the papyrus of the great poem on the battle of Kadesh, Erman has said that if we did not also have other versions of it which allow us to clear up innumerable mistakes, a good part would remain unintelligible.[1]

One short poem from the Nineteenth Dynasty gives ample proof that some would-be scribes (and not necessarily the least gifted ones) failed to make the grade, succumbing to laziness and the temptations of the big city. The erring student is being reprimanded:

> *They tell me that thou forsakest books,*
> *And givest thyself up to pleasure.*
> *Thou goest from street to street;*
> *Every evening the smell of beer,*
> *The smell of beer, frightens people away from thee.*
> *It bringeth thy soul to ruin. . . .*[2]

This glimpse of dissipation gives us an idea of the Egyptians' zest for life. The ancient peoples of the Nile were in love with life; their apparent preoccupation with death had nothing of the morbid or macabre that we associate with the civilization of the Mesopotamians, say, or of Old Mexico. Death, to the Egyptians, meant simply the hopefully awaited continuation of earthly existence into eternity. To be sure, every now and then there was the thought that the joys of life are perhaps more certain than those to come. At any rate, the wise man makes sure that his brief existence is lived to the fullest. The *carpe diem* philosophy—make merry today, for tomorrow you die—is a popular theme of Egyptian literature.

The Egyptians, who lived in the land of the plagues, had their share of hardships. Life was anything but easy for the majority of the people, as is explicitly stated in the "Satire of Trades." There are occasional hints of social protest and even of class struggle. In times of national crises, such as the political breakup of the Old Kingdom, we hear voices of anguish and despair—for example, as in the Leiden Papyrus I, in which the famous Ipuwer, a prophet, appears before the king to tell him (so he "may taste misery") of the ruin around him. Much of this work seems to express the disgust of a once well-to-do gentleman

---

[1] Erman: op. cit., p. xliii.   [2] Griffith: op. cit., p. 5344.

of the Old School with social change. The objects of his scorn
are the upstarts and the "carpetbaggers." There are vivid descriptions of the anarchy ("the land spins around like a potter's wheel")
that has befallen Egypt, at least in the jaundiced eyes of the old
aristocrat: "Nay, but the children of princes, men dash against
the walls. . . . Nay, but great and small say, 'I wish I were dead.' "
Murder and plunder are rife, and revolt is everywhere: "A man
looketh upon his son as an enemy." The virtuous go in rags, the
noble starve, while jewels "are hung about the necks of slave
girls. . . . Serfs become lords of serfs." It is the familiar refrain:
the scum, the parvenus ride in Rolls-Royces and eat at the fanciest
places. Worse still, foreigners ("who are not men") have moved
in and taken the best jobs.

The harangue is relieved, however, by a vision of a brighter
future. Jeremiah becomes Isaiah, and one sees the beginnings,
perhaps the first testimony, of a Messianic creed. Ipuwer rises
to prophetic eloquence when he announces the coming of the
savior prince: "He shall bring cooling to the flame. Men shall
say, 'He is the shepherd of all the people; there is no evil in
his heart. If his flocks go astray he will spend the day to search
them. The thought of men shall be aflame; would that he might
achieve their rescue. . . .' Verily he shall smite evil when he
raises his arm against it. . . . Where is he this day? Doeth he sleep
among you?"[3]

Fragments of poetry indicate the surprising range of Egyptian
literature, which, despite its strong religious orientation, experi-
mented with new secular forms, including the banquet song and
the love lyric. Songs of triumph celebrating the deeds of kings
form a category in themselves. Even the religious hymns tran-
scend the standard formulas of adoration and display a delight
in the physical universe and in its manifestations. Already, in the
Twelfth Dynasty (around 2000 B.C.), we hear the complaint that
it is hard to find any new subject to write about: "Would that I had
words that are unknown, utterances and sayings in a new language, that hath not yet passed away, and without that which
hath been said repeatedly—not an utterance that hath grown
stale, what the ancestors have already said."[4]

Only epic and drama are poorly represented, but even there
the lacunae may be due to the hazards of transmission rather

---

[3] J. H. Breasted: *A History of Egypt,* p. 205.
[4] Erman: op. cit., p. 109.

than to inherent limitations. A few passages from "passion" plays have survived; they were put on regularly in honor of Osiris at such Nilotic Oberammergaus as Abydos or Edfu. And the description of the Ramesside battle at Kadesh—erroneously called *Poem of Penaure,* after a copyist—has epic stature, though it cannot compare with *Gilgamesh* or the *Iliad.* Intensity of feeling, sensitivity to beauty and to the life-giving forces of nature, are superbly embodied in the great hymn to the sun god Aten (Aton)

Opening lines of the Poem of Penaure, which praises the dubious generalship of Ramses II at the battle of Kadesh against the Hittites. This copy is at the British Museum. Another version is incised into a Theban temple.

ascribed to the apostatic king Amenhotep IV (Ikhnaton) himself. But even this, perhaps the finest example of Egyptian poetic genius, is by no means unique. Several of the earlier hymns dedicated to Amon-Re rise to almost equal heights.

As compared with these solemn, rhapsodic songs, Egyptian love poetry is the quintessence of lightness, charm, and subtlety. There is nothing quite like it in ancient literature before the time of the Greeks. The Biblical Song of Songs echoes some of its Oriental sensuality but lacks its almost Alexandrine suppleness and elegance. Though literal translations cannot hope to capture the mood and polish of these poems, modern scholars have found them reminiscent of the wit and melancholy of Heine's romantic verses.[5] Most of the poems seem to have been written originally toward the end of the Empire, between 1300 and 1100 B.C. It is quite likely that they were meant to be accompanied by music,[6] perhaps by the lute. Note the grace of this piece from Harris 500:

> *The voice of the swallow speaks, saying,*
> *"The land is bright. What of thy way?"*
> *Prithee do not. O bird, scold me.*
> *I have found my brother in his bed,*

---

[5] Gardiner: op. cit., p. 77.
[6] D. Winton Thomas, ed.: *Documents of Old Testament Times* (New York: Harper Torchbooks; 1961), p. 187.

And my heart is pleased even more.
We have said (to one another),
"I shall not go far away
While my hand is in thine hand.
I shall stroll about
Being with thee in every beautiful place."
He has made me the chief of his lovely women
Lest he should wound my heart.[7]

If the Egyptians might well be considered the originators of lyric love poetry, the literary record is even clearer when it comes to the types of narrative they excelled in—the fairy tale, the short story, and the adventure novel. Many of their fantastic tales recall the Arabian Nights. However, despite the supernatural aspect of some of these writings, they have become a prime source for our knowledge of Egyptian life, society, and political history.

One of the great surprises of Egyptology came in 1852, when a French savant, the Vicomte Emmanuel de Rougé, to whom Mrs. D'Orbiney had entrusted her then recently acquired papyrus, published an article entitled *Notice sur un manuscrit égyptien en écriture hiératique, écrit sur le règne de Merienptah,* in which was included an Egyptian folktale. This was the first such publication, and it revealed a new dimension of Egypt's remarkably rich and varied literature. What is more, the story compared favorably with the tales of the Grimm brothers and Hans Christian Andersen, though it was written more than three thousand years ago. It was the *Tale of the Two Brothers,* a story of such humanity, and so rich in characterization, that it has delighted readers ever since. Among its greatest merits are the perceptive details of the daily life of Egyptian commoners in the New Kingdom. Indeed, many elements in the tale are reminiscent of the latter-day stories of other nations, some of whose plots and characters hint at an Egyptian original. Mrs. D'Orbiney's manuscript had the additional virtue of being intact and of coming from the workshop of an expert scribe whose name is known. It is no doubt one of the most beautifully written papyri in hieratic to have survived.[8] Even the owner of the papyrus could be identified. According to the colophon on the verso, the work belonged to an Egyptian crown prince who was later to rule under the name of Seti II.

The first part of the story touches us by its simplicity, but the second half employs so many devices of magic that, at least aes-

---

[7] Ibid., p. 189.   [8] Ibid., p. 168.

thetically, its effect is lessened. At the opening we meet the two brothers Anupu and Bata, who live under one roof and till the soil together. All goes well until Anupu's wife comes between them. Very much in the manner of Potiphar's wife, she tries to seduce Bata. One day, on the way home from the fields to fetch seed, Bata is propositioned by her: "Come, let's spend an hour sleeping together. This will do you good, because I shall make fine clothes for you!"[9] The wife is rejected outright and turns against her brother-in-law, accusing him to Anupu, with "feminine guile," of the very offense she had been guilty of. The enraged elder brother sets out to kill Bata. Forewarned by cows, who have the power of speech, Bata now takes flight, with Anupu on his heels. The sun god fortunately intervenes, making a river teeming with crocodiles to flow between them, and thus Anupu is kept from committing fratricide. Finally, from a safe distance, Bata is able to persuade his brother of his innocence, whereupon Anupu returns home and slays his treacherous wife. The rest of the story contains miracle upon miracle, and a series of marvelous transformations, all of which conspire to bring Bata close to the throne, with his faithful brother beside him. Eventually Bata becomes the father of a future pharaoh.

The *Tale of the Two Brothers* was only the beginning in the rediscovery of Egyptian fiction. Also, the story is among the least ancient of these compositions, the majority of which date from the Middle Kingdom, perhaps the most productive period in Egyptian secular literature. Papyrus Harris 500 yielded two beautiful pieces. One describes how Tahuti (Djehuti), a general of Thutmose III, took Joppa (ancient Jaffa) by a ruse reminiscent of both the Trojan horse and *Ali Baba and the Forty Thieves*. Tahuti was a historical person, and his sword and a present of gratitude from his royal master have survived. The story of his exploits may well be based on an actual incident.

Altogether removed from reality is the other tale in Harris 500, a beautiful story of the *Doomed Prince*, which takes place entirely in the realm of the supernatural but is told with superb art and compelling suspense. Flinders Petrie, who, like Maspero, Erman, and others, edited a collection of Egyptian fiction, has referred to the *Doomed Prince* as "an historical dictionary of the elements of fiction."[1] All the time-honored devices are used, includ-

---

[9] Pritchard: op. cit., p. 24.
[1] Baikie: *Egyptian Papyri and Papyrus-hunting,* p. 158.

ing a king's daughter who is locked away in a castle by her father, but they are used with great skill and, at least to our knowledge, for the first time. Whether the prince comes to a disastrous end, as foretold to his parents before his birth, or how the disaster comes, we have no way of knowing, for the final section in the Harris papyrus was destroyed.

One of the last hieroglyphic texts known, a fourth century A.D. papyrus

The First Sallier Papyrus has contributed a story that is also of inordinate historical interest, and though it is a pretty fanciful tale, it may be partly true. It takes us back to the time of the Hyksos kings, alien Asiatic sovereigns who ruled over the Nile delta. The scene is the outbreak of the Egyptian war of liberation. It seems that for Apepy, the Hyksos ruler, the native Theban prince was a thorn in the eye. Apepy was hard put to provoke the prince to war—which, we may be sure, he was going to fight on purely defensive grounds. So he made a strong protest about the hippopotamuses kept as sacred pets in water tanks at Thebes, whose splashing (some 350 miles away!) he said kept him awake at night. The studied insult, undoubtedly directed at the religious sentiments of the Thebans, did not fall short of its mark. Apepy got his war. As far as we are informed, he scored considerable success—we have the horribly battered skull of his antagonist, the Theban prince, now at the Cairo museum. However, hostilities flared up again and in the end the Theban's successors drove the Hyksos out of Egypt. This marked the rise of the great Eighteenth Dynasty and the beginning of the Empire, when Egyptians turned on the Asiatics with a vengeance.

The story of Wenamun, which comes from El Hibeh, rings so true that Egyptologists have not yet settled whether it is fact or fiction. Conceivably it was an embellished travel report made by

Wenamun, an official attached to the temple of Amon-Ra at Thebes, who undertook a mission to Syria to purchase cedarwood for the rebuilding of a ceremonial bark and suffered a veritable chain reaction of misfortunes. These are depicted with realism and humor. Poor Wenamun, who, Arthur Weigall says, "was not a traveller," brings to mind the solicitous effendi who roams about Near Eastern bazaars. The language is simple and direct, and the writer's descriptive power is of no mean order. There is, for example, a brief sketch of the local potentate of a Syrian port city on whom Wenamun called. It is unsurpassed in the literature of that early age: "I found him sitting in his upper room and his back leant against a window and the waves of the great Syrian Sea beat their spray against his neck."[2]

Again, the great value of the narrative lies in its numerous references to the life of the times. We get a clear glimpse of the breakdown of society in Ramesside Egypt, with its autonomous princelings in the North and the rising power of the Theban priesthood. Wenamun's difficulties in Syria are undoubtedly due to the decline of Egyptian prestige and power in these lands. In Syria–Palestine, near the modern Haifa, we meet newly arrived invaders (probably from Sicily) who can be linked to the population movement of the destructive Sea Peoples and of the Philistines, who occupied the Palestinian (i.e., Philistian) littoral. An interesting sidelight on the export of papyrus from Egypt is provided when the Syrian ruler demands a payment of five hundred sheets.

In the story of Sinuhe (Sanehat) we have a prototype of the adventure novel. This narrative, which is regarded as the finest product of Egyptian belles-lettres, takes place in the Middle Kingdom, in a realistic setting. Like Wenamun's tale, it takes us, during Sinuhe's self-imposed exile, to Syria. The popularity of the tale in ancient Egypt is borne out by the comparatively great number of fragments that have been found. Some passages even became part of the everyday language. We have it, for example, that sailors sent out by Queen Hatshepsut were greeted in a foreign port in precisely the same manner in which the barbarians welcomed Sinuhe, as we would say in jest: "Dr. Livingstone, I presume." Sinuhe's story was even set down in some tombs to entertain the dead.

Still another story, this one from the Ramesside era, takes us right into an Egyptian tomb, in the vein of Edgar Allan Poe.

---

[2] British Museum: *A General Introductory Guide to the Egyptian Collections* . . . , p. 70.

In one scene a royal prince plays draughts with the ghosts of the deceased, a chilling incident which, however, far from exhausts the other fascinations of the tale.

Thus has Egyptian literature risen from the dust of the ages during the past century and a half, revealing an ancient civilization with an enormous respect for writing and for letters. Several works of a religious or a secular nature enjoyed national popularity for centuries. As among the Chinese, the classics were highly appreciated. There was a conscientious effort to trace literary traditions to much earlier ages and to reevaluate them in the spirit of a renaissance. Older works were revived or rediscovered. The *Book of the Dead* claims to have incorporated a text that was itself "found" during the First Dynasty. Another such discovery was said to have been made by Prince Hordedef, a son of Khufu (Cheops), in the reign of Menkaure,[3] some fifteen hundred years before the compilation of the *Book of the Dead.*

It is fitting, then, that the hero of one ancient Egyptian tale anticipates living Egyptologists by some three millennia in his quest for a "lost" manuscript. This adventure story is preserved in a demotic copy from Ptolemaic times which is at the Cairo Museum. It describes the saga of Prince Setna (Setne Khaemwese, or Setme Khamuas), a son of Ramses II and a priest of Ptah at Memphis, as well as a keen student of ancient scrolls. Setna was famed in Egyptian legends for his explorations into the occult. An inscribed statue of the prince is now at the British Museum.

Setna is reported to have been hunting for a book, reputedly written by the god Thoth himself, which dealt with magic. After a long search, he managed to find the papyrus roll in a crypt in Memphis, where he entered into a contest with the ghosts of the deceased. He lost, but despite a warning, he took the coveted manuscript and eagerly set to study it. Soon, however, he was being haunted by the dead and was driven to the verge of insanity. His royal father, Ramses, finally counseled him to restore the book to the dead, and, to atone for the plundering of the tomb, Setna promised to transfer to it the mummies of the corpse's wife and son from their graves at Coptos. Manuscript hunting, then, proved an unrewarding, if not a dangerous, pursuit. Though in line to succeed Ramses, Setna died before his father, who outlived thirteen of his sons. Merenptah, the fourteenth in line, finally inherited the throne.

---

[3] Ibid., p. 80.

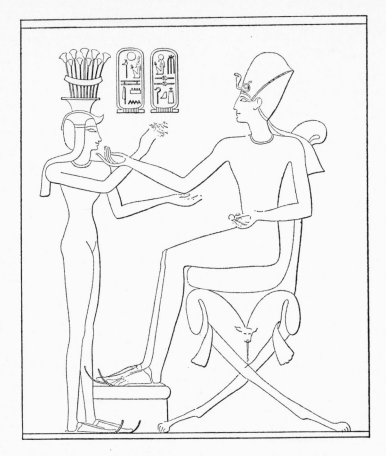

Relief of Ramses II, the long-lived pharaoh of the Nineteenth Dynasty, in a tender pose with one of his many children. Note the papyrus crown on the child's head.

Modern manuscript hunters and tomb robbers have fared better, though some too seem to have been pursued by demons. Every one, however, has helped to fulfill an age-old Egyptian prophecy, itself from a papyrus discovered in recent years: "As for those learned scribes who lived after the gods . . . their names will endure forever, though they are gone . . . and all their relatives are forgotten. They did not make for themselves pyramids of copper with tombstones attached of iron. . . . They gave themselves the papyrus roll as lector[chantry?]-priest, the writing board as a loving son; books of teachings were their pyramids, the reed-pen was their child, and the stone surfaces a wife. . . . More beneficial is a book than a carved stela or a solid tomb wall. . . . A man decays, his corpse is dust, and all his relatives are defunct; but the writings cause his name to be remembered in the mouth of the orator. More beneficial is a book than the house of the builder or a mortuary chapel in the west. . . ."[4]

---

[4] Quoted by Georg Steindorff and Keith C. Seele in *When Egypt Ruled the East,* second edition (Chicago: Chicago University Press; 1957), p. 123.

·XII·

THE BIBLE

OF THE CANAANITES

Thou also, Son of Man, take thee a tile, and lay it be-fore thee, and portray upon it the city, even Jerusalem.
EZEKIEL 4:1

LUCKLESS WENAMUN, the Egyptian official whom we accom-panied on his hazardous mission to Syria, delivered to a local prince a shipment of five hundred rolls or sheets of papyrus. This detail in the semihistorical narrative proves that the Syrians of the second millennium B.C. knew how to write, had a need for writing material, and consumed for this purpose profuse amounts of papyrus. In another passage of Wenamun's reportage the Prince of Byblos (Gebal), a prominent Syrian city on the Medi-terranean coast, actually sends for court records, kept on rolls, to check on business previously transacted by the Egyptians with his father and grandfather. Whatever happened to these Syrian archives? The answer is simple and disconcerting. No papyrus roll of such antiquity has ever been recovered from non-Egyptian soil. Would this mean that there is little likelihood that any sub-stantial Syrian documents have survived? Not necessarily so. Syrians and other civilized peoples of the eastern Mediterranean evidently used papyrus, but like the Egyptians themselves, they also wrote on other materials, including metal, animal hides, sherds, wood, and stone. And, above all, "they wrote on clay"[1]— a material far more durable than papyrus, parchment, or paper.

---

[1] Title of book by Edward Chiera (Chicago: Chicago University Press–Phoenix Books; 1956).

However, texts of any length in any media failed to turn up in Syria or Palestine for a long time. To Orientalists and Biblical scholars this was particularly distressing because this long strip of land—the abode of Canaanites, Phoenicians, and Hebrews and the link between Egypt and Mesopotamia—played a vital role in the history of the ancient Near East. Its literature would shed light on the cultural and religious environment encountered by the Israelites when they came into Canaan.

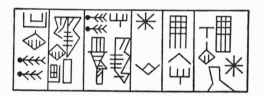

An early Sumerian inscription on clay from about 3000 B.C. The cuneiform (wedge-shaped) characters reflect their pictographic origin.

Throughout the nineteenth century, while neighboring Egypt and Mesopotamia so lavishly yielded documents and lost literary works on papyrus and clay, virtually nothing came out of the Syrian lands. In the absence of any evidence to the contrary, some learned men were quick to contend that written literature was unknown in these lands in the Bronze Age. And there were the extremists of the German "liberal" school of Bible studies (called Higher Criticism), like Julius Wellhausen, who insisted that the Hebrews did not practice any writing until at least their Age of Kings—a thesis which was meant to imply that all Biblical books were of late composition.

Wellhausen's and kindred arguments lost some ground with the appearance of the Tell el Amarna tablets in Upper Egypt in 1887, which included the correspondence of pharaohs of the Eighteenth Dynasty (about fourteenth century B.C.) with their Syrian vassals. Written in Akkadian, the international language of that time, these cuneiform records showed that Syrian rulers employed scribes. The Wenamun papyrus, found in the 1890's, added to this evidence. Yet no materials to speak of from Syria itself seriously challenged the Wellhausen thesis until 1929. Then, as a result of a chance discovery on the coast of northern Syria, French archaeologists uncovered a Canaanite temple library of clay tablets from the fourteenth or the fifteenth century B.C. All at once it became obvious that Syria–Palestine had an advanced literary tradition long before the coming of the Hebrews. From their contents, the Syrian tablets were soon recognized as representing an entirely new chapter of literature—indeed, as Cyrus H. Gordon, one of the leading American scholars in this field, has said, "the most important addition . . . since the decipherment of Egyptian hieroglyphics and Mesopotamian cuneiform in the last century."[2]

In March 1928, a peasant was plowing his field near Minet el Beida ("White Harbor") in northern Syria, when he struck a flagstone. After raising the heavy obstacle, he gained access to a well-laid-out underground structure. At the end of a passage was a vaulted burial chamber, and following a time-honored practice, the peasant looted the tomb. The precious artifacts, which he immediately unloaded on the antiquity market, could never be traced.

Meanwhile, news of the find—with the inevitable embellishments—spread like wildfire. Within a few days it reached the French governor of the territory, who in turn advised the Service of Antiquities for Syria and Lebanon at Beirut, then under the direction of Charles Virolleaud, a noted Orientalist. Virolleaud himself visited the site and then sent out an assistant to make a preliminary survey. Nothing very spectacular was taken from the plundered tomb, but the assistant dutifully collected a few potsherds and also drew a sketch of the subterranean vault. This material was dispatched to Paris to be examined by Monsieur René Dussaud, the curator of Oriental antiquities at the Louvre. By coincidence, Dussaud knew the area of Minet el Beida well. A few years earlier, he had carried out a historico-geographical study of Syria, and he had been impressed by the location of the harbor, with its fine natural bay lined by limestone cliffs and directly across from the "pointed finger" of Cyprus. Was this the Leukos Limen described by ancient Greek geographers, whose name was the exact equivalent of the present Arab name? Dussaud was almost certain of the importance of White Harbor in antiquity to overseas trade and to navigation in the eastern Mediterranean. Conceivably, it was also a hub on the historic road linking Asia Minor with Syria—Palestine and Egypt and with another road coming up from Mesopotamia, which joined the Persian Gulf with the Mediterranean. Here three continents converged. Its closeness to the Cypriote copper mines may well have given it

[2] Cyrus H. Gordon: *Adventures in the Nearest East* (Fair Lawn, N.J.: Essential Books; 1957), p. 104.

a kind of monopoly. How could the crafty mariners of Minoan Crete and Phoenicia have bypassed such a choice site?

Similar thoughts must have come to Dussaud when he saw the material just arrived from Minet el Beida. He also recalled that occasional finds of cuneiform seals had been made at a nearby hill, Ras Shamra ("Fennel Head"), thus named in modern times because of its growth of heavily scented herbs. And there had been persistent rumors that natives were collecting gold objects in the neighborhood. Virolleaud and his assistant had already noticed the strong resemblance of the tomb to non-Asiatic Minoan–Cypriote and Mycenaean structures. A glance at the sketch reminded Dussaud of the graves excavated by Sir Arthur Evans at Knossos in Crete. Likewise, the ceramic fragments betrayed a Cypriote and Mycenaean origin, perhaps of about the thirteenth century B.C. The evidence was unmistakable: for some time in the second millennium B.C., Minet el Beida had been under strong Mycenaean influence. No Mycenaean settlement had yet been traced on the Asiatic mainland, except for the "Ionian" coast, though the "Aegean" ware found by Petrie in Egypt in the 1880's in remains of New Kingdom age testified to the wide diffusion of Mycenaean elements.

Dussaud was gratified by such evidence of Mycenaean penetration of the Syrian littoral and was not discouraged by the meager returns from the trial dig. Instead, he persuaded the French Académie des Inscriptions et Belles-Lettres to mount a major campaign to get there before looters and antiquities dealers started their private operations. Dussaud was certain now that the

Claude F.-A. Schaeffer excavated this rython (drinking cup) of clay with painted octopus in the "White Harbor" area. The design closely resembles the "palace" style of vases found at Crete and other Aegean sites, and points to Mycenaean influence on the northern coast of ancient Syria.

tomb was not an isolated curiosity but part of a larger Mycenaean or Aegean burial ground connected with a once thriving metropolis. If only that maritime city could be located! He was already hopeful that the hill of Ras Shamra might yield the secret.

The Paris authorities acted with dispatch. Precisely one year after the native's find, a fully equipped French expedition started work near the White Harbor, some eight miles northwest of the Syrian town of Latakia. Excavation of the promising site was entrusted to a young Alsatian archaeologist, Claude F.-A. Schaeffer, of the Prehistoric Museum of Strasbourg. He chose as his assistant Georges Chenet, an archaeologist from the Argonne, who, like Schaeffer, had hitherto specialized in the prehistory of Western Europe. As soon as Schaeffer's party reached Minet el Beida, by the end of March 1929, and camped, it set to make an extensive survey of the area. Schaeffer had no doubt: here was an extensive necropolis, just as Dussaud had anticipated. But quite unexpectedly the soil turned out to be packed with a variety of relics. This was a major surprise: Syria had supposedly been thoroughly explored by archaeologists. Besides, the entire area had been trampled by invaders and conquerors for millennia—conditions that do not favor the survival of artifacts. The wealth of objects now excavated by the French suggested that the place had had multiple connections with the major Near Eastern civilizations of the latter half of the second millennium B.C., which the American Egyptologist, J. H. Breasted, once aptly called the era of the "First Internationalism."

Schaeffer and Chenet dug up delicate Minoan or Mycenaean vases resting side by side with immense native jars, "worthy of Ali Baba's hideaways." In some places they came across large, "very naturalistic"[3] phalli. At about the center of the burial ground —where so far they had only met with animal, not human bones —the Frenchmen discovered a cache of statuettes and other treasures of considerable artistry, including representations of Phoenician, Egyptian, and Minoan deities. When a golden plaque of the nude love goddess Astarte shone forth from amid the surrounding exquisite jewelry, Schaeffer cabled Paris in a paraphrase of Schliemann: "The treasure of Minet el Beida has been found."

Though gratified by the unexpected finds, the French archaeologists were puzzled about the cultural identity of this Syrian

---

[3] Claude F. A. Schaeffer: "A New Page Opens in Ancient History," *Illustrated London News*, Vol. 175 (November 2, 1929), p. 764.

necropolis. If anything, the tombs testified to a predominantly Aegean (i.e., non-Asiatic) influence. But there were signs of strong native elements and features of Egyptian and Hittite–Anatolian origin. No satisfactory solution to this multiculture puzzle would be possible until the actual city, to which the necropolis must

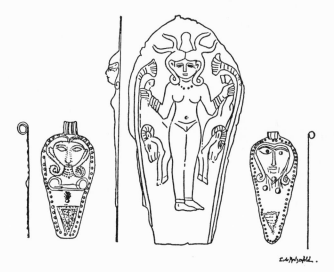

Golden pendants of nude Syrian goddess of fertility. Fifteenth to fourteenth century B.C.

have belonged, had been excavated. Would it simply turn out to be a colony of Mycenaean traders and shippers? The ancient seaport had yet to be found.

The hot Syrian summer was well on its way when Schaeffer decided to shift operations, for the closing weeks of the first campaign, to Ras Shamra, about a half mile inland from the bay. This was the hill that had already caught the eye of Dussaud. The sixty-five-foot-high elevation formed, at the top, a large rectangle of some 3,000 by 1,960 feet. It lay pleasantly between the conjunction of two rippling brooks, but geologically, it did not seem to fit into the topography of the coastal plain. It might be a mound or tell, such as those of Mesopotamia, which have risen to their present height as a result of long human occupation and intermittent destruction and abandonment. This suspicion was fully borne out not only by the immediate discovery of a sizable town connected with the Minet el Beida necropolis, but by Schaeffer's later penetration to the lowest level, which clearly indicated a Neolithic settlement contemporary with the Mesopotamian Tell Hassuna of the fifth to sixth millennium B.C. (Palaeolithic remains in the surrounding plain indicated that homo sapiens had roamed here ever since the appearance of the first men in Syria.)

Altogether the tell had five major strata, which, in the course of several excavations, helped to chart the town's evolution and its political and cultural affinities. The second lowest (stratum IV), like the bottom level (V), was of Neolithic age, roughly 4,000 to 3,500 B.C. It exhibited the el-Obeid (al-'Ubaid) type of pottery characteristic of Mesopotamian sites of that age. In stratum III there appeared an entirely new element, probably due to the arrival of Semitic Amorites, who were to form the dominant ethnic group in Syria from then on and who would be known as Canaanites or Phoenicians. Not much later, during the third millennium B.C., Egyptian infusions are registered. There are, for example, votive statues offered by pharaohs (and perhaps by their Syrian wives), some with hieroglyphic inscriptions. The picture becomes more complex in the second millennium, the period of the city's greatest flowering—when under the empire builders of the New Kingdom, chiefly Thutmose III, all of Syria was conquered by Egypt. The power struggle that took place in the Near East with the decline of the New Kingdom, so accurately depicted in the diplomatic correspondence from Tell el Amarna, left traces in the form of Hurrian, Mitanni, Hittite, and Assyrian inroads. In the fourteenth century, Ras Shamra may have been, for a brief time, subject to the Hittite ruler Suppiluliuma, after which Egypt once more asserted itself. The virtual end came with the landing of the Norsemen of antiquity, the mysterious "People of the Sea," who are sometimes thought to be the Philistines, at that time engaged in gaining a more solid foothold along the coast of southern Palestine. There is also a possibility that the final blow was dealt by Assyrian conquerors in the twelfth century. As to the Mycenaeans or the Minoans, their ascendancy was most likely of a commercial and cultural nature. These European merchants probably constituted an affluent foreign colony . . . in second-millennium Ras Shamra, which was a kind of ancient Shanghai.

This historical profile of Ras Shamra was to emerge over the years. For the first venture into the hill, in May 1929, Schaeffer selected the highest point on the side overlooking the harbor, where he believed the royal palace had stood. There was a rumor, moreover, that it was in the partly washed-out slope beneath that seals had been found. Schaeffer's diggers had removed only a thin layer of soil when the walls of a large edifice emerged (it later turned out to be a religious shrine). Ashes and soot had adhered to the ruined blocks and now blackened the excavators' hands. A bronze dagger and nails convoluted by exposure to great heat told the story: the building had been destroyed by a conflagration. Various implements and Egyptian statues established its age as of approximately the thirteenth century. A granite statue donated by a pharaoh carried an inscription in hieroglyphics that placed it clearly in the period of Egypt's imperial expansion during the New Kingdom. The statue was dedicated to the god "Seth of Sapouna." It became clear that ties with Egypt had been strong for many years. Later the Frenchmen noticed that a number of the Egyptian effigies appeared to have been willfully mutilated, a sign very possibly of Egyptian decline and international dissension.

At this early stage of excavation, the record of the city's past was necessarily vague. But one could be certain that Ras Shamra had had a long history and had been more than simply an Aegean or a Mycenaean colony. Since there were at that time no corroborative data from other sources, the spade had to supply the missing links. Then the excavators came upon a windfall. Schaeffer and his men were proceeding in a wide semicircle around the so-called palace. At its eastern flank they dug into another fairly large edifice, which later turned out to have, on either side, the two great temples of Baal and Dagon. Inside it were a number of small rooms of equal size grouped around a central patio. Schaeffer thought at first that the cells served as storerooms. But on May 14, 1929, he found in the corner of one of the cells, amid ashes and stones, a clay tablet covered with cuneiform writing. There was no doubt about it: this was a library.

Beside this find, all the splendid burial chambers, the fine jewelry, the statues, reliefs, and artifacts paled. Here, at long last, were dozens of clay tablets from the ancient Syrian land. Some were piled upon each other in orderly fashion; a few others had been immured in the wall, perhaps as building material. Special care had to be taken in removing the tablets because fire and other conditions had made them extremely brittle. After this delicate operation was successfully carried out, the French archaeologists could be sure that they had recovered the real treasure of Ras Shamra. More than fifty tablets were extricated before the end of the season, and a considerable number were brought out in the subsequent excavations undertaken annually until 1939 and resumed again in 1948. In 1953 Schaeffer found the main diplomatic archives when he was excavating the royal palace.

Neither Schaeffer nor his assistant Georges Chenet was an Orientalist, and the decipherment of the tablets had to wait until they reached Paris. Luckily, Charles Virolleaud, who was about to retire from his post at Beirut, was on hand to scan them. At first glance, all the tablets appeared to be physically identical with those brought from Assyria and Babylonia. Yet even a brief perusal by an expert showed undeniable signs of the ethnic and cultural variety, the conquests and colonizations, and the cosmopolitan conglomeration of an overseas port. The identity of the port was still in doubt. The clay tablets, it was hoped, would further disentangle its history, adding at the same time to our knowledge of a crucial age, in which great empires clashed and fell, "Sea Peoples" raided the coast, and "marginal" peoples such as the Hebrews, the Phoenicians, and the Aramaeans asserted their independence for a brief period.

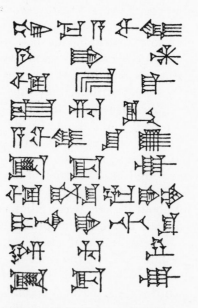

Section of the Law Code of Hammurabi (second millennium B.C.) in the syllabic cuneiform script of Babylonia

During the initial examination Virolleaud recognized tablets that were almost identical with those from Tell el Amarna. They were of about the same era, and like those, they contained diplomatic communications. In addition, there were letters of an official or a personal nature, accounts of taxes, temple records, a treatise on veterinary medicine (on the treatment of horses), a shipping list that brought to mind Lloyds of London, records of business transactions, and all kinds of other administrative documents. Most of these nonliterary materials were in the Akkadian ("Babylonian") language and could be easily read. The close links to the Mesopotamian civilization were further underscored by Sumerian legal and religious texts, as revered and studied in the Syrian town as in Nineveh or Babylon—and this more than a thousand years after Sumerian had ceased to be a living language. And then there were a number of word lists (of synonyms), bilingual tablets, dictionaries, etc., to aid scribes and to help apprentices learn composition and the various idioms in use. Clumsily written exercises indicated that the library had been a school for scribes as well as a college of learned priests of the kind attached to Egyptian and Mesopotamian temples.

As more material came in from later excavations, no doubt was left that the Mediterranean seacoast city was truly polyglot, though the basic Semitic–Mesopotamian roots of its native culture persisted with full vigor. In time, the library also yielded texts in Hittite, Egyptian, and Hurrian, and a few notations in Cypriote characters. Altogether, eight languages were counted. Charles Virolleaud, the first one to gauge the content and nature of the tablets, remarked: "C'est vraiment comme si toutes les civilisations de l'Orient, et celles aussi de l'Occident, s'étaient donné rendez-vous sur ce point de la côte syrienne, au cours du IIè millénaire."[4]

However, interesting and informative as these varied texts were, they were overshadowed by another type of clay tablet which constituted the great majority of the yearly finds. Physically indistinguishable from the rest, these tablets appeared to be written in a lost script, if not a lost language. Although they, too, consisted of wedge-shaped (cuneiform) signs carved into wet clay from left to right, Virolleaud soon noticed that the similarity to Mesopotamian script was only superficial. Instead of the five hundred and some syllabic symbols required to render a Sumerian, Babylonian, or Assyrian cuneiform text, the number in these tablets had been reduced to a fraction—some twenty-seven on first count,

---

[4] Charles Virolleaud: *La Légende Phénicienne de Danel* (Paris: P. Geuthner; 1936), p. 4.

later fixed at thirty. None of the fairly simple signs had a counter-part, apparently, in the traditional cuneiform syllabary.

Now, Virolleaud knew the basic tenet of epigraphy—that any script which could do with so few elements had to be alphabetic. The sudden confrontation with an alphabet from so early a period,

No.	Sign	Value	No.	Sign	Value
1		a	16		m
2		e(i)	17		n
3		u	18		s
4		b	19		s₂
5		g	20		ʿ
6		d	21		ġ
7		ḫ	22		p
8		w	23		ṣ
9		z	24		ẓ
10		ḥ	25		q
11		ḫ	26		r
12		ṭ	27		š
13		y	28		ŝ
14		k	29		t
15		l	30		ṯ

Cuneiform alphabet of Ras Shamra with equivalent values. Scholars now generally recognize thirty letters.

before the alphabet was supposed to have been invented, was stunning. The existence of a cuneiform alphabet in the second millennium had not been suspected by any scholar. True, the Egyptians had introduced quasi-alphabetic ("acrophonic") features into their script, but they were unable to implement them throughout and had to retain their complex, syllabic, ideogrammatic, and determinative (auxiliary symbols to indicate meaning) signs. In addition, there was the mysterious Sinaitic script discovered in 1908 by Petrie on rock carvings at Sinai. Some thought it was a Semitic adaptation of Egyptian hieroglyphs to alphabetic form, but in 1930 that was still an unsubstantiated hypothesis. Only a few years earlier, another French archaeologist had discovered at Byblos a sarcophagus with a Phoenician alphabetic inscription of a King Ahiram, whose date was much debated. The oldest well-established alphabetic document, found in 1868, was the Moabite Stone, in ancient "Hebrew" script, set up by King Mesha of Moab in the ninth century B.C. The consensus continued to be that the Phoenician alphabet, which became the alphabet of the West, was introduced not much earlier than the time of the Moabite inscription.

Schaeffer's telegraphic communication to Paris about the new alphabet excited scholars around the globe and brought Schaeffer, at his Syrian outpost, congratulations by radio and letter from England and America.[5] Orientalists the world over recognized that the tablets found at Ras Shamra contained the oldest alphabet yet known. Its age probably went far back beyond the time of the tablets, judging by the perfection of the script and the fact—soon to become known—that Ras Shamra scribes had already adapted it to another alien language, Hurrian. Since the Ras Shamra finds, two tablets written from right to left, Palestinian style, have been excavated in Palestine.[6] (Curiously, a specimen also cropped up later in Ras Shamra.) These two tablets are additional proof that the cuneiform alphabet was not conceived overnight at Ras Shamra by some unique genius, as some experts believed, but may well have had antecedents all over the Canaanite land, which, before the coming of the Hebrews, seems to have been distinguished by a remarkable cultural unity.

Even the proud title of "oldest alphabet" could not be defended for long. Other alphabetic, noncuneiform fragments discovered more recently in Syria-Palestine appear to be even older. In fact, they probably antedate the Sinaitic inscriptions, to which they appear to be related. However, the earliest list of alphabetic letters now known has come from Ras Shamra—in cuneiform. Schaeffer found it there twenty years after the first excavations, and it contained another surprise: the order is virtually the same as that of the Phoenician-derived alphabet taught in our elementary schools. Hence, we may assume that both the Phoenician and the cuneiform alphabets, with their corresponding consonantal values, were developed jointly or interdependently. There is also a probability, as scholars tend to hold at present, that the Phoenician alphabet came first. The contribution of the Canaanites is

---

[5] Schaeffer: "A New Alphabet of the Ancients Unearthed," *National Geographic Magazine*, Vol. LVIII, No. 4 (October 1930), p. 513.

[6] William Foxwell Albright: *The Archaeology of Palestine* (Harmondsworth: Penguin Books; 1951), p. 187.

not so much that they invented this or that script but that, some time in the second millennium B.C., they evolved the principle of alphabetic writing and carried it to its logical conclusion. This is no doubt among the greatest of all human achievements.

The oldest-known complete ABC. Values of letters and their sequence are surprisingly akin to the Western alphabet of our own school primers.

But how was one to read the new script? When the tablets in alphabetic writing appeared on the scene, no one could be certain what language they were in—particularly as Ras Shamra had been a multilingual seaside settlement. Nor did scholars think it then at all certain that the area of Canaanite–Phoenician settlement extended so far north toward Anatolia. Virolleaud's first impulse was to credit the Minoan–Cypriotes or even the Mitannis with the writing of these texts. The puzzle may well have appeared insoluble. Here were ancient texts in unknown characters. Few, if any, of the letters had even the slightest affinity to cuneiform syllabic signs. Nobody could tell which language they were written in. Knowledge of the idiom of the ancient Cypriotes and Minoans was extremely vague. And no bilinguals, which had played a major part in the decipherment of other scripts, had appeared. The alphabetic list was found, as we mentioned, much later. Was there any hope at all for decipherment? And if so, how was one to proceed?

Scholars have long maintained that an unknown script in an unknown language cannot be deciphered. Yet, put in this unspecific way, the statement is ambiguous and assailable. Much depends on the meaning of "unknown," particularly in the term "unknown language." Semantically speaking, there are various degrees of "unknown." The statement may simply mean, tautologously, that an "unknown" language cannot be known. An "unknown" language, however, may be related to a known (cognate) language; or the "unknown language" of an undeciphered text may turn out to be more or less familiar when it can be read. In the latter case, as has been proven once again by Ventris and Chadwick's decipherment of Linear B—which was nothing but an ancient form of Achaean Greek—success will come eventually. If the number of symbols are limited, as in an alphabet, the chances are greatly improved. Another case in point is the breaking of secret codes by cryptographers. Indeed, it was partly along such lines that three scholars, a German and two Frenchmen, arrived at the solution.

Unlike Sir Arthur Evans, who throughout his long life withheld Cretan clay tablets in the hope that he would decipher them all by himself, Charles Virolleaud transcribed meticulously all the alphabetic texts from Ras Shamra and for the benefit of colleagues had them published in April 1930 in the Orientalist review *Syria*, whose editor was René Dussaud. Virolleaud was in a way handicapped by what may be termed, in a Pickwickian sense, too much knowledge. He had been at the White Harbor and at Ras Shamra and had examined the archaeological remains at first hand, and had been perhaps overly impressed by the Mycenaean–Minoan features so prominent in the first discoveries at the Minet el Beida necropolis. It was an intelligent guess to associate the appearance of a strange script with an aggressive intruder into the native Syrian habitat, which, according to all evidence, had hitherto done quite well with the traditional cuneiform syllabary. In addition, Virolleaud had possibly not reconciled himself to the fact that a major coastal settlement in the northern extremity of Syria could be ascribed to Phoenicians or Canaanites. He may also have been influenced by the theory, then enthusiastically espoused, that our alphabet was ultimately of Aegean (quasi-Greek), not Asiatic Phoenician, origin.

Nevertheless, it was Virolleaud who offered the first clues, which his colleagues Professor Hans Bauer of the University of Halle and Père Paul (later Édouard) Dhorme put to good use. The first indication was the alphabetic nature of the script. Then Virolleaud noticed the vertical lines in the text, which very likely served as word dividers. Apparently the language in question consisted of rather short words, rarely exceeding three or four letters. This characteristic ruled out Greek or "Mycenaean." To these general insights Virolleaud added one more concrete detail.

By good fortune, right after unearthing the clay tablets, Schaeffer found at the foot of a stairway in the "library" a cache of seventy-four bronze weapons and tools. Five bronze axes were inscribed with the same alphabetic symbols. The length of the inscriptions varied, but several symbols, if not words, recurred. Virolleaud also found a longer word of six characters at the beginning of a tablet, where it was preceded by what was apparently a one-letter word. The latter, Virolleaud guessed, corresponded to the French *à* (the English *to*), or the Akkadian *ana*, conceivably used in an opening epistolary address or in a formula of dedication. By the same token, the second, longer word, common to both documents, was probably the name of a person, possibly the owner of the library. (It turned out to be the presiding priest's title.) Still another word recurred on two axes. It consisted of

One of the inscribed hatchets from Ras Shamra which helped in the decipherment of the hitherto unknown cuneiform alphabetic writing

four characters, and Virolleaud thought that it designated the object as "axe" in whatever language this happened to be. As it was, Virolleaud had correctly understood these words. With remarkable foresight he announced: "If it were possible to collect all the words in the various Oriental languages which mean 'axe,' one would undoubtedly be able to read this word on the Ras Shamra axes. In the absence of a bilingual, the determination of these four letters will probably be sufficient to decipher all the other texts."[7]

While Virolleaud worked quietly in Paris along the lines he had suggested, Dhorme, of the French-administered École Biblique in Jerusalem, and Hans Bauer at Halle, took up the challenge. They were both expert Orientalists and philologists and had also worked on cipher codes. Dhorme, who served with the French Intelligence at Saloniki (Thessalonike) during World War I, had been decorated for his accomplishments in decoding secret enemy messages. Though it is difficult to establish priority in scientific discoveries where three men have worked simultaneously along similar lines, and each one to some degree has benefited from the advances made by the others, Bauer is usually acclaimed as the first to develop the hypothesis that the unknown language was a northwestern, or simply a western, Semitic dialect akin to

[7] Virolleaud: "Les Inscriptions Cunéiformes de Ras Shamra," *Syria*, Vol X, No. 4 (1929), p. 307.

Canaanite and closely related to Hebrew. In any case, he made his announcement in a brief article in a Berlin daily, *Vossische Zeitung,* on June 4, 1930.

Bauer's feat of decipherment was the fastest on record. He himself proudly gave the time schedule: On April 22 he had received in Halle the issue of the journal *Syria.* In less than a week, on April 27, the decipherment was essentially completed, and on April 28 he informed René Dussaud of his success. On May 15 he dispatched his preliminary report to the *Vossische Zeitung.* Hans Bauer (1878–1937) was then one of Germany's leading students of Oriental languages. He had a command of Chinese and Malayan, but his specialty was the Semitic family of languages, including Aramaic, Amorite, Akkadian, and other variations. He had written several Aramaic and Hebrew grammars. On his own declaration, his recent study of the Sinaitic script had prepared him for Virolleaud's transcriptions of the alphabetic documents from Ras Shamra.[8] Naturally, he inclined toward a Semitic interpretation.

Bauer knew that his assumption that this was a western Semitic language was at best uncertain, but he thought it was worth testing. The brevity of the words strongly suggested the customarily vowel-less rendering of a Semitic text. At first glance, he had the uncanny impression that it was a Semitic language. Bauer proceeded to analyze the frequency of certain letters on the basis of his supposition that they would reveal Semitic characteristics. Western Semitic languages had three significant features: prefixes, suffixes, and one-letter words, all likely to be represented by certain consonants (and the "Hebrew" *aleph*) in various combinations. Bauer now postulated a corresponding incidence in the Ras Shamra idiom, and he went on (1) to detect and analyze the prefixes, suffixes, and single-letter words in the tablets, and (2) to equate the already familiar western Semitic phonetic values with corresponding cuneiform-alphabetic signs. The second step was crucial and required much more ingenuity than we would think necessary now that we know the solution. For one, though the choice had been narrowed, the number of letters liable to occur in the three categories was still considerable. Bauer set down these letters. Prefixes in western Semitic used *aleph, j* (Eng. *y*), *m, n, t,* and occasionally *b, h, k, l, w.* Suffixes included *h, k, m, n, t,* and possibly *w* and *j.* Single-letter words consisted of *l* and *m,*

---

[8] Hans Bauer: "Das Alphabet von Ras Schamra," *Vossische Zeitung,* No. 128 (June 4, 1930).

and in some instances *b, k,* and *w.* A comparison of the three categories showed that three letters—*k, m,* and *w*—appeared in all three categories. At this point, equating the Semitic characters and the Ras Shamra cuneiform signs became much more feasible. The outlook was further improved when the three letters were reduced to two: *m* and *w,* which had been widely used. At last Bauer was able to select, from the twenty-seven cuneiform signs (later it was established that there were really thirty), two that were likely to be the equivalents of *m* or *w.* By somewhat similar reasoning, he arrived at alternates for *n* and *t,* which were common to prefixes and suffixes.[9] But which were which?

Virolleaud's suggestions came to Bauer's aid. The single-letter symbol for "to" would correspond in a Semitic idiom to *l.* Once *l* was established, Bauer operated in the manner of algebraic equations, where *x,* the unknown, is a function of known quantities. In order to pin down *m,* Bauer thought of the Semitic word MLK, meaning "king." Very likely, this word occurred frequently. The German philologist was henceforth on the lookout for a three-letter word, the first letter of which, in the cuneiform alphabet, was *m/w,* the second *l,* and the third an unknown. The method worked. Bauer identified *m* (as well as *w*), and also *k.* From then on, the process became easier, as anticipated words helped to determine the value of various letters. Two signs repeated in what looked like a list of consecutive names (as in a Biblical genealogy) gave him BN, for "son." The name of the prominent Semitic god Baal (in Semitic B'L), who could be expected to be mentioned in the texts, was now comparatively easy to detect. And so on. In three days, Bauer was convinced that he had deciphered twenty letters with certainty and four with a high degree of probability.[1] His article in the *Vossische Zeitung* submitted the names of several Phoenician deities and the phonetic terms for numerals.

However, he had made some errors. Two wrong letters resulted from assigning the Hebrew spelling for axe, *grzn,* to the four symbols on the bronze tools singled out by Virolleaud. The Ras Shamra dialect, as was shown later, spelled the same word *hrsn.* Two wrong letters could easily have caused havoc in an alphabet of so few symbols. Actually, Bauer had read seventeen letters correctly. It was a considerable achievement, even though it did not yet make it possible to read the Ras Shamra texts.

---

[9] Bauer: "Die Entzifferung des Keilschriftenalphabets von Ras Schamra," *Forschungen und Fortschritte,* Vol. VI (1930), p. 306.
[1] Bauer, in *Vossische Zeitung,* June 4, 1930.

In the summer of 1930, Bauer's account in the *Vossische Zeitung* happened to come to the attention of a man who was destined to become one of the century's foremost Biblical archaeologists. The American W. F. Albright, who then, early in his career, was engaged in excavations at Tell Beit Mirsim near Jerusalem, took a keen interest in the excavations at Ras Shamra and eventually furnished some of the first English translations of the alphabetic cuneiform texts.[2] He knew of Dhorme's work on the Virolleaud transcripts and mentioned the German newspaper article to him. On the basis of Bauer's discoveries, Dhorme corrected one of his own errors (he had confused *n* with *t*). Then he went on to interpret twenty signs correctly, and generously briefed Bauer on these. Bauer in turn incorporated them in an improved version of his transcript, the so-called "Alphabet of October 5, 1930."[3]

From here on, the initiative was again Charles Virolleaud's. By then a professor at the Sorbonne, Virolleaud, though at a slower pace, had meanwhile arrived at similar conclusions.[4] He now eliminated some errors made by both Dhorme and Bauer (for example, the two incorrect consonants in "axe"), established three alternate values for *aleph* (Hebrew has only one), recognized thirty signs in the Ras Shamra alphabet, and completed the decipherment. Virolleaud also succeeded in making the first full-length translations. For years to come, he was the official editor of the Ras Shamra documents.

Was it fairly certain that the interpretation of the alphabet was correct? When Virolleaud started issuing coherent and intelligible translations of the texts, most doubts were dispelled. For those who needed more exacting proof, there was further corroborative evidence. Some tablets, for example, yielded the names of non-Semitic, Hurrian gods—completely unanticipated in this context. Separate lists of cities, in Mesopotamian Akkadian on the one hand and in the new alphabetic cuneiform on the other—though not identical, or in the same sequence—contained corresponding names. Akkadian syllabic spelling, by the way, also

---

[2] W. F. Albright: "New Light on Early Canaanite Language and Literature," *Bulletin of the American Schools of Oriental Research*, No. 45 (February 1932), pp. 15–20.

[3] Johann Friedrich: *Ras Schamra: Ein Überblick über Funde und Forschungen (Der Alte Orient,* 1933) (Leipzig: Hinrichs'sche Buchhandlung; 1933), p. 21.

[4] Godfrey Rolles Driver: *Canaanite Myths and Legends.* Old Testament Studies III (Edinburgh: T. & T. Clark; 1956), p. 2.

helped to reconstruct the likely pronunciation of the Ras Shamra idiom, otherwise highly uncertain because of the vowel-less manner of writing. The most precise demonstration was supplied by another list giving the number of vessels of wine delivered to Ras Shamra by several (subsidiary?) towns. After each place name there followed, written out in the Ras Shamra alphabet, the respective quantity. If these phonetic values for numerals were accurate, they would add up to 148 vessels. As it happened, the total put down in Akkadian was "1 *me'at* 48 *Dug Geŝtin*"—precisely "148 jugs of wine."[5]

While work on the decipherment was being carried out in 1930, Claude F.-A. Schaeffer and Georges Chenet had started the second excavation, accompanied by Schaeffer's wife. This time the sponsors were the Académie des Inscriptions, the Louvre, and the French Department of Education. Additional funds made it possible for Schaeffer to employ 250 native workers,[6] and he was able to unearth a considerable number of cuneiform tablets. The announcement of the newly discovered alphabetic script had turned world-wide attention on the new expedition. All eyes were on this town in northern Syria, so far known by the modern Arab name of the cape on which it lay, Ras Shamra (more accurately, Râs eš-Šhamrah), or by the name of a nearby harbor, Minet el Beida. From the start, the tell of Ras Shamra had appeared to be, to Schaeffer and his associates, the site of an ancient city of undeniable size and importance, probably the urban center of a fairly extensive city-state.

Unknown to Schaeffer at the time, scholars had been wondering for quite a while about a place name not yet accounted for: Ugarit. It had been mentioned in the Egyptian *Poem of Penaure* (Pentowere), dating from the age of Ramses II, whose doubtful military triumph over the Hittite host it eulogized. There were six references to it in the Tell el Amarna tablets. In one of the Amarna letters, the king of Tyre reported to Amenhotep IV: "Ugarit, the king's town, has been destroyed by fire. Half of the town has been burnt, the other half is no more."[7] This may well have been a reference to a destructive earthquake. Another letter makes clear

[5] Friedrich: *Extinct Languages* (New York: Philosophical Library–Wisdom Library; 1957), p. 86.
[6] Schaeffer: "Secrets from Syrian Hills," *National Geographic Magazine*, Vol. LXIV, No. 1 (July 1933), p. 99.
[7] Frederic G. Kenyon: *The Bible and Archaeology* (London: George H. Harrap; 1940), p. 164.

that the town had come under the influence of the Hittites, arch-enemies of the Pharaoh. Additional information about Ugarit was being uncovered in the cuneiform archives of the Hittites at Boghazkoi and in the letters of Hammurabi. A few years later, the records from Mari, an Amorite center in northern Mesopotamia, furnished further corroboration. All these data indicated that Ugarit had been a Canaanite city of consequence, probably on the coast of Syria, in the area hotly contested by the Hittite and the Egyptian empires.

Unlike other Canaanite–Phoenician cities such as Byblos, Beirut, Acre, Tyre, and Sidon, Ugarit seemed to have vanished from history at the time of the death struggle and decline of the two great Near Eastern empires and the beginning of the raids of the "People of the Sea" around 1200 B.C. What had become of it? Syria had been thoroughly investigated by archaeologists, and others, and the chances that any traces of it had been preserved were slim. Ras Shamra had not yet entered the picture. As a matter of fact, Schaeffer during the first expedition had thought that he had discovered the ancient name of Ras Shamra when the hieroglyphic inscription on the Egyptian votive stela already mentioned was read as a dedication to the Baal of Sapouna. The obvious conclusion was that the statue had been presented by the Egyptians to the patron god of the city called Sapouna (or Saphôn). For a while, French publications favored this designation.

W. F. Albright, a professor at the Johns Hopkins University, Baltimore, by then was not convinced. His keen insight, which was again dramatically in evidence during the early phase of the recovery of the Dead Sea scrolls, led him to question the conclusion of his French colleagues. In 1931, in an inconspicuous footnote to a learned article on another subject,[8] he reiterated the fact that Ras Shamra was by all evidence "a most important place," whereas a city by the name of Saphon (actually a mythological name for the Canaanite Mount Olympus) had never cropped up. How could a central site such as this fail to be mentioned in ancient records? On the other hand, there was a place that figured prominently in all kinds of second-millennium documents: UGARIT, a city that had not been located so far. Albright declared: "The identification with the Ugarit of cuneiform and Egyptian inscriptions of the second millennium seems exceedingly

---

[8] Albright: "The Syro-Mesopotamian God Šulmân-Ešmûn and Related Figures," *Archiv für Orientforschung*, Vol. VII (1931), Heft 4, p. 19.

likely."[9] He promised to deal with the question in a forthcoming publication, which was never released.

The reason was simple. One year later, in an article[1] dealing with the Ras Shamra texts, Albright announced that the tablets recently deciphered by Virolleaud made further pleas for the identification of Ugarit unnecessary. New evidence had appeared: several colophons appended to the alphabetic documents gave the name of Ugarit. One carried the actual date of the third year of the reign of the "King of Ugarit," whose name was NGMD.

Thereafter, the name Ugarit became even better known than Ras Shamra, and the presumably western Semitic language used there (its place within the larger Semitic group is still under debate) is usually referred to as Ugaritic. Any well-stocked university library will catalogue the ever-growing literature under "Ugarit," and by now we have such new fields of studies as Ugaritica, Ugaritic philology, Ugaritic mythology, grammar and epigraphy—to name but a few. Indeed, in the current curriculum of most theological seminaries Ugaritic has largely replaced Arabic as a linguistic basis for Old Testament Hebrew.[2] Yet the language and the place were totally unknown barely thirty-five years ago.

Ugaritic literature may very well be the most important subject in the catalogue of studies connected with Ugarit. To understand its significance, one should consider that until 1929 it was taken for granted that the entire literature of the highly literate Canaanites and Phoenicians had been irreparably lost.[3] A few fragments had survived, as quoted by Eusebius in the fourth century A.D. from a Phoenician historian by the name of Philo of Byblos. But they were quoted for polemical purposes. Even less reliable were the passages from a semilegendary Phoenician poet, Sanchuniathon, cited by Philo. That the clay tablets of Ugarit represented a lost literature, in a lost language in a lost script, was remarkable, but even more significant were the implications suggested by their contents. Serious scholars had long regretted our ignorance of the religious concepts, cults, liturgy, and poetry of the Canaanites, which would undoubtedly throw much light on the origin of certain Biblical books, particularly those of a later date,

---

[9] Ibid.

[1] Albright: "New Light on Early Canaanite Language and Literature," p. 19 n.

[2] G. Ernest Wright: *Biblical Archaeology*, abridged edition (Philadelphia: Westminster Press; 1960), p. 141.

[3] Albright: "The North-Canaanite Epic of 'Al 'Êyân Ba'al and Môt," *The Journal of the Palestine Oriental Society*, Vol. XII, No. 4 (1932), p. 185.

such as Psalms, Job, and some of the Prophets. To what extent had the Hebrews been dependent on Canaanite models?

On the other hand, were the earlier Biblical books attributable to pre-Canaanite, and hence quite ancient, Hebrew traditions? Familiarity with Canaanite texts would possibly reveal borrowings at least as extensive as those made by the Hebrews from Egyptian and Mesopotamian literature. In none of these expectations were the scholars disappointed, even though, admittedly, in the fever of discovery a number of sensational parallels and interrelationships were announced that could not be upheld later. These overly ambitious pronouncements resembled some of the first reactions engendered by the Dead Sea scrolls. René Dussaud, in his summary of the Ugarit finds (*Les Découvertes de Ras Shamra–Ugarit et l'Ancien Testament,* 1st edition, 1937), tried to identify Terah, Abraham's father, and attempted to trace the early history of the Israelites to Canaanite traditions.[4] The assertion was also made that most of the Ugaritic myths originated in the extreme south of Palestine, some four hundred miles away from Ras Shamra, in the Negev. This too cannot be substantiated. Despite such exaggerations—based on misreadings of difficult texts—the Canaanite mythological and religious texts disclosed a great deal that is of value.

Silver statuette (with golden apron) of a Canaanite deity, from Ras Shamra

Canaanite rituals and myths had been known only from Old Testament authors, who professed to despise these "idolatries," though it has long been surmised that the Hebrews owed more to them than they were willing to remember. Now, at last, the

---

[4] Arvid S. Kapelrud: *The Ras Shamra Discoveries and the Old Testament* (Norman, Okla.: University of Oklahoma Press; 1963), pp. 18–19.

Canaanites could have a hearing on their own. What they had to say was not only of vital concern to Biblical scholars and to students of comparative religion. Here was an impressive body of mythology that could stand with that of the Greeks. Some of the legends struck epic notes reminiscent of *Gilgamesh* and the *Iliad*. Moreover, their subject matter, imagery, and choice of words have shed light on obscurities in Hebrew and in Homeric literature. The mythological texts of the Canaanites help to elucidate the growth of European tragedy and comedy from rituals—staged as drama—celebrating a dying and rising vegetation god.[5]

To judge by the polished form in which this long-lost literature was inscribed around the first half of the fourteenth century B.C., its origins were considerably more ancient. Linguistically, its close affinity to Hebrew promised to advance tremendously our knowledge of Biblical vocabulary and to clarify Hebrew words that had been misunderstood or were of doubtful meaning. Some passages in the Old Testament now appeared to be verbatim borrowings from the Canaanites whose precise sense had so far eluded scholars. The same was true of metaphors, epithets, and mythological allusions which had been obscure and were now illuminated by the Canaanite counterparts. In the case of emendations and substitutions made by modern critics and translators of the Bible, Ugaritic usage could often act as a control. In quite a few instances in which scholars had proposed ingenious changes in wording and meaning, the Ugaritic sources indicated that the traditional text was nearer to the original.

The older, polytheistic Canaanite lore and the monotheistic, "divinely inspired" Hebrew writ are closely related and at the same time in strong opposition: Canaanite literature has both substantially influenced Judaism and inspired violent antagonism. The Hebrew religion, however unique in spirit, was nurtured, at least to some extent, in a Canaanite environment and cannot be fully comprehended apart from it. Moreover, the Old Testament itself gives ample evidence that the rigorous standards set up by its teachers were rarely maintained by the majority of the Israelites (many of whom were conquered proselytes), in whom the native Canaanite cults struck a responsive chord. The Bible is full of instances of the Israelite masses, and sometimes even their kings, adopting Canaanite idolatry as a kind of unofficial magic to sub-

---

[5] Theodor H. Gaster: *Thespis*, second edition (New York: Doubleday & Co.–Anchor Books; 1961).

sist side by side with their national cult of Yahweh. What is more, the Canaanite religion may have carried within itself the seeds of monotheism.

The Ugaritic texts make it amply clear that the Canaanite religion of the middle of the second millennium B.C. was outspokenly naturalistic. Its purpose was to explain and control the great natural forces: life-death-resurrection, rain, and, above all, fertility. In the manner of primitive religions, natural phenomena were personalized in anthropomorphic deities, and as in all cultures of a comparable level, from China to old Europe to Mexico, sex was unabashedly evident in effigies and rites. Whatever the aesthetic merits of Ugaritic mythologies—and they were considerable—Ugaritic religious poetry was not originally conceived as art, but as ritual to propitiate the gods and to insure that the vegetation cycle (annual or sabbatical) would proceed regularly. Religion was essentially functional, and man had a share and a responsibility in the scheme of things. Mortal man was in sympathetic communion with nature, not a supine outsider. Human rituals were effective aids in winning the battles waged by the gods. This is the light in which we must consider religious practices such as temple prostitution of both sexes, bestiality (sexual intercourse with animals), and child sacrifice, which were part of the fertility observances that the Hebrews found so repellent, even though they retained certain residues, such as "passing through fire," a euphemism for human sacrifice, as well as the worship of images and even some form of temple prostitution.

The Canaanite faith may have lacked an ethical dimension. Indeed, the gods of the populous Canaanite pantheon, like those of Mount Olympus (there is a family resemblance), behaved as raucously, lustily, jealously, and even murderously as some of their human counterparts. As in Homer, cunning was considered one of the most admirable traits of character. The "virgin" goddess Anath, a Canaanite Diana, was bloodthirsty and sadistic and was at her violent best when championing her beloved Baal, the young upstart who was ready to take the place of chief god, even if this meant threatening her father, the Canaanite super-god, mild El, who was supposedly in his dotage.

> And the Virgin Anath declared:
> "The Bull, God of my father, will yield
> He will yield for my sake and his own
> For I shall trample him like a sheep on the ground

Make his gray hair flow with blood
The gray of his beard with gore
Unless he grants Baal a house like the gods
Yea a court like the sons of Asherah!"[6]

Baal's clamor for a house of his own was a mythological precedent, as Cyrus Gordon has pointed out, for the construction of Yahweh's temple at Jerusalem. "The two accounts are organically related because of common background and attitudes. In both cases the god's interests had grown to a point where he could not condignly go on any more without a house. . . . Times had changed; Israel had arrived; with the added stature of Israel among the nations, the cultic requirements for Israel's God rose. . . . The Biblical and Ugaritic accounts of the building materials (cedars of Lebanon covered with metal) also link the mythical and historical houses of Baal and Yahwe, respectively."[7] Many such fascinating parallels exist between Ugaritic and Hebrew texts, starting with the very names of the Canaanite gods: Baal, and, much more frequently, El or Elohim, as synonymous for the Hebrew Yahweh, who also shares many divine attributes with his pagan namesakes.[8] Some scholars have even found a reference to Yahweh himself (as YW) as one of the Canaanite deities.

The underlying theme of victory over chaos, so pronounced in Ugaritic literature, is central in the Bible. It has conditioned the Biblical view of history, the moral order, and divine government.[9] Yahweh's triumph, like that of Baal, was to have established a cosmic balance. Like Baal, Yahweh is associated with the storm and announces himself by earth tremors, dark clouds, lightning, and thunder. "He who mounteth [or rides] the clouds" is a description of Baal transferred by the Hebrews to Yahweh.[1] It has been pointed out that, judging by its images and tone, Psalm 29 may have been originally a hymn to the Canaanite god which was taken over by worshippers of Yahweh. Much of Psalm 104 is unmistakably based on Canaanite mythology and can only be understood in the light of it. By the same token, when Psalm 48 refers, against all geographic reality, to the holy mountain

---

[6] Gordon, in Samuel Noah Kramer, *ed.*: *Mythologies of the World* (New York: Doubleday & Co.–Anchor Books; 1961), p. 204.

[7] Ibid., pp. 205–6.

[8] Wright: op. cit., p. 8.

[9] Rev. John Gray: *The Legacy of Canaan*, Supplements to *Vetus Testamentum*, Vol V (Leiden: E. J. Brill; 1957), p. 10.

[1] Ibid., p. 8.

of Zion in the recesses of the North (Hebrew *Saphon*), the point now becomes clear: Saphon was the Olympus of the Canaanite pantheon in the far north, a favored residence of Baal. One of Baal's foes was Leviathan—the seven-headed hydra common to both Canaanite and Greek mythology—whom Baal slew, just as Yahweh did in the Old Testament.

There are also similarities in religious observances, liturgy, and institutions. Canaanite Ugarit had its High Priest and its Holy of Holies. The Jewish Pentecost had a Canaanite model. And a close parallel can be seen in the Hebrew sacrificial system and purification ceremonies. Festivals and holy days such as the New Year, the Day of Atonement, and harvest feasts, with their agricultural connections (including the eating of unleavened bread), all have precedents in Canaanite traditions.[2]

Ugaritic texts have all the earmarks of being the product of a common Syrian heritage with strong Mesopotamian influence. The Old Testament, in the role of hostile critic or detached observer, mirrors facets of the Canaanite religion and society that the Israelites came in contact with during their stay in Palestine. However, the fact that Ugarit shared in a larger Canaanite civilization does not preclude a local literary development at the northern outpost which raised popular folklore to a poetic level beyond its ritualistic origins or intentions. Even though written as epic poetry, Canaanite texts bring to mind the style, rhythm, and repetitive pattern of Biblical verse. Closest of all are the triumphal songs of Miriam and Deborah. Thematically, some of the Canaanite legends and myths tally closely with those of Greece and Rome and have helped to underline the ties between the ancient Near East and the classical world. Our hackneyed manner of separating Greece from its Oriental matrix and sentimentally overplaying its unique characteristics and its innovations has blinded us to the obvious. There is a wide field for investigation here. By no means the least merit of the literary recoveries in Ugarit is that they have led to inquiries in this direction.[3]

The general character of the Canaanite religion is most clearly revealed in the Ugaritic version of the great Baal myths. However, because of the fragmentation of the tablets we have, the

---

[2] Gaster: "The Religion of the Canaanites," in Vergilius Ferm, ed.: *Forgotten Religions* (New York: Philosophical Library; 1950), p. 130.

[3] Gordon: "Homer and the Ancient Near East," in his *Introduction to Old Testament Times* (Ventnor, N.J.: Ventnor; 1953), pp. 89–99. See also Gaster: *Thespis*.

unity and sequence of the myths (in the manner of some recent "new wave" novels) remains a matter of debate. A powerful underlying theme is evident, nevertheless. Invariably, it deals with Baal's ascent to kingship among the gods, his struggle for leadership against his rivals, the sterile forces of Yamm (Poseidon–Oceanus) and Mot (Hades). Reverses and ultimate victory dramatize the cycle of death and resurrection, decay and flowering. Baal is accorded passionate support by Anath, whom El, cast in a King Lear role, addresses, with good reason:

> *I know thee to be impetuous, O my daughter,*
> *For there is no restraint among goddesses.*[4]

Altogether, we have some dozen damaged tablets dealing with Baal's tortuous career and Anath's forceful role as his helpmeet and sister-lover. The various episodes are enlivened by ferocious struggles; blood-curdling annihilation of humans; intrigues, deceit, and power politics among the gods; also by bucolic banquets (the consumption of wine is of astronomical proportions); reconciliations; and more combat. Baal may be put to death: Benign El, father of the gods, knows he will be brought back to life.

> *In a dream, Kindly El Benign,*
> *In a vision, Creator of Creatures,*
> *The heavens fat did rain,*
> *The wadies flow with honey!—*
> *The Kindly One El Benign's glad.*
> *His feet on the footstool he sets,*
> *And parts his jaws and laughs.*
> *He lifts up his voice and cries:*
> *"Now will I sit and rest*
> *And my soul be at ease in my breast.*
> *For alive is Puissant Baal,*
> *Existent the Prince, Lord of Earth!"*[5]

This is the message of hope: piety in the face of the dialectic processes of nature, and trust in the eternal return of its redeemer —the Prince of Plenty.[6]

A second genre in Ugaritic literature deals with legends of human heroes. Two major fragments have been recovered, those of Keret and Aqhat, who may have been historical personages.

---

[4] Gordon, in Kramer, ed.: op. cit., p. 204.
[5] Pritchard, ed.: op. cit., p. 140.
[6] Gordon, in Kramer: op. cit., pp. 212–13.

But the epics have absorbed so many of the elements of Canaanite mythology that they are considered part of the religious literature. They express a similar concern with fertility and ritual, though the emphasis is on human, or rather semidivine royal personages. Luckily, they offer some authentic glimpses of Canaanite life as well. In both poems the desire for male offspring is predominant. As with Abraham, god will announce to a man the fulfillment of his dynastic wish before the blessed event has been biologically initiated. Gods are also freely entertained by mortals, as in the Greek legend of Amphitryon. And, although the end of neither epic has so far been found, the miraculous rejuvenation or revival of the hero is almost certain to be the outcome.

The legend of Keret (KRT) is in three broken tablets bearing the colophon of a fourteenth-century king of Ugarit. It tells of a Job-like, Syrian sovereign who has lost all his family and is heartbroken. We see him retire to his inner chamber, crying with the copious abundance of Mediterranean heroes.

> *His tears do drop*
> *Like shekels to the ground.*
> *His bed is soaked by his weeping,*
> *And he falls asleep as he cries.*
> *Sleep prevails over him, and he lies;*
> *Slumber, and he reclines.*
> *And in his dream El descends,*
> *In his vision the Father of Man.*
> *And he approaches asking King Keret:*
> *"What ails Keret that he weeps,*
> *The Beloved, Lad of El, that he cries? . . ."*[7]

El then directs Keret to seek a bride, the fair daughter of powerful King Pabel, at distant Udum (Edom?), who shall bear him children. As instructed, Keret now assembles a large army to press his amorous claim against his prospective father-in-law. On the way, he pays respects at the shrine of Asherah, the supreme goddess, and promises her lavish tribute if his mission succeeds. Upon his arrival at Udum (with an army of several million men, to play it safe), Keret asks to wed the princess:

> *Whose fairness is like Anath's fairness,*
> *Whose beauty like Ashtoreth's beauty;*

---

[7] Pritchard, ed.: op. cit., p. 143.

> *Whose eyeballs are the pureness of lapis,*
> *Whose pupils the gleam of jets.*[8]

Pabel hates to give up his daughter, but yields under the pressure of Keret's unruly host, which threaten ruin to the land.

All goes well with Keret. In due time he brings up fine sons and daughters. But he has failed to keep his vow to the goddess Asherah, and toward the end of the story Keret becomes feeble and, in preordained synchronism, the land and its people decline and become impoverished. The king's own son rises like another Absalom against him and orders him to relinquish his power. The damaged tablet ends with Keret calling down the curse of the gods upon his rebellious son. There was probably still another tablet in which the wrath of the goddess is eventually assuaged and Keret returned to his former vigor, his land to prosperity.[9]

In the tale of Aqhat, gods and men mingle more freely. When it was first discovered, it was called the "Epic of Daniel" (or Dan'el), the father of the hero, but a line at the beginning, deciphered later, makes the former title more likely. Dan'el may well be identified with that Daniel to whom the prophet Ezekiel refers on several occasions as a wise and saintly man, and whom he even mentions in connection with the Canaanite city of Tyre. The Ugaritic Daniel, too, is one of the just and God-fearing, like Keret in his prime: "Judging the case of the widow, /Adjudicating the case of the fatherless." He is equally observant in his sacrificial duties to the gods. And at last Baal intervenes with El on behalf of the unhappy man, "who hath no son like his brethren." So Daniel is to be given a son. When divine messengers bring him the good tidings, he is beside himself. The blessing is to be celebrated in the most lavish style, with festivities that last for seven days. Food and wine are dispensed liberally, and entertainment is provided for all.

Daniel's son, Aqhat, grows up to be the apple of his father's eye. One day, while holding court outside the city walls, Daniel sees Kothar-wa-Khasis (an exact counterpart of Hephaestos-Vulcanus), the god of handicrafts, the divine smithy. Daniel invites the god to his home and has his wife cook him a special meal, thus obtaining from him a powerful bow as a gift for Aqhat. Then one day, while hunting with his new weapon, Aqhat is met by the maiden goddess Anath, who sees the marvelous bow and wants it.

---

[8] Ibid., p. 144.
[9] Gordon: *Adventures in the Nearest East*, p. 99.

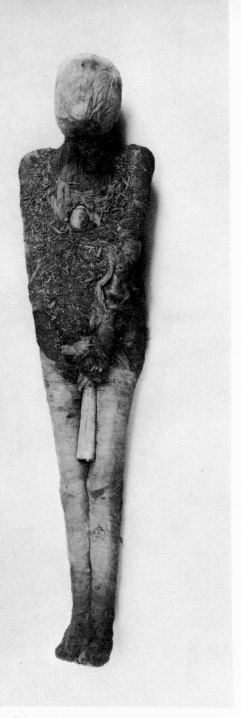

A sealed Aramaic papyrus from the Nile island of Elephantine near Aswan in Upper Egypt.

An Egyptian mummy from Deir el Bahri near Thebes. After archaeologists had removed its sarcophagus and had partly unwrapped it, a papyrus roll was found. One hand seems to be clasping it.

Buried in the ground for more than two millennia and then locked away in museum vaults, an Aramaic papyrus from Elephantine is at long last opened by an expert with the delicate techniques of the laboratory.

An Egyptian papyrus of considerable length photographed before it was unrolled and mounted in glass. Its outside is inscribed in handsome hieratic characters. The papyrus is in the Chester Beatty Library of Dublin.

Detail from a funerary papyrus of the Twenty-first Dynasty (1090–945 B.C.) excavated by the Metropolitan Museum of Art (New York) at Deir el Bahri, outside Thebes. Henttowe is seen here with an offering before Osiris, the God of the Dead.

Sorbonne papyrologists extracting written shreds from papyrus cartonnage with probes and spatulas. The fragment came from a mummy chest piece of the third century B.C., which had first been treated with hydrochloric acid to wash the plaster away and subsequently was put through a steam bath.

Ancient writing equipment from the Twelfth Dynasty or Middle Kingdom (c. 2000–1780 B.C.)—though essentially unchanged throughout three thousand years of Nilotic history. The narrow oblong pieces on the left and right are so-called palettes of wood used as cases for reed pens or writing brushes. An obsidian bowl in the center held water for mixing ink. The wooden box, right, is an inkwell. Wooden mallet was used for pounding papyrus sheets together. The letter by a mortuary priest, center, is written in vertical columns of hieratic of the Eleventh Dynasty.

Cuneiform clay documents of various shapes. The hexagonal piece on the left is the famous "Prism of Sennacherib" from Nineveh, now at the Oriental Institute of the University of Chicago. The two smaller, barrel-shaped cylinders date from Nebuchadnezzar (605–561 B.C.), and Sargon II (722–705 B.C.).

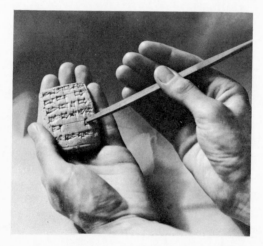

How to write on clay—a modern reconstruction.

A parchment leaf of the Codex Sinaiticus being stretched at the British Museum before rebinding.

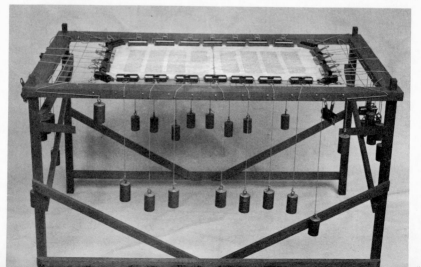

View of St. Catherine Monastery at the foot of Mount Sinai, Sinai Peninsula.

Infra-red photograph of a page from the difficult fifth-century Codex Ephraemi (Syri) Rescriptus, the parchment palimpsest of the Bibliothèque Nationale in Paris. Over it is a twelfth-century Greek translation of a work of St. Ephraem, a Syrian theologian.

Vellum fragment of the Diatessaron, excavated at the Hellenistic-Roman outpost Dura-Europos on the Euphrates. The tiny piece is considered the oldest text of New Testament material on vellum.

The Gnostic manuscripts of Chenoboskion from Egypt, discovered at about the same time as the Dead Sea scrolls, are virtually a library of extraordinarily well-preserved ancient books.

A general view by air over the partly excavated monastic buildings of Khirbet
Qumran atop the steep cliffs of the Qumran wadi in the Judean hills. Several cave
openings are visible in the foreground.

One of the Dead Sea scrolls is being opened by a scholar of the Hebrew University, Jerusalem.

The two Copper Scrolls as found *in situ* at Qumran Cave 3. The badly oxidized pieces may once have formed a continuous sheet. There were great technical problems to overcome in unrolling the scrolls.

Members of an international team of Old Testament scholars at work over fragments of Dead Sea scrolls in the so-called "Scrollery" of the Palestine Archaeological Museum of Jerusalem, in Jordan.

Sir Aurel Stein (1862–1943),
after a drawing by Sir William
Rothenstein.

A close-up view of a section of the Caves of the Thousand Buddhas near Tun Huang in China's Far West. Erosion of the soft rock has destroyed most of the front porches, but interior galleries still retain large shrines, often adorned with beautiful old frescoes and imposing stucco statues of the Buddha.

Non-Chinese documents from the walled-up library of the Caves of the Thousand Buddhas. The ancient manuscripts include: (1) a Sanskrit religious text on palm leaves; (2) a paper scroll with a Manichaean "Confession of Sin" in early Turkish; (3) a book in Runic Turkish; (4) and (6) Uigur texts in book form; (5) a *Pothi* (perforated oblong sheets in the shape of palm leaves) in a cursive Brahmi script of Central Asia; (7) a roll, also in cursive Brahmi, written on the back of a Chinese text; (8) a Sogdian roll; (9) a Pothi leaf from a Tibetan Buddhist text.

Opened roll of a copy of the Diamond Sutra, a sacred Buddhist text, from the Stein Collection at the British Museum. The oldest printed book in the world, it was commissioned in A.D. 868, half a millennium before Gutenberg.

El Yllmo. Sr. D. Fr. Diego de Landa, natural de Cifuentes, España, Obispo de Yucatan. Siendo Guardian de este Convento de S. Antonio, 1553, fabricó el primitivo claustro y esta Yglesia y Santuario de la Inmaculada Concepción Ntra. Sra. de Izamal, cuya milagrosa imagen inauguró trayéndola de Guatemala, costeada por el Pueblo Izamalense, año de 1559. Trajo á la vez otra igual que dejó en Mérida, y habiéndose aburado la una despues de 270 años, en el incendio de esta Yglesia el 17 de Abril de 1829, se repuso con la otra.

Portrait of Bishop Diego de Landa at the parish church of Izamal, Yucatán. During his ruthless campaign to stamp out Indian idolatries, he committed native manuscripts to the flames. Yet, ironically, it is to the bishop's own account that we owe much of our present knowledge of Maya culture.

An inscribed stela from Copán, Honduras, after a drawing by Frederick Cather-wood for J. L. Stephens' *Incidents of Travel in Central America, Chiapas, and Yucatan* (1841). Hieroglyphic monuments like these were erected by the Mayas at regular intervals to mark the passage of time.

But Aqhat won't be swayed, not even by the promise of fabulous riches. Instead he suggests, somewhat impudently, that the goddess go to Kothar and have him make her another bow. Anath persists, and even promises the youth eternal life. To such an offer Aqhat reacts with disdainful skepticism. How can a mere human attain immortality? Here the poem mirrors the pessimistic attitude toward man's ultimate fate which had already been expressed in *Gilgamesh*. Aqhat does not take seriously such an absurd pledge. He has no doubt that old age will eventually come to him; his hair will turn white. Cockily he shrugs off the goddess's vain offer and, adding insult to injury, asks what a woman

Anath, the fierce Canaanite goddess, depicted on an Egyptian stela

would want anyway with a weapon meant for a man, for a warrior. This is the final, unforgivable affront. Anath manages a wry laugh while already planning her revenge. She takes her complaint directly to her father El and regales him with another of her tantrums. As usual, he gives in to her. She thereupon hires a thug to carry out her plan. There is a hint in the garbled text that she intends a kind of mock murder and will bring Aqhat back to life after she has acquired the coveted bow. However, her hireling mismanages the whole business, and the slain hero is devoured by a vulture before he can be revived.

Aqhat's death brings about a catastrophic drought. Aqhat's

sister interprets the sad omen correctly and alerts her father, who sets out to find his son's body so he may bury it. He connects the vultures with the murder and asks Baal for help. The predatory beasts are brought down, one by one, so that Daniel can examine their insides. But none shows any trace of Aqhat, and Baal mercifully restores the birds to life. Finally, the mother vulture is downed, and lo, it was she who had devoured the flesh and bones of Aqhat. Daniel takes the remains of his son and buries them. Then he returns to the palace for seven years of mourning and weeping.

Pughat, Daniel's daughter, has in the meantime located her brother's killer, who, under the influence of wine, boasts of his detestable deed. At this point our text is broken off, but we may be sure that the murderer gets his just reward and the gods restore Aqhat to his father—at least, as Proserpina was restored to her mother Demeter, for part of the time.

The cuneiform tablets contain other Canaanite myths and legends. One cosmogonic account of the birth of the gods is presented in the form of a libretto, complete with stage directions. Another account, dealing with the love-struck moon god Yarih, who covets the goddess Nikkal, begins like the *Aeneid* and other Western epics: "I sing of Nikkal."[1]

The Canaanite literature of the cuneiform clay tablets of the Ras Shamra mound has added new dimensions to our knowledge of the ancient Near East. That it has given us the Canaanite antecedents of the Old Testament is only one of its many outstanding contributions. As literary creations, the texts are fascinating beyond their scholarly value as prototypes.

A few theologians, upon examining Ugarit mythology, claimed to be shocked by the violence and depravity of the Canaanite religion. They saw it as a crude form of polytheism, "the abominations of the Heathen," whose extermination by the Hebrews in Palestine was a pious and godly act, though unfortunately not quite thorough enough. This view, besides being morally dubious, ignores the fact that Judaism, both when it borrowed from the more primitive religion and when it reacted against it, was influenced by it. Many of the prerogatives of Yahweh were originally prerogatives of Baal or El; Daniel the Just was a Canaanite, not a Hebrew. Too, the spirit, if not the office, of prophet may well have been familiar to the Canaanites. In view of this, we must consider these

---

[1] Ibid., p. 96.

people with increasing respect, for, despite its crudities, Canaanite lore is a legitimate antecedent of the Judeo-Christian tradition. That an ancient people who are responsible for the invention of the alphabet can now also speak to us through their literature is a reason for rejoicing.

Book Three

THE PREVALANCE
OF PARCHMENT
A: *The New Testament*

·XIII·

TISCHENDORF
SEARCHES FOR THE
"BEST" NEW TESTAMENT

. . . the bush was burning, yet it was not consumed.
EXODUS 3:2

FOR SOME TIME in the early 1930's rumors had been rife that the Soviet government was considering the sale of valuable antiquities and art treasures. Hard currency was needed by the Communist regime to buy foreign machinery. Several American dealers and collectors had entered into negotiations with Amtorg, the Russian trading organization. The famous Abraham S. Wolf Rosenbach, prince of rare-book dealers, was in high hopes of closing the deal of his life. He had his eyes on a manuscript which even to so sardonic a man of the world ranked as "the most important, exciting, and valuable book in existence."[1] Though not unused to bidding in six figures, he told the Bolsheviks that their price was far too steep. But the door was left open and Rosenbach was confident that a compromise would be reached. Meanwhile, a colorful Texan state senator, Harry L. Darwin, had also been haggling with the Russians. He wanted to secure the ancient codex for the Church he was affiliated with, the Methodist Episcopal Church, South.[2]

Then the thunderbolt struck. Two days after Christmas, 1933,

---

[1] Edwin Wolf II, with John F. Fleming: *Rosenbach* (Cleveland: The World Publishing Co.; 1960), p. 367.
[2] "The Greatest Book Purchase on Record," *Literary Digest*, Vol. CXVII (January 6, 1934), p. 39.

the British Museum announced its acquisition of the Codex Sinaiticus from the Soviet Union for by far the highest amount ever paid up to that time for a manuscript, £100,000—somewhat more than half a million American dollars at the rate of exchange current at that time (but less than half the price asked by the Soviets when they offered the Codex to Rosenbach, as the stunned gentleman told the New York *Herald Tribune*).

Thus came to its conclusion a protracted and secretive transaction that was hailed as the greatest book purchase of all times. Despite the disappointment in America, Christians everywhere could take solace in the knowledge that a Biblical treasure had been rescued from an atheistic state. To the trustees of the British Museum the acquisition must have seemed an act of reverence and a boon to scholarship. A call for public subscription to defray the purchase price met with such enthusiastic response that it was soon over its mark, and the MacDonald government, pledged to match each donation by an equal sum—"£1 for every £1"—was able to save the Treasury a considerable amount.

Interest in the ancient parchment was greatly stimulated by a flood of articles in the daily papers, with some flamboyant and not always trustworthy accounts in the Sunday supplements. As soon as the manuscript was put on display in the museum, an endless stream of people filed past the glass-covered box to catch a glimpse of it. In the words of Sir Frederic Kenyon, who had taken a leading hand in the transaction, the response "proved once again the attachment of the English-speaking peoples to the Bible."[3] To a sophisticated man of letters like Aldous Huxley, it reflected fetishism: "If you regard idolatry as a good thing, then you will wholeheartedly approve the purchase of the Codex. I happen to regard idolatry as a very bad thing."[4]

The Laborite *Daily Herald* went so far as to call the whole bloomin' business, "the most vulgar ostentation of the most vulgar rich."[5] In a more ironic vein, the independent American weekly, *The Nation*, found that almost everybody should be pleased: "The Kremlin . . . at having exchanged a relic of 'the opiate of the people' for 510,000 pieces of good Christian money—a tidy sum which will aid the industrialization of Russia. . . . Ramsay MacDonald will be gratified at having proved to his conservative

[3] F. G. Kenyon: *The Story of the Bible* (London: John Murray; 1936), p. 1.

[4] Aldous Huxley: "Reflections on the Codex," *London Mercury*, Vol. XXIX (February 1934), p. 303.

[5] *Literary Digest*, Vol. CXVII (January 6, 1934), p. 39.

friends that even a Labor P.M. is no barbarian; and the Communists will find effective ammunition in the spectacle of a Labor P.M. buying a fourth-century Bible with one hand and cutting down the twentieth-century dole with the other."[6]

However, putting political resentments aside, few could dispute that here was one of the finest surviving specimens of fourth-century A.D. calligraphic art. Under then prevailing circumstances, the British Museum was undoubtedly a more sympathetic repository than the Leningrad library. In age and authenticity, only the Codex Vaticanus in Rome could compare with the Sinaiticus as a Biblical text. Actually, it was and remains the most complete New Testament of such great age.

The unique, little-known romance of its discovery is still one of the enthralling incidents of man's search for records of his past. In Lobegott Friedrich Constantin von Tischendorf, a seeker after ancient verities, the romance has a protagonist who was as stubbornly dedicated to the pursuit of his goal as his countryman and slightly younger contemporary, Heinrich Schliemann. His career, like Schliemann's, was picturesque and phenomenally successful. His explorations also led him to the Orient. In the course of his adventures he, likewise, came to taste the cultural decadence, administrative corruption, intrigue, and guile of the Ottoman-ruled lands of the Near East.

Schliemann dug through mounds with Homer as his bible, whereas all the efforts of Tischendorf, a theologian, centered on the Holy Bible itself, particularly the New Testament. Unlike Schliemann, Tischendorf was not prone in the slightest to mythomania. He was first and always a critical scholar who tried to unravel the mystery of the early Biblical texts. Yet Tischendorf was never shaken in his Christian beliefs. On the contrary, to him textual research and "criticism" were a formidable weapon against the arguments of the doubting Thomases of his day, who just then were gaining the ear of some of the leading German theologians, capturing university chairs, and enrapturing impressionable students with the siren song of enlightenment.

Ever since the classical scholar Friedrich August Wolf formulated the "Homeric question" and helped, toward the end of the eighteenth century, to found the modern science of philology, Germany enjoyed almost a monopoly in the critical study of ancient literature. Wolf had denied the existence of Homer and

---

[6] *The Nation*, Vol. CXXXVIII (January 3, 1934), p. 3.

attributed the authorship of the two great epics to several poets. His case was based on a rigorous, if not revolutionary, analysis of the transmitted texts. The method was further developed by new generations of German scholars.

There is no denying that German philological and historical research (the two were for some time virtually interchangeable) were among the towering achievements of the nineteenth century and helped to make the name of Germany synonymous with painstaking, brilliant scholarship. It was then that a German poet could bewail the fact that his beloved nation was so rich in thought (*gedankenreich*) but was wanting in action (*tatenarm*)—an exhortation which unfortunately did not fall on deaf ears.

St. Jerome and his pupils. From a woodcut in his *Epistolae* (Ferrara, 1497)

However, perhaps the finest trophies were won for German learning when the instruments forged and sharpened in the field of classical philology were applied to theology. There emerged a discipline of Biblical studies called "Higher Criticism" and "Lower Criticism," standing roughly for the thorough investigation of the content and text, respectively, of Holy Writ. Like everything else, it had its predecessors, and may be traced to Abélard and Spinoza, if not to Origen and St. Jerome.

Biblical criticism has often been ranked with agnosticism and skepticism as a lethal attack on the Christian traditions. Indeed, a good many nineteenth-century "critics" analyzed the Biblical text in order to challenge its ascribed authorship, the time and place of its origin, and its manner of transmission, collection, and canonization. The celebrated name of Julius Wellhausen is associated with a neat dissection *à la* Wolf of the Old Testament into several sections of different composition and background. Others went so far as to declare the evangelical origin of the apostolic documents as spurious. To them the Christian doctrine was little but a "syncretistic" combination of various Hellenistic cults and philosophies, in short, an "Alexandrine tutti-frutti," to use an irreverent phrase of Norman Douglas.

Against such tendencies in criticism, young Tischendorf protested from the beginning. But he did not choose the road of obscurantism to answer the rationalists and positivists. Quoting Tertullian, he reminded the timid that Christ has called Himself the Truth, not habit. Tischendorf was convinced that in all critical efforts the Christian religion would invariably be the winner. Negative criticism can only be rebutted by more criticism, he asserted. Analysis and doubt stood at the start of the scholar's path, fulfilling a methodological need. It was in this spirit that Tischendorf adopted as his motto:

> *Am Zweifel erstarkt die Wissenschaft,*
> *Doch nur der Glaube kann sie heiligen.*[7]
> (Doubt invigorates science,
> But faith alone can sanctify it.)

Tischendorf's achievement in scholarship and his search for manuscripts can only be fully understood in the light of his reaction to previous Biblical criticism. Since much of the critical debate in his college days fastened on the textual variations of the New Testament and the incongruities therein, which were supposed to cast a deep shadow on the truthworthiness of His message and the antiquity of the Christian tradition, Tischendorf turned his attention to these problems while still a student. He gave up all thoughts of entering the ministry and, though he occasionally preached, he thought he could serve God best by dedicating his life to constructive study of the holy texts. Even before taking his degree, he had set his aim: to demonstrate the genuineness of the Gospels and to restore the holy texts to their pristine evangelical wording.

The fulfillment of this goal did not confine him to the cloistered, well-ordered life of a typical German professor, made proverbial by Immanuel Kant. Instead, it led him on numerous trips to the great libraries of Europe, and far beyond, to high adventure in the Near East. The earnest theologian of modest, middle-class background had to turn into a mundane and resourceful traveler

---

[7] Hildegard Behrend: *Auf der Suche nach Schätzen. Aus dem Leben Constantin von Tischendorfs,* fifth edition (Berlin: Evangelischer Verlag; 1956), p. 8.

and hobnob with ecclesiastic dignitaries, Saxonian kings, and Russian grand dukes to succeed in his search. He had to learn the polished ruses of diplomacy.

Barely thirty, he was already an international celebrity. When, still a young man, he was introduced to a foreign colleague, the latter thought there must be two Tischendorfs. The youthful man in front of him could not have done this work, which might easily have made the reputations of several mature scholars. The king of Prussia at a reception was to compare him to Alexander von Humboldt. Like the latter, Tischendorf, the king said, could not help making discoveries wherever he went.

Constantin Tischendorf was born in 1815, the son of a physician, in the little town of Lengenfeld in the Saxon Vogtland. As a top-ranking student in his class at the Gymnasium of the nearby district capital, Plauen, he laid the foundation for his excellent command of Greek and Latin and of the ancient authors. To his knowledge of the classical languages, he was to add Hebrew, Aramaic, Syriac, and Coptic when he took up his theological studies at the University of Leipzig. Here he soon distinguished himself with prize essays in Latin on St. Paul and Christ. For a year he taught at a private school near Leipzig under the man who was to become his father-in-law. He was already immersed in research for his critical edition of the Greek New Testament, of which he was to publish eight versions throughout his life. A learned introduction to the first edition brought the twenty-five-year-old man an appointment, the "venia legendi," to the theological faculty of Leipzig University.

But the young scholar, though in love and engaged to be married, was not yet ready to settle down to the *gemütlich* and respected life of a Herr Professor. Scraping together some money, and with help from his brother and the skeptical Saxonian government, he went off to Paris on October 30, 1840. He was to be away for five years.

The immediate goal of Tischendorf's travels was as simple as it was sound, although it dumbfounded the dignified members of the older generation of scholars who either had not thought of it themselves or lacked Tischendorf's energy and self-confidence. They were also devoid of his palaeographic genius—for he was equally adept in finding valuable documents and in deciphering and dating them correctly.

When Tischendorf started work on his edition of the Greek

New Testament, he realized that the oldest documents from the fourth, fifth, and sixth centuries far exceeded in importance the much more numerous manuscripts from the tenth century onward which served as the basis of Erasmus' famed Greek New Testament and the translations from it into the vernacular languages, such as the Lutheran and King James versions. Erasmus' Greek New Testament (first edition, 1516) was in many respects a rather slipshod job, wanting in the discriminating standards of nineteenth-century scholarship. The great humanist had selected his manuscript sources haphazardly, had not inquired sufficiently into their origin, age, and accuracy, and had not investigated thoroughly the extent to which they might complement each other in the elimination of textual errors. Still more inexcusably, he retranslated a passage—for which he then lacked the Greek original—from the Latin into faulty Greek to fill the gap and meet the deadline of his printer-publisher, Johannes Froben of Basel. Unfortunately, Erasmus also ushered in a new tradition which tended to make his Greek edition sacrosanct, and even more so the great translations from it into the vernacular. This pious fixation on the "received" text (*Textus Receptus*) is with us still and is inevitably invoked every time a revised version or a new translation of the Bible is issued.

Erasmus of Rotterdam. After a contemporary woodcut

However, as early as the seventeenth century a few scholars had collected and collated variant readings they had found in a growing number of New Testament manuscripts, including several in the Coptic and Gothic languages. Simultaneously, an attempt was made to list and classify the manuscripts available in European countries and to gauge their relative reliability. When in the nineteenth century the mantle of Biblical scholarship passed largely to the Germans, doubt was cast on the accepted view that a comparison of the greatest number of manuscripts would make it possible to extricate from them the original apostolic text. Tischendorf wholeheartedly embraced this new approach. In fact, he made it a point to concentrate on texts from the first half of the Christian millennium. Only through them was it possible, he argued cogently, to get behind the officially "received" Byzantine New Testament, which he considered little more than a derivative and doctored version. But, when he began work on his Greek edition, he was surprised to see that, with rare exceptions, pitifully little philological and exegetic work had been done on the few truly ancient Biblical documents known to exist. What if study of these oldest evangelical texts, and any others that turned up, were to show that the Gospels originated within the living memory of Our Lord and His disciples and that surviving early versions faithfully transmitted the apostolic word? The need was, first, for a painstaking study of the small number of available ancient texts, and, second, for a search for additional, perhaps even older and more complete, manuscripts.

Tischendorf had found his challenge. His astonishing results were to prove that great discoveries are rarely a matter of sheer accident but happen, almost invariably, only to the prepared mind.

Before he left Leipzig in 1840, he drew up a list of the oldest New Testament manuscripts reportedly in European collections. His first stop was to be Paris, where several of these rare documents were, foremost the Codex Ephraemi (Syri) and the Codex Claromontanus. He concentrated largely on the Codex Ephraemi, a palimpsest on which the older handwriting had been effaced to make way for a newer text, a treatise by a fourth-century churchman, Ephraem, copied in the twelfth century over a much older, fifth-century New Testament, which had been carefully washed and soaked after being scraped with pumice stone. This was a standard practice in medieval monasteries, as parchment was expensive and relatively scarce. A good-sized codex would require a substantial herd of cattle or sheep. Little-used or obsolete volumes were therefore frequently turned to new use, somewhat as surplus or discarded books or a suppressed edition of a printed work will nowadays be made into pulp for reuse. As in the modern instance, the newer work was often far from being the more valuable.

Palimpsests from late antiquity and the Middle Ages—when much cheaper paper came into use—are, as we have seen, fairly common. By their very nature, they often harbor great mysteries and surprises. To a palaeographic gourmet, they are the true delicacies among manuscripts. Of course, not all palimpsests are readily recognized for what they are. Quite a few may still lurk undetected in library vaults.

As for the Codex Ephraemi, some of the faded and erased older lettering vaguely showed through the twelfth-century characters and had been first noticed in the seventeenth century. At that time it had been barely possible to establish the antiquity of the ancient text through a few brief excerpts, the nature of which palaeographers had been able to surmise. A chemical treatment of the parchments in 1834 had proved of little use and the consensus was that the Codex Ephraemi Syri was too far gone. It would never yield to decipherment. Hence the little enthusiasm with which the Saxonian government subsidized the unknown Tischendorf's ambitious project, on which another Leipzig professor had previously admitted defeat. When young Tischendorf went to see the custodian of the Bibliothèque Nationale upon his arrival in Paris, in order to get permission to inspect the codex, he was treated with good-humored skepticism. How could he hope to succeed in "solving one of the most difficult and important of scientific puzzles,"[8] when renowned experts had failed? But, bent over the manuscript day after day, from morning to night, Tischendorf mastered it. He had no optical aids such as are available today—no ultraviolet rays, polarized light, or quartzite lamps, which in many instances make the reading of palimpsests child's play now, provided one knows the script and the language. But Tischendorf was blessed with excellent eyesight and he had a superb knowledge of ancient uncials, and the supreme optimism of the young. Holding the parchment against the light, he came to notice, greatly facilitated the task.

In two years the work was done. With it his fame as one of the shining lights of palaeography was firmly established. By January 1843 he had the satisfaction of holding a printed edition of the deciphered text in his hands. He also worked on the Codex Claromontanus, an uncial manuscript of New Testament epistles. And he ransacked libraries in Utrecht, London (repository of the great fifth-century Codex Alexandrinus), Oxford, and Cambridge. After completing his work in Paris—he was there a total of twenty-seven months—he continued on to Strasbourg, Basel, Lyon, Marseille, and northern Italy, where valuable New Testament manuscripts were available. He visited the libraries of Venice, Milan, Turin, Modena, and Florence. But his road led invariably

---

[8] Ibid., pp. 110–11.

to Rome, where the papal library safeguarded the most ancient and complete of all the then known Biblical codices, the Codex Vaticanus, which had not yet been made fully accessible to textual critics. In Tischendorf's opinion, this Greek codex in capital letters was likely to outweigh in accuracy all the hundreds of later manuscripts in minuscule. The opportunity to examine and copy it would be of invaluable help to him in his efforts to resuscitate the original Greek text.

TEKNWNCOYTTEP·ITTATOYN
TACENAAHΘEIAKAΘWCENT
AHNEAABOMENATTOTOYПΓ̄C

A section of 2 John 4, from the Codex Alexandrinus. The fifth-century Biblical manuscript is written on parchment in double columns, in notably handsome and firm Greek uncials. Occasionally Coptic-type letters betray its Egyptian origin. The codex came to England as a gift to Charles I from the Patriarch of Constantinople. It is now at the British Museum.

Tischendorf expounded his plan in a private audience with Pope Gregory XVI (the archbishop of Paris and the Saxonian government had provided him with introductions), and he was pleasantly surprised to find the monarch of the Church sympathetic to his undertaking. The Pope graciously likened the young Protestant's labors to those of St. Jerome, and warned him that, like the illustrious father of the Church, he must bear it philosophically if his efforts should meet with lack of understanding and even with attacks from fellow Christians. Upon this occasion, the Pope also made him a knight of the Order of the North Star, the first of innumerable honors heaped on Tischendorf, who, it was later said, took a somewhat excessive pride in such distinctions, just as he enjoyed unduly his association with the great of the earth—statesmen and royalty.

However, his Vatican project soon faced an unexpected obstacle in the person of Angelo Cardinal Mai, who had discovered Cicero's *De republica* and unraveled other classical palimpsests, and was a Biblical scholar of some pretensions but somewhat doubtful accomplishments. He was just then engaged on his own edition of the Vaticanus. Tischendorf was permitted to examine the codex for only six hours, but he made good use of his time by surreptitiously copying a few salient passages.

And now, having for the time being exhausted the manuscript resources of Europe, Tischendorf in March 1844 set out for other shores across the Mediterranean. Once again his plan was bold and simple:"The Codex Ephraemi, like the great majority of the most ancient Greek documents which adorn European libraries, came from the Orient, that is to say, from those countries of the Orient in which Christian learning in particular had first flourished. Was it not possible that there, above all in the monasteries, with their libraries and hidden recesses, important additional literary treasures were still buried? In view of the few ancient documents available on which a restoration of the apostolic text could be based, I saw it as my duty to ascertain whether our resources were exhausted by the material which European libraries could offer."[9]

This daring effort to search the Near Eastern monasteries for New Testament manuscripts was crowned by singular success, yet it could hardly claim to be the first such attempt. Long before Tischendorf, travelers and scholars had been attracted by the alleged epigraphic wealth of these lands. Inspired by the Renaissance interest in lost classics, speculation on the buried treasures of the East cropped up as early as the fifteenth century. Thereafter, exploratory ventures were no rarity. Paris, the Vatican, and even Moscow received shipments of material from time to time, and expectations for signal discoveries were always high. Seventeenth- and eighteenth-century visitors to the monasteries of Mount Athos in Ottoman-held Greece and Saint Maria Deipara in Egypt expounded on the large collections of Christian texts they had seen, some of them "as old as the time of St. Anthony."[1] But such accounts were often accompanied by laments over the dismal condition of the manuscripts and their inaccessibility. Even at that time the local monks were inclined to discourage investigators and more than once purposely misled them. Unfortunately, the secretiveness of the clerics stood in inverse relation to the care they took of their legacy.

John Covel, one of the first English scholars to rummage through Eastern monasteries, heard in 1677 that "all books of humane learning" were burned at a Greek convent.[2] At Mount Athos and elsewhere, he wrote, he had seen "vast heaps of manu-

---

[9] Tischendorf: *Die Sinaibibel. Ihre Entdeckung, Herausgabe und Erwerbung* (Leipzig: Giesecke & Devrient; 1871), pp. 2–3.

[1] Edward Edwards: *Memoirs of Libraries. . . .* (London: Trübner & Co.; 1859), Vol. I, pp. 494–5.

[2] Hon. Robert Curzon, Baron of Zouche: *Visit to the Monasteries in the Levant,* with an introduction by D. G. Hogarth (London: Milford; 1916), p. xii.

scripts . . . of the Fathers, or other learned authors . . . all covered over with dust and dirt, and many of them rotted and spoiled."[3] Such accounts were enough to spur others on their search.

Shortly afterward, Robert Huntington, later Bishop of Raphoe, visited the Nitrian Desert of Egypt and acquired a few Syriac texts of moderate value for the Bodleian. The Vatican Library was well served by the two Syrian cousins, Joseph and Elias Assemani, who combed Egypt, Palestine, and Syria in the beginning of the eighteenth century, but who seem to have alarmed the monks by their high-handed operations.

For about one hundred years, repeated efforts by European emissaries were largely fruitless. Toward the turn of the century, another Englishman, William George Browne (1768–1813), who roamed all over Asia Minor, Armenia, Egypt, Syria, and Persia— and was murdered on the way to Teheran—was also drawn to the by now legendary monasteries of the Nitrian Desert, northwest of Cairo. In his *Travels* (1799), he narrates: "I inquired for manuscripts and saw in one of the convents several books in the Coptic, Syriac, and Arabic languages. The works of S. Gregory and the Old and New Testaments in Arabic. The Superior told me they had near eight hundred volumes, but positively refused to part with any of them; nor could I see any more."[4]

At last, in 1801, a surprise find by Edward Daniel Clarke caused considerable stir. It was a fine Plato manuscript from the island of Patmos. Once again expectations ran high. With the growth of Coptic and Syriac studies, naturally the libraries of Egyptian monasteries became prime targets. In this quest the British were much favored by their political ascendancy in the area, and for several decades they enjoyed a comfortable lead in their successive missions. Most of their efforts concentrated on the monasteries of Nitria, where the earliest Christian monks had settled and where, of a cluster of some three hundred and sixty once-flourishing institutions, a handful still subsisted.

In the forefront of the early nineteenth-century English visitors to Eastern libraries was Robert Curzon, later the Baron of Zouche. Born in 1810, he was just twenty-three years old when he first set foot in Egypt. His express purpose was to search the monasteries for buried books. In addition to Egypt, the Holy Land, Syria, and Greece were on his itinerary. Subsequently, he wrote

---

[3] Edwards: op. cit., 494, from John Covel: *Some Accounts of the Christian Church* (1675).
[4] Curzon: op. cit., p. x.

one of the age's most enchanting travel books, *Visit to the Monasteries in the Levant,* which has frequently been reprinted (in 1916, with an introduction by David G. Hogarth). It is also a classic of all time on the neglect and ruin of books. Curzon assembled a fine collection at Parham (Sussex), which was to illustrate the history and development of writing. But more important still, his detailed account whetted the appetites of others. He led the way to the formation of the matchless collection of Coptic manuscripts at the British Museum.

Curzon's lively narrative recalls the familiar conditions already met with by Boccaccio and Poggio on Western European soil. We can see him followed by half-starved monks as he enters an abandoned square tower. There, "in a large vaulted room with open unglazed windows, were forty to fifty Coptic manuscripts . . . lying on the floor, to which several of them adhered firmly, not having been moved for many years. . . ."[5] At the monastery of Caracalla at Mount Athos, Curzon was spirited enough to ask the abbot for a single vellum leaf of old uncials found in a dilapidated chamber they had entered.

" 'Certainly!' said the agoumenos [abbot], 'what do you want it for?' My servant suggested that, perhaps, it might be useful to cover some jam pots or vases of preserves which I had at home. 'Oh!' said the agoumenos, 'take some more'; and, without more ado, he seized upon . . . a thick quarto manuscript of Acts and Epistles, and drawing out a knife cut out an inch thickness of leaves at the end before I could stop him. It proved to be the Apocalypse, which concluded the volume, but which is rarely found in early Greek manuscripts of the Acts: it was of the eleventh century. I ought, perhaps, to have slain the *tomicide* for his dreadful act of profanation, but his generosity reconciled me to his guilt, so I pocketed the Apocalypse, and asked him if he would sell me any of the other books, as he did not appear to set any particular value upon them. 'Malista, certainly,' he replied; 'how many will you have? They are of no use to me, and as I am in want of money to complete my buildings, I shall be very glad to turn them to some account. . . .' "[6]

Tracking down a lead uncovered in Cairo, Curzon was able to gain access through a trap door to an old oil cellar in a Nitrian convent, whence later travelers carried away a precious load. Yet, quite unjustly, it was Curzon who was later to be accused by

---

[5] Ibid., 126.   [6] Ibid., p. 366.

the monks of robbing them of their cherished manuscripts. Such libel was apparently their favorite method of whitewashing their own failings. The pattern was to be repeated in the case of Tischendorf.

On the heels of Curzon there came to Nitria in 1838 Henry Tattam, Archdeacon of Bedford. He acted on behalf of the British Museum when he secured what has been called "the lion's share of the spoil," in excess of four hundred volumes. By now it was no longer lost Greek or Latin works that were sought, but, on the whole, evangelical and theological texts. Tattam himself was an Arabic and Coptic scholar of distinction, and his interests were largely lexicographic. It was among the cache of manuscripts he shipped back to England that the Reverend William Cureton discovered an ancient Syriac version of the Gospels. Named the Curetonian Syriac, this manuscript of the British Museum ranks as the most important Biblical discovery before Tischendorf's.

Undoubtedly, the success of the English pioneers encouraged Tischendorf to pursue his own designs. However, since he lacked the independent means of an English aristocrat or the backing of the vast resources of the British Museum, he had to attract munificent allies and sponsors. Luckily, the Saxonian ministry of education, at long last impressed by his achievements, liberally contributed to his foray into the Near East. Bankers from Frankfort and Geneva and an older colleague from Breslau also contributed. Tischendorf received the news "with tears of joy,"[7] as he wrote from Venice in November 1843 to his bride-to-be.

The trip from Livorno on the shaky French mailship *Lycurg,* during which he was miserably seasick, was a temporary letdown. Soon after his arrival in Alexandria—a memorable site for the student of early Christianity, though it is now an indifferent polyglot Mediterranean port city (or was, until its magic was rediscovered by Cavafy, Forster, and Durrell)—he continued by bark up the Nile to Cairo. From later accounts of Tischendorf's exploits (there is no serious biographical study available), one has the impression that from the outset he had marked the Monastery of St. Catherine, on the Sinai peninsula, as his principal goal. Some of the popular narratives—and Tischendorf produced several himself—suggest that as soon as he disembarked at Alexandria he rushed off on camelback in the footsteps of Moses—

[7] Behrend: op. cit., p. 12.

only with greater momentum—across the tidelands of the Red Sea to the foothills of the holy mountain. The implication is that all along he had an uncanny premonition of the treasures that awaited him at Sinai. There is little evidence for that. The Sinaitic sister establishment at Cairo, and above all the various Coptic monasteries in the Nitrian Desert, were at least as much on his mind and held out tangible hopes for great finds.

Sixteenth-century woodcut of Alexandria. From Pierre Belon: *Portraits d'Oyseaux, Animaux, etc. . . . . d'Arabie* (Paris, 1552)

On Tischendorf's tentative route were also Mar Saba on the Dead Sea, Laodicea, Patmos, and various other places in Syria and Asia Minor, as well as Mount Athos, and above all Constantinople, where rumors persisted that an alleged Hebrew text of the Gospel of St. Matthew was stored with other fabulous and unknown documents at the Serai (Seraglio) palace—survivors, perhaps, from the ancient Byzantine libraries and the Renaissance collection of Matthias Corvinus in Budapest. In fact, Tischendorf extricated an enormous number of manuscripts from many sources —and bought quite a few of unknown provenance, including papyri, from dealers—but they all came to be overshadowed by his windfall at Sinai.

At the Sinaitic monastery at Cairo his inquiries after manuscripts were referred to St. Catherine's, "where he would encounter a great many excellent specimens."[8] Thus the Cairo monks hoped to

---

[8] Tischendorf: *Reise in den Orient* (Leipzig: Bernhard Tauchnitz Jr.; 1846), Vol. I, p. 78.

rid themselves of the insistent foreigner. Simultaneously they sent a warning to their brethren on the peninsula to beware of the visitor's covetous appetites for parchments. The scheme backfired and helped, instead, to turn his attention to St. Catherine's. Tischendorf, by the way, was not that easily diverted, and urged the Cairo monks to open a wooden closet he just happened to notice. It took considerable time for the key to be found, but when it was, ancient texts galore were revealed, though, as was so often the case, they were in total disarray, having been left to molder. Apparently the monks were unaware of their contents, age, or even language.

Another bookcase, this one in the chapel of the Cairo convent, proved to be even better supplied with parchments, and Tischendorf was satisfied that, despite the warnings whispered into his ears at the outset by the professional pessimists of the Fatherland, he was on the threshold of exciting finds. He also gained confidence in his ability to outwit the monks and clergy, who still displayed a compulsive reluctance to let outsiders as much as look at their manuscripts. Like some negligent but perversely possessive parent, they could not tolerate an outsider's attention to their abused children. At one point these half-literate monks would be entirely oblivious of the hoary, rotting manuscripts, and at the next, when the foreign visitor expressed the slightest interest, they declared them to be of extravagant value. Tischendorf, although often exasperated and disgusted, and sometimes deceived, eventually acquired a measure of equanimity, together with a much needed proficiency in Levantine diplomacy which enabled him to carry away manuscripts from places adjudged by his colleagues to be barren or out of reach.

While in Cairo, he was repeatedly told of a fantastically rich hidden and sealed library there. It was supposed to be safeguarded by the Coptic archbishop of Alexandria (despite his title, for many centuries a resident of Cairo). The Coptic patriarch at that time was a man over ninety years of age, quite alert, charming, and vain. Tischendorf had managed to gain an audience with the old gentleman, whose elegant chatter reminded the visitor of a lady of the highest French society. When at last Tischendorf mentioned his wish to inspect the "secret" manuscript trove, the patriarch asked the reason. Tischendorf explained that he had set himself the task of restoring the original evangelical text and for this purpose was eager to consult ancient documents which were "as close as possible to the letter as it had come from the hand of the apostles."[9] This argument carried little conviction with the patriarch. He declared, quite straight-faced: "After all, we have all we need. We have the Evangelists, we have the apostles. What else would we want?"[1] Obviously, Tischendorf realized, the concept of textual criticism of the Bible had never even occurred to him during his ninety-odd years.

Even before this, the Coptic metropolitan's opinion of his visitor had cooled considerably when he asked him to read from a Greek book. Tischendorf's enunciation of the language of Sophocles horrified the old man. Be that as it may, Tischendorf and his eulogists seem to have been of the opinion that it was the archbishop's ignorance of classical Greek that accounted for this unjust impression. They never doubted that Greek pronunciation as taught at German Gymnasia—which sounded much like *Hochdeutsch* —had the authentic ring of the ancients.

From Cairo, Tischendorf set out in April 1844 for the Nitrian Desert, where there had once been several hundred monasteries before the rising tide of Islam encroached upon them, and the Christian fervor of the Copts declined. Tischendorf searched in several of them. He soon learned that no room in the building complexes "was safer from the visits of the monks than the libraries."[2] In some, these were relegated to attic alcoves high up in the towers. There, manuscripts lay piled topsy-turvy, or were strewn over the floor or stuffed into wicker baskets. A plethora of scraps and fragments covered the room.

The first two monasteries Tischendorf inspected failed to produce any Greek texts. The texts he found were in Coptic and Arabic, though of considerable age. At the third site he saw Syriac documents and extricated a few valuable Ethiopian fragments. The monks of the Nitrian monastery from which Englishmen had recently carried away several manuscripts after payment "of a very modest sum," treated the German scholar with utmost suspicion, professing to be smarting still from what they termed British trickery, which had deprived them of their treasures. Their suspicion was greater than their greed, and Tischendorf could not get them to agree to any sale, no matter how generous his terms. But in an unexpected flash of Oriental largesse, they let him take without any objection a few half-destroyed parchment leaves of sixth- and seventh-century Coptic vintage which Tischendorf had pulled out of a dust-laden mound. This good fortune

---

[9] Ibid., p. 82.   [1] Ibid., p. 82.   [2] Ibid., p. 124.

had to be expiated, however, by "several days of throat trouble caused by dust raised in the festering heat."[3]

In May 1844, after a twelve-day caravan trip through the desert, Tischendorf reached the Monastery of St. Catherine. It stands on a high, sandy plateau some 4,500 feet above the Red Sea, in a truly heroic landscape of precipitous granite cliffs culminating in Jebel Musa, where, according to a somewhat disputed tradition, God gave Moses the Ten Commandments. The monastery is a cyclopic, four-storied fortress of boulders, commissioned early in the sixth century by the Emperor Justinian as a refuge for monks of the area against marauding Bedouin. At that time St. Catherine's (the name is of a much later date) was consolidated into a single large monastery, absorbing scattered settlements of hermits and an already established, smaller convent centering on the Burning Bush chapel, which had been built by St. Helena, the mother of Constantine the Great, in the fourth century.

The Emperor Justinian. Sketch after
a mosaic at S. Vitale in Ravenna

Though physically in the midst of a desolate moonscape, Sinai is at the crossroads of the world's three great monotheistic religions. It is holy soil to all, but especially to Judaism, because of Moses' reception of the Law and the passage of the Israelites on their wanderings to the Promised Land. Moslems worship it because a rock near the summit shows the footprint of the camel which took off from here to transport the Prophet to heaven. The present monastery is a vivid testimony to this multifaceted religious and cultural legacy. It is named for St. Catherine, the Alexandrine Christian saint martyred during the persecutions of Emperor Maximius and said to be buried here. One of its twenty-two chapels is said to occupy the site where God revealed himself

[3] Ibid., p. 125.

to Moses in the Burning Bush. The visitor entering it is asked to take off his shoes.

Only in recent years, since a joint expedition in 1958 by the universities of Princeton, Michigan, and Alexandria was permitted to make a full inventory and to take color photographs, has the West gained an inkling of the fabulous art works housed within the walls of St. Catherine's. Its collection of two thousand-odd icons is the largest anywhere. The sixth-century mosaic of the *Transfiguration of Christ,* in the basilica's apse outshines anything in Ravenna and has been hailed as "among the most exalted blossomings of the Byzantine genius."[4]

That so much pictorial art has been preserved, even though the inconoclastic Emperor of Constantinople, Leo III, had ordered its destruction everywhere in his realm in 728, St. Catherine's owes to one of the endless ironies of history, the earlier conquest of the area by the Moslems. Despite the tendency of European histories to make the conquering soldiers of Mohammed the scapegoats for the ravaging of Christian sites—starting with the Library of Alexandria—Islam often helped to preserve and to save the Christians from each other.

As Tischendorf was quick to notice, St. Catherine's still reflects a spirit of tolerance by harboring in its midst a mosque, about whose origin there are a number of different stories. According to one version, it was built by the Prophet himself; another, recorded by Tischendorf, relates that the monks erected it to assuage the ire of the conquering Ottoman Sultan, Selim I (1512–20), over their failure to restore the health of a young Greek monk for whom the potentate had tender feelings. But such a romantic origin is invalidated by the fact that the mosque was already reported to exist two centuries earlier. One may be equally skeptical about the oft-repeated view that the monastery managed to survive solely because of the Arabs' respect for the little mosque. Surely its presence need not have distracted them from either destroying or converting the rest of the buildings. In any case, other monasteries and churches were allowed to stand during centuries of Arab or Turkish sovereignty, even without the protective proximity of minarets. The truth of the matter is that the coexistence of Christian and Moslem houses of worship was plainly a token of tolerance, which was far more common in the medieval Arab civilization than in the West.

---

[4] Kurt Weitzmann, quoted in *Time* magazine, Vol. LXXIII (April 3, 1959), p. 88.

After much shouting outside the forbidding walls to gain attention, Tischendorf and his men were granted entrance once his letters of reference, pulled inside by way of a basket suspended on a rope, had been duly examined and approved. The brethren asked for his recommendation from the prior of the mother institution in Cairo, but Tischendorf wisely declared that he had left it behind. He feared that advance notice about his anti-quarian proclivities might endanger his chances for a successful search for manuscripts. The monk now let down another basket, on which the visitor seated himself, as on a modern ski lift, in order to be heaved high up the wall and into a small opening.

"What a pleasant surprise," Tischendorf wrote in his popular travelogue *Reise in den Orient*, "to find oneself suddenly trans-ported from a desolate desert of rocks and sand to within these hospitable walls and into its small, tidy buildings and the company of serious, bearded men in black robes."[5] At once the prior showed Tischendorf to comfortable rooms and detailed a young Greek to attend him. The Greek wore a short, striped tunic and baffled Tischendorf by asking him whether his travels had also taken him to the sun and the moon. Obviously somewhat touched in the head, this "Signor Pietro," as the brethren called him, had been put away by his embarrassed relatives. Pathetically he waited every day for their visit. In spite of his mad caprices, he was un-usually bright, and spoke, besides his native Greek, Italian and French, and also some English, German, and Arabic. Tischendorf soon realized that he was the most spirited and ingenious of the eighteen inmates.

As a neighbor, the German scholar had Brother Gregorios, a dignified, benign-looking ancient of Biblical mien, who forty years ago had been a Mameluke general notorious for his atrocities. Tischendorf became most attached to the recently arrived librarian, Kyrillos, who had been transferred from Mount Athos because of a disagreement with the patriarch.

There was much to see in this mirage-like religious fortress. After a while Tischendorf found his way through the labyrinthine complex of houses, halls, workshops, cells, chapels, staircases, roller-coaster passageways, balconies, and balustrades—an accre-tion of 1,400 years of building and as bewildering as a medieval town. He noted the paintings, wood carvings, and mosaics, and let himself be guided by Signor Pietro through a subterranean

---

[5] Tischendorf: *Reise in den Orient,* Vol. I, p. 218.

passage into the delightful, well-watered garden outside the walls, where vegetables and luscious fruits were raised and rows of somber dark-green cypresses were silhouetted against the sky. In the garden was also the burial crypt, an ossuary where the bones of the dead were kept sorted out—ribs with ribs, arms with arms, skulls with skulls. Corpses were first left to desiccate in the dry desert climate and were broken up a few months later and distributed among the various piles. Only the skeleton of St. Stephanos, who died in A.D. 580, was left intact to stand watch in full garb at the entry, as had been his wish.

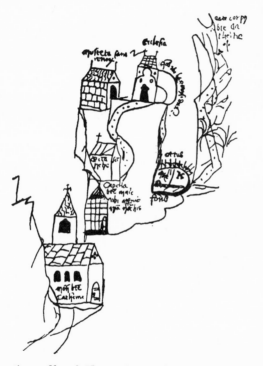

Schematic profile of Mount Sinai, sketched by a fifteenth-century pilgrim. From Jacques de Verona: *Liber Peregrinationis* (1420). The monastery of St. Catherine is at the bottom, and a chapel tops the mountain where the Law was given to Moses. The mosque is to the left of the chapel.

But foremost on the visitor's mind were manuscripts. Kyrillos was helpful and apparently trusting. He had himself made a beginning in wresting some order from the prevalent chaos by compiling the first catalogue. He had no objection—a professional phobia of some librarians even today—to seeing books being used, even if this temporarily upset his new arrangement of them. Tischendorf was permitted to take manuscripts to his rooms, to copy freely, and to compile lists of his own. Kyrillos, in fact. enjoyed the disturbance; no one else in the convent displayed any interest in the books. Occasionally he would hand Tischendorf a poem in modern Greek, on a handsomely illuminated page, which he had composed in his honor.

Tischendorf's travelogue on the Orient, published in two volumes soon after his return to Leipzig and written in the customary semipopular, somewhat hyperbolic, style of mid-nineteenth-century travelers—though more readable than most—is quite reserved about his palaeographic studies at Sinai, for reasons we will soon learn. But in private letters and notes Tischendorf gave vent both to his enchantment with the richness of the collections and to his dismay at the neglected state in which he found them, despite Kyrillos' incipient efforts. He began to despise the monks, who placidly ignored their store of Christian texts for the sake of silly chores and of stumbling mechanically through half-understood liturgy. To his fiancée he wrote: "It is now eight days since I came to St. Catherine's. But imagine this pack of monks! If I had the power and the physical strength, I would perform a work of piety by pushing the whole bunch over the wall. . . ."[6] When he asked for information on important manuscripts, the answers were usually evasive, often misleading and contradictory. Even Kyrillos was of little help. Indeed, he was quick to deny knowledge of any rare parchments rumored to have been seen by other monks.

Fortunately, Tischendorf was left pretty much alone on his sleuthing expeditions through the book and manuscript collections. St. Catherine's actually owned three libraries, quite separate from each other and kept in three different rooms. The smallest contained mostly printed works, arranged on shelves. The monastic library proper, on the first floor, carried the Greek sign ιατρεῖον ψυχῆς (the name which, according to Strabo, was inscribed on an ancient Egyptian library at Thebes), that is to say, "spiritual pharmacy" or "sanitarium of the soul." Tischendorf dryly commented: "As little as the rest of the desert inhabitants, paragons of health, are in need of the pharmacies of the towns, as little there

---

[6] D. Ludwig Schneller: *Tischendorf-Erinnerungen* (Lahr-Dinglingen, Baden, Germany: St. Johannis Druckerei–C. Schweickhardt; 1957), p. 39.

is among the brethren of the monastery a sick soul that would require help from this spiritual pharmacy."[7]

The third library also served as storage for priestly vestments, vessels, and the like. It too contained Bibles and patristic and liturgical texts, and had benefited from bequests by deceased Sinaitic archbishops. Here was kept a most magnificent, splendidly illuminated, uncial Gospel from the seventh or eighth century, which even the monks valued highly and which had attracted the attention of earlier travelers. Though its worth for textual criticism was negligible, Tischendorf was fully appreciative of its aesthetic merits.

Altogether, Tischendorf estimated that there were about five hundred manuscripts, mostly in Greek, but some also in Arabic, Syriac, Armenian, Georgian, and Slavonic. (A joint American Egyptian expedition under the auspices of the Foundation of Man was to find approximately 3,300 manuscripts, in twelve languages, more than two thirds of them in Greek.[8]) In content, the manuscripts were almost entirely theological, including copies of the Bible, missals, and patristic and liturgical literature. They testified to a time when serious religious studies still had a home in monastic cells. Some of the texts had probably once belonged to nearby monasteries which had been abandoned or destroyed. Tischendorf shuddered to think how much had been lost through "infamous negligence." He held in his own hands a manuscript which literally "teemed with fattened white mites." Another one, "adhering to a stone wall, had been compacted to such a degree that it should be counted among the petrified objects."[9]

None of the tomes and loose leaves Tischendorf had so far examined was of major interest for Biblical research. There was nothing to speak of that might help to trace the New Testament further back to early Christianity. And then, as in any true romance, the unforeseen came to pass. Tischendorf, on a browsing tour of the main library, happened to glance at a basket in the middle of the hall. It was filled with old parchments, and as Tischendorf made haste to examine them, Kyrillos, who by chance was

[7] Tischendorf: *Aus dem Heiligen Lande* (Leipzig: F. A. Brockhaus; 1862), p. 79.
[8] Aziz Suryal Atiya: *The Arabic Manuscripts of Mount Sinai*, American Founadation for the Study of Man, Vol. I (Baltimore: The Johns Hopkins Press; 1955), p. xi.
[9] Tischendorf: *Aus dem Heiligen Lande*, p. 80.

present, remarked that two heaps of similar material in a like state of decay had already been committed to the flames.[1] The present lot was marked for the same fate. Tischendorf was not dissuaded from taking a closer look. Before him were beautifully inscribed parchment pages of a four-column, uncial manuscript. It was a copy of the Greek Old Testament—the Septuagint—which, judging by the writing style, seemed to Tischendorf to antedate any he had ever seen: "The oldest Greek manuscripts in European libraries had been examined by me, and studied thoroughly, for the purpose of laying the groundwork of a new Greek palaeography. Some, among them part of the Vatican Bible, I had copied with my own hand. No eye could have been more familiar with ancient Greek written characters. Yet I had seen nothing that could be judged as of greater antiquity than these Sinaitic pages."[2]

There was no doubt that this manuscript ranked in age, and hence in its importance to scholarship, with those Biblical pearls of Europe—the uncial codices of Rome, Paris, London, and Cambridge. He counted 129 large parchment pages. All were from the Old Testament, though from only a part of it. Since Tischendorf was chiefly interested in the Greek New Testament, he may have felt a brief disappointment. But this did not diminish the magnitude of his discovery, which might well lead to more, perhaps even additional fragments of the Septuagint. There was no hint that a New Testament was attached to the codex, though indications pointed to a larger manuscript. And parts of it had already gone up in flames.

In view of the end intended for the basketful, Tischendorf had no difficulty in obtaining permission to keep forty-three sheets. Regrettably, he had not yet learned to assume the detachment of the skilled negotiator. His delight with the sudden find—some of which was now his to keep—was clearly reflected in his face. What a reward for the drudgery of deciphering faded palimpsests for months upon months; for compiling lists of virtually every shred of ancient Biblical manuscripts in European libraries, and following after them in tiresome trips across the continent; for living in cheap hotel rooms instead of getting married and settling down in his own home; for pleading for funds and cajoling wily officials, stuffy archivists, evasive ecclesiastics, and corrupt

---

[1] Tischendorf: *Codex Sinaiticus*, eighth edition (London: The Lutterworth Press; 1934), p. 23.

[2] Tischendorf: *Die Sinaibibel*, p. 3.

middlemen! How could a twenty-nine-year-old scholar who had just made what some have called the manuscript discovery of the century hide his emotions?

The monks realized the value of the scraps they had consigned to fire—some of which they had in ignorant generosity just handed over to a foreigner. Now nothing Tischendorf could say moved the prior to let him have the remaining eighty-six pages, even though, as Tischendorf noted, the old gentleman did not quite know what it was he was guarding. However, Tischendorf was permitted to examine the remaining pages, and he drew up a list of their contents and copied one page with at least three columns of Isaiah and also the first column of Jeremiah. He entreated Kyrillos to take good care of the precious pages withheld from him and to be on the lookout for any similar material that might turn up. Tischendorf also hinted that he might return to the monastery. Various projects already buzzed in his head. How might he gain possession of the pages that at the last minute had eluded him? Could he enlist outside support? What about the Russian Czar, who as patron of the Greek Orthodox Church and benefactor of Christian institutions in the Near East, was held in great reverence by the Sinaitic monks? Out of necessity, the palaeographer was on his way to becoming a crafty politician. About one thing he made up his mind: no one should know the origin of the Septuagint manuscript pages he was taking to Europe. All he would disclose was that they had been found "in or around the Egyptian desert." This was not a lie, though he was later to be accused of having lied. Indeed it was the truth . . . only, according to the time-honored precept of Talleyrand diplomacy, while he was telling the truth, and nothing but the truth, it was not the whole truth.

·XIV·

THE CODEX SINAITICUS

But that which I think more highly of than all these flattering distinctions is the fact that Providence has given to our age, in which attacks on Christianity are so common, the Sinaitic Bible, to be to us a full and clear light as to what is the real text of God's Word written, and to assist us in defending the truth by establishing its authentic form.

CONSTANTIN VON TISCHENDORF[1]

TISCHENDORF arrived in Leipzig in January 1845. He had not returned to Europe directly from Sinai, but had organized another caravan in Egypt, and eventually reached the Holy Land after a series of hair-raising incidents that involved him even in tribal warfare. We shall not follow him on his pilgrimage to monasteries in Palestine and Syria, and the extensive itinerary that brought him as far as Constantinople. At several places, his earlier experiences with suspiciousness and secrecy on the part of monks were repeated, as were his observations of the dismal state of monastic libraries, to which he would gain access only after tribulation and heartbreak. Nevertheless, his persistence and palaeographic instinct led him to acquire several valuable manuscripts, all of which were, of course, overshadowed by the forty-three pages from Sinai. He reached Leipzig heavily laden with Greek, Syriac, Coptic, Arabic, and Georgian documents, all of which he turned over to the Leipzig University library in gratitude for the government's assistance on his explorations. The material was catalogued as Manuscripta Tichendorfiana. Among them were three Greek palimpsets. The matchless Sinai fragments were kept apart, under the name their discoverer had given them

---

[1] Tischendorf: *Codex Sinaiticus*, p. 32.

in honor of the Saxonian sovereign: Codex Frederico-Augustanus. Tischendorf immediately got busy with the publication of a lithographic facsimile edition of the codex, to which he added a commentary.

On his return after an absence of more than four years, the thirty-year-old scholar, whose reputation as palaeographer and textual critic of the Bible was now firmly established, was promoted by Leipzig University to an associate professorship. He could now marry and start a family. He settled down to lecture at the university and to edit the texts he had discovered. A new edition of the Greek New Testament incorporated much of this new material and set another milestone in Bible criticism. Absorbed in his work and in his family, Tischendorf seemed to have terminated his wanderings. But the long university vacations invariably led him to the proximity of ancient libraries—in particular, Zurich and Saint Gall in Switzerland, which offered beautiful scenery as well as palaeographic attractions. Wherever he went, he was haunted by the thought of the pages he had had to leave behind. He had kept their existence secret because he did not want anybody else to get hold of them. Somehow he must find a way to acquire them. How could he induce the monks at St. Catherine's to change their minds?

He remembered the physician to the Egyptian viceroy, Pruner-Bey, whose friendship he had enjoyed in Cairo. Pruner-Bey was a man of considerable standing and connections and could be trusted to act discreetly. Tischendorf asked him to approach the Sinai monks and offer them a sizable sum of money for the Septuagint parchments. But Pruner had to report the failure of his mission: "Since your departure from the monastery," he wrote, "the monks there are fully aware of the treasure they possess. The higher the offer you make them, the less likely they will be to part with the manuscript."[2] It was clear that Tischendorf had to go himself. Even if he was not able to acquire the fragments, he would copy them, and they could then be published and put to use by Western scholars. Tischendorf let the Saxonian minister of education into his secret, and was granted a subsidy to finance the trip.

Tischendorf left Europe in mid-January 1853 and arrived at St. Catherine's early in February. His reception was friendly. Kyrillos, still in charge of the library, appeared pleased to see him. But all inquiries about the Greek parchments proved fruitless.

---

[2] Tischendorf: *Die Sinaibibel*, p. 5.

Kyrillos denied outright having any knowledge of what had happened to the fragments which Tischendorf had extricated from the wastebasket and had so strongly commended to his care. Tischendorf steadfastly believed in the librarian's sincerity and concluded that the manuscript had somehow been disposed of without Kyrillos' knowledge. He surmised that it had probably found its way to England or Russia. However, a clue turned up accidentally when Tischendorf was leafing through a collection of the *Lives of the Saints* in the library. He found a shred of a page, "not larger than half the palm of a hand,"[3] which had been used as a bookmark. It contained a few verses (eleven lines) from the twenty-third chapter of Genesis. Since it was from the opening part of the Bible—the first book of Moses—it served as further proof that this Greek Old Testament had originally been complete. But, Tischendorf had to admit sadly, "the greater part had long since been destroyed."[4]

The failure of this mission did not prevent Tischendorf from making valuable manuscript finds elsewhere during his brief stay in the Near East. This time he carried home sixteen palimpsests —old Syriac and Arabic parchments, and a substantial collection of Karaitic texts which had been set down by an early medieval Jewish sect. In addition, he had purchased a number of Greek, Coptic, hieratic, and demotic papyri. By May he was back in Leipzig.

He expected to hear any day of the appearance of the larger part of his rescued Septuagint in a European library or a private collection. But years went by and no such news was forthcoming. Tischendorf hoped to coax the presumed purchaser of the eighty-six pages into breaking his silence by printing in 1854 those passages of Isaiah and Jeremiah which he had copied in the monastery from the pages the monks had denied him. The excerpts appeared in his own series, the *Monumenta sacra inedita*, which he had set up to publish the manuscripts he had discovered, and any otherwise unavailable texts. An accompanying note to the passage from the Old Testament made it clear that he alone had discovered the original manuscript. Time passed. Apparently his apprehensions had been baseless; no one boasted of possessing the eighty-six pages. A Russian churchman, as Tischendorf learned a few years later, had been shown the coveted manuscript on a visit

---

[3] Ibid., p. 6.   [4] Tischendorf: *Codex Sinaiticus,* p. 25.

to Mount Sinai, but had failed at the time to realize its significance
and had not bothered to find out which texts it contained.

In the following years Tischendorf was occupied with extensive studies for his seventh critical edition of the Greek New
Testament. But the East was in his blood, and "the thought of renewed travels and research," he confessed, never left him; he
"refused to look on his first two trips as having in any way completed his mission."[5] Those who have been to the Orient, he
remarked, can never forget it. His expectations were raised again
when an English scholar who had been sent by the British government on an antiquarian tour of the Near East had purposely
omitted St. Catherine's from his itinerary, declaring: "At Mount
Sinai, after the visit of so eminent a palaeographer and critic
as Dr. Tischendorf, to say nothing of the visits of many other
literary men, there would be nothing which could justify the hope
of discovering anything which had escaped their practiced eye."[6]

Tischendorf wanted to be in a strong bargaining position
when he again faced the crafty monks of Sinai. Like Layard
and Mariette, who at that time were making revolutionary archaeological excavations in Mesopotamia and Egypt, he had
learned how much, in the face of Turkish obduracy and the
natives' callousness, political backing invested the foreign scholar
with the power and prestige to carry out successfully his digging
into the past. The Saxonian king would command relatively little
awe in the realm of the Khedive, but the patronage of the Prussian
government might be very useful. In the aged Alexander von
Humboldt he had a friend and ally of considerable influence at
the Berlin court. The Prussian minister of education, however,
was less enthusiastic. Tischendorf then reconsidered enlisting the
help of the Czar, whose name carried much greater weight in the
Levant. To the Czar's considerable political authority there was
added the charisma of his being the head of the Russian Church
and the champion of the Greek Church. Wasn't the Czar the successor of the former Byzantine Emperors and master of the
Third Rome in Moscow? Besides, the Sinaitic brotherhood had for
several centuries benefited from Czarist subsidies. Tischendorf
knew how to make the most of this.

---

[5] Tischendorf: *Reise in den Orient*, p. vii.
[6] Tischendorf: *Aus dem Heiligen Lande*, p. 15, quoting H. O. Coxe:
*Report to Her Majesty's Government on the Greek Manuscripts yet Remain-
ing in the Libraries of the Levant* (London, 1858).

In the fall of 1856 he handed over to the Russian ambassador at Dresden a memorandum for the Imperial minister of education, Abraham von Noroff. After setting forth his achievements in the recovery of lost manuscripts, Tischendorf stated: "These precious legacies of an age when scholarship flourished in monastic cells as much as it is now in abeyance, are, in my opinion, the sacred property of all learned men. What a rich spiritual life has Europe harvested from the dark and deserted monastic recesses of the East by transplanting significant medieval parchments, particularly parchments in Greek, to the seats of European culture and science! A great many of these documents, more than is commonly assumed, are still to be found today where they were originally deposited. This applies particularly to the fields of Greek literature and Byzantine history. . . ."[7]

Byzantine variations of the Christian monogram

Von Noroff was a man of "surprising erudition," who had himself gone on several journeys to the Orient. He was so enthusiastic about Tischendorf's project that he personally came to Leipzig to discuss plans, and even expressed a desire to join him on part of the trip. The virtues of Tischendorf's proposal did not fail to impress the Imperial Academy at St. Petersburg, which had been asked to give its opinion. However, the conservative Russian clergy was averse to entrusting a German Protestant with an embassy to their coreligionists in the Levant. Worse still, Von Noroff left his post. But the ex-minister retained access to the royal family, and the Czar's brother Constantine was won over. Eventually the Czarina Maria Alexandrovna and the dowager empress were brought into the little conspiracy.

Meanwhile Tischendorf was approached by the Saxonian government, which was ready to bear the costs if the Russians should withdraw their support. Now no longer dependent on the Russians, Tischendorf could act more boldly. He sent what was virtually an ultimatum to St. Petersburg, asking for a decision on his petition—one way or the other. Immediately Von Noroff and another intimate of the Grand Duke Constantine cabled that he need not wait much longer, that an Imperial endorsement

---

[7] Tischendorf: *Die Sinaibibel*, pp. 7–8.

would be granted in the very near future. The Empress had been approached again, just as she was about to board a train for Moscow with the Czar. The following night, instructions were given to advance Tischendorf the necessary funds (covering travel expenses and including a liberal allowance for purchases). These were handed over to him in Russian gold by the Imperial ambassador in Dresden. No commitments were attached. Neither was Tischendorf required to make out a receipt. "Thus, imperial munificence sealed the project as a matter of noble trust."[8]

His seventh edition of the Greek New Testament completed —it had taken three years of incessant labor—Tischendorf once more set sail for Egypt. This time he did not delay in the Nile Valley, but proceeded at once to the convent at Mount Sinai. His reception at the monastery was quite different from previous ones. He was now traveling on behalf of His Imperial Russian Majesty, and he was treated with deference and respect. The Russian flag was hoisted in his honor. No longer was he made to enter the monastery via an airborne contrivance, but was let in through a little door on ground level, which was opened only on rare occasions for guests of unusual distinction. The prior, apparently fully aware of the visitor's mission, received him with a little speech wishing him success in finding fresh support for the divine truth. Tischendorf later commented: "His kind expression of good will was borne out beyond his expectation."[9]

Whether the prior's speech was weighted with dramatic irony, as it seemed to Tischendorf and later German writers, or reflected a sincere intention on the monks' part to comply with the visitor's every wish, perhaps in the hope of commensurate Russian rewards, we lack evidence to decide. Whatever may have gone on behind the scenes—allowing for the possibility that the monks played a kind of cat and mouse game with Tischendorf—the course of outward events is clear. Tischendorf took another thorough look at the manuscript collections in the monastery. After three days, he was convinced that nothing had escaped him. There was little left for him to do but copy a few passages. He had decided not to ask any direct questions about the fate of the Bible manuscript, knowing only too well what the answer would be. Since he could not find any trace of it in any of the three libraries, he was more than ever convinced that it had been removed from St. Catherine's. On the fourth day of his stay, he made plans for his return to Cairo by the end of the week.

---

[8] Ibid., p. 10. [9] Tischendorf: *Codex Sinaiticus*, p. 27.

On the afternoon of that day, Tischendorf climbed to a nearby height and then down to the plain beyond, in the company of the monastery's steward (*oeconomos*), a young amiable Athenian and a pupil of Kyrillos, who called him his "spiritual son." On the way back, conversation turned to Tischendorf's editions of the Greek text of the Old and New Testament, copies of which he had presented to St. Catherine's. Toward sunset, upon their return, the steward asked Tischendorf to take some refreshment with him in his cell. Barely had they entered and begun to sip the date liqueur produced at the monastery than the steward resumed their earlier conversation: "And I too have read a Septuagint— a copy of the Greek Testament made by the Seventy."[1] After this remark, he walked across the room, took from a shelf a bulky object wrapped in red cloth, and laid it before his guest. Tischendorf untied the cloth. There was the same fourth-century uncial script, the same four-columned pages as in the Codex Friderico-Augustanus. And the parchments included not only the selfsame leaves Tischendorf had picked out of the basket some fifteen years ago, but much more besides.

To the eighty-six pages of the Old Testament he had seen earlier, were added a hundred and twelve more, together with the greatest treasure, the goal of all his endeavors, an apparently complete New Testament. Neither the Codex Alexandrinus nor the Codex Vaticanus contained such a full text. He counted the pages: there were 346. He glanced at the text to see whether all the Gospels, all the Epistles, were really there. He was examining the only New Testament that had been preserved in its entirety from an age this close to its actual composition. Could he believe his eyes when at the end of the New Testament text he caught a glimpse of the Epistle of Barnabas? This was the work of an apostolic disciple which a later canon, after much hesitation, excluded from the New Testament. A substantial part of it was considered lost, and the only surviving fragments had come down in faulty Latin translations. Tischendorf could hardly contain his joy. But this time he determined to act cautiously in order not to arouse the suspicions of the monks and lose his prize once again. Other monks had meanwhile gathered in the steward's cell, among them Kyrillos. They were witnesses of the German professor's "detachment" as he examined the bulky manuscript. Not knowing the full contents of the parchments, they could not, Tischendorf thought, possibly fathom their real signifi-

---

[1] Ibid., p. 27.

cance. He asked nonchalantly whether he could carry the pages to his room for further study, and the permission was freely granted. In a later account, he attempted to set down his feelings when at last he was alone: "There, by myself, I could give way to the transport of joy I felt. I knew that I held in my hand the most precious Biblical treasure in existence—a document whose age and importance surpassed that of all the manuscripts which I had ever examined during twenty years' study of the subject. . . ."[2]

The opening of the First Letter to the Romans, from the Codex Vaticanus, one of the two oldest and best-preserved uncial manuscripts of the Greek Bible. It was written on parchment in the late fourth century, at about the same time as Tischendorf's Codex Sinaiticus and a few decades earlier than the calligraphically more exacting Alexandrinus.

He proceeded to make a complete record of the contents of the 346 pages. In addition to twenty-two books of the Old Testament, most of them complete and comprising chiefly prophetic and poetic books, there were also parts of the Apocrypha. The New Testament had no gap whatsoever. When he leafed through it and read Barnabas, a thought flashed through his mind: could there be also another long-lost piece, the Pastor (Shepherd) of Hermas? He was almost ashamed to entertain "such ungrateful expecta-

---

[2] Ibid., pp. 27–8.

tions in the face of an already bountiful blessing."[3] Then his eye fell on a rather faded page before him. The caption read: THE PASTOR. He wept: "Thereupon I lost all control. Deep, deep in my heart I felt that which had not let me stay peacefully at home . . . the Lord's call. Though I had always told myself: I am traveling in the name of the Lord to seek treasures which will benefit His Church—now I knew it for certain and was truly in awe of the truth. The manuscript, entire, as it stands now, is for scholars and for the Christian Church an incomparable jewel."[4]

It was eight in the evening. On a night like this, it was impossible to sleep. Though the lamp gave only a dim light and there was no heat, Tischendorf sat down to transcribe the Epistle of Barnabas and the rescued part of the Pastor of Hermas.

Early next morning he sent for the steward. Mentioning the substantial amount of gold in his possession, he proposed to purchase the parchments for two handsome donations—one for the monastery and the other for the steward. The steward, he had to admit, "did well to reject the offer."[5] Tischendorf then explained that he simply must copy the manuscript. To this the steward raised no objection. But how could it be done? The manuscript included some 120,000 lines in a difficult ancient Alexandrine script. The work would take at least a year. Tischendorf was ill-prepared to stay at St. Catherine's for that length of time. Would the monks let him take the codex to Cairo, where he could get assistance? The brethren were ready to agree, except for old Vitalius, the *skevophylax* (guardian of church implements), from whose combined library and storeroom the manuscript had supposedly come in the first place. There was a further complication: the prior Dionysios, who would have had the last word in the matter, had left a few days earlier for Cairo to join the priors of other Sinaitic monasteries in electing a new archbishop to succeed the hundred-year-old Archbishop Constantine, who had died.

Tischendorf decided to follow the prior to Cairo, taking along warm letters of recommendation for his plan from Kyrillos and the steward. In Cairo he hastened to the Sinaitic convent where the synod of priors was meeting, and by evening he was granted permission to bring the manuscript to Cairo and a Bedouin sheik was dispatched to Sinai to fetch it. Ten days later, the manuscript arrived in Cairo by "dromedary express," speeded by the bonus

---

[3] Tischendorf: *Aus dem Heiligen Lande*, p. 111.
[4] Behrend: op cit., pp. 28–9 (letter of February 15, 1839).
[5] Tischendorf: *Die Sinaibibel*, p. 14.

promised by Tischendorf. It was now agreed that Tischendorf could borrow eight pages—a quaternion—at a time for the purpose of copying them. Before him was an immense labor—and it would be rendered obsolete by later developments. For two months Tischendorf labored in his room at the Hôtel des Pyramides, exposed to the ceaseless clamor and clatter of a Cairo street.

To reduce the chore, he enlisted two resident Germans who had some classical learning, a physician and a pharmacist. Under his supervision, they began to copy. But the task grew increasingly more formidable. In addition to the many faded passages, there were innumerable variants—about 14,000—entered by successive "correctors" of the text after its completion. Some pages contained more than a hundred such emendations. Furthermore, the text itself betrayed several handwritings of differing styles and peculiarities. At least six correctors had been at work, and most, it seemed, had made their entries more than a thousand years before.

When about half of the volume had been copied, Tischendorf learned, to his dismay, that due to an indiscreet remark of his to a German consular representative the secret had leaked to an English scholar who had just arrived. Moreover, the Englishman had been taken to the monastery where the codex was, and had lost no time in offering money to the monks. Tischendorf arrived at the monastery shortly after this and for once he lost his self-control. However, the prior soothed him with the words: "We would much rather present the manuscript to Emperor Alexander as a gift than sell it for English gold."[6]

Such a generous thought was not wasted on the shrewd Tischendorf, who was, he confessed, "happy at this expression of faith and would come back to it in the future."[7] More insistently now, he urged upon the Sinaites the magnificence of an action that would reflect their veneration for the Czar as protector of the Orthodox faith. At the same time, his irritation at the arrival of English competition and at the disclosure of his secret prompted him to make public the news of his recent discoveries. Like a victorious general, he composed a triumphant communiqué, directed it to the Saxonian minister of education, and had it published in mid-April 1859 in the scientific supplement of the *Leipziger Zeitung*.

The suggestion that the manuscript should be presented to the Czar evidently began to tempt the Sinaite brethren. But there

---

[6] Tischendorf: *Aus dem Heiligen Lande*, p. 117.
[7] Ibid., p. 117.

were unexpected complications. The newly elected archbishop, whose permission was required for the donation of so valuable an object as the Biblical codex, was opposed by the Greek Orthodox archbishop of Jerusalem, who refused to ordain him. In addition, he had yet to be confirmed by the Turkish government and the Egyptian viceroy. Both authorities took their time. Hence, his appointment could not be considered ratified and he refused to assume the responsibility of this decision. He hinted, however, that after he was fully invested with his high office, he would favor the transfer of the codex to the Czar.

Tischendorf shrewdly intervened in the crisis over the new archbishop. He was no longer the suppliant. Instead he let the monks know that he, an envoy of the Czar, would use his influence with His Orthodox Majesty on their behalf. The monks were greatly distressed by the episcopal interregnum, which brought both confusion and apathy to their community. When Tischendorf heard of the arrival of the Grand Duke Constantine in Jerusalem, he interrupted his work and chartered a ship that took him and three other men to Jaffa. And he became the constant companion of the Czar's brother throughout his stay in the Holy Land. Afterwards, he proceeded to Smyrna and Patmos, and on the way picked up several valuable manuscripts, which he sent as presents to Czar Alexander.

Back in Cairo, he learned that the election of the new archbishop had not been resolved, because of the obstinate position of the Metropolitan of Jerusalem. Finally, the archbishop-elect himself came to ask Tischendorf, whose prestige had increased considerably because of his association with the Grand Duke, to represent the interests of the community to the best of his abilities. Tischendorf accepted the mission gladly, because of, as he bluntly put it, "the close connection between its interests and my own."[8] In Constantinople, the second easily took precedence.

Tischendorf found in the Russian ambassador to the Sublime Porte, Prince Lobanov, a devoted ally who offered him the hospitality of his country home on the shores of the Bosporus. There, Tischendorf became more and more apprehensive about his own affairs. "To wait for months on end for the end of the monastic quarrel was hardly my way."[9] And he found a solution. He drafted an ingenious document, which he persuaded the Russian ambassador to sign. In it, the Russian government suggested that, in view of the fact that the investiture was still pending, the Biblical codex

---

[8] Tischendorf: *Die Sinaibibel*, p. 21.   [9] Ibid., p. 22.

might go to St. Petersburg on loan. It was to remain the property of the monastery until it was officially presented to the Czar. If for any unforeseen circumstance the gift was not made, the manuscript was to be restored, without any question, to the monastery. With this document in his possession, Tischendorf once again took ship for Egypt. Upon his arrival, the monks thanked him profusely for his efforts on their behalf, and signed the form that permitted him to carry the codex on loan to St. Petersburg, "there to have it copied as accurately as possible."[1]

At long last he could return to Europe with his precious cargo —a "rich collection of old Greek, Syriac, Coptic, Arabic, and other manuscripts, in the middle of which the Sinaitic Bible shone like a crown."[2] On the way, Tischendorf, who worshipped monarchs of any nationality, took time out to display his trophies to Emperor Franz Josef in Vienna, and a few days later to his own sovereign, King Johann of Saxony. He then continued on to Tsarskoe Selo, the imperial palace near St. Petersburg, where he presented the manuscripts to Their Majesties. Tischendorf now took the opportunity to propose to the Emperor "an edition of this Bible worthy of the work and of the Emperor, which should be regarded as one of the greatest enterprises in critical and Biblical studies."[3] There was, of course, no doubt who would direct the enterprise. Tischendorf was invited to settle in St. Petersburg for this purpose, but he declined for personal reasons and because of the advantage of the superior typographical facilities available at Leipzig.

The production of the facsimile edition of the codex, in four volumes, took three years. It turned out to be one of the most arduous tasks Tischendorf had ever undertaken, and probably in the end, it undermined his health. There was, for instance, the matter of having the precise Greek typefaces cut for the various uncial writing styles and for the still smaller corrections that were appended to the text and had to be incorporated. Tischendorf himself measured the distance between each two letters, to achieve the greatest possible verisimilitude. Since the lettering of the manuscript was uneven and partly faded, a photographic edition, with the methods and techniques then available, was not feasible. (The codex was eventually photographed in the early twentieth

---

[1] Tischendorf: *Codex Sinaiticus*, p. 31.
[2] Ibid., p. 31.
[3] Ibid., p. 31.

century by Professor and Mrs. Kirsopp Lake of Harvard and issued by the Oxford University Press: the New Testament in 1911, the Old Testament in 1922.) In addition, the corrections to the text had to be deciphered and inserted in the copy. Then there were the proofs to be read. When the work was done, a carload of heavy volumes—thirty-one boxes, with 1,232 folios, weighing some sixty tons—was shipped to St. Petersburg, to be issued in celebration of the thousand-year jubilee of the Russian monarchy, in the fall of 1862. The work bore the title:

CODEX BIBLIORUM SINAITICUS PETROPOLITANUS,
rescued from darkness under the auspices of His Imperial Majesty Emperor Alexander II, brought to Europe and edited for the advancement and glorification of Christian learning by C.T.

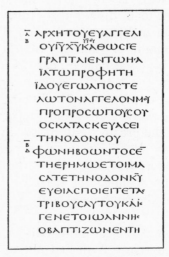

Page from Tischendorf's printed facsimile edition of the Sinaiticus, Mark 1:1–4

In a letter of dedication to his illustrious patron, Tischendorf emphasized the uniqueness of the manuscript, whose importance, "hopefully maintained by its discoverer from the beginning, has been splendidly confirmed. . . . There is no document of this kind which could present more valid evidence of its ancient nobility. Venerable Fathers of the Eastern and Western Church of remotest Christian antiquity bear testimony that the church of their time possessed the word of God in quite similar documents."[4]

---

[4] Tischendorf: *Die Sinaibibel*, pp. 39–40.

Rewards and honors were now his in plenty. The Emperor of Russia raised him and his descendants to noble rank. The Pope, upon receipt of a facsimile Sinaiticus, personally expressed his congratulations and his admiration. An English scholar of distinction greeted him with the words: "I would rather have discovered this Sinaiticus manuscript than the Koh-i-noor of the Queen of England."[5]

View of Mount Athos in northeastern Greece, with its cluster of Orthodox monastic communities long famed for their manuscript collections

Tischendorf's great triumph, however, was clouded by malicious attacks on his integrity and on the value of his find. In a sense, the adventure story continued. Now it had a picaresque sequel, with a rogue, the ingenious Greek Simonides, to enliven the scene. The sequel concerned the encounter between the greatest palaeographer of the age and the man who could aspire to a correspondingly lofty claim in his less creditable vocation of forging manuscripts. By coincidence, both scholar and knave bore the Byzantine name of Constantine.

Simonides was probably born in 1824 or 1819 (later he claimed 1815) on the small Aegean island of Syme. Orphaned at an early age, he was brought up by an uncle who was prior of one of the Mount Athos monasteries. There he was initiated into the arts of calligraphy, and had an opportunity to copy various ancient texts. He undoubtedly acquired an admirable knowledge

---

[5] Tischendorf: *Codex Sinaiticus*, p. 32.

of the early uses of writing materials, different styles of scripts, and peculiarities of language. After the death of his mentor, he turned up in Athens, where he sold the Greek government some parchments he had apparently taken as souvenirs from the hospitable monastery. Faced with a ready market, but with diminishing supplies, he set himself to the task of replenishing his stock. Within a short time, he caused a sensation with manuscripts supposed to have come from a hitherto totally unknown center of learning on, of all places, the obscure island of Syme. It seemed that Simonides' thirteenth-century forebears had anticipated virtually all technological innovations of the mid-nineteenth century, including the steamship. Another manuscript established its alleged author, a late medieval Greek monk, as the inventor of photography. These documents, meant to appeal to Hellenic patriotism and cleverly dedicated by their finder to the Greek statesman Mustoxydis, aroused doubts almost immediately. Mustoxydis, a scholar in his own right, declared them fraudulent. A commission of savants procrastinated. How, they said, could a youngster like Simonides, with such obvious gaps in his education, invent and fake so expertly?

Meanwhile, Simonides wisely moved on to Constantinople. There he obtained a concession to carry out archaeological excavations at the site of the old hippodrome. And in no time at all he came up with a bottle stuffed with manuscript pages. Unfortunately, somebody had seen him planting it during a lunch hour. The ubiquitous Symean had to go traveling once again. He cropped up all over the Levant, from Alexandria to Odessa. For a while he returned to Mount Athos, for obvious reasons, and then he gave England and Germany the benefit of his remarkable talents. Why did he choose these two countries? Was it because he considered Englishmen and Germans to be the most gullible of antiquarians, or were they the most liberal when it came to paying large sums to satisfy their passion for old parchments? In any case, these two countries were then the most active centers of palaeographic research. They were a ready market for manuscripts. That they also counted among their scholars some of the keenest minds must have been known to Simonides. But he was prepared to take risks, and he may have relied heavily on his agile Mediterranean wits to get the better of the Northern barbarians—at least for a time.

In Germany he offered a palimpsest of the long-lost *Uranios*, a Hellenist history of the Egyptian kings. A senior colleague of

Tischendorf, Professor Wilhelm Dindorf of Leipzig, declared the manuscript genuine. A Berlin board of scholars concurred and advised that it be purchased. Only Alexander von Humboldt remained skeptical. At the last minute, Dindorf showed Tischendorf a few pages. Tischendorf recognized it at once as a fake and cabled his expert opinion to Berlin. Threats of compromising disclosures and of scandal enabled Simonides to retain his liberty —but Tischendorf's intervention became a sore point. With the discovery of the Codex Sinaiticus, Simonides saw an occasion for revenge. Now he changed roles. No longer did he refute any suggestion that he had fabricated manuscripts. Instead, he suddenly confessed in September 1862 that it was he who had written the entire codex which Tischendorf had brought from Sinai. Simonides made up an intricate story to account for his having produced the manuscript, allegedly without any intention to deceive anybody about its age.

The startling disclosure caused confusion—and in England especially, it gained some credence. The press took up the scandal with relish. "Who is the deceiver, who is the deceived?"[6] one paper headlined its exposure of the German scholar. How is it possible, queried the writer of the article, that in the Sinai convent, where learned men of England had failed to find anything of note, Tischendorf should have extricated his precious parchments from a rag. . . . Who was this Tischendorf anyway? . . . Who was he, compared to his eminent countrymen Dindorf and Lepsius, who had both been ignominiously tricked by Simonides? Wasn't Tischendorf likely to have been tempted beyond endurance by the chance to see his name broadcast all over Europe, whatever the cost?

Some of these sentiments were echoed by enemies of Tischendorf in Germany. To him the whole business seemed a bad joke. That Simonides could have written the codex had about the same plausibility, he remarked, as someone suddenly exclaiming: "It is I who built London; or, I have placed Sinai at its present location in the desert."[7] And who indeed would believe a notorious cheat like Simonides?

However, it was internal evidence that exploded Simonides' tale. The Sinai manuscript was penned in at least three different hands, in addition to the various hands evident in the corrections, which revealed writing styles dating consecutively from the fourth to the twelfth centuries. There was no uncial document, and no

---

[6] Tischendorf: *Die Sinaibibel,* pp. 46–7.　　[7] Ibid., p. 45.

combination of documents, at Mount Athos or anywhere else, from which it could have been copied. Parts of the Epistle of Barnabas did not even exist in another Greek version. The codex itself bore evidence that it had been at Caesarea (in Palestine) in the seventh century. Furthermore, how was one otherwise to account for the fact that only approximately half of the manuscript had come down to us, whereas fragments turned up in bindings made centuries before? As a British Museum publication on the Sinaiticus was to observe: "The impossibilities of this story are almost too obvious to need demonstration."[8]

A scribe at work in front of a book closet. This drawing after a miniature in a Byzantine-Christian manuscript is supposed to be of the Prophet Ezra, but suggests an Eastern Father of the Church.

Simonides never took up the challenge to write one page in the Biblical uncials of the codex. Besides, he got himself caught in all kinds of contradictions. He asserted, for example, that he had seen the complete manuscript at Sinai in 1852, oblivious of the fact that Tischendorf had obtained forty-three pages some eight years earlier.

Still another battle raged over the parchments. This concerned not so much the authenticity of the codex but its authority. In brief, voices were raised by Russian orthodox priests who de-

---

[8] British Museum: *The Codex Sinaiticus and the Codex Alexandrinus* (London: British Museum; 1938), p. 9.

clared the manuscript to be heretic. "If the stake were still in vogue," wrote Tischendorf wryly, "the codex would run the risk of destruction by fire, which it had already barely escaped on an earlier occasion."[9] A pamphlet by a Russian archbishop, the Archimandrite Porfiri Uspenski—the same man who had previously seen the codex at St. Catherine's—pointed out that, in the Sinaiticus, Christ appeared neither as the Son of the Virgin Mary nor as the Son of God. Nor did the Sinaiticus refer to Christ's ascension. This was a serious accusation and it shocked Tischendorf, who saw his dearest ambition, to refute the skepticism of radical German theologians, challenged. Fortunately, at least to his own satisfaction, he was able to show with considerable exegetic and philological acumen that the Russian churchman's interpretation was fallacious. He found support in the fourth-century Fathers of the Church, St. Eusebius and St. Jerome, and even in the traditional versions of the Gospels according to Luke and Mark. The Russian ex-minister Von Noroff, Tischendorf's supporter, vigorously parried the attacks. The Orthodox Metropolitan of Moscow also came to the defense of the codex, and Uspenski admitted his error. Tischendorf answered his critics more extensively in 1863 with a tract entitled *The Attacks on the Sinai Bible,* in which he made the observation: "Great achievements in scholarship are rarely made without opposition. Indeed, one may consider it one of their characteristics that they provoke contention."[1]

And what about the proposed presentation of the codex to the Czar? The archiepiscopal crisis of the Sinai brotherhood lasted for years and eventually developed into an internal feud that ended only with the deposition in 1867 of the chosen candidate and the undisputed election of a successor. Only in 1869 could the transfer of the codex to the Russian monarch become official. The Czarist government's offer of nine thousand rubles was accepted by the Sinai monks, who hastened to seal the "donation" with a signed document. At last the codex was placed in the St. Petersburg Public Library. Tischendorf remained in friendly correspondence with the new archbishop. In fact, the prelate wrote him on July 15, 1869: "You know that this famous manuscript of the Bible has now been presented to the exalted Emperor and

---

[9] Tischendorf: *Die Sinaibibel,* p. 49.
[1] Tischendorf: *Die Anfechtungen der Sinai-Bibel* (Leipzig: Fleischer; 1863), p. 3.

Autocrat of all the Russias as a testimony of our and the Sinai Monasteries' eternal gratitude."[2] In later days, however, new generations of monks were wont to speak of the Tischendorf transaction with bitterness, and almost every writer who has visited St. Catherine's since, has come back with a story that puts Tischendorf in a bad light.[3]

An article in the January 1964 issue of the *National Geographic* announced dramatically that its author, George H. Forsyth of the University of Michigan, and fellow members of a recent expedition to St. Catherine's, had solved the century-old "whodunit of the academic world," whether Tischendorf stole the codex (which it is said he found in 1844!) or honestly bought it from the monks. The verdict: he was a thief! How did Forsyth and his colleagues come to this startling, and as they claim, definitive conclusion? They said they found new evidence. It so happened that they came across a letter written in Greek by Tischendorf himself in 1859, in which he promised to return the manuscript once his work was completed. A visiting Columbia University professor, Ihor Ševčenko, who was the palaeographer of the expedition, translated the letter. "Now the original and the English translation," reports the author of the article, "hang on the library wall without comment. None is needed."[4] None, indeed. Though the letter is not reproduced in the article, the evidence that Tischendorf confirmed that he had borrowed the codex—and borrowing implies return of the lent object, unless other provisions are later made—is not the least novel. It is precisely true to the facts as Tischendorf himself stated them. In 1859, the year of Tischendorf's discovery of the Sinaiticus, the codex was sent on loan to Cairo so that it could be copied. And the German theologian signed the pledge in good faith, whatever may have been his hopes for the eventual presentation of the codex to the Czar. As long as the donation was not made official, the manuscript remained on loan. Had the donation not been effected, the manuscript would undoubtedly have been returned. There is, of course, no legal or logical necessity for a borrowed object not to be transferred to new ownership eventually.

Why all this acrimony on the part of the Sinaites? To them

---

[2] R. Mercer Wilson, in his preface to the eighth edition of Tischendorf's *Codex Sinaiticus*, p. 8.

[3] See, for example, Louis Golding: *In the Steps of Moses the Lawgiver* (London: Rich and Cowan; n.d.), pp. 241–2.

[4] George H. Forsyth: "Island of Faith in the Sinai Wilderness," *National Geographic Magazine*, Vol. CXXV, No. 1 (January 1964), p. 91.

the Codex Sinaiticus has become a symbol of wounded pride—
a Sinaitic Alamo or Alsace-Lorraine. If the monks had only felt
so strongly about their codex in earlier times, instead of letting
it go to ruin and leaving it to an outsider to save its fragmented
remains! Quite understandably, they came to have second
thoughts, once they realized the uniqueness of the treasure they
had abandoned. And rather than blame themselves, they made
the dead Tischendorf their target. However, any declaration of the
monks of St. Catherine's that they had always known the value
of their codex (despite the evidence that as late as 1857 they were
unaware that they possessed a complete New Testament), and
had cherished it accordingly, does not require Tischendorf's word
to be utterly demolished. Conclusive proof to the contrary is
provided by the manuscript itself and the scattered bits which have
come to light from time to time in book bindings. The Russian
Archimandrite Uspenski found some, and so did others after
Tischendorf, for instance Heinrich Brugsch, the Egyptologist.

Byzantine variations of Christian monogram

Neither is Tischendorf's account invalidated by the observation that parchment is highly unsuitable for burning, as has been
insinuated. It goes without saying that the monks were not motivated by a need for combustible material when they threw the
manuscript pages into a basket for disposal by fire. Their purpose
was simply to get rid of them as waste, no matter how little heat
they might have generated. The decay of monastic libraries all
over the Near East and Greece serves to confirm the sad story.
One has only to read Robert Curzon to gain an idea of the way manuscripts were destroyed in the monasteries of the Levant. Entire
collections were ruined by exposure to rain. Others were depleted
by the sale of manuscripts to the Turks for the manufacture of
cartridges. Major Macdonald, an Englishman who had visited
St. Catherine's in Tischendorf's time, independently commented
on the monks' propensity for burning unwanted and torn manuscripts.[5]

---

[5] Samuel Prideaux Tregelles: *An Introduction to the Critical Study and
Knowledge of the Holy Scripture*, revised edition (London: Greenman,
Brown; 1856), Vol. 4, p. 775, quoted in Tischendorf: *Aus dem Heiligen
Lande*, p. 80. See also *Die Sinaibibel*, p. 22.

As with the Elgin Marbles, which were taken to England from the Athenian Parthenon, the debate on the rightful ownership of the codex has flared up again and again. It might indeed defy clear-cut settlement, since it lacks legal precedent and cannot be decided on the basis of an international statute. Is it wrong under any circumstances to remove works of art or documents from their original location? Who is to decide the local or national ownership of ancient objects that had been spirited away under the neglectful acquiescence or with the open connivance of the "natives"? Should all the obelisks, the Nefertitis and the Venuses, and all papyri be restored to their countries of origin, which once were quite insensitive to their worth? Are museums to be dissolved?

With the Codex Sinaiticus one cannot even be sure, in this light, of the proprietary rights of St. Catherine's because it was most likely acquired from an outside source (Caesarea, Alexandria?) in the first place. On the other hand, the manuscript was officially made over by the then owners to the Czar for a substantial sum, and to the satisfaction of the monks. As to Tischendorf's part in the transaction, no shred of evidence betrays any impropriety. His motives were the highest. Indeed, it must be credited to him alone that what was left of the precious manuscript was not thrown into the flames like the rest. In addition to the physical rescue, the German scholar contributed his learning and labor to make the codex available for Biblical studies. It has proved to be invaluable for the restoration of the apostolic text.

·XV·

TWO LADY SCHOLARS

IN THE LEVANT

Great was the consternation expressed by our friends at the idea of ladies venturing on so lengthened a pilgrimage alone. "Do you think they will ever come back? They are going amongst Mohammedans and barbarians," said some, who knew of our intention. But for what reason?

AGNES S. LEWIS, *Eastern Pilgrims*[1]

THE ENGLISH BOOK TRADE had never seen anything like the fanfare which greeted the publication of the Revised New Testament, a new English translation prepared under the auspices of top scholars. Both the Oxford and the Cambridge University Press, which had joined in the venture, were swamped. Before the publication date, one publisher alone had received orders in excess of one million copies. Bids went as high as £5,000 for an advance copy.[2] Precisely after the clock had struck twelve midnight, ushering in Tuesday May 17, 1881, distribution to stores began. Soon after, London's Paternoster Row was blocked by delivery carts and a milling crowd unable to repress its curiosity.[3] Meanwhile shipments of unbound sheets were being unloaded in American ports. Simultaneously, 800,000 volumes were coming off the presses in New York and Philadelphia, and two Chicago

---

[1] Agnes Smith Lewis: *Eastern Pilgrims* (London: Hurst & Blackett; 1870), p. 1.
[2] Kenyon: *The Story of the Bible*, p. 87.
[3] *The Times* (London), May 21, 1881.

newspapers reprinted the entire text, part of which had been telegraphed from England.

The Revised New Testament (it was followed three years later by the Revised Old Testament) was the crowning achievement of a great epoch in Biblical studies. It had received its main inspiration from Tischendorf's discoveries. Thanks to him, scholars were confident that a restoration of the ancient sacred texts of the Scriptures was at last becoming a possibility. Tischendorf's labors toward this end seemed to have reached fulfillment with his own edition of the Greek New Testament (based in part on the Sinaiticus he had recovered), and even more so with the celebrated 1881 edition of the New Testament in Greek by two English theologians, Bishop Brooke Foss Westcott and Professor F. J. A. Hort. Westcott and Hort had also played a major part in the Revised Version now being issued, which incorporated the results of nineteenth-century criticism and the manuscript finds that had been made to date.

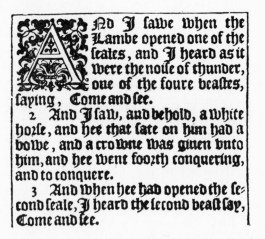

From the King James or Authorized Version of 1611. Revelation 6:1–3

Had the quest for the "best" Bible, the authentic New Testament, been brought to a conclusion? Many authorities, believing that ancient textual material had probably been exhausted, maintained that this was so: only a few minor philological points would have to be settled in the future. However, the Revised Version at once provoked violent controversy. There were some who insisted that the best Bible for all time was the King James, or Authorized, Version, while others, on the contrary, claimed that insufficient and unsatisfactory use had been made of the available critical apparatus. Similar arguments were raised in Germany and in every country where new translations of the Bible had been published. Yet only a few people had any inkling that textual criticism stood on the threshold of a new age. As was the case with the pronouncements made at about the same time to the effect that man's knowledge of physics and mathematics was virtually complete, revolutionary discoveries were soon to upset all such complacent estimates.

The appearance of the Revised Version was followed by more than half a century of spectacular manuscript finds. In due time these discoveries were incorporated in a number of new translations, several editions of the Greek New Testament, and at last, in 1961, *The New English Bible–New Testament*—which one day will undoubtedly have to be replaced in its turn.

The first significant addition to Biblical manuscripts since Tischendorf's discoveries—it also took place at Sinai—was the result of the efforts of two energetic, widely traveled ladies from Cambridge, England, the twin sisters Mrs. Agnes Smith Lewis and Mrs. Margaret Dunlop Gibson. They are numbered among the other admirable British ladies, such as Mary W. Montagu, Hester Stanhope, Gertrude Bell, Freya Stark, and Kathleen Kenyon, who have contributed so valiantly to our understanding of the Near East.

The daughters of a Scottish solicitor, John Smith of Irvine, Ayrshire, they lost their mother a fortnight after their birth. They had similar interests and talents, but the older of the two, Mrs. Lewis, was undoubtedly the senior member in their joint scholarly exploits. Both were married to men of learning, and both lost their husbands after only a few years of marriage. They had received the best private education and could hold their own with any university-trained Orientalist of the day. It is to the credit of the all-male academic world of those Victorian-Edwardian times that the two ladies were fully accepted as scholars of note. In 1915 the Royal Asiatic Society conferred on them its gold medal, and Mrs. Lewis was given honorary degrees by the universities of Halle, Heidelberg, Dublin, and St. Andrews.

In Cambridge, where Mrs. Lewis's husband, Samuel Savage Lewis, had been librarian of Corpus Christi College and an antiquarian of note, the sisters had occasion to meet with outstanding residents and visiting scholars. On their innumerable travels to Greece, Cyprus, Egypt, Syria, and the Holy Land, they crossed the paths of most of the contemporary archaeologists, theologians, and other students of the ancient Orient. They were equally well known to antique dealers in Cairo and to Greek abbots and archbishops from Athens to Aswan. Their proficiency in modern Greek proved to be a key to the Basilian convents of the Orthodox Church. In this respect, Mrs. Lewis and her sister had the advantage over Tischendorf, whose mishaps with the Alexandrine bishop will be remembered, and whose somewhat gruff, Teutonic manner may have been partly responsible for the vagaries and frustrations of his prolonged search. Feminine tact and forbearance helped the middle-aged ladies to get along with Greek, Bedouin, and Levantine alike. In the austere grounds of the desert monastery of St. Catherine's, they would give garden parties for visitors and their monastic hosts. Whereas the stern and self-righteous Tischendorf barely masked his scorn at the monks' reluctance to reveal their treasures and at their suspiciousness toward Europeans seeking lost manuscripts, the ladies were sympathetic and gracious.

Alluding to previous visitors to St. Catherine's, Mrs. Lewis wrote: "It is, perhaps, a habit of some learned men who visit Eastern monasteries to do so with a single eye to their own profit, and to show this perhaps a little too plainly, by giving the monks no information, either about their own work or about the value of their manuscripts; to treat them, in fact, as if they were the hopelessly stupid people which some travellers assume them to be. That this cause of trouble is not quite imaginary may be illustrated by the story which we heard in Cairo about the doings of a certain young Englishman, who went into a Coptic church and threatened the terrified priests with the vengeance of the British government because they declined to sell a beautifully worked silver censer to which he had taken a fancy.

"I cannot help thinking that one of our own countrymen, who had come into an inheritance of ancient coins and other objects which his education enabled him to appreciate only in a vague way, and who permitted a couple of experts to examine these, would behave in precisely the same fashion as the monks have done if he found that one of these gentlemen took copious notes for publication, treating the owner of the treasures merely as a person bound to provide him with coffee and stationery, and left without vouchsafing a word of explanation about anything he had examined. If he found the other full of human sympathy, and ready to communicate all that he wanted to know, so that without any great learning he might yet feel a genuine delight in his own property, it would only be natural for him to unlock all his secret cupboards and bring their contents under the eyes of his more generous visitor."[4]

With such an outlook, it is little wonder that library doors opened freely for the sisters, who showed no inclination whatsoever to purchase manuscripts or remove them to England unless these were offered on a free market by authorized dealers. In fact, when Cairo merchants showed them magnificent leaves from an ancient codex whose monastic provenance they suspected, they notified the police and the rightful owners. The monks, therefore, did not hide anything from them. On the contrary, they brought to the ladies' attention treasures whose existence had not been revealed to any previous visitors.

This was the dawn of a new age in manuscript hunting. The ladies desired above all to make these priceless documents available to modern research. They put little stock in the possession of the manuscripts and were only too happy to see them kept safely by their original proprietors. It is characteristic of this new approach that the two sisters contributed liberally to the upkeep and renovation of the Sinai libraries. They also devoted much time and energy to compiling catalogues.

To visit Mount Sinai had long been Mrs. Lewis's dream, kindled by the glowing reports of her future brother-in-law, who had traveled to Sinai and Petra when Mrs. Lewis was a young girl. A later voyage to Greece, and the ready hospitality of Greek ecclesiastics and monks, reawakened her desire to make the trip. Once she actually set out and had already reached the peninsula, but the illness of her companion forced her to turn back. And then she was married. Upon the death of her husband in 1891, she resolved to undertake the journey at long last, in the company of her sister.

As she herself confesses, she had given little thought to the library at St. Catherine's or to its manuscripts. But later in the same year, with the publication of the Syriac text of the *Apology of Aristides*, discovered by a young Cambridge Orientalist, J. Rendel Harris, at St. Catherine's in 1889, she became so intrigued that she decided to study Syriac, a form of Aramaic. She mastered it quickly because of her knowledge of its kindred languages, Arabic and Hebrew. Then, through a chance meeting of the sisters

---

[4] Lewis: *In the Shadow of Sinai* (Cambridge: Bowes & Macmillan; 1898), pp. 72–4.

with his wife, Dr. Harris heard of their impending visit to Sinai and of Mrs. Lewis's interest in Syriac studies. He called on them and encouraged the two ladies to search for Syriac texts "by vigorously expressing the opinion that something more might be got out of the early Estrangelo [the Syriac script] manuscripts in the convent library."[5] He also undertook to teach them the intricate art of photographing handwritten pages so that they would be able to take home prints of any significant finds.

Passage in Estrangelo (Estrangela) script from a manuscript of the Peshitta, the Syriac version of the Bible. Deuteronomy 19:2

Thus the pilgrimage to Sinai, conceived for its hallowed associations, gradually developed, to the sisters' amazement, into a voyage of scientific exploration. With it came a growing awareness that they were about to encounter something of value. "For several weeks," relates Mrs. Lewis, "I constantly dreamt of the dark closet so vividly described to me by Dr. Harris, in which lay two mysterious chests full of manuscripts, and to which access was only to be obtained by propitiating the revered recluses who owned them."[6] By the way, the secret manuscript recess, known to Rendel Harris, who however had not been able to investigate it, had never been disclosed to Tischendorf.

On the eve of the sisters' departure, when friends called to wish them farewell, some of the guests playfully speculated on the nature of their future discoveries. The brightest guess hinted at the *Diatessaron*, a long-lost, second-century compilation of the

---

[5] Margaret Dunlop Gibson: *How the Codex Was Found* (Cambridge: Bowes & Macmillan; 1893), p. 7.
[6] Lewis: *In the Shadow of Sinai*, p. iv.

Four Gospels. At the suggestion that, being women, they might be refused admission into a Greek monastery, the sisters showed no concern. On their previous trip through Greece, they had been freely received in various Greek monasteries and, as they put it with charming naïveté, "found intercourse with their inmates both pleasant and amusing."[7] After that trip, Mrs. Lewis had published a book, *Glimpses of Greek Life and Scenery* (1883), which was subsequently translated into Greek and earned its author the reputation of a philhellene. This distinction, together with their fluency in modern Greek and a warm recommendation from the vice-chancellor of Cambridge University, gained them ready access to St. Catherine's.

The prior and librarian of the Sinaite monastery were pleased to converse with the foreign ladies, especially as they spoke the Greek language. Asked what they wished to see at the convent, Mrs. Lewis—shocked by her own boldness—replied: "All your oldest Syriac manuscripts."[8] A few minutes later, her wish was granted. The ladies were taken to the dark, remote closet, and there saw boxes heaped with manuscripts. Of some six or eight codices carried to the daylight for further examination, Mrs. Lewis's eyes fastened on one of the least prepossessing of the lot. The incident is best told in her own words:

"It had a forbidding look, for it was very dirty, and its leaves were nearly all stuck together through their having remained unturned probably since the last Syrian monk had died, centuries ago, in the Convent. I had never before seen a palimpsest, but my father had often related to us wonderful stories of how the old monks, when vellum had become scarce and paper was not yet invented, scraped away the writing from the pages of their books and wrote something new on the top of it, and how, after the lapse of ages, the old ink was revived by the action of common air, and the old words peeped up again; and how the text of Plato had come to light in this curious way.

"I saw at once that this one contained two writings, both in the same ancient Estrangelo characters, which I had been studying; that the upper writing was the biographies of women saints, and bore its own date, which I read 1009 years after Alexander, A.D. 697; and that the under writing was the Gospels. The latter was written in two columns, one of which always projected on to the margin of the upper writing, so that many of its words

---

[7] Gibson: op. cit., p. 5.
[8] Lewis: *In the Shadow of Sinai*, p. vi.

could be easily read, and every such word distinctly belonged to the sacred narrative. I pointed this out to my sister, and, as if to make assurance doubly sure, I showed her also that at the top of almost every page stood the title 'Evangelium,' or 'of Mark,' or 'of Luke.' "[9]

The sisters spent the following days photographing the 358 pages of the palimpsest, some of which had to be separated by being held over a steaming kettle. Among the Arabic and Syriac manuscripts found by the sisters then, the most interesting was a Palestinian-Aramaic lectionary (a "lesson book" for public readings at church) written in the language spoken by Christ and the Apostles. It was the second of its kind to be discovered; the first and only one hitherto known to exist was in the Vatican. A third one was found at Sinai by Rendel Harris a year later.

The prize piece was undoubtedly the palimpsest, later to be variously known as Sinaitic Syriac, Syrus Sinaiticus, or Syriac Palimpsest. (Its colophon bore the subtitle: "The Gospel of the Separated Ones"—obviously to distinguish it from the *Diatessaron*, a then current "harmonized" version of the Gospels.) Mrs. Lewis seems to have realized its uniqueness at once, as she would not otherwise have insisted on photographing it so fully in the face of the dissuasions offered by her sister and the librarian, Galakteon. However, Mrs. Lewis was not yet as accomplished a Syriac scholar as she would later become, and she left the final verdict to her Cambridge friends, to whom she would show the films on her return.

In Cambridge in late spring—the end of the academic year— the two ladies met with a measure of skepticism and had difficulty in persuading learned Cantabrigians to examine the prints. A few scholars had their minds on vacation and were busy packing; others had already left. Later in July, the sisters used a ruse: they had Mr. and Mrs. F. C. Burkitt for lunch. Before the trip, Mr. Burkitt had instructed Mrs. Lewis in the reading of Estrangelo texts, and now she showed her guests the photographs she had taken. He became immediately absorbed and asked to take some dozen prints home for further study. Two days afterwards, the following letter was received from Mrs. Burkitt:

12, Harvey Road

My dear Mrs. Lewis,
Frank is in a state of highest excitement. He wrote down a

---

[9] Ibid., pp. vii-viii.

portion of the palimpsest last night, and has been in to Dr. Bensly with it, and they have discovered it is a copy of the Cureton Syriac. Do you know, only one copy exists! You can imagine Frank's glee! He has just been in to tell me, and has run back to Bensly's. I thought you would be interested and wrote at once.

I am yours affectionately,
A. Persis Burkitt[1]

Thus came to light an Old Syriac Gospel which had been only partly known from the Curetonian manuscript, found by Archdeacon Tattam at the monastery of Saint Maria Deipara in the Nitrian Desert in 1842, and taken to the British Museum, where it was identified by Dr. Cureton, for whom it was named. Cureton, by the way, believed that his manuscript represented the original text of the Gospels "as the Divine Author of our holy religion himself uttered in proclaiming the glad tidings of salvation."[2] This view never gained wide acceptance. But the same claim is sometimes made today for the Matthew of the Sinaitic Syriac.

Even as a translation—probably the oldest of any made from the Greek New Testament—the Old Syriac Gospels, surviving in just two incomplete copies, are of the greatest value. Further examination soon established that this version, though very likely taken from the same translation as the Curetonian, is definitely older and purer. Hence its superior authority.

The photographs made it clear that the Sinaitic contained passages that were missing from the Curetonian, as, for example, a great deal of St. Mark. This was particularly noticed by Robert L. Bensly, who, with Mr. Burkitt, had established the identity of the manuscript. Bensly was then the leading Cambridge expert in the field, and by coincidence was planning a new edition of the Curetonian text. Mrs. Gibson tells that the day he went over their photographs of the Sinaitic material, he became so excited that he forgot his dinner engagement for that evening. Largely at his urging, it was immediately decided that a full transcription of the earlier, or "underwriting," of the palimpsest should be made. Another journey to Sinai was in the offing. Professor Bensly, though already ailing, enthusiastically took the lead. (He was to die shortly after his return to England.) At Sinai he shared the work with his younger

---

[1] *Ibid.*, p. xi.
[2] William Cureton: *Remains of a Very Ancient Recension of the Four Gospels.* . . . (London: John Murray; 1858), p. xciii.

colleagues, Burkitt and Rendel Harris. Bensly and Burkitt were accompanied by their wives, and the two sisters naturally were of the party. It took forty days for the manuscript to be transcribed by the three men.

In 1894 the results of these labors were published by the Cambridge University Press as *The Four Gospels Transcribed from the Sinaitic Palimpsest,* by R. L. Bensly, J. R. Harris, and F. C. Burkitt, with an introduction by Agnes Smith Lewis. It contained about four fifths of the underwriting. The last portion, as yet undeciphered, prompted Mrs. Lewis to go on still another trip to Sinai, this time accompanied only by her sister. The additional material, together with a translation of the whole text into English, was published by Mrs. Lewis in 1896. She had now become a full-fledged Syriac scholar herself, and was responsible in 1910 for a complete edition of the Old Syriac Gospels, together with the variants of the Curetonian manuscript. Mrs. Gibson's increasing familiarity with the Syriac language was of inestimable assistance.

Meanwhile the literature on the Sinaitic Syriac proliferated; there were articles, lectures, monographs. Leading continental scholars, particularly in Germany—such as Wellhausen, Zahn, and Nestle—contributed. Authorities generally agreed on the age of the underwriting: late fourth or early fifth century. However, the age of this version of the Gospels is still disputed. It clearly preceded the fifth-century *Peshitta* (Syriac New Testament), but was it earlier or later than the mysterious *Diatessaron,* known to have been in use in Syria in the second half of the second century? On this point, too, there has been no agreement. Yet it would be invaluable to textual criticism to establish the age of this very early translation from the New Testament, which undisputedly preceded most of the Greek texts. It could then serve as a kind of checklist for the multiple versions and "families" of Bible manuscripts.

The Old Syriac Gospels have yielded much information on the wording and other peculiarities of the vanished Greek original on which they are based. In this respect they are hardly second to any of the other translations and are equaled by few of the Greek uncial and minuscule manuscripts, unless it be the remarkable Codex Arabicus palimpsest found at St. Catherine's in 1950 by an Arab member, Professor Aziz Suryal Atiya, of the American-sponsored Mount Sinai Expedition. This consists (a record!) of two Arabic, one Greek, and two Syriac layers—the oldest of the

Syriac layers being apparently another very ancient version of the Gospels in Syriac.[3]

The Old Syriac version owes its remarkable interest perhaps most of all to the fact that it is inevitably associated with Antioch, the cradle of Pauline Christianity, from which St. Paul set out on his great pilgrimage. One may safely assume that Antioch communities called for a translation of the evangelical writings at a very early date. If that was the case, the question arises whether such a translation was identical with the Sinaitic-Curetonian text, entirely different from them, or, as seems most likely, ancestral to them. Apart from all this, the Old Syriac Gospels may well be the prize among all known translations because they are in an Aramaic dialect closely related to the Galilean variety spoken by Christ. The fact that only two such texts survive, and of them the Sinaitic is the older and more complete, puts Mrs. Lewis's codex in the front rank of New Testament manuscript discoveries.

St. Catherine, fourth-century Alexandrian Christian martyr and patron saint of the Mt. Sinai monastery

It is beyond the compass of this book to expound the textual characteristics of the Sinaitic Syriac. However, it was the first

---

[3] Atiya: op. cit., p. xxvii.

new evidence that seriously challenged some of the distinctions made by Westcott and Hort between various "families" of New Testament texts, and their relative merits. The Sinaitic Syriac can no longer be classified among the so-called "Western" texts, previously considered the least creditable. Many of its readings (or versions) seem to place it back beyond some of the early Greek uncials. Either the concept of the "Western" family calls for revision or the whole division into fixed families, as accepted by Westcott and Hort and their predecessors, needs to be modified. Undoubtedly, the problem of early New Testament variants is of far greater complexity than it appeared to be in 1880.

In quite a few passages, the Sinaitic Syriac agrees with the "Neutral" Sinaiticus and Vaticanus rather than with the traditional "Western" variant. Thus, for example, it omits the word "first-born" in Matthew 1:25. Of still greater importance, the last twelve verses of St. Mark's Gospel are conspicuously absent; St. Luke follows immediately, on the same manuscript page. Rendel Harris pointed out in an influential article in 1894 that the Sinai palimpsest is peculiarly interesting for its lacunae ("a wealth of omissions is not too Hibernian a phrase").[4] The passages omitted are on the whole the very passages which critics had previously declared most likely to be spurious. Friedrich Blass, a German theologian, has proclaimed the Syriac palimpsest text, perhaps a bit too enthusiastically, as "almost a touchstone to determine what really belongs to each of the Four Evangelists."[5]

Like the Sinaiticus, Mrs. Lewis's codex did not escape insinuations of heresy. Most startling was a passage in Matthew 1:16 which contained the words: "Joseph, to whom was betrothed Mary the Virgin, begat Jesus, who is called the Christ." Mrs. Lewis, on her own confession, "was at first greatly shocked," and was tempted to regret "that I had unearthed such an heretical document."[6] There ensued a heated discussion in the *Academy*, a venerable scholarly journal, which was continued for several months. In the end most minds were put at ease, including Mrs. Lewis's, when it was pointed out that "begat" did not imply genetic descent, but simply "an official register of succession." Heretical interpretations of the passage, it was asserted, were in

---

[4] J. Rendel Harris: "The New Syriac Gospels," *Contemporary Review*, Vol. LXVI (1894), p. 655.

[5] Quoted in Lewis: *The Old Syriac Gospels or Evangelia Da-Mepharreshe. . . .* (London: Williams & Norgate; 1910), p. vi.

[6] Lewis: *In the Shadow of Sinai*, p. 102.

any event obviated by other readings of the palimpsest, foremost the following: "When Mary his mother was espoused to Joseph, when they had not come one near to the other, she was found with child of the Holy Ghost."

There was a happy aftermath to all these doubts. It came not from an omission in the text, or from a change of wording, but rather from an addition. When Mrs. Lewis took her third trip to Mount Sinai in 1895, in order to fill the gaps in the printed edition with so-far undeciphered passages, she discovered one unknown reading from which she derived a great deal of personal comfort. No matter how flimsy the brief entry may appear to others, for Mrs. Lewis, as a gentlewoman and a scholar, it meant not only the discovery of another New Saying [*logion*] of Jesus (this was the time of Grenfell and Hunt's sensational papyri finds), but a blessing bestowed on her sex. She puts it inimitably in her own words, in her account, *In the Shadow of Sinai:*

"The piece of my work on that occasion which has given me the greatest satisfaction consists in the decipherment of two words in John iv. 27. They were well worth all our visits to Sinai, for they illustrate an action of our Lord which seems to be recorded nowhere else, and which has some degree of inherent probability from what we know of His character. The passage is, 'His disciples came and wondered that with the woman He was *standing and talking*' . . .

"Why was our Lord standing? He had been sitting on the well when the disciples left Him, and we know that He was tired. However, sitting is the proper attitude for an Eastern when engaged in teaching. And an ordinary Oriental would never rise of his own natural free will out of politeness to a woman. It may be that He rose in His enthusiasm for the great truths He was uttering, but I like to think that His great heart, which embraced the lowest of humanity, lifted Him above the restrictions of His race and age, and made Him show that courtesy to our sex, even in the person of a degraded specimen, which is considered amongst all really progressive peoples to be a mark of true and noble manhood. To shed even a faint light upon that wondrous story of His tabernacling amongst us, is an inestimable privilege, and worth all the trouble we can possibly take."[7]

In this post-Freudian age, there is no longer any need to

---

[7] Ibid., pp. 96–8.

refute Madame de Staël's words, *les âmes n'ont pas de sexe*. Certainly, in the case of the Scottish twin sisters who have played
such a prominent role in latter-day discoveries of manuscripts,
the feminine element pervaded all their activities and was of inestimable value in their success. We shall meet the lady scholars
again.

·XVI·

THE ELUSIVE

DIATESSARON

His leaf also shall not wither
PSALM 1

N OW AND THEN a scrap of manuscript will win acclaim regardless of its brevity. In a previous chapter we mentioned the *Logia,* a tattered page torn from a papyrus booklet which Grenfell and Hunt excavated at Oxyrhynchus and which, immediately upon its discovery, electrified all students of early Christianity. A somewhat similar role was played by the Nash Papyrus, for long by far the oldest Hebrew manuscript of an Old Testament text. With these two, one might rank another fragment also associated with the Bible but written on parchment, not on papyrus. It represented a passage from the so-called *Diatessaron,* an ancient "harmony" or concordance assembled from the four canonical Gospels.

Before the *Diatessaron* made its reappearance, debate had raged over it for nearly a century. What was its form? What was its original language? Could it serve as evidence for the age and authenticity of the Gospels? One thing was certain: if a *Diatessaron* composed around the middle of the second century A.D. existed, then all the four Gospels had been completed at least several decades before it. To discover such an early text now became a vital task of Biblical scholarship. Until a tiny fragment of the *Diatessaron* was found in 1933, this search was rife with quixotic touches. It was also connected in its most successful phase with one of the outstanding archaeological ventures of the 1920's. Its track leads us once more into an area outside Egypt.

In the aftermath of World War I, when the Allies became embroiled in "police actions" against Arabs in the northern reaches of Mesopotamia and eastern Syria, British troops were stationed in a desolate spot along the upper Euphrates above a cluster of native hovels called Salahiyeh (Salihiyah). Captain Murphy, the commanding officer of the Sepoys, had chosen a ruined site on an easily defensible bluff which was cut by wadis and the river on three sides. Like so many other places in the Fertile Crescent, it showed obvious signs of former occupation. Its sand-covered ruins were surrounded by impressive walls which, together with its natural location, marked the site as a fortress. But its ancient name was unknown and it seemed so far to have escaped the archaeologist's spade.

Murphy had his men dig trenches and campsites inside the walled city. It was then that he came across a large hall near the northwest wall. Strong gusts of desert wind had partly freed it from the deep sand which once had buried it. Gazing at the walls, he saw brightly colored frescoes of a strange array of Oriental gods and worshippers. He could not have been more surprised than the chicle gatherers in Yucatán who came across the painted glories of Maya sanctuaries deep in the tropical jungle. Captain Murphy dutifully reported his discovery and sent sketches to the British authorities in Baghdad. Just at this time, the American Egyptologist James H. Breasted, who was visiting the Near East on a scientific mission for the Oriental Institute of the University of Chicago, happened to pass through Baghdad. Gertrude Bell, then in charge of archaeological operations in Mesopotamia, persuaded him to examine the paintings on behalf of the British High Commissioner. It was thus that the ancient fortress city came to be revealed to the modern world. Breasted presently established its identity from an inscription on one of the large murals. Its name was Dura-Europos, today a magic name in the history of Near Eastern art and culture.

Dura was never more than a second-rate frontier outpost, and lacks the glamour of the more ancient Assyrian, Babylonian, and Sumerian sites of the Tigris–Euphrates Valley—strangely, popular literature on archaeology has taken little notice of Dura—yet it turned out to be in many ways as remarkable. And this was not due to any intrinsic importance it may have had as a city in antiquity, but to its surprising state of preservation and its intricate, little explored cultural manifestations. It contained a faithful and so far unmatched record of the multiple influences at work in the Near East during the six hundred years after the conquest by Alexander. When it flourished, almost fifteen hundred years had passed since the fall of Ugarit in the twelfth or thirteenth century B.C. But the account it gave of its own cosmopolitan times was as faithful as the record left by the older Syrian city. Here too East and West had met. Dura amply deserved, as we shall see, the somewhat hackneyed epithet "Pompeii of the Syrian Desert."

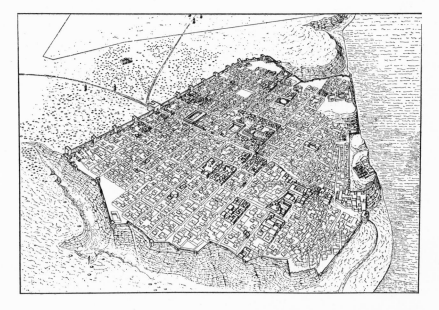

Isometric reconstruction of Dura-Europos. The Hellenistic city was built on a bluff above the Euphrates River, its western wall exposed to the Syrian desert.

It was founded about 300 B.C. at the site of an earlier settlement (hence its prefix Dura, Assyro-Babylonian for "burgh") by the Macedonian official Nicanor on behalf of Seleucos Nicator, and it was called Europos after Seleucos' native town in Macedonia, which was probably also the birthplace of some of its first colonists. The city may have been conceived as part of a chain of military strongholds along a strategic road of the Seleucid Empire. As such, it occupied an excellent position, roughly halfway between the Seleucid capitals of Antioch in Syria and Seleucia-on-Tigris (near modern Baghdad), at a point where the Euphrates could be easily crossed. Under the Seleucids, it was principally a colony of Macedonian soldiers. After its conquest during the latter part of the second century B.C., or early in the first century B.C., by the Parthians, Iranian kinsmen of the Persians and Medes, Dura grew as a caravan station, frontier fort, and garrison town. Thenceforth it became a prosperous emporium linked with the caravan trade to and from Palmyra.

During the Parthian period, the Iranian and particularly the Semitic peoples there intermarried with the established Greco-Macedonian families. Though Greek continued to be spoken and the Greek culture persisted, two of its principal ethnic components—Semitic and Iranian—aligned it with the East. In the first century A.D., it was a flourishing city, and most of its finest and largest temples date from that period. When Dura was taken by the Romans in A.D. 164–65 (it had been briefly held by Trajan around 117), its great days were over. Occupied by Roman colonial troops, it served now as a base for operations against the Parthians. During a soldiers' revolt in A.D. 244, the Roman Emperor Gordian III was killed there. Soon after, the Sassanian King Shapur, leading a great Persian offensive, took the city in his advance against Antioch. Despite Roman counterattacks and Aurelian's victory over Zenobia, Queen of Palmyra, Dura was evidently never reoccupied by Roman soldiers. Few additional buildings were put up in the Roman period, except for sanctuaries to new cults that mushroomed here as everywhere else in the soldier towns of the Roman frontier. "Dura was dying before the Sassanids killed it."[1] It was apparently abandoned some time after the middle of the third century A.D., since none of the thousands of coins excavated are of a later date than A.D. 256. All this was to be revealed by successive archaeological campaigns between the two world wars.

Breasted's mission was of short duration. In fact, on his way to Salahiyeh he was told that the British were about to evacuate the place. Before its abandonment to the Arabs, he had just one day to investigate the ruins and frescoes. "It was archaeology's biggest single day's work,"[2] said Jotham Johnson, the American archaeologist who took part in the excavations directed by Rostovtzeff at Dura a decade later.

Before the British withdrawal, troops under a sergeant were put at Breasted's disposal. It was not the first time in the annals

---

[1] Mikhail Ivanovich Rostovtzeff: *Dura-Europos and Its Art* (Oxford: Clarendon Press; 1938), p. 31.

[2] Jotham Johnson: "Written with the Archaeologist's Spade," *Scientific American*, Vol. CLVI, No. 6 (June 1937), p. 374.

of archaeological fieldwork that a dig profited from military support. With this help, Breasted cleared and photographed several of the large murals, making notes on everything he found. His brief stay was sufficient to convince him of Dura's significance and resulted in a pioneering study, *Oriental Forerunner of Byzantine Painting,* which "created a polite archaeological furore."[3]

Prophet of the cult of Mithras, which once rivaled Christianity. Sketch after a mural from a Dura sanctuary. Dura's many temples with their religious paintings reflect the profusion of religions that arose and mingled in the Near East during the Hellenistic and Roman eras.

On his return from the troubled Middle East, Breasted lectured on his discovery to the French Académie des Inscriptions et Belles-Lettres in Paris. Just then the site had been allotted for inclusion in the French mandate of Syria, and the French decided to launch a major archaeological campaign in Dura. The expedition was headed by the Belgian Franz Cumont, a member of the Académie renowned for his studies of Manichaeanism and other ancient mystery cults. Cumont was assisted in his work by a detachment of the French Foreign Legion. In two seasons he made remarkable finds, among which texts on parchment were perhaps the most sensational. Though their decipherment supplied some interesting data—mainly business records in Aramaic, Syriac, Pahlavi (Pehlevi), and Greek—the documents caused a stir in the scientific world for two reasons. First, it had become a virtual dogma that, except for Herculaneum, which had been sealed off, ancient texts on perishable materials could not have survived anywhere outside Egypt. Isolated evidence such as the vellum pieces discovered at Avroman in Kurdistan in 1909 were usually ignored. Second, since one of the vellum scraps from Dura was identified as having been written at the very beginning of

---

[3] Johnson: op. cit., p. 374.

the second century B.C., the traditional account that the king of Pergamum, Eumenes II, was the first to have introduced this material, to counter an Egyptian embargo on papyrus, was virtually invalidated on chronological and geographical grounds. For some time, however, few of the finds excited as much attention as the paintings in the temple of the Palmyra gods that had led to Dura's chance discovery. Unfortunately, soon after Breasted's departure the paintings had provoked the ire of roaming Arabs, who, in obedience to the Koran, ruthlessly disfigured or destroyed the faces.

The economic setbacks of the nineteen-twenties made it impossible for either the French Académie or the Syrian government to subsidize any further campaigns, and Cumont had to stop work after two seasons. When Rostovtzeff learned of this, he sought and obtained the consent of his French colleagues to raise American funds to reopen the Dura excavations. From then on, for ten consecutive annual expeditions (1928–37), Yale University, in friendly collaboration with the French Academy of Inscriptions, became the chief sponsor. Over-all supervision was now in the hands of Rostovtzeff, who was ably assisted by a number of French and American archaeologists, notably Professor Clark Hopkins of Yale.

What had already been intimated by Cumont's earlier excavations was now fully borne out by the large-scale Franco-American efforts. A wealth of artifacts bore in sumptuous detail the marks of Macedonian, Greek, Arab, Parthian, Palmyrene, Roman, and even Indian and Anatolian cultures. Dura provided a composite of the forces that had reshaped the Near East after the coming of Alexander and prepared the rise of a new world— that of resurgent Persia of the Sassanids, of Byzantium, and Islam, who in turn contributed to the European Middle Ages and Renaissance. It required an archaeologist of Rostovtzeff's historical grasp to trace the dimensions and differentiations of these various currents in the art, architecture, and religion of Dura. Here, as Rostovtzeff pointed out, scholars could understand for the first time the role of Mesopotamia as the meeting place of three great civilizations about which archaeology had previously been almost entirely silent: the Greco-Iranian of the Parthians, the Greco-Semitic of Babylonia, Syria, and Phoenicia, and the Greco-Anatolian of Asia Minor.[4]

---

[4] Rostovtzeff: op. cit., p. 9.

Pompeii had attracted Rostovtzeff early in his career (he wrote an undergraduate paper on it), and this interest never flagged throughout his long life. As in the case of Pompeii, Dura's archaeological importance overshadows her political or cultural role in antiquity. In both cities the ruins and the various objects found in them are excellently preserved. "The city, so far excavated, lies almost intact before us."[5] And, in addition, Dura was a veritable museum of wall paintings from which scholars could trace the evolution of ancient mural art and its development in the Near East. Also, as at Pompeii (and Herculaneum), the record is enhanced by numerous inscriptions, and by the ubiquitous graffiti and dipinti (rude inscriptions and sketches scratched on walls) which throw so much light on the life and attitudes of the inhabitants.

ϹΥΧΑΡΙϹΤѠ ΤΗ
ΤΥΧΗ ΔΟΥΡΑ

"I pray to (or I thank) the Fortune of Dura." The first inscription discovered by the Yale Expedition on the main gate at Dura was a good omen for the team of American and French scholars under the leadership of Mikhail I. Rostovtzeff.

After almost ten years of excavation, the American scholars were puzzled by the complete absence of Christian and Judaic places of worship in Dura. This seemed the more surprising because of the popularity of all kinds of religious cults during the Roman era; the spread of Christianity at this time; the proselytizing vigor of the Jews in Syria–Mesopotamia and the tolerance with which they were received. Several intricate explanations were advanced. But then the progress of excavation showed how misleading arguments *ex silentio* can be. In the 1931–32 campaign there was found a third-century Christian meeting place with a baptistry, now removed to the Yale Gallery of Fine Arts. Considered to be the oldest church in existence, it shows clearly its development from an informal sanctuary in the residence of a rich private citizen.

In the next season, even more startling discoveries were made.

---

[5] Ibid., p. 3.

One was a synagogue, rebuilt in the year A.D. 245 with contributions from the wealthy members of the Jewish community. This find, perhaps more than any of the earlier ones, brought Dura fame. The site was adorned with a series of excellent mural paintings illustrating incidents from the Old Testament and the Talmud. And except for mosaics in Palestine and certain Jewish decorations in catacombs in Rome, and in Alexandria, these were virtually the only major examples of Jewish art and antiquities from that period. Moreover, they belied the well-known injunction in Exodus 20:4 against the making of images. Obviously, in Hellenistic and Roman days, a more liberal interpretation was given to this iconoclastic position. However, it was not until the third century A.D. that such paintings were commissioned.

At least as remarkable as the synagogue was another find made in 1933. We have already mentioned that ancient written documents were preserved in Dura, as in Egypt and Herculaneum. Cumont turned up a number of texts, breaking Egypt's near-monopoly of these most precious of objects. He found bills of sale, contracts, deeds, and other miscellaneous records. A curious leather shield (a scutum) described in Greek the peregrinations of its owner. Rostovtzeff had high hopes that more items, perhaps of a literary nature, might be unearthed. And he was not disappointed. He and his associates were struck by the fact that most documents found so far came from one sector near the city's western wall. Before long, they brought up the first papyri—in an area that had already been explored by Jotham Johnson—and

"Anointing of David by Samuel." Ink drawing after a mural in the Dura Synagogue

Clark Hopkins, field director for that year, luckily dug right into what seemed to be the record office of the Roman prefect.

And then, in March 1933, Hopkins, excavating at the rampart north of the Palmyra Gate, not far from the Jewish synagogue and the Christian chapel, came up with a fragment from a Greek parchment roll, which "alone guaranteed Dura archaeological immortality."[6] It appeared to be a passage from a third-century New Testament written in noncursive characters, "not without some grace and vigour,"[7] and containing only fifteen lines, of which fourteen could be easily read. On the basis of its state and location, the Yale team could reconstruct the end of its career: "It had been crushed in the hand and thrown away as a piece of waste paper. But it fell, or was dumped afterwards, into a great embankment of earth, ashes and rubbish constructed along the inner face of the western city wall by the Roman garrison, in preparation for a siege. Here it was protected from the elements by the material heaped over and around it, by the layer of mud bricks with which the embankment was covered, and by the desert sand which eventually covered the whole city."[8] In expectation of a Persian onslaught, the Roman soldiery threw up a great embankment to strengthen the western wall on the one side of the city which lacked a natural defense. The embankment was built in or after A.D. 254, but not later than 257. We have thus a convenient date, or what logicians would call a *terminus ad quem*—that is, a limit beyond which the document could not have been written. Like the Themistoclean walls of Athens, a hastily built fortification making indiscriminate use of all kinds of handy materials proved a boon to archaeologists.

As to the origin of the writing itself, the ingenious Yale men ventured a sound guess; it might have come from the Christian sanctuary they had excavated the previous year. "It is inherently probable," wrote Carl H. Kraeling, who established the identity of the parchment, "that the roll to which our fragment belonged was used in the worship of the sanctuary. The probability is supported by the fact that the area in which the fragment was discovered is but two city blocks north of the chapel, which was demolished to permit the construction of the embankment in which the parchment came to light. The date of the chapel [shown

---

[6] Johnson: op. cit., p. 374.
[7] Carl H. Kraeling: *A Greek Fragment of Tatian's Diatessaron from Dura* (London: Christophers; 1935), p. 4.
[8] Ibid., p. 3.

to be between A.D. 225 and 235] may therefore be taken as the approximate date of our fragment, which possibly came from a roll ordered by the founder of the church. If so, it was a copy made about the year 222, and though there is, of course, no evidence as to the place where the archetype was, it is hard to prevent the imagination from turning to Edessa [the leading Christian center of the time in northern Mesopotamia]."[9]

At first sight, the Dura parchment was recognized as referring to the end of chapter 15, verses 40–43, of St. Mark, incorporating the well-known passage on Joseph of Arimathea's petition for Jesus' body. Further examination showed that the brief passage included material from all Four Gospels. That is to say, it was what New Testament scholars call a "harmony"—an integrated story pieced together from the canonical accounts of Christ's life. Kraeling's identification of the fragment with Tatian's *Diatessaron* was, despite such surprising and unexpected evidence, com-

Reconstruction of side gate of Hellenistic Dura-Europos

[9] Ibid., pp. 6–7.

pletely accepted by scholars everywhere. Though the parchment was pathetically brief, its appearance was an epochal event in New Testament studies—entirely out of proportion to its minute size and shoddy appearance.

But this is rather the last chapter (unless more are to be added in the future), and not the full story of a strange and elusive work of Christian literature that looms so large in all inquiries into the early history of the New Testament.

The *Diatessaron* was a composite Life of Christ compiled by Tatian, a second-century apologist of Assyrian origin and a long-time resident of Rome, where he was a disciple of Justin Martyr. Because of charges of heresy, he had to leave Rome and returned to his native East, where he later drifted into Gnosticism. He probably composed the *Diatessaron* in Greek during his stay in Rome and then translated it into Syriac himself. In any case, the *Diatessaron*, produced around A.D. 150–170, came to be adopted as the more or less official form of the Gospels by the Syriac-speaking churches, and most likely, it crowded out any rival texts. Then, in the fifth century, it was condemned by the Church— and rigorously hunted down and destroyed—and was replaced by the *Peshitta*. The *Diatessaron's* wide acceptance is evident from the exegetic literature of Syrian theologians, who were more likely to base their comments on Tatian's version rather than on the four "separate" Gospels.

The book's name is Greek and means "By Four," or "Through Four," a musical term reflecting its nature as a harmony—that is, a running story made up from the four Evangelists' memorabilia by a kind of "scissors and paste method."[1] Eusebius, in the fourth century, called it "a sort of patchwork combination of the Gospels."[2]

That the first three Gospels—Matthew, Mark, and Luke— are synoptic—revealing considerable agreement and overlapping in subject matter, arrangement, and wording—is well known. Such close correspondence and quasi-duplication (or triplication) among the Gospels is presumably due to the fact that there exists a certain genetic dependence among the three—St. Mark is held to be the oldest—and that in the early Church these evangelical

---

[1] H. G. G. Herklots: *How Our Bible Came to Us* (New York: Oxford University Press–Galaxy Books; 1957), p. 78.

[2] Kenyon: *Our Bible and the Ancient Manuscripts*, fifth revised edition (London: Eyre & Spottiswoode; 1958), p. 222.

writings, as well as others later lost or declared noncanonical, circulated separately. In addition, successive copies of each of the Gospels, including St. Mark, borrowed from each other, thus tending to become to some degree "harmonized." All this points to the likelihood that early generations of Christians had little concern for the verbatim integrity of Gospel texts. And Jerome, in a later age, could complain that there were as many texts as there were copies. Also, there were separate Gospels before there was a New Testament. Christians then knew only one Bible— the Old Testament. Poor communities, as a rule, were able to afford only one of the Gospels and maybe a few letters of Paul. But when Christian centers grew and became affluent enough to acquire several of the holy writings, there gradually developed the tendency to combine them in one volume. The *Diatessaron* may, in this light, be looked upon as a conscious effort to implement the forces at work, by, first, more drastically harmonizing the Four Gospels and, second, combining them in one book. A parallel stage, but probably for some time a less influential one, is marked by the two Syriac Gospels, the Curetonian and the Sinaitic, both bearing the description: "Distinct Gospels," to emphasize their difference from the synthetic *Diatessaron*.

The discovery of these two, and particularly of the Sinaitic Palimpsest, had raised the question of their relationship to the *Diatessaron,* long the most popular version of the Gospels in Syria. More generally, students of the New Testament have long considered the *Diatessaron* vital evidence because it was contemporaneous with the evangelical passages quoted by such second-century Church fathers as Justin Martyr and Irenaeus. A fusion of evangelical writings is, needless to say, in itself a proof that these writings were available as sources. In short, it establishes their priority of composition. This consideration is of utmost importance in the case of St. John, whose apostolic origin nineteenth-century scholars of the skeptical wing have frequently tried to dispute. In addition, a harmony based exclusively on the Four Gospels substantiates the thesis that by A.D. 170 these four were already considered the only canonical ones and an integral unit.

For all these reasons, the long-lost *Diatessaron* became one of the most coveted documents in Biblical studies, a kind of Prester John of Christian manuscripts. As late as 1925, Alexander Souter, a master of New Testament studies in England, wrote: "It may safely be said that the original Greek of Tatian's book is a more desirable possession for the textual critic of the Gospels than almost anything else yet undiscovered: the Syriac in its original form would be only less valuable."[3]

Nevertheless, attempts were made from time to time to discredit the missing *Diatessaron* or reduce it to a mere phantom. Indeed, it was hinted by some that the determined search for it was inevitably condemned to failure. The traditionalists, on the other hand, continued to invoke the evidence of Tatian's Harmony as proof that the Four Gospels were available at a date earlier than conceded by the Tübingen School and were already then "the recognized and authoritative records of the life of Christ."[4] Against this, the radicals, under the spell of Christian Baur, the head of the Tübingen School of Criticism attacked by Tischendorf, thought they had a devastating argument. Thus, the anonymous author of the once highly popular tract, *Supernatural Religion,* went so far as to declare categorically in 1876 that there had never been a Gospel harmony by Tatian. He stressed the ambiguity of Eusebius' testimony and declared that any allusion to the *Diatessaron* in ancient Christian literature was really a reference to the Gospel according to Hebrews, itself derived from Peter's Gospel. This, however, did not in any way end the search for the *Diatessaron,* or the debate. Neither party managed to score a conclusive point. And while the controversy dragged on, another chapter was being added to the mystery of this work, which, as Frederic G. Kenyon (on whom the present account leans heavily) has said, "is one of the romances of textual history."[5]

Much of the mystery depends on the paradoxical fact that, unknown to practically everyone, Tatian's Harmony had in a sense never been lost. This is a curious phenomenon that reappears throughout the history of ideas. There comes to mind the "lost" *Apology of Aristides,* discovered in a Syriac version by J. Rendel Harris in 1889 at St. Catherine's, which, upon publication, was recognized by Armitage Robinson as having been available all the time in the form of an unidentified insert in the medieval romance of *Barlaam and Josaphat.*

In 1836, the fathers of an Armenian monastery located in Venice had published in their language a commentary with extensive quotations from the *Diatessaron* by St. Ephraem, a fourth-century Syrian, some of whose work had appeared on the pal-

---

[3] Herklots: op. cit., p. 78.   [4] Kenyon: *Our Bible. . .* , p. 222.
[5] Ibid., p. 221.

impsest deciphered by Tischendorf in Paris. If any proof of the existence of the missing work was needed, here it was. But nineteenth-century theologians had apparently paid no attention to Armenian books, and the Armenians were seemingly oblivious of the whole controversy. What followed amounts to an even more puzzling breakdown in communication. Under the aegis of the Armenians, a version of St. Ephraem's work was issued in 1875, edited by an Austrian scholar. This, too, went unnoticed until an American, Ezra Abbot, turned the attention of his Western colleagues to it in 1880.

Only then did the news spread—and a great amount of disconnected evidence suddenly fell into place. Discovery brought about discovery, in quick succession. By 1888, two eleventh-century Arabic translations had been made available. One had been resting peacefully all the time in the Vatican library and had even been listed in a catalogue. When this translation was shown to a Coptic dignitary visiting Rome, he recalled having seen another Arabic manuscript of it in Egypt. In addition, it was realized that Bishop Victor of Capua, in the sixth century, had reported finding a Gospel harmony in Latin which he identified with Tatian's compilation mentioned by Eusebius. A copy of his own edition, based on the Vulgate, is preserved to this day at the German monastery at Fulda. In due time, English, German, Dutch, and French harmonies—and, as late as 1951, even a Persian harmony—said to be traceable to Tatian were located. (This line of research came to a head in 1958 with the announcement that two thirds of the Syriac original of St. Ephraem's commentary to Tatian's *Diatessaron* had been found. It had been acquired, through commercial channels, by one of the age's most prominent collectors, Sir Chester Beatty.[6])

These finds removed once and for all any doubts concerning Tatian's composition of a harmony, and its popularity in antiquity, but an original version of the work eluded the scholars. The Arabic version, and others, could hardly serve as substitutes since their texts had been accommodated to later "official" translations of the New Testament, the *Peshitta* and the *Vulgate*. Most of the burning textual problems raised in connection with the Syriac Gospels remained unsolved.

The breakthrough came, as we have seen, with the Dura

---

[6] Bruce M. Metzger: "Recent Discoveries and Investigations of New Testament Manuscripts," *Journal of Biblical Literature*, Vol. LXXVIII (March 1959), p. 16.

fragment. Admittedly, the evidence was pitifully slight. Yet it offered valuable insights—and hope for the future. First of all, it testified to the adoption and dissemination of the *Diatessaron* in early Christian Syria. As to textual aspects, even so short a passage revealed its dependence on all the Four Gospels, though it was too brief for gauging its affinities to the "Western" family, and its possible influence on the Old Syriac Gospels. One of the most crucial questions in textual criticism—whether the "Western" characteristics in Old Syriac and other Near Eastern texts can be immediately attributed to Tatian's transplantation from Rome—is as far from solution as ever.

The fact that the fragment was in Greek was first hailed as irrefutable confirmation of the traditional theory that Tatian had written his harmony originally in Greek. There was also the Greek name, Tatian's long stay in Rome, and the alleged Western characteristics of the text. But even this argument, added to the Dura evidence, is not entirely conclusive. Dura had a substantial Greek-speaking community which simply may have been unable to use a Syriac version.

Bilingual Dura inscription in Greek and Semitic Palmyrene (akin to Aramaic). Semitic and Hellenistic elements fuse in this votive offering by "Julius Aurelius Malochas, son of Soudai, of Palmyra, to the goddess of Nemesis."

In sum, the Dura discovery must be ranked as a dramatic link in a long line of studies devoted to the enigmatic *Diatessaron*. Only about one fifth of Dura had been excavated when the Yale team had to abandon work in 1937 because of the familiar "lack of funds." The likelihood is high, then, that this site may yet supply further clues. "Dura," Rostovtzeff said in 1938, "is as in spring and as full of promise as ever."[7]

What makes the recovery of the "lost" *Diatessaron* unique is not only that it involved several avenues of search, including dirt archaeology, but that it furnished a paradoxical case history of manuscript hunting in which the object, said not to exist at all, had never really disappeared. In fact, the *Diatessaron* episode,

---

[7] Rostovtzeff: op. cit., p. 1.

perhaps more clearly than other similar cases, points to the relativity of terms such as "lost" or "discovered." As in so many human activities, in manuscript hunting, too, there are moments when the pursuit is more rewarding than the accomplishment.

·XVII·

MORE LIGHT ON

THE NEW TESTAMENT

The doctrines of the school of Baur, which regarded the earliest Christian books as a tissue of falsifications of the second century, have been exploded. . . . Recent discoveries have only confirmed this conclusion.

FREDERIC G. KENYON[1]

T HE WEALTH of New Testament manuscripts has appeared to be, to several students of the Bible, a Christian miracle in itself. Be this as it may, both in age and in quantity, the New Testament textual tradition compares favorably with the works of classical authors, some of which have been transmitted in only one copy or are removed from their original composition by more than a thousand years. And the list is steadily growing. Whereas Erasmus had some eight Greek codices on which to base his edition, and Stephanus (Robert Estienne), printer of the improved Greek of the Received Text in 1550, used fourteen, today we have about three thousand Greek parchments and papyri of different length and value—not to speak of a plethora of translated "versions" in other languages. All these texts, embodying many variants as well as a number of errors, are a direct challenge to any arbitrary editorial dictates. They call for analysis, comparison, and further search.

The very attempt to reestablish the purity of the apostolic

---

[1] Kenyon: *Our Bible. . . ,* p. 155 *n.*

word has been a motivating force behind the quest for the earliest Biblical manuscripts. During the past century or so of New Testament studies, it is doubtful whether most of the manuscripts would have been found at all or would ever have been reported without this scholarly impetus. But one instance in the long chain of New Testament finds may be attributable to a less conscious effort, though it came to be closely associated with one of the epoch's leading palaeographers.

Passages from Ethiopic (Exodus 29) and Armenian (Mark 4) manuscript "versions" of the Bible

November 19, 1931, deserves to be remembered as a red-letter day in the epic of modern manuscript discoveries. On that day *The Times* in London carried a closely printed announcement of more than two columns. In the opening paragraph, which reviewed Biblical discoveries since the arrival of the Curetonian at the British Museum in 1842 and Tischendorf's first coup in 1844, the writer concluded: "In 1897 Messrs. Grenfell and Hunt found at Oxyrhynchus the papyrus fragment of the Sayings of Jesus, to which a second fragment was added in 1904. In 1906 Mr. C. L. Freer acquired a remarkable group of vellum manuscripts in Egypt, of which the most important is the fifth century copy of the Gospels, now known as W [the greatest Biblical treasure in the United States, it was bequeathed to the Smithsonian Institution], which contains an apocryphal addition in the last chapter of Mark. I have now after an interval of twenty-five years, the privilege of making known a discovery of Biblical manuscripts which rivals any of these in interest and surpasses them all in antiquity."[2] The article was signed by Sir Frederic Kenyon. The discovery consisted of a remarkably full collection of Old and

---

[2] Kenyon: "The Text of the Bible. A New Discovery," *The Times*, November 19, 1931, p. 13.

New Testament papyri, with certain apocrypha, dating in parts from the second century.

Sir Frederic George Kenyon was by that time England's grand old man of textual criticism and papyrology. We meet him at every step when surveying the major achievements of more than half a century. Kenyon may rightly be called one of the founders of papyrology as a separate discipline. He charted textual criticism, particularly of the New Testament, in a series of indispensable works of both a semipopular and a scientific nature. Though much of his energies went into the synthesis of complex and ever-evolving subjects, his original contributions were substantial enough to necessitate major revisions of his own manuals. His association with the British Museum (he was its director from 1909 to 1930) for more than forty years gave him first-hand contacts with the great manuscript finds of his age. Although Kenyon never went on field trips to dig up, literally or otherwise, lost works, his share in the recovery of manuscripts puts him in the front rank of this book's protagonists. As assistant and later director of the British Museum, as governing member of the Egypt Exploration Fund, of the British Academy, and other societies and institutions, he was a star witness and an instigator of note in major literary discoveries during some five decades. And he helped to identify them and restore them to their place in the history of man. When Kenyon retired from the British Museum, close to the Biblical age of three score and ten, he went back with full vigor to the studies of his earlier years, particularly textual criticism of the Bible. His critical ability and capacity for work were unimpaired. Indeed, while he was actively championing the purchase of the Codex Sinaiticus for the British Museum, he was also engaged in research on Biblical manuscripts.

The papyrus codices whose discovery Kenyon first announced to the world in the *Times* article, had, like the Freer parchments, reached dealers from undisclosed Egyptian sources. The great bulk of these had just been obtained by Alfred Chester Beatty, an American mining engineer then a resident in London, who made millions in copper mining on several continents. He became a naturalized British subject in 1933 and was later knighted. The British *Who's Who* of 1961 says that he has been engaged "for many years in collecting Oriental manuscripts, specializing particularly in manuscripts of artistic merit from the point of view of miniature and calligraphy." The Chester Beatty Biblical Papyri would hardly fall into this category, and *Who's Who* does not mention them. Yet, in the vocabulary of the Bible student, the words "Chester Beatty" have assumed a ring almost as familiar as that of the Vulgate or the Sinaiticus and the Dead Sea scrolls. The codices are now housed in a specially built library in Dublin, where the collector, twice an expatriate, has made his home since 1953.[3]

Παῦλος ἀπόστολος Χ(ριστο)ῦ Ἰη(σο)ῦ διὰ θελήματος
θ(εο)ῦ καὶ Τιμόθεος ὁ ἀδελφὸς τοῖς ἐν Κολασσαις
ἁγίοις καὶ πιστοῖς ἀδελφοῖς ἐν Χρ(ιστ)ῶ, χάρις ὑμῖν
καὶ εἰρήνη ἀπὸ θ(εο)ῦ πατρὸς ἡμῶν. Εὐχαριστοῦμεν

Opening lines of the Epistle to the Colossians, from a
Greek papyrus of about A.D. 230

Before news of Beatty's acquisition had reached the public, Kenyon, whose term as museum director had just ended, was asked to examine the cache of papyri. He made the identification and prepared a preliminary analysis. He was a natural choice as editor, and was given a free hand to publish the papyri in whatever form would be most useful to scholars. The papyri consisted of sizable portions of eleven codices (sometimes erroneously reported as twelve), the larger part of which came into the possession of Chester Beatty. Smaller but substantial sections reached the University of Michigan, Princeton, Vienna, and several private individuals. Because of the predatory and apparently surreptitious manner in which they were originally discovered and later disposed of, the likelihood cannot be entirely ruled out that some sections either were withheld by the dealers or drifted into hands as yet unknown. Luckily, Beatty acquired the great bulk. Later he added more leaves of the Pauline Epistles. The generous cooperation of the University of Michigan enabled Kenyon to include its papyri in his edition.

The actual provenance of the papyri has never been ascertained; the natives kept their secret well. For some time the papyri were rumored to have come from the Fayum, and then Carl Schmidt, a German papyrologist, stated that he had heard that the source was across the Nile near the ruins of ancient Aphroditopolis.[4] But no proof was forthcoming. It was also said that

---

[3] R. J. Hayes: "The Chester Beatty Library," *The Book Collector*, Vol. VII, No. 3 (Autumn, 1958), p. 253.

[4] Kenyon: *The Story of the Bible*, p. 112.

the various manuscripts were found in jars in a Coptic cemetery, a plausible account in view of previous discoveries. The general assumption, suggested by the condition and nature of the eleven codices, is that they once constituted the library of a church or monastery of not later than the fourth or the early fifth century. The manuscripts may all have been buried when the community was abandoned, or, according to another hypothesis, they may have been interred with the last Greek-speaking member of the community.

The ravages of time, and the greed and carelessness of the "rescuers," have inflicted great damage. None of the codices is intact. With the exception of the Pauline Epistles, there are enormous gaps. Nevertheless, considering their age, the treatment they have been subjected to, and the frailty of papyrus, a good many leaves are fairly well preserved. (Incidentally, the physical quality of the writing material—just as the manner of writing itself—varies considerably.) The codices consisted of parts of nine books of the Old Testament and fifteen of the New Testament. In addition, there were sizable sections of the apocalyptic Book of Enoch and the first part of a lost homily on the Passion by Bishop Melito of Sardis. The New Testament sections constituted three codices. Little was left of Matthew and John, but Mark and Luke had fared better. Of Acts, which belonged to the same codex as the Gospels, about half had survived. Of Revelation—interestingly enough a codex by itself, reflecting on the distinct position of this apocalyptic work—there remained about a third (ten of thirty-two leaves). The Pauline Epistles, yet another separate volume, had fared quite well: eighty-six somewhat frayed leaves had survived (thirty owned by Michigan), of a total of a hundred and four. Although none of the books of the New or the Old Testament in the batch of papyri acquired by Chester Beatty was complete, there were a number of lengthy, continuous passages—most notably the Pentateuch and the Prophets of the Greek Septuagint and portions of virtually all of the New Testament. These furnished ample material for the investigation of textual problems and eventually shed new light on the beginnings of the New Testament.

Fortunately, some manuscripts were in a relatively good state of preservation, and there was a great bulk of them. Moreover, their age ranged from the second to the fourth century A.D. With this, the sources for the Greek Bible were moved back by at least a century. The extensive codex of St. Paul's letters was apparently written only some hundred and forty years after the apostle's death. A hundred years may not seem much in the millennia of Judeo-Christian traditions or the span of Near Eastern civilizations, but in the history of the New Testament text, in which a link to the fourth century was for long the very best to hope for, it meant a momentous breakthrough.

This is not the place to go into the highly specialized problems of textual criticism and the related problem of families of ancient texts, for which the Chester Beatty New Testament papyri furnished quite unexpected evidence. Some of this will have become evident from Tischendorf's quest for the "best" New Testament and our brief discussion of the significance of the Syriac palimpsest. Suffice it to say that the goal of criticism is "restoration." It sets out to approximate the presumed original texts, the so-called "autographs." If we had the originals, textual criticism would of course be obsolete. Invariably, however, ancient works have come down to us in a number of variants. Through successive generations of copies, or copies of copies, all kinds of errors have been perpetuated. The text is said to have become "corrupted." Now, in order to establish a correct reading, scholars do not work on a single text at random, but take in all available materials, relate them to one another, and weigh their relative reliability. Very old manuscripts—the closer in age to the original the better —are the most desirable for this work. At an advanced stage of critical analysis, scholars will sort out divergent types of manuscripts into separate groups, or "families," according to mutual affinities and genetic dependencies. These families can often be traced to specific places or regions of origin. True to the name, a few families will turn out to be of a more noble and creditable lineage than others, and will claim special attention. In fact, the procedures of scholars when reconstructing a text from families of manuscripts may be likened to those of the modern geneticists who by scientific "backbreeding" from selected strains reproduce an extinct biological type.

It was particularly on the question of textual families that the Chester Beatty Papyri made a considerable contribution. Westcott and Hort had been the first, in the nineteenth century, to establish a number of families among the New Testament manuscripts then extant. These scholars favored the "Neutral" family, represented by Vaticanus and Sinaiticus, as the most genuine and the least tampered with. But their views were soon challenged.

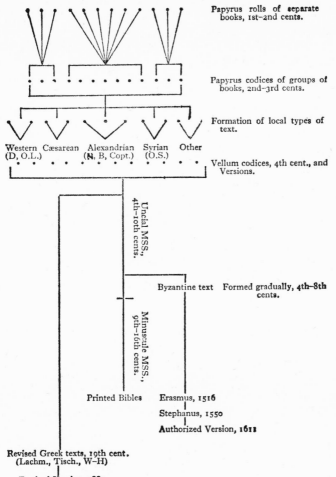

Papyrus rolls of separate books, 1st–2nd cents.

Papyrus codices of groups of books, 2nd–3rd cents.

Formation of local types of text.

Western Cæsarean Alexandrian Syrian Other
(D, O.L.) (ℵ, B, Copt.) (O.S.)

Vellum codices, 4th cent., and Versions.

Uncial MSS., 4th–10th cents.

Byzantine text   Formed gradually, 4th–8th cents.

Minuscule MSS., 9th–16th cents.

Printed Bibles   Erasmus, 1516

Stephanus, 1550

Authorized Version, 1611

Revised Greek texts, 19th cent. (Lachm., Tisch., W–H)

Revised Version, 1881

"Pedigree" tracing briefly the history of the New Testament text from early papyrus rolls through papyrus and vellum codices and the formation of "families" of texts to the modern "editions" of the Greek original (by Lachmann, Tischendorf, and Westcott and Hort) and the Revised Version of 1881 based on their critical work

Kenyon was able to show by comparative analysis that the Neutral text had not come down directly, and with little correction, from the autographs, but rather was "a text scientifically constructed from good materials." Several readings of the Chester Beatty, at variance with the Neutral, "are worthy of consideration."[5] In fact,

[5] Kenyon: "New Light on the Text of the Bible," *Discovery,* Vol. XIV (November 1933), p. 334.

the Chester Beatty Papyri reflected a period when the families of texts had not yet fully formed. They were early enough to be altogether free of Byzantine corruption and afforded therefore an unusual glimpse into the emerging textual traditions, when, as Kenyon put it pithily, "the object would be edification, not a punctilious preservation of the exact words of the original authors."[6] Furthermore, the evidence that fifteen books of the New Testament were distributed over three codices may in itself be taken as a sign that the unity and integrity of the New Testament had not yet been clearly realized. On the other hand, the combination, in one book, of the Four Gospels (and Acts) bears out Irenaeus' assertion, made in 180, that there are only Four Gospels, no more and no less, which belong together. The Beatty Papyri reveal more emphatically than the *Diatessaron* definite hints of a fixed canon.

The fragments from the Greek Old Testament, though less momentous in nature, were also important. Deuteronomy and Numbers, dating from early in the second century A.D., were acclaimed as the oldest copy of an Old Testament text in any language (with the possible exception of the mysterious Nash Papyrus). But this assertion could not be defended for long. Most interesting perhaps was the inclusion of the Book of Daniel, copied from the Septuagint version, which had been condemned and was replaced by the translation of Theodotion. The Septuagint text had been lost, except for a careless, eleventh-century copy at the Chigi Library in Rome.

Outside both Testaments stood the apocalyptic and apocryphal ("pseudepigraphic") Book of Enoch, for which the Chester Beatty Papyri contributed extensive missing passages of the Greek text, concluded by the Letter of Enoch. The Book of Enoch ties together several notable manuscript finds made over more than one hundred and fifty years. It had long been considered lost. But since it was quoted in the Epistle of Jude of the New Testament, its name had not been forgotten. Then James Bruce, the eighteenth-century Scottish traveler, brought back an Ethiopic version from Abyssinia, which was not published until fifty years later, in 1821. At that time, a translation in old Slavonic also came to the notice of theologians. Archaeology was brought into play when the French archaeological mission at Cairo excavated a tomb at Akhmim in 1886–87. In it was found a vellum codex of thirty-three leaves, containing, among others, the first thirty-two

---

[6] Ibid., p. 334.

chapters of the Book of Enoch in Greek. The missing eleven chapters were provided by the Chester Beatty Papyri and some of the material in the possession of the University of Michigan. Earlier, the Epistle of Barnabas, whose rediscovery is related to the Codex Sinaiticus, had furnished two quotations from Enoch. This is evidence of the popularity of the work among early Christians and makes it probable that both the Akhmim and the Chester Beatty fragments formed parts of ancient collections of Christian literature.

In origin, however, the Book of Enoch is pre-Christian and belongs undoubtedly to the same genre of apocalyptic texts as the latter section of Daniel in the Old Testament and the Second Book of Esdras in the Apocrypha.[7] The Dead Sea scrolls account for still another phase in the recovery of the lost Book of Enoch. In time, the Qumran caves were to yield some eight manuscripts of the book in Aramaic, which, however, differed widely from both Greek and Ethiopic versions and presented complex textual problems. But more fascinating still, the number of Enoch fragments, and the like, which were known to the Qumran sectarians has led to the suggestion that it was among this community that the book had been composed in the first place.

One aspect of the Chester Beatty Papyri remains to be mentioned. It has been widely commented on and has been the source of vital data on the history of books in general. It concerns their physical make-up rather than their content.

It has been recognized for some time that the codex—the modern type of book, consisting of sheets gathered in quires and bound together between two covers—came to be the prevalent form by the fourth century. According to this view, it then replaced the more cumbersome rolls, which had been in use for three millennia in Egypt and the Near East, and in classical antiquity. However, references in Latin literature make it likely that the codex was used in earlier centuries, particularly as a notebook. Genetically, it was preceded by wax tablets strung or hinged together like the leaves of a book. The surviving codices were all of parchment and suggested, therefore, that the change from roll to codex was accompanied by the simultaneous adoption of parchment or vellum. Thus, at least until the introduction of paper some six hundred years later, a codex was invariably identified

---

[7] Kenyon: *The Bible and Archaeology*, p. 246.

with parchment. It was thought that there had been a sudden revolution in bookmaking and that the Christians had led the way. Before the time of the Codex Vaticanus and the Codex Sinaiticus, which were roughly contemporaneous with Constantine's commission to Eusebius to produce fifty vellum Bibles in codex form, Christian literature, it was generally supposed, had circulated in papyrus rolls.

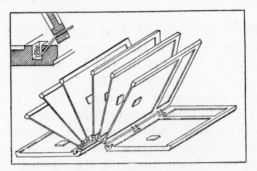

Reconstruction of a wax-tablet "book" from Herculaneum. This one, consisting of eight leaves, is a so-called *octoptych*. Wax-covered wooden tablets—the *pugillares* of the Romans—anticipated the form of codices and modern books. They were mainly used for taking notes and keeping accounts. Reconstruction by M. Paolini

As already mentioned, in classical times papyrus rolls rarely exceeded a length of thirty-five feet. One roll, then, would include no more than one Gospel or one book of Thucydides. Indeed, the length of a Christian text, as well as the fact that it circulated separately, may well have been conditioned by such external characteristics. The Christians' growing desire to collect their scriptures in a convenient form would make them favorably inclined toward the codex, which would be much more suitable for ready reference to precise passages of the divine message in sermons, missionary activities, or devotional tasks. In addition, a much larger body of text would be at the reader's fingertips. "A big book" in the guise of a long roll had previously been, as Paul said, "a big evil."

Early in this century, therefore, some scholars had put forth the interesting theory that the transition from papyrus roll to vellum codex should be attributed largely to the early Christians. That the Christians could effect, or at least considerably accelerate, this change may be ascribed to socio-psychological factors:

Christianity, being the religion of the "underdog," was not bound by literary conventions and formal traditions. Christians had no qualms about committing holy writs to the lowly codex form, quite unlike the Jews, who to this day produce handwritten Bible scrolls on leather for their services. The Christians, who represented in the patristic age a predominantly lower stratum of society, naturally chose the more practical and apparently cheaper codex. It is quite possible that the codex as such was originally considered the poor man's book and the notorious mandarin mentality of the well-born and well-heeled haughtily shied away from it, in the same manner as Italian aristocrats, after the invention of printing, would refuse to admit any printed book to their libraries.[8]

Papyrus texts of some value were wound around a stick (*umbelicus*), which had richly decorated knobs. Colored strings tied the roll together.

How does this mixture of fact and surmise fit in with the Chester Beatty Papyri? All these manuscripts turned out to be codices, but they were papyrus, not parchment. This was evidence that some hundred years before the sumptuous vellum codices, Christians were already collecting their scriptures in codices, and the material they used was papyrus. The papyrus codex, then, must have represented a stage between the papyrus roll and the parchment codex. Contrary to former belief, scribes and makers of books did not at once change both the material and the form of their medium. This was a landmark in our knowledge of the evolution of the modern book. Scattered pieces, such as the Oxyrhynchus *Logia* of Jesus, which turned out to be leaves from a papyrus codex, were no longer isolated instances. The Chester Beatty text of Numbers and Deuteronomy, dated not later than the second century A.D., indicated a very early use of the codex form. The new evidence showed that, for much longer than had generally been accepted, Christians had been in the habit of combining several works, such as the Four Gospels, in one book. More

---

[8] Jacob Burckhardt: *The Civilization of the Renaissance in Italy* (New York: Random House–Modern Library; 1954), p. 144.

precise corroboration of the Christians' preference for the codex was hardly necessary.

Documents found in Egypt provided statistical evidence that the papyrus codex was preponderantly and almost exclusively employed in Christian literature, whereas pagan manuscripts con-

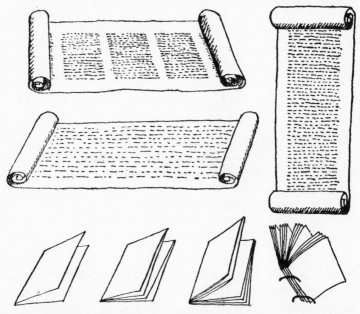

Various phases in the evolution of the book. The rolls are written in columns like pages, longitudinally, or in horizontal lines across their entire width. The four folded specimens, at bottom, show (left to right) a folio, a quarto (quaternion), an octavo, and four quartos joined together. Drawing by Ella Margules

tinued to appear in rolls. The Chester Beatty Papyri are a notable example of this intermediate stage in the history of bookmaking, just as their text and their organization in three volumes mark an intermediate phase in the emergence of the New Testament in word and canon. Another detail helps to illustrate the transitional groping for the new book form. The Pauline Epistles, though they consisted of more than one hundred leaves, were made up of one quire only (i.e., all sheets had the same center fold), whereas the Gospels were put together in a number of quires of just two leaves each, which may well account for their greater fragmentation. Book manufacturing was obviously still at an experimental stage. The arrangement in quires, however, was a boon to scholars. By judicious computation, they could gauge the length of missing passages and establish which portions—canonical or noncanonical—were likely, in view of the size of the lacunae, to be included or excluded.

The tattered Chester Beatty Papyri give only an incomplete idea of the ancient papyrus codex. The discovery of the Gnostic library of Chenoboskion, some fifteen years later, shed much more light on their physical make-up. Here, for the first time, were a number of neatly written papyrus books, virtually complete and superbly preserved. But the Christians who may have felt regret that these specimens were at best heretical had not long to wait their turn. In 1956, the collection of Martin Bodmer, a Swiss banker and high official of the Red Cross, who also brought to the world's notice the only complete Menander comedy, published the first fourteen chapters of the Gospel of John (provenance unknown) from an ancient papyrus codex that was at least as early as the Chester Beatty evangelical documents and supplemented them handsomely. They had yielded very little of John, for a long time the evangelist most poorly represented in ancient manuscripts. Now the Gospel of John was found in the oldest of all nearly intact Christian texts. Just two years later, in 1958, the Bibliotheca Bodmeriana of Cologny, near Geneva, announced the acquisition of substantial papyrus fragments of the last eight chapters of the Fourth Gospel from the same codex. The Bodmer John appeared to date from not later than A.D. 200 and belonged to a codex which originally consisted of 154 pages.[9]

The Bodmer John and the Chester Beatty Papyri were by no means the only major recoveries of ancient texts of the Scriptures. Somewhat like metropolitan buses, manuscripts rarely turn up alone after long lapses. Within a short time after Kenyon's press release, and while the veteran palaeographer was still at work on his edition, new discoveries were reported. On the whole, these failed to contribute measurably to textual criticism—they were mostly small finds—or to change in any radical way the views of scholars concerning the conditions under which the New Testament evolved (unless we take into account noncanonical, early Christian works such as the fragments from the Lost Gospel acquired at that time by the British Museum). But they did push back the time limit to a still earlier period. The Chester Beatty Papyri

---

[9] Metzger: op. cit., p. 13.

had taken the Scriptures back beyond the Sinaiticus by about one hundred years, and now the New Testament at least was definitely put into the first half of the second century A.D., if not to around 100. And a fragment of Deuteronomy in Greek came from the second century B.C., which brought it within range of the Septuagint translation.

These two notable finds, one of the Old Testament and the other of the New Testament, were made in a European library. As usual, the manuscripts had originally come from unspecified sites in Egypt, and for more than a decade and a half had remained unidentified, tucked away in the John Rylands Library in the city of Manchester. The Deuteronomy text had survived as a shroud for a crocodile mummy and had been bought by J. Rendel Harris in Egypt in 1917. The New Testament fragment, also from Egypt, was purchased on behalf of the library from dealers by Grenfell in 1920. Grenfell had been engaged by the library to sort and catalogue these and a number of other papyri, but he did not make much headway before he suffered another breakdown. Later Hunt was called to take up the job, but he was delayed, and then he died suddenly in 1934. A young Oxford papyrologist, Colin H. Roberts, who had assisted Hunt in the editing of the Oxyrhynchus texts, was then invited to complete the cataloguing.

Quite unexpectedly, our oldest testimony from the New Testament came from the Gospel of St. John, supposedly the last of the Four Gospels. Nineteenth-century skeptics had hoped to reduce John to a legendary evangelium, a mere romance concocted from the other three as late as the end of the second century. But the tiny fragment from the Rylands papyrus, some 2½ by 3½ inches and consisting of a few verses of John (from 18:31–33) written on both sides, had to be dated, on palaeographic grounds, as not later than A.D. 150. Indeed, it may have been copied, as Deissmann thought likely, closer to the year 100. The Chester Beatty manuscript of the Gospel was written some hundred and fifty years before the oldest of all vellum texts—and now we had another passage from the Gospel which was a hundred years older still. It was as much as two hundred and fifty years removed from the Vaticanus and Sinaiticus codices, which to Tischendorf, Hort (he had called them the "heavenly twins"), and a generation of Bible scholars who were still alive were as close to the Apostles as one could ever dare to get.

The excerpt from John was probably found in a rather remote part of Egypt, where Christianity had penetrated relatively late.

It would have taken several decades after the date of composition of the original for a copy to be disseminated to such a place; therefore the assumption that the Gospel according to John could not have been written much later than A.D. 80, and almost certainly before 100, seems to be sound.

St. John the Evangelist, after a tenth-century minature

An American scholar, Bruce Metzger of Princeton, has expressed vividly the significance of the Rylands fragment of John's Gospel: "Although the extent of the verses preserved is so slight, in one respect this tiny scrap of papyrus possesses quite as much evidential value as would the complete codex. As Robinson Crusoe, seeing but a single footprint in the sand, concluded that another human being, with two feet, was present on the island with him, so p⁵² [its international code name] proves the existence and use of the Fourth Gospel in a little provincial town along the Nile far from its traditional place of composition (Ephesus in Asia Minor) during the first half of the Second Century."[1]

Truly, the time gap between these manuscripts and the apostolic age has almost been closed. It has shrunk to as little, perhaps, as thirty or forty years. From the Codex Sinaiticus to the Chester Beatty Papyri and beyond them to the Rylands fragment, modern discoveries have, at least by implication, no more dramatic story to tell.

---

[1] Metzger: "Recently Published Greek Papyri of the New Testament," *Biblical Archaeologist*, Vol. X, No. 2 (May 1947), p. 38.

B : *Hebrew Writs*

·XVIII·

THE CAIRO GENIZA

The stone which the builders have rejected has become the cornerstone.

THE TALMUD

Most Hebrew synagogues, at least since the early Middle Ages, included a closet or lumber room, called a Geniza (genizah). This is a Hebrew word referring to hiding or burial. The Geniza served as a kind of morgue for the deposit and disposal of materials bearing writing.

It has been for a long time the custom of the Jews to discard worn-out holy books and scrolls. Since they contain the name of the divinity, the sacred *shemoth*, it was considered sacrilegious to simply cast them away and thereby expose them to possible defilement. The Geniza was designed as a temporary receptacle for these materials. And from time to time the accumulation was buried with religious ceremony, often beside a sage's grave—or occasionally with him—in the Jewish cemetery. To the Hebrews, says Solomon Schechter the Rabbinic scholar, a book was like a man: "When the spirit is gone, we put a corpse out of sight to protect it from abuse. In like manner, when a writing is worn out or disused, we hide the book to preserve it from profanation. The contents of the book go up to heaven like the soul."[1] Such burials still take place today, particularly in the East. Tischendorf's son-in-law, D. Ludwig Schneller, described one in Jerusalem in 1894. And we have a graphic report by a modern-day journalist, Richard Katz, on an interment at Prague in 1921, the first one there for 532 years.[2]

---

[1] Solomon Schechter: "A Hoard of Hebrew Manuscripts," *Studies in Judaism*, second series (London: A. and C. Black; 1908), p. 1.

[2] Richard Katz: "Seltsames Begräbnis," *Vossische Zeitung*, No. 22 (January 14, 1921, evening), pp. 2–3.

However, the Geniza came to receive not only used or mutilated texts but also faulty ones that were not permitted to circulate, either because they contained more errors or corrections by the scribes than the law permitted or because their contents were not considered suitable for the public eye, such as texts branded heretical and others excluded from the Biblical canon. The very term Apocrypha means hidden books and corresponds precisely to the Hebrew "geniza." Apparently much Hebrew literature of the Hellenistic and early Christian era was thus committed to limbo. When a sectarian literature arose, the conservative Rabbis would see that it was taken out of circulation. Once the official Masoretic text (the "traditional" form of the Scriptures) was established, no other types or editions were tolerated.

Until recently, no Hebrew Old Testament texts older than the ninth century—and these are rare enough—had come down to us, because of their purposeful elimination by way of the Geniza. As *The Jewish Encyclopedia* puts it, the Geniza had "the twofold purpose of preserving good things from harm and bad things from harming."[3] But both the good and the bad usually passed from Geniza to destruction by burial. They were not really meant to be preserved. "The People of the Book" have a long record as censors and destroyers of books.

Gradually, it seems, some Genizas took on additional functions. They came to be the community archives, though none of the documents stored there were catalogued nor were they held for permanent reference. Virtually everything of some significance —legal contracts, leases, marriage settlements, court decisions, even private letters and secular poetry—was sent to the Geniza to be eventually buried. Schechter explains this practice on the ground that, "as the Jews attached a certain sacredness to everything resembling the Scriptures [by virtue of having been written in Hebrew], either in matter of in form, they were loth to treat even these secular documents as mere refuse. . . . The Geniza of the old Jewish community thus represents a combination of sacred lumber-room and secular record office."[4] This, however, would hardly account for the fact that one Geniza whose contents have come down to us included quantities of secular material in languages other than Hebrew, mainly in Arabic, but also in Syriac (Aramaic), Greek, Coptic, Georgian, and even French.

---

[3] Elkan N. Adler: "Genizah," *The Jewish Encyclopedia* (New York: Funk & Wagnalls; 1916), Vol. V, p. 612.

[4] Schechter: op. cit., p. 9.

The Cairo Geniza is outstanding because much of its contents were untouched and perhaps even forgotten for the better part of a thousand years. That these manuscripts survived was entirely unintentional. This Geniza belonged to one of the oldest synagogues in one of the oldest Jewish communities of the Diaspora, and it had existed throughout the golden age of Arab civilization. Though occasionally considerable amounts of material were removed for burial, some of which has been actually dug up, the great bulk was left in the storeroom. And then, only the dry climate of Egypt could have so mercifully preserved it.

An Egyptian Fatimite coin bearing name
of Omar the Caliph. About A.D. 1000

The ancient synagogue, variously named for Ezra, Elijah, Jeremiah, or Moses, is located just south of Cairo in a section of Fostat, or Old Cairo, which was called Babylon in pre-Moslem days. Egyptian Babylon was the site of a Roman fort, and before that a sixth-century B.C. Persian fort. In this area a sizable Coptic and Jewish center developed. The synagogue was originally a Christian church dedicated to St. Michael, but had been transferred, according to some accounts, to the Jews during the brief Persian reoccupation in A.D. 616. A sale to the Jews in A.D. 882, after the Arab conquest, is recorded. After that, the synagogue's Geniza received all kinds of texts.

The first modern traveler who appears to have known of the Geniza was Heinrich Heine's great-uncle, Simon van Geldern, who visited it in the mid-eighteenth century and wrote in his diary of the likelihood that valuable manuscripts were buried there. Some hundred years later, the Hebrew scholar Jacob Saphir, known for his exploration in Yemen, paid the Geniza a visit. He had to use some persuasion to be allowed a glimpse of it. Despite the beadle's warning that "serpents and dragons" were lurking in the closed dark room, he braved the Nilotic beasts and plowed through the debris for two days, until he had his fill of dust and dirt. He did not find anything worthwhile, but remarked in his travelogue: "Who knows what may yet be beneath?"[5]

Leningrad Hebrew codex containing the Book of Prophets, A.D. 916. It was taken in 1839 by Abraham Firkovich from a synagogue in the Crimea. The codex ranked among the most ancient Hebrew Bible manuscripts of some size until the discovery of the Dead Sea scrolls.

At about this time, there also came to the Near East a Russian Jew who was a staunch adherent of the Karaite sect, Abraham Firkovich. He was among the oddest of nineteenth-century manuscript hunters, and it is due to him that the Leningrad Public Library possesses one of the most extensive collections of Hebrew manuscripts in the world. Firkovich has been described as a fascinating mixture of rogue, scholar, and fanatic. His explorations and acquisitions were primarily motivated by a desire to prove to the Russian Czarist government that the Karaites had been domiciled in the Crimea since pre-Christian times and were therefore, unlike Rabbinic Jews, innocent of both the execution of Christ and the authorship of the hated Talmud.[6] Though the chronology of such claims was dubious, his effort was successful. The Russian

---

[5] Adler: ". . . The Ancient Synagogue Near Cairo," *Jewish Quarterly Review*, Vol. IX (1897), p. 671.

[6] Hermann L. Strack: "Abraham Firkowitsch und der Wert seiner Entdeckungen," *Zeitschrift der Deutschen Morgenländischen Gesellschaft*, Vol. XXXIV (1880), p. 164.

Imperial government exempted Karaites from the discriminating measures against Jews. But to supply his proofs, Firkovich had
to falsify documents. He even went so far as to antedate inscriptions on tombstones in Karaite cemeteries in the Crimea. When
his practices became known, Firkovich's many manuscripts naturally became suspect. There is dissension among the experts to
this day as to which are genuine, which fakes. Like Simonides,
he was a forger, but he did not seem to have been impelled
primarily by materialistic considerations. He ruthlessly looted
synagogues and Genizas, including some in the Crimea and in
Bukhara, and he was probably among the first to grasp the
enormous value of these repositories. Since he operated secretly,
noboby knows his sources for certain. It is even doubtful whether
he ever personally entered the Cairo Geniza, whence several of
the most precious fragments of the Leningrad collection are believed to have come.

In 1888, Elkan Nathan Adler, the brother of the English
chief rabbi, made his first visit to the Old Cairo synagogue, but
was not able to see the Geniza. He was told that its books had been
buried in the cemetery. When the synagogue was redecorated in
1890, the Geniza's existence became better known, and the beadles
of the synagogue began to realize the propensity of dealers in
Cairo to purchase this "refuse" of centuries, for which foreign
eccentrics were willing to pay considerable sums. Thus, within a
few years masses of Geniza scraps filtered into the hands of private
collectors and the libraries of the West—the Bodleian, the British
Museum, the libraries of Frankfort, Berlin, Philadelphia, Budapest, and many more. For a while the source of all these treasures
remained guesswork. But the rumors brought to Cairo such avid
collectors and buyers as A. H. Sayce, Greville Chester, and the
Russian Archimandrite Antonin. In 1896, E. N. Adler revisited
the Cairo synagogue and was allowed to spend three or four hours
inside the Geniza and take away all he could carry in an old Torah
mantle (vestment for Pentateuch scrolls of Jewish services) which
he borrowed for the purpose.[7] Mrs. Lewis and Mrs. Gibson came
to Egypt that same year.

The two enterprising lady Orientalists had actually made up
their minds to brave the rigors of the English climate and stay at
home in Cambridge in the winter of 1895–96. They were looking
forward to productive months at work on the Palestinian-Syriac

[7] Adler: ". . . The Ancient Synagogue Near Cairo," p. 673.

texts they had previously photographed at Sinai. But in the midst of such work, intelligence from Egypt reached them through the archaeological grapevine indicating "that there might be a chance of our finding something there." Early in 1896 they were once again on the manuscript trail in the Near East, having decided to add a visit to Jerusalem to their Egyptian explorations. This, as Mrs. Lewis later wrote, was to be their only trip "unwillingly undertaken; and yet it has been not the least fruitful in results."[8]

Mrs. Lewis and Mrs. Gibson's visit in Cairo was cut short because of the outbreak of an epidemic and the threat that they might have to submit to ignominious quarantine regulations. However, they acquired some scraps of manuscript there. When they reached Jerusalem, they purchased a large Hebrew text of the Pentateuch, and when they passed through the Plain of Sharon near the coast, they were offered a bundle of various fragments, mostly in Hebrew, by a dealer. As they were about to take ship in Jaffa, they ran into unexpected difficulties at the customs house because of an embargo on the export of Palestinian antiquities, particularly of books. The Hebrew fragments, above all, drew the attention of officials. But the ladies' native guide, Joseph, who knew that as personal prayer books both the Bible and the Koran were exempt from any restrictive legislation, exclaimed indignantly, pointing to the leaves under scrutiny: "Do you not see they are Hebrew? The ladies say their prayers in Hebrew. Do you want to prevent them saying their prayers?"[9] This saved the day for the Scottish-Presbyterian ladies, and the pursuit of scholarship. They were allowed to depart with their manuscripts and reached England in May. Shortly after their return, they sorted out their various acquisitions. Those Hebrew portions which they could not ascribe to the Old Testament they put aside, thinking that they were probably from the Talmud or represented private Jewish documents. They had decided to submit these to a friend, the noted Hebraist Solomon Schechter, for further examination.

Schechter, the Reader in Talmudic and keeper of the collection of Hebrew manuscripts at Cambridge University, had been raised in a ghetto in Eastern Europe. Until he was well into his twenties, he had had no secular education. When at last, as an auditor at the universities of Vienna and Berlin, he encountered

---

[8] Agnes Smith Lewis: *In the Shadow of Sinai* (Cambridge: Bowes & Macmillan; 1898), p. 143.
[9] Ibid., p. 170.

Western learning, he did not, unlike so many gifted Jews of the time, abandon his beliefs or adopt the attitudes of the Western intelligentsia.

Schechter's religion owed something to the joyous mysticism of the Hassidic sect of eastern Jewry. He did not seem to bear any emotional scars from his ghetto life or from the severe discipline of Talmudic studies begun at the age of three. His massive physical frame and imposing leonine head with its shaggy auburn mane and beard commanded attention everywhere. The stream of brilliant impromptu sayings that flowed from his lips unfortunately never found a Boswell. An early associate recalled his first impression of the man: "He burst on us like an explosive bomb, and would bear down any rationalizing or cynical comment with his mixture of enthusiasm and indignation. I can see him rising from his chair, pacing up and down the room like a wounded lion and roaring retorts."[1]

The year of Schechter's birth is variously reported as 1847, 1849, or 1850. He was born in the little Rumanian town of Focsani in the Carpathian Mountains, to which his father, who occupied the humble office of ritual slaughterer, had migrated from Russia. Though reputedly the roughest boy in town, young Schechter was quickly recognized as a *Wunderkind,* a child prodigy in Talmudic learning. At the age of five he knew the Pentateuch by heart. There followed long years of study in religious schools and colleges, a drudgery that often exasperated the young romantic, yet never made him despise the sharp dialectic discipline of which he became a master. His thirst for greater knowledge drove him first to Poland, then to Vienna, and eventually to Berlin.

One of the great influences in his life was the incisive method of the German historical school. He was one of the first to apply meticulous textual study to Jewish religious literature. Simultaneously he acquired an abiding interest in the old manuscripts which were the basis of all such work. Thus began his lifelong enterprise of editing some of the ancient Tadmudic and Midrashic texts.

Schechter, never acclimatized to the German cultural environment, looked askance at the then flourishing school of Higher Criticism and its skeptical approach to the Old Testament. He abhorred the nationalistic arrogance and militarism of the Bismarck era, and was wounded by the anti-Hebraic position of

---

[1] Norman Bentwich: *Solomon Schechter* (Philadelphia: Jewish Publication Society; 1938), p. 60.

German scholars such as Harnack, Weber, and Delitzsch, who deprecated Jewish ethics and denied the Old Testament roots of Christianity. In Schechter's time, Paul de Lagarde, the celebrated theologian and Orientalist of Göttingen, had his books bound in pigskin so that "filthy Jew hands would not touch them," and Hugo Winckler, the great Semiticist, heavily endowed by Jewish sponsors, uttered anti-Semitic remarks while acclaiming Akkadians, Babylonians, and Phoenicians as pioneers of civilization. Academic Germany, as Schechter wrote, had lots of "learned bores who discuss in all earnestness whether a Semite has a soul or not."[2] He remembered being assaulted by Christian boys, but he was outraged even more by the bigotry and conceit of what he called "higher anti-Semitism," which "burns the soul though it does not hurt the body."[3]

For England and the Anglo-Saxon world in general, Schechter felt a warm affinity throughout his life. He also was certain that, in the future, Judaism would find its center of gravity in America. For this, among other reasons, he gave up the beloved academic groves of Cambridge to spend his last twelve years in New York as president of the Jewish Theological Seminary of America. England endeared itself to him not only because of the democratic ideals of its people and the relative lack of prejudice against the Jews among its academic leaders, but also because of its wonderful collections of Hebrew manuscripts. During his first years there, the British Museum and the Bodleian were his regular haunts. In England, Schechter engaged in serious research, out of which grew definitive editions of ancient texts. In 1890 he was appointed Lecturer and in 1892 Reader of Talmudic (Rabbinical literature) at Cambridge University. Two years later the university sent him to Italy to study Hebrew manuscripts. His long stay in Italy and his familiarity with its archival resources was to be an enduring inspiration. More fortunate than both Ranke and Tischendorf, Schechter was granted full access to the Vatican collections.

In the course of studying Saadia (Saady'a) and editing the *Abot of Rabbi Nathan,* a Talmudic work, Schechter became interested in the apocryphon Ecclesiasticus by Jesus ben Sira (ben Sirach), a book which until then had survived only in quite unsatisfactory translations. His long-lasting and, for a Jewish scholar, quite uncommon concern with noncanonical literature is

---

2 Ibid., p. 45.   3 Ibid., p. 30.

shown in an extensive article in the *Jewish Quarterly Review* of 1891; in it he discusses Hebrew quotations of Ecclesiasticus in Talmudic texts. He was fully prepared for what was now in store for him. Probably no other Jewish scholar alive at the time was as well qualified to identify an entirely unexpected Hebrew fragment from the Wisdom of Jesus ben Sira.

Shortly after Mrs. Lewis and Mrs. Gibson decided to get in touch with Schechter, Mrs. Lewis ran into him on King's Parade in Cambridge and told him about the manuscripts she wanted to show him. She continued her shopping trip in town, and when she went home she found Schechter already at work sifting through the fragments on her dining-room table. He held up a large parchment leaf and said: "This is part of the Jerusalem Talmud, which is very rare; may I take it away?"[4] Mrs. Lewis immediately gave her consent. Then he fastened on a rather dirty, torn piece of paper; paper as a writing material was a palaeographically late innovation, and so had been regarded by the ladies with little respect. "Who ever amongst scholars three years ago," Mrs. Lewis wrote later, "set any store whatever by Hebrew *paper*?"[5]

Schechter, however, was immediately struck by the passage. He had a hunch that it might be the Hebrew text of Ecclesiasticus, lost for nearly a thousand years, but he could not verify this right away, as the Bible in Mrs. Lewis's home did not contain the Apocrypha. Schechter asked Mrs. Lewis's permission to take the paper with him for identification. Somewhat skeptically, she gave her assent, saying: "Mrs. Gibson and I will only be too happy if you find that it is worth publishing."[6] Then he hastened to the Cambridge library, and from there he wrote a note to her the same afternoon, May 13, 1896: "I think we have reason to congratulate ourselves. For the fragment I took with me represents a piece of the *original Hebrew Ecclesiasticus*. It is the first time that such a thing was discovered. Please do not speak yet about the matter till to-morrow. I will come to you to-morrow about 11 p.m. [sic] and talk over the matter with you, and how to make it known. In haste and great excitement, yours sincerely, S. Schechter."[7]

Mrs. Lewis was soon to learn that in the excitement Schechter not only confused a.m. with p.m., but, despite his instructions to the ladies, spluttered the good news to the first people he met

---

[4] Lewis: op. cit., p. 173.   [5] Ibid., p. 179.   [6] Ibid., pp. 173–4.
[7] Ibid., p. 174.

at the library. Then, returning to his wife, he could hardly contain his elation. Essentially a humble man, but highly impulsive, he greeted her: "As long as the Bible lives, my name shall not die. Now telegraph Mrs. Lewis and Mrs. Gibson to come immediately."[8] The ladies received the telegram before the letter and promptly made their way to Schechter's small house in an unfashionable section of Cambridge. It was then agreed that Mrs. Lewis should advise the *Athenaeum* and the *Academy* of the find and give the size of the leaf, the type of writing, and other details.

Mrs. Lewis thought "with intense amusement and gratification" that the discovery had visited just judgment upon ben Sira, the Hebrew author of Ecclesiasticus. He was a misogynist and no woman—not Deborah, Ruth, or Judith—figures in his celebrated catalogue of Hebrew heroes. He only praised "famous *men*" in the well-known lines. Indeed, in one of his apothegms he says: "Better is the wickedness of a man than the goodness of a woman." Yet, here, as Mrs. Lewis pointed out with glee, his original utterances were "brought under the eyes of a European scholar, I might say a scholar of his own nation, by two women."[9]

The Book of Ecclesiasticus, or the Wisdom of Jesus ben Sira (Sirach), which had come down only in non-Hebrew versions, had been first translated into Greek by the author's grandson, who had freely admitted the difficulty of his task in his introduction. It had long been suspected that he was not qualified as a translator, that he badly misunderstood the meaning of some of the original passages, and that he took unnecessary liberties with the text. In 1895, just a year before Schechter's discovery, when the revisers of the Authorized Version published their new translation of the Apocrypha, they regretfully said in the preface of Ecclesiasticus that "considerable attention was paid to the text, but the material for correcting it was but scanty." And now the new discovery happily invalidated these regrets.

It so happened that like the *Diatessaron* in New Testament studies, Ecclesiasticus had become the focus of much speculation by Old Testament scholars in the latter part of the nineteenth century. For one thing, it was one of the Apocrypha definitely known to have been originally composed in Hebrew. St. Jerome mentioned that he had seen the book in the original Hebrew— *Hebraicum reperi.* And apparently Saadia, the tenth-century head of the Babylonian Rabbinic school, was familiar with it. But Maimonides no longer knew it.

---

[8] Bentwich: op. cit., p. 140.   [9] Lewis: op. cit., p. 180.

In addition, among all the Old Testament and apocryphal books, the authorship of this work was most clearly identified and the date of its composition could be pretty safely established. Ecclesiasticus was frequently cited by those Higher Critics who believed that much of the Old Testament had been composed at about the same time. Now, if it could be proven that the Hebrew of this work resembled that of the canonical books only superficially, the thesis of the Hellenistic origin of Old Testament books was about to collapse. Besides, if the original Ecclesiasticus, written about 200 B.C. if not earlier, included quotations from the Psalms, the whole hypothesis of the Maccabean origin of the Psalms—some time after 160 B.C.—would go up into thin air. For this reason, and particularly if one could prove that the Rabbinic idiom was used by ben Sira, it would consequently become certain that "between Ecclesiasticus and the books of the Old Testament there must lie centuries, nay, there must lie, in most cases, the deep waters of the Captivity, the grave of the Old-Hebrew and the old Israel, and the womb of the New-Hebrew and the new Israel."[1]

The recovery of the Hebrew original was to settle quite a few of the textual problems. Passages dropped or distorted in the translated versions were restored. At the same time, a blow was dealt once again to the Higher Critics. Schechter himself admitted that he had formerly believed that the Psalms were of Maccabean vintage, but upon the new evidence gladly abandoned this view. That the fragment represented the Hebrew original, Schechter did not doubt for a moment, though a few scholars disagreed: they maintained that it was a retranslation into Hebrew. However, internal evidence, marginal glosses, and, above all, recent finds in the Qumran caves (Cave II), which agreed completely with the Geniza copy, were to corroborate Schechter's views.

The badly mutilated scrap of some seventeen lines in two columns probably dates from the eleventh century, but points, of course, to a much older "archetype." To identify so brief a passage (Ecclesiasticus 39:15 to 40:8) from a work for whose variations in language there was no precedent in the Hebrew literature then accessible (linguistically, the entire period from roughly 250 B.C. to A.D. 150 was a *tabula rasa*) was in itself a great achievement. A contemporary of Schechter's, writing in the

---

[1] Schechter: "A Fragment of the Original Text of Ecclesiasticus," *The Expositor*, fifth series, Vol. IV (July 1896), p. 1.

Fortnightly Review, greeted the discovery as "A Romance in Scholarship." He commented: "After all its travels through the ages, and after traversing a whole continent, the insignificant fragment had, by the luckiest of chances, fallen into the hand of the one man prepared by his previous studies to identify it, and it was as if a lost page of the Bible has been restored by modern scholarship."[2]

Hebrew fragment of Ecclesiasticus 51 from the Cairo Geniza, now at the Taylor-Schechter Collection, University Library, Cambridge, England

Schechter could justly claim that the significance of the piece consisted "not only in what it offers, but also in the hope it holds out to us of fresh finds." And he added a chivalrous note expressing hope "that it may be again Mrs. Lewis and Mrs. Gibson, to whose zeal for everything relating to the Scriptures Semitic scholarship is already under such great obligations, whose further finds will prove the means of restoring to us the whole of Ecclesiasticus."[3] This gallant wish was not fulfilled. But in the meantime, and even before the release of Schechter's article, several additional leaves (nine in all) of Ecclesiasticus were found. Mrs. Lewis's communication to the *Athenaeum* prompted the Oxford Orientalist Adolf Neubauer to examine Hebrew documents recently acquired by A. H. Sayce in Egypt for the Bodleian Library. These were written in a similar type of Hebrew characters and also without vowel points (the post-Biblical system for adding

[2] Joseph Jacobs: "A Romance in Scholarship," *Fortnightly Review,* Vol. LXXII, N.S. 66 (1899), p. 697.
[3] Schechter: "A Fragment of the Original Text of Ecclesiasticus," p. 15.

vowels to the "nonvocalized" Semitic script). They were continuous with the Schechter leaf, and undoubtedly belonged to the same manuscript and were from the same deposit—somewhere in Egypt. Schechter now set out to determine the provenance of the Ecclesiasticus text. All the evidence pointed to the Cairo–Fostat Geniza, which, with his usual dynamism, he decided to investigate personally. Perhaps more leaves from Ecclesiasticus could be rescued.

Even though Schechter is often called the "Discoverer of the Geniza," he himself refused to take credit for it. When an anonymous letter writer to *The Times* later unjustly attacked him and claimed the honor for E. N. Adler, with whom Schechter was on good terms, Schechter answered: "The honor of discovering the Geniza belongs to the numberless dealers in antiquities of Cairo, who for many years have continually offered its contents to various libraries of Europe. . . . Mr. E. N. Adler spent half a day in the Geniza. I learnt from him that he had been presented with some manuscripts by the authorities. This is 'the key he gave me.' . . . Priority questions, however, are tedious, and I do not intend to become a burden to your readers."[4]

The search for the "first" inventor or discoverer may be left to those obsessed with a romantic approach to human achievement. Most of the ancient sites of Egypt or Mesopotamia had been known to the local inhabitants centuries before European archaeologists arrived with spade and camera. They had been visited first by the tomb robbers, those bold, ubiquitous rascals of the "second-oldest profession." The native fellahin knew the rock grave of Pharoah Seti much more thoroughly than Belzoni, who is supposed to have explored it first. In fact, they seem to have had knowledge of chambers and staircases which are only being opened up in the 1960's. And who can say for how many centuries the Dead Sea caves had been visited by roaming Bedouin?

Schechter's contribution is not lessened because he was preceded by others at the Geniza. He has the distinction of having traced to the Geniza of Cairo all the numerous Hebrew documents which had appeared on the market for some time. It was Schechter who put a stop to the arbitrary scattering of the precious manuscripts by unscrupulous synagogue attendants and dealers. To clear the entire Geniza and bring its contents to Europe was his

---

[4] *The Times* (London), August 7, 1897, p. 11.

grand design. A man of enthusiasm and persuasiveness, Schechter had no sooner conceived the project to spirit the Geniza away, than he obtained the backing of some of the top men in Cambridge University. His chief sponsor was Charles Taylor, Master of St. John's College, a mathematician of note who had also become one of the outstanding non-Jewish students of Rabbinic literature. A scion of wealthy London merchants, he supplied the funds for Schechter's expedition. The whole mission was planned in secrecy, though Schechter did not keep altogether silent, judging by the letters he exchanged with an American friend (who forecast great successes) before he had reached Cairo.

With these credentials and a considerable amount of social affability and drive, Schechter embarked in December 1896 on his journey to Egypt. The country of the Nile had for him none of the attractions that a few years earlier had enraptured him in Italy. "Now that the sources of the Nile are being visited by bicycles," he wrote prosaically, "there is little fresh to be said about Cairo and Alexandria."[5] He found Alexandria particularly disappointing. To his American friend he confided: "I spent one day at Alexandria. Of Philo-Judaeus [the Hellenistic-Jewish philosopher] not a trace is to be found. The present Jew is more interested in cotton and other rubbish than in the logos and eternal love."[6] When he paid the Chief Rabbi a call and told him of the purpose of his trip, he received little encouragement. The Rabbi assured him that he would find very little in Cairo but "a few loose sheets."

His doubts were increased when he reached Cairo, of which he observed: "Everything in it, calculated to satisfy the needs of the European tourist, is sadly modern, and my heart sank within me when I reflected that this was the place whence I was expected to return laden with spoils, the age of which would command respect even in our ancient seats of learning."[7] But a visit to the most Reverend Grand Rabbi of Cairo, Rafaïl b. Shim'on, to whom he submitted his introductory testimonials, soon restored his spirits. He was promised full support.

Since the belongings of the synagogue were held in trust by the Rabbi and the Wardens, Schechter also had to earn the good will of the lay president of the Jewish community in Cairo. But the Rabbi was the key man, and Schechter won him through

---

[5] Schechter: *Studies in Judaism*, second series, p. 4.
[6] Bentwich: op. cit., p. 128.
[7] Schechter: *Studies in Judaism*, second series, p. 4.

his brother, who was the Rabbi's chief adviser. Schechter wrote facetiously to his wife a few days later: "The Rabbi is very kind to me and kisses me on my mouth, which is not very pleasant." In the same letter he could also report that he was already at work in the Geniza and had just taken away two big sacks filled with fragments. Schechter, the most outgoing of men, made friends with everybody. Suddenly Cairo seemed a glorious place. It enjoyed, he observed, an Italian opera, French dancing masters, English administration, and Mohammedan houris. "The last are very ugly, and I do not wonder that they are very careful to cover their faces."[8]

The Geniza was located at the far end of the ladies' gallery at the western side of the synagogue. Entrance to the secret recess was through a hole high up in the wall, to which one had to climb on a crude ladder. Mrs. Lewis and Mrs. Gibson, who had joined Schechter in Cairo, were allowed to peek into the chamber, from which had issued "so many ragged scraps of writing to make glad the hearts of European scholars." They were shocked to watch an attendant jump through the small opening and hear, as they stood below, "the crash of ancient vellum beneath his feet."[9] As lovers of books, they were as outraged as we are when we read of Belzoni's exploits in the Thebes necropolis, where "every step I took crushed a mummy in some part or other." Mrs. Lewis thought that manuscripts had, on the whole, received more consideration at Sinai, where they had at least been packed in boxes or baskets and were not tossed around and buried under the debris of tumbled walls and sand blown in from the desert.

Schechter was taken to the synagogue by the Chief Rabbi himself. At first he was altogether awed by the enormous quantity of the material and by the state of confusion it was in. Though authorized to claim as much as he wanted, he also felt he had to use some discretion and decided to confine himself entirely to manuscripts and forego the more recent printed works, which had been accumulated in great profusion during the past four hundred years. He considered the newer material of limited interest in comparison to the much older, handwritten documents. In this he was perhaps unjust. Later students of the printed works, such as E. N. Adler and J. L. Teicher, found valuable volumes of in-

---

[8] Bentwich: op. cit., p. 129.
[9] A. S. Lewis and M. D. Gibson: *Palestinian Syriac Texts from Palimpsest Fragments in the Taylor-Schechter Collection* (London: C. J. Clay; 1910), p. viii.

cunabula (rare specimens of early printed books) that also throw much light on fifteenth-century printing in the Near East. But, under the circumstances, Schechter had little choice. In view of the abundance of the material, some selection had to be exercised. In an article published in *The Times,* after his return, on August 8, 1897, Schechter gave a lively description of the sight that filled his eyes:

"One can hardly realize the confusion in a genuine, old Genizah until one has seen it. It is a battlefield of books, and the literary productions of many centuries had their share in the battle, and their *disjecta membra* are now strewn over its area. Some of the belligerents have perished outright, and are literally ground to dust in the terrible struggle for space, whilst others, as if overtaken by a general crush, are squeezed into big, unshapely lumps, which even with the aid of chemical appliances can no longer be separated without serious damage to their constituents. In their present condition these lumps sometimes afford curiously suggestive combinations; as, for instance, when you find a piece of some rationalistic work, in which the very existence of either angels or devils is denied, clinging for its very life to an amulet in which these same beings (mostly the latter) are bound over to be on their good behaviour and not interfere with Miss Jair's love for somebody. The development of the romance is obscured by the fact that the last lines of the amulet are mounted on some I.O.U., or lease, and this in turn is squeezed between the sheets of an old moralist, who treats all attention to money affairs with scorn and indignation. Again, all these contradictory matters cleave tightly to some sheets from a very old Bible. This, indeed, ought to be the last umpire between them, but it is hardly legible without peeling off from its surface the fragments of some printed work, which clings to old nobility with all the obstinacy and obtrusiveness of the parvenu."[1]

Weeks of drudgery followed. Day by day, working in the windowless storeroom, Schechter inhaled the "dust of centuries." He even had to undergo medical treatment. His biographer, Norman Bentwich, says that the work in the Geniza lumber room turned the robust scholar into an old man and almost broke his health. Schechter himself wrote: "The task was by no means easy, the Genizah being very dark, and emitting clouds of dust when its contents were stirred, as if protecting against the dis-

---

[1] Schechter: *Studies in Judaism,* second series, pp. 6–7.

turbance of its inmates. The protest is the less to be ignored as the dust settles in one's throat, and threatens suffocation."[2]

Realizing that, under such difficult circumstances, he could not do the job himself, Schechter rather hesitantly had to accept the help so freely offered by the synagogue's attendants and their numerous kinfolk. After all, the synagogue keepers had had considerable experience, as a result of their earlier transactions, in removing manuscripts from the Geniza. (Excavators in the Judean desert, searching caves for scrolls, were likewise to hire the same Bedouin who had previously freebooted the coveted articles.) Schechter was thus initiated into the complex Oriental etiquette which under the name of "bakshish" calls for lavish remuneration and bribes, rudely demanded but ever so graciously accepted by the natives in return for little or no services rendered. In view of his "former course of life," Schechter was ill-prepared for this humiliating and inefficient practice. It meant much haggling, and loss of money and time. Yet he could also see its humorous side. The keepers, he wrote, "of course declined to be paid for their services in hard cash of so many piastres *per diem*. This was a vulgar way of doing business to which no self-respecting keeper of a real Genizah would degrade himself. . . . In fact, the whole population within the precincts of the synagogue were constantly coming forward with claims on my liberality—the men as worthy colleagues employed in the same work (of selection) as myself, or, at least, in watching us at our work; the women for greeting me respectfully when I entered the place, or for showing me their deep sympathy in my fits of coughing caused by the dust. If it was a *fête* day, such as the New Moon or the eve of the Sabbath, the amount expected from me for all these kind attentions was much larger, it being only proper that the Western millionaire should contribute from his fortune to the glory of the next meal."[3]

Acceptance of this dubious help caused additional problems, as Schechter was soon to find out. To his dismay, he heard that a dealer in Cairo was offering fragments from the Geniza for sale, and he had no choice but to buy them back at an exorbitant price. However, an appeal to the Jewish community stopped the vile practice—at least for the time being.

The hoard was packed into huge sacks whose number steadily increased. By the end of January there were thirty. Schechter wrote to a friend in England: "The work was done

---

[2] Ibid., pp. 7–8.   [3] Ibid., p. 8.

thoroughly, as it is written: 'And they despoiled the Egyptians.'"[4] To forestall any last-minute inconvenience or theft, he tried to have the load expedited to England as quickly as possible. The British Embassy at Cairo lent a hand in procuring export permits and speedy shipment. It remained to have the sacks transported from the synagogue to the forwarding agent. But even then, "there was a last grab at the fragments,"[5] as Mrs. Lewis found out when she saw and bought some of them on open display in the shops of Cairo dealers. Schechter, while on his way to Palestine to visit his twin brother, who had settled near Haifa, got the news that rival emissaries from the Bodleian had tried to obtain leftovers from the Geniza, material that had been buried outside the synagogue.

The Egyptian spoils reached England before Schechter, who spent a few weeks in Palestine and then traveled to Marseille on a boat that ran on a rock and nearly sank outside its destination. A fellow passenger whom he befriended was another "despoiler" of Egypt—Flinders Petrie. For Schechter the real work now began —and one man's lifetime was not enough. This was the task of assorting, identifying, and editing the vast material—some hundred thousand fragments, according to his estimate. Meanwhile, the manuscripts, henceforth to be known as the Taylor-Schechter Collection, were made over to the Cambridge University Library, which in 1898 officially announced the acquisition by publishing a list of some of the noteworthy treasures and setting down the conditions under which the unique collection had been offered by its donors. In accord with those stipulations, the Cairo Jewish community was regaled by the university's senate with a handwritten parchment address, ornately composed in three languages and conveying their obligation "not only on account of the goodwill with which you received our Reader in Talmudic, but also on account of the conspicuous liberality with which you permitted him to return laden with fragments." A verse from Proverbs was quoted to make the Cairo Jews aware of the universal gain caused by their partial loss (if they ever felt it as such): "There is one that scattereth and yet increaseth." As to Schechter, he was given the degree of Doctor of Letters from the university and was honored with another equally well chosen quotation, this one appropriately enough from Ecclesiasticus: "Search and examine, seek and find, hold her fast and let her not go."[6]

---

[4] Bentwich: op. cit., p. 130.
[5] Lewis: *In the Shadow of Sinai,* p. 186.
[6] Bentwich: op. cit., p. 134.

In Schechter's article of August 8, 1897, in *The Times,* and in the preliminary list of the collection issued by the Library Syndicate in June 1898, some of the most striking finds so far identified were made public. Though this was only a trickle compared to things to come, the finds were truly sensational. The same issue of *The Times* that carried Schechter's vivid report also printed a letter from his Cambridge colleague F. C. Burkitt, announcing his discovery, among the Geniza fragments just brought to England, of a leaf from Aquila's translation of the Hebrew Old Testament into Greek. This work, which was noted for its literalness and which had been entirely lost, had replaced the Septuagint among Greek-speaking Jews until Greek itself fell out of use during the Arab expansion. It then vanished.

In his remaining years at Cambridge, Schechter labored almost exclusively in the large room of the University Library set aside for the collection, which was first distributed among 184 boxes. There were also bound volumes, and some 1,800 fragments, which were put under glass. There, as his biographer relates, he "worked all the hours of daylight, clad in a dustcoat and wearing a nose and mouth protector. He sifted and classified himself the hundred thousand fragments which he had recovered. Around him were a row of common grocery boxes labeled Bible, Talmud, History, Literature, Philosophy, Rabbinics, Theology, etc. He would pick out from the mass each piece of paper or parchment, look at it with his magnifying glass, and then place it in its proper box 'with as much alertness as a housewife sifting different articles of laundry.' . . . Scholars came from Europe and America to see him at work."[7]

Understandably enough, his foremost interest was Ecclesiasticus, the "true begetter" of the Geniza miracle. And his hopes of finding additional leaves from it did not go unrealized for long. In Cairo he had come upon leaves from another manuscript, and gradually he found more. He announced several such happy discoveries from time to time in *The Times,* becoming increasingly enthusiastic about the wealth of his treasure trove. "A whole unknown Jewish world reveals itself to us," he wrote one day. A few days later, he had his "most glorious Genizah day," when he found a Greek text, a Syriac palimpsest, and "the most important portion of ben Sira" on the same afternoon.[8] In addition to the new leaves from Ecclesiasticus which Schechter kept finding, others from the same work turned up in the British Museum, in Paris, and among

---

[7] Ibid., pp. 147–8.   [8] Ibid., p. 146.

E. N. Adler's Geniza manuscripts (later bequeathed to the Jewish Theological Seminary in New York). Gradually, two thirds of Ecclesiasticus was recovered. Several critical editions were now undertaken, starting with that by Schechter and Taylor in 1899. Others followed, until a German scholar, Rudolf Smend, in 1906 and 1907, issued what was for long the definitive edition. Yet, leaves from ben Sira continued to appear for years afterwards and were later supplemented by fragments from the Dead Sea caves. At last, in 1953, an almost complete edition was issued by M. S. Segal of the Hebrew University.

The Aquila text identified by F. C. Burkitt was one of the many palimpsests from the Geniza which were overwritten by Hebrew hymns. Schechter passed on these manuscripts—with underwriting mostly in Greek and Syriac—to his Cambridge colleagues, who were more adept at deciphering them. Among others, Mrs. Lewis and Mrs. Gibson edited several of the Palestinian-Syriac palimpsests. Perhaps the most valuable of them (also published by Burkitt) was from the famous Hexapla, a polyglot third-century Bible containing six different versions of the same text in parallel columns, compiled by Origen and believed to have been lost when the Arabs took Caesarea in 638. This palimpsest contained Psalm 22. As so often happens in the annals of discovery, almost simultaneously another palimpsest section of the Hexapla, also of Psalms, had been located by Giovanni Cardinal Mercati at the Ambrosiana in Milan in 1894. Though Mercati's was a more extensive manuscript, it represented a late, less satisfactory copy in minuscule, and, unlike the Geniza leaf, was missing the Hebrew column.

It would be impossible to list the prodigious wealth of this collection of manuscripts, not all of which have been identified. Schechter's cherished plan of having a complete catalogue of all the materials, and a collection in print (Corpus), is today as far from fulfillment as ever. As late as 1959, Paul E. Kahle, author of the one comprehensive work on the Cairo Geniza, and himself a student of the collection for sixty years, wrote: "Even today thorough examination of the fragments results in the most outstanding discoveries. It will still be a long time before this great treasure can be used to its full advantage."[9] And shortly before his death, in a lecture on the Geniza, Schechter spoke of such subjects as "astronomy and astrology, fiction and legends, mathematics

---

[9] Paul E. Kahle: *The Cairo Geniza*, second edition (New York: Frederick A. Praeger; 1960), p. 13.

and medicine, the Koran and sufism—more subjects than there were letters in the alphabet"[1]—on which the documents cast light. Yet today, half a century after these remarks, those rich possibilities have barely begun to be looked into.

הִי עֲלִי עֲדִים וְקָנוּ מִמְנִי מֵעֲבַשִׁי
לְמְבוּרֶף בְּרִ קִיאֹם לְהְיוֹת בִּירֹן

צֹמַאנֶ אֲשְׂאֵחוּ יֻרְבְּחוּלָאֲחִיגוּ
לְבְקְרֶ וְלְדְרוֹשׁ וְלֻצְאֹת מֵהְפְקִיד

שְׁטָאה לָאְרֹן וַאֲנָשִׁים בָּאֹנֹה וַאֲשְׁעֵיהֹם מֵעַל יִישֵׁ קֵי
מִלְכֹת מְנֶ צְ מְוֹ תְּפֹוֹב בְּגְלֹוֹל חֹמֵט נָאֹנֹה: צֹה יְנָאֹה

שְׂדֵ בִּ בְּ וֹ לֹם לְאֹת חֹפֵיגַע
פֻנְ · בְּבֻ יִבְּיבֵּט וֹמֹשְׁאֹתֵיכֹם

Fragments of Hebrew manuscripts from the Cairo Geniza (top to bottom): a contract on vellum dated A.D. 980, British Museum; a letter dated A.D. 1055, British Museum; a copy of Ecclesiasticus, probably from the ninth century, formerly in the possession of E. N. Adler; a document dated A.D. 1033, British Museum

In Biblical studies alone, the Geniza started a new era— whose end is not yet in sight—comparable in significance and ramifications to that ushered in by the Dead Sea scrolls. With some justification, Hebraists have spoken of the Age of the Geniza, preceding, in their science, the Age of the Caves.[2] Comparisons with the Qumran rolls may appear to be farfetched, but they are eminently appropriate—as we shall see. Although none of the Geniza manuscripts is nearly as old as the Qumran material, their number as well as their range have assured them a place in Old Testament and Jewish scholarship which the scrolls, it is probably safe to say, have only temporarily eclipsed.

A vast proportion of the Geniza texts are Biblical and go back to the tenth, if not the ninth, century. No older Hebrew Old Testament (with the exception perhaps of the old Karaite Bible still

---

[1] Bentwich: op. cit., p. 161.
[2] Isaiah Sonne: "The Newly Discovered Bar Kokaba Letters," *American Academy for Jewish Research, Proceedings,* Vol. XXIII (1954), p. 76.

in the possession of the Cairo community) was known before the appearance of the Dead Sea scrolls and the tiny Nash Papyrus. Schechter thought it likely, judging from the palaeographic evidence, that a few of the Biblical manuscripts were even older than the British Museum Pentateuchs. One colophon indicated a date of origin earlier than the celebrated Leningrad Codex of the Prophets, which had come from the Crimea and which dates from 916. On one fragment Schechter detected traces of gilt letters; Hebrew manuscripts are usually singularly free of "ornamental arts," but nevertheless gilt lettering may have been an invention of the Jews, though one that was soon abandoned.

The Biblical manuscripts shed much light on textual variations, particularly through the marginal glosses, and on the development of vowel punctuation, which helped to elucidate formerly disputed questions of Hebrew vocalization and pronunciation. As Schechter examined Geniza Scriptures, he read with interest their colophons, which indicated when and where the copy was made, the name of the scribe, or the owner of the book. Frequently such memoranda included forceful curses on those who might sell or remove the Psalter or Pentateuch donated by God-fearing and generous Mr. So-and-so to such-and-such a synagogue. Pious incantations of that sort would bring a smile to the modern-day manuscript hunter. Schechter commented: "It is rather disconcerting to read these curses when you happen to know something about the person who removed the manuscript, but you have to make the best of such kind wishes if you want to get at its history. Perhaps my researches may, after all, prove helpful to the feeble efforts made by the pious donor to achieve immortality, in as much as his name will again be given to the world in the catalogue which will one day be prepared. His chances in the dustheap of the Genizah were certainly much poorer."[3]

Another curiosity were Biblical specimens written in an unusual shorthand, the so-called "Trellis" writing, in which every verse has the first key word or words in full and the rest only by first letters. In this manner, the first verse of the Bible might be written: "In the beginning G. c. h. a. e." This was a kind of *aide de mémoire* rather than a text, and was perhaps not unrelated to the original vowel-less Semitic writing, which, it is occasionally maintained, was not based on a true alphabet but made

---

[3] Schechter: *Studies in Judaism*, second series, p. 17.

use of a shorthand, semisyllabic system. The Geniza supplied the first such examples of Trellis writing (an old Rabbinic term) employed for entire texts.

This form of abridged script was intended for the mature scholar who was quite familiar with the sacred texts. There were also brief selections from the Pentateuch written carefully in large letters for the teaching of the young—in short, Bible reading made easy.

Together with the Bible, liturgical texts constitute a major portion of the collection. These texts reveal the oldest forms of Jewish service and greatly enhance our knowledge of the evolution of the Jewish prayer book. Still more important, numerous unknown old hymns, "by a whole series of latter-day psalmists," could be chanted once more in praise of the Lord.

The rediscovery of Yannai, a seventh-century A.D. Hebrew poet, constitutes a romance comparable to that of Bacchylides. Yannai lived in Palestine during the Byzantine rule, before the Arab conquest. A single poem of his was known to us. Israel Davidson, who taught at the New York Jewish Theological Seminary, discovered five additional poems among the Aquila and the Hexapla palimpsests. But this was just the beginning. By 1938, Menachem Zulay, of the Schocken Research Institute for Hebrew Poetry at Jerusalem, had examined more than ten thousand photographs of Geniza fragments scattered around the world. From these he assembled a volume containing some eight hundred poems of Yannai.[4]

This is one of the outstanding rediscoveries in poetry. Some of Yannai's poems were not entirely religious in subject matter. Here, as a recent student of the Geniza wrote, "were exquisite pictures of the Palestinian countryside, of tired farmers returning from work with songs of praise on their lips, of 'meadows clothed with sheep' and plants 'growing in the abundance of dew.' "[5] The new discoveries made it clear that Hebrew secular poetry had flourished all over the lands of Byzantine and Islam civilizations and not just in Moorish Spain, as commonly believed.

The range of poetic manuscripts is simply staggering. Nothing perhaps indicates this better than unexpected samples in French of the "Aliscans," a *chanson de geste*, which has drawn the attention of Romance scholars. Schechter said, rightly: "The

---

[4] Norman Golb: "Sixty Years of Genizah Research," *Judaism*, Vol. VI, No. 1 (Winter, 1957), p. 11.
[5] Ibid., pp. 11–12.

Genizah is a world, with all its religious and secular aspirations, longings and disappointments, and it requires a world to interpret a world."[6]

הוגה מספר · את
מאז כרב מיימון [...]

Autograph of the Hispano-Jewish scholar and physician Maimonides, from the Cairo Geniza

Some of the Talmudic fragments were older than any copies so far known, and included missing portions from the Jerusalem Talmud. Lost works by one of the most illustrious of Talmudists, Saadia ben Joseph (A.D. 892–942), the "Gaon" (teacher) of Sura in Babylonia, added to the knowledge of this versatile and controversial personality, who had astounded his contemporaries with the scope and variety of his theological, grammatical, and polemical works, but who was also noted for his combativeness against rivals, schismatics, and his own former patrons. Parts of his Hebrew grammar, believed to be the first of its kind, came to light. So did sections of his Arabic Bible commentary, an autobiographical "Apologia," and a number of private letters. The letters rank with autographs by Maimonides and the poet-philosopher Judah ha-Levi (Yehuda ben Halevi), as among the greatest treasures taken from the Geniza.

As Schechter and other scholars probed further into the dusty piles, more and more lost works emerged. Enough was found to suit any literary, historical, religious, or philological palate, and to launch many a budding scholar on a career. There was, for instance, a treatise by Philo, translated into Arabic, on the Ten Commandments, and a provocative work by an unknown Jewish skeptic of the tenth century, which Schechter edited as "The Oldest Collection of Bible Difficulties by a Jew." He was a rationalist predecessor of Abélard who found inconsistencies in composition and content in the Old Testament. Schechter was reminded of the Higher Critics and "the malice of the Encyclopaedists."[7]

The Geniza contained an almost unlimited fund of private letters by unknown persons, which offered a glimpse into the customs

---

[6] Bentwich: op. cit., p. 161.   [7] Ibid., p. 153.

and historical trends of centuries of life in the Near East. They may well be compared with the troves of private correspondence from Ptolemaic and Roman Egypt excavated from Egyptian rubbish heaps at the same time that the Geniza was emptied. The Geniza letters and miscellania are from a later period, but are full of the same trivia, humor, and sheer vitality. Some of them have been published and more are being readied for publication, particularly those of economic significance dealing with Mediterranean trade. Here one may expect counterparts to the Zenon letters, from which Rostovtzeff derived so much insight into the economic history of Hellenistic Egypt.

Egyptian Fatimite coin with name of
Caliph Othman

It was the second generation of Geniza students who began to look into the historical background of the Cairo documents, but sixty years after the opening of the Geniza, scholars admitted that they were just starting to tap the wealth of material available. So much of value is constantly being found that historians have to confine themselves to comparatively narrow aspects or periods. To grasp the magnitude of the task, it must be realized that the more than one hundred thousand-odd fragments from the Old Cairo synagogue which are in Cambridge and elsewhere reflect twelve hundred years of the Christian era as seen through an intellectually and economically flourishing community that was an integral part of the great Arab civilization of the Middle Ages. The documents bear on the most varied facets of Arab and Mediterranean history, much of which had been utterly obscured because of lack of evidence. For instance, some of our views about the Crusades appear to be in need of complete revision. Modern histories of the Crusades state that only Frenchmen participated in the First Crusade when it reached the Holy Land, but a letter from the Geniza, from that time, testifies to the presence of the "cursed ones who are called Ashkenazim [Germans]."[8] Another letter, found by Professor S. D. Goitein of the Jerusalem Hebrew University, now proves that these "pilgrims" did not massacre the entire Jewish population. Some prisoners were taken, to be ransomed—much more profitable—for glittering Oriental coins.[9] At the same time, local Jews were providing relief for their less fortunate brethren.

Before the opening of the Geniza, knowledge of Jewish history both in Palestine and in Egypt from the time of the coming of the Arabs (seventh century) to the twelfth century was virtually nonexistent. Now we have even minute details. Palestine itself continued to live an active Jewish life after the Crusades; visitors came from as far as Spain and Russia. Talmudic centers proliferated and attracted foreign scholars. At one religious academy, Jewish students, unhappy about their accommodations, staged a riot.[1]

Once again, it is private letters which breathe life into the scene. A woman finds herself stranded in Constantinople and implores her brothers in Egypt to come to her assistance.[2] A scribe is forced to ply his trade in the provinces while leaving his small son in the custody of a teacher. He is worried about the boy, fearful about the dangers of the Cairo streets, and appeals to the custodian's sympathy: "Though I am poor, my children are dear to me."[3] At Cambridge and New York, Professor Goitein uncovered original letters from the Geniza written by Judah ha-Levi in Spain to a friend in Cairo. In one the poet tells of his plan to visit Egypt and the Orient. Considerable light is now shed on the last years of his life.

Formerly blank areas of Near Eastern medieval history such as economic crises, business associations, price structures and currency fluctuations, shipping, and relations with India, South Arabia, and East Africa are today being studied from original documents in Arabic and Hebrew. In recent years we have learned of an important trading station at Kish, an island in the Persian

---

[8] Golb: op. cit., p. 15.
[9] Dov Shelomo (Solomon Dob Fritz) Goitein: "What Would Jewish and General History Benefit by a Systematic Publication of the Documentary Geniza Papers?" *American Academy for Jewish Research. Proceedings*, Vol. XXIII (1954), p. 35.
[1] Golb: op. cit., p. 15 n.
[2] Jacob Mann: "The Genizah: What It Means to Jewish Learning," *Menorah Journal*, Vol. VII (December 1921), p. 305.
[3] Ibid.

Gulf which maintained its own army and naval force.[4] Some of the Jewish merchants owned flotillas of merchant ships in the Indian Ocean. Others acted as accredited agents for compatriots in foreign cities, in the manner of the consuls later dispatched by European cities and states. In all these areas of life, we had few Arab documents until the Geniza yielded its treasures. The Geniza records reflect a society then far in advance of Europe, and have indicated thereby that many of the institutions and practices of the emergent West, particularly in trade, finance, and contractual law, were fully anticipated on the other side of the Mediterranean.

By its very nature, the Geniza could be expected to contain considerable portions of Apocrypha, pseudepigrapha, and kindred literature, which the Rabbis did their best to conceal. Ecclesiasticus is a notable example. By the time the Cairo Geniza was started, perhaps in the ninth century A.D., many of the noncanonical works had already been removed. However, quite a few fragments, in addition to the variant manuscript pages of Ecclesiasticus, found their way into the vault, intended for oblivion. Among them was an extensive Aramaic portion of what is generally considered a Christian apocryphon (the distinction between such Jewish and Christian works is by no means always clear, depending sometimes on Christian interpolations into Jewish texts), the *Testaments of the Twelve Patriarchs.* Jewish works included *Chapters of Rabbi Eliezer* and *The Seder Eliyahu,* the latter allegedly written by Elijah the prophet. Schechter hailed these texts as significant evidence of "the history of Jewish religious development between the two Testaments."[5]

Around the turn of the century, Schechter took a closer look at a short work in his Cambridge collection. The presumably sectarian text was to fascinate him for nearly a decade, until he gave it to the world in 1910, together with related pieces. Called by him *Fragments of a Zadokite Work,* it is now better known as the *Damascus Document.* The publication raised virtually an academic and doctrinal storm, and a long-drawn-out, frequently acrimonious debate ensued, but the general public took little notice of it.

A thorough study of the sectarian fragments had convinced Schechter that they dealt with the religious tenets of an ancient Hebrew sect. Various allusions in the text to what seemed actual

---

[4] Goitein: op. cit., p. 35.   [5] Jacobs: op. cit., p. 703.

events made it likely that the sect had exiled itself to Damascus. There its members were supposed to have formed a New Covenant. All this was most mysterious and apparently without precedent in Jewish tradition. Who could these strange sectarians be? When did their community flourish? Schechter at first looked for internal evidence. To his trained eye, it was obvious that the Geniza texts of the two separate pieces of the *Damascus Document* were approximately of the tenth and twelfth centuries A.D. But once he analyzed the Hebrew language, the quasi-historical references, and the content of the two pieces, he became convinced that the original must have been of far greater antiquity: probably from about 100 B.C. Concerning the general character of the schismatic group, Schechter stated in the introduction of the published version: "One thing is certain, that we have to deal here with a sect decidedly hostile to the bulk of the Jews as represented by the Pharisees. It was a sect of laws of its own, a Calendar of its own, and a set of laws of its own, bearing upon various commandments of the Scriptures."[6]

From a Hebrew magical treatise reassembled from fragments of Geniza provenance scattered in Leningrad, New York, and elsewhere, as announced in 1964

Meanwhile Schechter was on the track of other clues. Once again, he not only discovered an unknown manuscript, but was the one man most qualified to identify it and elucidate its contents. His analysis was to rely to a great extent on the study he had made of the Hebrew Ecclesiasticus. Of further help was the simultaneous discovery, also Schechter's, of another lost work, a large part of the *Commands* (written in Aramaic) by Anan, a Jewish reformer, who was active in Mesopotamia during the eighth century. The *Damascus Document*, Schechter noticed, had distinct affinities to both Ecclesiasticus and the *Commands*. Together, these three works were unmistakably connected with two Jewish sects, the Karaites and the "Zadokites."

---

[6] Schechter: *Documents of Jewish Sectaries*, Vol. I (Cambridge: Cambridge University Press; 1910), p. xxciii.

The Karaites were a schismatic group of Jews believed to have
been founded, or at least organized, by Anan ben David in
Mesopotamia in the eight century A.D. They were antirabbinical,
puritanical, opposed to Talmudic tradition and exegesis, and insisted on the right of the individual to interpret the Bible. Thus,
they resembled the Protestants of the Christian Reformation. The
"Zadokites" (or Sadducees) were a much more ancient priestly
caste bitterly oppressed and then eclipsed by the Pharisees. However, it is doubtful that the "Zadokites" alluded to in the sectarian
literature of the Geniza are to be equated with the Sadduceean
priests of New Testament Jerusalem.

Schechter first came across allusions to the Zadokites ("sons"
or "priests of the house of Zadok") in the Ecclesiasticus leaves.
What puzzled him from the start was the fact that Zadokites were
not mentioned at all in the translated version. The original had,
for instance, a lost hymn which glorified the house of Zadok. One
of its lines was: "O give thanks unto Him that chose the sons
of Zadok to be priests." How strange that any mention of the
Zadokites was dropped, apparently on purpose, by the author's
grandson, the translator into Greek. Schechter offered a plausible
explanation: within two generations, under the Seleucid and
later the Hasmonaean rule, and under pressure from the pro-
Hellenistic Pharisees, the Sadducees had become anathema and
Sira's descendant cautiously "edited" the book to avoid offense.
Sira's references to the Zadokites make it likely that he himself
had belonged to the anti-Phariseean Sadduceean party.

The Zadokites cropped up again and again in Schechter's
studies of the Cairo manuscripts. Banned, vilified, and suppressed,
their name ran like a red thread through several of the once
doomed Judean works. What was one to make of the persistent
attacks by the Babylonian Talmudist Saadia and other Rabbinical
teachers on their enemies, the Karaite sectarians, as "Zadokites"?
Was this just name-calling? Or did the slanders have a more concrete basis? But hadn't the Zadokites disappeared from the scene
centuries earlier? How did the *Damascus Document* fit into the
picture?

Like the passages deleted from the Greek version of Ecclesiasticus, the newly unearthed *Damascus Document* disclosed explicit and favorable references to Zadokite priests. The *Document*
obviously centered around the experiences and practices of an
unnamed ancient sect, whom Schechter now felt justified in
calling Zadokites. The correspondence between the two sects, the

Zadokites and the Karaites—though they were apparently separated by centuries—was striking. How they could have been related remained something of a mystery. However, Schechter was firm in his belief that the *Damascus Document* preceded the rise of the Karaites by several centuries.

Difficulties inherent in Schechter's own views gave his opponents ammunition. Some declared the sectarian fragments outright fakes. Several reversed Schechter's hypothesis that the Zadokites had influenced the Karaites, and held instead that the Karaites were the authors of the *Damascus Document*, disputing thereby the antiquity of the book and the very existence of a Zadokite sect of Jewish dissidents from the Jerusalem priesthood who had founded a separate brotherhood in the pre-Christian era. Louis Ginzberg, Schechter's colleague at the Jewish Theological Seminary, quite credibly maintained that, although there undoubtedly had been such a sectarian group, it had much in common with the Pharisees and next to nothing with the Sadducees of history. Some scholars acclaimed Schechter's recovery of the sectarian fragments as an achievement of even greater significance than the collating of the Hebrew text of Ecclesiasticus. Only a few men grasped the full implications of the *Damascus Document*, borne out so persuasively by the discovery of the Qumran community and its library some fifty years later. As Norman Bentwich, Schechter's biographer, aptly summarizes, the newly found sectarian fragments "opened novel aspects of Jewish life and thought in the critical period which preceded the birth of Christianity."[7] In a still bolder vein, in 1911, in a review in *The American Journal of Theology*, Kaufmann Kohler said that "the Document shows points of contact with many movements in Jewish and Judaeo-Christian history."[8]

But quite a few of the questions raised by the sectarian manuscripts and the Zadokite revival in the eighth or ninth century A.D. remained as perplexing as ever. If the documents are not themselves of Karaite origin, how are their affinities with that sect to be explained? How is it that after many centuries of eclipse, the Zadokites became, apparently quite suddenly, so important among the Jews of the Near East? How, indeed, did schismatic Zadokite fragments survive? If the references to the unpopular and

---

[7] Bentwich: op. cit., p. 264.

[8] Kaufmann Kohler: "Dositheus, the Samaritan Heresiarch, and His Relations to Jewish and Christian Doctrines and Sects," *The American Journal of Theology*, Vol. XV, No. 3 (July 1911), p. 435.

maligned "Sons of Zadok" were removed in the Greek text of Ecclesiasticus, how was it possible that they were retained in the outspoken passages of the Hebrew original—and this in spite of the ruthless practice of discarding heretic and apocryphal texts? True, copies were banished to the Cairo Geniza, perhaps around the twelfth century A.D. But how, short of a miracle, did they escape being entombed earlier in other genizas or graves? Did they really escape? Was there really any definitive proof of the existence of a Zadokite sect in the pre-Christian era? And if so, what was its relation to other known sects, particularly to the Pharisees, Sadducees, and Essenes? Was there any corroborative evidence for the antiquity of the *Damascus Document*?

These queries were left unanswered for several decades. But an ultimate solution is now possible as a result of the sensational manuscript discoveries made in the Judean desert in the 1940's and early 1950's.

Solomon Schechter no longer had a part in these developments—he died in 1915—but he had sensed as keenly as anyone the problems posed by the Geniza finds. Immersed in his labors, he wrote: "Looking over this enormous mass of fragments about me, in the sifting and examination of which I am now occupied, I cannot overcome a sad feeling stealing over me, that I shall hardly be worthy to see all the results which the Geniza will add to our knowledge of Jews and Judaism. The work is not for one man and not for one generation. It will occupy many a specialist, and much longer than a life time. However, to use an old adage, 'It is not thy duty to complete the work, but neither art thou free to desist from it.' "[9]

---

[9] Schechter: *Studies in Judaism*, second series, p. 29.

·XIX·

CAVES IN THE

JUDEAN WILDERNESS

In Stygian cave forlorn . . .
MILTON *l'allegro*

IT IS ONE of the most desolate areas of the globe—largely devoid of vegetation and inhospitable to human habitation. Steep, cragged, calcareous hills, cut by precipitous ravines and hollowed by caverns, make up the landscape. The rocky, whitish wasteland, a scurfy scar on the crust of the earth, vividly dramatizes tectonic pressures, convulsions from earthquakes, and the slow grind of erosion. Were it not for its location, it could have been one of the most forsaken spots anywhere. Barren and seemingly lifeless though it is, the desert of Judah lies just east of Bethlehem and Jerusalem. Jericho, the oldest town known, fringes on it in the north. Rising abruptly from the deep trench of the Dead Sea, this ancient land of the Hebrew tribe of Judah could not entirely escape history. Battles were fought here, at least since the days that Saul warred against his former minstrel David. Rebels, robbers, and saints sought sanctuary in its solitude. Yet through the ages it has been mostly a refuge of seminomadic tribes. Here they hunted or led their livestock in search of food. Occasionally they drifted into distant wadis and climbed the vertical cliffs. In more recent years the unpatrolled hills were a smugglers' paradise until even more lucrative enterprises claimed their skill.

One day a dog, in pursuit of another animal, suddenly vanished before his master's eyes. He apparently had jumped into one of the many natural caves, but the opening was probably too high above the ground and the dog was trapped. In order to rescue his pet, the Arab now lowered himself through the hole into the darkness. Once his eyes adjusted to the dim interior, he was amazed to discern strange objects which, after some rummaging, he realized were leather rolls covered with scrawls. We are told that the Arab huntsman thereupon went to Jerusalem and alerted Jewish residents to the fact that books were hidden in the Judean hills. Jews from Jerusalem came in droves into the wilderness, and at the site, near Jericho, they found a number of scrolls of the Old Testament and of non-Biblical texts, all in Hebrew.

Woodcut of Jerusalem, from Breydenbach's *Reise ins Heilige Land* (Mainz, 1486)

The incident sounds familiar enough. We have all heard of the circumstances: a Bedouin accidentally entering a cave while searching for a stray animal. We have heard of the place: the rugged hills northwest of the Dead Sea; and of the results: the discovery of ancient Hebrew manuscripts and literary fragments written on leather rolls. Only the date may come as a surprise. It happened about the year A.D. 800.

The episode is trustworthily reported in an undated letter by Timotheus I (726?–819?), Nestorian-Christian Patriarch of Seleucia-Ctesiphon, near Baghdad, to Sergius, the Metropolitan of Elam. When a German Orientalist, Oskar Braun, published this

and other Syriac letters of Timotheus in a German journal in
1901,[1] he caused hardly a stir. But half a century later, in 1949,
the long-forgotten article was brought to the attention of another
German scholar, Otto Eissfeldt, who promptly republished it.[2]
The world was thus made aware of this astonishing anticipation
of the Dead Sea scroll discoveries by some eleven hundred and
fifty years.

Was this just a coincidence, curious but otherwise of no
consequence? Is there any connection with the modern find? Do
we know what manuscripts were found in 800 and what happened
to them? Unfortunately we have nothing but the Nestorian's communication, but there are nevertheless quite a few clues. Timotheus related in his letter that he had been told about the discovery
by Jewish converts to Christianity from Jerusalem. According to
them, the books had been taken from the "rock dwelling" some
ten years earlier. There were "a great number," and they apparently included both canonical and noncanonical works. Among
the scrolls were more than two hundred hymns, referred to as
"Psalms of David." Timotheus was principally interested to know
whether the Biblical texts contained passages from the Old Testament quoted in the New Testament, "but which are not to be
found anywhere in it [the O.T.], neither amongst the Jews nor the
Christians." The patriarch's Hebrew informant, "a scribe well
read" in Hebrew literature, obligingly (he must have had a fabulous memory and remarkable powers of perception) assured him
that such passages were indeed included in the cave manuscripts.
But, understandably, Timotheus wanted further confirmation on
that point. As he tells his friend, he wrote about it "to the noble
Gabriel, and also to Shuvalemaran, Metropolitan of Damascus."
However, he did not get an answer. He ends his letter despondently: "I have no suitable person whom I can send. This is a fire
in my heart, burning and blazing in my bones."

It is interesting to note that Timotheus also pondered over
the origin and date of the "cave library" and the reasons for the
deposit of the rolls. Anyone who has delved into the enormous
literature on the Dead Sea scrolls will recall that these are some
of the most vexing questions in the case of the later discoveries.

---

[1] Oskar Braun: "Ein Brief des Katholikos Timotheos I über biblische
Studien des 9. Jahrhunderts," *Oriens Christianus*, Vol. I (1900), pp. 299–
313.
[2] Otto Eissfeldt: "Der gegenwärtige Stand der Erforschung der in
Palästina neugefundenen hebräischen Handschriften," *Theologische Literaturzeitung*, Vol. LXXIV (October 1949), pp. 595–600.

Timotheus thought he had the answer: the books from the cave had been placed there by either of the prophets Jeremiah or Baruch, who, informed "by divine revelation" of the coming conquest and exile, hid the holy scriptures "in rocks and caves . . . in order that they might not be carried off by plunderers." When the Jews returned from the Babylonian captivity, those who had buried the scrolls were no longer alive and the knowledge of the deposit had been forgotten. Timotheus may have attributed the burial of the books to the prophets because of a reference in Jeremiah 32:14 to "earthen vessels" as receptacles for books—"that they may continue many days." This would imply that the rolls had been found in jars, like the later scrolls from Qumran Cave I.

Earthen jars from Cave 1, Qumran

When the cave discoveries of A.D. 800 came to the notice of mid-twentieth-century scholars, they were immediately confirmed by other (circumstantial) evidence. Various hitherto somewhat puzzling phenomena, when considered in the light of these lost texts, were now explained.

The Jewish sect of the Karaites arose in the latter part of the eighth century in Mesopotamia, as we have mentioned. Its rapid growth in the ninth and tenth centuries had not been plausibly accounted for. And, surprisingly, the evidence from the Cairo Geniza was that it had evolved as the dominant sect in Jerusalem itself during this period, in the face of strong opposition from the Rabbinical sacerdotalists. In the ninth and tenth centuries the sect apparently drew on a new arsenal of ideas and arguments revealing, no doubt, quite remarkable affinities with the "Zadokite" fragments which are contained in the *Damascus Document*. In Karaite texts of the time we come across distinctly sectarian views that parallel the *Damascus Document* and are nowhere encountered in earlier Karaite or Rabbinical literature.

All of a sudden, Karaite authors openly appealed to Sadduceean (or Zadokite) books. And their enemies, the Talmudic rabbis, attacked them outright as "Zadokites."

The evidence is unmistakable. At this time an old sectarian calendar with its peculiar fixing of festival days was revived; it was identical with that of the noncanonical *Book of Jubilees* (by the way, one of the most profusely represented texts among the Qumran scrolls) and of the *Damascus Document*. Other clear-cut correspondences pertain to certain marriage, divorce, and purity rituals, and dietary laws. These reforms, as Karaite authors gleefully report, exerted some effect even on their Rabbinite enemies in Jerusalem, who partly adopted them. The impact of ancient sectarian concepts is perhaps best highlighted by a ninth-century Karaite reference to the "Teacher of Righteousness," a central figure of the Dead Sea–Damascus eschatology, who, as we now know, had not been alluded to for centuries.[3] The evidence could be easily amplified. In any case, it speaks persuasively for the immediate influence of "Zadokite" texts on Karaite teachings and for the likelihood that new sources greatly strengthened Karaite self-confidence and religious authority. But how had the Karaites come into possession of these ancient texts that had apparently been inaccessible for centuries?

One man who applied himself to the problem and contributed vigorously to its solution was Paul E. Kahle, the Anglo-German Old Testament scholar, who was also a long-time, avid student of the Geniza. He wrote: "How they [the Karaites] had come by such texts presented a real problem. The Sadducees had been dispersed when the Temple was destroyed and the Karaite movement began only in the course of the eighth century. So the handing down of Sadduceean teaching must have been achieved by literary means. But what literature was involved? All texts appertaining to Sadduceean literature had been destroyed by the Rabbis. . . . The connecting link was missing."[4] In Kahle's mind—and most scholars now share this view—there was no doubt that the texts had come to the Karaite community in Jerusalem from the cave hoard described by Timotheus I. The date of the discovery, around 800, fits well with the chronological evidence of the resurgence of the Karaites.

Kahle and his colleagues sedulously searched for and found

---

[3] John M. Allegro: *The Dead Sea Scrolls*, revised edition (Harmondsworth: Penguin Books; 1958), p. 167.

[4] Kahle: op. cit., pp. 23–4.

further proof in several contemporary Karaite and other writers. A principal source is a tenth-century Karaite by the euphonious name of Kirkisani (Yaʻqūb al-Qirqisānī), a prominent writer who expounded the Karaite Law and wrote a history of Jewish sects. In it he alludes to the so-called *Maghariyah*, an Arabic word meaning "Men of the Caves," whom he dates after the Pharisees and Sadducees, and before the Christians. He explains that they owe this name to the fact that their books were found in a cave. (The designation was probably given to them by the men who rediscovered them and does not represent their actual name.) That these "cave men" can be safely identified with the documents found near Jericho around A.D. 800 is further underlined by Kirkisani's enumeration of some of their works, foremost among them a *Book of Zadok*, and "many strange commentaries on the Scriptures." Additional information on the same sect and on cave finds is given by the Karaite authors Mirwan and Nahawendi, and even crops up in the correspondence between a Jewish statesman from Moorish Spain and a king of the Khazars (a Uigur-Turkic people in southern Russia who had been converted to Judaism and built a powerful kingdom).

A Moslem writer, Shahrastani (A.D. 1071–1153), also mentions the "cave sect" and, in agreement with Kirkisani, dates its origin "four hundred years before Arius," that is, about the first century B.C.—a date, one will remember, that comes close to the one Schechter suggested for the composition of the *Damascus Document*. As late as the thirteenth century, Moses Taku, an Eastern rabbi, recalled "that the heretic Anan [the Karaite leader] and his friends used to write down heresies and lies and hide them in the ground. Then they would take them out and say: 'This is what we found in ancient books.'" The rabbi's account is clearly a biased rendering of the Karaites' tradition that they owed some of their doctrines to lost books "taken from the ground."[5]

Do we know the cave from which this early hoard of manuscripts was taken? Though all this may sound like a "whodunit," there is good reason to believe that Timotheus' cave is in fact Qumran I, where the Bedouin shepherd boy Muhammad adh-Dhib found the first eleven Dead Sea scrolls. These scrolls probably were only a small fraction of the original deposit, to judge by the forty-odd broken jars, and by the many fragments of a total of perhaps 150 to 200 rolls. The scattered fragments unquestionably

---

[5] Saul Liebermann: "Light on the Cave Scrolls from Rabbinic Sources," *American Academy of Jewish Research, Proceedings*, Vol. XX (1951), p. 403.

came from scrolls previously carried off, more of which may have been taken away intact and thus have left no trace.

Several circumstances strengthen this thesis. For one, Timotheus' letter suggests that the earlier removal was a large-scale operation. Furthermore, various broken jars and leather fragments indicate by their chips and torn edges that this "plundering" took place a long time ago. And then the subject matter—Hebrew Old Testament texts, commentaries, hymns, and other noncanonical works—as well as the assumed sectarian character of several of the ninth-century manuscripts, implies a close affinity, if not the same origin, of the Qumran scrolls and the Timotheus texts. Even the way the animal got lost through an opening in the cave's ceiling rather than through a level entrance fits in with the physical layout of the Qumran I cave.

Passage from the "Midrash [commentary] on the Book of Habakkuk," from the Qumran caves

A few objections also come to mind. How was it that no material trace of the ninth-century visitors was found? To some people today it seemed odd that the eager manuscript hunters of 1,150 years ago would leave major scrolls behind, unless those had been hidden in a corner and were simply overlooked in the excitement. These points may weaken the argument that the cave discovered in 800 was indeed Qumran I, but they do not in the least undermine the likelihood of a connection between the A.D. 800 manuscripts and the Qumran cave deposits in general. Now that many more manuscript-bearing caves have been discovered in the same wadi, each with fragments from similar types of texts, Cave IV or VI or almost any other may be identified as the Timotheus cave. And there are possibly a number of caves in the vicinity which have not yet been explored but which may contain manuscripts and be the very one.

Do we have any way of telling what manuscripts were removed in Timotheus' time? Again, the evidence is only circumstantial, except for the somewhat vague hints given by Timotheus himself and by Kirkisani. We know for certain that, as with the modern Dead Sea scrolls, both canonical and noncanonical books were included. The "more than 200 Psalms of David" may have been akin to the Qumran Thanksgiving Psalms, just as Kirkisani's mention of "strange commentaries" recalls the Qumran I Commentary on Habakkuk, with its rather arbitrary interpretations of the Scriptures.

No doubt there must have been many Zadokite sectarian tracts among the Timotheus texts. Kirkisani not only referred to the *Book of Zadok* as one of the cave works, but in his own *Kitab al-Anwar,* or "Book of Lights," he expounded some of the sect's views, which he apparently took from the *Book of Zadok.* These beliefs and practices are in virtual agreement with the *Damascus Document.*

At last we have a plausible answer to the mysterious presence of the *Damascus Document* in the Cairo Geniza. The Damascus, or Zadokite, fragments must have been later copies of originals from the Jericho caves, as first proposed by Kahle. The discovery of schismatic texts around A.D. 800 explains why this sectarian literature could exert such influence so suddenly, after having been ineffective and forgotten for many centuries. In Timotheus' time these texts were revitalized; they were copied, disseminated, and commented upon. And then they were once more condemned and eliminated. Most were totally obliterated, but fragments of the *Damascus Document* survived in the Geniza of Old Cairo until rediscovered by Schechter.

The discovery of the Dead Sea scrolls, more than any ninth- or tenth-century references, compelled scholars to see the relationship between "Zadokite" fragments from the Geniza and the ancient Jewish sectarian literature, and also removed doubts concerning the authenticity and ultimate origin of the *Damascus Document.* If any further physical proof were needed, it was supplied by various manuscript scraps from old copies of this very document, all found in the Qumran Caves III and VI. The close connection between Schechter's Zadokite fragments and the sectarian books of the Dead Sea scrolls was recognized from the very beginning, even before their common origin in a cave was suspected. In fact, it has become customary to include the *Damascus Document* in most editions or translations of the Dead Sea texts.

In almost all of the numerous books about the Qumran cave literature, the *Damascus Document* is used to elucidate what little can
be surmised of the origin and historical background of the Dead
Sea scrolls. Presumably linked by common origin and contents,
but differentiated by conditions attending on their transmission
and recovery, each has contributed to our understanding of the
other.

The *Damascus Document* and the Dead Sea scrolls reflect
the same religious tenor, the same particulars of language—indeed, some passages agree word for word—and doctrines and
rules, and contain many allusions to what can only be the
same sect, though perhaps at different stages of development. The
identity of this sect with the Qumran community centered at the
Khirbet Qumran monastery is now fairly well established, even
though its name is not. An identification of the sect with the
Essenes is probably correct if one allows "Essenes" to be a collec-
tive term for a variety of puritanical groups who, like Zealots and
Pharisees, sprang from the earlier Hassidim and at one time had
more in common with the apocalyptic Pharisees than the Sadducees known from the New Testament.

Pre-Christian Palestine—not unlike eighteenth-century England, of which Voltaire remarked that it had as many denomina-
tions as France had sauces—was simply a hotbed of sects of
bewildering range. A third-century A.D. rabbi has said: "Israel was
not dispersed before it broke up into twenty-four sects of heretics."[6] Rabbinic conformism and calculated destruction of the literary evidence have unfortunately blurred the picture. The Geniza
and Qumran texts reveal aspects of a rich sectarian tradition in
the heterogeneous Jewish religious scene within which Christianity
arose. It would be presumptuous, if not wrong, however, to maintain that the Qumran community anticipated Christianity in any
of its vital doctrinal or eschatological concepts.

The *Damascus Document* was not the only text to be taken
from the Judean cave around A.D. 800 by Jerusalem Jews. What
happened to the other manuscripts? Here we can only speculate.
In all likelihood, most, if not all, of them were sooner or later committed once again to imprisonment at genizas. Those that did
not fall into the hands of the Karaites, or those with which even
the Karaites were not in sympathy, were perhaps quickly reburied.

---

6 Ibid., p. 404.

The few that survived may have vanished with the decline of the Karaites.

Even Old Testament manuscripts were unlikely to find much favor with the rabbis, who would not tolerate any challenge to the firmly established textual authority, fixed by the Synod of Jamnia (near Jaffa) in about A.D. 90. This is very much in line with the general practice of the Jews, who on the whole have shown little reverence for ancient manuscripts and have discarded writings as soon as they are considered worn out, provided of course that the exact transmission of the text was assured. Even in Schechter, one can see evidence of this insensitivity to ancient volumes. We are told that his rough handling of the Geniza manuscripts sent chills down the spine of the Cambridge University librarian. One can well imagine the fate of the Qumran scrolls had they fallen into the hands of Orthodox Jews.

While the *Damascus Document* is the one document we can trace with near certainty to the Qumran caves, a fairly good case can be made for the Hebrew version of Ecclesiasticus. This manuscript, which came from the Geniza, contains similar allusions to the Zadokites, and its Geniza text, too, can now be supplemented by fragments from the Qumran caves.

The cave brotherhood was attracted by noncanonical and pseudepigraphical works, and may even have written some of these. The possibility of the transmission of such works from the caves after A.D. 800 cannot be ruled out. Hugh J. Schonfield, an Anglo-Jewish scholar, has come up with the intriguing hypothesis that some books were taken from the caves and "either in copies or translation eventually reached Russia, and may in part be represented by Slavonic texts such as those of the *Book of the Search of Enoch, Apocalypse of Abraham, Testaments of the Twelve Patriarchs, Vision of Isaiah, Life of Adam and Eve,* and others. . . ."[7]

Does it not seem surprising that the world had to wait for more than a thousand years after the find in A.D. 800 until further manuscripts were quite accidentally uncovered in the same area? The answer is that the world has not been waiting all this time. Egyptian soil did not suddenly in the nineteenth century yield papyri when Egyptologists and papyrologists were ready for them. It would be against all the laws of probability that fellahin digging

---

[7] Hugh J. Schonfield: *Secrets of the Dead Sea Scrolls* (New York: A. S. Barnes–Perpetua Books; 1960), p. 56.

for *sebakh* during thousands of years have not occasionally dug up papyrus shreds or rolls. But there was no interest and hence no market. These were not genuine "discoveries," and the precious antiquities were unceremoniously discarded. A discovery is never merely a lucky find; it requires a sense of awareness of the significance of the object found, and a culture receptive to a potential addition to its knowledge.

Excerpt from a Biblical manuscript in Slavonic, tenth century

The Ta'amireh tribe has been roaming the Judean hills since the seventeenth century, and there were other Bedouin before them. The Hebrews who came into Canaan before and during the Exodus in the second millennium B.C. were their remote kinsmen. Shepherds and goatherds encamped in some of the very caves that show traces of former manuscript deposits. In several of the caves in which ancient Hebrew scroll fragments were stored, Arabic texts of a much later date (fourteenth and fifteenth century) have been found. Cave lore from many countries (for example, Altamira in Spain) tells of animals falling into natural caverns and of the good shepherd or loving master crawling to their rescue, thereby accidentally coming upon objects hidden there. Indeed, after the finding of Cave I, an old man of the Ta'amirehs turned the attention of his fellow tribesmen to an out-of-the-way cave which he had entered years before when following a wounded partridge. This was Cave IV, which turned out to be perhaps the richest of them all, and, according to some experts, the main library deposit of the Qumran sect.

We know that the Ta'amireh Bedouin, who for long looked upon these Judean hills as their private domain, have explored and exploited caverns before the discovery of the Dead Sea scrolls. In the early 1920's, at the Wadi Murabba'at, they collected the manure deposited there for centuries by birds and bats, and sold it to Jewish colonists. Some of it came from caves in which manuscripts were subsequently located. When asked later whether they had then seen any written scrolls or leaves, they did not recall any. In those days their main enterprise was the collection of fertilizer, so why should they even register the sight of rat-eaten scraps of writing of whose market potentialities they had no inkling? It is altogether possible, as Roland de Vaux suggested, that Jewish citrus plantations near Bethlehem were enriched by bits of manuscripts.[8]

The alert and enterprising Ta'amireh, always on the lookout for an easy way to make money, had recognized the value of antiquities long before the marketability of unappealing scraps of writing dawned upon them. In the 1930's and 1940's, this tribe was busy in the Wadi el-Tin, some three miles southeast from Bethlehem, searching systematically for prehistoric bronzes, which they offered to antique dealers.[9] Only by befriending the Ta'amireh could French archaeologists locate this rich mine of Chalcolithic art objects.

To this day, the Bedouin scour the cliffs for caves, search them diligently for artifacts, and then sell what they find on the Bethlehem market. Their principal agent has been an Assyrian Christian cobbler known as Kando. Scientific diggers only follow in the Bedouin's wake, and on the whole have come up with little more than secondary discoveries. With the exception of a single cave, all the others had already been opened and cleared by the Bedouin. The Jordan government has acquiesced in this practice, even giving the Ta'amireh a kind of monopoly over the manuscript trade by keeping other Bedouin out of the area. It is difficult to see how the whole business could be handled otherwise, since learned institutions lack the money to carry out continuous and systematic exploration, as does the Jordanian government, which

---

[8] Roland de Vaux, O.P.: "Les grottes de Murrabba'at et leurs documents," *Revue Biblique,* Vol. LX (1953), p. 247.

[9] L.-H. Vincent, O.P.: "Une grotte funéraire antique dans l'Ouady el-Tin," *Revue Biblique,* Vol. LIV (1947), p. 269.

has proved to be liberal enough. Indeed, Western scholars cannot be expected to compete in physical stamina and agility with the Ta'amireh, who know the hills as their backyard, and who, once they had tasted riches, could not be forced to desist from these "operations."

Naturally, a great deal of valuable archaeological data concerning stratification, identification *in situ*, manner of deposit, etc., are hopelessly lost. Moreover, some of the manuscripts are damaged by careless handling, and they have to be bought from the Bedouin, at high prices through shady middlemen. The team of international scholars now associated with the Palestine Archaeological Museum in the Jordanian section of Old Jerusalem, who are engaged in deciphering and editing of the manuscripts in the famous "scrollery," live in constant fear that documents will be sold to outsiders and thus scattered. Some illicit sales may already have taken place: nobody quite knows what is still in the possession of the crafty tribesmen. Scrolls exceeding in number and completeness those of Cave I have been rumored to exist.

Unfortunately, the Jordan museum is rarely able to pay the Bedouin. Foreign contributions toward the purchase of manuscripts have been made, but they are not nearly sufficient. Out of desperation the Jordanians, in an act of admirable but perhaps ill-advised self-denial, have even agreed to sell manuscripts. Some of these have been acquired by McGill, Manchester, and Heidelberg universities, on the pledge that the scrolls would be kept at the Palestine Museum until they had been fully edited. In view of the enormous interest generated by the Dead Sea scrolls, and the valuable contribution they make to our knowledge of Judeo-Christian backgrounds, it is sad indeed that funds are not available to acquire all the manuscripts from the Bedouin.

The story of the Dead Sea scrolls has been told in several highly seasoned, melodramatic versions. Fascinating in itself, it was largely acted out against the background of a shooting war in the holy city of Jerusalem, almost a reenactment of the apocalyptic War of the Children of Darkness against the Children of Light described in one of the scrolls. Only one cannot be quite sure which are which.

Many details in the standard account, particularly of the first cave discovery, not to speak of the sale of the scrolls, are greatly in doubt. To some skeptics, among whom Professor Solomon

Zeitlin of Dropsie College, Philadelphia, was the most vociferous, the story simply sounded too pat. There are, for example, considerable variations in the versions of G. Lankester Harding, John M. Allegro, and Millar Burrows, though they have all been in close touch with events in Palestine. Several implausibilities and contradictions have been pointed out by scholars, some of whom declared the scrolls to be either fakes or of medieval origin, and hence were eager to refute as much of the evidence as they could.

A few lines from the apocalyptic Qumran scroll, "The War of the Children of Darkness against the Children of Light"

For some time, no Westerner had seen Muhammad adh-Dhib, the boy discoverer. Did he really exist? Was it a sheep or a goat he was said to have been searching for? Did he throw a stone to alert the stray animal, or simply in boyish exuberance? Could he have heard the clatter of broken jars and have been startled by it? Did he enter the cave alone and right away? Did he come back with one of his two fellow herdsmen? Did they divide the loot? And so on. Further confusion was added by the Syrian Metropolitan, Mar Athanasius Yeshue Samuel, who at one time declared that the manuscripts he was showing to foreign experts had rested for long in the library of his monastery.

Several years after the discovery, in 1956, someone was able to get hold of Muhammad adh-Dhib in Bethlehem and had him recount his adventure. His words were taken down by an Arab scribe, and the document was signed by Dhib and published and translated into English by the noted American Orientalist William H. Brownlee, one of the original American team of the American School of Oriental Research, Jerusalem, which edited the Dead Sea scrolls in the possession of the Syrian Metropolitan. This "authorized version," if anything, obscured the matter still further. Most surprisingly of all, Dhib now said that the find was made in 1945 and not in 1947 as everybody had hitherto believed. He said he had hoped to find treasure when he opened the cave vessels, and when he saw only leather rolls, he seriously pondered whether he should take them at all. But he and his companions needed new leather straps for their sandals, so he took them after all. We are left in the dark as to why—or whether—the material was judged unsuitable for this purpose. Anyhow, Dhib now maintained that upon his return he put the rolls into "a skin bag and hung it up in a corner." There they apparently remained for more than two years, until an uncle of his noticed them and asked to show them to a Bethlehem dealer in antiquities.

Dhib's recollections differ considerably from earlier versions, and do not entirely tally with some fairly well established facts. For instance, he claimed there had been only ten jars, all of which he demolished before finding scrolls in the last one. (Scheherazade could not have improved on this.) Two other jars, he said, were filled with red seeds. But no trace of these has been found. We also know that Professor Sukenik of the Hebrew University acquired undamaged jars from the same cave. Dr. Brownlee was impressed by the "almost Biblical directness and beauty of this concise account," yet he freely admits that the story "had achieved precision and finesse through frequent retelling."[1]

And this brings us back again to the question whether the incident is on the whole credible, and whether the eleven Dead Sea scrolls were taken from the Qumran Cave I. Despite conflicting details, however, all serious doubts were dispelled when a joint expedition under G. Lankester Harding, Director of Antiquities in Jordan, Father Roland de Vaux, O.P., director of the Dominican École Biblique et Archéoligique Française in Jerusalem, along with a Belgian observer for the United Nations and an official of the Palestine Archaeological Museum in Jordan, found the cave. This was in 1949. Valuable time had elapsed, during which both the Bedouin and the Syrian Metropolitan had carried out illegal excavations in the most ruthless manner. The latter had even broken a new entrance into the cave, which had a natural window through its roof.

That this was indeed the same cave, no one could doubt. The modern-day plunderers had left incriminating evidence. There was, for instance, a cigarette lighter which had been accidentally dropped and whose owner was known. There were recently broken jars and a great many manuscript fragments—around six

---

[1] William H. Brownlee: "Muhammed ad-Deeb's Own Story of His Scroll Discovery," *Journal of Near Eastern Studies*, Vol. XVI, No. 4 (October 1957), pp. 236–9.

hundred were collected by carefully combing the soil—some of which fitted the scrolls removed earlier. The scientists also found bits of linen in which the scrolls had been wrapped. These proved invaluable for a later determination of the manuscripts' approximate age by the Carbon-14 method.

Writing desk excavated at Khirbet Qumran. It belonged to the monastic scriptorium where the Dead Sea scrolls were probably written.

This was the beginning of Qumran archaeology. The location and antiquity of the Hebrew cave library was established. The next step was the excavation, also by Lankester Harding and Father de Vaux, of the nearby Khirbet Qumran ruins, which were identified after several digs as the monastic center of the sectarian community most likely responsible for the writing and deposit of the cave scrolls. As to the age of the scrolls, palaeography and archaeology rule out a medieval or a later origin. Only Professor Zeitlin and a few of his pupils remain unconvinced. The heterogeneous subject matter of the cave documents as well as their lack of textual uniformity make it quite certain that they must have been written before the end of the first century A.D., that is, before the rabbis firmly established the texts and canon and suppressed nonconformist variants.

Debate on the meaning and significance of the Dead Sea scrolls still rages. It involves such questions as the nature, creed, and rules of the Qumran community; the age of the scrolls; the date of their composition and deposit; the identity of the Wicked Priest and the Teacher of Righteousness; the Essenes and their affinities with the Qumran Covenanters; the sect's supposed exile in Damascus; possible connections with John the Baptist, Christ, and His brother James; and the most burning issue of all— whether, and how, the Qumran sect was a forerunner of Christianity? Did its Messianic views, its ritual, dogma, and theology closely resemble those of the early Christians? Is the uniqueness of Jesus challenged? Unfortunately, in these matters there has been much sensationalism on the one hand ("The most vigorous debate in Christianity since Darwin," "Qumran rather than Bethlehem as cradle of Christianity") and undue timidity on the other.

One of the outstanding things about the scrolls is that they are Hebrew manuscripts some one thousand years older than any previously known. This may well be their most lasting contribution. They have already shed much light on the history of the Hebrew language, on Hebrew palaeography (a science that has only now come into its own), the growth of the Biblical canon, and the textual traditions of the Old Testament. When the scrolls were first examined, it was announced that they were in almost complete agreement with the officially recognized Masoretic text of the Scriptures. This can no longer be maintained. Further study and additional fragments clearly indicate that the Masoretic text, though of considerable authority, represents just one of several traditions. It is not the exclusive descendant of *one* "archetype." Some ancient Hebrew passages from the caves, for example, favor the Greek Septuagint rather than the Masoretic form. As a matter of fact, what had been occasionally suspected is now well established: namely, that the Septuagint is based on a sound and authoritative variant Hebrew text which in many instances may well be preferable to the Masoretic one. Similar observations can be made about the Samaritan Pentateuch. The implications for new editions of the Hebrew Old Testament and for translated versions are momentous. This may well spur an entirely new branch of textual criticism that will occupy coming generations of Old Testament scholars. Indeed, as additional ancient texts become available, we may have to borrow the concept of "families" of manuscripts from the Greek New Testament in order to trace systematically the relationships among the variant texts and arrive at sound editorial decisions.

As editors, the Masoretes may have done their work extremely well; but they did not do as well in establishing a monopoly for their Old Testament text when they rigorously suppressed rivals. As recently as 1939, Sir Frederic Kenyon said in the third edition of *Our Bible and the Ancient Manuscripts:* "There is indeed no possibility that we shall ever find manuscripts of the Hebrew text going back to a period before the formation of the text we call Masoretic [i.e., before the second century A.D.]." But one can never be sure. The new knowledge derived from the

Dead Sea scrolls so far is likely to be overshadowed by many more discoveries. Even material recovered previously, like the texts taken from the Cairo Geniza, will not be fully available for a number of years, and then it will take much longer to be assimilated. By that time the popular interest may have died down and with it exaggerated claims and overspeculative assessments.

Facsimile of square Hebrew characters impressed into the copper scroll and traced by Professor K. G. Kuhn of Göttingen University even before the oxidized sheets were opened and fully deciphered.

Meanwhile other finds, greeted with less fanfare, have been steadily forthcoming since the clearing of Cave I. No longer does it make much sense to talk of Dead Sea scrolls, if one understands by this term the leather rolls from Cave I which were acquired almost in their entirety by the Hebrew University and the Israeli government. The alternative name "Qumran scrolls" has been proposed, because of the valuable finds from some ten or eleven additional caves in the wadi, particularly those of Cave IV, with its tens of thousands of fragments, and the famous copper scroll (actually two strips) from Cave III with its list of fabulous treasures of precious metal and their hiding places. The proposed name also indicates the connection of the scrolls from all these caves with the sectarian center at nearby Khirbet Qumran.

But even the Qumran label is inadequate now. Almost equally important discoveries have been made in four caves of the Wadi Murabba'at, eleven miles south of the Qumran Cave I. Documents from these range from a Hebrew papyrus palimpsest of the sixth (or possibly eighth) century B.C., in the ancient "Phoenician" cursive script, to a scroll of the Minor Prophets and personal letters apparently by Simon ben Kosebah, or Bar Kokhba (Kochebah), the second-century A.D. Jewish rebel leader and would-be Messiah. The letters are written, surprisingly, in Hebrew, which was supposed to have become a dead language by that time. The Murabba'at documents also include Aramaic, Greek, and even Latin and Arabic fragments. Systematic excavations of these caves, again directed by Harding and De Vaux, have shown that they were occupied as far back as 4000 B.C. Well-preserved implements from the Chalcolithic age have been collected from these sites.

None of the manuscripts taken from the Murabba'at caves have any connection with the Qumran community, or with a third area at Khirbet Mird, site of a ruined Christian monastery, also opened by the tireless Ta'amireh tribesmen. Here mainly Byzantine-Christian documents have been unearthed. They are, on the whole, of a considerably later date than the Qumran and the bulk of the Murabba'at manuscripts. But the finds are valuable enough and include parts of Greek uncial codices from the Old and New Testament as well as nonliterary Greek and Arabic papyri and a fragment of the *Andromache* by Euripides. Meanwhile, in the 1960's, Israel's archaeologist-general, Yigael Yadin, has opened up a promising new mine of manuscripts at Masada, above the western shore of the Dead Sea. In addition to these sites, Bedouin seem to have tapped other sources, whose location they have not disclosed.

The Dead Sea scrolls, then, have inaugurated an altogether new phase in Palestinian archaeology. In subject matter, date, and provenance, the manuscript harvest has now gone far beyond the Qumran confines and sectarian connotations. Documents are coming forth from all over the honeycombed cliffs of the Judean wilderness. Others have been cropping up for some time to the south, in the Negev.

The biggest stumbling block for discoveries was the tacit assumption that no manuscripts of any age and consequence could ever be expected from Palestine, "where climate and history alike have been unfavorable to documentary survival."[2] That spell has now been broken. "The greatest manuscript discovery in modern times," as William F. Albright called it—and by the

---

[2] Frederic G. Kenyon: *Our Bible and the Ancient Manuscripts* (London: Eyre & Spottiswoode; 1958), p. 31.

same token the most valuable in the archaeology of the Hebrew Bible—was made on Palestinian soil. Suddenly the Holy Land was raised to a par with Egypt as a treasure house of papyri and parchments.

It is difficult to decide which of the documents from the Judean wilderness is most noteworthy: the superbly preserved Isaiah scroll, the sectarian Manual, the mysterious copper scroll, the Daniel manuscripts (only a few decades removed from the composition of the originals), the actual letters of the Hebrew hero Bar Kokhba, or, most unexpected and ancient of all, the palimpsest from the otherwise palaeographically and documentarily blank period of the Hebrew Kings. And this may be only the beginning.

·XX·

THE SHAPIRA MYSTERY

A Hair perhaps divides the False and True;
Yes; and a single Alif were the clue—
Could you but find it. . . .

OMAR KHAYYÁM

CONTROVERSY over the relative value of the Dead Sea scrolls, including one that was labeled a forgery seventy years ago, disturbed the scholarly calm."[1] Thus reported *The New York Times* correspondent on the stormy 92nd meeting of the Society of Biblical Literature and Exegesis. Some three hundred Biblical scholars had come together on December 27, 1956, at the Union Theological Seminary of New York City. The Society's president, Dr. J. Philip Hyatt of Vanderbilt University, referred in his address to the leather scrolls which M. W. Shapira had offered to the British Museum in 1883, and expressed hope that "recent discoveries" might authenticate the once discredited Hebrew documents. Hyatt had been preceded as speaker by Professor Menahem Mansoor, chairman of Hebrew and Semitic Studies at the University of Wisconsin and the principal champion for the rehabilitation of Shapira. Pandemonium almost broke loose when Dr. Zeitlin, who had entered the hall only toward the end of Mansoor's review of the Shapira manuscripts, challenged the speaker's thesis by violently denouncing the genuineness of these texts. The chairman had to rule that the subject had been sufficiently covered and closed the meeting. Nevertheless, the crossfire over Shapira was continued in the corridor, and has been pursued ever since in various learned journals with unusual

---

[1] *The New York Times*, December 28, 1956, p. 14.

partisanship and fervor. The discussion over Shapira highlighted a crucial issue of virtually all manuscript discoveries.

Invariably, when old manuscripts appear on the scene, the question arises: are they genuine? Most of the great finds in archaeology have met with skepticism on the part of some members of the learned world. The doubts may not die down for decades. In some instances they will suddenly flare up again, to the shock and surprise of a credulous public. Are the acclaimed objects really witnesses to a mute antiquity? Or are they indifferent remains of a much later age? Have they been incorrectly dated and identified by the extravagant imagination of a wishful antiquarian? Were they perhaps "planted" by a deceitful explorer to gain attention or to demonstrate his pet theory? Is the much admired artifact a fraud foisted on affluent museums or private collectors by an unscrupulous dealer? Is it a hoax engineered by some odd character of unusual skill but questionable morality to mislead his academic colleagues and to make fools of stuffed shirts?

An 1883 sketch of a section of one of the Shapira leather strips made at the time they were on exhibit in London. Above it is a facsimile line in ancient Phoenician-Hebrew ("non-square") characters. The manuscripts have since vanished.

No expert wants to risk exposure as a gullible ignoramus. Hence, a renowned authority may often coolly dismiss as spurious any objects that do not fit into the present frame of knowledge. Discoveries made by outsiders are immediately suspect to the guild. Schliemann's explorations and claims were received with scorn by the German academic archaeologists, including the illustrious Curtius and Furtwängler. But no expert wants to miss a good thing either. This may be his great opportunity to achieve immortality. Thus, poised between the fear of slighting a discovery and the terror of being taken in, the antiquarian scholar may lose his critical bearings and fall into Scylla while trying to avoid Charybdis. Little does the average amateur know of these trials. And once the truth is out and the popularizers—who by the nature of their métier must be simplifiers—get busy, it is easy to ridicule the specialists who have been duped. How could they have fallen for "the Piltdown man" and hailed him as "the first Englishman"? Suddenly the habitual doubters are heroes, though conceivably they distrusted Dawson, fabricator of the Piltdown skull, for trivial reasons. Ironically, those who suspected a fake from the very beginning may have been the less able scientists. They could have been right for the wrong reasons.

On the other hand, admirable ingenuity and meticulous scholarship may go into the vain attempt to prove the genuine work a fraud. In the 1890's, two scholars neatly demonstrated that Tacitus' *Annals*, said to have survived in only one medieval manuscript, had really been composed by Poggio Bracciolini, who rediscovered it. They made a good and impressive case. Yet chances are that they are wrong.

There are some works whose authenticity has not been conclusively established—some of Plato's letters, several of the Pauline Epistles, or the Tao Tê Ching, a great Chinese classic, for example. Here final judgment may have to be suspended. But nobody can tell when a work of art or a piece of writing that has long been accepted as the work of a master will rightly, or wrongly, be branded as spurious. We have to be grateful to the doubters, no matter how irritating, who refuse to be overawed by authority and reputation. Yet how are we to separate the genuine from the false? Scholars cannot always comfortably defer a judgment. Once a discovery is announced, they have to take a stand, though they may live to regret it. And truth so often has a disconcerting way of remaining elusive and inconspicuous. "O, what a goodly outside falsehood hath," said Shakespeare.

Fortunately, the faking of manuscripts is such an exacting art and demands such a rare combination of talents in order to be successful—that is, to remain undetected—that relatively few ever undertake it. The cruder productions never find acceptance for long, and with advances in textual criticism, palaeography, and chemical and physical analysis, faking may soon become a dying art. However, the issue still hangs heavily over many manuscript discoveries of the past. Forgeries of literary works are legion. For the sake of national self-glorification and religious dogmatism, deception has been widely practiced. The systematic study of manuscripts may be said to owe its inception to the growing need, in the late Middle Ages, to establish the spuriousness of false deeds and other "legal" documents. This need decisively stimulated palaeography, the science of determining the age and origin of a piece of writing. Nicolaus Cusanus, the cardinal, and Lorenzo Valla, the papal secretary, contributed enormously to textual criticism and philology—and to the scientific method itself—by unmasking false Church documents.

We have met with forgeries and the long shadow cast by suspicions of them at almost every turn of our story. In the nineteenth century there were such colorful practitioners as Constantine Simonides and the Karaite fanatic, Abraham Firkovich. There have been a host of others before and after. Recent scandals of this nature, among them the Van Meegeren fakes of Vermeer and the false statues of Etruscan warriors in New York's Metropolitan Museum of Art, have created considerable awareness of forgery in the arts and in archaeology.

Although the Dead Sea scrolls are now almost universally accepted as genuine, it would be wrong to think they were endorsed from the very beginning. The men to whom the Syrian Metropolitan first showed the manuscripts were all doubtful of their age and authenticity. Several declared them utterly worthless. Unfortunately, they were misled also by the bishop's distorted account of the documents' origin. The Metropolitan Athanasius himself firmly believed all along that they were two thousand years old, though his knowledge of Hebrew and of manuscripts in general was rather rudimentary. His belief may have been inspired more by the hope that they were indeed of immense value than by an informed guess. He desperately sought confirmation of his hopes.

For Bishop Athanasius, the change in fortunes came when he communicated with the American School of Oriental Research in Jerusalem. As chance would have it, only a junior member, an American, was there at the time. Maybe his youth and relative inexperience served him in good stead and kept him from pondering over the fact that such a find was "impossible." At any rate, Dr. John C. Trever was reminded of the Nash Papyrus and sent photographs of the manuscripts to Professor William F. Albright of Johns Hopkins, who did not hesitate to commit himself. Within a few days he wrote Trever by airmail: "My heartiest congratulations on the greatest manuscript discovery of modern times. There is no doubt in my mind that the script is more archaic than that of the Nash Papyrus. . . . What an absolutely incredible find! And there can happily not be the slightest doubt in the world about the genuineness of the manuscript."[2]

This tipped the scale. But it did not by any means silence attacks on the age and authenticity of the scrolls. Professor Solomon Zeitlin was the most insistent. He insinuated that the scrolls were a hoax or, at best, medieval documents written by "very ignorant men," and he has poured forth article after article since 1948 in his own journal, the *Jewish Quarterly Review,* which has proved hospitable to a number of other dissenting opinions on the origin, genuineness, and interpretation of the cave documents. Again and again Zeitlin attacked opponents, questioning their scholarship in no uncertain terms. Repeatedly and repetitiously he discussed "The Fiction of the Recent Discoveries near the Dead Sea," "The Alleged Antiquity of the Scrolls," "The Propaganda of the Hebrew Scrolls and the Falsification of History," etc. In 1950 he wrote an article fifty-eight pages long, "The Hebrew Scrolls: Once More and Finally." And then he went right on. After the Piltdown story broke in 1953, he wrote a twenty-nine-page exposé: "The Antiquity of the Hebrew Scrolls and the Piltdown Hoax: A Parallel." In fact, when Athanasius came to the United States to sell his scrolls—he is said to have asked one million dollars for one of them alone—he found unexpected wariness on the part of American institutions which had formerly seemed eager to acquire the documents. It may have been out of despair at not finding a ready customer, while Zeitlin's charges were gaining ground, that he put an advertisement in the *Wall Street Journal.* Professor Albright is of the opinion that the Israeli government picked up the invaluable scrolls for a mere $250,000 or $300,000 thanks to Zeitlin's influence on the market price. Zeitlin, by the way, thinks the Israelis were outrageously overcharged: some $10,000 to $15,000 would have been ample compensation.

This is not to ridicule Zeitlin. His arguments, buttressed by the learning of a renowned Hebraist, are for scholars to settle. Suffice it to say that the majority of palaeographers, archaeologists, textual critics, Orientalists, and New and Old Testament scholars accept the scrolls as ancient. The Dead Sea scrolls, they have assured us, will not turn out to be another Piltdown hoax or a "Shapira forgery." Shapira's name, so often brought into the controversy over the Dead Sea scrolls, remains in dubious repute.

---

[2] John C. Trever: "The Discovery of the Scrolls," *The Biblical Archaeologist,* Vol. XI, No. 3 (Steptember 1948), p. 55.

For long it has been associated with one of the most impudent of nineteenth-century manuscript frauds, and to Zeitlin and his followers, the Dead Sea scrolls were little else but a repetition of that notorious trick. Among those who recognized the authenticity of the Judean documents, however, a few thought that the recent finds called for a reexamination of the Shapira manuscripts. Had Shapira, who died by his own hand in a Rotterdam hotel room in 1884, been sinned against?

What then is the evidence?

Top section of Moabite Stone, a stela discovered in the nineteenth century, bearing cursive characters akin to those used by the Hebrews before—and on occasion long after—the introduction of their square script

In the summer of 1883 London was excited over the announced discovery of two variant ancient Hebrew manuscripts of Deuteronomy written in the old cursive Phoenician-Hebrew ("Palaeo-Hebrew") characters known from the Moabite Stone and held to date from about the ninth century B.C. There were some fifteen or sixteen long leather strips, apparently originally folded, like some Far Eastern and pre-Columbian Mexican books, rather than rolled up. The manuscripts had been brought from Palestine by M. W. Shapira, who offered them to the British Museum for "a cool million sterling." A contemporary of Shapira's wrote in his autobiography: "For weeks the 'discovery' of this precious manuscript was discussed at every dinner table high and low."[3] The English press published daily articles which covered every phase and detail. Reporters laid siege to the British Museum, where some of the fragments were displayed under glass. Past the exhibition cases filed a host of curious Londoners.

Charles Clermont-Ganneau, the brilliant French Biblical archaeologist, hastened to the scene from Paris, and observed that when he arrived "l'émotion du publique avait atteint son

---

[3] A. C. R. Carter: *Let Me Tell You* (London: Hutchinson & Co.; 1940), p. 216.

paroxysme."[4] Official blessings were conferred upon the exhibit when the Prime Minister, Gladstone, a man of considerable anti-quarian interests, appeared at the Museum and chatted amiably with the "discoverer," Mr. Shapira, and with Dr. Christian Gins-burg, to whom the British Museum had entrusted the examination of the manuscripts. Ginsburg's translations of the texts were appearing in installments in *The Times* and in the *Athenaeum*. Provincial papers carried reprints.

Obviously, the British Museum would not have displayed the manuscripts and leading papers would not have reproduced excerpts if forgery had been suspected. Ginsburg delayed final judgment, but betrayed enthusiasm by his meticulous translations. The London correspondent of the *Liverpool Daily Post* wrote, on August 16, 1883: "Dr. Ginsburg is still busily engaged at the British Museum in deciphering Mr. Shapira's latest antiquarian find; and the reticence Dr. Ginsburg displays leads many to put faith in the original assertion that these scraps of leather are hundreds of years older than the Christian era. It is argued by these believers that, if the skins had been forgeries, such an acute scholar as Dr. Ginsburg would have been able, long before this, to have detected the fraud."[5] Meanwhile, rumors had it that the purchase was held up only by the need for vast sums. Names of private benefactors were hinted at. Some said that the Treasury was advancing the huge amount to the British Museum from the Civil Contingencies Fund.

Moses Wilhelm Shapira, a Polish Jew, but a convert to Christianity married to a German Lutheran deaconess, had been for many years a dealer in antiquities and manuscripts at Jeru-salem. He had supplied the libraries of Berlin and London with valuable Hebrew texts, chiefly from Yemen. He found a com-mentary to the Midrash by Maimonides, subsequently sold to Germany, that was hailed as a remarkable contribution, even after his exposure. His reputation was somewhat tarnished after the sale to the Berlin Museum of obnoxiously crude "Moabite idols," whose manufacture Charles Clermont-Ganneau, then French Consul at Jerusalem, was able to trace to the local workshop of one of Shapira's associates.

---

[4] Charles Clermont-Ganneau: *Les Fraudes Archéologiques en Palestine* (Paris: Leroux; 1885), p. 191.
[5] Menahem Mansoor: "The Case of Shapira's Dead Sea (Deuteronomy) Scrolls of 1883," *Transactions of the Wisconsin Academy of Sciences, Arts and Letters,* Vol. XLVII (1958), p. 195.

Some have seen in Shapira the innocent, almost saintly victim of Palestinian fakers. Others, chiefly writers of memoirs with the benefit of hindsight, such as Walter Besant or Bertha Stafford Vester, have depicted him as the propagator of fiendish frauds. In any case, the Moabite fiasco did not seem to have harmed him permanently. He continued to sell antiquities and documents to European collectors. Several of his manuscripts were bought by Mayor Alfred Sutro of San Francisco and are now in that city's Public Library. Possibly it was taken for granted that no dealer in antiquities could help offering fakes, unknown to himself, for sale. Shapira had amply made up for these by other undoubtedly genuine articles. And Palestine, in the age of the great discoveries of the Moabite Stone and subterranean Siloam inscription, and of a Biblical renaissance in general, simply teemed with all kinds of forgeries which were impossible to detect all at once. Clermont-Ganneau, an ingenious uncoverer of sham antiquities, has devoted a delightful book to the subject, *Les Fraudes archéologiques en Palestine* (1885), in which, however, Monsieur Shapira is one of the villains.

According to his own account, Shapira had been in possession of the Deuteronomy manuscripts for several years before he decided to sell them. He claimed that he had taken them to Europe only after assuring himself of their genuineness. The circumstances of the discovery had an odd resemblance to the finding of the Dead Sea scrolls. In a letter Shapira wrote to a German friend, he stated that in July 1878 he had visited the house of an Arab sheik, Mahmud el-Arakat. There he conversed with several Bedouin who told him of Arabs who had taken refuge in a cave of the Wadi el-Moujib near the east bank of the Dead Sea, in the ancient land of the Israelite tribe Reuben. In one of the caves they noticed "several bundles of very old rugs." Peeling off the cotton or linen wrapping, they encountered "black charms" inside. The caves were described as remarkably dry and hence suggested to Shapira conditions that, "like the Egyptian soil," would preserve old documents. Guessing the nature of the black charms, Shapira says he enlisted the help of the sheik and thereby gained possession of the "embalmed leather" fragments, which he eventually deciphered as a rendering of "the last speech of Moses in the plain of Moab."[6]

During his visit to London, Shapira sent a memorandum

---

[6] Quoted, from the British Museum dossier, by Mansoor: op. cit., p. 189.

to Dr. Ginsburg, which was published in the *Athenaeum* on August 11, 1883, wherein he freely admitted that doubts had been raised regarding the treasure he was now offering to the British Museum. He confessed that Professor Konstantin Schlottmann of the University of Halle, to whom he had forwarded copies of the "Deuteronomy" manuscript in 1878, had declared it a fabrication and had berated Shapira for calling it a sacred text. Schlottmann also informed the German Consul at Jerusalem, Baron von Münchhausen, so that Shapira would be prevented from announcing the find publicly. Schlottmann, by the way, was the one who had endorsed the German acquisition of the Moabite monstrosities, and his apprehension at becoming associated with another fraud was quite understandable. Shapira told Ginsburg that upon Schlottmann's warning he deposited the documents in a Jerusalem bank. He also informed another savant, to whom he had submitted a transcript of the text, of this unfavorable judgment.

But eventually he had second thoughts. In his own words: "Subsequently I began to reconsider Schlottmann's objections and found that they were partly grounded on mistakes I had made in deciphering the writing. I felt better able to judge them myself because I had more experience in manuscripts. It was before Easter of the present year that I reexamined them, and deciphered them a second time. Professor Schroeder, Consul in Beyrouth, saw them in the middle of May, 1883, and pronounced them genuine. He wanted to purchase them. I took the writings to Leipzig at the end of July to have them photographed. Professors there saw them. Dr. Hermann Guthe, who intends to write about them, believes in them. The manuscripts have been smeared with asphalt originally as a kind of embalmment. They became subsequently further darkened by the use of oil and spirit. The oil was used by the Arabs to counteract the brittleness, and to prevent their suffering from wet."[7]

This seems to be an admirably frank statement, though it could also be looked upon as a clever device to gain confidence and forestall rumors and accusations. Unfortunately, Shapira left out a significant detail: during his previous visit to Germany he had submitted the scrolls to the Royal Museum of Berlin, where a committee presided over by Professor Richard Lepsius, on July 10, after one and a half hours of deliberation pronounced the

---

[7] *Ibid.*, pp. 191–2.

goat-skin manuscripts a forgery. Shapira had not wished to prejudice his case. He himself believed in the genuineness of his articles and was confirmed in this by the positive stand of Schroeder. He wanted a fair trial from British experts.

When what had happened in Berlin was later disclosed by *The Times* in London, Shapira declared in his defense that the Berliners, despite their pronouncement, had expressed willingness to buy the manuscripts for a nominal price. Were they just trying to get hold of his texts at a pittance? Since it was inconceivable that a museum would waste public funds on forgeries, Shapira took the offer as an unmistakable sign that the manuscripts were in fact considered genuine. Thereupon he proceeded to London. Like so many details in Shapira's story, it is still a mystery why the German authorities remained silent when the English acclaimed the sensational manuscript find. "If the [German] professors," asked the *Athenaeum*, "detected the forgery, why should they have offered to buy the fragments? And while they read in German and English papers sensational news from London, why did they keep quiet? Not a word to the British Museum?"[8]

Upon his arrival in London, Shapira generally met with good will, though his association with the dubious Moabite pottery was noted. It would be erroneous, however, to think that everybody in England believed in the authenticity of the Deuteronomy skins. There were skeptics from the beginning. Walter Besant, the popular Victorian novelist, who was at the time secretary of the Palestine Exploration Society, was apparently the first to be approached by Shapira. He has recorded the meeting in his posthumously published autobiography, which does not lack venomous asides, though he predates the Shapira scandal by six years. In 1877 (Besant wrote), "a Polish Jew converted to Christianity but not good works" had called on him mysteriously. "He was a man of handsome presence, tall, with fair hair and blue eyes; not the least like the ordinary Polish Jew, and with an air of modest honesty which carried one away." It seemed that the man had a "contemporary copy" of Deuteronomy. Besant was allowed to see a piece. And behold: "It was written in fine black ink, as fresh after three thousand years as when it was laid on." Still more startling, the Jew insisted it had been deposited "in a perfectly dry cave in Moab."[9]

---

[8] *Athenaeum*, September 8, 1883, pp. 304–5.
[9] Walter Besant: *The Autobiography of Sir Walter Besant* (New York: Dodd, Mead & Co.; 1902), p. 161.

These circumstances—well-conserved inking and cave deposit—are the two great improbabilities which likewise confounded the first scholars to learn of the Dead Sea scrolls at the Syrian monastery seven decades later. From what we know today, they are actually in Shapira's favor and are the least deserving of Mr. Besant's sneers. A "competent" forger, one may argue, would not have presented conspicuous fresh ink, nor would he have invented an improbable detail that was bound to arouse suspicion. In claims of discovery, it is often the improbabilities rather than the commonplaces that ring true. Another detail mentioned by Shapira, the linen wrappings of the manuscripts, raised even graver doubts. The London *Times* was later to declare: "The mention of linen seems somehow a mistake since believers in leather can hardly be expected to assign equal staying power to mere flax."[1] Yet, linen bits adhering to the Deuteronomy manuscripts were pronounced ancient by a Leipzig expert. And the scrolls from Qumran I were bundled in linen.

Walter Besant arranged for a consistory of scholars to meet on the next day. Shapira consented to show them all the Pentateuchal fragments. Besant writes that Shapira "unfolded his manuscripts amid such excitement as is very seldom exhibited by scholars." The procedure took three hours. One professor of Hebrew was heard to exclaim: "This is one of the few things which could not be a forgery and a fraud!" Besant makes us think, however, that he was never really taken in, and he recalls the low opinion of "the worthy Shapira, Christian convert," held by William Simpson of the *Illustrated London News* and by Captain Claude R. Conder, surveyor of Western Palestine. Conder assured Besant, after the meeting, that all the caves of Moab were damp and earthy. "There is not a dry cave in the country."[2] Later, Conder assailed any thought that manuscripts of perishable leather could have been buried for more than two thousand years in a land with a twenty-inch rainfall. This to him was conclusive proof that the documents were fakes. Nevertheless, whatever their opinions, the skeptics did not voice their views. Captain Conder himself was wary. After the private exposition, therefore, the manuscripts were allowed to go on display at the British Museum, and for three weeks the scrolls basked in celebrity. Then the bubble burst. With it went Shapira's hopes for recognition and reward.

---

[1] *Times Weekly Edition*, August 22, 1883, p. 12.
[2] Besant: op. cit., p. 163.

Among the first in England to declare (on August 18) his conviction that the manuscripts were forged was Adolf Neubauer, Hebrew scholar of Oxford, who had been in touch with one of Lepsius's team in Berlin. The final blow was dealt by the French archaeologist Clermont-Ganneau, Shapira's nemesis since the exposure of the Moabite effigies. The Frenchman had been refused permission to examine the documents by Shapira, but Ginsburg had allowed him a brief glance at some of the leather strips. Clermont-Ganneau had also joined the stream of curiosity seekers swarming around the glass cases in the British Museum. And whereas others labored for days on end over the language, writing, style, usage, textual form, etc., a few cursory glances were enough for him. An English colleague admiringly paid tribute to the unmasker. Despite the harassments that kept him from closer examination, he—his colleague said—could now proudly proclaim: "*Veni, non vidi, vici.*"[3]

The Frenchman's initial skepticism had been intensified when he had heard that Shapira was offering the manuscripts for sale. Clermont-Ganneau made no bones about his feelings. In a communications to *The Times* of August 21, 1883, he stated his opinion after first setting down his past connections with Shapira and the difficulties and limitations that had attended his work at the British Museum. He concluded: "The fragments are the work of a modern forger. This is not the expression of an a priori incredulity, a feeling which many scholars, like me, have experienced at the mere announcement of this wonderful discovery. I am able to show, with the documents before me, how the forger went to work. He took one of those large Synagogue rolls of leather, containing the Pentateuch, written in the same square characters, and perhaps dating back two or three centuries, rolls which Mr. Shapira must well be acquainted with, for he deals in them, and has sold to several public libraries in England sundry copies of them, obtained from the existing Synagogues of Judaea and Yemen. The forger then cut off the lower edge of this roll— that which offered him the widest surface. He obtained in this way some narrow strips of leather with an appearance of comparative antiquity, which was still further heightened by the use of proper chemical agents. On these strips of leather he wrote with ink, making use of the alphabet of the Moabite stone, and introducing such 'various readings' as fancy dictates, the passages from

---

[3] Clermont-Ganneau: op. cit., p. 229.

Deuteronomy which have been deciphered and translated by M. Ginsburg, with patience and learning worthy of much better employment."[4]

Caricature in *Punch*, September 8, 1883. "Semitic"-looking Shapira is apprehended outside the British Museum by nice Mr. Ginsburg, the English scholar. (Both were converts to the Christian faith.)

There is undoubtedly a note of malice in these remarks, and an indirect insinuation that Shapira had actually fabricated the strips. Clermont-Ganneau boldly announced that it would be child's play for him to manufacture a companion piece that might "make a fitting sequel to the Deuteronomy of Mr. Shapira," besides having "the slight advantage over it of not costing a million sterling."[5] The Frenchman's cocky airs did not appeal to all Englishmen. The immediate public reaction to his letter to *The Times* was open war on Clermont-Ganneau rather than on Shapira, for whose manuscripts the British had apparently formed a proprietary affection which they hated to see destroyed by a flippant foreigner. Several papers rejected Clermont-Ganneau's verdict and maintained that Shapira's leather was much thicker than the type in use for synagogue rolls. The Frenchman was taken to task for his initial bias as much as for his callous offer to manufacture a Moabite scroll. Editorial writers castigated what they termed "Gallic self-glorification." The *Manchester Guardian* on September 6 accused Ganneau himself of having "shown the hand of the critic a little too soon for British notions of fair play."[6]

---

[4] *The Times*, August 21, 1883.　　[5] Ibid.
[6] Mansoor: op. cit., p. 197.

The experts, however, were impressed by Clermont-Ganneau's elegant proof, and by the description of how the forger must have proceeded. Ginsburg, who had hesitated for some time, now came up, virtually overnight, with a wholesale indictment of the Shapira manuscripts and fully endorsed the external evidence given by his sharp-eyed French colleague. To it he added, like Neubauer and Albert Loewy, an impressive catalogue of internal evidence. It was on those grounds that the fragments were ultimately condemned as forgeries.

Shapira partisans, then and now, direct their fire almost exclusively at Clermont-Ganneau. They claim that the other critics simply followed him and reiterated his arguments. By questioning the Frenchman's motives and logic, they seek to explode any doubts cast on the authenticity of the Shapira Deuteronomy. But this is only wishful thinking. The far weightier internal evidence has to be accounted for before a good case can be built up in defense of Shapira. Here, however, we cross into a highly technical field in which the nonspecialist is at a loss. Most scholars in 1883 judged the evidence furnished by Ginsburg and others as absolutely conclusive.

There is no need to detail the specific grammatical, linguistic, textual, and theological issues. It is noteworthy, however, that the Reverend Albert Loewy, one of the first in England to doubt the genuineness of the Shapira documents, also employed internal criticism to discredit the Moabite Stone, whose authenticity is not at all in question. Also, several of the linguistic inconsistencies and anomalies in the usage of ancient Hebrew that disturbed Ginsburg might well have parallels in the various texts from the Judean caves found in recent years. In a number of instances in which Ginsburg, Neubauer, or German critics maintained that they had located late Rabbinic words, Mansoor was able to prove them wrong or to establish the incidence of the words in such an ancient document as the Siloam inscription. In addition, slipshod writing and grammatical errors—quite frequent in some of the Dead Sea fragments—can no longer be considered sufficient proof of spuriousness.

Ginsburg had made the point that "the compiler of the Hebrew text was a Polish, Russian, or German Jew, or one who learned Hebrew in the North of Europe."[7] Of this he sees evidence in peculiar misspellings. But, again, Professor Mansoor has made

---

[7] *The Times,* August 27, 1883.

clear that similar confusions of phonetic values are common errors in Qumran and Old Testament texts whose Oriental origin is not in doubt. As to the contents of the abridged Deuteronomy text, with its unusual version of the Decalogue and its interpolations, it may be compared to a Qumran fragment such as the *Sayings of Moses,* which also consists of a compilation of various parts of the Pentateuch. Judging by remains from the Judean caves, Deuteronomy was probably the most popular work of Scripture among the Qumran community. Hence, the fact that Shapira's documents are also a rendering of Deuteronomy tends to speak for their authenticity. There is a likelihood, then, that the controversial scrolls belong with those pseudepigraphic works that proliferated in the last two centuries before Christ. If this is the case, the use of Rabbinic Hebrew words is no longer an embarrassment.

Maccabean coins (140–135 B.C.) inscribed
in the old Phoenician-Hebrew script

Ginsburg had declared in one of his earlier communications to the *Athenaeum:* "It is pretty clear that, whatever the age of the leather, the writing must either date from somewhere about B.C. 800 or from A.D. 1880. There is no middle term possible."[8] This was an apodictic either/or alternative which was not subscribed to by all his fellow academics. It introduced an unwarranted barrier by stamping everything as forgery that did not appear to belong to the period about the ninth century B.C. The archaic Phoenician-Hebrew cursive script, as we now know from the Qumran scrolls, was in use at a much later date, possibly into Christian times. More justly, a London paper, *The Standard,* reported on August 14, 1883, ten days after Ginsburg's dogmatic declaration: "Among those who hold that the manuscripts are genuine . . . some incline to the time of the eighth century [B.C.] . . . others

---

[8] *Athenaeum,* August 4, 1883.

to the period of Captivity, while a third party places the documents as late as the Maccabees."⁹

This is not to say, however, that there are exact palaeographic parallels between Qumran and Moabite Pentateuchal documents. No one has yet removed all the difficulties that stand in the way of our acceptance of the Shapira leather strips as genuine. But they deserve, as Professor Mansoor has so cogently pleaded, a thorough reexamination. As far as internal evidence goes, it may not be points once considered crucial, but rather the accumulation of many unusual or incongruous features that tip the scale against the Shapira texts.

Professor Mansoor, who says that from the day he first heard of Shapira's tragedy he spent many sleepless nights, wisely has refrained from proclaiming himself outrightly in favor of the Shapira documents. Instead he insists that "neither the internal nor the external evidence, so far as yet published, supports the idea of a forgery."¹ More emphatically pro-Shapira is the English Hebrew scholar J. L. Teicher, whose article "The Genuineness of the Shapira Manuscripts" appeared in *The Times Literary Supplement* of March 22, 1957. He asserts: "On re-examining the evidence on which the manuscripts were pronounced to be forgeries, one realizes with a shock that the verdict was unfounded and that the manuscripts were in fact ancient and genuine."² Unfortunately, Teicher refutes only some of the weakest arguments of Shapira's opponents and dismisses others wholesale as logical non sequiturs. "The text of the Shapira strips," he admits, "is the real stumbling block." But once this is viewed as a redrafting of the Book of Deuteronomy "for liturgical and catechetic purposes, in the Jewish-Christian Church," all the obscurities and difficulties are supposed to be magically removed. Teicher, one may recall, is the lone advocate of an identification of the Qumran sect with the Jewish-Christian Ebionites. It can hardly be said that he furthered the cause of the Shapira documents by involving them in his pet theory. To my knowledge, no other scholar of repute has embraced his views on the Dead Sea scrolls, and it is probably safe to say that Teicher will not gain many followers in his quixotic attempt to validate the Shapira texts.

According to Oskar K. Rabinowicz, no "Biblical scroll mystery" attaches to the condemned manuscript. The mystery was solved

---

⁹ Quoted by J. L. Teicher: "The Genuineness of the Shapira Manuscripts," *The Times Literary Supplement*, March 22, 1957, p. 184.
¹ Mansoor: op. cit., p. 225.   ² Teicher: loc. cit.

as far back as August 1883. In an article in the *Jewish Quarterly Review* in 1957, Rabinowicz furnishes a cogent résumé of the history of the fragments and of the persuasive arguments of Ganneau and Ginsburg, but he has little to add that is new. Only at the end does he arrive at a conclusion as strange as Teicher's: the discovery of a passage in the Dead Sea scrolls identical with one from Shapira's strips would automatically prove that the Dead Sea scrolls are also a hoax.

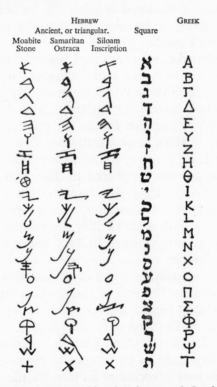

HEBREW				GREEK
Ancient, or triangular.			Square	
Moabite Stone	Samaritan Ostraca	Siloam Inscription		

A comparative table of Hebrew and Greek alphabets. The first three columns give cursive (or "angular") Hebrew letters from old inscriptions of the first half of the first millennium B.C.

The literature of the Shapira affair sometimes refers to the autobiographical novel of his daughter, *La petite fille de Jérusalem* (1914), written in French under the pseudonym Myriam Harry. By now it has become an axiom that the daughter herself was convinced of her father's guilt. Thus, the *Palestine Exploration Quarterly* in 1957 editorialized on the reawakened interest in the Shapira manuscripts: "One piece of evidence, however, which carries considerable weight on the other side, is the fact that Shapira's daughter . . . seems to be quite sure that Clermont-Ganneau was right in charging Shapira with forgery."[3] No evidence is given for such a preposterous claim by this scientific publication. Yet it is put down as a solid argument against Mansoor's efforts to have the case reexamined. Anyone who has read Miss Harry's book will be convinced that she worshipped her unworldly, romantic father, called Benedictus in the novel. Not once does she cast on him the slightest suspicion of dishonesty.

Much is made by still another critic, M. H. Goshen-Gottstein, of the following passage in Miss Harry's autobiography: ". . . she would watch her father as he copied each inscription carefully on large white sheets, sometimes writing the same word twenty or even one hundred times, and trying to arrange the signs into different combinations."[4] But this incident depicts the antiquarian's efforts to decipher inscriptions on ancient pottery. That he had some familiarity with ancient Phoenician and Nabataean letters, Shapira never tried to hide. He had genuine antiquarian interests. But there is no hint that his knowledge of the old Phoenician-Hebrew script served him for the fabrication of fake documents. In the light of Shapira's own assertion that he spent much time in deciphering the Deuteronomy fragments, there is nothing suspicious in learning from his daughter that he actually did so.[5]

Whatever one may make of Shapira's dexterity with ancient scripts, it is sheer nonsense to attribute to his daughter the charge that her father was a forger. Mr. Goshen-Gottstein has tried to bolster his hunch with further passages from *The Little Daughter*, and sums up: "It is possible that his desire to prove his learning and to improve his material status so as to marry off his daughter, drove him into being involved into forgery."[6] The marriageable daughter, by the way, was not Myriam Harry, who was very young at the time, but her elder sister. All these flimsy and farfetched arguments do not add up to an indictment. Even Mr. Goshen-Gottstein had to admit that the forgery "could not be accomplished by one person."[7]

---

[3] *Palestine Exploration Quarterly*, Vol. LXXIX (1957), p. 96.
[4] M. H. Goshen-Gottstein: "The Shapira Forgery and the Qumran Scrolls," *Journal of Jewish Studies*, Vol. VII (1956), p. 189.
[5] Myriam Harry (Mme Émile Perrault): *La petite fille de Jérusalem* (Paris: A. Fayard; 1914), p. 112. English edition: *The Little Daughter of Jerusalem* (New York: E. P. Dutton; 1914).
[6] Goshen-Gottstein: op. cit., p. 189.
[7] Ibid.

With all these claims and counterclaims, and with the introduction of the Shapira case into the debate over the Dead Sea scrolls, we seem to be as far removed from a solution as ever. And there is another mystery. Nobody knows where the manuscripts are. Mansoor believes they are somewhere in the vaults of the British Museum, though the museum authorities deny this. However, since the manuscripts were reexamined there in 1884 after Shapira's death, it is impossible, even if the British Museum people and Rabinowicz consider it likely, that they were returned to Shapira and vanished with him in Holland. A letter from Shapira's widow inquiring about the manuscripts is in the files of the British Museum, but it is not known what the reply was, if there was a reply, or whether any action was taken.

A. C. R. Carter, the former editor of *The Year's Art*, in his memoirs *Let Me Tell You* (1940) states that "after the exposure he [Shapira] wrote a piteous letter of regret for the trouble and unrest which he had caused, and he thankfully accepted a few pounds from the British Museum for his once 'priceless' manuscript to be kept as a warning to others. With this small sum he went to Amsterdam [sic], and died by his own hand in an obscure inn."[8] This evidence would indicate that the British Museum gained legal title to the manuscript, but would the museum retain something that was deemed worthless? On the other hand, the reliability of this recollection by Carter, who devoted a whole chapter to "Shapira, the Bible Forger," may well be questioned. If Shapira had made such a bargain, involving his own acknowledgment that the manuscripts were fraudulent, he would hardly have sent a last appeal from Holland to the Principal Librarian of the British Museum to summon a group of unbiased scholars to reexamine the scrolls.

Shall we ever see again the physical evidence that would perhaps with one stroke end the mystery? Professor Mansoor has been told that some Shapira fragments have been sold by the well-known London book dealer Bernard Quaritch, but Mansoor has been unable to trace them. Conceivably, these were other manuscripts that Shapira had taken with him to London on his last visit there. One lead has, to my knowledge, not been explored. Mrs. Shapira mentions in her letter that she had found two fragments from Deuteronomy among her husband's papers and had sent them to Professor Konstantin Schlottmann in Halle. The

---

[8] Carter: op. cit., pp. 218–19.

possibility that these fragments were retained by Halle University should not be ruled out and may well be worth investigating. There is still another possibility: the Transjordanian Wadi el-Moujib on "the other side" of the Dead Sea. Are these caves really as wet as Captain Conder asserted? Are there any traces of manuscripts? And if so, would some of them resemble in makeup, writing, language, and content the Shapira scrolls?

It seems reasonably certain that the circumstances related by Shapira in connection with the finding of the Deuteronomy documents could not have been altogether an invention. Cave burials of manuscripts in general, and such details as the linen wrappings and the not immediately recognizable "black charms" inside—all these suggest too close a parallel to the Qumran finds to have been anticipated by seven decades without any precedent or material basis. Even if Shapira's documents are not genuine, the conclusion seems warranted that their fabricators must have known or heard of previous manuscript discoveries in Moabite or other "Dead Sea" caves.[9]

---

[9] The author wishes to note that *The Shapira Affair* by John Marco Allegro (New York: Doubleday & Co.; 1965) was published after he had completed this volume.

Book Four

A PROFUSION OF SILK, BARK, AND PAPER

A : *Inner Asia*

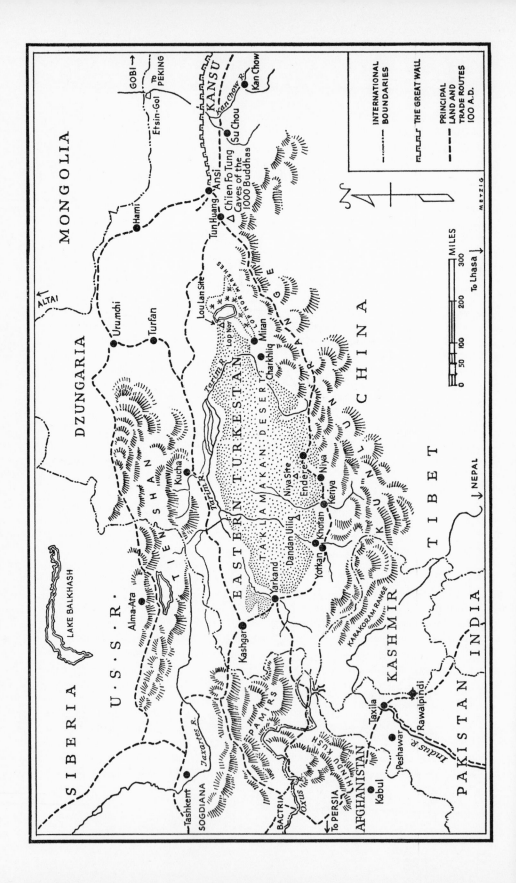

·XXI·

IN THE STEPS

OF MARCO POLO:

AUREL STEIN

Do you know the world's white roof-tree—do you know
    that windy rift
    Where the baffling mountain-eddies chop and
    change?
Do you know the long day's patience, belly-down on
    frozen drift,
    While the head of heads is feeding out of range?
It is there that I am going, where the boulders and the
    snow lie,
    With a trusty nimble tracker that I know. . . .
        RUDYARD KIPLING, The Roof of the World

IN THE 1870's a schoolboy at a Dresden Gymnasium was captivated by the romantic epic of Alexander the Great. He read
voraciously of his idol's lightning campaigns that swept over half
the known world and subdued the proud empires of the East. Most
of all he immersed himself in Alexander's thrust across the Hindu
Kush into India. Here was high adventure after his own heart:
unexplored, rugged mountains; physical courage and mental
alertness; and a gateway that led deep into the exotic world of
Asia. But when the boy sought information on the actual routes
taken by Alexander, the passes he crossed, the sites where he
fought some of the most crucial and brilliant battles of his career,
the books failed to furnish him with sufficient answers. Right then
he conceived the plan to follow Alexander, and to chart his exact

route through ancient Bactria and his later retreat from the Indus delta to Persia.

For many years, even after he had grown to manhood and achieved international recognition, he was refused permission by the authorities of Afghanistan, the modern kingdom that occupies ancient Bactria, to carry out any investigations. Three viceroys of India intervened on his behalf. Once he sent the Afghan ruler a two-volume set of one of his masterly works on Asiatic exploration, but the king wrote back that he knew no English and would have to have the books translated before he would be in a position to express his appreciation, and this might take years. All seemed in vain. And then, in the fall of 1943, when Aurel Stein was past eighty, a personal friend from Harvard, at the time American minister at Kabul, was able to obtain the necessary permission. Within a few days Stein, as vigorous and enterprising as ever, left his favorite retreat high up in Kashmir and quickly made his way to Kabul, where he stayed at the minister's residence. Two days after his arrival, he caught a chill on a visit to the local museum. A stroke and death followed in less than a week. Before the end, he told his American friend: "I have had a wonderful life, and it could not be concluded more happily than in Afghanistan which I have wanted to visit for sixty years."[1]

In the sixty years between his youthful dreams and the threshold of their fulfillment, Sir Aurel Stein came to be regarded as "the greatest explorer of Asia since Marco Polo."[2] Though he remained an admirer of Alexander all his life, the conqueror's route was only one of the royal roads into the mysterious continent. In later years Sir Aurel chose as guides his Venetian precursor, Marco Polo, and, above all, a seventh-century A.D. Chinese Buddhist monk, Hsüan Tsang, to whom he loved to refer as his "patron saint." Stein would never tire of invoking the memory of this pilgrim, an acute observer of Indian, Gandharan, and Turkestani sites. Hsüan Tsang led the way to Inner Asia. He was witness and symbol of the link between China and India, which Stein reconstructed in his explorations. Fittingly, Hsüan Tsang had ventured from China into India to settle obscurities and discrepancies in Buddhist texts. He returned years later with a load

---

[1] Quoted by C. E. A. W. Oldham: "Sir Aurel Stein," *British Academy. Proceedings*, Vol. XXIX (1943), p. 341.

[2] Geoffrey Grigson, ed.: "Stein, Marc Aurel," *Peoples, Places, Things, Ideas*, Vol. I (London: Grosvenor Press; 1954. New York: Hawthorn Books; 1957). Also Percy Sykes: *A History of Exploration* (New York: Harper Torchbooks; 1961), p. 254.

The oldest known Chinese image of
Buddha—a gilded statue cast in
bronze and dated A.D. 338

of sacred books. Proceeding in the opposite direction after an
interval of twelve hundred years, Stein was to emulate his "gentle
master."

Marcus Aurelius (later Sir Aurel) Stein was born in 1862
in Budapest. He came from a middle-class Hungarian-Jewish family of merchants and intellectuals, and he spoke German and
Hungarian from childhood. After pursuing Oriental languages
and archaeology at several universities on the Continent—culminating in a Ph.D. from Tübingen in Indo-Iranian studies at the
age of twenty-one—Stein came to England in 1884 to continue
research at Oxford and the British Museum. There intervened
a year of military training in Hungary, during which he received
valuable instruction in surveying and topography. Upon his return
to England, which became his adopted country after the death
of his parents and brother in Hungary, Stein gained the attention
of Sir Henry Yule, the learned editor of Marco Polo's works, and
Sir Henry Rawlinson, the soldier-scholar who helped to decipher
cuneiform. To his English mentors Stein owed his appointment
in 1888 as principal of Oriental College at Lahore and registrar
of the Punjab University. So, at the age of twenty-six, Stein had
found his way to Asia.

His stay in India brought Stein physically closer to the historical highways and byways which crisscrossed the continent's
little-known interior. But for a long time he was tied down by
official duties; and he began to doubt whether he would ever escape

the drudgery of a career in education. Rare and brief were the intervals of hard-earned leisure which he could devote to antiquarian pursuits. And he had to do without public patronage or subsidy. That the Indian administration should support archaeological explorations was considered absurd at the time. Antiquarian investigation of Inner Asia or even of India was virtually nonexistent. To European officialdom and the general public, archaeology was almost synonymous with the excavation of Homeric Greece and Near Eastern sites linked to the Holy Scriptures. Troy and Knossos had Schliemann and Evans, men of wealth who could finance their own projects, and various societies for the promotion of Christian knowledge were dispensing funds liberally for excavations in the Bible lands. Stein's chosen area did not intrigue any of these. Then, when Stein was thirty-seven, his opportunity finally came.

Within a few years of Stein's arrival in Asia, several fragments of inscribed birchbark leaves had reached collections in the West and in India. Some had been purchased by the ill-fated French traveler M. Dutreuil de Rhins. Best-known and most extensive of all was the so-called Bower manuscript, named for L. H. Bower, the British officer who came into possession of it in 1890. It was actually a fairly voluminous package of fifty-one leaves, consisting of seven distinct, though incomplete, texts. The manuscript, first declared to be illegible, was deciphered by an Anglo-German Orientalist, A. F. Rudolf Hoernle, and was found to contain unknown tracts on medicine and divination. The script was of the Gupta variety of northern India, datable to the fourth to sixth centuries A.D. There was little doubt that the manuscript had been written by native Indians—possibly Buddhist monks— as the language, the writing, and the typical Indian *pothi* format (imitating the shape of loose talipo palm leaves) indicated. No written work of such antiquity had survived anywhere in India.

The surprisingly well-preserved leaves of the Bower manuscript, and others like it, had been acquired in the distant desert uplands of Chinese Turkestan through local treasure seekers or their intermediaries. A land capable of harboring such treasures for more than twelve hundred years surely deserved closer investigation, and Stein was the first to realize the full implications of these finds and to act on them. Modern travelers had entered Inner Asia, but no part of it had been scientifically explored. Stein was much encouraged in his plan to launch a large-scale expedition by the reports of visitors, such as Sven Hedin, that there were indeed ancient ruined sites in the region and that these were relatively accessible and could be excavated. Stein adroitly and persuasively presented his plan to the Indian government in 1898. It was finally approved, thanks largely to the intervention of the Viceroy of India, Lord (George Nathaniel) Curzon, himself an eager student of Asian history.

Luckily, Stein had at least one other objective besides archaeology, and that was geography. Even vigilant administrators would dispense government money for a project which promised to survey entirely uncharted mountains and plateaus in the Indian borderlands. Stein was fortunate enough, then, to be sponsored by the Survey of India. The assignments he carried out as a topographer in the heart of Asia were a labor of love as well as an important achievement. In order to gather all the geographical data he could, he made it a point never to take the same road twice from India to Turkestan or any other region. He traversed the Takla Makan Desert at its greatest width and climbed up and down the snow-covered massifs of the highest Asian ranges. Crossing passes above 15,000 feet became almost routine for him.

Stein was a wiry little man of incredible endurance and a frame of iron. Once he requested the government to assign to him a hardy native soldier for his surveys along the North-West Frontier. The request was passed on to the military authorities in the region, and they carefully selected a young Pathan tribesman from the hills. When the mission was completed, the Pathan soldier was asked by his superior officer how he fared on the journey. "Stein Sahib," exclaimed the young man, "is some kind of supernatural being, not human; he walked me off my legs on the mountains; I could not keep up with him. Please do not send me to him again, Sir."[3] At that time Stein was well over sixty. Years earlier, in 1907, he had lost all the toes of his right foot to frostbite when mapping areas of the Kunlun, at an altitude of 20,000 feet. On another occasion he was severely lacerated when his horse threw him while crossing a river, and fell on him. He broke his collarbone several times, and barely escaped drowning in the Persian Gulf.

Stein avoided a large retinue and cumbersome equipment on his expeditions, and preferred the company of Sikhs and Pathans to Europeans. Invariably he took along Dash, his agile Scottish

---

[3] Oldham: op. cit., p. 346.

terrier, or rather, successive members of that species (numbered I to VII) who were temperamentally attuned to the nimbleness of their master.

The sandy, windswept waste of innermost Asia, which was the object of Stein's most vital archaeological explorations, comprises largely what is today Chinese Turkestan, or Sinkiang. The area stretches eastward for about 1,500 miles from the headwaters of the Oxus in the Hindu Kush to China proper, and is 500 miles at its widest. The drainageless Tarim basin and the Takla Makan Desert occupy the central part of the area. In the north it is bounded by the Tien Shan, the "Celestial Mountains," and in the south by the mighty Kunlun ranges, across which lies Tibet. In the west tower the Pamirs, "Roof of the World." Unless one is attracted to the metaphysical charms of endless undulating sand mounds and shifting dunes, one will be hard put to find appealing a series of windswept altiplanos. In the absence of moisture in the atmosphere, and almost total lack of salt-free water, human, animal, and plant life cannot be sustained there for any length of time except at a string of oases confined to a narrow fringe near the piedmont, which are watered by glacier-fed streams.

Artificial irrigation supports life in a larger area during times of political stability. Evidence points to progressive desiccation, however, which has led to the shrinking of most settlements and even to their abandonment to the encroaching desert sea. One frequently comes across shriveled whitish stumps and skeletal branches of dead trees, indicating past habitation and in shrill surrealistic accents suggesting the existence of sand-buried edifices nearby. Other characteristic landmarks of the dried-up oasis belt are tamarisk cones, accumulations of sand around decayed tamarisk shrubs, which through the years have been piled up to considerable heights.

Despite the visible advance of the desert dust bowl on villages and towns, there is no reason to assume that Chinese Turkestan, except for a marginal zone, was ever fertile enough for settlement. Nature has apparently raised here one of its most formidable bastions. But like any natural barrier—ocean, river, mountains—it is potentially also a bridge, and as such it has played a vital role in Asian history. It was never really inaccessible. Though forbidding, it served as a natural corridor between eastern and western Asia, with connecting links to Tibet in the south and, via the Gobi, to Mongolia and Siberia in the north.

To judge by Paleolithic and Neolithic artifacts, the long trail across the desert may be one of the world's oldest roads, perhaps associated with the birth of Chinese civilization itself. Long before it became a silk road, it was a jade road, for over it jade may have reached Troy, thousands of miles away, in the second millennium B.C. Chinese Turkestan was also a source of the lapis lazuli cherished by Sumerians and Babylonians.

For a very long time, however, China and the Near East had no direct contact and only the haziest knowledge of each other. Great empires rose in both, but China, building a splendid civilization and realm of her own, remained oblivious of the West, of Persia, even of India, and they of her, until the second century B.C. When the meeting of East and West took place, it was due to Chinese initiative. The Chinese, on their westward drive across Inner Asia, faced appalling hardships; yet in truth the East discovered the West.

The movement was started by the great second-century B.C. Emperor Wu Ti of the Han Dynasty, who sought help against the marauding hordes of the Hsiung-nu, known to Europeans as Huns. Thereafter, for several centuries the road across the deserts broadened into a highway joining distant worlds. China now made contact with three great civilizations, the Indian, the Greco-Roman, and the Persian. Traffic flowed in both directions along the roads of Inner Asia. Caravans transporting Chinese silks, merchants of many races, conquering armies, and embassies filed through the oasis belts. Most important of all, the trade and military route soon became an artery for the dissemination of artistic, linguistic, and religious influences. The heterogeneous strands were merged in the polyglot culture of the oasis towns, which, in turn undergoing transformation and adaptation, reached China herself.

Buddhist missionaries were the main agents of cultural influence. Through them Buddhism gained a lasting foothold in China, and beyond it, in Korea and Japan. This was one of the signal events in world history. Buddhist art, already an eloquent blend of classical, Indian, and Iranian elements, was thoroughly assimilated by the Far East, where it became as formative a force as Christianity in Europe. The main route of the Buddhist missionaries was the Inner Asian highway charted initially by Chinese rulers advancing in the opposite direction. Not for the first time was an imperial aggressor opening the way through which his domain was to be conquered by foreign intellectual and spiritual forces. This is one of the quasi-Hegelian ruses of history. *Graecia capta ferum captorem cepit* (Captured Greece took its uncouth capturer captive). Similarly, the excellent communications and the peace and unity of the Roman Empire permitted the relatively easy spread of the Christian faith.

Christian crosses engraved in Chinese monuments testify to the penetration of the Nestorian Christian faith across Central Asia into China. Jesuit missionaries rediscovered this one in the seventeenth century.

The decline of the Hans and disillusionment with official credos, what Gilbert Murray has called a "failure of nerve," created in China a responsiveness to Buddhism—and other cults—analogous to developments in the Mediterranean world under Roman rule. However, Buddhism in the generally more tolerant and pluralistic environment of the Middle Kingdom never became an exclusive religion. It coexisted side by side with Confucianism and Taoism, and on a smaller scale with Manichaeanism, Nestorian Christianity, and perhaps even Judaism. But Buddhism was thoroughly transformed by the Chinese, who took it upon themselves to spread the new religion zealously in other countries. At least one of their missions, if we are to believe the official Chinese annals, may have reached the American west coast in pre-Columbian days.[4]

For some thousand years after Wu Ti's breakthrough from China and the arrival of the first Buddhist missionaries from the Gandhara across the Pamir, the Inner Asia desert of Eastern Turkestan, with its flourishing oasis towns, was the stage for the interpenetration of the great civilizations of Europe and Asia. Yet only since the advent of Sir Aurel Stein in Central Asia, and of

---

[4] Vilhjalmur Stefansson, ed.: *Great Adventures and Explorations* (New York: Dial Press; 1947), pp. 109–15.

the German, French, Russian, and Japanese expeditions which followed in his wake, have we begun to comprehend its variegated cultural, religious, economic, ethnic, and political aspects.

Stein's foray had one immediate purpose: to trace the source of the manuscripts which recently had reached the West, and possibly to add to their number. He also hoped that ancient documents would untie the skein of that region's tangled history and lead him to physical evidence of the cultures that once flourished there. The stage was thus set for what Leonard Woolley has called "the most daring and adventurous raid upon the ancient world that any archaeologist has attempted."[5]

From 1900 to 1916, Stein was engaged in three major expeditions into Central Asia, which kept him in the field for seven years. During the second, and perhaps most important, campaign, undertaken from 1906 to 1908, he was on the move for two and a half years. Altogether he covered, mostly on foot, some 25,000 miles. At least in a spatial sense, Stein practiced extensive rather than intensive archaeology. He did not concentrate on a single rich site, but searched out an entire civilization in its widest range and physical setting. Typically, Stein was absorbed in tracing the ancient routes—particularly those of Hsüan Tsang and Marco Polo—by which several civilizations met.

All three journeys covered roughly the same ground. Stein would set out from Kashmir, explore little-known valleys of the Hindu Kush and Pamir, and then follow the oasis belt from Kashgar in the west, along one of the two edges of the Takla Makan Desert. From present-day towns he would venture into the desert to abandoned sites, where he excavated. He visited several of these ruins on successive expeditions, and between seasons he undertook his cartographic surveys of the high mountains.

Stein's first journey, covering seven months in 1900–1, centered largely on the city of Khotan, the long-time capital of a native kingdom at the southern fringe of Eastern Turkestan. Stein was convinced that Khotan had been a significant link in the exchange of goods and cultural influences. He already knew of scattered passages in the Chinese Annals which mentioned Khotan as a way station on the road to the Oxus. During the

---

[5] Leonard Woolley: *History Unearthed* (New York: Frederick A. Praeger; n.d.), p. 116.

Later Han Dynasty and the Tang Dynasty it was apparently under direct Chinese political control. Some artifacts (including manuscripts) which displayed affinities with ancient Indian objects had already been discovered in the Khotan area at the ruined sites by native treasure seekers. As most of these places had been thoroughly ransacked, Stein decided to move on to more remote areas on the ancient desert road to China. But there was a puzzling problem he had to answer first.

Since 1895, several paper manuscripts and block prints in strange and confusing characters had been purchased on behalf of the Indian government by its representative in Chinese Turkestan. Considerable quantities of documents of a similar kind had drifted into Russia and into public collections in Europe. Every one of these was supposed to have been excavated in the desert area near Khotan, and all of them could be traced to one man, a Khotan treasure seeker by the name of Islam Akhun. A few years earlier, the Indian representative had been able to persuade him to disclose the location of the sand-buried ruins from which he had allegedly obtained the manuscripts. Yet Stein had some doubts about the genuineness of these strange texts and he set himself the task, while he was still in India, of getting to the bottom of the mystery. He resolved to visit the old sites named by Akhun. On the road from Kashgar to Khotan he stopped at a place called Guma, which had been listed by the treasure seeker. Local dignitaries assured him that no "old books" had ever come to light there. Of the number of nearby ruins mentioned by Akhun, only two were known to them. They took Stein to these, but it was obvious that the ruins had been abandoned in relatively recent times. None could have furnished any antiquities whatsoever.

In Khotan, Stein vainly waited for a visit from Islam Ahkun peddling his dubious ware, which he usually offered to recent arrivals. But the man, for reasons best known to himself, shunned prospective customers from India just then. Meanwhile Stein made the acquaintance of a Russian Armenian who was the proud possessor of a birchbark manuscript in the same writing. The Armenian, who had bought the book as a speculative investment, wanted to have it appraised. Stein could not be very reassuring, however; an examination of the book only increased his suspicions. None of the birchbark leaves had received the careful preparation known to Stein from his analysis of such materials in Kashmir. Neither was the ink of the type traditionally used for writing on bark.

Unfortunately there was still no sign of Islam Akhun. Every time Stein came back to Khotan from excursions into the adjacent mountains or desert, Akhun was absent. A confrontation took place finally, but only during Stein's last trip to Khotan at the end of his first expedition. Though the evidence of fraud was pretty conclusive, Stein was "anxious for a personal examination of that enterprising individual whose productions had engaged so much learned attention in Europe."[6] The local Mandarin governor volunteered his assistance and Islam Akhun was at last seized.

At first the suspect presented himself as only the docile sales agent for other "old book" dealers, who conveniently had either run away or passed on to their just reward. Akhun seemed convinced that there was no direct evidence to implicate him in fraud and made a great show of his respect for the law. But he overreached himself. Not knowing that a report published in India contained in indelible print the account he had given to the British resident of his "discoveries," he now told Stein that he himself had never been to any of the places from which the books had supposedly come. Stein promptly put the report before him. And, as Stein wrote in an amusing chapter of his personal narrative on the rascal, "the effect was most striking. Islam Akhun was wholly unprepared for the fact that his lies told years before, with so much seeming accuracy of topographical and other details, had received the honour of permanent record in a scientific report to Government. He was intelligent enough to realize that he stood self-convicted, and that there was nothing to be gained by further protestations of innocence."[7] Gradually the whole truth came out.

Islam Akhun had indeed once engaged in collecting genuine antiques from neighboring ruins. Then an Afghan trader alerted him in 1894 to the new lucrative market for ancient manuscripts among the "Sahibi" of India. It seems, "the idea of visiting such dreary desert sites, with a certainty of great hardships and only a limited chance of finds, had no attraction for a person of such wits as Islam Akhun. So in preference he conceived the plan of manufacturing the article he was urged to supply the Sahibs with."[8]

---

[6] Aurel Stein: *Sand-buried Ruins of Khotan* (London: Hurst & Blackett; 1904), p. 472.
[7] Ibid., p. 475.
[8] Ibid., p. 449.

Several specimens of his illegible workmanship appeared in the British Museum. Sven Hedin appended a reproduction of one to the German edition of his *Through Asia*.

With little coaxing from Stein, the forger became rather voluble, and in fact boasted of his accomplishments. He even showed Stein one of his artful implements for the creation of fakes, about which Stein remarked: "How much more proud would he have felt if he could but have seen, as I did a few months later, the fine morocco bindings with which a number of his . . . forgeries had been honored in a great European library!"[9] So pleased was Islam with himself that he considered his talents wasted in the Turkestan hinterland—he had the effrontery to ask Stein to take him to Europe. Stein on his part was well satisfied that he had solved the case without any "resort to Eastern methods of judicial inquiry." Moreover, he deemed that his own investigations had in themselves disposed of Islam Akhun's ware as clumsy fabrications. None of the sites he searched along the several hundred miles from Khotan east to Endere, the end point of his first expedition, had disclosed any scripts even remotely related to Akhun's specimens.

The unmasking of these forgeries was merely a byproduct of Stein's first exploratory venture; yet it reveals the critical acumen he brought to bear on antiquities. He had won a test against the crafty treasure seekers, but then it occurred to him that he could put to good use their knowledge of sand-buried ruins. Before setting out from India, he was haunted by the fear that the infinite desert might swallow him up in an aimless search for abandoned settlements. There was no literature, and no map, that could give precise information on ancient settlements. He knew of several place names from the Chinese Annals and from the writings of Hsüan Tsang and Marco Polo, whose footsteps he wanted to follow part of the way to China. But, except for a few still inhabited oasis towns, which because of their continuous occupation were unlikely to yield any artifacts, the identity and location of these places was unknown. How far from the modern roads in the waterless sand waste were they? Were they at all visible? Undoubtedly many more ancient settlements, not mentioned by Chinese or Venetian travelers, were slumbering in the desert.

Stein devised a simple scheme to resolve the problem. Whenever on his eastward progression he reached an oasis town, he

---

[9] Ibid., p. 454.

tracked down native rumors of nearby treasures. Occasionally treasure seekers would approach him first. His own Turkestani men acted as an intelligence force and could be counted on to strike up useful acquaintances among the local men, one of whom Stein then chose as a guide. A few of these became his trusted companions throughout all his expeditions.

Stein owed the discovery of the most promising buried towns to native sources of information. With the exception of the Caves of the Thousand Buddhas near Tun Huang (Tunhwang or Tunhuang), his crowning archaeological achievement, Stein did not seek out a specific place so much as make his way to wherever he suspected the existence of treasures of respectable antiquity. In this way he came upon the so-called Dandan Uiliq ("the Houses with Ivory"), as it was known to treasure hunters, the Niya site, and Endere, principal digs of his first expedition. On his next two trips to Inner Asia, he made further use of the knowledge he had meanwhile acquired. At the Lop Desert he followed the description of Sven Hedin, who had previously visited the ruins of Lou Lan.

Stein had refined his method while still at Khotan. He realized that much time and labor might be lost by following up vague information elicited from treasure hunters. Even reliable men

Brahmi inscription from a decree by King Piyadasi on a rock in northwestern India

would not always understand just what he was after. He decided, therefore, to send out simultaneously a number of scouts to gather specimens from various sites. While this operation was in progress, Stein left Khotan on a surveying mission into the Kunlun range. On his return, he established that the ancient site of Khotan was the nearby village of Yotkan. Just then one of the parties he had dispatched came back with pieces of a fresco inscribed in Indian Brahmi characters, and an old paper document in cursive Brahmi of a Central Asian variety. The samples were undoubtedly genuine. They had been secured by Turdi, a former treasure hunter who became one of Stein's faithful scouts. Thus, the choice fell on Dandan Uiliq, some sixty miles to the northeast of Khotan, as the first target for excavation. With thirty laborers and supplies for four weeks, Stein now ventured deep into the desert. Winter, the only time when work in the sandy wastes is feasible, had set in with full vigor. Night temperatures dropped to below zero Fahrenheit. In his tent at night, Stein was forced to give up his regular writing chores and retire to his heavily blanketed cot, where little Dash had already sought refuge.[1]

Turdi had guided the party well. Within the extensive ruins, buildings of considerable antiquity were recognizable. The fresco fragments Turdi had brought to Khotan led the way to a Buddhist shrine appropriately termed by Stein's Mohammedan men, "Temple of Idols." Stein cleared large mural paintings, whose composition and figures were strongly reminiscent of the Ajanta cave paintings in central India. Little of this art had survived elsewhere in India. Here, then, was unmistakable evidence of the flourishing of Indian culture and religion far from its native soil.

But manuscripts were what Stein hoped for most of all. He took it as a good omen that the Buddhist frescoes depicted Indian *pothis*, the characteristic manuscript form, in which a number of oblong leaves are bundled together, perforated with a circular hole, and tied together with string. During the first three days, no such documents turned up, but on the fourth day one of the men discovered a narrow strip of paper with the sorry remnants of what appeared to be a Sanskrit text. Stein offered a reward in silver to the man who found the first real manuscript, and within less than an hour, he heard a cry from an adjacent structure. Someone had found an oblong leaf of paper 13 by 4 inches, perforated like *pothis*, and inscribed with Brahmi characters, but in what Stein identified as a non-Indian language.

From then on, manuscript scraps turned up more frequently. The majority were written in Brahmi on paper *pothis* and were from three Sanskrit texts of the Buddhist canon. Soon whole manuscript bundles turned up, some so brittle that they could not be

---

[1] Ibid., p. 276.

separated until they arrived at the British Museum. The longer manuscripts dealt with the Buddhist *Dharma*. A. F. R. Hoernle, the philologist who deciphered and published all of Stein's Brahmi materials, recognized among the *pothi* stacks a nearly complete Sutra of Mahayana Buddhism, copied about the seventh century A.D. This wealth of religious literature made it quite probable that Stein had found a Buddhist monastic library.

On Christmas Day, Stein busied himself with further excavation at an edifice half a mile away from the camp. It yielded documents of a different kind, quite a few ancient texts of the type that had caused scholars almost as many headaches as Islam Akhun's productions. These were manuscripts in a distinctive cursive Brahmi script but in an unknown language. All of them were on rolled-up paper. Stein had a hunch that they might have been written in the native, long-extinct language of the Khotan region.

While he examined these texts, his workers took from the same room which contained the "Khotan" pieces a few more Christmas surprises: the first Chinese texts. One was a long stick of tamarisk wood on which faded Chinese letters had been inscribed in vertical lines. The second document was nearly intact. It was on thin, water-lined paper neatly folded up, and was later identified as a trivial official document, but of considerable historical significance. Someone had filed a petition concerning a donkey that had been borrowed ten months earlier and had not been returned. An exact date was given, the sixth day of the second month of the sixteenth year of the Tali period, which would be our A.D. 781. The petitioner had also set down the locality, a place named Li Sieh. Thus, in one stroke, Stein had discovered the probable identity of the site, or at least its Chinese name.[2] All the Chinese documents ranged in date from A.D. 781 to no later than 790. From the way they had been deposited in living quarters the inference could be drawn that the site was abandoned soon after. This conclusion was borne out by the presence of Chinese copper coins issued no later than A.D. 760. And there is an account in the Chinese Annals that control over the Tarim basin during the Tang era came to an end about A.D. 791.

These finds helped Stein to pass Christmas Day in good spirits. With his sociable little terrier sharing his Christmas din-

---

[2] Stein: *On Ancient Central-Asian Tracks* (London: Macmillan & Co.; 1933), p. 67.

ner, he doubted "whether even the friends whose kind thoughts turned toward me that evening from the distant South and West, could realise how cheerful is the recollection of the Christmas spent in the solitude and cold of the desert."[3] Early in January, he moved on. He had gathered a substantial quantity of documents in various languages, several fine pieces of Buddhist art, and a great many artifacts, including writing utensils. He had not confined himself to excavation, but had also studied the layout, physical setting, and conditions of life of this desert outpost. The shriveled orchards, decayed more than a thousand years before, indicated that the town had once been fed by irrigation canals carrying water for many miles from distant streams. Were internal disorders in China responsible for the desolation of this outpost?

From Dandan Uiliq, Turdu guided Stein to other ruined places in the neighborhood. In mid-January the caravan reached Keriya, a modern oasis, where Stein could rest and write his reports for a scientific journal. He did not neglect to inquire for antiquities, however, and on the very day of his arrival he gleaned information about promising ruins farther east in the desert around Niya and beyond the termination of the Niya River. When the rumors were confirmed by several people, Stein decided to extend his itinerary a greater distance from Khotan than originally planned, and include Niya, the more attractive to Stein because Hsüan Tsang had passed through the settlement on his way to the Lop Nor and China. The Chinese traveler had then described it as the easternmost outpost of the Khotan Kingdom.[4]

Kharoshthi writing. An ancient Indian alphabetic script widely used during the Kushana Empire for official and business transactions. This inscription is dated from 38 B.C.

One of the alert young men on the expedition had lost no time at Niya and had become friendly with a villager who owned two inscribed wooden tablets from the ruined site Stein planned to investigate. The tablets were produced and revealed still an-

---

[3] Stein: *Sand-buried Ruins of Khotan*, p. 314.
[4] Ibid., p. 342.

other phase in the wide epigraphic range of ancient Turkestan. These documents were novel in both makeup and writing. Stein saw before him an ancient script—Kharoshthi—used in the extreme northwest of India a few centuries before and after the beginning of our era. It had first become known in 1837 from inscriptions which closely connected it with the Kushana rulers of ancient India. Some early coins from Khotan dating from the first or second century A.D. carried Kharoshthi letters. And a birch-bark codex acquired in 1892 in Khotan was written in the same script. The Kharoshthi documents indicated the great antiquity of the ruins Stein was about to visit.

Further inquiries at Niya revealed that another villager, an enterprising miller and part-time treasure hunter, Ibrahim, had been the finder of the Kharoshthi tablets. During the previous year he had carried away several of them, but judging them useless, he threw some away on the road. Others he gave to his children to play with; naturally they were soon destroyed. Poor Ibrahim now was grieved by his carelessness, the more so when he saw the European gentleman remunerate his fellow villager who had picked up two of the discards. As it worked out, Stein secured the services of Ibrahim as his guide. Some ten days later, marching under a clear sky along an old river course, Stein's caravan reached the ruins. A preliminary inspection showed it to be a much more imposing site than Dandan Uiliq, and considerably more ancient. The proof came from one of the first houses Stein entered when he caught a glimpse of richly carved sculptures of the early Gandhara type.

The next morning Stein hastened to inspect the building from which Ibrahim said he had taken the Kharoshthi tablets. Stein was apprehensive, however. Maybe Ibrahim was a mere braggart, or perhaps he had had second thoughts and had decided to keep the discovery to himself, knowing now the high value Europeans set on the wooden tablets. But, as Stein wrote, "the mingled feelings of expectation and distrust with which I now approached it [Ibrahim's site] soon changed to joyful assurance. About a mile to the east of the camp I sighted the ruins towards which Ibrahim was guiding us, on what looked like a little terrace rising high above the depressions of the ground caused by the erosive action of the wind. On ascending the slope I picked up at once three inscribed tablets lying amidst the débris of massive timber that marked wholly eroded parts of the ruined structure; and on reaching the top, I found to my delight many more scattered about within one of the rooms, still clearly traceable by remains of their walls."[5]

Stein's men cleared one room inside the building, and found no less than eighty-five tablets before the day had ended. Most of them were excellently preserved. They were all wooden, with distinctive features, and were written in Kharoshthi characters from right to left. The majority consisted of two pieces. Nearly all the ones found on the first day were wedge-shaped pairs held together by a string tied around their widest edges and through a hole at the tapered ends. Those with the string still intact had a clay seal on one side, "which had been inserted over the string in a specially prepared square socket." The inner surfaces of the matching pairs were covered with writing, and the outside, like some modern envelopes, carried only a brief entry, which at once suggested the address or name of the sender.[6] It was likely, then, that the sealed twin documents had served as official records, contracts, or letters. Further excavation yielded more of these texts, and also others of a considerable range in size and shape. Many single oblong wooden tablets had writing on both sides, and were provided with a handle. Other oblong or rectangular paired tablets consisted of a lower piece with raised edges into which the smaller top could be fitted like a drawer. These too were kept closed by strings overlaid with clay seals.

The clay seals in themselves were extraordinary: they were of pure classical Greco-Roman design, and impressed on them were recognizable Hellenic deities such as Pallas Athene and Eros. Here, among third-century A.D. ruins, halfway between the Mediterranean and the Pacific Ocean, was more evidence of the diversity and mingling of cultural influences.[7]

The entire Niya site failed to yield one scrap of paper: clearly an indication that the town had been abandoned relatively early. Although paper had already been invented in China, it took considerable time to spread into Eastern Turkestan.

The houses showed plainly that they had not been haphazardly destroyed. The exodus of the inhabitants must have been orderly, since comparatively little of material value had been left behind. But the houses were not Stein's only source; like Grenfell and Hunt at Oxyrhynchus, he now turned to the rubbish heaps. They yielded additional epigraphic novelties such as a wooden

---

[5] Ibid., p. 355.
[6] Stein: *On Ancient Central-Asian Tracks*, p. 77.
[7] Stein: *Sand-buried Ruins of Khotan*, p. xvii.

document, this time written in Chinese; and a folded Kharoshthi document on leather. That a scribe of Indian language and religious ties should use ox or cowhide was, to say the least, surprising. However, systematic excavation of the rubbish heaps produced mostly wooden tablets—in the end more than two hundred, scattered among all kind of detritus. Wood was undoubtedly the most common stationery, and its peculiar shapes had been introduced to Turkestan by the Chinese.

The compactness of the unsavory refuse conglomerate had helped to shield its contents from the erosive action of desert winds. This was the compensation for such unceremonious burial. The thought consoled Stein as he worked for three days, his fingers benumbed by cold, assorting, cleaning, and tabulating each piece carefully in order to facilitate the later decipherment of connected pieces and to ascertain their chronological order. It was not exactly a pleasant task. With "a fresh north-east breeze raised from the dug-up refuse heap" he had "to inhale odours, still pungent after so many centuries, and to swallow in liberal doses antique microbes luckily now dead."[8]

Stein had heard at Niya of another site, the Endere ruins some four hundred miles east of Khotan. Here an ancient Buddhist temple became the scene of new manuscript finds. Since this was not as old as the Niya ruins, paper predominated. Stein extracted Sanskrit manuscripts as well as cursive Brahmi texts in the non-Indian ("Khotan") idiom he had found earlier. He discovered at the feet of one of the statues various Buddhist scriptures, apparently deposited as religious offerings. Other pieces of what had once been a manuscript were curiously distributed in front of a number of images. The devout owner had, it seems, tried to propitiate more than one divinity by spreading thin his mutilated gift. When later examined and assembled at the British Museum, the fragments were found to belong to a Tibetan version of a Buddhist philosophical treatise, whose Sanskrit original had been lost. Once again, Stein's excavations had enlarged the scope of our literary and linguistic documentation from Central Asia. Tibetan was now added to the polyglot picture. For good measure, the manuscript not only was a lost religious work but represented the oldest specimen of Tibetan writing known.

Time was running short before the season of sandstorms would set in and excavation would become impossible at exposed

---

[8] Ibid., p. 388.

desert sites. Endere thus came to be the eastern terminus of Stein's first campaign. It seemed a logical stop; Stein then thought he had very likely reached the borderline beyond which Indian influence yielded to Chinese.[9] Later expeditions led him to revise this concept. The influence of India, and even of the classical West, had penetrated far beyond: into the Lop desert and deep into China proper.

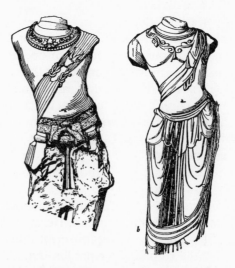

Two supple Bodhisattvas—one from India, the other from China—unmistakable links in the spreading of Gandhara art and Buddhist culture across Central Asia

No sooner had Stein completed his first expedition in Central Asia than he was planning a second. The precise purposes of this one was the tracing of further archaeological and topographical evidence for the spread of Indian Buddhism into Kansu, the northwestern province of China.[1] That he also meant to follow the tracks of Hsüan Tsang and Marco Polo goes without saying. And he was going to make use of what a Hungarian friend had told him years earlier about China's western gateway, the oasis of Tun Huang. On this venture, which was partly sponsored by the British Museum, Stein had more time and more means at his disposal. He was already a seasoned explorer, and besides, he had enlisted the assistance of a Chinese secretary, who "with the

---

[9] Ibid., p. 422.
[1] Stein: *On Ancient Central-Asian Tracks*, p. 193.

true historical sense innate in every educated Chinese . . . took to archaeological work like a young duck to water."[2] Stein dug at some of the places he had investigated earlier and also carried out a good deal of additional research. On approaching the Niya site, he had the joyful sensation of finding himself among the now familiar "shrivelled trunks of poplars and fruit trees which had flourished when there was still an Imperial Rome."[3] Again he reaped a rich harvest in Kharoshthi documents. In one building he struck what must have been an entire record office. As elsewhere, "manuscript finds became so frequent that . . . [he] soon had to give up the attempt to number all the fragments individually."[4] Everywhere, in the furniture, plaster works, wood panels, and art objects, he recognized the Greco-Buddhist style of Gandhara. From so much detail—the finely built houses, utensils, orchards, and avenues, not to mention the wealth of documents—the conditions of life could be reconstructed. There was no doubt in Stein's mind that an advanced civilization had once flourished here, inspired by the Buddhist religion but highly susceptible to Hellenistic influences.

After revisiting Niya, Stein moved eastward, past Endere and the ancient oasis of Charkhliq (Charkhlik), across the desert some thousand miles beyond the limit of his previous travels. The forbidding territory of Lop beckoned him. This salt bed left from a largely dried-up prehistoric sea, part perhaps of the giant Thetis Sea proposed by geologists, which swallows the dying Tarim River, had been crossed by Marco Polo, and over it the Chinese had ventured into Central Asia. Yet no one had attempted to retrace the exact route, and some of the northern sections of the Lop had never been explored.

The first destination was the Lou Lan ruins described by Sven Hedin. But on the way to the Lop, some fifty miles northeast of Charkhliq, Stein camped at the ruins of Miran. It was too good a spot to bypass. As icy gales blew fiercely and the thermometer dropped to subarctic temperatures, Stein and his men began to dig. A giant rubbish heap became a prime target and proved rich in archaeological treasure, and remarkable, too, as Stein observed, for dirt. It was full of Tibetan records, unmistakable proof of Tibetan occupation of the area about the eighth or

---

[2] Ibid., p. 48.
[3] Stein: *Ruins of Desert Cathay* (London: Macmillan & Co.; 1912), Vol. I, p. 270.
[4] Ibid., p. 270.

ninth century A.D.[5] After the eclipse, in the eighth century, of Chinese control in the Tarim basin, Miran had apparently become a Tibetan fort guarding the road between Tun Huang in western China and the southern oasis towns of Inner Asia.

Stein confessed to some mixed feelings about his familiarity with rubbish heaps. Those of Miran were appalling in their filth. "Nothing but absolute indifference" to dirt could have induced the Tibetan occupants to turn their very living quarters into mounds of refuse, some piled right to the roof. "I have had occasion," wrote Stein mordantly, "to acquire a rather extensive experience in clearing ancient rubbish heaps, and know how to diagnose them. But for intensity of sheer dirt and age-persisting smelliness I shall always put the rich 'castings' of Tibetan warriors in the front rank. More than a year later, when clearing the remains of a small ruined fort on the Mazartagh hill north of Khotan, more than 500 miles away, I correctly diagnosed its Tibetan occupation by the smell of the refuse even before finding antiquarian evidence."[6]

No matter how unappetizing their manner of deposit, the Tibetan documents were a welcome find. In the end, Stein collected more than one thousand, the majority undoubtedly commonplace. But their everyday language, of which little had been known previously, since virtually all Tibetan literature is of an elevated religious nature, was a boon to scholars. From similar deposits was to come an even rarer and unexpected find, a packet of papers in so-called "Runic" Turkish, which were similar in script and language to the famous inscriptions at Orkhon, south of Lake Baikal. This was the earliest known Turkish writing and had been deciphered in 1893 by a Danish scholar, Vilhelm L. P. Thomsen. On his return, Stein dispatched his Runic-Turk documents to Thomsen.

Miran, however, had not yet yielded up all its treasures. There were structures of a far greater age, some of which had probably been in ruins when the Tibetan invaders arrived. Among them Stein made some of the most astonishing discoveries of his forty years of exploration. First, against all his expectations he beheld large torsos in the pure Greco-Buddhist style of Gandhara. At the foot of one statue he picked up a manuscript of palm leaves written in Brahmi script in Sanskrit. It could not have been

---

[5] Stein: *On Ancient Central-Asian Tracks*, p. 112.
[6] Ibid., p. 114.

written anywhere but in India, and must have been carried all the way across the badlands of innermost Asia to the fringe of China. Its style indicated that it was at least as old as the fourth century A.D.

Stein then noticed a small, badly eroded Buddhist stupa, most of it buried under a mound. Remains of painted stucco showed up as the digging progressed, and when a greater depth was reached, Stein was completely taken by surprise by the beautiful winged angels on the wall. "How could I have expected by the desolate shores of Lop Nor, in the very heart of innermost Asia, to come upon such classical representations as Cherubim! And what had these graceful heads, recalling cherished scenes of Christian imagery, to do here on the walls of what beyond all doubt was a Buddhist sanctuary?"[7] There were echoes of the Egyptian-Greek girls and youths of the Fayum wax panels, and of Byzantine art. Pompeii now did not seem too far away. Had Stein known the paintings of Dura, a striking parallel to their hybrid Mediterranean-Asiatic style would surely have occurred to him.

As he uncovered more and more murals depicting the life story of Buddha, but quite Western in the physical types painted, Stein perceived a suggestion also of Semitic traits and the possibility of influence from early Christian iconography. For a moment he thought he had been transported to some ancient villa in Syria or an eastern province of the Roman Empire. Then in a passage in the same shrine Stein made another discovery, which helped to date the frescoes: remains of silken votive banners with inscriptions in Kharoshthi of exactly the same type as the wooden documents from the Niya site, which had been abandoned in the third century A.D.[8]

Most of the manuscripts found in Eastern Turkestan recorded the penetration of Indian influence across Central Asia toward China. These frescoes, however, more so even than the Gandhara style of Buddhist sculpture, were evidence of the transplantation of classical influences, which evidently had been carried out under Buddhist auspices.

The road to Lou Lan was arduous, hard on men and animals both. Strong gusts of wind swept down incessantly from the Mongolian plateau in the north. The temperature rarely rose above

---

[7] Stein: *Ruins of Desert Cathay*, Vol. I, p. 457.
[8] Stein: *On Ancient Central-Asian Tracks*, p. 119.

zero Fahrenheit. Camels were packed with four to five hundred pounds of ice to supply sufficient water for weeks in the waterless salt waste. The caravan had to cross sharp-edged, wind-eroded clay terraces, which were cut by deep trenches. The poor camels developed sore feet and, according to an old practice, were "re-soled" with pieces of leather stitched onto the live skin. The beasts responded with kicks to this crude bit of surgery. But it worked.

Shortly after entering the Lop, along Marco Polo's track, Stein noticed stone-age weapons and coarse pottery on the old lake bed. Farther on, he picked up a succession of Chinese copper coins of Han imprint, which apparently had fallen out of a leaking money bag being transported across the old route some two millennia before. Even in this most inhospitable of regions, man had left traces.

The caravan stayed at Lou Lan for eleven days. Stein wisely pitched his tent at the foot of a ruined stupa, but even then it was almost blown away in the middle of the night. Excavations

Chinese documents on paper and wooden slips from Lou Lan, third century A.D.

brought forth Chinese documents on wood and paper, as well as Kharoshthi records, also on wood and paper. The Kharoshthi documents were further evidence of the wide use of this Indian script in the early centuries of our era. They manifested the considerable linguistic homogeneity prevailing at that time from Khotan to Lou Lan at the extreme eastern edge of the Tarim basin. Chinese imperial documents from here were to offer administrative and military details of considerable importance. An imperial order to reduce food rations for the soldiers stationed at this army camp indicated the rapid decline of Chinese power during the Later Han period. Virtually all these documents were dated between A.D. 263 and 270. By means of these, the French Sinologist Édouard Chavannes was to prove conclusively that Lou Lan had been a fortified garrison of Chinese troops who, like the Tibetans five hundred years later at Miran, had watched over the vital Inner Asia route.

In addition to texts on wood and paper, Lou Lan also yielded documents on silk, which bore out the ancient Chinese tradition that before the invention of paper silk was one of the chief writing materials. Another curiosity, taken from the first ruin, was a small bale of yellowish silk. Additional artifacts enabled Stein to show that the bale was of standard size and represented "the actual form in which that ancient and most famous product of Chinese industry used to be carried to the classical West."[9] Nothing of its kind had come to light before.

Epigraphically, the most interesting trophy was a strip of paper covered with still another unknown script. Stein noticed right away that it was written in the Semitic manner, from right to left, and he perceived a faint resemblance to the Aramaic of the Near East. It later came to be identified as Sogdian, a language once native to the region of Samarkand and Bukhara.

From Lou Lan (Stein established that its original name had been Kroraina—obviously unpronounceable to a Chinese) Stein now crossed the length of the Lop Desert—some 380 miles—toward Tun Huang. This span had been traversed by Marco Polo in twenty-eight stages; Stein managed it in seventeen marches. Luckily, he had to face fewer hardships than on the way to Lou Lan. His caravan did not meet a single human on the entire road: all around them was utter desolation. No wonder, then, that Messer Marco and his Chinese predecessors dreamed up a miscellany of spirits to populate it and to lead travelers astray. Stein, however, was given to more sober thoughts. At first sight, this uninhabitable territory offered little to challenge the archaeologist's scrutiny. But there was ample room for observations of another kind. For one thing, Stein could study the changes in retreating lake beds and river courses. The shores of some terminal salt marshes were more than one degree of latitude farther east of the limits given on available maps. Stein envisioned the

---

[9] Ibid., p. 138.

geological past, when the now dried-up bed of the Sulo (Su-lo) was joined with the great Lop Sea. In those days the drainage area of the Tarim River no doubt extended from the Pamir across the central core of Asia to the watershed of the Pacific Ocean.[1]

Lost in these geographical speculations, Stein could hardly have suspected that he stood on the threshold of two momentous archaeological discoveries. He knew from the ancient annals of the Han Dynasty that Chinese traffic to Lou Lan had once started at the famous "Jade Gate," a fortified station whose location had been lost. Before entering the Lop Nor, he had hoped that he could be led to it by other posts or lookouts. Some scattered ruins had been mentioned by an earlier French traveler. If those existed, could they be found in the endless waste? And would they be on the ancient road? Were they indeed of sufficient antiquity to be connected with the Han Gate of two thousand years ago?

Stein had been on the Lop Desert for two weeks when one evening he and his men crossed a gravel plateau. About a mile from the traditional caravan trail, he noticed a small mound, to which he made his way. It turned out to be a quite well-preserved watchtower twenty-three feet high. Its distinctive solid build of sun-dried clay and layers of tamarisk branches indicated great antiquity. Its shape as well as its location along a deep, easily defensible river bed (now dry) marked it as a military outpost. Adjacent to it were ruins of the soldiers' or watchmen's quarters. Then more and more towers were found, many, however, almost completely eroded. One day, as Stein was looking down from one of these stations, his eyes fell on what seemed a regular line of reed bundles on the flat terrain. Following this line a short distance along the edge of the plateau, he saw to his delight that it "stretched away perfectly straight towards another tower visible some three miles to the east and assumed the form of an unmistakable wall where it crossed a depression."[2]

He had discovered a Chinese wall, an old frontier rampart— or limes, as Stein called it by its Roman name—which petered out beyond what Stein later identified as the Jade Gate near the ancient desert road. On his third expedition, Stein was to follow it for some six hundred miles to Etsin Gol in Kansu. Much of the fortified line had of course been eroded. Stein's studies fixed not only its extent, but its purpose and approximate date of origin. The limes had obviously been constructed to protect the trade and

---

[1] Ibid., p. 166.   [2] Ibid., p. 169.

military road into Inner Asia against marauding barbarians from
the Gobi in the north. It was coeval with China's first great western expansion in the second century B.C. Whereas the Great Wall
of China served a wholly defensive purpose, however, the limes
was an instrument of Chinese advance. Like the Romans from
Scotland to Syria, but at an earlier date, the Chinese of the Han
age protected their newly gained marches with a chain of military
posts. Reminiscent too of the Romans was the practice of recruit-
ing the bulk of the frontier soldiers stationed in the guardhouses
from "barbarian" peoples. This was determined from buried
records.

Archaeological spadework carried out at and near the watchtowers led to notable epigraphic discoveries which yielded a
wealth of data on armed ventures, troop movements, Chinese
military and civil administration, the clothing and feeding of
the men, and trade. Stein was naturally on the lookout for any
evidence that would establish the age of the wall. A clue cropped
up shortly in the form of a wooden Chinese tablet with the modest
inscription: "The clothes bag of one called Lu tingh-shih." The
wooden material itself spoke for its considerable age, and so did
the type of writing. And this was only the first morsel.

Again, Stein found refuse heaps to be a rewarding source.
They contained numerous Chinese records written on narrow slips
of wood, usually with only one vertical line of writing. A number
of these were dated, and Stein, with the assistance of his Chinese
secretary, deciphered them. They went back to the first century
A.D. The date of one of the rods corresponded to the year of
Christ's birth.

Stein derived immense satisfaction from holding in his
hand what was the oldest manuscript of a Chinese literary text
(the *Chi-chiu-chang*) so far recovered anywhere.[3] Even more rewarding were small rolls containing neatly folded letters on paper.
These were remarkable in several respects. First, they were written in the same, apparently Aramaic, type of script Stein had
found in Lou Lan, and second, they were probably not later than
the middle of the second century A.D., judging from the other
datable records with which they had been buried in the refuse
heaps. They would be, then, the oldest pieces of paper known,
produced perhaps within a generation or two of the invention
of this new writing material (according to Chinese tradition, in

---

[3] Stein: *Ruins of Desert Cathay*, Vol. II, p. 155.

A.D. 102 or 105). In recent years, however, several experts have challenged the age of these paper sheets and relegated them to the third century. The identification of the language in which the letters were written as Sogdian, an extinct Iranian-Scythian idiom, was accomplished by an English friend of Stein's, Arthur Cowley. Even if there are doubts today that these are the oldest paper documents known to us, these letters have the distinction of having been written in an ancient Indo-European tongue in a Semitic script on Chinese material by what may have been members of a kind of Chinese foreign legion. The writers were probably of the Buddhist faith. On the basis of these finds, and other texts and documents such as the silken Kharoshthi fragments, Stein could justly declare: "It seemed as if three civilizations from the East, West and South had combined to leave their written traces at this lonely watch-station in the desert, and with them to demonstrate also the earliest writing materials."[4]

This observation fittingly sums up the accomplishments of the first phases of Stein's "daring raid" on Chinese Turkestan. Records of this kind would show the connections, influences, and undercurrents of a thousand years of history, when innermost Asia was the meeting ground of religions, languages, races, and cultures. More than a lost chapter of the Asian past was coming to light. Here was an object lesson to demolish the parochial concepts of European-centered history and historians. The record was plainly written in the sand. Stein had extracted, from sites abandoned for centuries to the desert, written evidence of a cosmopolitan civilization with a notable wealth of languages and scripts. His Kharoshthi documents were the earliest records on wood in an Indian writing. They multiplied the available specimens of this script and suggested that Eastern Turkestan had been settled by people from northern India before the beginning of our era, perhaps in connection with the Kushana Empire and the spread of Buddhism. Official records in Kharoshthi in addition yielded a chronology for the Khotan region, giving names and dates of consecutive rulers. The language most commonly used was the early Prakrit of India, but some Kharoshthi texts were entirely in Sanskrit.

Likewise, the long-lost indigenous tongue of Khotan, an Iranian idiom, was restored. Khotanese texts included Buddhist scripture and religious poems, folk tales, and materia medica.

---

[4] Ibid., Vol. II, p. 115.

Eventually, manuscripts in other allied "Tokharian" dialects, once spoken in the Tarim basin, were identified. Another entirely forgotten Irano-Scythian language, that of the Sogdians, came to life from documents that could be deciphered. Nothing to speak of had been known of it before Stein's second expedition. Yet its ubiquitousness made it likely that it had once been a *lingua franca* throughout much of Central Asia. The Uigurs, native to Siberia, had adapted the Sogdian alphabet to their Turkic language.

As diverse as the languages were the scripts. Whether used by Turk, Indian Buddhist, Tibetan monk, or Iranian warrior, they were ultimately—though through complex intervening stages—derived from the Phoenician-Aramaic alphabet, which originated in ancient Mediterranean Syria. Only Chinese stood by itself.

The range of materials represented in these texts was considerable and included well-preserved samples of little or unknown

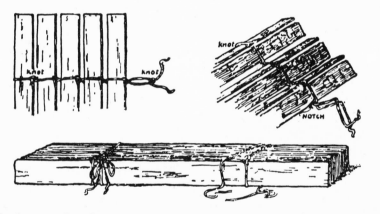

Books from wooden slips. Stein's discoveries furnished many details for tracing the history of Chinese writing materials and bookmaking before the invention of paper. After silk, wood was the favorite stationery. Narrow slips of wood (originally of bamboo) were used for all kinds of documents and communications. From Stein's finds it was possible to gauge the manner in which slips were joined to form a coherent sequence of texts. The sketches above show a set of slips from a calendar of A.D. 63. Upper left, open. Upper right, concertina method of folding. Below, a closed "book"

modes of writing. The people of Eastern Turkestan used tree bark, palm leaves, leather, bamboo strips, tamarisk wood, silk, and, far earlier than anywhere in the West, paper. Several of these materials had become associated with a standardized form according to the kind of communication they conveyed. Stein's recovery of thin rods, paired rectangular and wedge-shaped records in wood, and silken and paper leaves along China's frontier shed light on the evolution of Chinese books and writing, about which little concrete evidence had been available. Some of the wooden slips contained probably the oldest Chinese manuscripts, among them extracts from dictionaries and magical and medical works.[5] Eastern Turkestan had done for Buddhist India and China proper what Egypt had done for the classical world and Christianity: it had preserved some of its lost books.

The preservative characteristics of the sands and climate of innermost Asia are, if anything, superior to those of Egypt. As Stein has noted: "The thinnest layer of gravel sufficed to preserve in absolute freshness the most perishable objects."[6] When the explorer returned to a remote site he had visited seven years before, he could still distinguish the imprints left by him and his canine companion, Dash II. One trail, as we have seen, was clearly marked by Han copper coins shining as if they had just come from the mint. In one grave Stein found neatly shaped pieces of pastry about 1,300 years old. His animals nibbled straw that was equally ancient.

As a rule, deserts are far from being the most likely sites for a flourishing cultural life to evolve, though, paradoxically, they are ideally suited to enshrine and perpetuate its remains. In archaeology, cultural productivity and its testimonies do not necessarily coincide. Arid zones that might have the required physical properties must also have had proximity to and connections with literate societies of the past to qualify as potential sources of buried texts. Egypt and Chinese Turkestan, each in its own way, fulfilled these conditions admirably.

In desolate Chinese Turkestan, Stein had been faced with a region not only much different but considerably larger than the Nile Valley of Egypt or Mesopotamia. The terrain was of such vastness that meaningful investigation, of necessity, required a coverage commensurate with it. Since Stein was the first scientific explorer to arrive on the scene, he had to compress in his person and within a few years the efforts carried out in Egypt by several generations of travelers and excavators. Stein rose to this challenge, becoming the Alexander of Asiatic archaeology in the swiftness of his campaigns, the extent of the ground covered, and the brilliance of his triumphs. Yet, when Stein emerged in March

---

[5] David Diringer: *The Hand-produced Book* (London: Hutchinson & Co.; 1953), pp. 401–2.

[6] Stein: *Ruins of Desert Cathay*, Vol. II, p. 105.

1907 from the Lop, with his successes at the Niya site, at Miran, and at the limes behind him, he could hardly have anticipated that the deserts of Inner Asia were to bestow upon him still another find which would excel all his former discoveries.

·XXII·

AT THE
THOUSAND BUDDHAS

Infinite riches in a little room.
CHRISTOPHER MARLOWE

AMONG ALL THE OASIS TOWNS strung across the deserts of Inner Asia, Tun Huang ("Blazing Beacon") or Sha Chou ("The City of the Sands") is easily the most important. Since the age of the Hans, some two thousand years ago, it has been the center for China's incoming and outgoing land traffic with the West. Another route crosses it from north to south, joining India via Lhasa in Tibet to Mongolia and southern Siberia. Tun Huang lies in Kansu Province in China proper, though its geographical and climatological affinities are clearly with Turkestan. The town and its surroundings were one of Stein's goals on his second expedition.

A Hungarian geologist friend of Stein's, Professor L. de Lóczy, had been there on a geographical expedition as early as 1879. He was captivated by the little-known Buddhist grottoes, some twelve miles southeast of Tun Huang, named the "Caves of the Thousand Buddhas," or Ch'ien Fo Tung. It was he who turned Stein's attention to this extraordinary shrine, whose large paintings had suggested to him a connection with the art of India. The professor's enthusiastic description and the possibility of encountering major pieces of Indian-inspired mural art and stucco sculpture had motivated Stein to plan his expedition to penetrate so far across Turkestan and into China.

Sketch of an Indian pagoda after a
mural at Buddhist caves near Tun
Huang in western China

Before he continued his exploration at the newly discovered
limes and excavated at a number of locations along the wall,
Stein made his way to Tun Huang. From there he paid a quick
visit to the fantastic site and skirted the vicinity of the cave
temples. His first impression exceeded in excitement all hearsay
descriptions. Along a broad, barren valley there stretched a steep
conglomerate escarpment. For a length of about half a mile it
was honeycombed by dark openings which glared at the traveler
like a multitude of gaping mouths. Some of the cavities were
close to the top of the cliff. It was difficult to visualize how they
could have been entered from the ground. Those Stein noticed first
were on the whole quite small. The man-made caverns suggested
to him "troglodyte dwellings of anchorites retired to a distant
Thebais."[1] But none seemed inhabited. Was the whole area deserted?

Conceivably, the enormous hive had been started by an early
Buddhist pilgrim who was later joined by other pious men or
monks. Eventually, the holy men made the grottoes the abodes of
divine images and themselves dwelled outside, as did perhaps
some of the brethren connected with the Judean caves. A monastic community (or communities) developed, dedicated above all
to building temples in the rock and decorating them lavishly
with fresco (actually, tempera) paintings and statuary. Though
rock-carved shrines were a feature of Buddhism in northwestern
India and in the Afghan and Iranian borderlands, they proliferated nowhere as luxuriantly as in the western Chinese marches.
Stein later came across similar, beautifully painted rock shrines at
the so-called "Valley of the Myriad Buddhas" and elsewhere. But

[1] Stein: *On Ancient Central-Asian Tracks*, p. 194.

none could compare with the grottoes of the Thousand Buddhas in sheer quantity and physical dimensions.

When Stein traveled farther along the escarpment, he saw that the man-made caves became ever more numerous, and varied considerably in size. There was no regular arrangement. Several were large enough to contain gigantic stucco statues of Buddha, usually surrounded by groups of Bodhisattvas. The number of caves, some five hundred altogether, was astonishing, and all showed traces of wall paintings. There had apparently been porches outside which in most instances had broken away, baring the murals inside.

Closer examination revealed how the exquisite cave art had fallen on bad days. The weathering and collapse of the soft carved rock was only one of the causes of decay. Most devastating, and also more painful to Stein, were obvious signs of the wanton passion of iconoclasts, spread into Central Asia by the rising tide of Islam. Worse things were to happen after Stein's time, however, when White Russian soldiers who had fled from the Bolsheviks took refuge in the grottoes, smeared obscenities on the murals, and blackened them with smoke from their fires.

A secular theme from a Tun Huang cave mural. This farm scene was painted during the early Sung period, around A.D. 1000.

A surprising number of walls remained in excellent condition, owing, as Stein observed, to the complete dryness of the caves as well as to "the strength and tenacity with which the plaster bearing the frescoes clings to the conglomerate surface."[2] Like other objects that Stein excavated in Turkestan, these

---

[2] Ibid., p. 195.

Buddhist paintings revealed Indian and Gandharan inspiration in subject matter and in the human features and poses. "No local taste had presumed to transform the dignified serenity of the features, the simple yet impressive gestures, the graceful richness of folds with which classical art, as transplanted to the Indus, had endowed the bodily presence of Tathagata and his many epiphanies."[3] Yet the Chinese influence had wrought a thorough and miraculous transformation. The unmistakable style of China is evident in the intense coloring, the delicate texture, and the vivid detail. Landscapes, floral designs, cloud formations, and the free movement and realism of some of the human figures owed little to outside influence. The finest of the frescoes were probably painted during the regime of the Wei in the fifth century and in the great age of the Tangs when Buddhism flourished. It was then that Tun Huang enjoyed imperial protection.

Stein rushed in amazement from grotto to grotto, followed by his Chinese secretary. Then a young local priest appeared and stayed with the visitors as their guide. So the caves were not entirely deserted! In Tun Huang, Stein had heard of a Taoist monk who, despite his different faith, had come to Ch'ien Fo Tung several years earlier and had decided to dedicate his life to the care and restoration of this noble monument. It came to Stein as a surprise that these caves were still the object of religious observances, despite their visible decline and partial destruction. As an archaeologist, he could not help feeling disappointed that the site was not completely abandoned and left to his impious spade. Would he be able to overcome the apprehensions of the small resident priesthood? Could they, in the usual manner, be propitiated by material "offerings" to let him investigate and "to close their eyes to the removal of any sacred objects?"[4] A still greater obstacle might be the lay people of the area, who took a superstitious pride in the cave temples as a place of pilgrimage. One had to wait and see.

Actually, the valley was soon to receive its annual flood of Tun Huang people. Noisy throngs of tens of thousands would infiltrate into the cliffs and stage a colorful kind of religious fiesta. This occasion was more appropriate "for studying modern humanity than for searching out things of the past."[5] Stein, then, limited

[3] Stein: *Ruins of Desert Cathay*, Vol. II, p. 25.
[4] Ibid., p. 30.
[5] Ibid., p. 159.

his first visit to one day. But before he left, he tried to verify a rumor that had reached him at Tun Huang by way of a Mohammedan trader who was fleeing from his creditors in Turkestan and who "like the versatile person he was . . . had kept an eye open everywhere for possible treasures."[6] The story went that a few years earlier a great hidden deposit of manuscripts had been accidentally discovered in one of the grottoes when the Taoist monk undertook to clear a cave temple that had been blocked by fallen rock and drifted sand. Workmen noticed a crack in a frescoed wall. Their curiosity aroused, they examined the wall, which turned out to be made of bricks rather than of natural rock. By widening the crack, they found a small rock chamber filled with manuscripts. According to rumor, all the rolls were supposedly written in Chinese characters but, somewhat implausibly considering the ideogrammatic nature of the Chinese script, in a non-Chinese language. The Taoist priest was said to be keeping the whole treasure trove under lock and key upon official orders of the viceroy of the province, who, the Moslem tradesman related, had been let into the secret.

First, the existence of the manuscripts had to be confirmed. Then, if they did indeed exist, an attempt had to be made to gain access to them, and—the chances seemed indeed remote—to obtain permission for the removal of at least a few of the documents. The enterprise was indeed vague, and quite unlikely to succeeed. Moreover, the Taoist priest was absent on one of his frequent begging tours on behalf of the projected renovation of the shrine. Stein now intimated to his Chinese secretary that he should speak to the young monk who was acting as their guide, while Stein went on a promenade to inspect cave inscriptions. The secretary soon got the salient facts and established the exact location of the deposit. As luck would have it, Stein also had tangible evidence of the nature of the manuscripts from the young monk's spiritual adviser, a Tibetan, who had been given one of the manuscripts on loan as a sort of ornamental relic for his small private chapel. This was a beautifully written roll of paper, which Stein and his secretary were permitted to unfold. However, the antiquity of the text and script made it impossible to read it in so short a time; it appeared to be quite an old Buddhist document in Chinese. The excellent preservation of the ancient roll testified to the dryness of the well-sheltered rocky

---

[6] Ibid., p. 19.

recess. Further speculation, Stein concluded, had to be deferred until the great but hypothetical day when the whole of the hidden library would be open to him.

Several weeks later, he returned from his profitable excavation at the limes to the somber valley of the caves for an extended stay. No longer was it only the frescoes and statues which drew

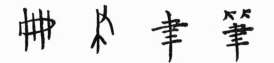

Chinese symbols for "writing." The first two are pictograms from ancient oracle bones and depict wooden slips strung together and a hand holding a brush. The third and fourth glyphs give the modern equivalents.

him to the grottoes. He did not doubt that the caves harbored a hidden collection of ancient manuscripts. The thought had kept his "heart buoyant for months, and was now drawing . . . [him] back with the strength of a hidden magnet."[7] Stein realized that everything depended on tact, prudence, and studied patience. So the morning after his arrival he made quite clear that his main purpose was to survey the dimensions and locations of the grottoes and to photograph the finest of the murals and statues. When the Taoist custodian came to pay his respects, Stein purposely kept the interview short. But he took a good look at the man who stood between him and what may well have been a top prize in Asiatic archaeology. The impression was anything but favorable. It confirmed information gathered independently by Stein's secretary. "He looked a very queer person, extremely shy and nervous, with an occasional expression of cunning which was far from encouraging. It was clear from the first that he would be a difficult person to handle."[8]

Later in the day, as he was taking photographs near the shrine where the manuscripts had been discovered, Stein glanced furtively at the blocked passage to the recess. He was shocked to see that it was no longer barricaded by a wooden door, as on his first visit, but had been sealed by a layer of brickwork. His heart sank and he mentally prepared himself "for a long and arduous siege."[9]

The changed situation called for a new approach. He was

---

[7] Ibid., p. 164.   [8] Ibid., p. 165.   [9] Ibid., p. 165.

still determined to gain permission to see all the manuscripts in their actual place of deposit. Only thus could the nature and approximate date of deposit be ascertained. The next morning Stein sent Chiang, his secretary, on a scouting operation. Chiang, being Chinese, might more easily befriend the Taoist monk. The maneuver proved moderately successful: it was a relief to learn that the library was walled up as a temporary precaution against the thousands of pilgrims who had come on their annual visit to the caves. Chiang then asked to see the manuscript collection, but the priest would not make any promises. However, when Chiang held out the likelihood of a "liberal donation" to the shrine, he noticed that the priest seemed more receptive. Still, he would permit Stein to examine just a few of the specimens from the library, and then only those he might select. The secretary, encouraged by the partial success of his mission, overstepped his instructions and the boundaries of diplomatic reticence by alluding to Stein's wish to purchase some manuscripts. To this the Taoist reacted with "perturbation, prompted equally, it seemed, by scruples of a religious sort and fear of popular resentment."[1] And the secretary quickly dropped the issue.

In Stein's opinion, his incurably optimistic secretary overestimated the results of this talk. The priest's temperament would undoubtedly continue to present all kinds of problems. Money alone would not overcome his fear and obstinacy. At this point Stein decided to press his case personally and sought out the Taoist in the company of his secretary, who would interpret. With diplomatic finesse he asked Wang Tao-shih to show him over the restored cave temple, knowing well that the site was the pride of the priest's life. As anticipated, the request met with a ready response. Of the guided tour Stein later wrote: "As he took me through the lofty antechapel with its substantial woodwork, all new and lavishly gilted and painted, and through the high passage or porch giving access and light to the main cella, I could not help glancing to the right where an ugly patch of unplastered brickwork then still masked the door of the hidden chapel. This was not the time to ask questions of my pious guide as to what was being guarded in that mysterious recess, but rather to display my interest in what his zeal had accomplished in the clearing of the cella and its sacred adornment."[2]

It was obvious to Stein that the restoration was far too thor-

---

[1] Ibid., p. 166.   [2] Ibid., p. 167.

ough. But he wisely kept this reaction to himself. Some of the new images were hideous and showed only too plainly to how dismal a level art had sunk in this part of China since the Tangs. Yet Stein could not help feeling something akin to respect for the queer little figure by his side, "whose devotion to this shrine and to the task of religious merit which he had set himself in restoring it, was unmistakably genuine. As a poor shiftless mendicant he had come from his native province of Shan-hsi some eight years before . . . settled down at the ruined temple caves, and then set about restoring this one to what he conceived to have been its original glory. . . . It was clear from the way in which he lived with his two humble acolytes, and from all that Chiang had heard about him at Tun-huang, that he spent next to nothing on his person or private interests."[3]

A mutual regard developed between the archaeologist and the priest. But how was Stein to communicate to this unlearned man his need to study the ancient texts? Stein had easily obtained the support of Chinese officials, whose high level of education enabled them to appreciate archaeological and antiquarian research. Then Stein had an inspiration. Often before he had conjured up the image of Hsüan Tsang, his "patron saint," whose popularity among both the literati and the common people rarely failed to gain him a friendly ear. Even Wang would be familiar with the great Chinese traveler-monk. So Stein told the Taoist of his admiration for the Chinese saint, whose steps he had traced all the way across the backbone of the continent to his native land. To mention Hsüan's revered name was almost like summoning a jinni. Stein quickly became aware of the "gleam of lively interest . . . in Tao-shih's eyes, otherwise so shy and fitful." Opportunely, the secretary filled in the gaps in Stein's colloquial Chinese and answered some of the priest's questions about the saint's travels. Stein then realized that Wang Tao-shih, "though poorly versed in and indifferent to things Buddhist, was quite as ardent an admirer in his own way of . . . the great monk of the Tang period" as Stein was.[4] The Hsüan Tsang of Chinese folklore whom Wang adored was not quite Stein's historical scholar; indeed, his alleged exploits bore some resemblance to the supernatural adventures of Baron Munchausen. But this mattered little. A common bond had been established.

Stein was given tangible proof of the priest's great regard

---

[3] Ibid., p. 168. [4] Ibid., p. 169.

for Hsüan in a series of pictures of the life of Hsüan Tsang which the Taoist had commissioned and which he now showed his visitor. It was then Stein's turn to listen. One of the recently painted frescoes depicted a scene of particular interest to Stein, because it showed an odd parallel to his own aspirations. It pictured the saint's difficulties in transporting across a turbulent river the twenty pony-loads of sacred books he was said to have brought from India. "But would the pious guardian read this obvious lesson aright," Stein thought to himself, "and be willing to acquire spiritual merit by letting me take back to the old home of Buddhism some of the ancient manuscripts which chance had placed in his keeping?"[5] Stein decided that for the time being the wisest course would be not to put this question directly. He left Chiang behind to press the issue, should Hsüan's magic continue to work.

Apparently the priest was not yet ready to make a loan of the manuscripts, however. "Later, later," he promised Chiang. Yet, late the same night, Stein heard a rustling in his tent. It was Chiang, loaded with a bundle of rolls which the Taoist priest had just taken to him secretly, tucked under his priestly gown. Stein saw immediately that the rolls were ancient versions of Buddhist canonical texts. Chiang spent the night poring over them and early next morning announced triumphantly that these Chinese translations of Buddhist sutras bore notes stating that they had been taken to China and translated by Hsüan Tsang himself. Stein would now be able to suggest to Wang that Hsüan wished to have the results of his labors, buried for many centuries in a rock cavern in China's farthest West, brought to the notice of the learned world. Had not Hsüan revealed the hiding place of the precious manuscripts to Wang so that he could play a part in aiding the master's latter-day disciple from distant India? Chiang hurried to bring the monk the exciting news.

"The effect," Stein wrote, "was most striking. . . . Some hours later . . . [Chiang] found the wall blocking the entrance to the recess of the temple removed, and on its door being opened by the priest, caught a glimpse of a room crammed full to the roof with manuscript bundles. I had purposely kept away from the Tao-shih's temple all the forenoon, but on getting this news I could no longer restrain my impatience to see the great hoard

---

[5] Ibid., p. 170.

myself. . . . I found the priest there evidently still combating his scruples and nervous apprehensions. But under the influence of that quasi-divine hint he now summoned up courage to open before me the rough door closing the narrow entrance which led from the side of the broad front passage into the rock-carved recess, on a level of about four feet above the floor of the former. The sight the small room disclosed was one to make my eyes open. Heaped up in layers, but without any order, there appeared in the dim light of the priest's little lamp a solid mass of manuscript bundles rising to a height of nearly ten feet, and filling, as subsequent measurement showed, close on 500 cubic feet. The area left clear within the room was just sufficient for two people to stand in. . . . All the manuscripts seemed to be preserved exactly in the same condition they were in when deposited. Some of the bundles were carelessly fastened with only rough cords and without an outer cloth wrapper; but even this had failed to injure the paper. Nowhere could I trace the slightest effect of moisture. And, in fact, what better place for preserving such relics could be imagined than a chamber carved in the live rock of these terribly barren hills, and hermetically shut off from what moisture, if any, the atmosphere of this desert valley ever contained? Not in the driest soil could relics of a ruined site have so completely escaped injury as they had here in a carefully selected rock chamber where, hidden behind a brick wall and protected by accumulated drift sand, these masses of manuscripts had lain undisturbed for centuries."[6]

Obviously, no work could be done inside the "black hole," but Wang was still wary of having anybody at Tun Huang know that he had granted Stein access to a hidden library, lest he lose support among his patrons for the holy work of restoration and maintenance. Stein had to agree to have the priest carry out of the chamber a bundle or two at a time for inspection. While the priest extricated manuscripts, Stein and Chiang began their work in a recently built porch nearby, where they would not be noticed by outsiders. But first Stein briefly examined the rock chamber, and the remains of frescoes that had formerly covered its entrance. There were indications from these paintings that the deposit could not have been sealed later than the eleventh century, in itself a guarantee of the importance of the hoard of manuscripts. But

---

[6] Ibid., pp. 174–6.

only the documents themselves could yield more precise information about when they were written and when they must have been deposited.

To Stein it was the least surprise that the desert had preserved the manuscripts so well. However, they showed signs of much use, and the scripts, arrangement, materials, and other features were a clear indication of considerable age. Eventually, the colophons of a number of works yielded exact dates: some of the Chinese texts went back to the early fifth century A.D. Virtually all were written on paper, and thick paper rolls, on the average about a foot in height and of considerable yardage, were prevalent. Many were rolled on a wooden stick, in the manner of some papyri.

Tomb tile of a Chinese scribe. He is holding in his arms a bundle of writing slips, the traditional form of ancient Chinese "books." Han Dynasty

Stein was handicapped by his limited knowledge of Chinese. He had to rely on his Chinese secretary, who unfortunately was not too familiar with Buddhist literature. The more reason, Stein decided, for the manuscripts to be carried away for systematic study by international scholars. In the meantime, Wang was heaping more and more bundles on him. Stein was particularly elated over an ancient Chinese roll which carried a Buddhist text in the Brahmi script of India on its reverse side. Since it closely resembled documents he had come across in the Khotan region, it could serve as proof that the Ch'ien Fo Tung Buddhist establishment had been connected with India via the Tarim basin. It also demonstrated that the bulk of the manuscripts probably dated from a period "when Indian writing and some knowledge of Sanskrit still prevailed in Central-Asian Buddhism."[7]

Along with the Chinese material, there were a number of Tibetan manuscripts: long rolls written in horizontal lines, forming part of the extensive Buddhist canon of Tibet. These rolls were undoubtedly left from the Tibetan occupation of the area in the ninth century. No Tibetan manuscripts of such length and state of preservation had turned up in Stein's previous explorations. In the first bundle examined by Stein and his assistant, there were also texts in languages other than Chinese and Tibetan. One of the many surprises was a large package found to contain delicate paintings on linen and silk gauze: banners and ex-votos (votive offerings) illustrating scenes from Buddhist legend. This material in itself constitutes one of the finest treasures of ancient Serindian (Sino-Indian) art.

Curiously, it was with remains of this kind that the priest hoped to divert Stein from the Chinese canonical texts which he considered the only things of value. Stein was quite pleased with the arrangement: the most unusual articles came from the disorderly piles that Wang heaped before him. There were rolls in the still undeciphered, presumably indigenous languages of Turkestan, written in Indian characters. Stein concealed his enthusiasm as he put the precious items away for further inspection. Everything depended on keeping up the good humor of the priest, who betrayed signs of flagging dedication. From time to time Chiang had to administer doses of genial persuasion, while Stein would once again invoke Hsüan.

Night fell and only a small portion of the enormous hoard had been examined. After the day's work, Stein had no choice but to leave behind a large stack of documents and paintings on cloth which he had sequestered in the hope that he would eventually be permitted to take them away. Would Wang ever agree to the removal of the documents? If he could be swayed at all, Stein decided, it would not be with vulgar insinuations of sale or payment. Also, to judge by the priest's fears for his reputation, the

---

[7] Ibid., p. 176.

transaction had to be handled under the strictest secrecy. Though worn out by the labors and excitement of the day, Stein reopened the subject of "our common hero and patron saint, the great Hsüan Tsang." This time he made it a point to discuss at length the mural of Hsüan's return from India with his book-laden animals. Its prophetic suggestion was unmistakable, and the painting was the most effective advocate for his own efforts to rescue the relics. Certainly "the priest in his more susceptible moods could not help acknowledging that this fate of continued confinement in a dark hole was not the purpose for which the great scholar-saint had let him light upon these precious remains of Buddhist lore, and that he himself was quite incompetent to do justice to them by study or otherwise."[8] Chiang added "all the force of his soft reasoning," pointing out that it would be an act of genuine religious merit if the priest were to make the fruits of what was surely a divinely guided discovery available to the wise men of the West. He hinted subtly that if the priest listened to the heavenly voices he would be compensated handsomely, to the benefit of the shrine.

Stein must have felt as if he were wrestling with an angel, so elusive was the Taoist at times. One could never be sure whether he had been won over or whether fear and doubts had got the better of him and he was wavering once more. In the end, Stein appeared to have won. The priest asked him to leave Chiang with him to work out details of the surrender of the articles singled out, in diplomatic understatement, "for closer examination." The priest's condition was that no one know of the transaction until the materials had been removed from Chinese soil. Hence the goods had to be carried in darkness from the temple to Stein's tent. Chiang graciously assumed the task, and for seven nights he made his way, at the witching hour, to the tent, "his slight figure panting under loads which grew each time heavier, and ultimately required carriage by instalments."[9]

This is not to say that it was smooth sailing from then on. The Taoist had recurrent fits of doubt and "timorous contrariness." Time after time he had to be propitiated with silver ingots. Occasionally he would reproach himself for betraying the trust of his lay patrons of Tun Huang. At one time he locked away the material sorted out by Stein, and then disappeared for several days. He had to reassure himself that the secret had not leaked

---

[8] Ibid., p. 180.   [9] Ibid., p. 181.

out. Fortunately, his spiritual reputation was untarnished. After his return he was more cooperative and even allowed an additional twelve bundles to be taken out. In the end, Stein had to obtain help from two of his trustworthy servants to remove to his tent what still remained to be packed.

When four months later Stein returned to the shrine from further explorations into China, he was well received by Wang, who agreed to part with some two hundred more bundles of Chinese and Tibetan manuscripts. The good Taoist was at last at ease, and when Stein took leave of the Thousand Buddhas, the priest's "jovial sharp-cut face had resumed once more its look of shy but self-contained serenity."[1] But for Stein full peace of mind came only when twenty-four cases of manuscripts and five filled with paintings and art treasures had arrived at their destination, the British Museum in London, sixteen months later.

Afterwards, scholars safely ensconced in European museums or immersed in their studies criticized Stein's selection of documents, holding that he had acquired too many copies of the same Buddhist sutras in Chinese and had allegedly overlooked some canonical and noncanonical works. This disparagement ignores completely the difficulties under which Stein worked and which dictated fast, haphazard, and improvised action. Again and again Stein refers to the great haste with which he had to examine an avalanche of manuscripts, while constantly in fear that the Taoist monk would change his mind. In most instances there was no opportunity to make a closer examination on the spot.[2] And he freely and overmodestly admitted his lack of Sinological training. Yet these gaps in learning could not have made much difference under the circumstances. They were amply compensated for by Stein's extraordinary linguistic and epigraphic grasp of the variegated polyglot material. His detailed knowledge of the Indian background of Buddhism and its spread from the Indian borderlands through Irano-Scythian channels across Inner Asia was unsurpassed. He was also familiar with the beginnings of Chinese Buddhism because of his study of the Chinese Annals and the memoirs of Hsüan Tsang.

Stein's selection could hardly be expected to be systematic and scientific. All along, he hoped eventually to persuade the Taoist monk to part with the entire collection so that it could be reassembled and studied at a temple of learning in Ta-Ying-kuo

---

[1] Ibid., p. 194.   [2] Ibid., p. 188.

(England). As it was, his was one of the most extensive single recoveries on record. Leonard Woolley, who once assisted at the British Museum in cataloguing the Stein collection, has justly called it "an unparalleled archaeological 'scoop.'"[3]

The fate of the remaining manuscripts is quickly told. Like Stein's excavations in Turkestan, his 'scoop' at the Thousand Buddhas brought other scholars to the scene who benefited from his spadework and hence could proceed with greater foresight and at a less hurried pace. A year after he left Tun Huang, an eminent French Sinologist and a friend of Stein's, Paul Pelliot, reached the Caves of the Thousand Buddhas. With his specialist's eye, he examined the bulk of the Chinese materials Stein had had to leave behind. Wang, having no reason to regret the deal with Stein, was easily persuaded to allow the acquisition of 15,000 more scrolls and fragments. These, together with the Stein collection in England, constitute the main surviving body of the once buried library.

However, when Pelliot departed, the rocky niche had by no means given up all its treasures. During Pelliot's stay at Peking in 1909, Chinese authorities seem to have gotten wind of the important source of manuscripts. They ordered the transfer of what was left of the library to the capital city—an ill-fated move, transacted in what Stein called *more Sinico*. A considerable sum of money set aside to compensate the shrine never reached its destination: presumably it disappeared in the quicksand of officials' pockets. Orders were carried out that the collection be duly packed for shipment to Peking, but comparatively little ever reached there. Years later, Stein was to come across precious Tang bundles, of undoubted cave origin, offered for sale at Tun Huang, in Turkestan, and all along the way to Kan Chow.

In 1914, on his third expedition to Central Asia, Sir Aurel revisited the Caves of the Thousand Buddhas and was received by Wang as a trusted old friend and benefactor. From the priest, Stein learned of the sad fate of the library. Wang bitterly reproached himself for not having accepted Chiang's suggestion to let the whole collection go to England. But he had been astute enough, in the face of the pilfering ordered by Peking, to put away some six hundred Buddhist manuscripts. For a commensurate contribution, Stein was permitted to take them away, packed into

---

[3] Woolley: *History Unearthed*, p. 127.

five cases. They made valuable additions to his collection. Thus, Stein says in a later summary of his explorations, "ended on my part the 'Prieste's Tale' from the Caves of the Thousand Buddhas."[4] In fact, however, there was at least one epilogue when thirty years later, in the 1940's, an additional hideaway—probably another of Wang's caches—was discovered in the cave shrine.

Stein's rescue operation, and the accompanying diplomatic wrangles, left little time to undertake any full-scale investigation of his prize. Such research demanded the leisure of the study and had to wait. Nevertheless, Stein possessed the instincts of a gifted archaeologist for the unique and valuable. In many instances he anticipated the results later arrived at by specialists.

Merely by selecting and superficially examining these documents, he discerned further evidence that Buddhism had linked the ancient civilizations of East, West, and South across the desert corridor of Asia.[5] Like the limes and the sand-buried ruins of the Tarim basin, the walled-up temple library, with its manuscripts and artworks, recorded a great cultural melting pot—only here the Chinese ingredient was much stronger. Several important details connected with the grottoes of the Thousand Buddhas and with the general area came to light immediately. But it took Stein, whose extraordinary capacity for sustained hard work was extolled by all, almost fifteen years to publish the scientific report of his second expedition. It consisted of five magnificent volumes: *Serindia*. And even this formidable opus was in a sense only preliminary.

The archaeological finds from this expedition filled close to a hundred large cases, a substantial portion of them manuscripts. Material from the cave library alone made up twenty-nine boxes, including about nine thousand books and inscribed fragments. The decipherment, analysis, and interpretation of this textual material was a titanic job calling for the specialized knowledge, skill, and endurance of many scholars over many years. Several learned men were to spend a lifetime in the study of just a small fraction of the documents, as for instance the Abbé Boyer, who published the wooden Kharoshthi records in a number of large tomes. The complete catalogue of the Chinese manuscripts of the

---

[4] Stein: *On Ancient Central-Asian Tracks*, p. 211.
[5] Stein: *Ruins of Desert Cathay*, Vol. II, p. 211.

Stein collection at the British Museum was issued in 1957 under the direction of Lionel Giles, who said that much of his labor of decades consisted in going through some ten to twenty miles of closely written Chinese rolls.[6]

Leading Orientalists from a score of countries were enlisted. The roster of names includes some of the greatest Oriental linguists, philologists, historians, and scholars of Asiatic art and religion from the early twentieth century. And the work is still being carried on today. Like the Cairo Geniza, the Buddhist library, though seemingly devoted to the literature of one religion, touches on many subjects and covers several previously obscure centuries. To an even greater degree than the Geniza, it mirrors the cross-roads of a civilized world—and in a far less known area.

The cross-cultural interchange between so many lands and peoples was focused at the Buddhist temple deposit in a score of different languages—known, partly known, or entirely unknown. The cave manuscripts complemented the records Stein had found in desert ruins. In addition to the Chinese texts, there were docu-

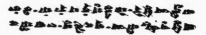

Excerpt from a Kuchean *pothi* manuscript. The writing is based on Brahmi Gupta characters of India, and the language is a native Indo-European idiom (long extinct) of Turkestan.

ments (among the oldest that have survived) in the languages of India, such as Sanskrit and the more colloquial Prakrit (Prakhtri), and in Tibetan, Iranian, Sogdian, Uigur, "Runic" Turk, the indigenous Indo-European idioms of Eastern Turkestan (Khotan, Kuchean), unknown Tibeto-Burmese languages, and a host more. The library even included selections in Hebrew from the Old Testament.

In many instances, the manuscripts not only furnished lost texts or important "new" versions of surviving works, but by their very existence threw light on the spread of cultural influences and their mode and intensity of transmission. Thus, to give just one example, the Sogdian literature revealed that Iranian influence had traveled much farther into China proper than even Stein had sus-

---

[6] Lionel Giles: *Six Centuries at Tunhuang.* . . . (London: The China Society; 1944), p. 6.

pected. Secular documents, particularly those in Chinese, bore on geography, topography (even that of the Caves of the Thousand Buddhas themselves), administration, historiography, and poetry.

Sample of Sogdian writing. The script was widely disseminated over Central Asia and even into Mongolia. It was used by an Iranian people, who had adapted it from the Aramaic alphabet. The oldest examples of the script were found by Stein on letters from the watchtowers of the Chinese "limes."

Though the great mass of manuscripts was Buddhist—and it was essentially a cosmopolitan Buddhist civilization which had been so brightly illuminated—other religious faiths were also represented. This was in a sense a testimony to the relative tolerance and religious latitude of the Chinese, which made it possible even in the twentieth century for a humble Taoist priest to champion the restoration of a Buddhist shrine. But, more important, it demonstrated that Buddhism was only the strongest of many religious movements crossing Central Asia into China. Most prominent among the secondary spiritual forces was undoubtedly Manichaeanism, which penetrated deep into the Middle Kingdom and Mongolia. The finds from the cave temple amplified those made by Russian and German teams at Turfan in northeastern Sinkiang, and included a Manichaean version of the *Shepherd of Hermas,* which Tischendorf had recovered from the Codex Sinaiticus. They helped to restore some of the virtually lost sacred literature of that strange hybrid Persian faith which originated in Babylon, and whose adherents at one time spread across the Roman Empire— St. Augustine in his youth had been a Manichaean—and which left its traces in medieval heresies.

Some scholars cherish most the many versions of canonical and noncanonical Buddhist texts, which constitute in several instances by far the oldest copies of such scriptures, and are comparable in importance to the ancient Bible codices, and the Qumran scrolls of the Old Testament, for the critical restoration of archetypal texts. In addition, the sacred rolls in Chinese, Tibetan, and Sanskrit have aided in reconstructing the different types of Buddhist canons, knowledge of which had been lost. Thus, a Japanese scholar, the Reverend K. Yabuki, has been able to identify hitherto missing texts of the Buddhist canon of China. Research of a similar kind among Stein's manuscripts contributed to the recovery of the Taoist canon.

The prodigious wealth of religious manuscripts made it possible to undertake a quasi-statistical study of the frequency of certain Buddhist sutras according to the dates when they were copied. In this manner, one could gauge their popularity at one time or another. One of the remarkable features of the collection is the dating of so many items, which range from A.D. 406 (January 10, between seven and nine o'clock) to 997. Internal evidence makes it likely that the deposit was sealed around 1035, perhaps due to the imminent invasion of the barbarian Hsia Hsia. Then, like the Qumran cache, whose abandonment was conceivably occasioned by similar motives, the cave library was forgotten for nine centuries.

The enumeration of the lost or unknown works which came to light would make a long list indeed. In addition to the Chinese and Turkish Manichaean texts and Buddhist scriptures, we should mention the Uigur (the idiom of a once powerful Turk people) translation of a Buddhist metaphysical classic, a collection of stories written in "Runic" Turkish, several apocryphal sutras, and, above all, Chinese historical, lexicographic, biographical, and geographic works. The Chinese manuscripts include such other varied texts as an early fifth-century census, a topographic description of the Tun Huang region with its holy caves, and romances. Giles has described as "perhaps the most romantic discovery among the Tunhuang manuscripts"[7] a poem of 238 lines, entitled *The Lament of the Lady Ch'in*. A celebrated Tang author and statesman was reputed to have composed in his youth a ballad by that name which had caused some displeasure in high quarters and had been suppressed. Here it was, rediscovered a thousand years later. It appears to be a work of considerable merit, portraying with a Goyaesque touch the never outdated miseries of war when a rebel army takes a city, sets fire to it, and converts the residents into pitiful refugees. The siege and storming of the city is told to the poet by the Lady Ch'in:

Supporting the infirm and leading the children by the hand,
  fugitives are calling to one another in the turmoil:
Some clamber on to roofs, others scale walls, and all is in
  disorder. . . .

---

[7] Ibid., p. 21.

Our northern neighbour's womenfolk, trooping all together,
Dash wildly about it in the open like stampeding cattle.
Heaven and earth shake with the rumbling of chariot wheels,
And the thunder of ten thousand horses' hoofs re-echoes
 from the ground.
Fires burst out, sending golden sparks high up into the firma-
 ment,
And the twelve official thoroughfares are soon seething with
 smoke and flame.[8]

Several works are reminiscent of Near Eastern didactic literature, particularly a book entitled *Teachings of a Father*. Among the most curious items are collections of model letters. One, from the year 856, is divided into such useful categories as "Laymen's letters to Buddhist and Taoist monks" or "Private letters to relatives on the father's or mother's side." There is also "A letter of apology for a breach of decorum after getting drunk":

> Yesterday, having drunk too much, I was so intoxicated as to pass all bounds; but none of the rude and coarse language I used was uttered in a conscious state. The next morning, after hearing others speak on the subject, I realized what had happened, whereupon I was overwhelmed with confusion and ready to sink into the earth for shame. It was due to a vessel of small capacity filled for the nonce too full. I humbly trust that you in your wise benevolence will not condemn me for my transgression. Soon I will come to apologize in person, but meanwhile I beg to send this written communication for your kind inspection. Leaving much unsaid, I am yours respectfully.[9]

How was one to answer such an embarrassing communication? Another collection comes up with an appropriate, though hardly forbearing, sample:

> Yesterday, Sir, while in your cups, you so far overstepped the observances of polite society as to forfeit the name of gentleman, and made me wish to have nothing more to do with you. But since you now express your shame and regret for what has occurred, I would suggest that we meet again for a friendly talk. Respectfully yours.[1]

Easily the most famous of all the documents brought by Stein to England is a text existing in many copies and not even handwritten: a Chinese copy of the Diamond Sutra. Though its contents offer nothing new, it is one of the most treasured books anywhere because it is the first printed book on record, made more

---

[8] Ibid., p. 21.   [9] Ibid., pp. 33–4.   [1] Ibid., p. 34.

than half a millennium before Gutenberg, in the year A.D. 868. Typically of the chronologically minded Chinese, its colophon gives an exact date (May 11), in addition to the name of the man who commissioned and distributed it. (He was not, however, the world's first printer of books as is sometimes said.) The book was dedicated by one Wang Chieh to the memory of his parents.

The printed work is actually a roll sixteen feet long, consisting of six separately block-printed sheets and a fine woodcut, all glued together. No one knows where it was printed, but its excellence leaves little doubt that it was not the first such effort and must have had many predecessors. As in Europe at a later date, printing did not immediately take the place of the more arduous production of manuscripts. There are only twenty-six printed documents in the Stein collection—some curiously reminiscent of the block-printed Christian *Heiligen* and indulgences of late medieval Europe. However, it has been asserted that printing, if not actually invented by Buddhist priests, served as an influential agent of Buddhist propaganda across the Far East—the million-odd charms printed upon the order of the Japanese Empress Shotoku in the eighth century being a case in point. That no earlier Chinese printed specimen has come down may well be due to the wave of anti-Buddhist persecution and civil wars during the decline of the Tang Dynasty in the mid-ninth century. The stages by which printing, as well as paper, China's other bequest to bookmaking, reached Europe have not yet been fully traced. But the oldest block prints of the Mediterranean region have been found in the Fayum of Egypt, the earliest dating from about A.D. 900.[2]

Between Egypt and Inner Asia the road is long, but the affinities and contacts are not as slight as was once thought. Hellenistic influences affected both profoundly. Semitic scripts and Iranian languages were not unknown in either land, and it is not an accident that substantial portions of the lost Manichaean scriptures have been recovered in the sands of Inner Asia and Egypt—so alike in the manner in which they have preserved buried texts. Moreover, the oldest samples of printing in East and West were found in China's far-western desert and along the Nile. Thus printing, invented in the Far East, came to add a new

---

[2] Thomas F. Carter: *The Invention of Printing in China* . . . , second edition revised by L. Carrington Goodrich (New York: Ronald Press; 1955), pp. 176–81.

dimension to the interchange of civilizations. In a way it closes the circle in the long cultural road between East and West across the backbone of Asia.

Chinese ornamental motif. From a bronze brick of the Chou period

B: *The New World*

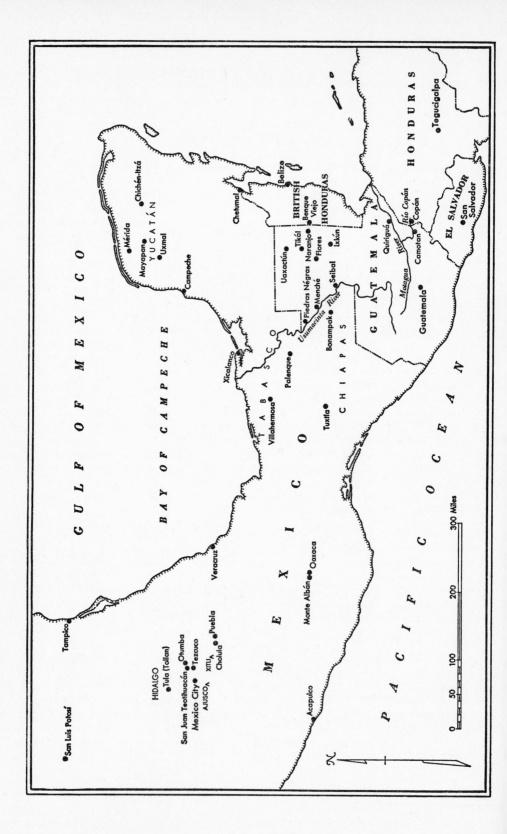

·XXIII·

THE SPELL OF THE MEXICAN PICTURE BOOKS: FROM HUMBOLDT TO KINGSBOROUGH

> *Imagine our great libraries all destroyed by invaders from a different universe and only seventeen books saved—those seventeen books consisting of almanacs, astronomical drawings, a book on black magic, a text on religious festivals and national holidays, an astrological horoscope, a text on the conquests of the First World War and a genealogy of a prominent family! What would the invaders think of our civilization when their historians began to analyse it through the contents of those seventeen documents?*
>
> FREDERICK PETERSON, *Ancient Mexico*[1]

A decorative pattern of ancient Middle America. From an El Tajín (state of Vera Cruz) stone carving

HOW IS IT POSSIBLE to doubt that a part of the Mexican nation had arrived at a certain degree of cultivation, when we reflect on the care with which their hieroglyphical books were com-

---

[1] Frederick Peterson: *Ancient Mexico* (New York: G. P. Putnam's Sons–Capricorn Books; 1962), p. 240.

posed?"[2] At the beginning of the nineteenth century a reference such as this to the cultural advancement of ancient Mexico was unusual. It was made by Alexander von Humboldt, a German baron, whom his age celebrated as the last universal man and who was the author of the first comprehensive work on American antiquities.

When Humboldt in 1799 started on travels that were to take him throughout the Western Hemisphere, knowledge of pre-Columbian civilizations was at a minimum. Among learned Europeans it was then the fashion to debunk any allusion to the relatively high level of culture reached by aboriginal Indian societies. Savants described America in earnest as a continent physically adverse to the increase of animals and men, and once inhabited only by savage hordes.[3] A case in point was William Robertson, the eminent eighteenth-century Scottish historian, who flatly declared that nowhere in New Spain was there "a single monument or vestige of any building more ancient than the Conquest."[4] Was it really true that early man in America had left no traces of his art and ingenuity? Or had the white masters made such a clean sweep that, even if Robertson's assumption was mistaken, there was no proof to the contrary? Strange to say, until Humboldt appeared on the scene, opinions pro and con depended on little but hearsay.

During Humboldt's five years of exploration he found a great deal to demonstrate once and for all the absurdity of what he called the "absolute skepticism" of his contemporaries regarding the achievements of aboriginal America. In both New Spain (Mexico) and Peru he had occasion to visit enormous ruins. The pyramid of Cholula, which he thoroughly surveyed and sketched, exceeded even that of Cheops (Khufu) in volume. What impressed him most, however, was the fact that, at least in Mexico, the skill of writing and keeping records had been known—the very touchstone of civilized life, according to historians of the Enlightenment. The question was whether any inscriptions or books

---

[2] John Taylor, ed.: *Selections from the Works of Baron De Humboldt, Relating to . . . Mexico* (London: Longmans; 1824), p. 63.

[3] Alexander von Humboldt: *Researches Concerning the Institutions and Monuments of the Ancient Inhabitants of America, with Descriptions and Views of Some of the Most Striking Scenes in the Cordilleras* (London: Longmans; 1814), Vol. I, p. 4.

[4] Quoted by Justin Winsor: *Narrative and Critical History of America* (Boston: Houghton Mifflin Co.; 1884), Vol. I. p. 76.

with authentic writing had survived and could be produced. Fortunately Humboldt had various guides to assist him in his search.

First there were the memoirs of the Spanish Conquistadores. These men were by no means oblivious to signs of literacy among the Mexican Indians, though they reacted to them with a characteristic mixture of curiosity, contempt, and destructiveness. As soon as Cortés had disembarked near Vera Cruz, he was presented by emissaries from the Aztec ruler Montezuma with two books, or codices (as they are now customarily labeled), which he dispatched to his sovereign, Charles V, together with other splendid gifts, and a few jugglers whom he had freed from the cages where their captors were fattening them for sacrifice. Peter Martyr (d'Anghiera), the Italian historian of the Ocean Seas, ever alert to the fascination of the New World, had an opportunity at the court of Charles V to revel in the strange scrolls which had been sent to Spain. One of Cortés' agents suggested that they represented some kind of pattern for embroidery or jewelry, but Peter Martyr was certain they were authentic books in an unknown script. The pictorial characters reminded him of hieroglyphs which he had seen when traveling in Egypt, and he expressed genuine appreciation for the neat, skillful execution of the pictures and symbols. He suggested that the books dealt with laws, religious ceremonies and festivals, astronomical observations, and the affairs of ordinary life.[5]

Several early colonial writers were aware that writing in some form or other was known to the Indian peoples of Mexico and Yucatán. But many of the early colonial treatises on the subject were suppressed by the Spanish government and not published for centuries. They suffered a fate not unlike that of the native literature which some of them had tried to preserve. The conquerors themselves came across books, records, and other pictorial documents everywhere. When Cortés asked Montezuma about port facilities along the Gulf of Mexico, he was given a map delineating the whole coast down to the Isthmus or Tehuantepec.

---

[5] *De orbe decades octo,* decade IV, chapter 8, quoted by Daniel G. Brinton: *Essays of an Americanist* (Philadelphia: Porter & Coates; 1890), p. 233.

Later, when he went on the historic march to Honduras, he also made use of a native map.

All the cities through which the Spaniards passed had substantial archives attached to temples and palaces. These did not escape the perceptive Bernal Díaz del Castillo, a member of

Outline of the temple complex in Tenochtitlán (Mexico City). The major shrines are to Huitzilopochtli, Tlaloc, and Xipe. From Codex Florentino

Cortés' original four hundred, who wrote down his personal recollections in his old age. In the Totonac temple of Cempoala near Vera Cruz he saw "many paper books doubled together in folds like cloth of Castile."[6] The reminiscence made him pensive in his charmingly unpretentious, semi-articulate manner: "There

[6] Bernal Díaz del Castillo: *The Discovery and Conquest of Mexico, 1519–21*, translated by A. P. Maudslay (New York: Farrar, Straus and Cudahy), p. 86.

is so much to think over that I do not know how to describe it, seeing things as we did that had never been heard or seen before or even dreamed about." Later, after entering the capital, he was taken to the royal record office, "the steward of which was a great chief to whom we gave the name of Tapia, and he kept the accounts of all the revenue that was brought to Montezuma in his books, which were made of paper, which they call *amatl*, and he had a great house full of these books."[7] It was these archives, together with the temple library, that inadvertently went up in flames just when the last Aztec emperor Cuauhtémoc's resistance against Cortés was about to collapse.

Whatever may be said of the Spaniards' wanton destructiveness, few of their learned men were indifferent to the picture books. The codices' almost tropical riot of luminous colors, their tapestry of intricate shapes, grotesque figures, confusing arrangement, and unusual makeup both attracted and repelled them. To what strange uses were they put? Unfamiliar or half-understood books were liable to frighten the timid and bigoted as they do self-appointed guardians of public morals in the twentieth century. And the stench of heresy was in Spanish nostrils. Not altogether unjustly, they associated Mexican books with magic and pagan rites. Yet men like Father Alonzo Ponce, the Pope's commissioner-general, singled out the natives of Yucatán as especially deserving of praise: "First, that before the Spaniards came they made use of characters and letters, with which they wrote out their histories, their ceremonies, the order of sacrifices to their idols, and their calendars, in books made of bark of a certain tree."[8] Their other virtues were, according to Ponce, freedom from sodomy and from cannibalism.

By an odd twist of fate, it was the possession of books that helped to accelerate the ruin of Aztec political power and civilization. The natives responded to the coming of the pale-faced, hirsute strangers by recalling ancient myths. Their books proclaimed that one day Quetzalcoatl, the benevolent, deified prophet-king of old, would return from the East, where the sun rises. The Quetzalcoatl myth turned Montezuma, the once bold Aztec ruler, into a wavering, unspirited, indecisive leader. Other pronouncements based on the native divinatory and astrological literature no doubt added to Montezuma's loss of heart. Moreover, forebodings

---

[7] Ibid., p. 210.   [8] Quoted by Brinton: op. cit., p. 234.

of the empire's imminent downfall had been culled from sacred texts even before any Spaniard had been sighted.

Barely a generation after the Conquest, all the record offices and temple libraries of the major Mexican cities had vanished. The destruction was almost complete. Even the skill to write the native "script" and the ability to read it were eventually lost. Later a reputedly liberal colonial governor of New Spain sold ancient documents remaining in Mexican archives as "wrapping-paper, to apothecaries, shopkeepers, and rocket-makers."[9] Despite the searches of the past hundred and fifty years, there are left from the warfare, the autos-da-fé, and the neglect of centuries just a few scattered pieces: no more than three codices (and those incomplete) of Maya origin and some fourteen of pre-Columbian lineage from central and southern Mexico, in addition to a few scraps and maps. Only one of these, the Codex Borbonicus of the Chamber of Deputies in Paris, is definitely Aztec, and its antiquity has recently been questioned.[1] Much less was known when Humboldt completed his explorations.

By the eighteenth century, the few Mexican documents preserved in European collections were virtually forgotten. No one took an interest in them, and scarcely a single scroll was recognized for what it was. It was almost too late when their recovery, preservation, and interpretation was at last undertaken by a line of dedicated men—and one woman—for whom the exotic picture books became a passion. Toward the end of the last century, Americanist studies began to interest scientists in North America and Germany. Before that, the field had attracted a fair number of eccentrics and mythmakers. On the whole, these men together constitute a not undistinguished mixture of savants and amateurs whose persistence and ingenuity solved many mysteries. However, the riddle of the Maya script still awaits complete solution.

In the forefront was Alexander von Humboldt, friend of Jefferson and of Bolívar, adopted son of several American republics, a "second Columbus," whose prodigious studies revealed the hemisphere to its own inhabitants as much as to the Old World. He called himself half-American. Bolívar, who was encouraged in his struggle for liberation by Humboldt's liberal ideas,

---

[9] William H. Prescott: *History of the Conquest of Mexico* (New York: Random House–Modern Library; n.d.), p. 60 *n.*

[1] Peterson: op. cit., p. 239.

proclaimed him "the true discoverer of South America. The New World owes more to him than all the conquistadores put together."[2]

Here was a man to match a continent. In his five years of travel (1799–1804) he covered nearly the length and breadth of it. He spent many more years on analyzing and publishing the wealth of material he had gathered. He described ocean currents, one of which was named after him, suggested the exploitation of guano from the Peruvian islands for fertilizer, drew maps, computed the surface area of Mexico, made the first profile of any large land mass when he outlined a cross section of Mexico from the Gulf to the Pacific, established the geographical location of Acapulco, was the first to climb Chimborazo in Ecuador, verified the natural link formed by the Casiquiare between the Amazon (Rio Negro) and the Orinoco, discovered mineral deposits and surveyed them, copied petroglyphs in the Brazilian jungle, collected hundreds of new botanical specimens, formulated revolutionary theories on vulcanism and geological formations, gathered population statistics of colonial Mexico, wrote the first books on political geography (on Cuba and Mexico), learned several native languages from Quechua to Nahuatl, examined minutely all kinds of archives, made sensitive drawings of llamas, mountain peaks, balsa rafts, pyramids . . . and that is not all.

Humboldt was primarily a naturalist and had started out as a mining engineer, but there was little that he did not assimilate and make his own. To the Americas he brought a fresh, undogmatic, inquiring mind, and was an inspiration both to John Lloyd Stephens, the explorer of Mayan ruins, and to William H. Prescott, the historian of Mexico and Peru, who did so much to arouse curiosity in pre-Columbian civilizations. No one before Humboldt had examined America systematically and set its nature and culture into a sound, rational framework. A true cosmopolitan, without the slightest trait of racial bigotry, he had full, and unpatronizing, sympathy for the indigenous people and their accomplishments and aspirations. He never entertained a doubt that the Negro slaves were the equals of their keepers in everything but law.

Fresh from his journey through the wilderness of the Amazon basin, he encountered by chance in the Peruvian backlands a sixteenth-century manuscript written in a native language but in

---

[2] Herbert Scurla: *Alexander von Humboldt. Sein Leben und Wirken* (Berlin: Verlag der Nation; 1955), p. 218.

Latin alphabetic script. It stirred his imagination, and thereupon he resolved to track down Indian antiquities. To his brother, Wilhelm von Humboldt, the celebrated philologist, he confided: "The discovery of this manuscript revived in me the wish to study the early history of the aborigines of these countries, a desire first aroused in me by the traditions I collected at Parime, and by the hieroglyphs [actually, rock drawings] encountered in the jungle of the Casiquiare River."[3]

Plan of early colonial Mexico City, occasionally attributed to Hernando Cortés. It shows Tenochtitlán as in island, with the temple area in the center. The map was first published in 1524 in Nuremberg.

He entered Mexico in March 1803 at Acapulco on the Pacific coast, passing through Taxco and Cuernavaca, and on the way to the capital he inquired about "hieroglyphic paintings," as he called ancient Mexican documents. He was elated when a native

---

[3] Quoted by Helmut de Terra: *Humboldt. The Life and Times of A.v.H. 1769–1859* (New York: Alfred A. Knopf; 1955), p. 134.

showed him a pre-Columbian map. At last, in Mexico City, which was built on the ruins of the Aztec metropolis, Humboldt was able to picture Tenochtitlán, with its sacrificial altars, royal palaces, and temple pyramids, from the few surviving artifacts and from old sketches and records. Only a few years earlier various important archaeological finds had been made near the great square, when workmen dug a subterranean aqueduct. Most notable among these treasures was the celebrated Calendar Stone, which Humboldt examined thoroughly and drew with great precision. It was the beginning of his study of the Mexican calendar. He had also heard of the finding of a formidable, two-headed Aztec idol made of porphyry, which he was eager to sketch. He was told that when it was excavated, the viceroy had had it taken to the University of Mexico, the proper haven for the magnificent works of the country's past, but the professors, who were members of the Dominican order, would not expose such a monster to the sight of impressionable youths. Humboldt enlisted the aid of the bishop of Monterrey, whom he had befriended and who was just passing through the capital. The stratagem was successful and the rector of the university ordered the idol taken out from underneath one of the passageways of the learned institution.

Humboldt was a scientist, and not one to jump at fantastic theories concerning the origins of American civilizations. The men who for another hundred years were to proffer the tired phantoms of Israel, Atlantis, and the rest, might have taken a warning from Humboldt. "Some, allured by splendid hypotheses, built on very unstable foundations," he wrote, "have drawn general consequences from a small number of solitary facts: they have discovered Chinese and Egyptian colonies in America; recognized Celtic dialects and the Phoenician alphabet."[4] On the other hand, he was not timid when after careful examination he arrived at a hypothesis. Indeed, he made the brilliant guess, borne out by excavations at a later date, that the pyramid builders had probably been preceded by a farming people who expressed themselves in modest clay effigies.[5]

He was convinced of the considerable racial homogeneity of all American aborigines except those in the far north, and of their predominantly Mongolian stock, but he did not exclude a possible relationship between Old and New World artifacts and

---

[4] Humboldt: op. cit., Vol. I, p. 10.
[5] Terra: op. cit., p. 169.

styles. Particularly in the Mexican calendar, and in its signs, he believed he recognized definite Chinese and Tibetan affinities too close to be accidental. Striking analogies such as these, whether in myths, systems of chronology, architecture, or artifacts, could not be ignored. "It is the duty of the historian to point out these analogies, which are as difficult to explain as the relations that exist between Sanskrit, the Persian, the Greek, and the languages of German origin; but in attempting to generalize ideas, we should learn to stop at the point where precise data are wanting."[6]

Humboldt had heard of a tradition that the Toltecs in their sacred literature traced their invasion of Mexico from a migration out of Asia. He hoped therefore that the study of Mexican texts would throw light on the origin of the American Indians. But he suspended judgment as long as the evidence remained obscure. In

Aztec migration record. Drawn after a Mexican picture codex

Mexico City he began his search for pre-Conquest manuscripts; he visited private collectors and went to the national archives. Soon he became only too keenly aware of the scarcity of codices in New Spain and registered the sorry fact that "the greater part of the well-informed men who reside there have never seen any."[7] It was then that he heard of a predecessor, the Cavaliere Lorenzo Boturini Benaduci, a Milanese of gentle birth, whom Humboldt and W. H. Prescott both insisted on calling "the unfortunate Boturini." His misfortunes were indeed many.

---

[6] Humboldt: op. cit., p. 11.   [7] Ibid., p. 190.

Boturini had gone to Mexico in 1735 to settle some personal matters for the Countess of Santibáñez, a direct descendant of the Aztec ruler. There Boturini found two loves, Our Lady of Guadalupe (the Madonna who had appeared to a humble Indian peasant in 1531) and the Mexican past. His labors to collect material in order to authenticate the Virgin's apparition and to promote papal sanction for the coronation of her image at the Guadalupe shrine led him unintentionally into other realms, and he embarked on an ambitious program of research that he hoped would eventually enable him to write a comprehensive history of the indigenous nations based on primary sources. He did not depend on the limited and familiar evidence available in the capital but roamed all over Mexico, always alert for some old picture book or manuscript. For eight years Boturini led a life of deprivation, "living much with the natives," as Prescott writes, "passing his nights sometimes in their huts, sometimes in caves, and the depths of the lonely forest."[8] Slowly he gained the confidence of the natives, learned their language, and patiently added document by document to his growing collection. On his return to Mexico City, he had some five hundred pieces of writing from both pre-Columbian and post-Columbian times, probably the largest number of these codices ever assembled.

Boturini had not forgotten his Madonna—and she was to be his downfall. He now thought he had sufficient evidence to advance her case in Rome. But by this very step he seems to have antagonized the viceroy, who felt that he had been bypassed. Some of Boturini's unguarded remarks fell on malicious ears, and the ever suspicious Spanish authorities were alarmed. In 1743 Boturini was imprisoned, his documents were confiscated, and he was unceremoniously expelled from the country he had chosen to serve and glorify. At Vera Cruz he was put on a ship bound for Spain—without the bulk of his priceless collection, his "Museum," as he called it, "the only property which he possessed in the Indies, and which he would not change against all the gold and silver in the New World."[9] These he had to leave behind to an uncertain fate.

In mid-ocean the Spanish ship was boarded by English privateers and Boturini was robbed of the few manuscripts he had managed to take with him. (Their fate is unknown.) When he reached Spain, he vigorously pleaded his case before the Coun-

---

[8] Prescott: op. cit., p. 91 *n.*   [9] Humboldt: op. cit., p. 188.

cil of the Indies and was absolved of any legal transgression he had been charged with. To his *Idea de una nueva historia de la América Septentrional,* written in Spain without the benefit of his materials, he appended from memory a catalogue of his collection of manuscripts. The work came to the attention of the king, who named Boturini official Historiographer General of the Indies, at a salary that was too meager, however, for him to contemplate returning to New Spain. He died shortly afterward without reclaiming possession of his beloved "Museum." The confiscated papers had meanwhile been carelessly deposited in the damp basement of the viceregal palace. It was there that Humbolt saw the remains: three small packages, utterly neglected and partly decomposed by humidity.

As chance would have it, during Humboldt's stay at the Mexican capital, the library of Antonio de León y Gama, a Mexican antiquarian, was auctioned off. Among the pieces were a few pre-Columbian documents and some from early in the Conquest, probably originally part of Boturini's collection. Humboldt managed to purchase these scraps and later took them to Berlin. The sixteen fragments are far from the most spectacular of Mexican manuscripts, though along with the Dresden Codex and a Hamburg manuscript they represent the only such items in German possession and later in the century led to important investigations by Eduard Seler, the German Mexicanist. The majority of the pieces deal with nonreligious matters such as litigations, bills for work and commodities, land titles, and some historical miscellanea, including a map of Texcoco, the ancient cultural capital of the Valley of Mexico. Among the most interesting is an early pictorial rendering of the Ten Commandments, which bears out the tradition that Spanish missionaries, particularly the Frenchman Jacques Testera, were engaged at one time in adapting Mexican picture writing to the spread of the Gospel.

Humboldt's contribution to the preservation of the pre-Columbian codices, however, consisted not so much in his acquisition of scattered fragments but in the sustained study he devoted to them. They posed many puzzling problems. What was their exact makeup and purpose? How did they compare to European books and other Old World books? What did they contain? How were they written? Did the "paintings" represent a script in our sense?

Although Humboldt did not get beyond superficialities in deciphering any of the codices, he nevertheless gained a thorough comprehension of the nature and mode of Mexican picture writing. Some of his knowledge came from early colonial accounts and from the studies of the recently deceased Mexican scholar, Antonio de León y Gama. How strange these native books were! No wonder that Europeans, if they did not see the devil's handiwork in them, found them unusual. And yet, many things about them seemed familiar.

Each codex, unless it consisted of just one sheet or map, was made up of a continuous strip folded like an accordion or fan. When intact, its beginning and end were attached to wooden boards or leather, occasionally inlaid with precious stones, which gave the closed codex the appearance of a sumptuous medieval manuscript of the West. Their characteristic folds reminded Humboldt of the manuscripts from Siam he had seen at the Paris Na-

Mexican bookmaking, after Codex Mendoza. A professional scribe or "painter" of codices at work. To the right of him, a hieroglyph representing the figure 8,000, with paper attached to it; hence, 8,000 rolls or sheets of paper. Below, the traditional, "folding-screen" pre-Columbian book.

tional Library. As in some Far Eastern books, one would read first all the consecutive pages of one face before proceeding in reverse order on the other. The sequence of the characters would vary from left to right, right to left, horizontal or vertical, even circular or in zigzag. Red guidelines occasionally helped one to find one's way.

The manuscripts, just as in the Old World, were made either of parchment or of a kind of vegetable fiber that was not true paper but looked much the same. This "paper" was prepared from several species of native fig trees, from which the inner bark was detached. It was then treated by pressing and beating. Some kind of gum or starch was probably used for sizing, and the flattened sheet was given a thin white coating of lime or gesso. The papermaking process, by the way, was quite similar in South America, the Pacific Islands, Southeast Asia, and parts of Africa. As in those areas, "paper" was widely used for ritual offerings and clothing. Parchment from deer, and perhaps jaguar skin, was also whitened and appears to have been a favorite with the Mixtecs of southern Mexico. Cotton cloth was used for shorter documents, particularly maps and genealogical tables.

Most nineteenth-century authors, including Humboldt and Prescott, claimed that the paper was a product of the maguey, or agave, but analysis of extant specimens has not borne this out. In some parts of Mexico the traditional papermaking art is still practiced. In ancient Mexico it was a major industry and, as we know from Aztec documents, paper was a leading item of tribute

Preparation of paper (*amatl*) from tree bark

and trade. An annual tax of 24,000 bundles from a subject people is recorded. Like the ancient Egyptians and Romans, Mexicans distinguished between various types of paper, and some places, such as Amacoztitlán and Itzamatitlán, in Morelos, were noted for the fine quality of their product.[1]

The physical makeup of ancient Mexican books was rather

---

[1] Victor von Hagen: *The Aztec: Man and Tribe* (New York: New American Library–Mentor Books; 1958), p. 190.

different from what the West had been used to, and the writing was considerably more outlandish. Parallels to Egyptian hieroglyphics were only superficial. Indeed, the question has been endlessly pondered to this day whether these documents really can be called books. Did they carry writing in conventional characters and communicate a precise message? In a way, the picture books of the Mexicans have a strong resemblance to the pictorial records of their kinsmen of the North American plains. Humboldt saw parallels to the paintings on wood made by the Iroquois and the Hurons. "In America," as Paul Radin, the University of California anthropologist, has more recently observed, "there was a well developed tendency to represent selected events pictographically on bark or skin."[2] Yet there is an essential difference. Those who still see in the Mexican or Mayan codices little but an attempt to represent an event by reproducing its action pictorially miss the point. Mexican books are not counterparts of the Bayeux tapestries, or a sinister form of comic strip. They do not simply provide a portrayal of an incident in its entirety, but contain an analysis of individual acts and aspects of them. Neither are they, in the manner of the *Biblia Pauperum* of the Middle Ages, picture books for illiterates. All the evidence indicates that Mexican books were composed and written by highly trained priests or professional guildsmen and were readily understandable to only a select few.

Undoubtedly, the Mexicans had advanced beyond mere pictorialization to writing in pictures. That is to say, their pictures were not necessarily realistic representations, but signs. To a large degree, and increasingly so, they were formalized. They could express a statement and store and convey data and, perhaps, even ideas. They retained figurative elements, however, and even today we do not know exactly how far they advanced beyond pictorialization. It is doubtful whether, with rare exceptions, a word for word reading could be made, unless the symbols served as mnemonic notations for orally transmitted texts, as they probably did in some cases. We know that the Aztecs maintained schools, one of whose purposes was to train young men in the memorizing of copious religious, historic, and poetic literature. In short, the Mexican script reached neither the conventionalization nor the exactness of the Phoenician or the Mesopotamian or

[2] Paul Radin: *The Sources and Authenticity of the History of the Ancient Mexicans,* University of California Publications in American Archaeology and Ethnology, Vol. XVII (1920–26), p. 6.

even the Chinese system of writing. Among the peoples who had picture writing, the Egyptians of 3000 B.C., as Prescott noted pointedly, "were at the top of the scale, the Aztecs at the bottom."[3] Where the Mayas stood is a matter of doubt, but they were certainly ahead of the Aztecs and Mixtecs.

Mexican script, then, was neither a syllabary nor an alphabet, and cannot be reduced to a fixed number of symbols. For this reason there can never be a master key to it: there is no overriding principle. You may rightly identify one pictogram or "read" a passage, yet it will fail to give you a clue to another symbol or passage. One has to start all over again with each one. Nevertheless, many features are standardized. The Mexicans were familiar with elements of the three main types of scripts—as they are customarily classified—the pictographic, ideogrammatic, and phonetic. Their system is a fossil, genetically older than the writing of any known civilization, past or present. Indeed, one of the interests of the Mexican documents is that, in the words of a modern Americanist, "it is possible to find in the Mexican manuscripts illustrations of all the steps in the early history of writing."[4]

Briefly, pictographic writing implies the figurative rendering of a tangible object or scene. It limits writing to the depiction of items that can be visualized and precludes a continuous, coherent narrative. Ideograms enormously broaden the scope by symbolizing objects as well as abstract concepts, relations, activities, and so on. Phonetic signs, the most advanced form of writing, confine themselves to one language, but permit the codification of any word in that language, in complete disregard of its meaning, simply by sounds. There is no verbalized thought or occurrence they cannot express unambiguously, within the limitations of the human intellect. In a developed script, phonetic elements can be reduced to a minimum of syllables, as in a syllabary, or of letters, as in an alphabet, consisting of standard signs.

The Mexicans were familiar with all three methods, but in varying degree. Their number symbols were completely ideogrammatic, as they are with us. They were indicated by the signs of a vigesimal (counted by twenties) rather than a decimal system.

---

[3] Prescott: op. cit., p. 56.
[4] Alfred M. Tozzer: "The Value of the Ancient Mexican Manuscripts in the Study of the General Development of Writing," *American Antiquarian Society. Proceedings*, Vol. XXI (April 1911), p. 3.

For example, 20 was indicated as a flag or war banner, 400 by what may have been a feather or a branch of leaves (some say a plait), 8,000 by a bag used to carry copal grains (incense) or cocoa beans, which served as a kind of legal tender. The Mayas used two different types of figures, as we use Roman and Arabic numerals. Their units progressed from 20 to 360 (18 x 20), and then through multiplication by 20 to 7,200. Like Hindu and Arab mathematicians of the early Middle Ages (and probably the ancient Sumerians), they were familiar with zero, which was written usually as a shell, and could multiply large figures by position. Every one of the 260 days (13 x 20) of the complex sacred calendar, common to all advanced cultures of Middle America and used in the black art of prognostication (*Tonalpohualli*), had its fixed combination of signs.

Mexican (that is, Aztec and Mixtec) ideograms usually reflect pictorial origins. Thus, walking is indicated by a sequence of footprints, talking by a wagging tongue, and seeing by an upturned eye. The conquest of a city is shown by a temple set afire, with the city's name attached. The capturing of a prisoner is equated with dragging someone by the hair—curiously reminiscent of the famous Egyptian pictogram on the Narmer Palette from the beginning of the Dynastic period (about 3100 B.C.). In hieroglyphic scripts, a part or an aspect may stand for the whole. In this way pictograms become abstractions.

Most charming is the symbol for singing, which shows the wagging tongue ("speaking") surrounded by flowers. Death is usually depicted as a bundled-up corpse, and such a bundle with a name and date signs, followed by an open-eyed figure also with date and name—both figures with a crown—means roughly that such and such a ruler died at a certain date and was succeeded by such and such an individual.

The Spanish marveled at finding signs for the cross and a symbol that looked like a Roman capital letter A. In both cases

The Mixtec year symbol in three variations, from pre-Columbian Codex Nuttall

the similarity was coincidental. The cross stood for one or all of the four cardinal points of the compass. Enthusiasts of cultural diffusion announced that the Mixtec "A" was an abbreviation for the Latin *annus* or the Spanish *año,* but in reality it was an inverted sun ray, a life-giving symbol for a year, which was overlaid by a rectangle in which the actual year was inscribed.

The phonetic aspect is the least prominent. Among the Aztecs and Mixtecs, in particular, it is almost exclusively of the rebus kind, which relies on identifiable pictures. A rebus, so familiar from children's games, is a kind of pun on the approximate phonetic similarity of a word or syllable with another one whose pictorial image is easily recognizable and may be substituted for the former. All sorts of compounds can thus be formed by combining various pictures. Among the Mexicans the device, analogous to medieval heraldry, had its widest application in names of persons and places, which, as among many primitive peoples, usually consisted of concrete, identifiable elements. Humboldt was well aware of this: "They knew how to write names by writing signs associated with sounds."[5] In such manner, a man born on the eighth day of the month Deer is named 8 Deer (Mixtec: 8 *mazatl*) and his hieroglyphic will consist of a string of eight beads beside the head of a deer. The Aztec ruler Itzcoatl was depicted as a snake with obsidian knives projecting from it (*itzli* = obsidian knives; *coatl* = snake). Montezuma, or more correctly Mo-quauh-zoma, was represented by a mousetrap (*mo*ntli), an eagle (*quauh*tli), a lancet (*zo*), and a hand (*ma*itl). Here we get an incipient syllabary. In some of the place names a symbol may even stand for one sound corresponding to a single Western letter, as *atl* (water) for just "a," *etl* (bean) for "e," and *otli* (road) for "o." There is the possibility, however, that the latter were post-Columbian refinements.

To cite examples of place names, the Aztec capital Tenochtitlán was compounded by a stone (*tena*) resting on a cactus (*nochtli*); Chapultepec, by a grasshopper (*chapul*) on a hill (*tepec*).

The fact that the Mexicans were aware of phonetic elements made Humboldt wonder whether they had not been on the threshold of the discovery of a syllabary. "It might have brought them to alphabetize their simple hieroglyphics."[6] But shrewdly assessing

---

[5] Quoted in *American Antiquarian Society. Proceedings*, No. 70 (1878), p. 94.
[6] Ibid.

the innate conservatism of all races, and considering that the more advanced Egyptian script failed to reach that stage in three thousand years, he thought the chances slim that the Mexicans would have evolved an alphabet in a short time. In any case, the vested interests of priests and scribes would have offered a serious obstacle.

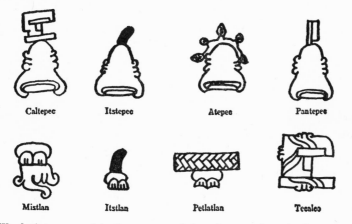

Caltepec	Itstepec	Atepec	Pantepec

Mistlan	Itstlan	Petlatlan	Tecalco

Word pictures, used in the manner of the rebus as phonetic elements, are combined to form glyphs of Mexican place names.

In addition to the three types of writing described, color, too—as in Byzantine iconography—could be expressive of meaning; "for even colors speak in the Aztec hieroglyphics."[7] Together with design, illumination had been put to uses that would delight Rimbaud. Brilliant polychrome patterns triumphed over lack of perspective and superficially primitive shapes. Even in the few surviving codices we can distinguish differences in the use of design, color, and symbols. Particularly impressive are the strong, well-defined, audaciously archaic tapestries of the Mixtecs.

Humboldt and most of his successors well into the second half of the nineteenth century failed to make any noticeable headway in deciphering Mexican writing. A Rosetta Stone was not likely ever to be found. Prescott, who studied Humboldt's treatise thoroughly, concluded sadly: "It is impossible to cast the eye over this brilliant assemblage of forms and colors without feeling how hopeless must be the attempt to recover a key to the Aztec mythological symbols."[8] Humboldt nevertheless acquired considerable

---

[7] Prescott: op. cit., p. 56.   [8] Ibid., p. 91 *n.*

knowledge of the scope of Mexican books. He knew that native records on landholding continued to be used in litigation for some time after the Conquest. Spanish rulers had also shown an interest in the tribute lists of the Aztecs and had copied several of them and added explanations in Spanish. Early colonial writers mentioned the wide range of topics dealt with in the scrolls. The magic purpose of some of the surviving codices was obvious to the untutored eye; much of the contents was devoted to astronomical and astrological matter. From the Calendar Stone and the codices Humboldt gained considerable insight into Mexican astral concepts, the calendar, cyclical counts, and the numerical system, and he took a special interest in the complex intercalations of the civil and religious years.

Humboldt had little doubt that the Aztecs possessed annals which "exhibit the greatest method, and astonishing minuteness."[9] It appeared to him likely that central valley records went back to the sixth century A.D. He agreed with Boturini that before that the Mexicans, like the Peruvians and, it seems, the ancient Chinese, had employed quipus (knot) records, which were called *nepohuatltzitzin.* They were related, perhaps, to the wampum strings and belts used in North America. In A.D. 660 a Toltec sage is said to have compiled at Tula the *Teoamoxtli,* a divine book of all Nahuatl people which dealt with the creation of the universe and man, time divisions and the stars, mythology, the migration of nations, and perhaps moral philosophy. Humboldt gloomily reflected that this Toltec bible probably had still been in existence when the Spanish landed and systematically stamped out all traces of native idolatry.

After Humboldt returned to Europe in 1804, the magic books of Mexico remained on his mind. Unexpectedly, the Old World offered ample opportunity to pursue the subject. On his wide travels to the Vatican, to Velletri and Florence, and to libraries all over Western Europe he was able to locate and examine many more manuscripts than had been available in Mexico. When in 1810 he published his two-volume work on American monuments, he devoted a large part of the text to a discussion of the pre-Columbian scrolls and the Mexican calendar. One third of all the illustrations consisted of sections from the codices. This material had never before been brought together, nor had such a succinct summary been given of what was known about Mexican writing.

---

[9] Humboldt: op. cit., p. 137.

All the manuscripts Humboldt had been able to trace were listed, with accompanying notes on their hazardous survival.

It is anything but an accident that the majority of the Mexican codices are to be found today not in Mexican but in European hands. After Cortés received two manuscripts which he dispatched to his emperor, Mexican picture books were for a while a fairly popular commodity in the curio traffic. They were regarded in Europe as oddities rather than instruments of Satan, and were not willfully destroyed. Indeed, according to contemporary reports, they circulated in considerable numbers. We probably owe the preservation of several to Spanish soldiers who sent them home as souvenirs. As is the fate of souvenirs, however, many were soon forgotten and perished. Those which were put away in European closets more often than not remained unknown to their owners and to the learned world in general. From time to time someone would inspect a scroll and would be struck by its bizarreness and imagery. Often it was not even known that they contained true writing.

Virtually every one of the mere handful of scrolls that survived, after lingering in some alcove, or worse, had to be rediscovered—several not before the twentieth century. Ragged, faded pieces retaining scant traces of their former brilliance and delightful designs turn up now and then. And the little we know of the migrations and hairbreadth escapes of these codices is in the adventurous tradition of Old World manuscripts.

Alexander von Humboldt, after years of searching in Mexico and in European collections, was not aware of the existence of the Dresden Codex until he was about to go to press with his study of American antiquities. Even then, the Dresden Codex remained the only known Maya book for another half century. The provenance of this manuscript is as obscure as any. Some think it may originally have been in the possession of the Habsburg emperors. In any case, in 1739 the director of the Dresden Library, Johann Christian Götze, visited Vienna on his way from Italy, and there he was given the manuscript by its owner (unknown) as a curiosity, seemingly "ununderstandable and hence valueless."[1] Götze in turn donated it to the Royal Library of Dresden in 1744. Through Humboldt's publication of five of its pages it became more widely

---

[1] Humboldt: op. cit., Vol. II, p. 48. See also William Gates: *The Dresden Codex*, Maya Society Publications, No. 2 (Baltimore, 1932), n.p.

known, but it was decades before it came to be recognized as fundamentally different from the other Mexican picture books, and still longer before it was declared "the greatest intellectual achievement of pre-Columbian America."

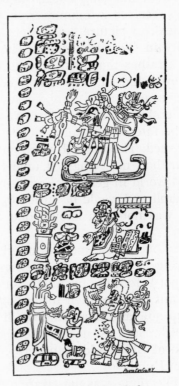

From the Dresden Codex

The Codex Borgia, one of the most important if not the most sumptuous of Mexican manuscripts, had its share of adventures. It was a deerskin book containing a pictorial narrative of the birth of Mexican deities, and had once been in the possession of the Giustiniani family of Venice, to whom it may have been bequeathed by a seafaring ancestor. A satanic document whose like had once frightened the Spanish inquisitors, it became a plaything—a nursery book—of the servants' children and barely escaped being burned up when a child set it playfully on fire. It was rescued by a Roman cleric, and it still bears signs of the singeing it received. The codex was given to the Borgias and housed in their library at Velletri, and eventually it passed to the Vatican Library of Propaganda. Humboldt was charmed by its rainbow colors and deemed that it deserved to rank high among the exotic books.[2] Later scholars agreed with him.

Humboldt was also the first to sense that the Dresden Codex, with its characters of standard size, differed from all the others. Today we consider the Dresden Codex the most remarkable of

Representation of the Jaguar god in animal and human shape in the Codex Borgia

the pre-Columbian manuscripts. Here is a subtle, baroque art that shuns blank spaces and delights in extravagant forms and flamboyant tracery. Several of the figures are drawn with a macabre elegance worthy of the Yellow Book. Quite fetchingly, though not quite correctly, Humboldt compared the Mexican scrolls to the ribbon of relief sculptures winding around Trajan's Column in Rome. His conclusion: "Notwithstanding the extreme imperfection of the hieroglyphical writing of the Mexicans, their paintings were good substitutes for books, manuscripts, and alphabetic characters."[3]

An eccentric Anglo-Irish lord executed one of Humboldt's projects with splendor and aristocratic munificence: the publication of all known pre-Columbian manuscripts.[4] Theretofore, few people had had the opportunity to examine the scattered codices at their places of deposit in two hemispheres and in several coun-

---

[2] Humboldt: op. cit., Vol. I, pp. 206–7.
[3] Humboldt: op. cit., Vol. I, p. 162.
[4] Prescott: op. cit., p. 74.

tries. Besides, the survival of the codices had to be assured. What was needed were painstaking, detailed facsimiles which could circulate widely. Humboldt had expressed the hope that a government would step in and undertake the costly work "at its own expense." But none did. So it fell upon the Right Honorable Edward King, Viscount of Kingsborough, to sponsor and carry out the great project. It was he who assembled the manuscripts that had eluded the bonfires.

The large tomes he published gave the world its first broad view of these remains of ancient American civilizations, and opened up a new era in pre-Columbian research by making the material widely available. The major nineteenth-century Mexicanists expressly acknowledge their debt to these volumes. Kingsborough tracked down codices that had previously been little known and probably preserved some that might have been lost or destroyed. Friends assisted him in his search in places as far away as Hungary, and today several codices are reproduced nowhere but in his volumes. In honor of this work, one of the Mexican manuscripts was named Codex Kingsborough.

Kingsborough was an untrained layman, as were practically all the early students of pre-Columbian manuscripts. Enthusiasm rather than any preconceived scholarly purpose moved them, and the brilliant designs of the codices kept their imagination on fire. Indeed, it has been said of Kingsborough that this pursuit became a mania.[5] Edward King, a scion of the Anglo-Irish nobility, was born in 1795, the eldest son of the Earl of Kingston. "Viscount of Kingsborough" was a courtesy title he was given in 1799. He entered Exeter College, Oxford, in 1814, and was there until 1818 without taking a degree. It was during this time that he fell under the Mexican spell.

Judging by the suddenness and intensity of his interest, it was close to a mystical experience. It was set off by the Codex Mendoza, which Kingsborough came upon at the Bodleian Library—a post-Columbian codex compiled in 1549 by native craftsmen on the orders of the first viceroy of New Spain, Don Antonio de Mendoza. The codex is a unique catalogue of Mexican customs, based on older records, and includes a list of tribute rendered to Montezuma. Its story is hard to match in sheer drama. Mendoza

---

[5] S. Austin Allibone: "Kingsborough, Rt. Hon. Edward King, Viscount," *A Critical Dictionary of English Literature. . . .* (Philadelphia: J. B. Lippincott Co.; 1871), p. 1033.

had it completed in ten days to send by outgoing fleet to his sovereign, who wanted to familiarize himself with his new subjects. The manuscript never reached its destination, for the ship fell into the hands of French pirates. The book was acquired by a French historian, André Thevet, and, according to one version (usually the French one), was given on loan to an Englishman for publication. But the son of perfidious Albion failed to return it.[6] According to another version, Richard Hakluyt, then attached to the English legation in Paris, bought it for twenty crowns. Later owners were Samuel Purchas and John Selden. Selden donated

Pictograms from the Codex Mendoza recording the conquest of two towns in southern Mexico by an Aztec king. Note Spanish explanations.

it to Oxford in 1664. Then it was lost sight of for more than a century, but somehow it reappeared before or during Kingsborough's student days. Shortly before the outbreak of World

---

[6] Cottie A. Burland: *Art and Life in Ancient Mexico* (Oxford: Bruno Cassirer; 1948), p. 102.

War II, an English Americanist, James Cooper Clark, completed a first-rate three-volume edition of the codex. An air raid made short shrift of most of the copies stored in a London warehouse.[7]

Other Mexican manuscripts in the Bodleian must have come to Kingsborough's attention soon after. There was, for one, the Codex Laud, which was inscribed by one of its former possessors as *Liber Hierogliphocorum Aegiptorum MS*.[8] This pre-Conquest manuscript once belonged to William Laud, the famous archbishop of Canterbury who, though also noted as a book burner, gave his collection of some 1,300 manuscripts in eighteen different languages to Oxford. The codex has been in England at least since the seventeenth century. Yet Robertson, the historian and a contemporary of David Hume, who wrote a once popular history of America, stated that not a single ancient picture scroll was deposited in England. He was patently wrong: in those days, not only old monastic libraries or Spanish repositories were cemeteries of books. England is today the proud possessor of the lion's share of pre-Columbian codices. But already in Robertson's time it had several prize specimens hidden somewhere in the Bodleian.

About the Selden Roll, still another of Oxford's treasures of Mexicana, all kinds of romances have been spun, none fully substantiated. C. A. Burland, a twentieth-century English Americanist who published an edition of it in 1955, thinks that it too may have been seized by French privateers or may have reached England directly through Britain's own adept practitioners of high-sea robbery on the Spanish Main. Another possibility is that it was given to Prince Charles (the later "Good King Charles I" of unhappy memory) when he went unsuccessfully to woo a Spanish infanta.[9]

The older and more valuable Codex Bodley 2858 was reported in the Bodleian Library between 1603 and 1605. There is some evidence that it was once in the collection of the learned Portuguese bishop of Faro, Jerónimo Osorio. But how did it reach England? Scholars have looked to the freebooting operations of the Earl of Essex, Elizabeth's favorite, who it seems included among his other not too creditable exploits the sacking of the bishop's palace and library. Essex bestowed on his friend Sir Thomas Bodley the items he had thus obtained.[1]

It was these Oxford codices which introduced Kingsborough

---

[7] Peterson: op. cit., p. 242. [8] Ibid., p. 238.
[9] Burland: *The Selden Roll* (Berlin: Gebr. Mann; 1955), p. 9.
[1] Alfonso Caso: *Interpretación del Codice Bodley 2858* (Mexico, D.F.: Sociedad Mexicana de Antropología; 1960), p. 11.

to the Mexican enigma. To what extent his lordship inquired into the meaning of the records at that time is not known. Did he venture an interpretation even then? His contemporaries are all agreed that from the first the exotic picture books haunted him. One witness alleged that "he thought of nothing else."[2]

After leaving Oxford, he first considered a public career. Twice he was elected to Parliament as the member from County Cork, but in 1826 he resigned in favor of a younger brother. The preparation of his great work, *Antiquities of Mexico,* required all his attention, all his funds, and eventually even his life. To execute facsimiles, he employed an Italian draftsman, Agostino Aglio, who had done the etchings for Belzoni's Egyptian drawings, and he kept him busy for five years entirely at his own expense. Three years were spent on copying codices in collections on the Continent, mainly at Vienna, Rome, and Dresden. Obadiah Rich, the American bibliographer, who was then living in England, went twice on his behalf to Spain to search for manuscripts. Kingsborough also subsidized that man of obscure nationality and title, Count Jean-Frédéric Maximilien de Waldeck, on several archaeological forays into Mexico and Yucatán.

Kingsborough himself wrote copious, and on the whole helpful, notes to all the illustrative material. Scattered among them, however, are learned paragraphs by his lordship expounding his "Arguments to shew that the Jews in early ages colonized America." The first four volumes contained nothing but plates of the codices, in addition to sketches of monuments at Palenque and elsewhere, some of which have since been razed, so that these drawings are the only record extant. The rest of the work contained various accounts of Mexico accessible until then only in manuscript form, above all a long selection from one of the most valuable sixteenth-century descriptions of the indigenous civilization, the manuscripts of the friar Bernardino de Sahagún, which had been lost for nearly three centuries and had just then been rediscovered. Sahagún's great work has been tapped in more recent years as a prime source for pre-Columbian Mexican literature, which the friar transcribed in Nahuatl, the predominant language of ancient Mexico.

Seven volumes were issued in 1831, in Kingsborough's lifetime. Two more followed in 1846, but the tenth and final one never came out. Their reception was in general exceedingly favor-

---

[2] Allibone: op. cit., p. 1033.

able. The London *Athenaeum* reported: "This work, in its magnificence, recalls to mind the patronage of crowned heads and the splendour of the princely patrons of literature."[3] At a cost of approximately £3,000 each, Kingsborough donated a copy on parchment to the British Museum and another to the Bodleian Library—certainly a grand manner in which to bring out books. The oversized volumes were printed in imperial folio, to reflect adequately his lordly passion for the exotic subject. Prescott, a New Englander of more Puritanic tastes, caustically remarked that "it is not uncommon, in works on this magnificent plan, to find utility in some measure sacrificed to show."[4]

Nine copies, printed on especially selected drawing paper, were presented to crowned heads. The sets that were put on sale were originally offered at £210 (a small fortune then) for the hand-colored, and £140 for the ordinary edition. At that sum the market was small, and the price soon fell to £63 and £36, respectively.[5] The two posthumous volumes sold for just 25 pounds 4 shillings.

The fall in price meant the financial ruin of Kingsborough, whom the enterprise had cost over £32,000. His family had never approved of the venture, and he obtained no financial aid from his wealthy father. Soon his creditors began to close in. Printers and paper manufacturers clamored to be paid. There was the widow Cranston who preferred charges and caused him to be detained. Other claimants followed suit. The dogma of the sanctity of money and property did not spare a nobleman in the England and Ireland of the Reform Bill. Three times Lord Kingsborough was taken to the sheriff's prison in Dublin, and none of his kin made a move. During his third prison term he contracted "jail fever," an euphemism for typhus, and died within a few days, in November 1837. Had he lived a few months longer, he would have succeeded to the earldom of Kingston and a comfortable annuity of £40,000. Kingsborough, after all, did not fare any better than Boturini. It was as though doom were attached to the Mexican books and had been visited on their compassionate rescuers.

When he died, Kingsborough was only at the beginning of his pre-Columbian studies, and there is every likelihood that, in the manner of other nineteenth-century antiquarians burdened by Biblical preconceptions, he might eventually have outgrown some

---

[3] Ibid., p. 1034.   [4] Prescott: op. cit., p. 74.
[5] Allibone: op. cit., p. 1033.

of his odd theories and made genuine advances in the knowledge of the Mexican past. Kingsborough believed, for example, that Mexico had been settled by one or several of the lost tribes of Israel, a grotesque hypothesis which has now and again turned the heads of a number of respectable scholars. He hoped to prove his point as part of his ambitious undertaking. "To this," writes Prescott, "the whole battery of his logic and learning is directed. For this, hieroglyphics are unriddled, manuscripts compared, monuments delineated."⁶

Kingsborough traced Hebraic origins in names and institutions where nobody else had suspected them. The lost *Teoamoxtli* of the Toltecs was etymologically derived from *teo* (divine), *amotl* (paper, book), and *moxtli*. The latter, he declared, "*appears* to be Moses." Hence the name means "Divine Book of Moses."⁷ It is of course easy to deride this today. We rarely stop to consider the remarkable parallels between the Biblical and the Mexican accounts of the Deluge, or a Mayan legend that is uncomfortably close to the Biblical story of the Tower of Babel. There was also the ever present specter of Quetzalcoatl, the bearded white man from the East who had brought moral law and had sailed away again into the Atlantic. Several early Spanish writers shared Kingsborough's views, including Diego Durán, the chronicler of New Spain who went to Mexico within a few years of the Conquest. And so did Cotton Mather, Roger Williams, and William Penn in the American colonies. Colonial writers, more or less unintentionally, may have introduced elements to validate the Hebraic thesis, but it is not always possible to recognize the insertions and distinguish them from original traditions. Historical criticism and anthropology and archaeology—not to mention the new chronological concepts of geology and evolution—were in their infancy. And men of Humboldt's stature are rare in any age. Half a century after Kingsborough, Flinders Petrie, the pioneer of scientific archaeology, began his career in Egypt with a belief in the mystical mathematical properties of the pyramids. Still later, the New Englander, Edward H. Thompson, famous for his work at Chichen Itzá and its *cenote*, had hoped to discover Atlantis in Yucatán.

The final words have been said by Prescott, himself the proud owner of one of Kingsborough's "colossal" sets: "It would be unjust, however, not to admit that the noble author, if his logic is

---

⁶ Prescott: op. cit., p. 75.   ⁷ Ibid., p. 63.

not always convincing, shows much acuteness in detecting analogies; that he displays familiarity with his subject, and a fund of erudition, though it often runs to waste; that, whatever be the defects of arrangement, he has brought together a most rich collection of unpublished materials to illustrate the Aztec, and, in a wider sense, American antiquities; and that, by this munificent undertaking, which no government, probably, would have, and few individuals could have, executed, he has entitled himself to the lasting gratitude of every friend of science."[8]

---

[8] Ibid., p. 75.

·XXIV·

BRASSEUR

DISCOVERS LANDA AND

THE ANTEDILUVIANS

. . . magic casements, opening on the foam
Of perilous seas, in faery lands forlorn.

KEATS

IN 1863, the American Antiquarian Society of Worcester, Massachusetts, could look with pride upon its first fifty years. Since its founding, with the blessing of Alexander von Humboldt, men everywhere had learned to contemplate the New World's past with growing awe and curiosity. Much of the popularity of the subject was stimulated by two American authors: John Lloyd Stephens of New Jersey, a lawyer who around 1840 had ventured into the jungles of Yucatán, Honduras, and Guatemala to track down long-forgotten cities of exotic splendor; and his contemporary, William H. Prescott, the Boston historian, who had created a vivid canvas of the melancholy decline and conquest of the Aztecs and the Incas. Now, in 1863, the year of the semi-centennial, recent finds promised to vindicate the "maturity of mankind" in the western lands and "establish a position of equality with the most ancient nations." Such claims, the secretary of the society stated, were above all due to a discovery made in 1863, and destined, perhaps, "to unlock the mysterious records that are concealed beneath the hideous hieroglyphs of Mexico and Central America."[1] A French scholar, the Abbé Brasseur de Bourbourg, had found in Spain an unpublished description of Yucatán, which supposedly included the lost phonetic alphabet of the Mayas. Though this was not precisely true, the early colonial manuscript was to provide a breakthrough in our knowledge of Maya civilization.

The Abbé Brasseur de Bourbourg was already known to antiquarians. Less than ten years earlier, he had treated his colleagues to another, though less creditable, surprise. In a letter from Guatemala to the *New York Tribune* of 1855, and in similar communications to the French press, he declared that the languages spoken by the native peoples of Central America revealed unmistakable affinities to the Germanic, and particularly Scandinavian, tongues. In Guatemala City, he had devoted several months to the analysis of centuries-old manuscripts written in local languages. There he found a confirmation of his thesis. The ancestors of the natives were said in one of the narratives to have come across the sea from a cold and snowy land. Their original home, the Abbé affirmed, was the Scandinavian peninsula, and the fantastic palaces and temples in the jungles of America were built by men who were ultimately descended from the Germanic races. "The Toltecs, Mexicans, Quichés, Kakchiquels, and Zutugiles," he wrote with a rhetorical flourish, "will they turn out to be your brothers? Are they Scandinavians?"[2]

This was the age in which the wildest theories about American origins were promulgated, despite the warnings of Humboldt and the fate of Lord Kingsborough. Through the dark mists of oblivion, clairvoyant observers were constantly receiving messages from the mysterious ruins and inscriptions in the tropical forests. The greater their ignorance, the higher their flights of fancy. A few scholars were becoming weary of such inquiries, but the champion of the Scandinavians was a man to be reckoned with. His colleagues were agreed that, although he might be among the least reliable when it came to elucidating the roots of the native civilizations of Mexico and Central America, he nevertheless was one of the foremost students of American antiquities. In Brasseur, however, the ability to find and salvage lost and neglected documents was unfortunately coupled with visionary tendencies, which may

---

[1] Samuel F. Haven: "Report," *American Antiquarian Society. Proceedings,* No. 55 (October 1870), p. 46.

[2] Charles Étienne Brasseur de Bourbourg: "Notes d'un voyage dans l'Amérique Centrale," *Nouvelles Annales des Voyages,* Vol. I, Sér. 6 (August 1855), p. 158.

have obscured his genuine achievements. To him more than anyone we owe the knowledge that the ancient peoples of Central
America possessed a literature.

Whereas Lord Kingsborough never saw an Indian in the flesh,
the French Abbé undertook five extensive trips to the New World
and resided and traveled for long periods in Mexico and Guatemala, where he acquired fluency in native tongues, an enormous
store of data on aboriginal life, and a unique collection of native
documents written soon after the Conquest. He was born in 1814
as plain Charles Étienne (or Étienne-Charles) Brasseur (the em
bellishing title was of his own making) in Bourbourg, a little
Flemish town between Calais and Dunkerque in northern France.
His passion for the past was awakened early. Characteristically,
the history of ancient Egypt, Persia, and India captured his interest first. He thought, as did most people of the time, that
America before Columbus had no culture and no history. Then in
1832 he read a newspaper report of the alleged discovery of a
grave in Brazil in which a warrior was buried with Macedonian
arms and within a casket inscribed in Greek. The bizarre notice
excited his imagination, suggesting possible links between America and the Old World. As with Kingsborough, his first impression
was decisive and, in a way, fatal. From then on, he read avidly
all the news of American exploration he could lay his hands on.

Soon after, destiny blew a copy of the *Journal des Savants*
his way. It contained an abridged account by Antonio del Río, a
Spanish army officer who had been commissioned in 1785 by
Carlos III (the Bourbon king who had begun his monarchical
and archaeological career in the kingdom of Naples) to investigate
the ruins of Palenque in Chiapas, Mexico. Much later, Brasseur
was to recall the encounter, "a wonder mixed with pleasure. . . .
It settled my future in archaeology. A vague presentiment showed
me, in the distance, I know not what mysterious veils, which a
secret instinct urged me to lift. And on hearing of Champollion,
whose fame had begun to penetrate even the colleges of our province, I asked myself whether the Western continent would not one
day also be susceptible to the same scientific work then carried
out in Europe. . . ."[3] The emulation of Champollion became another persistent motive in his pre-Columbian studies.

After leaving school, he turned for a while to politics and
journalism, and wrote a novel in the romantic style of Chateau-

---

[3] Brasseur: *Histoire des Nations Civilisées du Mexique et de l'Amérique
Centrale. . . .* (Paris: A. Bertrand; 1857), Vol. I, p. iii.

briand, *La dernière vestale*. He then entered a Catholic seminary and was ordained in Rome in 1845. The same year, he was given a professorship in Quebec to teach ecclesiastic history and to write a life of Monsignor Laval, the first bishop of Quebec. Within another year he was transferred to Boston, and there he renewed his interest in American Indians. He took up English and buried himself in Prescott's *Conquest of Mexico*. "This delightful and instructive work," he later confessed, sealed his lifelong dedication to things American.

Panoramic view of Palenque, a Maya temple city famed for its wealth of hieroglyphic inscriptions

Back from his first stay in the New World, Brasseur devoted himself for two years to the study of American antiquities in the Vatican libraries. There he absorbed Kingsborough's "great work," and immersed himself in the Vaticanus and the Borgia codices, already familiar to him from references in Humboldt's book. During his studies he conceived a longing to return to America and to visit the sites of the hemisphere's greatest cultural flowering. As Rome went through the turmoils of civil war and nationalist risings, the Abbé found the moment ripe to escape to what he hoped would be more peaceful lands, and in 1848, a year of revolutions in Europe, he crossed the Atlantic once more. Leaving the east coast of the United States, he traveled down the Ohio and the Mississippi. In New Orleans he took a ship to Vera Cruz. Aboard he had the good fortune to make the acquaintance of the French minister to Mexico, whose interest was awakened by the Abbé's enthusiasm. When they arrived in Mexico City, the minister secured him the office of almoner of the French legation, a sinecure which permitted the Abbé to pursue his studies of aboriginal civilizations freely.

Brasseur's American education could at last be continued on native soil. Because of his position and his natural affability, his labors were greatly eased. He befriended the director of the national museum, Don Rafael Isidoro Gondra, and was introduced by him to the rare copies of early colonial authors, among them a manuscript containing a part of a seventeenth-century translation from a native Quiché (Guatemalan) religious-historical work which was virtually unknown. The Abbé began to collect old documents relating to pre-Columbian antiquity. The first he acquired was an incomplete Spanish version of a *Historia Tolteca* which had once belonged to Boturini. Through the good services of the Mexican foreign secretary he also gained access to the viceregal archives, and he virtually haunted the neglected libraries of church-affiliated institutions. From time to time, he traveled into the interior. He visited Tula, "celebrated as a metropolis in the antique annals," and ventured north into California as far as San Francisco. His collection of native materials was growing and so was his knowledge of Mexico before the Conquest. In order to read original accounts, he took up the study of Nahuatl, the ancient language of the Aztecs and their neighbors. His teacher was Don Faustino Chimalpopoca Galicia, a professor of law at the College of San Gregorio, who claimed to be a direct descendant of Montezuma's brother. Brasseur "de Bourbourg" could hardly doubt the title.

The Abbé then extended his search to the San Gregorio library, where he made his first capital find: an old manuscript in Nahuatl dating from after the Conquest. Brasseur, who liked to concoct fanciful names, called it Codex Chimalpopoca in honor of his teacher and mentor. The codex (now also called Annals of Cuauhtitlan) is one of our prime sources for the pre-Columbian history of the kingdom of the valley of Mexico. Written by an anonymous author and probably based on ancient picture scrolls, it throws light on Toltecs, Chichimecs, and Aztecs. Its record reaches back several centuries before the ascendancy of the Aztecs, and centers largely on Culhuacán, once an important city-state and political power.[4]

Shortly thereafter, in 1851, Brasseur rushed into print with four *Lettres pour servir d'instruction à l'histoire des anciens nations civilisées du Mexique*. He had them published in Mexico City in both Spanish and French. These jottings were more a chart

---

[4] George C. Vaillant: *The Aztecs of Mexico* (Harmondsworth: Penguin Books; 1960), p. 84.

of the tentative progress he had made in his own learning than a mature summary of the subject, and they betrayed his unbridled and not always wise enthusiasm. The failings in scholarship which grew more pronounced in later years were already evident, for example in a penchant for etymological derivations that prove almost any ethnic or linguistic relationship, and in a dogmatic preoccupation with tracing American-Indian civilization to outside sources. At this stage he was certain of its origin in ancient Oriental cultures. Later he propounded a Scandinavian origin, first having considered a Phoenician, Hindu, Arab, and antediluvian Atlantean ancestry, and a host of others. To the bafflement of his contemporaries, he would change his views with dizzy speed or would hold several simultaneously. At one time he seriously considered whether the Egyptians might not have received their civilization from Central America rather than the other way around.

Etymology, so often the last refuge of pretentious but superficial scholarship, remained one of his chief weapons throughout his career. Shortly before his death, when he had an inkling of his errors, he still insisted that "of 15,000 words in the Maya vocabulary, at least seven thousand exhibit a striking resemblance to the language of Homer."[5] He found Germanic word roots everywhere. *Nawal*, meaning "intelligent" in one of the Mexican dialects, he derived in all earnestness from the English *know all*. *Calar*, to make manifest, is of course—*solis luce clarius*—the same as *clear* in English, or *klar* in German. The ancient center of Mexican traditions, Tula, is none other than the legendary *ultima Thule* of European geographers. Such notions were enough to startle any responsible philologist.[6]

No matter how jejune some of the views in his first effort of 1851, the work proved his serious absorption in Mexican antiquities and entitled him to a place among the small band of pre-Columbian students. It served as an introduction to Ephraim George Squier in New York, the American archaeologist, who was making significant contributions to our knowledge of Indian prehistory in the United States and Nicaragua. Back in France, Brasseur met J. M. A. Aubin, then the leading interpreter of Mexican picture books. Originally a physicist, Aubin had come to Mexico

---

[5] Brasseur: *Bibliothèque Mexico-Guatémalienne* (Paris: Maison Neuve; 1871), p. xxiii.
[6] Daniel G. Brinton: "The Abbé Brasseur de Bourbourg and His Labors," *Lippincott's*, Vol. I, No. 1 (January 1868), p. 81.

in 1830 with Arago's scientific expedition, but, having lost the instruments necessary to carry out physical observations, he turned to ancient documents and managed to find some of Boturini's codices, which Humboldt had considered lost.

From 1851 to 1853 Brasseur stayed in Europe. He then spent some time at the Vatican libraries, and issued his two-volume *History of Canada,* for which he had done research during his first stay at Quebec. The work was anything but well received. In Paris he had to earn his living writing popular tales and novels, some of them under the Gothic-sounding name of Étienne-Charles de Ravensberg. His historical novel, *Le Khalife de Bagdad,* a colorful Oriental romance of the eleventh century, fared well with the critics but was soon forgotten. The financial rewards were disappointing. His thoughts were on the countries across the Atlantic, but he lacked the means to carry out the extensive exploration he had planned—nothing less than to trace the lost civilization of Guatemala and Yucatán, and to gather ancient records from which its history could be reconstructed. Throwing caution to the wind, however, he sailed in the fall of 1854 to New York, arriving penniless.To pay for his passage to Central America, he sold some of his precious manuscripts.

When he landed in Greytown, the Caribbean port of Nicaragua, he found the town in shambles from a recent bombardment by an American cruiser. Under the circumstances, foreign visitors were not exactly welcome. A few days later, on the road to the interior, Brasseur and his companions were stopped at gunpoint by a detachment of uniformed men, who took them prisoners. Protests against this violation of international law were of no avail. In vain, Brasseur flaunted his passport, signed by the minister of Nicaragua at Washington. He was moved to a nearby hacienda, and there the commanding officer showed him a letter from the president of the republic ordering the arrest of any foreigners who passed through the Camino Real. They were to be sent to the capital or, in case of the slightest resistance, to be summarily shot. However, after the officer's temper had cooled and he had persuaded himself of the harmlessness of the French Abbé, he allowed the party to proceed.

On February 1, 1855, Brasseur entered Guatemala. This country, too, had suffered periods of unrest. Brasseur was chagrined to learn that religious and political upheavals had led to the dispersal, if not the destruction, of manuscript collections housed for centuries in the now disbanded Catholic monasteries. A number of pieces had weathered the storm, however, and some had been taken to the library of San Carlos University. Would these documents throw light on aboriginal Guatemala-Yucatán, whose prominent, if not decisive, part in the cultural evolution of the hemisphere the Abbé had long suspected?

Unlike most students of antiquities, Brasseur was never unduly tormented by doubts—neither about the existence of lost documents with which to reconstruct a civilization, regardless of how utterly it had vanished; nor about his own capacity to locate this evidence where others had not succeeded. He was equally confident that ancient records, once found, would answer almost any question put to them. The epistemological ambiguity of his "loaded" interrogations escaped him—a strange failing in a man who was described by his contemporaries as a worldly skeptic who took his ecclesiastic commitments lightly.[7]

In Guatemala, Brasseur met with good will everywhere. A local collector, Mariano Padilla, bestowed on him a manuscript in one of the Maya dialects, which he generously renamed the Codex Padilla. Brasseur found support in it for his Scandinavian doctrine. Within a few months, he made a vastly more important acquisition, the so-called *Popol Vuh*, a superb work of aboriginal Indian literature, which has been compared to the *Rig-Veda* and the *Edda*. There was some question at the time whether Brasseur was the actual "discoverer" of the work, which he acquired from the library of San Carlos University at Guatemala City through the good services of a "young and zealous Guatemalan archaeologist, Don Juan Gavarrete, one of the notaries of the ecclesiastical court."[8] In a sense it did not need a discoverer.[9]

That it had survived at all was almost miraculous. It was itself a copy in the Quiché language, to which was added a translation made around 1700 by a Spanish Dominican monk, Father Francisco Ximénez. Curiously, in Central America the Dominicans were much more tolerant than the Franciscans, and Father Ximénez conceived a genuine interest in native traditions and records, of which he compiled several volumes. While he was serving as parish priest in the village of Santo Tomás Chichicastenango, he heard of a sacred book kept hidden by the Indians.

[7] Herbert B. Adams: "The Abbé de Bourbourg," *American Antiquarian Society. Proceedings*, Vol. VII (April 1891), p. 283.

[8] Adrián Recinos, ed.: *Popol Vuh. The Sacred Book of the Ancient Quiché Maya* (Norman, Okla.: University of Oklahoma Press; 1950), p. 42.

[9] Nicolaus Trübner: "Central American Archaeology," *Athenaeum*, No. 1492 (May 31, 1856), p. 683.

Eventually he was able to borrow it for copying. It turned out to be a transcription in the Roman alphabet, which Ximénez thought must have been made soon after Pedro de Alvarado had invaded Guatemala. Moreover, it probably had not been copied directly but had been compiled from memory. It stated that it was based on a more ancient lost version ("its sight is hidden to the searcher and the thinker"[1]), the *Popol Vuh* proper, which was "painted" before the Conquest. The alphabetic version in turn was later lost, and only the copy made by Ximénez remains.

Opening lines of Father Ximénez's manuscript of the *Popol Vuh*, with his translation into Spanish. The manuscript was acquired by the Abbé Brasseur in Guatemala City and is now at the Newberry Library of Chicago.

Brasseur, on his previous visit to Mexico City, had seen a section of the Ximénez translation of the *Popol Vuh* incorporated in another colonial compendium. In his *Letters* of 1851 Brasseur expressed concern over the possible loss of the *Popol Vuh,* which, as he knew, had been familiar in its entirety to Félix Cabrera, a Mexican scholar, in the late eighteenth century. An Austrian traveler, Carl Scherzer of Vienna, was, it seems, alerted by Brasseur's reference and decided to look for the work. The trail led him in 1854 to Guatemala City, where he saw the manuscript at the university library. It had been transferred there in 1830 from the convent of Chichicastenango. Scherzer thus preceded Brasseur by nearly a year, though the Abbé could claim priority because of the excerpt he had seen in Mexico City. In any case, it was Brasseur who was fully cognizant of the uniqueness of the sacred book of the ancient Quichés, a Guatemalan people of Maya speech. Brasseur translated it and took along the Ximénez transcript, which had been moldering in Guatemala City. From his estate it eventually reached the Newberry Library in Chicago.

The *Popol Vuh* ("Book of the Community")—the name given to it by Brasseur, though it is occasionally disputed—is a kind of

---

[1] Recinos: op. cit., p. 80.

national scripture, like those possessed by a number of peoples around the world. In this way it is related to the *Nihongi* of the Japanese, and even to the Pentateuch, and presents a rich kaleidoscope of legends, migration traditions, folklore, religious beliefs, theology, prayers to the gods, and history. It combines cosmogony with the sagas of culture heroes and with the authentic annals of the Quiché people (until A.D. 1550), and throws light on many facets of the pre-Columbian civilizations of Middle America. It is a primary source for both Maya and Mexican myths and divinities. The work is divided into four parts, the first of which gives an imaginative rendering of creation: "There was not yet a single man, not an animal. . . . Like a fog, like a cloud, was its formation: like huge fishes rise in the water, so rose the mountains; and in a moment the high mountains existed."[2] Included are accounts of cyclical destructions of the universe, and of the gods' various experimentations with the human form (monkeys are one such stage). A chronology emerges in the later parts of the book, with references to actual persons and to the alien rule of the Toltecs from the Mexican plateau, and the record is brought down to the Spanish Conquest. In addition to this priceless repertory of anthropological, religious, and historical data, the *Popul Vuh* impresses the modern reader by the eloquent tenor of its faith. Considering the date of its writing, there is little likelihood that any but minor Christian influences could have gone into it. Authorities generally agree that the diction, imagery, and ideas are wholly aboriginal. The *Popol Vuh has* restored the stature of the American Indian and silenced ignorant talk of the innate savagery of the people of the Western Hemisphere. Thenceforth, it was possible to discuss the mythology, institutions, and moral teachings of the ancient inhabitants of Central America.

Sylvanus G. Morley, the prominent American Maya scholar and co-translator of the first complete English version of the sacred book of the Quiché (it had to wait until 1950) has praised "the elegance of the language and literary style of the *Popol Vuh,* the lofty philosophy it expresses, coupled with the rich and varied life it reveals." He goes on to say that such high caliber only helps to emphasize "the magnitude of the losses we have suffered in the almost complete annihilation of Quiché learning brought about through the Spanish Conquest."[3] Indeed, there must have existed

---

[2] Brinton: "The Abbé Brasseur . . . , pp. 82–3.
[3] Sylvanus Griswold Morley: *The Ancient Maya* (Stanford: Stanford University Press; 1946), p. 304.

an extensive literature, not only of the Quichés, but of all the other Maya people. And a great deal might well have survived the Spanish furor, only to fall by the wayside in later days of indifference and intolerance. Ironically, the anticlericalism of the nineteenth century was also harmful to what remained of the native religions.

Some of the Spanish priests in Mexico and the lands of the Maya had encouraged their wards to write down the ancient traditions and legends in their native tongues, using the Latin alphabet. The Mayas responded avidly, as if obeying a deeply ingrained impulse of their own to keep written records. The alphabetic texts they produced were probably close approximations of the ancient codices. Almost every Maya town in Yucatán came to have its own book of Chilam Balam ("Jaguar Priest"), like the *Popol Vuh* a kind of chronicle mixed with religious and legendary matters, and greatly revered. Some were begun almost immediately after the Conquest, when, as one book puts it, strangers roamed about like "strutting turkey cocks." Another recalled the days before the coming of the Spaniards, when "there was no robbery by violence, there was no greed and striking down one's fellow man in his blood, at the cost of the poor man, at the expense of the food of each and everyone." Afterward "it was the beginning of tribute, the beginning of church dues, the beginning of strife with purse snatching, the beginning of strife with guns, the beginning of strife by trampling people, the beginning of robbery with violence, the beginning of debts enforced by false testimony, the beginning of individual strife, a beginning of vexation."[4]

Unfortunately, most of the books of Chilam Balam, some of which were moved to the public library of Mérida (Yucatán) early in the twentieth century, are considered lost today. Several are said to have turned up in Boston, where they were auctioned off.[5] John Lloyd Stephens appended one to the second volume of his *Incidents of Travel in Yucatan* (1843). Several related works vanished during the revolutions that beset Central America and Mexico after the liberation from Spanish rule in the first half of the nineteenth century. Luckily, the *Popol Vuh* survived. Many other manuscripts which were not transferred to the university and ecclesiastic libraries of the Guatemalan capital were destroyed, but even the materials stored in Guatemala City did not fare too well.

---

[4] J. Eric S. Thompson: *The Rise and Fall of Maya Civilization* (Norman, Okla.: University of Oklahoma Press; 1954), p. 134.
[5] Peterson: op. cit., p. 242.

They were described at the time of Brasseur's visit as "in a wretched condition; nobody cares for them; and it is to be feared that fifty years hence they will have utterly perished."[6] How else would a foreign visitor like Brasseur have been permitted to carry off the *Popol Vuh* manuscript, which one would expect to be guarded as a national treasure?

Brasseur recovered other valuable texts in Guatemala, among them the *Annals of Cakchiquels* or, as he called it, the *Memorial of Texpán-Atitlán*. It had evidently been composed in the colonial period but, like the *Popol Vuh*, it contains many references to earlier times. It deals mainly with the history of the Cakchiquels, a Maya people closely related to the Quiché. The narrative was begun by a member of the ruling Cakch family, one of whose descendants brought it down to 1604. Its climax is a description of the Spanish invasion and Alvarado's atrocities. The *Annals of Cakchiquels* is second in importance only to the *Popol Vuh*,[7] which it parallels to some degree. Although it lacks the mythological richness and poetic loftiness of that work, it contains more historical information. Unlike the *Popol Vuh*, none of it had ever been made known to the world.

Brasseur learned of the book through Juan Gavarrete. Some ten years earlier, in 1844, Gavarrete had been commissioned by the archbishop of Guatemala City, Francisco García Pelaez, to reorganize the archives of the monastery of San Francisco. In the course of these labors he had noticed a manuscript of forty-eight folded leaves, written in a native tongue, and in a Spanish hand of about the sixteenth century. Gavarrete had the document examined by various persons, but no one managed to produce a satisfactory translation. Then in 1855 Brasseur set to work on it himself. In Gavarrete's own words, Brasseur, "having had in his hands the manuscript in question, devoted himself to its translation, using the knowledge he already possessed of the Mexican language and the primitive traditions of the peoples of this continent, and utilizing in addition the ancient dictionaries of the Quiché and Cakchiquel tongues . . . succeeded in completing the work of translating it from the Cakchiquel into French. . . ."[8] In 1873 Gavarrete issued a Spanish translation based on Brasseur's French version. Brasseur in turn appropriated the original text "with the

---

[6] Trübner: op. cit., p. 683.
[7] Recinos and Delia Goetz, eds.: *The Annals of Cakchiquels* (Norman, Okla.: University of Oklahoma Press; 1953), p. vii.
[8] Ibid., p. 7.

same facility with which he acquired other similar documents."⁹
After Brasseur's death, it was bought from a subsequent owner by
Daniel G. Brinton, a North American scholar, who made the first
English-language translation and donated the original to the Uni-
versity of Pennsylvania. The Guatemalans appear not to have
questioned the removal of this manuscript, or of the *Popol Vuh.*

Brasseur enjoyed the friendship of the archbishop of Guatemala, Monsignor Pelaez, who was sympathetic to his archaeological efforts and may have spread a protective mantle over his
fellow cleric's acquisitions. The archbishop appointed him ecclesiastic administrator of the parish of Rabinal, a large community
in Quiché-speaking territory. Brasseur was never happier. At Rabinal he spent more than a year among pure-bred Indians and
spoke nothing but Quiché with them and learned to write the language. In this congenial environment he labored over the translation of his newly acquired manuscripts. He delighted in the
scenery of the lush valley, with its banana plantations and cane
fields, and the fragrant orange trees, whose branches shaded the
tumuli in which ancient chiefs were buried. Over his parish
towered a Moorish-style church, "larger than a cathedral,"¹ which
the Dominican missionaries had built. From Rabinal he sallied
into the tropical wilderness along the Usumacinta River and discovered several ruined cities buried in the jungle.

Before his return to Europe, he made still another literary
recovery, a rather unusual one inasmuch as it did not involve a
moldering manuscript. He owed it to his intimacy with the Indians.
"I gained their confidence," he wrote, "by talking to them about
their past. By and by the interest I had shown them led them to
relate to me their traditions. In this manner I obtained the wonderful stories of their king Qikab the Enchanter, the Carbuncle of the
Black Mountains, the heroic deeds of the wars of Rabinal against
the Pokomans and the princes of the Quiché, and at last the
famous spoken ballet *Xahoh-Tun,* which one of their old men
dictated to me for twelve days from beginning to end in the
Quiché tongue."² The "ballet" was in fact a historical drama, dating
back perhaps to the twelfth century, whence it had been passed
down orally like the Greek sagas of Homer. It showed not the
slightest European influence. With the exception of the Peruvian
drama of *Ollanta* or *Ollantay* (whose antiquity is doubtful) and

---

⁹ Ibid., p. 7.
¹ Brasseur: *Histoire des Nations.* . . . Vol. I, p. xxvii.
² Ibid., xxviii.

one or two minor pieces, it is the only example of its genre to come down from pre-Columbian America. The text, which Brasseur transcribed under the title *The Hero of Rabinal,* is complete. Moreover, when the natives saw Brasseur's delight, they were so pleased that they staged a special performance of the drama in ancient costumes. This gave the Abbé a chance to jot down stage directions and note the accompanying music.

With his collection enriched by so many valuable additions, Brasseur returned to Europe in 1856 and embarked on the magnum opus of his career, his *Histoire des Nations Civilisées du Mexique et de l'Amérique-Centrale, durant les siècles antérieurs à Christophe Colomb.* . . . The four-volume work began to appear in 1856 and was completed in 1859. It made almost exclusive use of original native and Spanish documents pertaining to pre-Conquest times, many of which had been gathered by Brasseur himself. Probably no one before had had sufficient material and knowledge to undertake a consecutive account of pre-Columbian America. Indeed, few had thought that such a work was possible. It was the first of its kind and greatly expanded our knowledge of Mexico before the coming of Cortés.

For once nobody could question Brasseur's competence. Wisely, he had abstained throughout from drawing any comparisons between the peoples of the Old and the New World. There were bound to be flaws. As to be expected, his bibliographic research was superior to his interpretation. And he had not overcome his tendency to take all mythological references as clues to actual events. H. H. Bancroft, the American historian, who years later was to cover more or less the same ground, said that Brasseur "rejects nothing, and transforms everything into historic fact."[3] In this respect he was like Heinrich Schliemann. But Schliemann worked a narrower, less risky field, in which the results of his explorations dwarfed his naïve motivations and interpretations.

In addition to his *History,* Brasseur issued a series of great value, the *Collection de documents dans les langues indigènes par servir à l'étude de l'histoire et de la philologie de l'Amérique ancienne,* between 1861 and 1864. Libraries and institutions everywhere now felt honored to play host to him, and the French government assisted him in his research. Spanish archivists, noted for the jealousness with which they guarded their possessions, invited him to examine their resources. Yet it was, quite naturally, on

---

[3] Quoted by Winsor: op. cit., Vol. I, p. 171.

American soil that Brasseur continued to search for a solution to the enigmas of Central American civilization. After his first visit to Mexico, his studies were concentrated more and more on the ancient people who inhabited the lands beyond the Isthmus of Tehuantepec, mainly in the states of Yucatán and Chiapas in Mexico and the Petén region of northern Guatemala. There Stephens and Catherwood had visited some forty-four ruined temple cities, many abandoned long before the Spanish came. At the time, the aboriginal peoples of this vast area were not referred to as Maya, which was the name of only one of the many nations of kindred speech. In fact, the name as well as the concept of an all-embracing Maya civilization was unknown to Humboldt and Prescott. Brasseur was among the first to point out the kinship of the Central American peoples and to recognize their distinctiveness from the peoples of the Mexican plateau in the north. This made him "the real founder of Maya research"[4] as a separate discipline. He was greatly impressed by the similarity of the strange characters used in the Dresden Codex (the only one of its kind known until 1859) and the inscriptions on stairways, lintels, walls, murals, stelae, and vases of the buried cities of Central America. For some time he had been convinced that they represented not just pictograms but a phonetic script.[5] Now that he had recovered authentic remains of the literature of this ancient race, he inevitably returned to his dream of becoming the Champollion of the Americas and of recording the muffled voices of Palenque and Copán.

In 1859 and 1860 Brasseur roamed again over the tropical lands of Central America, visited the ruins, and gathered more rare manuscripts from colonial times. He was bewitched by the hieroglyphic inscriptions whose meaning had so far eluded everybody. Three years later, in 1863, he was in Madrid, where he made the most of the freedom granted to him to examine library collections and leaf through documents that nobody had beheld in centuries. One day, while fingering with his customary bibliographic zest through the manuscripts stored at the library of the Royal Academy of History, his eyes fell on a sixteenth-century manuscript written by Diego de Landa, who had been bishop of Yucatán. Today, to anyone the least familiar with Maya research the name of Landa has a magic, though dissonant, ring. Bras-

---

[4] William Gates: op. cit.
[5] Brinton: "The Abbé Brasseur and His Labors," p. 81.

seur's discovery of Landa's *relación de las Cosas de Yucatán* compares in importance with the finding of the Rosetta Stone, and the resemblance, as we shall see, is anything but superficial.

Who was Diego de Landa, who rose to such posthumous fame as *historiador primordial* of Yucatán?[6]

"Tablet of the Slaves," a glyph-covered slab from Palenque, drawn by Miguel Covarrubias

In 1549, some eight years after Montejo the Younger (II) had finally succeeded in conquering most of Yucatán and had begun a permanent settlement at Mérida, a boatload of Franciscan monks landed at the coast. Among them was a young man of twenty-five, of noble lineage, Diego de Landa, who at the age of sixteen

---

[6] Tozzer, ed.: *Landa's Relación de las Cosas de Yucatán*, Papers of the Peabody Museum of American Archaeology and Ethnology, Vol. XVIII (1941), p. 44 ff.

had joined the Franciscan order in Toledo. In Yucatán he entered the monastery of Izamal as an ordinary friar.

Already then the Franciscans were a power in the new country, at constant odds with the Spanish governors and settlers who confiscated the land of free Indians and reduced the natives to little better than indentured serfs. The Franciscans pursued a policy of their own which was almost as ruthless. It meant, as has been said by a contemporary, the turning of the entire country into a great monastery.[7] For that purpose Indians were uprooted and native villages were left to decay, while their inhabitants were made wards of the friars in their monastic manors. Monks and lay people—both posing as "protectors" of the natives —accused each other of inhumanity toward the Indians, and both, no doubt, had a good case. Given these conditions and conflicts, a man of young Landa's caliber was certain to make headway. Whether because of his abilities or because of his fanatic zeal, or both, his rise in the order was rapid. Within twelve years he was head of the order in Yucatán.

He had one consuming ambition: to stamp out all vestiges of pagan rites and religion. On his initiative, native shrines and idols were destroyed mercilessly, and recalcitrant or lapsed converts were harshly punished. Landa's fervor had been forged in the white heat of the Spanish Inquisition, and he pursued idolators with Christian hellfire. His career came to a head with the famous incident at Maní, when someone discovered indelible signs of pagan worship and sacrifice at a nearby cave. Landa responded with the mass imprisonment of native notables and had thousands tortured, including women. Several died while their tormentors tried to make them confess to their alleged transgressions; others were maimed for life. At last, on July 12, 1562, he staged the auto-da-fé of Maní, at which Mayans of the old faith were burnt, together with some five thousand idols and the priceless native picture books that had been sedulously rounded up by the inquisitors. Of the books Landa himself said: "These people also made use of certain characters or letters, with which they wrote in their books their ancient affairs and their sciences, and with these and drawings and with certain signs in these drawings, they understood their affairs and made others understand them and taught them. We found a great number of books in these characters, and,

---

[7] Gates, ed.: *Yucatan before and after the Conquest, by Friar Diego de Landa . . .* , Maya Society Publications, No. 20 (Baltimore, 1937), p. v.

as they contained nothing in which there was not to be seen superstition and lies of the devil, we burned them all, which they regretted to an amazing degree and caused them affliction."[8]

Landa's book burning has come down to us as a great catastrophe in the history of Mayan culture. Had it not been for his bonfire, it is maintained, a knowledge of the Maya script, and of their literature, history, and science—all believed to have been dealt with in the scrolls—would have survived. This is perhaps an overstatement, as Landa threw into the flames only twenty-seven codices. Moreover, a collection of Maya manuscripts was reported to exist as late as 1697, in the possession of an isolated tribe of the Itzá, who had retreated to Tayasal, an island of Lake Petén in northern Guatemala. And these people, it is said, had the ability to read and write the ancient script.

Nevertheless, Landa's fanaticism was responsible for an ignoble act of destruction, and may have set an evil example for others. Several religious leaders of Landa's time deplored his intolerant fervor. José de Acosta, who wrote a history of the Indies in 1590, declared that after the Maní book burning "not only the Indians but many eager-minded Spaniards who desired to know the secrets of the land felt badly. . . . This follows from a stupid zeal. . . ."[9] In addition, Francisco Toral, the bishop of Yucatán, who had been absent at the time of the Maní outrage, was in total disagreement with Landa's practices. When he returned to his diocese from Mexico City, he released the prisoners taken by Landa in his crusade, and ordered a thorough investigation. Persuaded of Landa's injustices and unlawful usurpation of authority, he referred the case to the Council of the Indies in Spain. In a letter to the king, he said of Landa and his Franciscan helpmates that they were men of "pocas letras y menos caridad" (little learning and even less charity).

Landa was forced to go to Spain, where he was taken into custody and reprimanded by the Council. However, a few years later, the case was decided in his favor on the ground that, according to a Papal bull of 1535, he had been in his full rights to assume judicial power in the absence of his bishop. It was a triumph for Landa. Not only was he completely exonerated, but he was sent back to the New World as Bishop of Yucatán in 1573.

The new bishop had apparently not been shaken by his ex-

---

[8] Morley: op. cit., p. 295.
[9] Tozzer: *Landa's Relación de las Cosas de Yucatán*, p. 77.

perience and continued on his course of repression. Indians repeatedly appealed over his head to the government of New Spain, but met with only slight success. A measure of relief came only with Landa's death, in 1579. Students of Spanish colonial history still discuss whether the man was a pathological zealot or a dedicated soldier of Christ and a true friend of the Indians. As a mark of sophistication, they will usually settle on the golden middle: he was a little of both.

Modern-day Americanists are faced with the paradox that the brutal, bigoted destroyer of Mayas, their idols, and their books is also our principal source for information on all facets of the vanished Maya civilization. Such a double role is probably without precedent in all history. Compared to him, Julius Caesar, the butcher of the Gauls, was an indifferent recorder of the mores of his transalpine victims.

There was actually no contradiction in Landa's double role. It is almost certain that he wrote his *Relación* in 1566 in Spain while preparing his defense. What better way to justify his harsh ways in stamping out idolatry? Apart from the legal technicalities, he could buttress his position most effectively through an unimpassioned description of the "revolting" habits and rituals of the Indians. The facts were to speak for themselves. Who could then doubt that he had waged a holy crusade against the devil himself and his obstinate disciples?

In the course of this undertaking, Landa wrote what is nearly a treatise on social and cultural anthropology. In the manner of a practiced modern researcher, he had obtained the material by direct observation and in-person questioning of the natives in Yucatán. A principal source were Indian nobles such as Nachi Cocom, whose bones Landa later exhumed and scattered on the mere suspicion that he might have remained true to the faith of his fathers. In all likelihood, Landa would never have written the *Relación* had he not found in Spain the need and leisure to do so. The work is thus, by a trick of fate, a direct outcome of the Maní outrage and of Bishop Toral's intervention.

To paraphrase George Bernard Shaw, the way to the kingdom of knowledge is on occasion paved with bad intentions and anything but sweet reasonableness. No matter how hard he tried to obliterate native culture, Landa the book burner and inquisitor has become its preserver. His *Relación*, which has come down to us in a later, incomplete transcript, is by far the best colonial account of ancient Yucatán, worthy to stand with the work of

Sahagún on the valley of Mexico. Like the latter, it is extraordinarily rich in details of folklore, religion, rites and ceremonies, history, customs, and daily life. It was a reading of Landa that led E. H. Thompson to dredge the Chichen Itzá *cenote* for votive treasures. Indeed, Landa leaves no doubt that the Indians whose souls he tried so diligently to save were the builders of magnificent cities that even then had already been swallowed up by the jungle. It is through Landa that we gain an insight into events in Yucatán after the fall of the Old Empire (about A.D. 900).

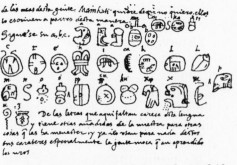

Landa's "Maya Alphabet." From the Madrid manuscript of the Spanish bishop's *Relación de las Cosas de Yucatán*

Some eight different editions in various languages have been published of the *Relación* since its discovery. And it has been claimed that in the long run we owe almost all our knowledge of the Mayans to Brasseur's discovery in Madrid.[1] The *Relación* has become the fountainhead of all serious study of the Mayas.

As a key to the Maya inscriptions, the *Relación* is only partly successful. Landa, to be sure, devoted considerable space to the native script, but his explanations are not very clear or intelligible and have given rise to nearly as much speculation over what he could have meant as the hierogylphs themselves. Landa gives a complete list of twenty-nine characters of what he calls an alphabet, with corresponding Spanish vocal values. It has never been settled whether he intended this to be a European phonetic notation for the Maya language, or whether he was taken in by his native informants. One scholar declared outright that the list of alphabetic letters was a "Spanish fabrication."[2] Despite Landa's

---

[1] Gates: *Yucatan*, p. iii.

[2] Philip J. J. Valentini: "Landa's Alphabet a Spanish Fabrication," *American Antiquarian Society. Proceedings*, No. 75 (April 1880), pp. 59–91.

obscurity, however, he seems to have been convinced that the natives were capable of writing word elements phonetically, though we do not know to what degree. This vagueness renders Landa's alphabet almost entirely useless. The discussion of the real nature of the script has continued to this day. Confident announcements of a final solution have been made from time to time, and several would-be Champollions have insisted that it was truly phonetic. But if such were the case, it has been argued, it is highly improbable that the understanding of a script in a known idiom could have been delayed for so long. Indications point rather to a mixture of ideogrammatic and phonetic elements, with a residue of pictographic signs and further complicated by the use of determinants.

It is nevertheless thanks to Landa that today about one third of all hieroglyphs can be read. Aware of the focal position the calendar and astronomical computations had in Maya religious and civil life, Landa devoted much space to this topic, though he only dimly realized its intricacy. He sketched with great care the symbols for the days and months of the sacred (260-day) calendar, or *tzolkin*, and, partly due to his efforts, each of these ideograms, identified with individual godheads, can now be read. By ingenious deductions, a number of scholars from many lands advanced suggestions for a full decipherment of all the symbols connected with the calendar. Brasseur himself was the first to disentangle the dot and bar system used in mathematical notation. After that, analogous pictographic symbols could be determined. Ernst Förstemann, a librarian of Dresden, took a decisive step when he wrested from the Dresden Codex the secret of the Maya time counts and interlocking cycles, including a calendar of Venus. Independently, an American newspaperman, J. T. Goodman, famed as Mark Twain's erstwhile boss on the *Virginia City Enterprise,* worked out the principles of Maya dating (particularly the "Initial Series," so-called because they appear at the start of inscriptions) from reproductions of the stelae and other monuments and objects.

At last it dawned on the world that the Mayas had perfected astronomy, and especially planetary observations, to a remarkable degree. For instance, they had determined the length of the solar year with greater precision than is evident in the Gregorian calendar, which was adopted by Spain after the death of Landa. They knew more about the revolution of the heavenly bodies than was known in the ancient Near East. In their chronological system they could fix exact dates within the range of 374,400 years. In addition to the Venus year, which had its particular religious significance, the Mayas had devised four different calendars. These were used side by side and could be coordinated. Through insights of this nature, scholars increased their respect for the scientific abilities of this ancient people. More important, modern-day man now had a glimpse of Maya philosophy, which was concerned with astrology and divination and, to an obsessive degree, with time, the burden it places on man, its cyclical nature, and its enormity. When most educated Europeans believed that the world was no older than some 5,000 years, the Mayas conceived of periods of time within the range of hundred millions of years, but for them a concern with time was not a tyranny of time. Past and future were in a way indistinct. This world would come to an end, but it would have a new beginning.

Maya glyphs for the twenty days of their eighteen-month year

Maya dates, no matter how precise, had to be correlated with the Gregorian calendar to be meaningful—a problem that is only now being solved. A relationship was worked out between Mayan dates and the data on pre-Columbian events given by Landa, and on this basis, scholars were able to outline periods of Mayan history: the flourishing of cities, the arrival of Toltec invaders, and the decline and fall of the Old Empire, or the classical age.

As the dates on various artifacts were read, the temporal horizons of Middle America were pushed further back. The celebrated jade Leyden Plate found in Guatemala at Puerto Barrios near the Atlantic coast in 1864, but probably originating in Tikal, gave a Mayan date of A.D. 320. Then at Tikal's sister city, Uaxactún, also in the Petén lowlands of northern Guatemala, where classical Mayan civilization reached its apogee, Sylvanus G. Morley, a leading American authority, found in 1916 a stela (Stela 9) that had what was for long considered the oldest date on any Maya monument, calculated as April 9, 328. After 1958, when the University Museum of Philadelphia launched its large-scale expeditions at Tikal, still earlier dates were obtained.

The broken slab of Tres Zapotes (La Venta culture) in the state of Vera Cruz. It shows a jaguar mask on one side and a date column, believed to be 31 B.C., on the other. Drawn by Miguel Covarrubias

Landa's key to Mayan chronology eventually was to lead to greater knowledge of other areas, just as the Assyrian archives helped us to discover the lost Sumerians. There was, for instance, the quaint Tuxtla statuette—a tiny duck-billed jadite figure that looked curiously like a Chinese sage—some of whose inscribed marks could now be read. It carried a date which, in the generally accepted Goodman-[Martínez] Hernández-Thompson (GMT) scale, was worked out as A.D. 162, more than a century and a half earlier than that of the Leyden Plate. Moreover, it did not come from traditional Maya territory, but from the Vera Cruz area, far to the northwest. Later the antiquity of this date was exceeded by a date on a broken stone slab discovered at Tres Zapotes, a site of the La Venta culture in the lowlands along the Gulf of Mexico, also outside the Maya area. It was 31 B.C., hailed as the earliest date recorded in America. (However, excavations in the 1960's at Chiapa de Chorzo in central Chiapas appear to have produced dates of a yet greater age.)

The La Venta discovery was a clear indication that the Mayan chronology was in use considerably earlier by another people, a mysterious race now usually called Olmecs, or "Rubber People." Were they perhaps the cultural innovators of Middle America, the Sumerians of the New World? Did they create the script which the Mayas then carved into their monuments all over the Yucatán peninsula? Did they also have books? Would the Olmecs one day help us to solve the riddle of "Mayan" writing? Or were the Olmecs in turn, just like the Zapotecs, the Totonacs (Tajín), the builders of Teotihuacán, and the Mayas themselves, benefactors of still another race, unknown to us, which bequeathed its legacy to all of Middle America? Only future archaeological spadework can tell. Meanwhile there is little doubt that, no matter what their origins, these New World cultures had reached their finest fruition among the Mayas.

Thus far we have considered a few of the results of Brasseur's recovery of Landa's work. It is time to get back to the Abbé himself, who was fully aware of the significance of his lucky find at Madrid. But, as was his habit, he read more into it than was warranted. His edition of the book carried the ponderous subtitle: "S'il existe des sources de l'histoire primitive du Mexique dans les monuments égyptiens, et de l'histoire primitive de l'Ancien Monde dans les monuments américains?" As to Landa's alphabet, Brasseur never had any doubt that it was an alphabet in the true sense. In the preface to his edition (unfortunately further truncated), which included a French translation, Brasseur announced categorically that it was the key to the inscriptions.

The Abbé's work was now deservedly gaining greater attention. Recognition as France's leading *américaniste* came to him in 1864, after the publication of the Landa book. He was named a member of the Commission Scientifique du Mexique, which Napoleon III, "le petit," emulating the equally ill-fated enterprise of his uncle in Egypt, had called into being as a cultural counterpart to his political venture. In Mexico, under the short-lived regime of Maximilian, Brasseur was offered the high office of General Superintendent of Museums and Libraries and Minister of Public Education, but he wisely declined. Ever since the revolutions of 1848, he had cultivated a healthy habit of shunning the political arena—and indeed what was now in the offing was no minor conflict. However, he traveled in Mexico on behalf of the

Commission and edited a volume on the country's ancient monuments, illustrated by the Count de Waldeck, who was still very active, though approaching a hundred years of age. His main concern was, as always, the hieroglyphics, which he yearned to read. For that purpose he revisited the Palenque ruins: here, somewhere among the inscriptions on the sculptured temples, must lie the solution. He examined the inscriptions on the walls again and again, and made various attempts to read them, but to no avail. Yet he was not discouraged.

Ironically, although he did not accomplish his purpose in Yucatán, when he returned to Mexico City and was not looking for anything in particular, he added, almost absentmindedly, to the stock of knowledge about the Mayas. He was rummaging through a second-hand bookstall and pulled out an old colonial manuscript, which he bought for four pesos. The manuscript turned out to be the only extant copy of a Maya-Spanish dictionary compiled by a Franciscan friar around 1580. Now generally known as the Motul Dictionary, in memory of the Yucatán friary where it was written, it has become an indispensable tool of Maya research and a prized possession of the John Carter Brown Library at Providence, Rhode Island. A modern-day Maya explorer, J. Eric S. Thompson, has called it "a mine of information on the Yucatan-Maya language and on the customs and practices of the Maya," whose preservation is "little short of a miracle." In his autobiography (1963) Thompson, who has been able to decipher some non-calendrical symbols on Maya inscriptions, tells how he kept his copy "in constant use as he tried to match hieroglyphs with Maya words."[3]

On his return from Maximilian's Mexico in 1865, Brasseur sailed to Cádiz and then made his way to Madrid. There he called at the library of the Royal Academy of History, the source of his greatest triumph. Conversation with a friend connected with that institution put him on the track of a curious manuscript then in the possession of a Madrid professor and palaeographer, Juan de Tro y Ortolano. Brasseur was given permission to examine the relic. A first glance bore out his fondest hopes: it was written in the same pebble-like shapes (*calculiform,* for "pebble," was the elegant term he contrived for the exotic script) as the inscriptions of the Central American ruins he had just visited and as

---

[3] Thompson: *The Rise and Fall of the Maya Civilization,* p. 35. Also *Maya Archaeologist* (London: R. Hale; 1963), p. 18.

Landa's sketches of Maya letters and calendrical symbols. The learned world had not the slightest inkling of its existence. It had to be named immediately, and Brasseur's baptismal talents rose to the challenge: he called it Troano, a contraction of the owner's Iberian compound appellation. And then he went to work on the decipherment. What he had sought in vain in America, he was confident would now be revealed to him.

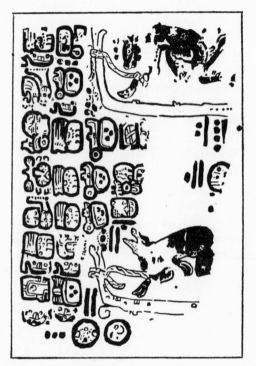

A section of the Codex Troano showing game caught in snares, Yucatán

He thought he recognized an account of one of the religious ceremonies described by Landa, and had the bright idea that it might contain a kind of farmer's almanac. But for two years he was unable to wrest any consecutive reading from the manuscript. At times he came to doubt whether the symbols were really phonetic and whether they were even in the Maya language. Yet, "by sheer dint of persistent labor," as he wrote, "of groping and comparisons of all kinds," he at last gained enlightenment. Deeper and deeper he penetrated into the mysteries of the bizarre characters, and gradually words, and full sentences, emerged. All doubts vanished. He was able to read the text from beginning to end. Upon his own admission, one of the reasons for his success was that he "had beforehand an idea of what it could contain." He had been "firmly convinced from the reading of Mexican texts and the documents published by Lord Kingsborough that it must have dealt with a cataclysm which tore the Old World from the New. . . . In short, a narrative of a catastrophe like the one Plato has left us on the destruction of Atlantis."[4] As to the manner of reading, he had no doubt the symbols had to be read from bottom to top and from right to left.

In 1869, the Abbé submitted to the world the fruits of his long labors. The two oversized volumes, including a colored facsimile of the Troano, had been liberally subsidized by the French Imperial government. They constituted the first installments of a projected series on the *Mission Scientifique au Mexique et dans l'Amérique Centrale*. The work contained the entire text of the Madrid codex in a more or less flawless French, but to any reader, except for Brasseur himself, it still sounded like abracadabra. One may consider just the opening lines of the translation, called by Brasseur a *traduction libre:*

> The earth of the crescent, aquatic land, was swallowed up by the waters, bloated as it was like a frog. Just when the volcanic blast was about to shake it, it rose to its level. Its track is what it has piled up under the wrinkled surface of the uplifted earth; its movement is lava in front, the glazed surface of raised lands; its track is the lava pushing the deceptive surface basin of the raised lands.[5]

Such terrestrial and oceanic upheaval and confusion supposedly bore out Brasseur's singular theories. "Now nothing is wanted," he declared. "I am master of all the inscriptions, in spite of the numerous variations in each character, and the same key which has enabled me to read the Manuscript Troano has served for the Dresden Manuscript, and the Mexican Manuscript No. 2 of the Bibliothèque Impériale, as well as the inscriptions of Palenque and the monoliths of Copán."[6] The Abbé went on to proclaim that had the Spaniards not destroyed the ancient pictorial records in the erroneous belief that they referred to idolatrous ceremonies,

---

[4] Brasseur: *Manuscrit Troano* (Paris: Imprimerie Impériale; 1869), p. 223.

[5] Ibid., p. 156.

[6] Quoted from letter to Léon de Rosny, in S. F. Haven: op. cit., p. 47.

the geological and human history of the antediluvian world would stand clearly before us. Fortunately, enough was left of these records to enable him to bring forth the truth. The subject of the Troano was the great cataclysm, so decisive to both the Old and the New World. Here, the Abbé continued, "you will find the entire history of the rise of the mountains and the sinking of the ancient land."[7]

From then on, the applications of his revolutionary epigraphic discovery assumed grotesque proportions. *Four Letters on Mexico,* an octavo volume of 463 pages, which came from the presses even before the Troano deluxe edition had been completed, was designed to give, as its subtitle declared: "An absolute explanation of the Hieroglyphic system of Mexico, the end of the Stone Age, the temporary Glacial Epoch, the commencement of the Age of Bronze, the origin of the civilization and the Religions of Antiquity, derived from the Teo-Amoxtli [the lost Toltec bible Brasseur had meanwhile equated with the *Popol Vuh*] and other Mexican documents."

To dwell longer on Brasseur's speculations, which took in all "the mysterious history engraved upon the antediluvian palaces of Palenque"[8] and traced the first society of men to the Great Antilles, would be unkind. Once he raised his historical superstructure on cataclysmic fantasies, for which the Mayan hieroglyphs served as little more than a pretext, his reputation collapsed. He persisted in his theories, however, though in a footnote to a work published in 1871 he admitted his error in the decipherment of the Troano, which should have been read from left to right, not right to left. In the end he was like an old actor who continues to recite after the last person in the audience has left and as the lights are being turned off. His remaining years were greatly embittered by his disappointment over the refusal of the Collège de France to nominate him in 1872 to a chair in American philology and archaeology. He began selling his library and died shortly after, in January 1874, in Nice—another tragic figure in the reconquest of America's ancient civilizations.

Since the Abbé's death, our store of Maya writing has not been substantially increased. Only one other fragment of a Maya codex has come to light. It had reached Madrid fifteen years after the discovery of the Troano, from a private owner in Estremadura.

---

[7] Ibid., p. 49.   [8] Ibid., p. 47.

The manuscript was first named "Cortés," because it was supposed to have been owned by the conquistador himself, though there was no evidence to support this claim. Léon de Rosny, a Paris philologist, was shown photographs of it and recognized it as a part of the Troano. The original scroll had been neatly cut in two and could be rejoined with considerable ease, though it had suffered some damage. Its contents seem to center on rituals, and on New Year, farming, and hunting ceremonies. Léon de Rosny brought out a lithographed edition of this fragment. It was, by the way, Léon de Rosny's father, also an eminent philologist, who discovered the third extant Maya codex—beside the Dresden and the Madrid—in 1859 or 1860 among a discarded pile of papers in the cellar of the Bibliothèque Nationale in Paris. The name Pérez was scribbled on the wrapping, hence its current Latinized designation: Peresianus. It is the least well preserved of the three. Large parts of the Peresianus, or Paris, were missing and much of its stucco sizing had peeled off.

Despite additions in the nineteenth century, the entire volume of Mayan manuscripts remains infinitesimal, and the chances of any further finds are slim. Nevertheless, not all possibilities have been exhausted. Once more it is Landa who suggests another interesting avenue. In his *Relación* he reported on the Mayan custom of burying a chief with "idols, and, if he was a priest, with some of his books."[9] One cannot discount Landa's testimony, even though nothing has turned up so far to bear out his observation. And although archaeologists are on the whole skeptical that any of the texts could have weathered centuries of interment in the moist tropical climate of Central America, some hopes cling to the fact that remains of paper with some colored specks of lime flakes strewn among them have been taken from graves on a few occasions.[1] They were too poorly preserved to permit identification with any book or writing. Nevertheless, an unusual combination of circumstances may one day repeat the miracle of the Dead Sea scrolls somewhere in Maya country, to give us further light on that vanished civilization.

The pre-Columbian Maya manuscripts we have deal almost certainly with calendrical, astronomical-astrological, and divinatory-ritualistic matters. They are, however representative of the Maya outlook, of limited scope, which in itself has been a serious

---

[9] Tozzer: *Landa's Relación de las Cosas de Yucatán*, p. 130.
[1] Ibid., p. 130 *n*. See also E. H. Thompson: *People of the Serpent* (Boston: Houghton Mifflin Co.; 1932), pp. 8–9.

obstacle to a successful decipherment of the script. History proper, which Landa mentioned as a chief topic of Maya books, does not appear to be included. At least, this was long the opinion of the experts. They agreed that even if the texts of the three Maya codices and the lengthy inscriptions on the sacrificial steps of Copán and the walls of Palenque were read one day, not much new data would emerge.

And then came a startling discovery announced in 1961 by Tatiana Proskouriakoff,[2] whose specialty is Maya art and the restoration of buildings and structures through her exemplary drawings.

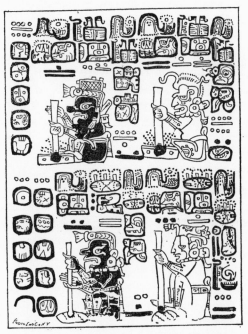

"Page" of glyphs from the Codex Troano

Her study of sculptural motifs on Maya monuments, particularly those at Piedras Negras, suggested a connection with the accompanying inscriptions. Where everybody had hitherto seen divine figures and religious allusions, she found definite references to actual rulers and their families. As J. Eric S. Thompson, the leading Maya epigrapher of our time, said in a preliminary sum-

---

[2] Tatiana Proskouriakoff: "The Lords of the Maya Realm," *Expedition*, Vol. IV, No. 1 (Autumn, 1961), pp. 14–21.

mary: "A few years ago no one dreamed that such information would ever be recovered."[3]

It is still too early to assess this possibility. However, for unexpected light on ancient American history we can turn again to the non-Maya codices of Mexico.

---

[3] J. Eric S. Thompson: "Invocation Address, 75th Anniversary of the University Museum . . . ," *Expedition*, Vol. IV, No. 3 (Spring, 1962), p. 16.

·XXV·

THE DEVIL EXORCISED:

FROM ZELIA NUTTALL

TO ALFONSO CASO

But what priest, what prophet shall explain the words of the books . . . ?
                    The Book of Chilam Balam of Chumayel

WELL KNOWN as the Mayas and the Aztecs are to us today, they were by no means the only important peoples in pre-Columbian Middle America. The Maya achievements more and more are losing their aura of uniqueness and are being examined within the larger context of the entire area. The Aztecs owe their prominence in the popular mind mainly to the timing of Cortés' conquest rather than to any outstanding accomplishments of their own. Indeed, by 1519 they had barely emerged from savagery, and had been politically dominant for only a few generations before the coming of the Spanish. They owed their thin veneer of civilization almost entirely to other peoples, particularly to their kindred Nahuatl-speaking neighbors and their predecessors as rulers in central Mexico, the Toltecs and Chichimecs. Most of "Aztec" art and handicraft was probably imported wholesale. Modern archaeologists have come to suspect that the master artisans the Aztecs employed were Mixtecs ("Cloud-People"),[1] a gifted race then

---

[1] Miguel Covarrubias: *Indian Art of Mexico and Central America* (New York: Alfred A. Knopf; 1957), pp. 326–7.

living in what are today the states of Puebla, Guerrero, and Oaxaca in southern Mexico.

Nearly all the pre-Columbian codices which are not Mayan are Mixtec. But how do we know that they are Mixtec, since it has been impossible to verify the actual source of any manuscript? They do not, it need hardly be said, carry colophons. However, as is the case with the Mayas, details in the style of the picture books and their glyphs closely parallel frescoes, altar paintings, polychrome ceramics, and other decorative media. Archaeological investigation in recent years has made it possible to establish sources with considerable precision.

Animal drawings from Mixtec codices

The Mixtecs were consummate graphic artists who composed semipictorial chronicles of their remote past. How these codices came to be partly deciphered, without a master key, by several generations of scholars is one of the little-known success stories of American archaeology. The groundwork was laid by a remarkable woman of great stamina and ingenuity. Undeservedly by-passed in popular accounts, she has been so much forgotten that a recent book on Mexican archaeology by a scholar from the United States identifies this daughter of the American West as British. Few of our encyclopedias have caught up with her.

Zelia Maria Magdalena Nuttall has been called "one of the most diligent and most erudite students of Mexico in all its aspects,"[2] an outstanding "example of nineteenth century versatility."[3] She was born in San Francisco in 1857 and was taken to Europe as a child and educated in France, Germany, Italy, and her father's native England. But she had Mexico in her blood.

---

[2] Philip Ainsworth Means: "Zelia Nuttall: An Appreciation," *Hispanic American Historical Review*, Vol. XIII (November 1933), p. 489.

[3] Tozzer: "Zelia Nuttall," *American Anthropologist*, N.S., Vol. XXXV (September 1933), p. 480.

Her mother, who was of Mexican birth, had given her the volumes of Lord Kingsborough, and ever since, she had been drawn to Mexican antiquities. For close to fifty years, she was a dominant figure in the archaeology of America, which she helped to raise to a level with the ancient Near East. During her long residence in Mexico, she became a center of the intellectual life of the capital. The University of Mexico named her an honorary professor in 1908. Yet, although Miss Nuttall's discoveries place her among the leading pioneers of the American past, in later years her theories, which combined brilliant research with speculation, estranged her from the new, "specialist" generation of scientifically minded archaeologists, who, however, owed her more than they were willing to acknowledge.

Zelia Nuttall was married in 1880 to Alphonse-Louis Pinart, a French anthropologist, who had bought Brasseur's manuscript collection a few years before. In 1883 he published a catalogue of its Mexico-Guatemalan items. Pinart's own studies concentrated in the main on the ethnology and languages of Panama. Quite probably he encouraged his wife's enthusiasm for studying American aboriginals; yet the marriage was brief and unhappy. After the couple's separation in 1884, Zelia Nuttall resumed her maiden name and embarked on a career of her own. In the same year she went on a prolonged visit to Mexico with her mother and young daughter. There she took up serious work at the National Museum of Mexico City.

She made her archaeological debut in 1886 with a paper on terra-cotta heads she had gathered at the old cultural metropolis of Teotihuacán. Her subsequent study of the famous feather headdress at Vienna, one of the articles in Cortés' original shipments to Charles V, was among the first on the subject and inaugurated her lifelong association with Harvard University's Peabody Museum of American Archaeology and Ethnology. It was the first in the museum's distinguished series of *Papers*, Volume I, Number 1, in 1888. Miss Nuttall soon became fluent in Nahuatl and developed a superb command of the vast literature produced in that language and in Spanish during the early colonial era. All of ancient America from the Zuñis of the American Southwest to the advanced peoples of Middle America and Peru came within her compass. However, in the manner of her age, she remained throughout most of her career primarily concerned with American origins.

Like Brasseur, but on a more scholarly plane, Miss Nuttall

devoted herself to the problem in her longest and most ambitious work, *The Fundamental Principles of New and Old World Civilizations* (1901), on which she labored for thirteen years. It was written during her residence at Dresden, the German city of the celebrated Maya codex, which was just then stimulating much valuable research. Dresden before World War I was a favorite of the international set. Renowned for its lively cultivation of the arts and for its fine baroque architecture, it was hailed as a German Florence; but its unmelodious local dialect had no resemblance to the graceful Tuscan Italian. Zelia Nuttall may have imbibed some of the gravity, if not the presumption, of Teutonic scholarship of the Wilhelminian era. At any rate, it was with infinite learning that she tried to find the one basis common to all civilizations. As it turned out, this underlying principle was revealed to her in the swastika, a universal astronomical symbol for the North Star. Miss Nuttall lived long enough (she died in 1933) to see modern savages gather under its banner, though they hardly shared her cosmopolitan claims for the mystic emblem. Alfred M. Tozzer, the American Maya scholar and long-time friend of Miss Nuttall, regretted the book's "archaic" character, but thought it had a "considerable influence in attracting several students to the Middle American field."[4]

When Zelia Nuttall had finished her formidable treatise, she happily returned to more concrete subjects. In 1902 she settled permanently in Mexico, in a house at Coyoacán a few miles south of Mexico City, which had once belonged to the tough conquistador Pedro de Alvarado. This house in some form or other had been occupied as far back as the fifth century A.D. and was perhaps the oldest continuously inhabited house of the hemisphere. She rebuilt it into one of the most beautiful in America, filled its rooms, galleries, and patios with exquisite antiquities, and surrounded it with delightful gardens. Presiding over it as a gracious and lively chatelaine, Miss Nuttall made the Casa Alvarado a haven for a host of international visitors. On its grounds she carried out "the first complete study of Aztec pottery in a given site."[5]

Nearby, from layers buried under lava she dug up primitive clay figurines which had no resemblance to the plastic art of Aztecs, Toltecs, or Mayas. They could only have belonged to a much older, prehistoric time. Her excavations in other parts of

---

[4] Ibid., p. 477.   [5] Ibid., p. 478.

the country also added to our knowledge of that period, and led Miss Nuttall to postulate an archaic Mexican culture that had preceded the great urban civilizations—as Humboldt had vaguely anticipated. The recognition of such a stage was a milestone in Mexican archaeology, comparable to Petrie's and De Morgan's discoveries of the pre-Dynastic cultures of Egypt. It was Miss Nuttall's outstanding accomplishment as a practicing archaeologist.

Terra-cotta figurines from the archaic (or "pre-classic") horizon of central Mexico

Singularly fruitful as her strictly archaeological studies were, Zelia Nuttall achieved prominence among Americanists by her discoveries of ancient manuscripts. Two native codices, several Spanish works, and lost papers of Sir Francis Drake are known thanks to her. She searched ardently in the libraries of the Old and the New World and was as much at home in the archives of Simancas (Spain), in the London Public Records Office, or in the Vatican. In 1911 she extricated from the National Library at Madrid an original, mid-sixteenth-century account of the Conquest, probably by Cervantes de Salazar, a personal friend of Ludovico Vives, the Spanish humanist, and of Cortés. Several years earlier she had made her prize find, a document which at the insistence of the director of the Peabody Museum was named Codex Nuttall.

Zelia Nuttall learned of its existence at an informal reception in Florence from a renowned Italian historian, Pasquale Villari, biographer of Machiavelli and Savonarola and a former minister of education. The conversation had turned to a topic of vital interest to both scholars, as Miss Nuttall relates in the introduction to the facsimile edition of her codex:

"We were soon deep in a discussion of the marvellous wealth

of Florentine libraries, in one of which, the Mediceo-Laurentian Library, the original manuscript of the most valuable work in existence on Ancient Mexico, by Friar Bernardino de Sahagún, was preserved. In another, the Biblioteca Nazionale Centrale, I had just discovered an important Hispano-Mexican manuscript [the Codex Magliabecchi XIII-3, or "The Book of Life of the Ancient Mexicans"]. At this juncture, Senator Villari communicated some facts to me which caused my keenest interest and made an indelible impression on my memory. He told me that, more than thirty years previously, he had spent some time examining and studying historical documents preserved in the library of the Monastery of San Marco, around which cluster so many memories of Fra Angelico and Fra Savonarola. It was by chance that, about this time, Signor Villari first became acquainted with an ancient Mexican codex. One of the friars of San Marco brought it to a salon frequented by Florentine literati and scholars, in order to obtain opinion about it. He asked Pasquale Villari, the future historian, whether he could understand and explain the curious manuscript. The friar stated that neither he nor the other monks could make anything out of it. They had already sent it to be examined by a member of the institution known as the Propaganda Fide in Rome. His reply had been 'that the document was probably intended for the amusement of children, but was so foolish that it could only bore them.' With the eye of a connoisseur, Signor Villari saw at a glance that the despised manuscript was of great value and interest, being an ancient Mexican codex, with occasional words [in Spanish] inserted, as if to explain the hieroglyphics. Subsequently, whilst studying in the old library Signor Villari would now and then pause at the case where the curious document was kept, to look wonderingly at its pages, covered with figures and signs. He examined it with interest and attention, and begged the friar, its custodian, to guard it with utmost care. Later, a disturbed political period supervened and the monastic orders were suppressed throughout Italy. The library of San Marco became the property of the state and was thrown open to the public. On revisiting the library Signor Villari made inquiries about the Mexican manuscript, but in vain, for it had vanished. He subsequently learned that it had been sold to a wealthy Englishman residing in Florence. On applying to the latter for permission to see the manuscript again, Signor Villari was informed that it was no longer in his possession, and had been given to a friend in England. 'So there the matter ended,' said my host, with an expression of deep regret that Florence should have thus lost so rare a treasure, and one which has doubtlessly been preserved within its walls for centuries."[6]

Human figures from Mixtec codices

But where was the manuscript now? Had the Englishman's friend—whose name Villari did not know—kept it? If not, to whom had he passed it on? That had been over thirty years before, and no one in Florence was likely now to have the answers. Probably the work had been taken to England. There was also the possibility that it had continued to change hands. Or the codex might have come to the notice of scholars, been acquired by a museum, and published. Miss Nuttall, who was quite familiar with the codices in European and Mexican collections, was almost certain that this had not been the case. Signor Villari's amazingly detailed recollections did not fit any codex she knew. Those with which "Codex X" seemed to have the closest affinities were not of the same length, and did not have explanatory notes in Spanish. To make quite certain, Miss Nuttall spent almost a year investigating the background of all known or reported codices, but evidently none could have come from the San Marco library. More than ever she believed that the manuscript Villari had seen three decades before had remained unknown. Furthermore, it "must have been an original and of incalculable importance."[7] How was it to be reclaimed from oblivion? Letters of inquiry went out everywhere. One clue led to the Honorable Robert Curzon, the fourteenth Baron of Zouche, and he turned out to be the man to whom the manuscript had been given as a gift.

Robert Curzon, the 14th Baron of Zouche, is already known to us as the author of a travel narrative that vividly described

---

[6] Zelia Nuttall, ed.: *Codex Nuttall. Facsimile of an Ancient Mexican Codex Belonging to Lord Zouche of Harynworth, England* (Cambridge, Mass.: Peabody Museum–Harvard University Press; 1902), pp. 1–2.

[7] Ibid., p. 2.

his visits to the dilapidated libraries of the Levant, where he found a number of valuable manuscripts. On his estate in Sussex he had brought together a collection of rare manuscripts "to illustrate the history of the art of writing." No doubt, a Mexican codex would have rounded off that record nicely. Curzon had even put out a catalogue of his collection, limited to fifty copies and awkwardly but descriptively titled "Materials for Writing, Early Writing on Tablets, Stones, rolled and other manuscripts, Books and Oriental manuscripts, in the library of the Hon. Robert Curzon." The catalogue was published in London in 1849, but even if Curzon had come into the possession of the Mexican codex, it would have been at a later date and the codex would not have been listed. Direct application to the heir, the fifteenth Baron of Zouche, was to dissolve all of Miss Nuttall's doubts: "It was in these surroundings that, during one third of a century, the codex remained undisturbed and so lost to view that not even a rumor of its existence reached the outer world."[8]

Permission to study and publish the rare treasure was promptly granted by the owner. In June 1898, Miss Nuttall had the codex before her at the British Museum: eagerly she scanned the folded deerskin. The Spanish notes, appended later to the unmistakably pre-Columbian document, were not as extensive as she had hoped and did not furnish a translation, but the codex itself far surpassed her expectations. It was perfectly preserved, and its colors were fresh and of exacting artistry. Zelia Nuttall thought it was "the most superb example" of an ancient manuscript of its kind she had ever seen. Further examination persuaded her that in wealth of detail it excelled the closely related Codex Vindobonensis (Vienna Codex), which was believed to be the first sent by Cortés to Europe. Was it possible that the newly found codex had been with it? An inscription bore the date *1 Acatl* (year) *1 Cipectli* (day)—which, by coincidence, Miss Nuttall had shown four years earlier to be the very day of the vernal equinox corresponding to March 12, 1519, of the Julian calendar.

There now began the lengthy and highly uncertain job of "reading" the Mexican manuscript, while preparing it for publication. By the late eighteen nineties some substantial progress had been made in deciphering Mexican codices. The concept of the character of the Mexican hieroglyphics had not significantly changed since Humboldt had surveyed them, and no one had

---

[8] Ibid., p. 3.

offered an over-all scheme for translation. In view of the rudimentary and hybrid nature of this quasi-script of the non-Maya Mexicans, chances were that nobody ever would. What was brought into play now, patiently and piecemeal, was a growing body of knowledge, not only of chronology, but of Mexican customs in general, and specific rites, social institutions, trades, deities, astronomy, astrology, and magic. Little by little, pictorial representations as well as symbolic abstractions (ideograms) of these subjects, and their meaning in particular settings and sequences, were understood. The insights had come from study of accounts of early post-Conquest times, especially of Sahagún, and of post-Columbian codices such as the Mendoza and Zelia Nuttall's Magliabecchi, which contained an excellent pictorial register of characteristic incidents of Mexican life and religion. Some of these records included comments in Spanish. All kinds of artifacts from Mexico, and data on non-Mexican Indian cultures and mores, also helped clarify the glyphs. Aubin and others had made advances in the recognition of additional rebus features. The greatest strides were made as a result of comparisons, extrapolations, and trial substitutions of familiar meanings and references, on the basis of the vast store of information available from archaeological, historical, and anthropological literature. A prerequisite for this work was a command of Mexican languages, place names, and a host of related data. Mexicanists steeped in the science, such as Eduard Seler, made the most substantial contributions.

Eduard Seler (1849–1922) was a teacher of botany at a Berlin Gymnasium before he became one of the founding fathers of modern Mexican archaeology. In 1887 he had gone to Mexico for reasons of health. He returned again and again to study the ancient civilizations and to carry out excavations. In the course of his new career he became director of the Berlin Museum of Ethnology. His specialty was Mexican languages and texts, and he was the first to furnish extensive commentaries on a number of codices. These publications were sponsored by the Duc de Loubat, the Frenchman who had inherited Kingsborough's mantle as lord protector of the Mexican scrolls.

Seler's studies concentrated on some six closely related manuscripts of pre-Columbian age, which he designated as the Borgia group, after its most sumptuous and valuable member. They were all clearly of a religious-magical nature, and dealt with the sacred calendar and other related matters such as the Venus Year, divination, lucky and unlucky days, mystical numbers, rituals, and the lore of the gods. In addition to this set of codices, there was another group, definitely distinct and of even greater homogeneity both in style and apparently in subject matter. But scholars had not been nearly as successful in interpreting it as in interpreting the Borgia manuscripts. Its brilliant imagery, highly reminiscent in its formalized character and continuity of the technique of the modern comic strip, was still a puzzle. What was it about? The usual concern with the passing of time, number magic, and stellar movements appeared to be minor here, but there was evidence of rituals, even of human sacrifice, and of the supernatural. Seler and his German colleagues maintained that the codices in this group also were of a religious nature and probably dealt with mythological themes.

The Mexican god of war Texcatlipoca ("Smoking Mirror") as he appears in ornate regalia in the Codex Borgia, his right foot replaced by a mirror. This American Mars was the foe of peace-loving Quetzalcoatl, whom he defeated. Redrawn by Miguel Covarrubias

It was to this group that Zelia Nuttall's newest discovery belonged. It seemed almost to have been painted by the same hand as the Vindobonensis, hitherto the most important of the group. Vienna owned two more fragments of the same kind: the Becker I and II, which had been taken from Mexico in recent years by a German of that name. The Codex Colombino, or Dorenberg, of Mexico City probably had once been part of Becker I.

England was favored as much as Vienna: there were two, the Selden and the Bodley, at the Bodleian Library at Oxford; and the Nuttall, or Zouche, was eventually acquired by the British Museum. Alfonso Caso, the Mexican archaeologist, who has become the undisputed mid-twentieth century authority on pre-Columbian Mexican codices, has given this group the name Mixteca because of their origin, which is now certain. It should be remembered that the Borgia codices are also Mixtec or, to be more precise, Tlaxcala-Puebla.

Zelia Nuttall broke new ground when she took up her work on the codex in England, first at the British Museum and then at the Bodleian. A case might be made for the intuitive grasp of a woman scholar, where systematic efforts had so far borne little fruit. The preliminary reading of relative dates and names of people and places was somewhat routine, and not too revealing as such. However, "a prolonged course of close study" impressed upon Miss Nuttall certain striking elements which seemed to recur, particularly in the case of personal names. What did they indicate? Could they be fitted into a pattern? At last, there emerged from the multicolored canvas a set of well-defined personalities, with hints of rank, age, and clan associations. "The present codex," Miss Nuttall realized, "acquaints us with a series of events in the lives of several personages, and shows us the great variety of costume and insignia they adopted as they rose in rank or performed ceremonial rites."[9] Then Miss Nuttall began to detect the threads of individual careers, and she perceived a certain progression or evolution among the sequences of pictures. In several instances she was able to follow some person all the way "through the winding and crowded text on its obverse." Now she knew: the codex was historical.

In what seemed to her the most important section, she followed the history of a hitherto unknown person, a conqueror named Eight Deer, or Tiger's Claw. He had as his closest companion Twelve Ollin, or Tiger's Head. When Eight Deer first appears, he shows by dress and body paint that he is a priest. Later he embarks on military ventures and is seen participating in the council of tribal chieftains. As must have happened to so many Mexican heroes, he is finally sacrificed and has his pulsating heart torn out. Other persons could also be identified and followed in skeleton biographies, among them a Lady Three Flint.

[9] Ibid., p. 20.

Zelia Nuttall was the first to point out the prominent role that women played in ancient Mexico, even though it was a warrior society. In several instances they appeared as military leaders, heading what she called "gyneocracies."

"Eight Deer," the Mixtec conqueror resurrected from pre-Columbian manuscripts. He wears a feline helmet, familiar in both ancient China and America. From Codex Nuttall, redrawn by Miguel Covarrubias

In view of all the data we can now "read" in the codex, Zelia Nuttall's work was just a beginning. But she had established the historical character of the manuscript and pointed the way for others to follow, and she had contributed considerable new information about the mores and institutions of ancient Mexico. She was also the first to notice that most persons had second names, or nicknames, in addition to their official names, which were identical with their date of birth. Miss Nuttall wisely warned that a codex of this kind could not be taken as a consecutive written text in our sense. She accepted the hypothesis that an ancient Mexican might have read her codex "by reciting in beautiful language and metrical verse, composed by himself or by oral tradition, the list of native heroes whose deeds are pictured, accompanied by hieroglyphs recording the names of persons or localities only."[1] According to this not altogether unfamiliar conception of the Mexican records, the codices served as mnemonic devices for the bard, annalist, and priest, rather than as a word for word codification of a fixed text. Conceivably, the native historians of the sixteenth century, whether they were writing in Spanish or in the Nahuatl—such as Ixtlilxochitl, and to some degree Sahagún too—simply translated these "shorthand" picture records into a complete narrative with the aid of oral tradition. Sahagún said: "All the information that I obtained, they made known to me by means of their paintings."[2]

In later years, Zelia Nuttall's novel suggestions about the historical picture manuscripts were supplemented by a number of British and American scholars. Others, notably Germans, refused to be convinced for a long time. As late as 1929, Walter Lehmann rejected all historical explanations in his commentary on the Vienna Codex. He believed that the recurrent dates were astronomical references and that the persons mentioned were gods, not men, and he declared that all codices of the Vindobonensis-Nuttall class dealt with astronomical and theological topics only. However, in 1912 Miss Nuttall's opinions had already been corroborated and expanded by James Cooper Clark, a British major, in the *Story of Eight Deer in the Codex Colombino.* Cooper Clark had found that Eight Deer was mentioned in several other manuscripts, and now, with the Colombino as his principal evidence, Cooper Clark reconstructed in surprising detail, from cradle to sacrificial block, the events in the life of the pre-Columbian hero and conqueror. Cooper Clark's emphasis on the parallelism and coordination of the data in the various codices proved very useful.

More significant still was the reexamination by Richard C. E. Long, another English Americanist, of the Codex Nuttall in 1926.[3] Long, according to Alfonso Caso, made fundamental discoveries. He distinguished five divisions within the codex relating to dynastic lines, and he suggested a chronology for the codices. He thought that the Codex Nuttall dealt with a period of 478 years. However,

---

[1] Ibid., p. 21.
[2] Quoted in Recinos, ed.: *Popol Vuh*, p. 17.
[3] Richard C. E. Long: "The Zouche Codex," *Journal of the Royal Anthropological Society*, Vol. LVI (1926), pp. 239–58.

because of the peculiarity of the Mexican calendar, which, like that of the Tibetans, lacks a fixed point, yet runs through recurrent cycles, Long's time scale was only relative.

Military exploits of "Eight Deer," pictorial detail from the Codex Nuttall showing him as he takes "Four Wind" prisoner. Undoubtedly "Four Wind" was marked for human sacrifice, a fate to which "Eight Deer" himself submitted in the end. Redrawn by Miguel Covarrubias

Next to enter the field was Herbert J. Spinden, a scholar from the United States known chiefly for his Maya research, with a succinct paper on "Indian Manuscripts of Southern Mexico" in the *Smithsonian Report of 1933,* the year of Zelia Nuttall's death. A study of the manuscripts at the Bodleian had given him unexpected proof, which, he thought, "fixes once and for all the fact that human beings and mundane affairs form the principal subject of these ancient records."[4] He had noticed in the Selden Codex that whenever a pictograph of a person appeared for the first time he was attached by a crinkly line to a year sign. The

---

[4] Herbert J. Spinden: "Indian Manuscripts of Southern Mexico," *The Smithsonian Report for 1933,* Publication 3279 (Washington, D.C.: Government Printing Office; 1935), p. 432.

undulating line Spinden assumed to represent an umbilical cord, which, by tying an individual to the year sign, referred to the year of his birth. The accompanying day of his birth gave his conventional name. Spinden supplied an impressive roster of incidents in the lives of several persons who must have played major roles in the pre-Columbian history of southern Mexico. He retraced the life of One Monkey throughout his sixty-five years. Interesting sidelights were gained on marriage customs, initiation ceremonies into knightly orders, murders for the sake of succession to the throne, brother-sister marriages, political alliances, conquests, and ritual wars to gather victims for the anthropophagous appetites of the planet Venus. The historical record is richly interspersed with mythology. In one gruesome scene, Eight Deer, whom Spinden verified as "the most thoroughly documented individual" in this part of Mexico, was seen officiating at the sacrifice of his own brother.

In the cast of characters of the Selden Codex there was the prepossessing Princess Six Monkey, who outlived her three brothers and forced her way to the throne. According to Spinden, this Mixtec Hatshepsut was truly an "Amazon queen." The life of Lady Six Monkey, amply dealt with in the Selden, was also covered in the Bodley and Nuttall codices. It exemplified the "militant feminism" of women in southern Mexico, and their high position. Zelia Nuttall was right when she maintained that they had great power and prominence. Indeed, Spinden was amazed by the skill and authority with which Lady Six Monkey "could handle both martial and marital situations." She is seen leading the way into battle, and taking dreadful vengeance on rebellious cities. Like Queen Elizabeth I, she will not be hurried into selecting a consort and turns procrastination to political advantage. Going beyond Richard C. E. Long's more limited study, Spinden collated the genealogies of several prominent families from all the codices. In the course of this work, he reached the conclusion that the records started around the first quarter of the thirteenth century and comprised some ten generations.

The tentative nature of all these hypotheses became evident when Alfonso Caso showed that the seventh century of the Christian era, not the thirteenth century, had seen the beginning of the dynasties recorded in the picture books. J. Cooper Clark thought that the conqueror Eight Deer was born in 1439; Alfonso Caso worked out his dates as 1011–63.

Alfonso Caso has been Mexico's leading archaeologist since he took up his explorations at Monte Albán, an ancient Zapotec-Mixtec center. His interest in this culture was aroused by its hieroglyphic inscriptions on stelae, which he thought might shed light on an obscure phase of Mexican history before the coming of the Aztecs. His subsequent investigations of the inscriptions revealed affinities between Mayan and Aztec systems of writing. Caso then decided to undertake actual excavation with the hope of further elucidating the Zapotec-Mixtec culture and its historic role within the Middle American complex in general.[5] All these goals were fulfilled in the course of his successful spadework at Monte Albán. To a surprising degree, these findings confirmed and amplified the results of his study of the codices. But first there came an archaeological windfall on the scale of Woolley's at Ur. This was Caso's widely acclaimed discovery in 1931 of the now famous Tomb 7, with its magnificent jewelry and gold pieces.

Incised stelae from Monte Albán, attributed to the earliest ("Olmec"?) period of the Zapotec-Mixtec center in sourthern Mexico. The undeciphered glyphs are probably dates.

Dr. Caso has long been a professor at the University of Mexico and director of Mexico's National Institute of Indian Affairs, besides being a distinguished man of letters who has

[5] Philip Dark: *Mixtec Ethnohistory* (Oxford: Oxford University Press, 1958), p. 9.

always taken a special interest in Mexican hieroglyphs and codices. It was he who first identified the two main groups of pre-Columbian manuscripts as Mixtec by their similarity to Mixtec ceramics. The Borgia series he traced to the areas of Puebla and Tlaxcala because of their close resemblance to the paintings of Tizatlán in Tlaxcala. The other group, he ascertained, came from the two ancient capitals of the Mixtecs, Tilantongo and Teozacoalco, and, as he was eventually to show, they referred to the ruling houses of these two centers. The Mixtecs even had a name for that kind of genealogical record: *tonindeye*, or *naandeye*.[6] Zelia Nuttall had been of the opinion that they were either Aztec or pertained to their neighbors and kin, the lords of Texcoco, whereas Cooper Clark, closer to the truth, had thought them Zapotec.

Alfonso Caso's identification was corroborated by his excavations at Monte Albán. Incised bones taken from Tomb 7 revealed historical dates in the same manner as the codices. Could there be a connection between the royal or priestly mausoleums and the manuscripts?

Four years later, in 1935, Caso began an exhaustive study of the genealogical picture texts for the purpose of compiling a kind of biographical dictionary of all the Mixtec persons mentioned. For years he made no significant progress, and then, at a historical congress held at Guadalajara in 1944, a colleague, Jiménez Moreno, turned Caso's attention to a "map" of Teozacoalco, Oaxaca, which was owned by the University of Texas in Austin. This post-Columbian document was done in native style, with notes appended in Spanish. It is believed to owe its origin to local surveys ordered by Philip II in 1580. On its margin was a vertical column of human figures, arranged like a sketch for a gigantic totem pole.

On examining this map, Caso was startled to find that the figures and glyphs contained names strongly reminiscent of those in the Mixtec manuscripts he was studying. What if by chance they were related? Indeed, this proved to be the case: some names overlapped. By virtue of the Christian dates given on the map, a chronological correlation could be worked out for all the codices. Caso's extraordinary luck held: the pre-Columbian princely persons on the map reappeared in the manuscripts' more extensive dynastic histories.

Though the map of Teozacoalco was, even less than Landa's

---

[6] Caso: *Interpretación del Codice Bodley 2858*, p. 13.

Relación, a key to the unknown script, it deserved to be called by Caso the Rosetta Stone of the Mixtec historical codices.[7] With its aid, a more or less extensive "translation" could now be undertaken, in which the chronology was worked out, the historical nature of the records was verified, and the dynastic lines were correlated with those of the Mixtec centers of Tilantongo and Teozacoalco. A Spanish note even named the then living lineal descendants of the fourth dynasty of Teozacoalco, which was founded by a prince of Tilantongo. It all worked out neatly: the codices were historical; the people mentioned were, in the words of Caso, "real and terrestrial," though, in the manner of chronicles of early peoples, the rulers were considered of ultimately divine ancestry. As in *Faust,* there had to be a "Prologue in Heaven." Whatever the religious concepts of the Mixtecs, however, their "writers" had a considerable grasp of history and set down their royal annals with utmost care and in rational order. In addition, the data, despite a strange and awkward way of transmission, were of surprising detail, just as Humboldt had predicted. They reflected a hitherto unsuspected range of ancient Mexican life and lore. Much of it, even then, remained open to varying interpretation.

From a handful of codices barely saved from ruin and once judged to be little more than barbaric oddities, scholars had extricated a remarkable wealth of knowledge. Pre-Columbian Mexico, so close in time and yet so far removed from the historical awareness of the European West, had been declared "prehistoric" and impenetrable. "The traditions of Chichimecs, Colhuas and Nahuacs," wrote the nineteenth-century Anglo-German Orientalist, Max Müller, "are no better than the Greek traditions about Pelasgians, Aetolians, and Ioanians, and it would be a mere waste of time to construct out of such elements a systematic history, only to be destroyed again, sooner or later, by some Niebuhr, Grote or Lewis."[8] What lay beyond the single fixed date, the founding of Tenochtitlán in 1325, was considered forever outside historical grasp. Scholars despondently faced a blank of several hundred years intervening between the eclipse of Teotihuacán and the ascension of the Aztecs. For Yucatán and Central America, a dent had already been made with the decipherment of the Maya

---

[7] Caso: "El Mapa de Teozacoalco," *Cuadernos Americanos,* Vol. VIII, No. 5 (1949), p. 145.
[8] Max Müller: *Chips from a German Workshop* (New York: Charles Scribner & Co.; 1870), Vol. I, p. 327.

chronology, though its correlation with the European calendar caused difficulties, particularly since the Maya dates we had were all from the Old Empire and disconnected and void of concrete reference.

Mixtec records, unlike the Initial Series on Mayan stelae, had helped to fill out Middle American history. The data had come directly from aboriginal records and not from transcripts or tendentious narratives by Christian missionaries. Admittedly, the decipherment did not entirely exclude other hypotheses, and some scholars maintained that it was hardly definitive.[9] However, through persistent investigation, patient comparison, inspired guesses, and lucky finds, the symbolism of the picture books was gradually reduced to intelligible data. The majority of Americanists concurred that in general the Mexican historical documents could now be read in all but the strictest sense of the word. As in Ras Shamra and Nineveh, lost books and a lost writing literally made history.

Animal motif from Mixtec codex

What was more, the past, not so much of the Aztecs, who were, after all, newcomers, but of one of Mexico's older and most advanced civilizations, had been penetrated. A first, fairly dependable date of A.D. 692 was given in the Codex Bodley, furnishing a historical continuity of some eight hundred years. With the addition of a codex from post-Conquest times, the pictorial chronicle of the Mixtec dynasties was extended to 1642—a time span of close to a thousand years. This was a historical record equaled by few of the ancient nations of the Old World, and attested clearly to the effectiveness of the graphic devices used in the New World and to the skillful renderings of its scribes.

A great woman scholar had made a start with the discovery

[9] Dark: op. cit., p. 9.

of a rare pre-Columbian codex, and now, thanks to the crowning labors of Alfonso Caso, the world's most unusual historical annals were on the verge of full decipherment. The mysterious picture scrolls had almost become open books. If scant remains of the once vast number of Mexican picture scrolls could yield so much, however, our satisfaction must be tempered by the thought of all that was lost with the destruction of the rest.

EPILOGUE

THE DEDICATED SEARCHES of our scholar-adventurers have taken them almost full circle around the globe—from Italy to Egypt and the Near East, from Central Asia to Middle America. But their true frontier was time.

Each discovery of a long-lost text, important or trivial, has helped to push back that curtain in time beyond which all human activities are dim and obscure. Each discovery tells us more about our past, about how we came to be what we are. That is why the searches of the scholar-adventurers were so powerfully motivated, and why they will continue, for there is much yet to be done.

Tomorrow or the day after may yield the next surprise, but no one can say where it will come from. Will it be from the abandoned early Christian monasteries on the Sinai peninsula, from the desert sands of North Africa, from the binding of a medieval manuscript in a European collection, or from the hidden library of the Russian Czar Ivan? We can be sure only that there will be many more discoveries. Experience indicates that the soil of Herculaneum, and most certainly the ancient lands of Egypt, Palestine, Syria, and Mesopotamia, have yielded far from all of their buried documents. And elsewhere, even in climates most unfavorable to survival, such as the jungles of Middle America, there is no reason categorically to rule out future textual recoveries.

The outlook thus remains auspicious. "When I sincerely compute the lapse of ages," wrote Gibbon in meditating on the Alexandrian libraries, "the waste of ignorance, and the calamities of war, our treasures, rather than our losses, are the object of my surprise."[1]

Yet Gibbon, at the end of the eighteenth century, was aware of only a fraction of the astonishing retrievals this book has described. Casting a nostalgic glance at the Byzantines before their

---

[1] Edward Gibbon: *The History of the Decline and Fall of the Roman Empire*, J. B. Bury, ed., ninth edition (London: Methuen & Co.; 1932), Vol. V, p. 455.

crusading Christian brothers from the West fell upon them, he remarked: "In the enjoyment or neglect of our present riches we must envy the generation that could still peruse the history of Theopompus, the orations of Hyperides, the comedies of Menander, and the odes of Alcaeus and Sappho."[2] In Gibbon's time, these writers were known by little but their names; nevertheless, miraculous as it may seem, modern scholars and archaeologists have been able to find something by virtually every one of them.

But what about entire literatures that have been wiped out—the literatures, for instance, of the Eruscans, the Khmers of Cambodia, or the Phoenicians of Tyre and Sidon? What about the Carthaginians, whose books the Romans gave away to their Numidian allies, with whom they vanished? A people from whom the Romans took a young slave who became famous as Terence, the accomplished Latin playwright, must have had literary talent of no mean sort. But who knows whether we may not still find Carthaginian works? A hundred and fifty years ago the literature of the Egyptians or of the people of Mesopotamia seemed equally beyond our reach. Yet we now have Gilgamesh and the Rhind Papyrus and the hymn of Ikhnaton, as well as invaluable legal, social, and historical documents from the ancient Near East.

Indeed, had scholars since the early Renaissance despaired of adding to the scanty remains of ancient literature, they might never have embarked on their adventures and we would lack the excitement and rewards of the continuing search for the testaments of time.

---

[2] Ibid., Vol. VI, p. 106.

BIBLIOGRAPHY

The following list of books and articles, arranged according to the main subdivisions of this work, makes no attempt whatever to be exhaustive. It simply presents a few of the entries which I have found most useful in the preparation of my book—itself dealing selectively with a well-nigh inexhaustible subject and ranging over many ages and civilizations of man.

As mentioned in the foreword, no other book of similar scope has come to my knowledge, unless it be Frederic G. Kenyon's very brief *Ancient Books and Modern Discoveries,* which was delivered as a lecture before the Caxton Club of Chicago in 1927. There is also a fairly recent (1962), fine magazine article relevant to our topic, by a renowned classical scholar, Gilbert Highet.

It goes without saying that I have consulted a great many more sources than could be indicated here, among them all kinds of journals and bibliographies, and such standard reference works as Pauly-Wissowa's *Realencyclopaedie der Classischen Altertumswissenschaft, The Oxford Classical Dictionary, The Encyclopedia of Religion and Ethics, The Enciclopedia Italiana, The Dictionary of National Biography,* and a host of others. Quite a few of the books cited below will provide further bibliographical guidance.

The reader who wishes to keep abreast of manuscript discoveries cannot do better than to peruse specialized journals (for example, *The Journal of Egyptian Archaeology* and *The Journal of Biblical Literature*), several of which regularly feature articles or lists of the newest finds. Various national and international palaeographic and papyrological societies have their own organs. An examination of the papers read at their meetings can be particularly rewarding. For the Dead Sea scrolls, and all questions connected with them, we have virtually complete bibliographies, foremost Christoph Burchard's in the *Beihefte zur Zeitschrift für die Alttestamentliche Wissenschaft* (Berlin). News of manuscript discoveries in that area are also likely to reach nonprofessional publications, and unexpected finds such as those made in 1964 in Italy of golden tablets covered with Etruscan inscriptions will even arouse the daily press.

The titles given here in one category will not be repeated in another. As a rule, I have listed that edition of a work which I consulted, and where known and available to me, I have given preference to paperback editions. Occasionally I have also included information on reprints or on recent revisions. It goes without saying that such "classical" works of the nineteenth century as those by Burckhardt, Prescott, and Symonds went through many earlier editions.

GENERAL

Altick, Richard D.: *The Scholar Adventurers*. New York: The Macmillan Co.–Macmillan Paperbacks; 1960.

Birt, Theodor: *Die Buchrolle in der Kunst*. Leipzig: B. G. Teubner; 1907.

Blumenthal, Walter Hart: *Bookman's Bedlam of Literary Oddities*. New Brunswick, N.J.: Rutgers University Press; 1955.

Ceram, C. W.: *Gods, Graves, and Scholars*. New York: Alfred A. Knopf; 1951.

———: *The March of Archaeology*. New York: Alfred A. Knopf; 1958.

Clark, John Willis: *The Care of Books*. Cambridge: Cambridge University Press; 1901.

Cleator, P. E.: *Lost Languages*. New York: New American Library–Mentor Books; 1962.

Cramer, Frederick H.: "Bookburning and Censorship in Ancient Rome." *Journal of the History of Ideas*, Vol. VI (1945), pp. 147–96.

Curtis, Georgina Pell: "Some Lost Manuscript Treasures." *Catholic World*, Vol. LXXIII (July 1901), pp. 447–52.

Daniel, Glyn E.: *A Hundred Years of Archaeology*. London: Gerald Duckworth & Co.; 1950.

Diringer, David: *The Hand-produced Book*. London: Hutchinson & Co.; 1953.

Doblhofer, Ernst: *Voices in Stone. The Decipherment of Ancient Scripts*. New York: Viking Press; 1961.

Edwards, Edward: *Memoirs of Libraries*. 2 vols. London: Trübner & Co.; 1859.

Gelb, I. J.: *A Study of Writing*. Second revised edition. Chicago: University of Chicago Press–Phoenix Books; 1963.

Gibbon, Edward: *The History of the Decline and Fall of the Roman Empire*, J. B. Bury, ed. Ninth edition. 7 vols. London: Methuen & Co.; 1923–32.

Hessel, Alfred: *A History of Libraries*. New Brunswick, N.J.: The Scarecrow Press; 1955.

Highet, Gilbert: "The Wondrous Survival of Records." *Horizon*, Vol. V, No. 2 (November 1962), pp. 74–95.

Jackson, Holbrook: *The Anatomy of Bibliomania*. New York: Charles Scribner's Sons; 1932.

James, M. R.: *The Wanderings and Homes of Manuscripts*. New York: The Macmillan Co.; 1919.

Jensen, Hans: *Die Schrift in Vergangenheit und Gegenwart*. Glückstadt and Hamburg: J. J. Augustin; 1935. Second edition, 1958.

Kenyon, Frederic G.: *Ancient Books and Modern Discoveries*. Chicago: The Caxton Club; 1927.

————: *The Bible and Archaeology.* London: George H. Harrap; 1940.

————: *Books and Readers in Ancient Greece and Rome.* Second edition. Oxford: Clarendon Press; 1951.

————: "Papyrus: Alte Bücher and Moderne Entdeckungen." *Philobiblion*, Jahrg. XI, Heft 1 (1939), pp. 1–30.

Macaulay, Rose: *The Pleasure of Ruins.* London: Weidenfeld and Nicolson; 1953.

McMurtrie, Douglas C.: *The Book: The Story of Printing and Bookmaking.* Third revised edition. New York: Oxford University Press; 1943.

Madan, Falconer: *Books in Manuscript.* London: Kegan Paul; 1920.

Milkau, Fritz, ed.: *Handbuch der Bibliothekswissenschaft.* Second revised edition, by Georg Leyh. 2 vols. Wiesbaden: O. Harrassowitz; 1952–55.

Moorhouse, Alfred C.: *The Triumph of the Alphabet.* New York: Henry Schuman; 1953.

Prescott, William H.: *History of the Conquest of Mexico* and *History of the Conquest of Peru.* New York: Random House–The Modern Library; n.d.

"Recovery of Lost Writings." *Edinburgh Review.* Vol. IIL (1828), pp. 348–89.

Sahl, Svend: *History of the Book.* New York: The Scarecrow Press; 1958.

Schreiber, Hermann and Georg: *Vanished Cities.* New York: Alfred A. Knopf; 1957.

Targ, William, ed.: *Bouillabaisse for Bibliophiles.* Cleveland: The World Publishing Co.; 1955.

Thompson, James Westfall: *Ancient Libraries.* Berkeley: University of California Press; 1940.

Woolley, Leonard: *History Unearthed.* New York: Frederick A. Praeger; n.d. London: Ernest Benn; 1958.

————: *Spadework in Archaeology.* New York: Philosophical Library; 1953. London: Butterworth Press; 1953.

BOOK ONE: A RENAISSANCE PRELUDE

Artz, Frederick B.: *The Mind of the Middle Ages.* Third revised edition. New York: Alfred A. Knopf; 1959.

Bolgar, R. R.: *The Classical Heritage and Its Beneficiaries.* Cambridge: Cambridge University Press; 1954. Harper Torchbooks, 1964.

Burckhardt, Jacob: *The Civilization of the Renaissance in Italy.* New York: Random House–Modern Library; 1954. London: Phaidon Press; 1951.

Clark, Albert C.: "The Literary Discoveries of Poggio." *The Classical Review,* Vol. XIII (1899), pp. 119–30.

————: "Sabbadini's 'Finds of Latin and Greek Manuscripts.'" *The Classical Review,* Vol. XX (1906), pp. 224–9.

568 · *Bibliography*

————: "The Trau Manuscript of Petronious." *The Classical Review,* Vol. XXII (August 1908), pp. 178–9.

Clark, James Midgley: *The Abbey of St. Gall as a Centre of Literature and Art.* Cambridge: Cambridge University Press; 1926.

Cosenza, M. E., tr.: *Petrarch's Letters to Classical Authors.* Chicago: Chicago University Press; 1910.

Curtius, Ernst Robert: *European Literature and the Latin Middle Ages.* New York: Pantheon Books–Bollingen Series; 1953.

D'Israeli, Isaac: *Curiosities of Literature,* Vol. I. New York: Widdleton; 1865.

Durant, Will: *The Renaissance.* New York: Simon and Schuster; 1953.

Gilmore, Myron P.: *The World of Humanism: 1453–1517.* New York: Harper & Brothers; 1952. Harper Torchbooks, 1962.

Gutkind, Curt Sigmar: "Poggio Bracciolinis geistige Entwicklung." *Die Vierteljahrsschrift für Literaturwissenschaft und Geistesgeschichte,* Vol. X (1932), pp. 548–96.

Hallam, Henry: *Introduction to the Literature of Europe,* Vol. I. London: John Murray; 1873.

Harbison, Harris E.: *The Christian Scholar in the Age of the Reformation.* New York: Charles Scribner's Sons; 1956. The Scribner Library, n.d.

Hutton, Edward: *Giovanni Boccaccio: A Biographical Study.* London: J. Lane; 1910.

Jebb, Richard C.: "The Classical Renaissance." *Cambridge Medieval History,* Vol. I. Cambridge: Cambridge University Press; 1902.

Jerrold, Maud F.: *Francesco Petrarca. Poet and Humanist.* London: J. M. Dent; 1909.

Koerting, Gustav: *Boccaccios Leben und Werke.* Leipzig: Fues; 1880.

————: *Petrarca. Leben und Werke.* Leipzig: Fues; 1878.

Kristeller, Paul Oskar: *Renaissance Thought.* New York: Harper & Brothers–Harper Torchbooks; 1961.

Loewe, Elias Avery: "The Unique Manuscript of Tacitus 'Histories.'" *Casinensia* Year 1929, Vol. I, pp. 257–72.

MacManus, Francis: *Boccaccio.* London: Sheed & Ward; 1947.

Nolhac, Pierre de: *Petrarch and the Ancient World.* Boston: Humanists' Library; 1907.

Robinson, James Harvey, and H. W. Rolfe, eds.: *Petrarch. The First Modern Scholar and Man of Letters.* Second revised edition. New York: G. P. Putnam's Sons; 1914.

Roscoe, William: *The Life of Lorenzo de' Medici.* Tenth edition. London: George Bell; 1902.

Rubinstein, Nicolai: "An Unknown Letter by Jacopo di Poggio Bracciolini on Discoveries of Classical Texts." *Italia Medioevale e Umanistica,* Vol. I (1958), pp. 383–400.

Sabbadini, R.: *Le Scoperte dei Codici Latini ed Greci ne' Secoli XIV ed XV.* 2 vols. Florence: Sansoni; 1905–14.

Sandys, John Edwin: *Harvard Lectures on the Revival of Learning.* Cambridge, Mass.: Harvard University Press; 1905.

————: *History of Classical Scholarship*, Vol. II. Cambridge: Cambridge University Press; 1908.

Schneider, Karl: "Die Bibliothek Petrarcas und ihre Schicksale." *Zeitschrift für Bücherkunde*, N.S., Vol. I (1909), pp. 157–60.

Shepherd, Rev. William: *The Life of Poggio Bracciolini*. Liverpool: J. Cadell; 1802.

Symonds, John Addington: *Renaissance in Italy*, Vol. II of *The Revival of Learning*. New York: G. P. Putnam's Sons–Capricorn Books; 1960.

Tatham, Edward H. R.: *Francesco Petrarca. The First Modern Man of Letters*. 2 vols. London: Sheldon Press; 1925.

Thompson, James Westfall, et al.: *The Medieval Libraries*. Chicago: Chicago University Press; 1939.

Tièche, Édouard: "Die Wiederentdeckung der antiken Bücher im Zeitalter der Renaissance." *Bibliothek der Schweizer Bibliophilen*, Ser. III, Heft 7. Berne 1936.

Traube, Ludwig: *Vorlesungen und Abdhandlungen*, Vol. I. Munich: C. H. Beck; 1909.

Voigt, Georg: *Die Wiederbelebung des classischen Alterthums*. Fourth edition. 2 vols. Berlin: W. de Gruyter; 1960.

Walser, Ernst: *Poggius Florentinus. Leben und Werke*. Leipzig: B. G. Teubner; 1914.

Wilkins, Ernest Hatch: *Life of Petrarch*. Chicago: Chicago University Press; 1961.

Wilkinson, L. Patrick, ed.: *Letters of Cicero*. London: Arrow Books; 1949.

BOOK TWO: THE PERMANENCE OF PAPYRUS AND CLAY

(A) Classics

Baikie, James: *A Century of Excavation in the Land of the Pharaohs*. London: Religious Tract Society; 1924.

————: *Egyptian Antiquities in the Nile Valley. A Descriptive Handbook*. London: Methuen & Co.; 1932.

————: *Egyptian Papyri and Papyrus-hunting*. London: Religious Tract Society; 1925.

Barker, Ethel Ross: *Buried Herculaneum*. London: A. and C. Black; 1908.

Bell, H. I.: "Arthur Surridge Hunt, 1871–1934." *British Academy. Proceedings*, Vol. XX (1934), pp. 323–33.

————: *Egypt. From Alexander to the Arab Conquest*. Oxford: Clarendon Press; 1948.

————: "The Historical Value of Greek Papyri." *Journal of Egyptian Archaeology*, Vol. VI (1920), pp. 234–46.

————: "Hunt, Arthur Surridge." *Dictionary of National Biography, 1931–40.* London: Oxford University Press–Geoffrey Cumberlege; 1949.

————: "Papyrology in England." *Chronique d'Égypte,* Vol. VII, Nos. 13/14, pp. 134–6.

————: *Recent Discoveries of Biblical Papyri.* Oxford: Clarendon Press; 1937.

————: Review of *"Papiri greci e latini." Journal of Egyptian Archaeology,* Vol. VI (1920), p. 129.

————: "Sir Frederic Kenyon, 1863–1952." *British Academy. Proceedings,* Vol. XXXVIII (1952), pp. 269–94.

————: "Some Private Letters of the Roman Period." *Revue Egyptologique,* N.S., Vol. I (1919), pp. 199–209.

Beloch, Julius: *Campanien. Topographie, Geschichte and Leben der Umgebung Neapels im Altertum.* Berlin: S. Calvary; 1879.

Belzoni, Giovanni: *Narrative of the Operations and Recent Discoveries within the Pyramids, Temples, Tombs, and Excavations in Egypt and Nubia.* . . . London: John Murray; 1820.

Breasted, Charles: *Pioneer to the Past. The Story of James Henry Breasted.* New York: Charles Scribner's Sons; 1943.

Brion, Marcel: *Pompeii and Herculaneum. The Glory and the Grief.* New York: Crown Publishers; 1960.

Budge, Ernest Alfred Wallis: *By Nile and Tigris.* 2 vols. London: John Murray; 1920.

Černý, Jaroslav: *Paper and Books in Ancient Egypt.* London: University College; 1952.

Comparetti, Domenico: "La Bibliothèque de Philodème" in *Mélanges Chatelain.* Paris: Champion; 1910; Pp. 118–29.

————, and Giulio de Petra: *La Villa Ercolanese dei Pisoni, i suoi Monumenti e la sua Biblioteca.* Turin: Ermanno Loescher; 1883.

Corti, Egon Caesar Conte: *The Destruction and Resurrection of Pompeii and Herculaneum.* London: Routledge & Kegan Paul; 1951.

Cottrell, Leonard: *The Mountains of Pharoah.* New York: Rhinehart & Co.; 1956.

Crönert, Wilhelm: "Über die Erhaltung und die Behandlung der Herkulaneischen Rollen." *Neue Jahrbücher,* Vol. V (1900), pp. 586–91.

David, M., and B. A. Groningen: *Papyrological Primer.* Third edition. Leyden: E. J. Brill; 1952.

Deissmann, Adolf: *Light from the Ancient East. The New Testament Illustrated by Recently Discovered Texts of the Graeco-Roman World.* Revised edition. London: Hodder & Stoughton; 1937.

Denon, Dominique Vivant: *Travels in Upper and Lower Egypt* . . . . 2 vols. New York: Heard and Forman; 1803.

Ebers, Georg: "The Papyrus Plant." *Cosmopolitan,* Vol. XV (1893), pp. 677–82.

Egypt Exploration Fund. Graeco-Roman Branch: *Archaeological Reports*, 1904/5, 1905/6, 1906/7, etc.

Emery, Walter Bryan: *Archaic Egypt.* Harmondsworth, Middlesex: Penguin Books; 1961.

Erman, Adolf: "Die Herkunft der Fayum Papyri." *Hermes*, Vol. XXVI (1886), pp. 585–9.

Finegan, Jack: *Light on the Ancient Past.* Princeton: Princeton University Press; 1946. Second edition, 1959.

Gallavotti, Carlo: "La Libreria di una Villa Romana Ercolanese." *Bolletino del R. Istituto di Patologia del Libro.* Fasc. IV (1941), pp. 129–45.

Glanville, S. R. K., ed.: *The Legacy of Egypt.* Oxford: Clarendon Press; 1942.

Gomperz, Heinrich, ed.: *Theodor Gomperz: Briefe und Aufzeichnungen,* Vol. I. Vienna: Gerold; 1936.

Goodspeed, Edgar Johnson: "Papyrus Digging with Grenfell and Hunt." *Independent,* Vol. LVII (1904), pp. 1066–70.

Grenfell, Bernard P.: "The Oldest Record of Christ's Life. The First Complete Account of the 'Sayings of Our Lord,'" with an introduction by F. G. Kenyon. *McClure's,* Vol. IX (1897), pp. 1022–30.

———: "The Present Position of Papyrology." *John Rylands Library. Bulletin,* Vol. VI (1921), pp. 142–62.

———: "The Value of Papyri for the Textual Criticism of Extant Greek Authors." *Journal of Hellenic Studies,* Vol. XXXIX (1919), pp. 16–36.

———, and Arthur S. Hunt: "Excavations at Oxyrhynchus." *Archaeological Reports* of Egypt Exploration Fund. Graeco-Roman Branch, 1904/5, 1905/6.

———: "A Large Find of Papyri." *The Athenaeum,* No. 3785 (May 12, 1900), pp. 600–1.

———: *The Oxyrhynchus Papyri,* Vols. I–XXV. London: Egypt Exploration Fund. Graeco-Roman Branch; 1898–1959. (Later volumes by different editors.)

———, and J. Gilbart Smyly, eds.: *The Tebtunis Papyri.* 3 vols. University of California Publications: Graeco-Roman Archaeology, I–IV. London: H. Frowde–Oxford University Press; 1902–38.

Grenfell, Bernard P., Arthur S. Hunt, and D. G. Hogarth, with J. Grafton Milne: *Fayum Towns and Their Papyri.* London: Egypt Exploration Fund; 1900.

Hadas, Moses: *Ancilla to Classical Reading.* New York: Columbia University Press–Paperback; 1961.

Headlam, Cecil: *The Story of Naples.* London: J. M. Dent—Everyman Library; 1927.

Highet, Gilbert: *The Classical Tradition.* New York: Oxford University Press–Galaxy Books; 1957.

———: "'The Dyskolos' of Menander." *Horizon,* Vol. I, No. 6 (July 1959), pp. 78–89.

Howorth, H. H.: "Literary Discoveries in Egypt." *Quarterly Review,* Vol. 176 (April 1893), pp. 344–72.

Hunt, Arthur S.: "B. P. Grenfell." *Aegyptus,* Vol. VIII (1927), pp. 114–16.

——: "Bernard Pyne Grenfell, 1869–1926." *British Academy. Proceedings,* Vol. XII (1926), pp. 357–64.

——: "J. P. Mahaffy." *Aegyptus,* Vol. I (1920), pp. 217–21.

——: "The Oxyrhynchus Papyri." *The Classical Review,* Vol. XII (1898), pp. 34–5.

——: "Papyri and Papyrology." *Journal of Egyptian Archaeology,* Vol. I (1914), pp. 81–92.

——: "Twenty-five Years of Papyrology." *Journal of Egyptian Archaeology,* Vol. VIII (1922), pp. 121–8.

——, and C. C. Edgar, eds.: *Select Papyri.* 2 vols. Cambridge, Mass.: Harvard University Press—Loeb Library; 1932.

Jacobs, E.: "Winckelmann and Bianconi." *Jahrbuch des Deutschen Archaeologischen Institutes. Beiblatt,* Vol. 47 (1932), pp. 563–97.

Jensen, Christian: "Die Bibliothek von Herculaneum." *Bonner Jahrbücher,* Heft 135 (1930), pp. 49–61.

Johnson, J.: "Antinoë and its Papyri. . . ." *Journal of Egyptian Archaeology,* Vol. I (1914), pp. 168–81.

Justi, Carl: *Winckelmann und seine Zeitgenossen,* Vol. II. Fifth edition. Constance: Phaidon; 1956.

Kenyon, Frederic G.: "Aristotle's Treatise on the Constitution of Athens." *Review of Reviews,* Vol. III (February 1891), pp. 175–7.

——: "Fifty Years of Papyrology." *Actes du Vᵉ Congrès International de Papyrologie.* Brussels, 1938.

——: "Greek Papyri and Their Contribution to Classical Literature." *Journal of Hellenic Studies,* Vol. XXXIX (1919), pp. 1–13.

——: "Greek Papyri and Recent Discoveries." *Quarterly Review,* Vol. 208 (1908), pp. 333–52.

——: "Hyperides." *Quarterly Review,* Vol. 178 (1894), pp. 531–52.

——: "The Library of an Oxyrhynchite." *Journal of Egyptian Archaeology,* Vol. VIII (October 1922), pp. 3–4, 129–38.

——: *The Poems of Bacchylides.* . . . London: British Museum; 1897.

——, ed.: *Classical Texts from Papyri in the British Museum* . . . . London: British Museum; 1891.

Liebich, Werner: "Aus der Arbeit an den Papyri von Herculaneum." *Deutsche Akademie der Wissenschaften. Wissenschaftliche Annalen.* Jahrg. II (1953), pp. 304–13.

Ludwig, Emil: *The Nile.* New York: Pyramid Books; 1963.

MacKendrik, Paul: *The Mute Stones Speak. The Story of Archaeology in Italy.* New York: St. Martin's Press; 1960.

Mahaffy, John Pentland: "Further Gleanings from the Papyri." *New Review,* Vol. IX (1893), pp. 526–35.

————: "On the Flinders Petrie Papyri." *Cunningham Memoirs,* Vols. VIII, IX, XI. Dublin: Royal Irish Academy; 1891, 1893, 1905.

————: "The Petrie Papyri." *New Review,* Vol. VII (1892), pp. 549–61.

Maiuri, Amadeo: *Herculaneum.* Guide Books to Museums and Monuments of Italy's Ministerio della Pubblica Istruzione, No. 53. Rome: Istituto Poligrafico dello Stato–Libreria dello Stato; 1956.

Makarónas, Harálambos: "The Dherveni Crater." *Greek Heritage,* Vol. I, No. 1 (Winter, 1963), pp. 5–8.

Martin, Victor, ed.: *Papyrus Bodmer IV. Ménandre: Le Dyscolos.* Cologny–Geneva: Bibliotheca Bodmeriana; 1958.

Mason, Edward G.: "Greek Papyri in Egyptian Tombs." *The Dial,* Vol. XIII (June 1892), pp. 49–50.

Maupassant, Guy de: *The Collected Works.* Vol. XII: *La Vie Errante.* Alliance Française edition. New York and London: M. Walter Dunne; 1903.

Mitteis, L., and U. Wilcken: *Grundzüge und Chrestomathie der Papyruskunde.* 2 vols. Leipzig: B. G. Teubner; 1912.

Murray, Margaret A.: "William Matthew Flinders Petrie." *Religions,* Vol. XXXXI (October 1942), pp. 21–4.

Newberry, Percy E.: "William Matthew Flinders Petrie. . . ." *Journal of Egyptian Archaeology,* Vol. XXIX (December 1943), pp. 67–70.

Oldfather, C. H.: *The Greek Literary Texts from Graeco-Roman Egypt.* University of Wisconsin Studies, No. IX. Madison, 1923.

Partsch, Joseph: *Papyrusforschung.* Leipzig: Veit & Co.; 1914.

Petrie, W. M. Flinders: *Hawara, Biahmu, and Arsinoe.* London: Field & Tuer; 1889.

————: *Illahun, Kahun and Gurob. 1889–90.* London: David Nutt; 1891.

————: *Methods and Aims in Archaeology.* London: Macmillan & Co.; 1904.

————: *Seventy Years in Archaeology.* London: Sampson Low, Marston; 1931.

————: *Ten Years' Digging in Egypt, 1881–1891.* Second edition. London: Religious Tract Society; 1893.

Powell, James Underhill, and E. A. Barber, eds.: *New Chapters in the History of Greek Literature.* First, second, and third series. Oxford: Clarendon Press; 1921, 1929, 1933.

Praz, Mario: "Herculaneum and European Taste." *American Magazine of Art,* Vol. XXXII (December 1939), pp. 684–93, 723.

Preisendanz, Karl Lebrecht: "Abriss der Papyruskunde," in Fritz Milkau, ed.: *Handbuch der Bibliothekswissenschaft,* Vol. I, pp. 163–248.

————: *Papyrusfunde und Papyrusforschung.* Leipzig: Hiersemann; 1933.

Radice, Betty, ed.: *The Letters of the Younger Pliny*. Harmondsworth, Middlesex: Penguin Books; 1963.

Rehm, Walter, ed.: *J. J. Wincklemann Briefe*. 4 vols. Berlin: W. de Gruyter; 1952–57.

Roberts, Cecil Henderson: "The Codex." *British Academy. Proceedings*, Vol. XL (1953), pp. 169–204.

————: "The Greek Papyri," in S. R. K. Glanville, ed.: *The Legacy of Egypt* (Oxford: Clarendon Press; 1942), Ch. X, pp. 249–82.

————: *An Unpublished Fragment of the Fourth Gospel*. Manchester: Manchester University Press; 1935.

Rostovtzeff, Mikhail I.: "The Foundations of Social and Economic Life in Egypt in Hellenistic Times." *Journal of Egyptian Archaeology*, Vol. VI (1920), pp. 161–78.

————: *A Large Estate in Egypt in the Third Century* B.C.: *a Study in Economic History*. University of Wisconsin Studies in the Social Sciences and History, No. VI. Madison, 1922.

————: *Out of the Past of Greece and Rome*. New Haven: Yale University Press; 1932.

Sayce, Archibald Henry: "The Greek Papyri," in W. M. F. Petrie: *Illahun, Kahun and Gurob*, pp. 34–7.

————: *Reminiscences*. London: Macmillan & Co.; 1923.

Schmid, Wolfgang: "Zur Geschichte der Herkulaneischen Studien." *La Parola del Passato. Rivista di Studi Antichi*. Fasc. XLIV and XLV. Naples, 1955.

Schubart, Wilhelm: *Das Alte Aegypten und seine Papyrus*. Berlin: W. de Gruyter; 1921.

————: *Einführung in die Papyruskunde*. Berlin: Weidmann'sche Buchhandlung; 1918.

————: *Die Papyri als Zeugen Antiker Kultur*. Berlin: Akademie Verlag; 1949.

Scott, Walter: *Fragmenta Herculensia*. . . . Oxford: Clarendon Press; 1855.

Smith, Sidney: "Sir Flinders Petrie." *British Academy. Proceedings*, Vol. XXVIII (1942), pp. 306–23.

Tarn, W. W.: *Hellenistic Civilisation*. Third revised edition, in collaboration with G. T. Griffith. Cleveland: The World Publishing Company—Meridian Books; 1961.

Thompson, R. Campbell: "Ernest Alfred Wallis Budge." *Journal of Egyptian Archaeology*, Vol. XXI (September 1935), pp. 68–70.

Tyrell, Robert Y.: "The New Papyri." *The Quarterly Review*, Vol. CLXXII (1891), pp. 320–50. Reprinted in R. Y. Tyrell: *Essays in Greek Literature*. London: Macmillan & Co.; 1909.

————: "The Poems of Bacchylides." *The Quarterly Review*, Vol. CLXXXVII (1898), pp. 422–7.

Waddell, W. G.: *The Lighter Side of Greek Papyri*. Newcastle: Cutter; 1932.

————: "Some Literary Papyri from Oxyrhynchus." *Études de Papyrologie*, Vol. I (1932), pp. 11-18.

————: "A Teacher of Classics in Egypt." *The Classical Journal*, Vol. XXVIII (1933), pp. 489–96.

Waldstein (Walston), Charles, and Leonard Shoobridge: *Herculaneum: Past, Present and Future.* London: Macmillan & Co.; 1908.

Wheeler, Sir Mortimer: "Flinders Petrie." *Antiquity*, Vol. XXVII (June 1943), pp. 91–2.

Winckelmann, Johann Joachim: *Critical Account of the Situation and Destruction by the First Eruptions of Mount Vesuvius, of Herculaneum, Pompeii, and Stabiae . . .* ["Sendschreiben"]. London, 1771.

————: *Nachrichten von den Neuesten Herculaneischen Entdeckungen an Heinrich Fuessli in Zurich.* 1764. Vol. II in *Werke*, C. L. Fernow, ed.

————: *Werke* (Collected Works), C. L. Fernow, ed. 8 vols. Dresden: Walther; 1808–34.

(B) The Ancient Near East

Adams, J. McKee: *Ancient Records and the Bible.* Nashville: Broadman Press; 1946.

Albanèse, Léon: "Notes sur Ras Shamra." *Syria*, Vol. X, No. 1 (1929), pp. 16–20.

Albright, William F.: *The Archaeology of Palestine.* Harmondsworth: Penguin Books; 1951.

————: *From the Stone Age to Christianity.* New York: Doubleday & Co.–Anchor Books; 1957.

————: "New Light on Early Canaanite Language and Literature." *Bulletin of the American Schools of Oriental Research*, No. 45 (February 1932), pp. 15–20.

————: "The North-Canaanite Epic of 'Al 'Êyân Ba'al and Môt." *The Journal of the Palestine Oriental Society*, Vol. XII, No. 4 (1932), pp. 185–208.

Bauer, Hans: "Das Alphabet von Ras Schamra." *Vossische Zeitung*, No. 128 (June 4, 1930).

————: "Die Entzifferung des Keilschriftenalphabets von Ras Schamra." *Forschungen and Fortschritte*, Vol. VI (1930), pp. 306–8.

————: *Entzifferung der Keilschrifttafeln von Ras Schamra.* Halle: Max Niemeyer; 1930.

Birch, Samuel, ed.: *Facsimiles of Two Papyri Found in a Tomb at Thebes* (with account of discovery by A. Henry Rhind). London: Longmans; 1863.

————: *Papyrus Harris No. 1.* London: British Museum; 1876.

Breasted, James Henry: *Ancient Records of Egypt. . . . ,* Vol. III. Chicago: Chicago University Press; 1905.

————: *A History of Egypt.* New York: Charles Scribner's Sons; 1937. Bantam paperback, 1964.

British Museum: *A General Introductory Guide to the Egyptian Collections.* . . . London: British Museum; 1930.

————: *A Guide to the Babylonian and Assyrian Antiquities.* Third revised edition. London: British Museum; 1922.

Budge, E. A. Wallis: *The Book of the Dead. The Papyrus of Ani, Scribe and Treasurer of the Temples of Egypt about* B.C. *1450.* 3 vols. New York: G. P. Putnam's Sons; 1913.

————: *The Rise and Progress of Archaeology.* London: M. Hopkinson; 1925.

Charles-Picard, Gilbert and Colette: *Daily Life in Carthage at the Time of Hannibal.* New York: The Macmillan Co.; 1961.

Chiera, Edward: *They Wrote on Clay.* Chicago: Chicago University Press–Phoenix Books; 1956.

Childe, Gordon V.: *New Light on the Most Ancient East.* Revised edition. New York: Grove Press–Evergreen Books; n.d.

Driver, Godfrey Rolles: *Canaanite Myths and Legends.* Old Testament Studies III. Edinburgh: T. & T. Clark; 1956.

————: *Semitic Writing. From Pictograph to Alphabet.* The Schweich Lectures of the British Academy 1944. London: Geoffrey Cumberlege–Oxford University Press; 1948. Revised edition, 1954.

Erman, Adolf: *The Literature of the Ancient Egyptians.* London: Methuen & Co.; 1927.

Ferm, Vergilius, ed.: *Forgotten Religions.* New York: Philosophical Library; 1950.

Frankfort, Henri: *Ancient Egyptian Religion.* New York: Harper Torchbooks; 1961.

————: *The Birth of Civilization in the Near East.* New York: Doubleday & Co.–Anchor Books; 1956.

Friedrich, Johann: *Extinct Languages.* New York: Philosophical Library–Wisdom Library; 1957.

————: *Ras Schamra. Ein Überlick über Funde und Forschungen.* (*Der Alte Orient,* Vol. XXXIII, Nos. 1–2, 1933.) Leipzig: Hinrichs'sche Buchhandlung; 1933.

Gadd, C. J.: "A New Script from Ancient Syria." *Discovery,* Vol. XII (1931), pp. 42–5.

Gardiner Alan H.: *Egypt of the Pharaohs.* Oxford: Clarendon Press; 1961.

————: "New Literary Works from Ancient Egypt." *Journal of Egyptian Archaeology,* Vol. I (1914), pp. 20–36, 100–6.

————: "Writing and Literature," in S. R. K. Glanville, ed.: *The Legacy of Egypt.*

Gaster, Theodor H.: *Thespis.* Second revised edition. New York: Doubleday & Co.–Anchor Books; 1961.

Gordon, Cyrus H.: *Adventures in the Nearest East.* Fair Lawn, N.J.: Essential Books; 1957.

————: *Introduction to Old Testament Times.* Ventnor, N.J.: Ventnor; 1953.

————: *The Living Past.* New York: John Day; 1941.

————: *Ugaritic Literature*. Rome: Pontif. Inst. Bibl.; 1949.

Gray, Rev. John: *The Legacy of Canaan*. Supplements to *Vetus Testamentum*, Vol. V. Leyden: E. J. Brill; 1957.

Griffith, Francis Llewellyn, ed.: *The Petrie Papyri: Hieratic Papyri from Kahun and Gurob*. London: Bernard Quaritch; 1898.

————, and Kate B. Griffith: "Egyptian Literature," in Charles Dudley Warner, ed.: *Library of the World's Best Literature*, Vol. XIII. New York: The International Society; 1896.

Gunn, Bathiscombe: *The Instruction of Ptah-Hotep and the Instruction of Ke'gemni: The Oldest Books in the World*. London: John Murray; 1918.

Hartleben, Hermine: *Champollion. Sein Leben und Sein Werk*. 2 vols. in one. Berlin: Weidmann; 1906.

Hitti, Philip K.: *History of Syria*. London: Macmillan & Co.; 1951.

Jirku, Anton: *Die Ausgrabungen in Palaestina und Syrien*. Halle (now Tübingen): Max Niemeyer; 1956.

Kapelrud, Arvid S.: *The Ras Shamra Discoveries and the Old Testament*. Norman, Okla.: University of Oklahoma Press; 1963.

Keller, Werner: *The Bible as History*. New York: William Morrow; 1956.

Kramer, Samuel Noah: *History Begins at Sumer*. New York: Doubleday & Co.–Anchor Books; 1959.

————, ed.: *Mythologies of the World*. New York: Doubleday & Co.–Anchor Books; 1961.

Moscati, Sabatino: *Ancient Semitic Civilizations*. London: Elek; 1957. Capricorn Books, 1960.

————: *The Face of the Ancient Orient*. New York: Doubleday & Co.–Anchor Books; 1962.

Murray, Margaret: *The Splendour That Was Egypt. A General Survey of Egyptian Culture and Civilisation*. New York: Philosophical Library; 1949. New and revised edition, Hawthorn Books, 1963.

Osgood, Howard: "The Oldest Book in the World." *Bibliotheca Sacra*, Vol. VL (1888), pp. 629–68.

Owen, G. Frederick: *Archaeology and the Bible*. Westwood, N.J.: Revell; 1961.

Petrie, W. M. Flinders: *Egyptian Tales Translated from the Papyri*. 2 vols. London: Methuen & Co.; 1895.

Pritchard, James B., ed.: *Ancient Near Eastern Texts*. Second edition. Princeton: Princeton University Press; 1955.

Schaeffer, Claude F.-A.: *The Cuneiform Texts of Ras Shamra–Ugarit*. The Schweich Lectures of the British Academy 1936. London: British Academy–Oxford University Press; 1939.

————"Discoveries at Ras Shamra. . . ." *Illustrated London News*, Vol. CLXXVII (November 29, 1930), pp. 968–72.

————: "Discoveries in Northern Syria." *Illustrated London News*, Vol. CLXXV (November 2, 1929), pp. 764–7, 784.

————: "Les Fouilles de Minet-el-Beida et de Ras Shamra." *Syria*, Vol.

X, No. 4 (1929), pp. 285–97. (Additional "Note" by René Dussaud, pp. 297–303.)

——: "A New Alphabet of the Ancients is Unearthed." *National Geographic Magazine,* Vol. LVIII, No. 4 (October 1930), pp. 476–516.

——: "Secrets from Syrian Hills." *National Geographic Magazine,* Vol. LXIV, No. 1 (July 1933), pp. 96–126.

——, and M. G. Chenet: "Des Tombeaux Royaux et un Palais du 2ᵉᵐᵉ Millénaire avant J.-C." *L'Illustration,* No. 4519 (October 12, 1929), pp. 401–13.

Smith, George: "A Chaldean Account of the Deluge," read 3rd December, 1872. *Transactions of the Society of Biblical Archaeology,* Vol. II, pt. 1 (July 1873), pp. 213–34.

Steindorff, George, and Keith C. Seele: *When Egypt Ruled the East.* Second edition. Chicago: Chicago University Press; 1957. Phoenix paperback, 1963.

Thomas, D. Winton, ed.: *Documents of Old Testament Times.* New York: Harper Torchbooks; 1961.

Ungar, Meril F.: *Archaeology and the Bible.* Grand Rapids: Zondervan; 1954.

Virolleaud, Charles: "Les Inscriptions Cunéiformes de Ras Shamra." *Syria,* Vol. X, No. 4 (1929), pp. 304–10 (followed by plates with transcripts).

——: *La Légende Phénicienne de Danel.* Paris: P. Geuthner; 1936.

Weigall, Arthur E. P. B.: *The Treasury of Ancient Egypt.* London: Blackwood; 1911.

Wiseman, D. J.: *Illustrations from Biblical Archaeology.* London: Tyndale Press; 1958.

Wright, G. Ernest: *Biblical Archaeology.* Abridged edition. Philadelphia: Westminster Press; 1960.

BOOK THREE: THE PREVALENCE OF PARCHMENT
(A) The New Testament

Atiya, Aziz Suryal: *The Arabic Manuscripts of Mount Sinai.* American Foundation for the Study of Man, Vol. I. Baltimore: The Johns Hopkins Press; 1955.

——: *The Monastery of St. Catherine in Mount Sinai.* Cairo: Misr; 1950.

Behrend, Hildegard: *Auf der Suche nach Schätzen. Aus dem Leben Constantin von Tischendorfs.* Fifth edition. Berlin: Evangelischer Verlag; 1956.

Bensly, R. L., J. R. Harris, and F. C. Burkitt, eds.: *The Four Gospels in Syriac Transcribed from the Sinaitic Palimpsest,* with an introduction by Agnes Smith Lewis. Cambridge: Cambridge University Press; 1894.

Bonner, Campbell: "Biblical Papyri at the University of Michigan."

The Harvard Theological Review, Vol. XXV, No. 2 (1932), pp. 205–6.

Bratton, Fred Gladstone: *A History of the Bible.* Boston: Beacon Press; 1959.

British Museum: *The Codex Sinaiticus and the Codex Alexandrinus,* with a preface by H. J. M. Milne and J. C. Skeat. Second revised edition. London: British Museum; 1955.

Bruce, F. F.: *The Books and the Parchments.* London: Pickering & Inglis; 1950.

Burkitt, F. C.: "The Chester Beatty Papyri." *Journal of Theological Studies,* Vol. XXXIV (1933), pp. 363–8.

Clark, Kenneth W.: "Exploring the Manuscripts of Sinai and Jerusalem." *Biblical Archaeologist,* Vol. XVI, No. 2 (May 1953), pp. 22–42.

"Codex Sinaiticus Goes to England." *Christian Century,* Vol. LI (January 3, 1934), p. 8.

Cureton, William: *Remains of a Very Ancient Recension of the Four Gospels.* . . . London: John Murray; 1858.

Curzon, Hon. Robert (Baron of Zouche): *Visit to the Monasteries in the Levant,* with an introduction by D. G. Hogarth. London: Milford; 1916.

Enslin, Martin Scott: *The Literature of the Christian Movement.* New York: Harper Torchbooks; 1956.

Forsyth, George H.: "Island of Faith in the Sinai Wilderness." *National Geographic Magazine,* Vol. CXXV, No. 1 (January 1964), pp. 82–103.

Gibson, Margaret Dunlop: *How the Codex Was Found. A Narrative of Two Visits to Sinai, from Mrs. Lewis's Journals, 1892–93.* Cambridge: Bowes & Macmillan; 1893.

Golding, Louis: *In the Steps of Moses the Lawgiver.* London: Rich and Cowan; n.d.

Goodspeed, Edgar J.: "The Four Gospels and Shenute of Atripe." *The Biblical World,* N.S., Vol. XXXIII (1909), pp. 201–6.

———: *How Came the Bible?* Nashville: Abingdon Press; 1940. Apex Books, n. d.

———: "Was the Codex Sinaiticus Stolen?" *Christian Century,* Vol. LI (February 7, 1934), p. 197.

———: "The World's Oldest Bible." *Journal of Biblical Literature,* Vol. LIV, pt. II (June 1935), p. 126.

"The Greatest Book Purchase on Record." *Literary Digest,* Vol. CXVII (January 6, 1934), p. 39.

Harris, J. Rendel: "The New Syriac Gospels." *Contemporary Review,* Vol. LXVI (1894), pp. 654–73.

Hayes, R. J.: "The Chester Beatty Library." *The Book Collector,* Vol. VII, No. 3 (Autumn, 1958), pp. 253–64.

Herklots, H. G. G.: *How Our Bible Came to Us.* New York: Oxford University Press–Galaxy Books; 1957.

Howard, Wilbert F.: "The Romance of the Recovery of Early Christian

Writings." *London Quarterly Review*, Vol. CLX (January 1935), pp. 1–16.

Hunt, Arthur S.: "Codex Sinaiticus and Others." *Spectator*, Vol. CLII (January 5, 1934), p. 8.

Huxley, Aldous: "Reflections on the Codex." *London Mercury*, Vol. XXIX (February 1934), pp. 302–5.

Johnson, Jotham: "Written with the Archaeologist's Spade." *Scientific American*, Vol. CLVI, No. 6 (June 1937), pp. 374–7.

Kenyon, Frederic G.: *The Chester Beatty Biblical Papyri*. London: Emery Walker; 1933–36.

———: *Handbook of the Textual Criticism of the New Testament*. Second revised edition. Grand Rapids, Mich.: Eerdmans Publishing Co.; 1953.

———: "New Light on the Text of the Bible." *Discovery*, Vol. XIV (November 1933), pp. 332–4.

———: *Our Bible and the Ancient Manuscripts*. Fifth revised edition, by A. W. Adams, with an introduction by G. R. Driver. London: Eyre & Spottiswoode; 1958.

———: *Recent Developments in the Textual Criticism of the Greek Bible*. The Schweich Lectures of the British Academy 1932. London: Oxford University Press–Humphrey Milford; 1933.

———: *The Story of the Bible*. London: John Murray; 1936.

———: "The Text of the Bible. A New Discovery." The London *Times*, November 19, 1931, p. 13.

Kraeling, Carl H.: *A Greek Fragment of Tatian's Diatessaron from Dura*. London: Christophers; 1935.

Lewis, Agnes Smith: *Eastern Pilgrims. Travels of Three Ladies*. London: Hurst & Blackett; 1870.

———: *In the Shadow of Sinai. A Story of Travel and Research from 1895–97*. Cambridge: Bowes & Macmillan; 1898.

———: "Notes. . . ." *Royal Asiatic Society. Journal*, N.S., Vol. VL (1893), pp. 647–9.

———, ed.: *The Old Syriac Gospels or Evangelion Da-Mepharreshe*. . . . London: Williams & Norgate; 1910.

McCown, C. C.: "The Earliest Christian Books." *Biblical Archaeologist*, Vol. VI, No. 2 (May 1943), pp. 21–31.

Margoliouth, D. S.: "Agnes Smith Lewis." *Royal Asiatic Society. Journal*. April 1926, pp. 385–7.

Martin Victor, ed.: *Bibliotheca Bodmeriana V: Evangile de Jean*. 2 vols. Cologny–Geneva: Bibliotheca Bodmeriana; 1956–58.

Metzger, Bruce M.: "Recent Discoveries and Investigations of New Testament Manuscripts." *Journal of Biblical Literature*, Vol. LXXVIII (March 1959), pp. 13–20.

———: "Recently Published Greek Papyri of the New Testament." *Biblical Archaeologist*, Vol. X, No. 2 (May 1947), pp. 25–44.

Milligan, George: *The New Testament and Its Transmission*. London: Hodder & Stoughton; 1932.

Mould, Elmer W. K.: *Essentials of Bible History.* Revised edition. New York: Ronald Press; 1951.

The New English Bible. N.T. New York: Oxford University Press and Cambridge University Press; 1961.

Oulton, J. E. C.: *The Chester Beatty Biblical Papyri.* Dublin: Trinity College Press; 1951.

Rau, Arthur: "Bibliotheca Bodmeriana. Part I: Manuscripts." *The Book Collector,* Vol. VII, No. 4 (Winter, 1958), pp. 380–95.

Rostovtzeff, Mikhail I.: *Caravan Cities.* New York: Oxford University Press; 1932.

———: *Dura-Europos and Its Art.* Oxford: Clarendon Press; 1938.

Sanders, Henry A., ed.: *A Third-Century Papyrus Codex of the Epistles of Paul.* University of Michigan Studies. Humanities Series, XXXVIII. Ann Arbor: University of Michigan Press; 1935.

Schlisske, Otto: *Der Schatz im Wüstenkloster.* Third edition. Stuttgart: Kreuz-Verlag; 1957.

Schneller, D. Ludwig: *Tischendorf-Erinnerungen.* Lahr-Dinglingen, Baden, Germany: St. Johannis Druckerei–C. Schweickhardt; 1957.

Schonfield, Hugh J.: *A History of Biblical Literature.* New York: New American Library–Mentor Books; 1962.

Scrivener, F. H. A.: *A Plain Introduction to the Criticism of the New Testament for the Use of Biblical Students.* Fourth edition. 2 vols. London: G. Bell & Sons; 1894.

Tischendorf, Constantin von: *Die Anfechtungen der Sinai-Bibel.* Leipzig: Carl Fr. Fleischer; 1863.

———: *Aus dem Heiligen Lande.* Leipzig: F. A. Brockhaus; 1862.

———: *Codex Sinaiticus . . . Tischendorf's Story and Argument Related by Himself.* Eighth edition. London: The Lutterworth Press; 1935.

———: *Reise in den Orient.* 2 vols. Leipzig: Bernhard Tauchnitz Jr.; 1846.

———: *Die Sinaibibel. Ihre Entdeckung, Herausgabe und Erwerbung.* Leipzig: Giesecke & Devrient; 1871.

Vogels, Heinrich Joseph: *Die Altsyrischen Evangelien.* Freiburg, Germany: Herder; 1911.

Vööbus, Arthur: *Studies in the History of the Gospel Text in Syriac.* Louvain: L. Dusberg; 1951.

Weitzmann, Kurt: "Mount Sinai's Holy Treasures." *National Geographic Magazine,* Vol. CXXV, No. 1 (January 1964), pp. 109–27.

Wolf, Edwin II, with John F. Fleming: *Rosenbach.* Cleveland: The World Publishing Co.; 1960.

(B) Hebrew Writs

Adler, Elkan N.: ". . . The Ancient Synagogue Near Cairo." *Jewish Quarterly Review,* Vol. IX (1897), pp. 669–81.

582 · *Bibliography*

————: "Genizah." *The Jewish Encyclopedia,* Vol. V, p. 612. New York: Funk & Wagnalls; 1916.

Allegro, John M.: "The Copper Scroll of Qumran: A Story of Hidden Treasure in a Dead Sea Scroll." *Illustrated London News,* Vol. CCXXXVIII (January 7, 1961), pp. 16–19.

————: *The Dead Sea Scrolls.* Revised edition. Harmondsworth: Penguin Books; 1958.

Bentwich, Norman: *Solomon Schechter.* London: G. Allen & Unwin; 1931.

————: *Solomon Schechter.* Philadelphia: Jewish Publishing Society; 1938.

————: "Solomon Schechter," in Simon Noveck, ed.: *Great Jewish Personalities.* New York: B'nai B'rith; 1916.

Besant, Walter: *The Autobiography of Sir Walter Besant.* New York: Dodd, Mead & Co.; 1902.

Braun, Oskar: "Ein Brief des Katholikos Timotheos I über Biblische Studien des 9. Jahrhunderts." *Oriens Christianus,* Vol. I (1900), pp. 299–313.

Brownlee, William H.: "Biblical Interpretations Among the Sectaries of the Dead Sea Scrolls." *The Biblical Archaeologist,* Vol. XIV, No. 3 (September 1951), pp. 54–76.

————: "A Comparison of the Covenanters of the Dead Sea Scrolls with pre-Christian Sects." *The Biblical Archaeologist,* Vol. XIII, No. 3 (September 1950), pp. 50–72.

————: "Muhammed ad-Deeb's Own Story of His Scroll Discovery." *Journal of Near Eastern Studies,* Vol. XVI, No. 4 (October 1957), pp. 236–9.

Burrows, Millar: *The Dead Sea Scrolls.* New York: Viking Press; 1955.

Carter, A. C. R.: *Let Me Tell You.* London: Hutchinson & Co.; 1940.

Clermont-Ganneau, Charles: *Les Fraudes Archéologiques en Palestine.* Paris: Leroux; 1885.

De Vaux, Roland, O.P.: "Fouille au Khirbet Qumran." *Revue Biblique,* Vol. LX (1953), pp. 83–106.

————: "Les grottes de Murrabba'at et leurs documents." *Revue Biblique,* Vol. LX (1953), pp. 245–67.

————: "A Propos des Manuscripts de la Mer Morte." *Revue Biblique,* Vol. LVII (1950), pp. 417–29.

Driver, G. R.: *The Hebrew Scrolls.* Oxford: Oxford University Press; 1950.

Eissfeldt, Otto: "Der gegegnwärtige Stand der Erforschung der in Palästina neugefundenen hebräischen Handschriften." *Theologische Literaturzeitung,* Vol. LXXIV (October 1949), pp. 595–600.

Ginzberg, Louis: *Students, Scholars and Saints.* Philadelphia: Jewish Publication Society; 1928.

Goitein, Dov Shelomo (Solomon Dob Fritz): "From the Mediterranean to India." *Speculum,* Vol. XXIX, No. 2 (April 1954), pp. 181–97.

————: "What Would Jewish and General History Benefit by a Systematic Publication of the Documentary Geniza Papers?" *American Academy for Jewish Research. Proceedings.* Vol. XXIII (1954), pp. 29–39.

Golb, Norman: "Sixty Years of Genizah Research." *Judaism,* Vol. VI, No. 1 (Winter, 1957), pp. 3–16.

Goodspeed, Edgar J.: *The Story of the Apocrypha.* Chicago: University of Chicago Press; 1939.

Goshen-Gottstein, M. H.: "The Shapira Forgery and the Qumran Scrolls." *Journal of Jewish Studies,* Vol. VII, Nos. 3 & 4 (1956), pp. 187–93.

Grégoire, Henri: "Les Gens de la Caverne, les Quaraïtes et les Khazares." *Le Flambeau,* Vol. XXXV, No. 5 (1952), pp. 477–85.

Harding, G. Lankester: "The Dead Sea Scrolls." *Palestine Exploration Quarterly,* Vol. LXXXI (July–October 1949), pp. 112–16.

————: "The Dead Sea Scrolls: Excavations Which Establish the Authenticity and pre-Christian Date of the Oldest Bible Manuscripts." *Illustrated London News,* Vol. CCXV (October 1, 1949), pp. 493–5.

————: "Khirbet Qumran and Wadi Murabba'at." *Palestine Exploration Quarterly,* Vol. LXXXIV (May–October 1952), pp. 104–9.

————: "Recent Discoveries in Jordan." *Palestine Exploration Quarterly,* Vol. XC (January–June 1958), pp. 7–18.

Harrison, R. K.: *The Dead Sea Scrolls. An Introduction.* New York: Harper Torchbooks; 1961.

Harry, Myriam (Mme Emile Perrault): *La petite fille de Jérusalem.* Paris: A. Fayard; 1914. (*The Little Daughter of Jerusalem.* New York: E. P. Dutton; 1919.)

Hillaby, John: "American Revives the Biblical Scrolls Case." *The New York Times,* August 13, 1956, pp. 1, 6.

Hyatt, J. Philip: "The Dead Sea Discoveries: Retrospect and Challenge." *Journal of Biblical Literature,* Vol. LXXVI, No. 1 (1957), pp. 1–12.

Jacobs, Joseph: "A Romance in Scholarship." *Fortnightly Review,* Vol. LXXII, N.S. Vol. LXVI (1899), pp. 696–704.

Kahle, Paul E.: *The Cairo Geniza.* Second edition. New York: Frederick A. Praeger; 1960.

————: "The Karaites and the Manuscripts from the Cave." *Vetus Testamentum,* Vol. CXI (January 1953), pp. 82–4.

Katz, Richard: "Seltsames Begräbnis." *Vossische Zeitung,* No. 22 (January 14, 1921, evening), pp. 2–3.

Kohler, Kaufmann: "Dositheus, the Samaritan Heresiarch, and His Relations to Jewish and Christian Doctrines and Sects." *The American Journal of Theology,* Vol. XV, No. 3 (July 1911), pp. 404–35.

Kraeling, Carl H.: "A Dead Sea Scroll Jar at the Oriental Institute." *Bulletin of the American Schools of Oriental Research,* No. 125 (February 1952), p. 6.

Lewis, A. S., and M. D. Gibson: *Palestinian Syriac Texts from Pal-*

impsest Fragments in the Taylor-Schechter Collection. London: C. J. Clay; 1910.

Liebermann, Saul: "Light on the Cave Scrolls from Rabbinic Sources." *American Academy of Jewish Research. Proceedings,* Vol. XX (1951), pp. 395–404.

Mann, Jacob: "The Genizah: What It Means to Jewish Learning." *Menorah Journal,* Vol. VII (December 1921), pp. 298–308.

Mansoor, Menahem: "The Case of Shapira's Dead Sea (Deuteronomy) Scrolls of 1853." *Transactions of the Wisconsin Academy of Sciences, Arts and Letters,* Vol. XLVII (1958), pp. 183–225.

Marcus, Ralph: "Pharisees, Essenes and Gnostics." *Journal of Biblical Literature,* Vol. LXXIII, pt. 3 (September 1954), pp. 157–61.

Marx, Alexander: *Essays in Jewish Biography.* Philadelphia: Jewish Publication Society; 1948.

———: "Genizah." *Universal Jewish Encyclopedia,* Vol. IV (1948), pp. 531–3.

———: "The Importance of the Genizah for Jewish History." *American Academy for Jewish Research. Proceedings,* Vol. XVI (1947), pp. 183–204.

Nemoy, Leon: "Al-Qirqisani's Account of the Jewish Sects and Christianity." *Hebrew Union College Annual,* Vol. VII (1930), pp. 317–97.

Rabinowicz, Oskar K.: "The Shapira Forgery Mystery." *Jewish Quarterly Review,* Vol. XLVII, No. 2 (October 1956), pp. 170–82.

Reed, William L.: "The Qumran Caves Expedition of March 1952." *Bulletin of the American Schools of Oriental Research,* No. 135 (October 1954), pp. 8–13.

Roberts, B. J.: "Some Observations on the Damascus Document and the Dead Sea Scrolls." *John Rylands Library. Bulletin,* Vol. XXXV (1952–53), pp. 366–87.

Rowley, Harold H.: "The Covenanters of Damascus and the Dead Sea Scrolls." *John Rylands Library. Bulletin,* Vol. XXXV (1952–53), pp. 111–54.

———: *The Zadokite Fragments and the Dead Sea Scrolls.* London: Macmillan & Co.; 1955.

Schechter, Solomon: Communications on Ecclesiasticus MSS. in *The Athenaeum,* May 16, 1896, p. 652; June 27, 1896, p. 846.

———: *Documents of Jewish Sectaries.* 2 vols. Cambridge: Cambridge University Press; 1910.

———: "A Fragment of the Original Text of Ecclesiasticus." *The Expositor,* 5th Ser., Vol. IV (July 1896), pp. 1–15.

———: "A Hoard of Hebrew Manuscripts." London *Times,* August 7, 1897, p. 13.

———: "The Lewis-Gibson Hebrew Collection." *The Jewish Quarterly Review,* Vol. VIII (October 1896), pp. 115–21.

———: "The Original Ecclesiasticus." London *Times,* July 5, 1897.

———: *Studies in Judaism.* Second Series. London: A. and C. Black; 1908.

——, and C. Taylor, eds.: *The Wisdom of Ben Sira*. . . . Cambridge: Cambridge University Press; 1899.

"Scholars Dispute Scrolls' Validity." *The New York Times*, December 28, 1956, p. 14.

Schonfield, Hugh J.: *Secrets of the Dead Sea Scrolls*. New York: A. S. Barnes–Perpetua Books; 1960.

Sellers, O. R.: "Excavation of the 'Manuscript' Cave at 'Ain Fashka." *Bulletin of the American Schools of Oriental Research*, No. 114 (1949), pp. 5–9.

Sonne, Isaiah: "The Newly Discovered Bar Kokaba Letters." *American Academy for Jewish Research. Proceedings*, Vol. XXIII (1954), pp. 75–108.

Strack, Hermann L.: "Abraham Firkowitsch und der Wert seiner Entdeckungen." *Zeitschrift der Deutschen Morgenländischen Gesellschaft*, Vol. XXXIV (1880), pp. 163–5.

Sutcliffe, Edmund F.: *The Monks of Qumran as Depicted in the Dead Sea Scrolls*. Westminster, Md.: The Newman Press; 1960.

Teicher, J. L.: "The Genuineness of the Shapira Manuscripts." *The Times Literary Supplement*, March 22, 1957, p. 184.

Trever, John C.: "The Discovery of the Scrolls." *The Biblical Archaeologist*, Vol. XI, No. 3 (September 1948), pp. 46–57.

Van der Ploeg, J., O.P.: *The Excavations at Qumran*. London: Longmans, Green; 1958.

Vester, Bertha Stafford: *Our Jerusalem. An American Family in the Holy City, 1881–1949*. New York: Doubleday & Co.; 1950.

Vincent, C.-H., O.P.: "Une grotte funéraire antique dans L'Ouady el-Tin." *Revue Biblique*, Vol. LIV (1947), pp. 269–82.

Wilson, Edmund: *The Scrolls of the Dead Sea*. New York: Meridian Books; 1955.

Zeitlin, S.: "The Dead Sea Scrolls: A Travesty on Scholarship." *Jewish Quarterly Review*, Vol. XLVII, No. 1 (July 1956), pp. 10–36.

——: "Revealing Data on the So-called Discovery of the Dead Sea Scrolls." *Jewish Quarterly Review*, Vol. XLVII, No. 2 (October 1956), pp. 183–7.

BOOK FOUR: A PROFUSION OF SILK, BARK, AND PAPER
(A) Inner Asia

Andrews, F. H.: "Sir Aurel Stein: The Man." *Indian Art and Letters*, N.S., Vol. XVIII, No. 2 (1944), pp. 65–74.

British Museum Guide to the Exhibition of Paintings, Manuscripts, and other Archaeological Objects Collected by Sir A. Stein in Chinese Turkestan. London: British Museum; 1914.

Cable, Mildred, and Francesca French: *The Gobi Desert*. London: Hodder & Stoughton; 1942.

Carter, Thomas F.: *The Invention of Printing in China*. . . . Second edition revised by L. Carrington Goodrich. New York: Ronald Press; 1955.

Chakravarti, N. P.: "Sir A. M. Stein." *The Journal of the Greater India Society*, Vol. XI, No. 1 (January 1944), pp. 1–6.

Crum, W. E.: "A 'Manichaen' Fragment from Egypt." *Royal Asiatic Society. Journal*. April 1919, pp. 207–8.

Cumming, Sir John, ed.: *Revealing India's Past*. London: The India Society; 1939.

Dames, Longworth M.: "Christian and Manichaean Manuscripts in Chinese Turkestan." *The Royal Asiatic Society. Journal*, 1907, pp. 1055–7.

Giles, Lionel: *Six Centuries at Tunhuang. A Short Account of the Stein Collection of Chinese Manuscripts in the British Museum*. China Society Sinological Series, No. 2. W. Perceval Yetts, ed. London: The China Society; 1944.

Hudson, Geoffrey F.: *Europe and China: A Survey of Their Relations from the Earliest Times to 1800*. London: E. Arnold & Co., 1931. Beacon paperback, 1961.

Le Coq, Albert von: *Buried Treasures of Chinese Turkestan*. London: George Allen & Unwin; 1928.

Luders, H.: "Über die Literarischen Funde aus Ost-Turkestan." *Internationale Monatsschrift*, Vol. VIII (1914), p. 1439.

MacLagan, Sir Edward: "Marc Aurel Stein." *The Hungarian Quarterly*, Vol. IV, No. 2 (Summer, 1938), pp. 273–9.

Oldham, C. E. A. W.: "Sir Aurel Stein." *British Academy. Proceedings*. Vol. XXIX (1943), pp. 329–48.

Parsons, Desmond: "The Caves of the Thousand Buddhas. A Storehouse of T'ang Buddhist Painting. . . ." *Illustrated London News*, Vol. CLXXXVIII (May 30, 1936), pp. 969–71.

Stefansson, Vilhjalmur, ed.: *Great Adventures and Explorations*. New York: Dial Press; 1947.

Stein, Sir Aurel: *On Ancient Central-Asian Tracks*. London: Macmillan & Co.; 1933.

———: "On Ancient Tracks Past the Pamir." *Himalayan Journal*, Vol. IV (April 1932), pp. 1–24.

———: *Ruins of Desert Cathay. Personal Narrative of Explorations in Central Asia and Westernmost China*. 2 vols. London: Macmillan & Co.; 1912.

———: *Sand-buried Ruins of Khotan*. London: Hurst & Blackett; 1904.

———: *Serindia*. 5 vols. Oxford: Clarendon Press; 1951.

Sykes, Percy: "Aurel Stein." *American Journal of Archaeology*, Vol. XLVIII (April 1944), pp. 178–9.

———: *A History of Exploration*. New York: Harper Torchbooks; 1961.

Vincent, Irene Vongehr: *The Sacred Oasis*. Chicago: Chicago University Press; 1953.

Warner, L.: *The Long Old Road in China*. New York: Doubleday, Page & Co.; 1926.

(B) The New World

Adams, Herbert B.: "The Abbé de Bourbourg." *American Antiquarian Society. Proceedings*, Vol. VII (April 1891), pp. 274–90.

Bernal, Ignacio: *Mexico before Cortez: Art, History, Legend*. New York: Doubleday & Co.–Dolphin Books; 1963.

Bitterling, Richard: "Alexander von Humboldts Amerikareise in zeitgenössischer Darstellung." *Petermanns Geographische Mitteilungen*, Vol. XCVIII, No. 3 (1954), pp. 161–71.

Brandon, William: *The American Heritage Book of Indians*. New York: American Heritage; 1961. Dell–Laurel edition, 1964.

Brasseur de Bourbourg, Charles Étienne: *Bibliothèque Mexico–Guatémalienne*. Paris: Maison Neuve; 1871.

————: *Histoire des Nations Civilisées du Mexique et de l'Amérique Centrale, durant les Siècles Antérieures à Christophe Colomb, Écrite sur des Documents Originaux et entièrement inédits, Prises aux Anciennes Archives des Indigènes*. 4 vols. Paris: A. Bertrand; 1857.

————: *Manuscrit Troano*. 2 vols. Paris: Imprimerie Impériale; 1869–70.

————: "Notes d'un voyage dans l'Amérique Centrale." *Nouvelles Annales des Voyages*, Vol. I, Sér. 6 (August 1855), pp. 129–58.

————: *Relation des Choses de Yucatan de Diego de Landa. . . .* Paris: A. Bertrand; 1864.

Brinton, Daniel G.: "The Abbé Brasseur de Bourbourg and His Labors." *Lippincott's*, Vol. I, No. 1 (January 1868), pp. 79–86.

————: *Essays of an Americanist*. Philadelphia: Porter & Coates; 1890.

————: "A Notice of Some Manuscripts in Central American Languages." *Historical Magazine*, Ser. 2, Vol. V (May 1869), pp. 305–9.

————, ed.: *The Maya Chronicles*. Brinton's Library of Aboriginal American Literature, No. 1. Philadelphia: D. G. Brinton; 1882.

Burland, Cottie A.: *Art and Life in Ancient Mexico*. Oxford: Bruno Cassirer; 1948.

————: *Magic Books from Mexico*. Harmondsworth: King Penguin Books; 1953.

————: *The Selden Roll*. Berlin: Gebr. Mann; 1955.

Caso, Alfonso: *The Aztecs. People of the Sun*. Norman, Okla.: University of Oklahoma Press; 1950.

————: "The Codices of Azoyu." *Dyn*, Nos. 4–5 (December 1943), pp. 3–6.

————: *Interpretación del Codice Bodley 2858*. Mexico, D.F.: Sociedad Mexicana de Antropología; 1960.

————: "El Mapa de Teozacoalco." *Cuadernos Americanos*, Vol. VIII, No. 5 (1949), pp. 145–81.

Charency, H. de: "Note sur M. l'Abbé Brasseur de Bourbourg." *Société de Géographie. Bulletin*, Vol. VII (1874), pp. 508–10.

588 · *Bibliography*

Cornyn, John Hubert: "Finding a Lost Literature." *Pan American Magazine*, Vol. XLIII (August 1930), pp. 124–6.

Covarrubias, Miguel: *Indian Art of Mexico and Central America*. New York: Alfred A. Knopf; 1957.

————: *Mexico South*. New York: Alfred A. Knopf; 1946.

Currier, Charles Warren: "Discovery of Historic Manuscript of Mexico." *Pan American Union. Bulletin*, Vol. XXXV (1912), pp. 542–8.

Dark, Philip: *Mixtec Ethnohistory*. Oxford: Oxford University Press; 1958.

Díaz del Castillo, Bernal: *The Discovery and Conquest of Mexico, 1519–21*, translated by A. P. Maudslay. New York: Farrar, Straus and Cudahy; 1956.

Gallenkamp, Charles: *Maya*. New York: Pyramid Books; 1962.

Gates, William E., ed.: *The Dresden Codex*. Maya Society Publications, No. 2. Baltimore, 1932.

————: *Yucatan before and after the Conquest, by Friar Diego de Landa*. . . . Maya Society Publications, No. 20. Baltimore, 1937.

————: *The Madrid Codex*. Maya Society Publications, No. 21. Baltimore, 1933.

Hagen, Victor von: *The Aztec: Man and Tribe*. New York: New American Library–Mentor Books; 1958.

————: *World of the Maya*. New York: New American Library–Mentor Books; 1960.

Haven, Samuel F.: "Note on Alexander von Humboldt and His Services to American Archaeology." *American Antiquarian Society. Proceedings*, No. 70 (1878), pp. 91–100.

————: "Report of the Librarian." *American Antiquarian Society. Proceedings*. No. 55 (October 1870), pp. 42–60.

Humboldt, Alexander von: *Researches Concerning the Institutions and Monuments of the Ancient Inhabitants of America, with Descriptions and Views of Some of the Most Striking Scenes in the Cordilleras*. 2 vols. London: Longmans; 1814.

Jijón y Caamaño, Jacinto: "Edward King, Vizconde de Kingsborough, 1795–1837." *Boletín de la Sociedad Ecuatoriana de Estudios Históricos Americanos*, Vol. I, 1918 (Quito, 1919), pp. 2–9.

Joyce, Thomas A.: *Mexican Archaeology*. New York: G. P. Putnam's Sons; 1914.

Long, Richard C. E.: "The Zouche Codex." *Journal of the Royal Anthropological Society*, Vol. LVI (1926), pp. 239–58.

The Maya and Their Neighbors. New York: D. Appleton-Century; 1940. University of Utah Press reprint, 1962.

Means, Philip Ainsworth: "Zelia Nuttall: An Appreciation." *Hispanic American Historical Review*, Vol. XIII (November 1933), pp. 487–9.

Molé, Harvey E.: *The Abbé Brasseur de Bourbourg*. Summit, N.J.: The Monday Night Club; 1945 (typescript).

Morley, Sylvanus Griswold: *The Ancient Maya*. Stanford: Stanford University Press; 1946. Third edition revised by George W. Brainerd; Stanford, 1956.

——: "This Historical Value of the Books of Chilan Balaam." *American Journal of Archaeology*, 2nd Ser., Vol. XV, No. 2 (1911), pp. 195–214.

Müller, Max: *Chips from a German Workshop*. Vol. I. New York: Charles Scribner & Co.; 1870.

Nowotny, Karl A.: *Tlacuilolli. Die Mexikanischen Bilderhandschriften. Stil und Inhalt*. Monumenta Americana III. Berlin: Gebr. Mann; 1961.

Nuttall, Zelia, ed.: *The Book of the Life of the Ancient Mexicans, Containing an Account of Their Rites and Superstitions* (Codex Magliabecchi). Berkeley: University of California Press; 1903.

——: *Codex Nuttall. Facsimile of an Ancient Mexican Codex Belonging to Lord Zouche of Harynworth, England*. Cambridge, Mass.: Peabody Museum–Harvard University Press; 1902.

Peterson, Frederick: *Ancient Mexico*. New York: G. P. Putnam's Sons –Capricorn Books; 1962.

Proskouriakoff, Tatiana: "The Lords of the Maya Realm." *Expedition*, Vol. IV, No. 1 (Autumn, 1961), pp. 14–21.

Radin, Paul: *The Sources and Authenticity of the History of the Ancient Mexicans*. University of California Publications in American Archaeology and Ethnology, Vol. XVII. Berkeley, 1920–26.

Ramírez, Fernando: "Cronología de Boturini." *Anales del Museo Nazional*, Vol. VII (1903), pp. 167–94.

Recinos, Adrián, ed.: *Popol Vuh. The Sacred Book of the Ancient Quiché Maya*. Norman, Okla.: University of Oklahoma Press; 1950.

——, and Delia Goetz, eds.: *The Annals of Cakchiquels*. Norman, Okla.: University of Oklahoma Press; 1953.

Rivet, Paul: *Maya Cities*. London: Elek Books; 1960.

Schellhas, P.: "Fifty Years of Maya Research." *Maya Research*, Vol. III, No. 2 (August 1936), pp. 129–39.

Scurla, Herbert: *Alexander von Humboldt. Sein Leben und Wirken*. Berlin: Verlag der Nation; 1955.

Seler, Eduard: *Gesammelte Abhandlungen zur Amerikanischen Sprach- und Altertumskunde*. 5 vols. Berlin: A. Asher; 1902–23.

——, ed.: *Historische Hieroglyphen der Azteken im Jahr 1803 im Königreich Neu-Spanien Gesammelt von A. v. Humboldt*. 2 vols. Berlin, 1893.

Spence, Lewis: *The Civilisation of Ancient Mexico*. New York: G. P. Putnam's Sons; 1912.

——: "The Papyri of Central America." *The Open Court*, Vol. XLII, No. 4 (April 1928), pp. 193–207.

——: "The Popol Vuh: America's Oldest Book." *The Open Court*, Vol. XLII, No. 11 (November 1928), pp. 641–58.

Spinden, Herbert J.: "Indian Manuscripts of Southern Mexico." *The*

Smithsonian Report for 1933, Publication 3279, pp. 429–51. Washington, D.C.: Government Printing Office; 1935.

Stoddard, Richard Henry: *The Life of Alexander von Humboldt.* New York: Rudd & Carleton; 1859.

Taylor, John, ed.: *Selections from the Works of Baron De Humboldt, Relating to . . . Mexico.* London: Longmans; 1824.

Terra, Helmut de: *Humboldt. The Life and Times of A.v.H., 1769–1859.* New York: Alfred A. Knopf; 1955.

Thompson, J. Eric S.: *The Civilization of the Mayas.* Chicago Natural History Museum Popular Series, Anthropology No. 25. Sixth edition. Chicago: Chicago Natural History Museum Press; 1958.

———: *Maya Archaeologist.* London: R. Hale; 1963.

———: *Mexico Before Cortez.* New York: Charles Scribner's Sons; 1933.

———: *The Rise and Fall of Maya Civilization.* Norman, Okla.: University of Oklahoma Press; 1954.

Tozzer, Alfred M., ed.: *Landa's Relación de las Cosas de Yucatán.* Peabody Museum Publication, Vol. XVIII. Cambridge, Mass.: Peabody Museum–Harvard University Press; 1941.

———: "The Value of the Ancient Mexican Manuscripts in the Study of the General Development of Writing." *American Antiquarian Society. Proceedings*, Vol. XXI (April 1911), pp. 1–24.

———: "Zelia Nuttall." *American Anthropologist*, N.S., Vol. XXXV (September 1933), pp. 475–82.

Trübner, Nicolaus: "Central American Archaeology." *The Athenaeum*, No. 1492 (May 31, 1856), pp. 683–5.

———: "The New Discoveries in Guatemala." *The Athenaeum*, No. 1472 (January 12, 1856), pp. 42–3.

Vaillant, George C.: *The Aztecs of Mexico.* Harmondsworth: Penguin Books; 1960. Revised edition by Suzannah B. Valliant; Doubleday & Co.; 1962.

Valentini, Philip J. J.: "Landa's Alphabet a Spanish Fabrication." *American Antiquarian Society. Proceedings*, No. 75 (April 1880), pp. 59–91.

Wauchope, Robert: *Lost Tribes & Sunken Continents: Myth and Method in the Study of American Indians.* Chicago: Chicago University Press; 1962.

Winsor, Justin: *Narrative and Critical History of America*, Vol. I. Boston: Houghton Mifflin; 1884.

INDEX

LEO DEUEL was born of Swiss parentage, but has been an American citizen for many years. He has lived in Europe, Australia, Latin America, and the Near East, holds a master's degree from Columbia University and a Ph.D. in philosophy from Zurich University in Switzerland. From 1948 to 1954 he served on the editorial staff of the Columbia University Press and the *Encyclopedia Americana*. In 1955 he was a technical assistant for the World Health Organization in Geneva, and from 1958 to 1961 he was a member of the History Department of New York's City College. Mr. Deuel's first publications appeared in the *Neue Zürcher Zeitung* and *Weltwoche*, in Switzerland. He wrote the introductions to the German-language editions of Alfred North Whitehead's *Science and the Modern World* and John Dewey's *How We Think*. His anthology, *Teacher's Treasure Chest*, was published in 1956, and *The Treasures of Time* (1961) has been published in the United States, England, and Germany.

July 1965

A NOTE ON THE TYPE

THE TEXT of this book was set in a typeface called *Primer,* designed by RUDOLPH RUZICKA for the Mergenthaler Linotype Company and first made available in 1949. Primer, a modified modern face based on Century broadface, has the virtue of great legibility and was designed especially for today's methods of composition and printing.

Primer is Ruzicka's third typeface. In 1940 he designed Fairfield, and in 1947 Fairfield Medium, both for the Mergenthaler Linotype Company.

Ruzicka was born in Bohemia in 1883 and came to the United States at the age of eleven. He attended public schools in Chicago and later the Chicago Art Institute. During his long career he has been a wood engraver, etcher, cartographer, and book designer. For many years he was associated with Daniel Berkeley Updike and produced the annual keepsakes for The Merrymount Press from 1911 until 1941.

Ruzicka has been honored by many distinguished organizations, and in 1936 he was awarded the gold medal of the American Institute of Graphic Arts. From his home in New Hampshire, Ruzicka continues to be active in the graphic arts.

Composed, printed, and bound by
The Haddon Craftsmen, Inc., Scranton, Pa.
Typography and binding design by
ANITA KARL